Lecture Notes in Computer Science 1243
Edited by G. Goos, J. Hartmanis and J. van Leeuwen

Springer
Berlin
Heidelberg
New York
Barcelona
Budapest
Hong Kong
London
Milan
Paris
Santa Clara
Singapore
Tokyo

Antoni Mazurkiewicz Józef Winkowski (Eds.)

CONCUR'97: Concurrency Theory

8th International Conference
Warsaw, Poland, July 1-4, 1997
Proceedings

Springer

Volume Editors

Antoni Mazurkiewicz
Józef Winkowski
Institute of Computer Science, Polish Academy of Sciences
Ordona 21, 01-237 Warsaw, Poland
E-mail: (amaz/wink)@ipipan.waw.pl

Cataloging-in-Publication data applied for

Die Deutsche Bibliothek - CIP-Einheitsaufnahme

Concurrency theory : 8th international conference ; proceedings / CONCUR '97, Warsaw, Poland, July 1 - 4, 1997. Antoni Mazurkiewicz ; Józef Winkowski (ed.). - Berlin ; Heidelberg ; New York ; Barcelona ; Budapest ; Hong Kong ; London ; Milan ; Paris ; Santa Clara ; Singapore ; Tokyo : Springer, 1997
(Lecture notes in computer science ; Vol. 1243)
ISBN 3-540-63141-0

CR Subject Classification (1991): F.3, F.1, D.3, D.1, C.2

ISSN 0302-9743
ISBN 3-540-63141-0 Springer-Verlag Berlin Heidelberg New York

Typesetting: Camera-ready by author
SPIN 10550358 06/3142 – 5 4 3 2 1 0 Printed on acid-free paper

Preface

The purpose of the CONCUR conferences is to bring together researchers, developers, and students in order to advance the science of concurrency theory and promote its applications. Interest in the conference is continuously growing, as a consequence of the importance and ubiquity of concurrent systems and applications, and of the scientific relevance of their foundations. The first two meetings were held in *Amsterdam* in 1990 and 1991, the following ones in *Stony Brook*, *Hildesheim*, *Uppsala*, *Philadelphia*, and *Pisa*. The proceedings have appeared in Springer LNCS, as Vols. 458, 527, 630, 715, 836, 962, and 1119. The *steering committee* of CONCUR consists of

Jos Baeten (chair, Eindhoven),	Ugo Montanari (Pisa),
Eike Best (Hildesheim),	Scott Smolka (Stony Brook),
Kim Larsen (Aalborg),	Pierre Wolper (Liège).

The conference CONCUR'97 was held in Warsaw on July 1-4, 1997. This volume contains 4 invited papers and 24 papers selected from 41 submitted papers. The invited talks were delivered by *Jeremy Gunawardena* (Hewlett-Packard Labs, Bristol), *Michael Shields* (University of Surrey), *Scott A. Smolka* (SUNY at Stony Brook), *P. S. Thiagarajan* (SPIC Mathematical Institute, Madras), and *Glynn Winskel* (Aarhus University). The members of the *program committee* of CONCUR'97 were

Samson Abramsky (Edinburgh)	Ugo Montanari (Pisa)
Ralph Back (Åbo)	Rocco De Nicola (Firenze)
Jos Baeten (Eindhoven)	Doron Peled (Bell Labs)
Marek Bednarczyk (Gdańsk)	Wojciech Penczek (Warsaw)
Eike Best (Hildesheim)	Ernst R. Olderog (Oldenburg)
Gérard Boudol (Sophia Ant.)	Wolfgang Reisig (Berlin)
Ursula Goltz (Hildesheim)	Joseph Sifakis (Grenoble)
David Harel (Rehovot)	Bernhard Steffen (Passau)
Gerard Holzmann (Bell Labs)	Colin Stirling (Edinburgh)
Maciej Koutny (Newcastle)	Józef Winkowski (Warsaw, co-chair)
Kim Larsen (Aalborg)	Pierre Wolper (Liège)
Antoni Mazurkiewicz (Warsaw, co-chair).	

The program committee discussion was held electronically in February 1997. The conference CONCUR'97 was organized by the Institute of Computer Science of the Polish Academy of Sciences. The conference office was run by

Ewa Gąsiorowska-Wirpszo.

The organizers would like to thank the invited speakers, the authors of the papers, the members of the steering and the program committees, and the referees of the papers. They are also indebted to Springer-Verlag for publishing this volume.

Warsaw, 1997

Antoni Mazurkiewicz and Józef Winkowski

Referees

L. Aceto
R. Amadio
R. Back
E. Badouel
J. Baeten
M. A. Bednarczyk
E. Best
M. Bialasik
J. Blanco
A. Borzyszkowski
G. Boudol
J. Bradfield
O. Burkart
I. Castellani
F. Corradini
P. Darondeau
R. Devillers
H. Dierks
C. Dietz
J. Esparza
G. Ferrari
C. Fischer
H. Fleischhack
P. Gastin
T. Gehrke
R. van Glabbeek
U. Goltz
D. Graves
O. Grumberg
D. Harel
N. Heintze
M. Hennessy
Y. Hirshfeld
B. Hohberg
G. Holzmann
D. Howe
H. Huttel
A. Ingolfsdottir
D. Janin
L. J. Jagadeesan
E. Kindler
S. Kleuker
B. Konikowska
M. Koutny
K. J. Kristoffersen
O. Kupferman
T. Laan
A. Labella
Y. Lakhnech
R. Langerak
K. Larsen
G. Lüttgen
A. Maggiolo-Schettini
O. Maler
A. Mateescu
S. Mauw
M. Mendler
K. McMillan
L. Mounier
M. Müller-Olm
U. Nestmann
R. De Nicola
P. Niebert
D. Niwinski
E.-R. Olderog
P. Paczkowski
D. Peled
W. Penczek
S. Peuker
M. Pinna
M. Pouzet
J. Power
R. Pugliese
A. Puri
R. Ramanujam
M. Reniers
A. Rensink
G. Ristori
D. Sangiorgi
V. Sassone
R. Segala
E. Sekerinski
S. K. Shukla
J. Sifakis
A. Simpson
S. Sokolowski
M. Srebrny
B. Steffen
P. Stevens
I. V. Tarasyuk
L. Urbina
B. Venneri
I. B. Virbiskaite
T. Vesper
H. Voelzer
W. Vogler
M. Voorhoeve
A. Votintseva
I. Walukiewicz
H. Wehrheim
P. Wolper
M. Yannakakis

Table of Contents

Invited talks

Contributions

Recent Developments in the Mathematics of Reactive Systems (Extended Abstract)

Jeremy Gunawardena

Basic Research Institute in the Mathematical Sciences
Hewlett-Packard Laboratories, Bristol BS12 6QZ, UK.
http://www-uk.hpl.hp.com/brims/

A reactive system, when coupled with its environment, is an example of a *dynamical system*. That is, at any particular instant the system is in one of a collection of possible states and this state changes over time. Mathematicians have studied dynamical systems for nearly a century but have largely concentrated on systems arising from physics: planetary systems, fluids, elastic solids, etc, [11]. By constrast, much less is known about so-called *discrete event dynamical systems* (or reactive systems) which arise in computer science, communications, operations research, manufacturing, etc.

A number of models have been proposed for studying such systems, including (timed or stochastic) Petri nets, Jackson networks, Generalised Semi-Markov Processes and forms of process algebra. A good overview of such models appears in a special issue of the IEEE Proceedings, [12]. For the most part, these models are mathematically intractable in the following sense: it is hard to find any theorem about them which engineers would wish to learn as an aid to designing reactive systems.

In this talk I will discuss some recent ideas which take a different approach. They have emerged through the independent work of several people coming from different standpoints, [1, 2, 9, 13, 17]. A more detailed overview can be found in [6, §4].

Suppose that the set of states of the system can be represented by $\mathbf{R}^n$. For instance, if the system has n possible events labelled $1, \cdots, n$, then $(x_1, \cdots, x_n) \in \mathbf{R}^n$ might represent the times of occurrence of each event, relative to some arbitrary origin of time. Suppose further that the time evolution of the system is represented by a function $F : \mathbf{R}^n \to \mathbf{R}^n$ so that if the system is currently in state $\mathbf{x}$ then it evolves in the next time step to state $F(\mathbf{x})$. These may seem like absurdly restrictive assumptions but let us proceed with them for the moment.

What assumptions should we make about F? The following are very natural. Firstly, the origin of time should be irrelevant. Hence, F should be *homogeneous*: for all $\mathbf{x} \in \mathbf{R}^n$ and $h \in \mathbf{R}$,

$$F(\mathbf{x} + h) = F(\mathbf{x}) + h \ .$$

(We use here the convention that when a vector and a scalar appear together in a binary operation or relation then the operation is performed, or the relation is required to hold, on each component of the vector. Hence, $(\mathbf{x}+h)_i = x_i + h$ for all i, while $\mathbf{x} = h$ means that $x_i = h$ for all i.) Secondly, if we delay the times of occurrence of each event, then the next occurrences should not be faster than they were before. That is, F should be *monotonic*: for all $\mathbf{x}, \mathbf{y} \in \mathbf{R}^n$,

$$\mathbf{x} \leq \mathbf{y} \implies F(\mathbf{x}) \leq F(\mathbf{y}) \ ,$$

where $\mathbf{x} \leq \mathbf{y}$ denotes the product ordering on $\mathbf{R}^n$, $x_i \leq y_i$ for all i. This axiom is perhaps less immediately compelling than the first one but it has a clear intuition and can be seen to hold in practice in a wide variety of systems.

Functions with both properties are called ***topical functions***, [9]. We want to understand the dynamics of the corresponding system, so we shall study the trajectories $\mathbf{x}, F(\mathbf{x}), F^2(\mathbf{x}), \cdots$. This emphasis will allow us, hopefully, to answer such questions as *"does the system attain an equilibrium or cycle indefinitely or blow up?"*, *"how sensitive is the system to a change of its parameters?"*, *"how fast does the system operate?"*, etc. Questions like these are often very much in the minds of engineers when designing reactive systems but, for the most part, they have not had the tools to answer them.

It turns out that there are real-life systems which can be represented even by the simple model above. For instance, the problem of *clock schedule verification* in synchronous digital circuits has been solved by finding the equilibrium points of a suitable topical function, [7, 16]. Furthermore, the model can be extended in various ways to accommodate nondeterminism, stochasticity and more complex states. These extensions suggest that some of the other models in current use can be incorporated within this framework, although our understanding of this important question is still rudimentary, [2, 4]. I will not discuss such extensions here, for fear of putting the cart before the horse. As we shall see, the horse has not yet been tamed and already presents us with some difficult problems.

The first remark to make about topical functions is that they are nonexpansive in the ℓ_∞ (or supremum) norm. Let $\|\mathbf{x}\| = \max_{1 \leq i \leq n} |x_i|$. This defines a norm on $\mathbf{R}^n$, so that $\|\mathbf{x} - \mathbf{y}\|$ is a metric. F is nonexpansive if

$$\|F(\mathbf{x}) - F(\mathbf{y})\| \leq \|\mathbf{x} - \mathbf{y}\| \ .$$

This property has an important effect on the dynamics of F and constrains it in ways that are still not fully understood. For instance, it limits the extent of cyclic behaviour in the dynamics of F, [15]. Of course, if F was contractive then the Banach Contraction Principle would tell us that the dynamics of F were straightforward: there is an unique equilibrium point and all trajectories converge to it. When F is merely nonexpansive, its dynamics are much more subtle, [5].

The space of topical functions, $\mathsf{Top}(n, n)$, includes a number of important examples studied in optimal control, game theory, mathematical economics and operations research, [10]. In particular, nonnegative matrices can be considered as topical functions. The dynamics of such matrices has been extensively studied under the name of Perron-Frobenius theory, [3]. From this perspective, topical functions lead the way towards a nonlinear generalisation of Perron-Frobenius.

One of the interesting results to emerge from this is that any topical function can be approximated by so-called min-max functions. These latter functions are topical functions which are built recursively from the operations max, min and addition. The approximation is similar to the way in which polynomials approximate continuous functions but has the added feature that some of the dynamics of the topical function are inherited by its approximating min-max functions, [10]. For nonnegative matrices, these approximations are new and they probably would not have been found if not for the introduction of topical functions. It is a welcome development that topical functions are interesting both through their applications to reactive systems and through their intrinsic mathematical qualities. Perhaps this will encourage more mathematicians to think about the problems of reactive systems.

I will concentrate in the talk on two related questions. How do we measure the speed of the underlying system? When does the system have an equilibrium point? For the former question, the limit

$$\lim_{k \to \infty} F^k(\mathbf{x})/k$$

turns out to be the appropriate measure. It can be thought of as the asymptotic average slowness of each event. This limit does not exist for all topical functions—it is an important open problem to identify those for which it does—but if it does exist, it is independent of $\mathbf{x}$. Hence it associates to F a vector, called *the cycle time vector*, $\chi(F) \in \mathbf{R}^n$. We are starting to understand the properties of χ as a (partial) functional, $\chi : \mathsf{Top}(n,n) \to \mathbf{R}^n$. These properties allow us to calculate χ in the case of min-max functions and hence to estimate it when we do not know how to calculate it exactly. It turns out that the cycle time is closely related to the existence of equilibrium points. If F has an equilibrium point, so that $F(\mathbf{x}) = \mathbf{x}$, then it is easy to see that $\chi(F) = \mathbf{0}$. Conversely, if F is a min-max function and $\chi(F) = 0$, then F has an equilibrium point.

There are a number of unsolved conjectures and open problems in this area which I will try and point out.

The work reported here draws upon joint research with Jean Cochet-Terrasson, Stéphane Gaubert, Michael Keane and Colin Sparrow and upon discussions with Geert-Jan Olsder, François Baccelli, Vassili Kolokoltsov, Sjoerd Verduyn Lunel, Jean Mairesse and Roger Nussbaum. It was partially supported by the European Commission through the TMR network ALAPEDES.

References

1. F. Baccelli, G. Cohen, G. J. Olsder, and J.-P. Quadrat. *Synchronization and Linearity.* Wiley Series in Probability and Mathematical Statistics. John Wiley, 1992.
2. F. Baccelli and J. Mairesse. Ergodic theorems for stochastic operators and discrete event systems. Appears in [8].
3. A. Berman and R. J. Plemmons. *Nonnegative Matrices in the Mathematical Sciences.* Classics in Applied Mathematics. SIAM, 1994.
4. G. Cohen, S. Gaubert, and J.-P. Quadrat. Algebraic system analysis of timed Petri nets. Appears in [8].

5. K. Goebel and W. A. Kirk. *Topics in Metric Fixed Point Theory*, volume 28 of *Cambridge Studies in Advanced Mathematics*. Cambride University Press, 1990.
6. J. Gunawardena. An introduction to idempotency. Appears in [8].
7. J. Gunawardena. Timing analysis of digital circuits and the theory of min-max functions. In *Digest of Technical Papers of the ACM International Workshop on Timing Issues in the Specification and Synthesis of Digital Systems*. ACM, 1993.
8. J. Gunawardena, editor. *Idempotency*. Publications of the Isaac Newton Institute. Cambridge University Press, 1997.
9. J. Gunawardena and M. Keane. On the existence of cycle times for some nonexpansive maps. Technical Report HPL-BRIMS-95-003, Hewlett-Packard Labs, 1995.
10. J. Gunawardena, M. Keane, and C. Sparrow. In preparation, 1997.
11. M. W. Hirsch. The dynamical systems approach to differential equations. *Bulletin of the American Mathematical Society*, 11:1–64, 1984.
12. Y. C. Ho, editor. *Special issue on Dynamics of Discrete Event Systems*. Proceedings of the IEEE, 77(1), January 1989.
13. V. N. Kolokoltsov. On linear, additive and homogeneous operators in idempotent analysis. Appears in [14].
14. V. P. Maslov and S. N. Samborskiĭ, editors. *Idempotent Analysis*, volume 13 of *Advances in Soviet Mathematics*. American Mathematical Society, 1992.
15. R. D. Nussbaum. Periodic points of nonexpansive maps. Appears in [8].
16. T. Szymanski and N. Shenoy. Verifying clock schedules. In *Digest of Technical Papers of the IEEE International Conference on Computer-Aided Design of Integrated Circuits*, pages 124–131. IEEE Computer Society, 1992.
17. J. M. Vincent. Some ergodic results on stochastic iterative DEDS. To appear in Journal of Discrete Event Dynamics Systems.

Partial-Order Reduction in the Weak Modal Mu-Calculus*

Y.S. Ramakrishna and Scott A. Smolka

Department of Computer Science
SUNY at Stony Brook
Stony Brook, NY 11794–4400, USA

Abstract. We present a partial-order reduction technique for local model checking of hierarchical networks of labeled transition systems in the weak modal mu-calculus. We have implemented our technique in the Concurrency Factory specification and verification environment; experimental results show that partial-order reduction can be highly effective in combating state explosion in modal mu-calculus model checking.

1 Introduction

Model checking [CE81, QS82, CES86] is a verification technique aimed at determining whether a system specification possesses a property expressed as a temporal logic formula. Model checking has enjoyed wide success in verifying, or finding design errors in, real-life systems. An interesting account of a number of these success stories can be found in [CW96].

Despite these successes, many applications lie beyond the reach of today's generation of model checkers due to the *state explosion* problem. State explosion occurs when a system specification gives rise to an excessively large state space. This problem is particularly compelling in the case of concurrent systems, where a system of n concurrent processes, each with a local state space of size k, can potentially generate a global state space of size k^n. Somewhat mitigating the problem is the fact that, in general, the entire space need not be reachable, since interactions between individual processes may rule out certain evolutions.

Even when the size of the reachable state space is formidable, *local model checking* [SW91] may allow a property to be established without having to explore this state space in its entirety. Nonetheless, the worst case remains exponential in n, and this is illustrated by the simple network of $2n$ processes depicted in Figure 1. Now consider the formula $\nu X. [a] X \wedge \langle\langle - \rangle\rangle \mathtt{tt} \wedge [-a] \mathtt{ff}$ of the weak modal mu-calculus, which states that the visible component of every computation of the system is an infinite sequence of a actions.

A naive algorithm for model checking this formula on the network of Figure 1 would result in the exploration of each of the 2^n reachable global states and $(n+1) \cdot 2^{(n-1)}$ global transitions of the system. Most of these states result from interleaving the system's n τ-transitions in all possible orders, where each τ-transition is the result of a bi-party synchronization. Alternatively, one could exploit the fact that

* Research supported in part by NSF grants CCR–9505562, and AFOSR grants F49620-95-1-0508 and F49620-96-1-0087. Email: {ysr,sas}@cs.sunysb.edu

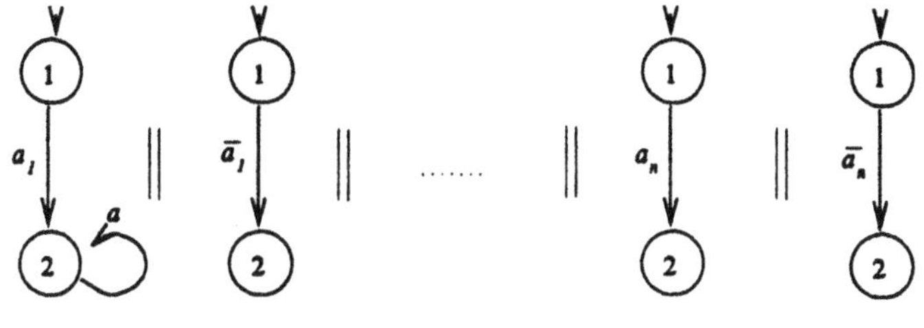

Fig. 1. A simple network of $2n$ processes. Actions a_i and $\bar{a}_i$ may synchronize, CCS-style, giving rise to a τ-transition. Action set $\{a_1, \cdots, a_n\}$ is restricted so that only action a is externally visible.

the τ-transitions are "independent" of one another, and thereby avoid exploring redundant interleavings. This yields a method in which no more than $n+1$ of the reachable states, and $n+1$ of the global transitions need be explored. This observation provides the basis for the partial-order reduction technique we present in this paper.

Partial-order techniques were first introduced for checking simple properties such as absence of deadlock [Val88, GW93]. Subsequently, they were extended to more elaborate properties, in particular, to the model checking of linear-time temporal logic (LTL), without the next-time operator [Val92, Val93, GW94, Pel96]. Recently, several of the techniques for LTL were extended to CTL* [GKPP97, WW96], representing the first application of partial-order reduction to branching-time temporal logic model checking.

Here, we continue this trend by presenting a partial-order reduction technique for the weak modal mu-calculus, a very expressive branching-time temporal logic subsuming, for example, CTL and CTL* (without the next operator) in expressive power. The weak modal mu-calculus can be seen as a variant of the (strong) modal mu-calculus [Koz83]. The essential difference is that the strong modalities $[a]$ and $\langle a \rangle$ (meaning necessarily after a and possibly after a, respectively), are replaced by their weak counterparts $[\![a]\!]$ and $\langle\!\langle a \rangle\!\rangle$. A weak modal mu-calculus formula of the form $[\![a]\!]\,\phi$ means that after performing the observable action a, preceded by and followed by zero or more unobservable τ actions, formula ϕ necessarily holds; similarly for $\langle\!\langle a \rangle\!\rangle\phi$.

The main innovations of our partial-order reduction method for the weak modal mu-calculus are the following:

- It is the first partial-order technique technique to be proposed expressly for a modal mu-calculus, and hence the first technique applicable to event-based models such as labeled transition systems (LTSs). In contrast, LTL, CTL, and CTL* are interpreted over state-based models such as Kripke structures.
- To bridge the gap between partial-order methods for event-based and state-based models, we consider a hybrid model called *doubly labeled transition systems* (DTSs), and proposed originally in [DNV95]. A DTS has action-labeled transitions, like an LTS, and proposition-labeled states, like a Kripke struc-

ture. Within the DTS framework, we show that our partial-order technique is applicable to both the weak modal mu-calculus and nextless CTL/CTL*.

- Unlike previously proposed techniques, our partial-order method requires no information about the semantics of transitions; in particular, there is no need to associate transitions with source-level program operations, and no need to provide an independence relation among operations. Given a hierarchical network of interacting DTSs, our method uses only the structural information present in the network topology and the transition labels on the DTSs. This point is particularly relevant in a modular verification setting, where processes, or concurrent compositions of processes, may be minimized under an equivalence relation before being submitted to model checking. In this case, any association of transitions with program operations may be lost.
- Our notion of independence between transitions is a dynamic one and not, as in previous approaches, fixed at compile time. This distinction is significant as the dynamic approach can lead to greater reductions in the state space explored. Moreover, our check for independence is a purely local one, requiring no transition lookahead. It essentially amounts to checking for the presence of an *inert* transition out of a global state. An inert transition preserves the observable behavior of the system and therefore allows one to "delay" the model checking procedure until the target state of the inert transition is reached. Analogous to previous approaches, care must be taken with cycles of inert transitions.
- We have implemented our technique in the Concurrency Factory specification and verification environment [CLSS96] via a relatively small modification to the code of the existing local model checker for the strong modal mu-calculus. This was made possible by the local nature of our check for inert transitions, and by a translation we provide of the weak modal mu-calculus into the strong modal mu-calculus. Preliminary experimental results show that our method can produce large savings in time and memory when model checking weak modal mu-calculus formulas.

The remainder of this paper is organized as follows. Section 2 introduces the computational model: hierarchical networks of doubly labeled transition systems. Section 3 defines weak bisimulation and inert transitions. Section 4 presents the weak modal mu-calculus. Section 5 then gives a local model checking technique that uses inertness information to cut down on the explored state space. Section 6 presents our experimental results, while Section 7 concludes.

2 Hierarchical Networks of DTSs

In this section, we present a general model of finite-state concurrent composition based on the notion of doubly labeled transition systems (DTSs), and hierarchical networks of DTSs. We use DTSs, proposed originally in [DNV95], to bridge the gap between partial-order methods for state-based models, such as Kripke structures, and event-based models, such as labeled transition systems. Networks of DTSs will be parameterized by a "synchronization algebra" which will allow us to capture many of the extant models of synchronous communication.

In the sequel, we fix a finite set of atomic actions Act, containing a distinguished action τ, and a finite set of primitive propositions $Prop$, containing the logical constants tt and ff.

Definition 1. A *doubly labeled transition system* (DTS) is a tuple $\langle S, \Lambda, \longrightarrow, s_0\rangle$ where S is a finite set of states, $\Lambda : Prop \hookrightarrow 2^S$ is a (partial) valuation function, $\longrightarrow \subseteq S \times Act \times S$ is a transition relation, and s_0 is a distinguished initial state.

A DTS has actions labeling transitions, and propositions labeling states. The proposition valuation function Λ maps propositions to the set of states in which they hold. This function is partial, its domain being the set of propositions "controlled" by the DTS.

DTSs will simultaneously serve as a model for the (weak) modal mu-calculus and CTL/CTL*. We also define hierarchical networks of DTSs; the structural information present in these networks is used by our partial-order method to detect inert transitions. Networks are constructed according to the following grammar:

$$N ::= D \mid \Pi_{\mathcal{A}}\langle N_1, \cdots, N_n\rangle \mid N[f]$$

where D is a DTS; $\Pi_{\mathcal{A}}$ is a parallel composition operator, parameterized by a synchronization algebra $\mathcal{A}$; and f is a relabeling operator, a partial function sending actions to actions, and propositions to propositions, and satisfying $f(\tau) = \tau$, and f restricted to $Prop$ is injective. We denote by $\mathcal{N}$ the class of all network expressions generated by the above grammar. For n a natural number, we shall also write $[n]$ for the set $\{1, 2, \cdots, n\}$.

A synchronization algebra specifies the permitted synchronizations in a network, and is given by a set of identities of the form $\beta = a_1 \cdot a_2 \cdots a_k$, with $a_i \in Act \setminus \{\tau\}$, $\beta \in Act$. We also need the notion of the observable propositions $\mathrm{prop}(N)$ of a network N, defined inductively as follows:

$$\begin{aligned}
\mathrm{prop}(D) &= \mathrm{dom}\,\Lambda, \text{ for a DTS } D = \langle S, \Lambda, \longrightarrow, s_0\rangle \\
\mathrm{prop}(\Pi_{\mathcal{A}}\langle N_1, \cdots, N_n\rangle) &= \biguplus_{i\in[n]}\mathrm{prop}(N_i) \\
\mathrm{prop}(N[f]) &= \{ f(p) \mid p \in \mathrm{prop}(N) \cap \mathrm{dom}\, f \}
\end{aligned}$$

We require that the observable propositions of the operands of a parallel composition are pairwise disjoint.

Synchronization algebras allow us to capture many of the extant models of synchronous communication, and therefore increase the overall applicability of our partial-order method. For example, synchronization algebras can be devised for the binary communication of CCS and the n-ary communication of CSP. They also permit simultaneous synchronizations at different levels of the composition hierarchy. Asynchronous bounded-buffer communication can be modeled by explicitly introducing "buffer processes" between the communicating entities. Synchronization algebras play a role similar to that of the communication function of ACP [BK84].

If $\bar{s} = \langle s_i\rangle_{i\in[n]}$ is an n-tuple, we write $\bar{s}[t/s_j]$ for $\bar{s}$ with s_j replaced by t. To give semantics to network expressions, we associate with each $N \in \mathcal{N}$, a DTS $[\![N]\!]$ defined inductively as follows.

- $[\![D]\!] = D$

- if $[N_i] = \langle S_i, \Lambda_i, \longrightarrow_i, s_i^0 \rangle$, $i \in [n]$, then $[[\Pi_{\mathcal{A}} \langle N_i \rangle_{i \in [n]}]] = \langle S, \Lambda, \longrightarrow, s^0 \rangle$, where

$$
\begin{aligned}
S &= S_1 \times \cdots \times S_n \\
\Lambda(p)(\langle s_1, \cdots, s_n \rangle) &= \Lambda_i(p)(s_i), \text{ if } p \in \mathrm{prop}(N_i) \\
s^0 &= \langle s_1^0, \cdots, s_n^0 \rangle
\end{aligned}
$$

and $\longrightarrow$ is the least relation satisfying the following rules:

$$
\frac{\forall i \in I \subseteq [n].\ s_i \xrightarrow{a_i}_i t_i}{\langle s_j \rangle_{j \in [n]} \xrightarrow{\beta} (\langle s_j \rangle_{j \in [n]})\,[t_i/s_i]_{i \in I}} \quad [(\beta = \Pi_{i \in I} a_i) \in \mathcal{A}]
$$

$$
\frac{s_i \xrightarrow{a_i}_i t_i}{\langle s_j \rangle_{j \in [n]} \xrightarrow{a_i} (\langle s_j \rangle_{j \in [n]})\,[t_i/s_i]}
$$

- if $[N] = \langle S, \Lambda, \longrightarrow, s^0 \rangle$, then $[N[f]] = \langle S, \Lambda', \longrightarrow', s^0 \rangle$ where

$$
\Lambda'(p) = \Lambda(f^{-1}(p)), \text{ if } p \in (\mathrm{ran}\ f \cap \mathit{Prop})
$$

and $\longrightarrow'$ is the least relation satisfying the following rule:

$$
\frac{s \xrightarrow{\alpha} t}{s \xrightarrow{\beta}' t} \quad [f(\alpha) = \beta]
$$

The first $\Pi_{\mathcal{A}}$ rule states that a subset of the processes in a parallel composition can take a joint step, giving rise to a β-transition, provided that this is permitted by the synchronization algebra, and that each of the participating processes can perform the requisite a_i-transitions. The second $\Pi_{\mathcal{A}}$ rule states that components in a parallel composition may also interleave their transitions. The rule for $[f]$ gives the semantics of relabeling; because relabeling functions may be partial, they also provide CCS-style restriction.

3   Weak Bisimulation and Inert Transitions

Our partial-order method will rely on the fact that inert transitions do not change the observable behavior of a network of DTSs. That is, the source and target states of an inert transition are weakly bisimilar. In order to define weak bisimulation on DTSs, we first extend $\longrightarrow$ to the *weak transition relation* $\Longrightarrow$ in the usual way:

$$
\begin{aligned}
\Longrightarrow &= (\xrightarrow{\tau})^* \\
\xLongrightarrow{\alpha} &= \Longrightarrow \xrightarrow{\alpha} \Longrightarrow, \text{ for } \alpha \in Act
\end{aligned}
$$

For an action $\alpha \in Act$, define

$$
\hat{\alpha} = \begin{cases} \alpha & \text{if } \alpha \neq \tau \\ \epsilon & \text{otherwise} \end{cases}
$$

where ϵ denotes the empty string.

Definition 2. Given a DTS $D = \langle S, \Lambda, \longrightarrow, s^0 \rangle$ and $\mathcal{P} \subseteq Prop$, a finite set of primitive propositions, a relation $R \subseteq S \times S$, is a *weak $\mathcal{P}$-bisimulation* if $\langle s, t \rangle \in R$ implies:

- for every $p \in \mathcal{P}$, $\Lambda(p)(s) = \Lambda(p)(t)$
- for every $s' \in S$, $\alpha \in Act$, such that $s \stackrel{\alpha}{\Longrightarrow} s'$, there is a state $t' \in S$ such that $t \stackrel{\hat{\alpha}}{\Longrightarrow} t'$ and $\langle s', t' \rangle \in R$
- for every $t' \in S$, $\alpha \in Act$, such that $t \stackrel{\alpha}{\Longrightarrow} t'$, there is a state $s' \in S$ such that $s \stackrel{\hat{\alpha}}{\Longrightarrow} s'$ and $\langle s', t' \rangle \in R$

Two states s and t are *weakly $\mathcal{P}$-bisimilar*, denoted $s \approx_{\mathcal{P}} t$, if there exists a weak $\mathcal{P}$-bisimulation relation containing the pair (s, t).

Our partial-order technique detects inert transitions in a local fashion, i.e., with no transition lookahead in the network under investigation. The following definitions are needed to formulate the local detection criteria for inert transitions. Let $N \in \mathcal{N}$ be a network of DTSs. Every *global transition* T of N (i.e., a transition of $[\![N]\!]$) is either a transition in some DTS in N or the result of synchronization involving two or more of the DTSs in N. We refer to this set of DTSs as proc(T). Moreover, with each $D \in$ proc(T), we can identify the *local transition* D contributed to this synchronization. This transition is denoted T_D.

Similarly, with each *global state* s of N (i.e., a state of $[\![N]\!]$), we can identify a *local state* s_D, for each DTS D in N. Also, for s a global state of N, we denote by enabled(s) the set of global transitions emanating from s; i.e., global transitions of the form $s \stackrel{a}{\longrightarrow} s'$.

Given a network N with DTSs $\langle D_i \rangle_{i \in [n]}$, it will be convenient to identify a global transition T of N with the tuple $\langle T_{D_i} \rangle_{i \in [n]}$; i.e., the local projections of T on to the DTSs D_i. In the case that a projection T_{D_k} is null, we write "$-$" for that component of T.

Given a local transition T_l of some DTS D in N, define the *neighborhood* of T_l as the collection of DTS sets (each of which includes D) that can possibly synchronize to give rise to a global transition T with $T_D = T_l$. We are only interested in synchronizations involving two or more DTSs, so the size of a DTS set in the neighborhood of T_l is at least two. In general, calculating the exact neighborhood of a local transition entails exploring the entire reachable state space of N. For our purposes, however, an over-approximation of this set suffices. For each DTS D in N, define sort(D) to be the set of action labels on D's transitions. The sort of a DTS can be computed easily from its static structure (its "program text"). Using the sorts of the DTSs of N and N's synchronization algebra, it is now possible to define nbhd(T_l), our approximation to the neighborhood of T_l. The following example should suffice to clarify the definition of nbhd(), and many of the other concepts introduced above.

Example 1. Consider the network $N = (\Pi_{\mathcal{A}} \langle D_1, D_2, D_3, D_4 \rangle)[f]$ of four DTSs depicted in Figure 2, with $\mathcal{A} = \{\tau = a \cdot b, \tau = a \cdot b \cdot c, \tau = a \cdot d, e = c \cdot d\}$ and $f = [\tau \mapsto \tau, e \mapsto e]$. The initial state $\langle 1,1,1,1 \rangle$ of N has three enabled transitions:

$$T_1 : \quad \langle 1,1,1,1 \rangle \stackrel{\tau(=a \cdot b)}{\longrightarrow} \langle 2,2,1,1 \rangle$$

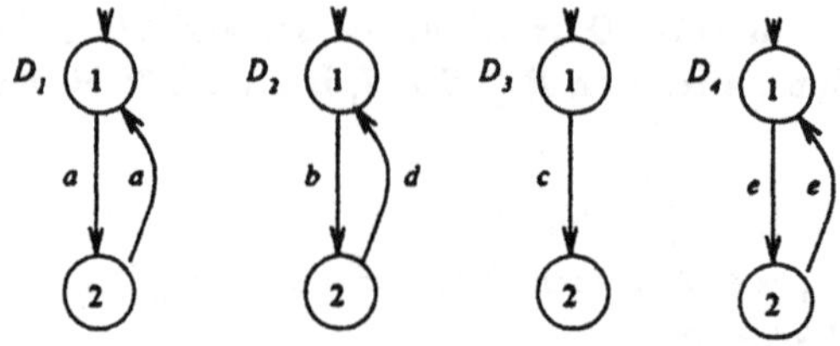

Fig. 2. An example network.

$$T_2: \quad \langle 1,1,1,1 \rangle \xrightarrow{\tau(=a \cdot b \cdot c)} \langle 2,2,2,1 \rangle$$
$$T_3: \quad \langle 1,1,1,1 \rangle \xrightarrow{e} \langle 1,1,1,2 \rangle$$

with $\mathrm{proc}(T_1) = \{D_1, D_2\}$ and T_1 having projections $(T_1)_{D_1} = 1 \xrightarrow{a} 2$ and $(T_1)_{D_2} = 1 \xrightarrow{b} 2$ on D_1 and D_2, respectively. Identifying T_1 with the tuple of its local projections yields $T_1 = \langle 1 \xrightarrow{a} 2, 1 \xrightarrow{b} 2, -, - \rangle$, where "$-$" represents the null projection. Note that, according to this convention, it makes sense to say, for example, that T_1 is enabled in state $\langle 1,1,1,1 \rangle$ as well as in state $\langle 1,1,2,2 \rangle$. In general, a global transition T is enabled in any global state s such that for every $D \in \mathrm{proc}(T)$, local transition T_D is enabled in local state s_D.

The neighborhoods of local transitions can be obtained from the synchronization algebra and the sorts of the DTSs. For instance, since $\tau = a \cdot b$, $\tau = a \cdot b \cdot c$, and $\tau = a \cdot d$ are the only synchronizations possible for a transition with label a, and since $\mathrm{sort}(D_1) = \{a\}$, $\mathrm{sort}(D_2) = \{b, d\}$ and $\mathrm{sort}(D_3) = \{c\}$, it is easy to see that the neighborhood of local transition $(T_1)_{D_1} = 1 \xrightarrow{a} 2$ of DTS D_1 is the set $\{\{D_1, D_2\}, \{D_1, D_2, D_3\}\}$. Similarly, the neighborhood of transition $(T_2)_{D_3} = 1 \xrightarrow{c} 2$ of D_3 is $\{\{D_1, D_2, D_3\}, \{D_2, D_3\}\}$.

In the sequel, we shall sometimes write $s \xrightarrow{T} s'$ to denote the fact that the execution of transition T in state s results in state s'. We are now ready to formally define inert transitions.

Definition 3. Let $N \in \mathcal{N}$ be a network expression such that $[\![N]\!] = \langle S, \Lambda, \longrightarrow, s^0 \rangle$, and let $T = s \xrightarrow{\alpha} s'$ be a global transition of N. Moreover, let $\mathcal{P}$ be a subset of *Prop*, the set of primitive propositions. Then T is $\mathcal{P}$-*inert* if the following conditions hold:

1. $\alpha = \mathrm{action}(T) = \tau$
2. $\forall p \in \mathcal{P}. \ \Lambda(p)(s) = \Lambda(p)(s')$
3. $\forall T' \in \mathrm{enabled}(s). \ T' \neq T \ \Rightarrow \ \mathrm{proc}(T') \cap \mathrm{proc}(T) = \emptyset$
4. $\forall D \in \mathrm{proc}(T). \ \forall T'_D \in \mathrm{enabled}(s_D). \ \forall \mathcal{D} \in \mathrm{nbhd}(T'_D).$
   $\qquad \mathcal{D} \setminus \mathrm{proc}(T) \neq \emptyset \ \Rightarrow \ \exists D' \in \mathcal{D}. \ \mathrm{enabled}(s_{D'}) = \emptyset$

Conditions 1 and 2 are self-explanatory. Condition 3 stipulates that T does not share a common component with T', thereby ensuring that T can neither disable, nor be disabled by, any other global transition enabled in s. Finally, condition 4 ensures that the occurrence of T does not preclude any *future* observable behavior of the system. To see this, let D be a DTS in proc(T) contributing local transition T_D to the execution of T. Now let T'_D be another local transition of D enabled in s_D. Condition 4 states that if T'_D could potentially be part of some future global transition T', then the occurrence of T' is ruled out by a deadlock in some other component DTS of T'.

Note that condition 4 can be weakened. For example, instead of requiring some component DTS of T' to be deadlocked, we could merely ask that this DTS never be able to execute a transition with a label needed for T' to occur.[2]

Example 2. Recall the network of Example 1 and the three transitions T_1, T_2, T_3 enabled in its initial state $\langle 1,1,1,1\rangle$. None of these transitions is inert: T_1 and T_2 violate, for instance, condition 3, while T_3 violates condition 1.

In state $s = \langle 2,2,2,1\rangle$ there are two enabled transitions: T'_1: $\langle 2,2,2,1\rangle \xrightarrow{\tau(=a.d)} \langle 1,1,2,1\rangle$ and T'_2: $\langle 2,2,2,1\rangle \xrightarrow{e} \langle 2,2,2,2\rangle$. The reader can verify that T'_1 is inert. If D_3 is modified to include two new local transitions, $2 \xrightarrow{\tau} 3$ and $3 \xrightarrow{c} 1$, then state s would have one more enabled transition, T'_3 : $\langle 2,2,2,1\rangle \xrightarrow{\tau} \langle 2,2,3,1\rangle$. T'_1 would no longer be inert in this modified system, since it would violate condition 4. However, if the second of the two newly added transitions was removed, then, although by Definition 3 T'_1 would still not be inert, it would be deemed inert by the weakened version of condition 4 discussed above.

Proposition 4. *If $T \in$ enabled(s) is $\mathcal{P}$-inert in global state s, then $T \in$ enabled(t) is $\mathcal{P}$-inert in global state t, where t is any state reachable from s by the execution of a transition $T' \neq T$.*

From Proposition 4, we can conclude that an inert transition cannot be disabled by any other transition. It is also easy to show, along similar lines, that an inert transition cannot disable any other transition. We therefore have:

Proposition 5. *An inert transition can neither disable, nor be disabled by, the execution of any other transition.*

The conditions of Definition 3 ensure that the effect of an inert transition is felt only at a subset of the DTSs comprising a network, and that this subset remains "frozen" until the inert transition occurs, irrespective of any other activities in the system. As a consequence, we can show the following:

Proposition 6. *If T is an inert transition enabled in state s, and $\mathcal{T}$ is any finite sequence of transitions not containing T such that $s \xrightarrow{T}\xrightarrow{\mathcal{T}} t$, then for any splitting of the sequence $\mathcal{T}$ into sequences $\mathcal{T}_1$ and $\mathcal{T}_2$, where either of $\mathcal{T}_1$ or $\mathcal{T}_2$ could be the empty sequence, it is the case that $s \xrightarrow{\mathcal{T}_1}\xrightarrow{T}\xrightarrow{\mathcal{T}_2} t$.*

[2] An approximation to this condition can be obtained by checking that such a transition will never be *locally* possible. Observe that we need only examine the local state space of a DTS in order to check this condition, and in practice the state space of a single DTS is usually not very large. However, since the check is in a strict sense not local, requiring the generation of the entire state space of the DTS, we have not used this weaker condition in Definition 3.

We can now present the main result of this section.

Lemma 7. *Let $N \in \mathcal{N}$ be a network with $[N] = \langle S, \Lambda, \longrightarrow, s_0 \rangle$, such that T is a $\mathcal{P}$-inert transition of N from s to t, $s, t \in S$. Then $s \approx_{\mathcal{P}} t$.*

Proof. It is enough to show that the relation R defined by:

$$R = \mathbf{Id}_S \cup \left\{ \langle u, v \rangle \;\middle|\; u, v \in S, T' : u \xrightarrow{\tau} v, T' \text{ is } \mathcal{P}\text{-inert} \right\}$$

is a weak $\mathcal{P}$-bisimulation. Consider a pair $\langle u, v \rangle \in R$, such that there is a $\mathcal{P}$-inert transition T' from u to v. We prove below that R satisfies the three conditions of weak $\mathcal{P}$-bisimulation.

1. By condition 2 of Definition 3, $\Lambda(p)(u) = \Lambda(p)(v)$ for all $p \in \mathcal{P}$.
2. Let $u' \in S$ such that $u \stackrel{\alpha}{\Longrightarrow} u'$. Aiming to show that there is a v' satisfying $v \stackrel{\hat{\alpha}}{\Longrightarrow} v'$ and $\langle u', v' \rangle \in R$, we consider two cases:
   [CASE 1] Let T' be part of the sequence $\mathcal{T}$ of transitions in $u \stackrel{\alpha}{\Longrightarrow} u'$. Consider the first occurrence of T' in $\mathcal{T}$, and let $\mathcal{T}_1$ be the sequence of transitions preceding and $\mathcal{T}_2$ the sequence succeeding that occurrence, i.e. $u \xrightarrow{\mathcal{T}_1} \xrightarrow{T'} u'' \xrightarrow{\mathcal{T}_2} u'$. Proposition 6 allows us to conclude that $u \xrightarrow{T'} \xrightarrow{\mathcal{T}_1} u'' \xrightarrow{\mathcal{T}_2} u'$. But $u \xrightarrow{T'} v$, so we have $u \xrightarrow{T'} v \xrightarrow{\mathcal{T}_1} u'' \xrightarrow{\mathcal{T}_2} u'$. Since action$(T') = \tau$, and $u \stackrel{\alpha}{\Longrightarrow} u'$, we have $v \stackrel{\hat{\alpha}}{\Longrightarrow} u'$. Since $\langle u', u' \rangle \in R$, we are done.
   [CASE 2] Now consider the case when T' is not part of the sequence $\mathcal{T}$ constituting $u \stackrel{\alpha}{\Longrightarrow} u'$. By Proposition 5, $T' \in$ enabled(u'), so let $u' \xrightarrow{T'} v'$. By construction, we have $\langle u', v' \rangle \in R$. Since $u \xrightarrow{\mathcal{T}} u' \xrightarrow{T'} v'$, using Proposition 6, we have $u \xrightarrow{T'} \xrightarrow{\mathcal{T}} v'$. But since $u \xrightarrow{T'} v$, and action$(T') = \tau$, we can conclude that $v \stackrel{\hat{\alpha}}{\Longrightarrow} v'$.
3. Let $v' \in S$ such that $v \stackrel{\alpha}{\Longrightarrow} v'$. Since $u \xrightarrow{T'} v$, and since action$(T') = \tau$, by condition 1 of Definition 3, we have $u \stackrel{\hat{\alpha}}{\Longrightarrow} v'$. But $\langle v', v' \rangle \in R$ by construction.

■

4 The Weak Modal Mu-Calculus

In this section, we present the syntax and semantics (w.r.t. DTSs) of the modal mu-calculus, and its variant, the weak modal mu-calculus. There are several different presentations of the modal mu-calculus, and we use here the equational version [BC96].

To define the syntax of the equational mu-calculus of [BC96], assume that we have a set *Var* of propositional variables, with X,Y ranging over *Var*, and (recall) a set *Prop* of primitive propositions, with p,q ranging over *Prop*. The set of ***basic formulas*** of the equational mu-calculus is given by the following:

$$\phi ::= p \mid \neg p \mid X \mid X \vee Y \mid X \wedge Y \mid \langle \alpha \rangle X \mid [\alpha] X$$

Note that negation may only be applied to primitive propositions and that the proper subformulas of a basic formula are variables. An *equational system* E is a finite set of equations $\{X_i = \phi_i\}_i$, where the X_i are distinct and each ϕ_i is a basic formula. Let $\mathrm{lhs}(E) = \{X_i\}_i$ denote the set of variables defined in E, and $\mathrm{rhs}(E, X_i) = \phi_i$ the right-hand side of X_i in E.

A *block* B has the form νE or μE, where E is an equational system. B is called a *ν-block* in the former case and a *μ-block* in the latter. Let $\mathrm{lhs}(B) = \mathrm{lhs}(E)$, and for $X \in \mathrm{lhs}(B)$, let $\mathrm{rhs}(B, X) = \mathrm{rhs}(E, X)$. A *formula* has the form X in $\mathcal{B}$, where $\mathcal{B} = \langle B_1, \cdots, B_n\rangle$ is a list of blocks such that $\mathrm{lhs}(B_i) \cap \mathrm{lhs}(B_j) = \emptyset$ whenever $i \neq j$. We denote by $L_\mu(\mathcal{P})$ the set of all equational mu-calculus formulas over the set $\mathcal{P} \subseteq Prop$ of primitive propositions, and simply write L_μ when $\mathcal{P}$ is $Prop$.

The semantics of basic formulas is defined with respect to a given DTS $D = \langle S, \Lambda, \longrightarrow, s_0\rangle$, and *environment* $e : Var \rightarrow 2^S$ assigning meaning to propositional variables. Let $\mathrm{env}(D)$ be the set of functions $Var \rightarrow 2^S$. The semantic function $[\![\cdot]\!]_D\,(e)$ maps a basic formula ϕ to the set of states satisfying ϕ.

$$
\begin{aligned}
[\![\mathrm{tt}]\!]_D\,(e) &= S\\
[\![\mathrm{ff}]\!]_D\,(e) &= \emptyset\\
[\![p]\!]_D\,(e) &= \{\, s \in S \mid p \in \Lambda(s)\,\}\\
[\![\neg p]\!]_D\,(e) &= \{\, s \in S \mid p \notin \Lambda(s)\,\}\\
[\![X]\!]_D\,(e) &= e(X)\\
[\![X_1 \vee X_2]\!]_D\,(e) &= [\![X_1]\!]_D\,(e) \cup [\![X_2]\!]_D\,(e)\\
[\![X_1 \wedge X_2]\!]_D\,(e) &= [\![X_1]\!]_D\,(e) \cap [\![X_2]\!]_D\,(e)\\
[\![\langle a\rangle X]\!]_D\,(e) &= \left\{ s \in S \;\middle|\; \exists s'.\, s \stackrel{a}{\longrightarrow} s' \text{ and } s' \in [\![X]\!]_D\,(e) \right\}\\
[\![[a] X]\!]_D\,(e) &= \left\{ s \in S \;\middle|\; \forall s'.\, s \stackrel{a}{\longrightarrow} s' \text{ implies } s' \in [\![X]\!]_D\,(e) \right\}
\end{aligned}
$$

To define the semantics of formulas, we first lift the semantic function $[\![\cdot]\!]_D\,(e)$ to block lists; the meaning of a block list $\mathcal{B}$, defined inductively on the length of $\mathcal{B}$, will be an environment in $\mathrm{env}(D)$. If $\mathcal{B}$ is empty, we take $[\![\mathcal{B}]\!]_D\,(e) = e$. If $\mathcal{B} = \langle B_1, \cdots, B_n\rangle$ is nonempty and B_1 is a ν-block, then $[\![\mathcal{B}]\!]_D\,(e)$ is the greatest fixed point of a certain function $f_{\mathcal{B},e}$ interpreted over the lattice obtained by ordering environments using pointwise set inclusion. Dually, if B_1 is a μ-block, then $[\![\mathcal{B}]\!]_D\,(e)$ is the least fixed point of $f_{\mathcal{B},e}$. The existence of these fixed points follows from the Knaster-Tarski theorem.

Let $\mathcal{V} \subseteq Var$. To define $f_{\mathcal{B},e}$, we shall write $e[e'/\mathcal{V}]$ to denote environment e updated such that the variables in $\mathcal{V}$ are interpreted according to e'; i.e.

$$
e[e'/V](X) = \begin{cases} e'(X) & \text{if } X \in \mathcal{V}\\ e(X) & \text{otherwise} \end{cases}
$$

Function $f_{\mathcal{B},e} : \mathrm{env}(D) \rightarrow \mathrm{env}(D)$ is defined as follows for $X \in \mathrm{lhs}(\mathcal{B})$, $\mathcal{B} = \langle B_1, \cdots, B_n\rangle$:

$$
f_{\mathcal{B},e}(e')(X) = \begin{cases} [\![\mathrm{rhs}(B_1, X)]\!]_D\,([\![\langle B_2, \cdots, B_n\rangle]\!]_D\,(e[e'/\mathrm{lhs}(\mathcal{B})])) & \text{if } X \in \mathrm{lhs}(B_1)\\ [\![\langle B_2, \cdots, B_n\rangle]\!]_D\,(e[e'/\mathrm{lhs}(\mathcal{B})]) & \text{otherwise} \end{cases}
$$

A formula X in $\mathcal{B}$ may now be interpreted as follows: $[\![X \text{ in } \mathcal{B}]\!]_D(e) = ([\![\mathcal{B}]\!]_D(e))(X)$. If the formula is closed—all variables used in rhs($\mathcal{B}$) appear in lhs($\mathcal{B}$)—then its meaning is independent of e; in this case we write $[\![X \text{ in } \mathcal{B}]\!]_D$.

Given a DTS $D = \langle S, A, \longrightarrow, s_0\rangle$ (or, alternatively, a network $N \in \mathcal{N}$ with $[\![N]\!] = \langle S, A, \longrightarrow, s_0\rangle$), and an L_μ formula X in $\mathcal{B}$, the *model checking* problem is to determine whether $s_0 \in [\![X \text{ in } \mathcal{B}]\!]_D$.

The weak equational mu-calculus (the equational variant of the weak modal mu-calculus) is obtained from L_μ by replacing the modalities $[\alpha]$ and $\langle\alpha\rangle$ with the "weak" modalities $[\![a]\!]$ and $\langle\!\langle a\rangle\!\rangle$, $a \in (Act\setminus\{\tau\})\cup\{\epsilon\}$. Notice that there are no weak counterparts to $[\tau]$ and $\langle\tau\rangle$, but there are the "empty" modalities $[\![\,]\!]$ and $\langle\!\langle\,\rangle\!\rangle$. We denote by $L^w_\mu(\mathcal{P})$ the set of all weak equational mu-calculus formulas over the set $\mathcal{P} \subseteq Prop$ of primitive propositions, and write L^w_μ when $\mathcal{P} = Prop$.

The semantics of the weak modalities is given by means of the $\Longrightarrow$ relation introduced in Section 2:

$$[\![\langle\!\langle a\rangle\!\rangle X]\!]_D(e) = \left\{ s \in S \;\middle|\; \exists s'.\, s \overset{a}{\Longrightarrow} s' \text{ and } s' \in [\![X]\!]_D(e) \right\}$$

$$[\![\,[\![a]\!]\, X\,]\!]_D(e) = \left\{ s \in S \;\middle|\; \forall s'.\, s \overset{a}{\Longrightarrow} s' \text{ implies } s' \in [\![X]\!]_D(e) \right\}$$

As observed in [Liu92], the weak modal mu-calculus is actually a fragment of the strong calculus. That is, we can show that for every L^w_μ formula X in $\mathcal{B}$ and every DTS D, there exists an L_μ formula X in $h(\mathcal{B})$ such that $[\![X \text{ in } \mathcal{B}]\!]_D = [\![X \text{ in } h(\mathcal{B})]\!]_D$. The essential idea of the translation is to capture the semantics of the weak modalities with an additional fixed point computation, and concomitantly replace weak modalities with their strong counterparts. For example, the L^w_μ formula ψ given by X_0 in $\langle \mu\{X_0 = [\![a]\!] X_1,\;\; X_1 = X_2 \wedge X_0,\;\; X_2 = p\}\rangle$ translates to the following L_μ formula ψ':

$$\begin{aligned} X_0 \text{ in } \langle\, &\mu\{\, X_0 = X_3,\;\; X_1 = X_2 \wedge X_0,\;\; X_2 = p\},\\ &\nu\{\, X_3 = X_4 \wedge X_5,\;\; X_4 = [a]\, X_6,\;\; X_5 = [\tau]\, X_3,\\ &\quad X_6 = X_7 \wedge X_1,\;\; X_7 = [\tau]\, X_6\}\rangle \end{aligned}$$

Note that the translation may increase the number of variables (and equations) by at most a factor of six, the number of blocks by at most one, and the alternation-depth [EL86] of the formula by at most one. In particular, an alternation-free formula in L^w_μ may translate into an L_μ formula having alternation depth two (as in the example).

Because DTSs are finite-state, two states are weakly bisimilar precisely if they satisfy the same set of weak modal mu-calculus formulas [Sti92]. Combining this result with Lemma 7, we obtain the following "Preservation Lemma."

Lemma 8. *Let $N \in \mathcal{N}$ be a network expression with $[\![N]\!] = \langle S, A, \longrightarrow, s^0\rangle$, and let T be a $\mathcal{P}$-inert transition from s to t, $s, t \in S$. Then for all $\phi \in L^w_\mu(\mathcal{P})$, $s \in [\![\phi]\!]_{[\![N]\!]}$ if and only if $t \in [\![\phi]\!]_{[\![N]\!]}$.*

5 A Partial-Order Model Checking Algorithm

In this section, we first present *LMC*, our "semi-local" model checking algorithm for L_μ. We then present LMC_{PO}, an extension of *LMC* for model checking L^w_μ formulas, which achieves partial-order reduction through the detection of inert transitions. A version of *LMC* for the alternation-free fragment of L_μ appeared in [Sok96].

5.1 LMC: Semi-Local Model Checking for the Modal Mu-Calculus

Given a network N with $[N] = \langle S, \mathcal{A}, \longrightarrow, s_0\rangle$, and an L_μ formula $\phi = X_0$ in $\mathcal{B}$, *LMC* determines if ϕ holds in s_0 by constructing a *dependency graph* $G_{N,\phi}$: a kind of and-or graph whose vertices are from $S \times \mathcal{V}$, where $\mathcal{V} \subseteq Var$ are the variables in ϕ. The vertices of $G_{N,\phi}$, and therefore the states in S, are constructed in a lazy, demand-driven fashion, using the rules given in Table 1 and starting with the initial vertex $\langle s_0, X_0\rangle$. For example, for a vertex $w = \langle s, X\rangle$, if X is defined in ϕ to be $[a]Y$ and s can reach $\{s_i\}_{i\in[k]}$ via a-labeled transitions, then w has k successors $\{\langle s_i, Y\rangle\}_{i\in[k]}$. The graph itself, however, is explored in a depth-first fashion starting with the initial vertex; thus, at any point during the execution of the algorithm, only some of w's successor vertices may actually have been constructed.

$$\wedge\!: \frac{\langle s, X\rangle}{\langle s, X_1\rangle \quad \langle s, X_2\rangle}\ [X = X_1 \wedge X_2] \qquad\qquad \vee\!: \frac{\langle s, X\rangle}{\langle s, X_1\rangle \quad \langle s, X_2\rangle}\ [X = X_1 \vee X_2]$$

$$\wedge\!: \frac{\langle s, X\rangle}{\langle s_1, Y\rangle \quad \cdots \quad \langle s_k, Y\rangle}\ \left[X = [a]Y,\ \ s \xrightarrow{a} s_1, \cdots, s \xrightarrow{a} s_k\right]$$

$$\vee\!: \frac{\langle s, X\rangle}{\langle s_1, Y\rangle \quad \cdots \quad \langle s_k, Y\rangle}\ \left[X = \langle a\rangle Y,\ \ s \xrightarrow{a} s_1, \cdots, s \xrightarrow{a} s_k\right]$$

Table 1. Rules for constructing the dependency graph.

Associated with each vertex v of $G_{N,\phi}$ is a *type*, denoted $\text{type}(v) \in \{\wedge, \vee, \lambda\}$, as shown to the left of each rule in Table 1. For instance, for the vertex w considered above, its type is $\wedge$. For a vertex for which none of the rules in Table 1 apply, its type is λ, indicating a "leaf node."

Also associated with each vertex v is a *value*, denoted $\text{value}(v) \in \{0, 1, U\}$, which is computed (and kept updated) based on v's type. If $\text{type}(v) = \wedge$ (respectively, $\vee$), then value(v) is the conjunction (respectively, disjunction)[3] of the values of v's successors (if any); otherwise, i.e. if $\text{type}(v) = \lambda$, v is a leaf node with no successors, and its value is defined by:

$$\text{value}(\langle s, X\rangle) = \begin{cases} 1 & \text{if } X = \mathit{tt} \\ 0 & \text{if } X = \mathit{ff} \\ \mathcal{A}(p)(s) & \text{if } X = p \\ 1 - \mathcal{A}(p)(s) & \text{if } X = \neg p \end{cases}$$

[3] Let $Val = \{0, 1, U\}$. The conjunction of a sequence in Val^* is 0 if it is in $Val^*0\,Val^*$, 1 if it is in 1^*, and U otherwise. Dually, the disjunction of a sequence in Val^* is 1 if it is in $Val^*1\,Val^*$, 0 if it is in 0^*, and U otherwise.

When a vertex that is not of type λ is first constructed, it is assigned value U, since its value depends upon those of its successors, which have not yet been determined. The algorithm maintains an up-to-date value for a vertex as new vertices are constructed in the graph. Whenever a new vertex v is constructed whose type is λ, the values of some or all of the U-vertices that are immediate predecessors of v may change; this change may, in turn, affect the values of the next level predecessors. Such backwards propagation of updates is accomplished by lines 8 and 17 of the pseudo-code for the algorithm, which appears in Table 2; a "one-step" back-propagation is performed at line 22. The back-propagation procedure itself, which is not shown in Table 2, merely traverses *backwards* from v, in depth-first fashion, along the edges in the graph modifying values of the vertices as required, and backtracking as soon as it encounters a vertex whose value remains unchanged.

The presence of cycles in $G_{N,\phi}$ complicates the algorithm somewhat. Cycles are possible since ϕ may, in general, involve recursive variable definitions, and the transition relation of $[N]$ may be cyclic. To determine the values of U-vertices lying on cycles, we build $G_{N,\phi}$ in a depth-first fashion, using Tarjan's algorithm [Tar72] to identify maximal strongly connected components (SCCs) of U-vertices. Call such an SCC a U-SCC. As soon as a U-SCC $\mathcal{U}$ is found, a "global" iterative technique, for instance Emerson-Lei [EL86] or Cleaveland-Klein-Steffen [CKS92], is invoked to determine the values of the vertices in $\mathcal{U}$.

The number of vertices in $G_{N,\phi}$ is bounded by $|S| \cdot |\mathcal{V}|$ and thus finte. It is then easy to see that *LMC* will terminate provided that the global iterative technique invoked at line 16 terminates. But a global iterative technique such as [EL86, CKS92] is guaranteed to terminate on finite boolean graphs, which each SCC of $G_{N,\phi}$ is. The following lemma ensures that *LMC* produces the correct result when it terminates.

Lemma 9. *In LMC, if the final value given to a vertex* $\langle s, X\rangle$ *is* 1, *then* $s \in [X \text{ in } \mathcal{B}]_{[N]}$, *and if its final value is* 0, *then* $s \notin [X \text{ in } \mathcal{B}]_{[N]}$.

Let the *SCC-graph* of a dependency graph $G_{N,\phi}$ be the directed graph induced by collapsing the SCCs of $G_{N,\phi}$ into single nodes. Clearly, an SCC-graph is acyclic. *LMC* processes the SCCs of $G_{N,\phi}$ in post-order of $G_{N,\phi}$'s SCC-graph. Thus, the values of vertices in a given SCC can depend upon the values of vertices in the same SCC and, at most, on SCCs earlier in the post-order. The lemma can thus be proved by induction on the "post-order number" of the SCC in which the vertex $v = \langle s, X\rangle$ occurs. It is clear that the algorithm assigns correct values to vertices of type λ (which are singleton SCCs). For the case of non-λ vertices, the correctness follows from the induction hypothesis, the soundness of the rules for assigning values to $\wedge$ and $\vee$ vertices, and the correctness of the global algorithm (EL/CKS) for computing fixed points of boolean graphs.

Time and Space Complexity. Let $|S|$ and $|\longrightarrow|$ denote, respectively, the size of N's reachable state space and transition relation. Let $|\mathcal{V}|$ be the number of variables in ϕ. The number of vertices in $G_{N,\phi}$, then, is bounded by $|S| \cdot |\mathcal{V}|$ and the number of edges is bounded by $(|\longrightarrow| + 2|S|)\,|\mathcal{V}|$. Assume that the visited vertex table *VT* is implemented as a balanced binary tree, allowing insertion and membership operations in time logarithmic in its size. *LMC* then requires time at most $O((|\longrightarrow| + |S|)\,|\mathcal{V}| \log(|S| \cdot |\mathcal{V}|))$, but for the calls to the global algorithm at line 16.

```
0  procedure LMC (N: network with [N] = ⟨S, ⟶, A, s0⟩, X0 in B: Lμ formula)
1      Initialize the DFS stack D := ⟨⟨s0, X0⟩⟩;
2      Initialize the visited vertex table VT := {⟨s0, X0⟩};
3      Initialize the Tarjan stack to TS := ⟨ ⟩;
4      while D is not empty do
5          let v = ⟨s, X⟩ be the top vertex in D;
6          if value(v) ∈ {0, 1} then {
               /* type(v) = λ or value known through back-propagation */
7              pop D;
8              transitively propagate v's value backwards via its U-predecessors;
9          }
10         else {   /* value(v) = U */
11             obtain the next successor v' of v, using the rules in Table 1;
                   /* v' is set to null if v has no more successors */
12             if v' = null then {
13                 pop D;
14                 push v on TS;
15                 if v is the root of an SCC C then {   /* ask Tarjan */
16                     pop the vertices in TS that belong to C,
                           and run a global iterative algorithm (EL/CKS) on C;
                           /* the values of the vertices in C are now determined */
17                     transitively propagate v's value backwards via its U-predecessors;
18                 }
19             }
20             else if value(v') ∈ {0, 1} then {   /* type(v') = λ or v' visited before */
21                 add v' to VT;
22                 update value(v);
23             }
24             else if v' ∉ VT then {   /* value(v') = U and first visit of v' */
25                 add v' to VT;
26                 push v' on D;
27             }
28         }
29     endwhile
30     return value(⟨s0, X0⟩);
31 end   /* LMC */
```

Table 2. Basic algorithm for semi-local model checking in L_μ. At line 11, the successors of v are examined one after the other in, say, left-to-right order, so that each call returns the leftmost successor that has not yet been examined; *null* is returned when all successors have been examined. "EL/CKS" at line 16 represents a call to Emerson-Lei [EL86] or Cleaveland-Klein-Steffen [CKS92].

In particular, this gives us the time complexity for the case of alternation-free formulas, for which a call to the global algorithm is unnecessary.[4]

Consider now a call to the global procedure at line 16 on an SCC of n nodes and e edges, involving $k > 1$ alternations of fixed points. EL takes $O\left(n^{(k+1)}\right)$ time [EL86], while CKS does somewhat better at $O\left(e\,(n/k)^{(k-1)}\right)$ [CKS92]. LMC_{PO}'s worst case behavior manifests when the entire dependency graph is one big SCC, giving an overall upper bound, if using CKS, of $O\left((|\longrightarrow| + |S|)\,|\mathcal{V}|\,(|S| \cdot |\mathcal{V}|/ad)^{(ad-1)}\right)$, where $ad > 1$ is the alternation depth of the L_μ formula. Using EL, instead of CKS, yields $O\left((|S| \cdot |\mathcal{V}|)^{(ad+1)}\right)$.

Since EL and CKS require space linear in the size of the SCC, the overall space complexity of the algorithm is easily seen to be bounded by $O\,(|\longrightarrow| + |S| \cdot |\mathcal{V}|)$.

5.2 Modifying LMC for Partial-Order Reduction

We now present LMC_{PO}, our partial-order-based extension of *LMC* for the local model checking of L_μ^w formulas. By virtue of our procedure for translating any L_μ^w formula into a logically equivalent L_μ formula (discussed in Section 4), LMC_{PO}, like *LMC*, accepts and L_μ formula as input; it differs from *LMC* mainly in its ability to detect and subsequently exploit inert transitions for the purposes of partial-order reduction.

LMC performs on-the-fly construction of the portion of the state space S of $[\![N]\!]$ needed to determine the truth-value of the given L_μ formula. The partial-order technique employed by LMC_{PO} results in on-the-fly construction of a *dynamically reduced* state space S', in which the truth-value of L_μ^w formulas is preserved.

The modifications to *LMC* that yield LMC_{PO} are given in Table 3. The main idea is that whenever a newly constructed vertex $v = \langle s, X\rangle$ is not of type λ (so its value is U) then, instead of using the rules in Table 1 to compute its successors, we try to "postpone" the model checking until reaching a single successor state s' via an inert transition. Intuitively, this partial-order modification attempts to avoid exploring portions of the state-space arising from arbitrary interleaving of inert transitions with other transitions in enabled(s).

To guarantee the soundness of our technique, we first check the "loop non-inertness condition" at line 11.3, which prevents "postponing forever" the evaluation of a subformula X. In the absence of such a check, the evaluation of X could be postponed indefinitely if $[\![N]\!]$'s transition relation contained, at an appropriate point, a cycle consisting only of inert transitions. Thus, a reduction step is permitted only if it does not result in such a cycle of inert transitions in the dependency graph constructed by the algorithm.

If the loop non-inertness condition is met, then $v' = \langle s', X\rangle$ is made the only successor of v, and the construction proceeds with v'. The type of v is ι and its

[4] The global algorithm is not required on any SCC that contains no fixed point alternation. This might be the case even if the original formula does involve alternating fixed points. Observe, also, that the logarithmic factor above drops out if, like in [VL94], we assume the use of a direct-access structure to store VT. We do not, however, make this assumption since the initialization of such a structure goes against the local spirit of the algorithm.

value is defined by value(v) = value(v'). If, however, an inert transition satisfying the loop non-inertness condition is not found, the construction proceeds as usual, by trying to obtain a successor of v using the rules in Table 1. Observe that when evaluating the inertness of a transition for the vertex $\langle s, X\rangle$, we require only $\mathcal{P}$-inertness, where $\mathcal{P}$ = prop(X) is the set of primitive state propositions mentioned on the right-hand sides of the variables that X transitively depends upon.

Modify procedure *LMC* of Table 2 as follows:

- replace line 0 of procedure *LMC* with the following:

```
0   procedure LMC_PO (N: network with [N] = ⟨S, ⟶, A, s₀⟩,
                      X₀ in B: L_μ formula obtained by translating
                               an L_μ^w formula as outlined in Section 4)
```

- replace line 11 of procedure *LMC* with the following:

```
11.1        P := prop(X);
11.2        if type(v) = ι then {
11.3            if ∃T ∈ enabled(s) s.t. T is P-inert, s —T→ s', and
                    either ⟨s', X⟩ ∉ D or else
                    the induced loop has some non-inert transition then {
11.4                v' := ⟨s', X⟩;
11.5                make v' a successor of v;
11.6            }
11.7            else set type(v) according to Table 1;   /* type(v) ≠ ι now */
11.8        }
11.9        if type(v) ≠ ι then
11.10           obtain the next successor v' of v, using the rules in Table 1;
```

- insert the following line between lines 24 and 25 of procedure *LMC*:

```
24.1            type(v') := ι;   /* each non-λ vertex is a potential candidate */
```

Table 3. Modifications to procedure *LMC* required to obtain LMC_{PO}, a model checking algorithm with partial-order reduction. The text describes how prop(X) at line 11.1 is computed, and how the "loop non-inertness" condition at line 11.3 is checked.

Concerning the loop non-inertness condition at line 11.3, it is easy to see that an inert cycle can result only if v' lies on the depth-first stack D. Information about whether a vertex is on D is kept in a single bit with each vertex, which is set when the vertex is pushed on D (lines 1 and 26) and reset when it is popped from D (line 13). When v' is on D, we perform an inexpensive check of the following "Tarjan condition," which when true guarantees that the resulting cycle C has a non-inert transition. Let w be the vertex at the top of the Tarjan stack TS, which is used to accumulate SCCs. If the depth-first number of w is greater than that of v', there must be a branch from some vertex $u \in C$ that leads to w. Therefore, type(u) $\neq \iota$, as vertices of type ι cannot have more than one successor, and C does not constitute an inert cycle. When the Tarjan condition fails to hold, we have the choice of either exhaustively checking C to see if it has a non-ι vertex, or of pessimistically assuming that it does not. In practice, the situation where the Tarjan condition fails and C has a non-inert transition is so rare that either choice appears to make little difference in running time or memory usage (the Concurrency Factory implementation uses the former strategy).

The main sublemma required to prove the counterpart of Lemma 9 for LMC_{PO}, is the following.

Lemma 10. *Let* $v = \langle s, X\rangle$ *be a vertex of* $G_{N,\phi}$ *with* type(v) $= \iota$ *when* LMC_{PO} *terminates. Then there is an* L_μ^w *formula* ϕ *that is logically equivalent to the* L_μ *formula* X in B, *i.e. for every DTS* D, $[\![\phi]\!]_D = [\![X \text{ in } B]\!]_D$.

Since the construction of the reduced dependency graph $G_{N,\phi}$ by LMC_{PO} avoids inert cycles, we can now invoke the Preservation Lemma (Lemma 8) to prove a version of Lemma 9 for LMC_{PO}.

As an illustration of Lemma 10, recall (Section 4) the translation of the example L_μ^w formula ψ into the L_μ formula ψ'. If in the course of model checking ψ' LMC_{PO} applies a partial-order reduction step at vertex $\langle s, X\rangle$, then X is either the main variable X_0 (the reduction step was applied at the initial state), or *a variable immediately following an action modality* in ψ' (the reduction step was applied following a change in the state component of a vertex, and this can happen only when an action modality is expanded). Since each variable X in ψ' that was also present in ψ is already equivalent to an L_μ^w formula, we can restrict our attention to variables X_3 and X_6, which are new variables introduced by the translation and which immediately follow some action modality in ψ'. X_6 is logically equivalent to $[\,]X_1$, and X_3 is logically equivalent to $[a]X_6$, which is equivalent to $[a]X_1$.

5.3 The Case of CTL*\X

In [BC96], Bhat and Cleaveland give a translation from CTL* into the alternation-depth-two fragment of L_μ. We use this result to apply our partial-order reduction technique to the nextless fragment CTL*\X of CTL*.

Suppose that we modify the definition of inertness of a transition so that the first condition of Definition 3 is dropped. It can be shown that a version of the Preservation Lemma holds for CTL*\X formulas under this weakened notion of inertness. The reason the first condition is not needed is that a CTL*\X formula cannot "name" the action on a transition. In this sense, the labels on global transitions are irrelevant, and may all be replaced by a single action label "·" as in [BC96]. Note, however, that the labels on local transitions are still needed to detect inert transitions. Now, for any CTL*\X formula ϕ, an equivalent L_μ formula ϕ' can be obtained using the Bhat-Cleaveland translation. We can then show that invoking LMC_{PO} on ϕ' and the "·"-transition-labeled global DTS correctly model checks ϕ.

6 Experimental Results

LMC_{PO} has been implemented in the Concurrency Factory and has proved quite effective in reducing the time and space requirements for model checking. Table 4 shows the reduction in the size of the explored dependency graph (and thus the size of the explored state space) and in memory usage when partial-order reduction is applied. The examples are from the SPIN benchmark suite.

Leader is a leader election protocol in a unidirectional ring, due to Dolev, Klawe and Rodeh. We checked several properties of four instances of the protocol for ring sizes ranging from two to five processes. The capacity of the links is assumed to be 10. DFS is an instrumentation run that constructs the entire reachable state space of the system, which, in the case of partial-order reduction, is a reduced state space. LFP is a formula that asserts that in every run at least one leader is elected. NST is a nested fixed point formula asserting that in every run precisely one leader is elected.

Sieve is the primality testing system known as the sieve of Eratosthenes, for which we checked instances ranging from an array of two to six processors, with a link capacity of one. Observe that the growth in the size of the dependency graph, and in the space requirements, goes from being exponential in the number of processes to linear.

7 Conclusion

We have presented a partial-order reduction technique for the weak modal mu-calculus, which we have incorporated into the Concurrency Factory's local model checker. The main change required was the insertion of code to detect and subsequently exploit inert transitions for partial-order reduction. Initial experimental results indicate that appreciable savings in time and memory usage can be obtained for many applications.

As we have indicated, the weak modal mu-calculus is a fragment of the (strong) modal mu-calculus. It would be interesting to see what other useful fragments can be handled by an inert-transition-based approach to partial-order reduction.

Acknowledgements. We thank Xinxin Liu for valuable comments on this work, and Gerard Holzmann and Doron Peled for providing us with the SPIN benchmarks, and for making available [GKPP97].

References

[AH96] R. Alur and T. A. Henzinger, editors. *Computer Aided Verification (CAV '96)*, volume 1102 of *Lecture Notes in Computer Science*, New Brunswick, New Jersey, July 1996. Springer-Verlag.

[BC96] G. S. Bhat and R. Cleaveland. Efficient model checking via the equational μ-calculus. In Clarke [Cla96], pages 304–312.

[BK84] J. A. Bergstra and J. W. Klop. Process algebra for synchronous communication. *Information and Computation*, 60:109–137, 1984.

[CE81] E. M. Clarke and E. A. Emerson. Design and synthesis of synchronization skeletons using branching-time temporal logic. In D. Kozen, editor, *Proceedings of the Workshop on Logic of Programs*, Yorktown Heights, volume 131 of *Lecture Notes in Computer Science*, pages 52–71. Springer-Verlag, 1981.

[CES86] E. M. Clarke, E. A. Emerson, and A. P. Sistla. Automatic verification of finite-state concurrent systems using temporal logic specifications. *ACM TOPLAS*, 8(2), 1986.

Formula	Program	No P.O. Reduction		With P.O. Reduction	
		Vertices	Memory (MB)	Vertices	Memory (MB)
DFS	leader2	36	0.057	24	0.049
	leader3	134	0.189	62	0.098
	leader4	633	1.106	272	0.361
	leader5	2196	5.710	547	0.934
LFP	leader2	128	0.082	39	0.049
	leader3	478	0.344	82	0.115
	leader4	2254	2.220	313	0.410
	leader5	7748	11.665	577	0.965
NST	leader2	108	0.057	49	0.049
	leader3	402	0.213	122	0.139
	leader4	1899	1.229	239	0.647
	leader5	6588	6.177	1086	1.753
DFS	sieve1	204	0.090	91	0.058
	sieve2	699	0.352	117	0.107
	sieve3	2481	1.646	134	0.131
	sieve4	8481	7.741	149	0.155
	sieve5	26868	33.571	162	0.189
	sieve6	70645	115.237	173	0.213
LFP	sieve1	362	0.107	93	0.058
	sieve2	2597	0.721	122	0.107
	sieve3	9109	3.473	139	0.131
	sieve4	30753	16.286	154	0.163
	sieve5	95885	70.091	167	0.189
	sieve6	248811	238.100	178	0.221
GFP	sieve1	612	0.115	95	0.058
	sieve2	2097	0.451	126	0.107
	sieve3	7443	1.966	143	0.131
	sieve4	25443	8.839	158	0.155
	sieve5	80604	37.462	171	0.189
	sieve6	211935	125.452	182	0.221

Table 4. Illustrating the effect of partial-order reduction.

[CKS92] R. Cleaveland, M. Klein, and B. Steffen. Faster model checking for the modal mu-calculus. In G.v. Bochmann and D.K. Probst, editors, *Computer Aided Verification (CAV '92)*, volume 663 of *Lecture Notes in Computer Science*, pages 410–422, Montréal, June/July 1992. Springer-Verlag.

[Cla96] E. M. Clarke, editor. *11th Annual Symposium on Logic in Computer Science (LICS '96)*, New Brunswick, NJ, July 1996. Computer Society Press.

[CLSS96] R. Cleaveland, P. M. Lewis, S. A. Smolka, and O. Sokolsky. The Concurrency Factory: A development environment for concurrent systems. In Alur and Henzinger [AH96], pages 398–401.

[Cou93] C. Courcoubetis, editor. *Computer Aided Verification (CAV '93)*, volume 693 of *Lecture Notes in Computer Science*, Elounda, Greece, June 1993. Springer-Verlag.

[CW96] E. M. Clarke and J. M. Wing. Formal methods: State of the art and future directions. *ACM Computing Surveys*, 28(4), December 1996.

[DNV95] R. De Nicola and F.W. Vaandrager. Three logics for branching bisimulation. *Journal of the ACM*, 42(2):458–487, March 1995.

[EL86] E. A. Emerson and C.-L. Lei. Efficient model checking in fragments of the propositional mu-calculus. In *Proceedings of the First Annual Symposium on Logic in Computer Science*, pages 267–278, 1986.

[GKPP97] R. Gerth, R. Kuiper, W. Penczek, and D. Peled. A partial order approach to branching time model checking. *Information and Computation*, 1997.

[GW93] P. Godefroid and P. Wolper. Using partial orders for the efficient verification of deadlock freedom and safety properties. *Formal Methods in System Design*, 2:149–164, 1993.

[GW94] P. Godefroid and P. Wolper. A partial approach to model checking. *Information and Computation*, 110(2):305–326, May 1994.

[Koz83] D. Kozen. Results on the propositional μ-calculus. *Theoretical Computer Science*, 27:333–354, 1983.

[Liu92] X. Liu. *Specification and Decomposition in Concurrency*, Technical Report No. R 92-2005. PhD thesis, Department of Computer Science, Aalborg University, 1992.

[Pel96] D. Peled. Combining partial order reductions with on-the-fly model-checking. *Formal Methods in System Design*, 8(1):39–64, January 1996.

[QS82] J. P. Queille and J. Sifakis. Specification and verification of concurrent systems in Cesar. In *Proceedings of the International Symposium in Programming*, volume 137 of *Lecture Notes in Computer Science*, Berlin, 1982. Springer-Verlag.

[Sok96] O. Sokolsky. *Efficient Graph-Based Algorithms for Model Checking in the Modal Mu-Calculus*. PhD thesis, Department of Computer Science, SUNY at Stony Brook, April 1996.

[Sti92] C. Stirling. Modal and temporal logics. In S. Abramsky, D. Gabbay, and T. Maibaum, editors, *Handbook of Logic in Computer Science*. Oxford University Press, 1992.

[SW91] C. Stirling and D. Walker. Local model checking in the modal mu-calculus. *Theoretical Computer Science*, 89(1), 1991.

[Tar72] R. E. Tarjan. Depth-first search and linear graph algorithms. *SIAM Journal of Computing*, 1:146–160, 1972.

[Val88] A. Valmari. Error detection by reduced reachability graph detection. In *Proc. 9th European Workshop on Application and Theory of Petri Nets*, pages 95–112, Vencie, 1988.

[Val92] A. Valmari. A stubborn attack on state explosion. *Formal Methods in System Design*, 1(4):297–322, December 1992.

[Val93] A. Valmari. On-the-fly verification with stubborn sets. In Courcoubetis [Cou93], pages 397–408.

[VL94] B. Vergauwen and J. Lewi. Efficient local correctness checking for single and alternating boolean equation systems. In *Proceedings of ICALP'94*, pages 304–315. LNCS 820, 1994.

[WW96] B. Willems and P. Wolper. Partial-order methods for model checking: From linear time to branching time. In Clarke [Cla96].

Cyclic Vector Languages

M. W. Shields
Department of Mathematical and Computing Sciences
University of Surrey

Abstract

Vector languages may be used to model the non-sequential behaviour of systems of co-operating sequential processes. This report presents some preliminary results of an investigation into the following. Given that all the processes are cyclic, in what circumstances will the system as a whole be (asynchronously) cyclic? The question is of interest because many real-world systems are composed partially of cyclic sequential processes and have behaviour which is conceived of as being made up of transactions, which in our case are the asynchronous cycles.

1. Introduction.

Consider a set of n processes, each of which proceeds cyclically in the sense that the set of sequences of actions which it might execute is of the form $\downarrow(V^*)$, the set of string prefixes of V^*.

This is characteristic of processes involved in communications protocols. For example, a telephone call may be described in terms of a cycle which proceed from and return the state 'onhook'.

Let us assume further that these processes synchronise on shared actions. Thus, an action a may be performed if and only if *all* the processes which are eligible to perform a may do so, and if a is performed all those processes which are eligible to perform a do so. This is the mechanism for combining path expressions in the COSY notation [JaL92] and combining CSP programs using the || combinator [Hoa85].

A behaviour of such a system may be described by an n-tuple of sequences, in which the entry in the ith co-ordinate describes the sequence of actions that have been carried out by process i. Each co-ordinate must therefore be an element of some set of the form $\downarrow(V^*)$. Each vector must also somehow reflect the synchronisation rule. The set of all n-tuples satisfying the rule will belong to a set of n-tuples denoted by $A_\alpha{}^*$ and so the set of behaviours of the system may be described by a set of the form

$$A_\alpha{}^* \cap (\downarrow(V_1{}^*) \times \cdots \times \downarrow(V_n{}^*)).$$

As we shall see, $A_\alpha{}^*$ may itself be regarded as a monoid and partial order, so that if $V \subseteq A_\alpha{}^*$ then we may define a 'language' of vectors by $L = \downarrow(V^*)$. Such a language has a particularly simple form, it describes a system in which the processes combine to produce behaviour which is 'globally cyclic', made up of a set of 'transactions'.

For example, the behaviour of a telecommunications system may partly be represented by a vector with co-ordinates corresponding to subscribers; in this case, V is the set of all possible telephone calls, and for each $\underline{v} \in V$, two co-ordinates will be non-null, consisting of a sequence of actions cycling from the 'onhook' state and back to it again.

The designer of a system may envisage its desired behaviour in terms of global cycles, in which each participant has executed a local cycle. Technically, this would mean that

$$A_\alpha{}^* \cap (\downarrow(V_1{}^*) \times \cdots \times \downarrow(V_n{}^*)) = \downarrow(V^*)$$

where $V \subseteq A_\alpha{}^*$ has the property that if $(v_1, \cdots, v_n) \in V$, then $v_i \in V_i \cup \{\Omega\}$, each i (Ω denotes the empty sequence). In such a case, we shall call the system 'cyclic'.

In this paper, we present some preliminary results on cyclic systems.

In section 2, we quote the principal properties of vector languages that we shall be using in the sequel. In section 3, we derive some necessary conditions for cyclicity for vector languages based on sets V_i satisfying a certain unique decipherability property. In section 4, we show that these conditions are sufficient in the case $n = 2$, and are equivalent to local conditions which allow cyclicity to be verified. In section 5, we show that a particular strengthening of the necessary conditions is sufficient.

2. Preliminaries.

In the situation described in the introduction, we have a set of processes, each of which is associated with some set of actions, those which it may execute. Such a system determines an indexed cover, where the indexing set is the set of processes and the set associated with each process is the set of actions it may execute.

Definition 2.1 An *indexed cover* for a set A, is a map $\alpha: I \rightarrow \wp(A)$ such that

$$\bigcup_{i \in I} \alpha(i) = A$$

A behaviour of such a set of processes may be described by a tuple of sequences of its actions, which we may think of as a function associating processes to suitable sets of sequences.

Definition 2.2 If $\alpha: I \to \wp(A)$ is an indexed cover, then an α-*vector* is a mapping $\underline{v}: I \to A^*$ such that

$$\forall i \in I: \underline{v}(i) \in \alpha(i)^*$$

$\underline{\Omega}_\alpha$ is defined to be the vector $\underline{v}$ satisfying $\forall i \in I: \underline{v}(i) = \Omega$.

If $I = \{1, \cdots, n\}$, then we shall write α-vectors $\underline{x}$ in the form $(\underline{x}(1), \cdots, \underline{x}(n))$.

Definition 2.3 If $\alpha: I \to \wp(A)$ is an indexed cover and $\underline{x}, \underline{y} \in M_\alpha$, then:

1• $\underline{x}.\underline{y}$ is defined to be the α-vector $\underline{z}$ such that $\forall i \in I: \underline{z}(i) = \underline{x}(i).\underline{y}(i)$;
2• $\underline{x} \leq \underline{y} \Leftrightarrow \forall i \in I: \underline{x}(i) \leq \underline{y}(i)$.

Proposition 2.1 If α is an indexed cover, then:

1• M_α is a monoid with identity $\underline{\Omega}_\alpha$;
2• M_α is a poset with respect to $\leq$, with bottom $\underline{\Omega}_\alpha$.

■

A particular submonoid of M_α is of interest to us, namely that generated by the event vectors of the following definition. The idea is that when an event a occurs, it occurs for precisely those processes which are eligible to execute that action; the other processes do nothing at all.

Definition 2.4 If $\alpha: I \to \wp(A)$, is an indexed cover then for each $a \in A$, the α-*event vector* of a, denoted by $\underline{a}_\alpha$, is the α-vector such that

$$\underline{a}_\alpha(i) = \begin{cases} a \text{ if } a \in \alpha(i) \\ \Omega \text{ otherwise} \end{cases}$$

Let $A_\alpha = \{\underline{a}_\alpha \mid a \in A\}$ and let $A_\alpha{}^*$ denote the submonoid of M_α generated by A_α. We call $A_\alpha{}^*$ the set of behaviour vectors associated with the cover α.

If we define $\iota_\alpha \subseteq A \times A$ by $a\,\iota_\alpha\,b \Leftrightarrow \forall i \in I: a \in \alpha(i) \Rightarrow b \notin \alpha(i)$, then ι_α is an independence relation in the sense of [Maz77] and there is a natural monoid and poset isomorphism between A_α^* and the set $A_{\iota_\alpha}^*$ of Mazurkiewicz traces ([Shi97, Maz97]).

The following results will be of use when we wish to reason about or manipulate behaviour vectors. Most of them were first presented in [Shi82] and all of them are demonstrated in [Shi97].

Lemma 2.1 If $\underline{m} \in M_\alpha$ and $a \in A$, then $\underline{m}.\underline{a}_\alpha \in A_\alpha^* \Rightarrow \underline{m} \in A_\alpha^*$.

■

The next result says that we can define the length of vectors.

Proposition 2.2 There exists a function $|\ |: A_\alpha^* \to \mathbb{N}$ - and we shall write $|\underline{x}|$ instead of $|\ |(\underline{x})$ - which satisfies

1• $|\underline{x}| = 0 \Leftrightarrow \underline{x} = \underline{\Omega}_\alpha$;

2• $\forall a \in A: |\underline{a}_\alpha| = 1$;

3• $\forall \underline{x}, \underline{y} \in A_\alpha^*: |\underline{x}.\underline{y}| = |\underline{x}| + |\underline{y}|$.

■

The next result relates the order theoretic structure of monoids A_α^* with their monoid theoretic structure.

Proposition 2.3 If $\underline{x}, \underline{y} \in A_\alpha^*$, then $\underline{x} \le \underline{y} \Leftrightarrow \exists \underline{z} \in A_\alpha^*: \underline{y} = \underline{x}.\underline{z}$

■

If $\underline{x}.\underline{z}_1 = \underline{x}.\underline{z}_2$, then $\underline{x}(i).\underline{z}_1(i) = \underline{x}(i).\underline{z}_2(i)$ each $i \in I$. and so $\underline{z}_1(i) = \underline{z}_2(i)$ each $i \in I$ and so $\underline{z}_1 = \underline{z}_2$. Hence, the vector $\underline{z}$ of proposition 2.3 is unique; we denote it by $\underline{y}/\underline{x}$. We shall use the same notation for sequences; if $x \le y$, then y/x is defined to be the unique string such that $x.(y/x) = y$.

The relationship of this next definition is central to the study of behaviour vectors. If two vectors are independent in the following sense then they represent behaviours which may take place concurrently.

Definition 2.5 If $\underline{x}, \underline{y} \in M_\alpha$, then $\underline{x}$ and $\underline{y}$ are *independent*, and we write $\underline{x}\ ind\ \underline{y} \Leftrightarrow \forall i \in I: \underline{x}(i) > \Omega \Rightarrow \underline{y}(i) = \Omega$.

The next lemma shows how independence interacts with ordering.

Lemma 2.2 If $\underline{x}, \underline{y}, \underline{z} \in A_\alpha^*$, such that $\underline{x}, \underline{y} \le \underline{z}$, then $\underline{x}\ ind\ \underline{y} \Rightarrow \underline{y} \le \underline{z}/\underline{x}$.

■

The next results are concerned with upper and lower bounds. Such order theoretic constructions turn out to be very important in the handling of languages of behaviour vectors.

Proposition 2.4 If $\emptyset \subset X \subseteq A_\alpha{}^*$, then $\sqcap X$ exists. Consequently, if $X \subseteq A_\alpha{}^*$ is bounded above, then $\sqcup X$ exists.

■

Proposition 2.5 Suppose $\underline{x}, \underline{y} \in A_\alpha{}^*$, $\underline{x}' = \underline{x}/(\underline{x} \sqcap \underline{y})$ and $\underline{y}' = \underline{y}/(\underline{x} \sqcap \underline{y})$, then $\underline{x} \sqcup \underline{y}$ exists $\Leftrightarrow$ $\underline{x}'$ *ind* $\underline{y}'$ and then

$$\underline{x} \sqcup \underline{y} = (\underline{x} \sqcap \underline{y}).\underline{x}'.\underline{y}' = \underline{x}.\underline{y}' = \underline{y}.\underline{x}'.$$

■

The next result shows that where least upper bounds exist, they may be computed co-ordinatewise.

Proposition 2.6 Let $X \subseteq A_\alpha{}^*$, then $\sqcup X$ and equals $\underline{x} \in A_\alpha{}^*$ $\Leftrightarrow$

$$\forall i \in I: \underline{x}(i) = \sqcup\{\underline{y}(i) \mid \underline{y} \in X\}$$

■

No equivalent result holds in general for greatest lower bounds, but in particular cases greatest lower bounds may be calculated co-ordinatewise, namely when the vectors concerned are consistent in the sense of the following definition.

Definition 2.6 If $\underline{x}, \underline{y} \in A_\alpha{}^*$, then we define $\underline{x} \leftrightarrow \underline{y} \Leftrightarrow$

$$\forall i \in I: \underline{x}(i) \leq \underline{y}(i) \vee \underline{y}(i) \leq \underline{x}(i).$$

Proposition 2.7 Suppose that $\underline{x}, \underline{y} \in A_\alpha{}^*$ with $\underline{x} \leftrightarrow \underline{y}$, then

1• $\forall i \in I: (\underline{x} \sqcap \underline{y})(i) = min(\underline{x}(i), \underline{y}(i));$

2• $\underline{x} \sqcup \underline{y}$ exists.

■

In the analysis of cyclic vector languages, we shall be confronted with a situation in which every vector $\underline{x}$ is the prefix of a concatenation of global cycles. The following result will help us to factorise $\underline{x}$ as a concatenation of prefixes of the cycles.

Proposition 2.8 (Factorisation Lemma). Suppose that $\underline{x}, \underline{y}, \underline{z} \in A_\alpha{}^*$ such that $\underline{x} \le \underline{y}.\underline{z}$, then there exists unique $\underline{u}, \underline{v} \in A_\alpha{}^*$ such that

1• $\underline{x} = \underline{u}.\underline{v}$;
2• $\underline{u} \le \underline{y}$ and $\underline{v} \le \underline{z}$;
3• $\underline{v}$ *ind* $\underline{y}/\underline{u}$.

■

3. Parallel Composition and Cycle Systems.

We are interested in the following situation. We have a set of processes or agents and each process or agent is cyclic in the sense that it's possible behaviour is described by a set of sequences of the form $\downarrow V^*$, where V is a set of non-null strings over a set of action names which we may think of as compound tasks, so that a process progresses by performing such tasks. We are interested in situations in which the whole system's behaviour is of the form $\downarrow V^*$, where V is a set of vectors whose ith co-ordinates are either empty or an element of the set of tasks of process i.

We begin by defining the set of behaviours of an arbitrary system of sequential processes. Each process is associated with a sorted string language, that is a pair (A,L) with $L \subseteq A^*$. The behaviours of the whole system is a parallel composition of these sorted string languages.

Definition 3.1 If $\mathcal{L} = (A_i, L_i)_{i \in I}$ is a family of sorted string languages then we define

$$\| \mathcal{L} = \{ \underline{x} \in A_\alpha \mid \forall i \in I : \underline{x}(i) \in L_i \}$$

where (A,α), the *sort* of $\mathcal{L}$, is given by.

- $A = \bigcup_{i \in I} A_i$;
- $\alpha : I \to \wp(A)$, given by $\alpha(i) = A_i$.

We call $\| \mathcal{L}$ the parallel composition of $\mathcal{L}$.

Definition 3.2 If $V \subseteq A_\alpha{}^*$, then we define $\downarrow V = \{ \underline{x} \in A_\alpha{}^* \mid \exists \underline{v} \in V : \underline{x} \le \underline{v} \}$. If $V = \downarrow V$, then V will be said to be *left closed*.

Proposition 3.1 If $\mathcal{L} = (A_i, L_i)_{i \in I}$ is a family of sorted string languages then

1• If each L_i is left-closed then $\| \mathcal{L}$ is left-closed;

2• If $X \subseteq \| \mathcal{L}$ and $\sqcup X$ exists, then $\sqcup X \in \| \mathcal{L}$.

Proof. (1) follows immediately from definition 3.1 and (2) follows by definition 3.1 and proposition 2.6.

■

Definition 3.3 If $V \subseteq A_\alpha{}^*$, then we define $V(i) = \{\underline{v}(i) \mid \underline{v} \in V\}$.

Proposition 3.2 Suppose that $\mathcal{L} = (A_i, L_i)_{i \in I}$ is a family of sorted string languages with sort (A, α) and that $V \subseteq A_\alpha{}^*$, such that

$$\forall i \in I \; \forall v \in V(i) \; \forall x \in A_i{}^*: v.x \in L_i \Rightarrow x \in L_i \qquad (3.1)$$

then $\| \mathcal{L} = \downarrow(V^*) \Leftrightarrow$

1• $\downarrow(V(i)^*) \subseteq L_i$, all i;

2• $\forall \underline{x} \in \| \mathcal{L} - \{\Omega_\alpha\} \; \exists \underline{v} \in V: \underline{x} \leftrightarrow \underline{v} \wedge \neg \underline{x} \; ind \; \underline{v}$.

Proof. Suppose first of all that $\| \mathcal{L} = \downarrow(V^*)$,

If $x \in \downarrow(V(i)^*)$, then $x \leq y$, some $y \in V(i)^*$ and hence $y = \underline{y}(i)$, some $\underline{y} \in V^*$, and $x = \underline{x}(i)$, some $\underline{x} \leq \underline{y}$. Thus, $x = \underline{x}(i)$, where $\underline{x} \in \downarrow(V^*) = \| \mathcal{L}$, and thus $\underline{x} \in L_i$, so that (1) holds.

Next, suppose that $\underline{x} \in \| \mathcal{L} - \{\Omega_\alpha\}$, so that $\underline{x} \in \downarrow(V^*)$. Let $\underline{v}_1, \cdots, \underline{v}_r \in V$ such that $\underline{x} \leq \underline{v}_1 \cdots \underline{v}_r$ and r is minimal in this respect. Since $\underline{x} \neq \Omega_\alpha$, $r \geq 1$. If $\underline{x} \; ind \; \underline{v}_1$, then $\underline{x} \leq \underline{v}_2 \cdots \underline{v}_r$, by lemma 2.2, contradicting the minimality of r so $\neg \underline{x} \; ind \; \underline{v}_1$. Since $\underline{x}, \underline{v}_1 \leq \underline{v}_1 \cdots \underline{v}_r$, the sets $\{\underline{x}(i), \underline{v}_1(i)\}$ are totally ordered, each i so $\underline{x} \leftrightarrow \underline{v}_1$. Here, we are using the property that the set of prefixes of a sequence is totally ordered.

Next, suppose that (1) and (2) hold.

If $\underline{x} \in \downarrow(V^*)$, then $\underline{x}(i) \in \downarrow(V(i)^*) \subseteq L_i$, each i, by (1), and so $\underline{x} \in \| \mathcal{L}$ and we have shown that $\downarrow(V^*) \subseteq \| \mathcal{L}$.

Finally, suppose that $\underline{x} \in \| \mathcal{L}$. If $\underline{x} = \Omega_\alpha$, then certainly $\underline{x} \in \downarrow(V^*)$, so suppose that $\underline{x} \in \| \mathcal{L} - \{\Omega_\alpha\}$. By (2), there exists $\underline{v} \in V$ such that $\underline{x} \leftrightarrow \underline{v}$ and $\neg \underline{x} \; ind \; \underline{v}$. By (1), $\underline{v} \in \| \mathcal{L}$. By proposition 2.7 and (2) of proposition 3.1, $\underline{y} = \underline{x} \sqcup \underline{v}$ exists and belongs to $\| \mathcal{L}$. By (3.1), whether or not $\underline{v}(i) \neq \Omega$, we must have $(\underline{y}/\underline{v})(i) = \underline{y}(i)/\underline{v}(i) \in L_i$. Now $\underline{y}/\underline{v} = \underline{x}/\underline{w}$, where $\underline{w} = \underline{x} \sqcap \underline{v}$, by proposition 2.5, and since $\neg \underline{x} \; ind \; \underline{v}$ and $\underline{x} \leftrightarrow \underline{v}$, $\underline{w} \neq \Omega_\alpha$. Thus, $|\underline{y}/\underline{v}| < |\underline{x}|$ and so by induction, $\underline{y}/\underline{v} \in \downarrow(V^*)$. As $\underline{v} \in V$, $\underline{y} \in \downarrow(V^*)$, and as $\underline{x} \leq \underline{y}$, $\underline{x} \in \downarrow(V^*)$.

■

We shall be interested in the case in which the languages in a given family are of the form $\downarrow(V_i^*)$. For such languages, the following property will guarantee that (3.1) will hold.

Definition 3.4 A set $V \subseteq A^*$ will be said to have the *prefix property* $\Leftrightarrow$ $\Omega \notin V$ and

$$\forall u, v \in V : u \leq v \Rightarrow u = v.$$

Lemma. 3.1 If $V \subseteq A^*$ has the prefix property then

$$\forall v \in V \; \forall x \in A^* : v.x \in \downarrow(V^*) \Leftrightarrow x \in \downarrow(V^*)$$

Proof. The backward implication always holds. Suppose $v \in V$ and $x \in A^*$ such that $v.x \in \downarrow(V^*)$, then $v.x.u \in V^*$, some $u \in A^*$, so $v.x.u = v'.w$, some $v' \in V$ and $w \in V^*$, as $v.x.u \geq v > \Omega$. But now, either $v \leq v'$ or $v' \leq v$ and so $v = v'$ by the prefix property, whence $x.u = w \in V^*$, and so $x \in \downarrow(V^*)$.

■

Definition 3.5 By a *cycle system*, we mean an indexed family $\mathcal{V} = (V_i)_{i \in I}$ of sets of sequences in which each V_i has the prefix property.

If $\mathcal{V}$ is a cycle system, then let $\mathcal{L}_\mathcal{V}$ denote the family of sorted string languages $(A_i, \downarrow V_i^*)_{i \in I}$, where for each $i \in I$, A_i is the smallest set such that $V_i \subseteq A_i^*$ and let

$$V_\mathcal{V} = \{\underline{x} \in A_\alpha^* \mid \underline{x} \neq \underline{\Omega}_\alpha \wedge \forall i \in I : \underline{x}(i) \in V_i \cup \{\Omega\}\}$$
$$L_\mathcal{V} = \| \mathcal{L}_\mathcal{V}$$

where (A, α) is the sort of $L_\mathcal{V}$.

We shall define $\mathcal{V}$ to be *cyclic* $\Leftrightarrow$ $L_\mathcal{V} = \downarrow(V_\mathcal{V}^*)$.

Proposition 3.3 If $\mathcal{V}$ is a cycle system, then $\mathcal{V}$ is cyclic $\Leftrightarrow$

$$\forall \underline{x} \in L_\mathcal{V} - \{\underline{\Omega}_\alpha\} \; \exists \underline{v} \in V_\mathcal{V} : \underline{x} \leftrightarrow \underline{v} \wedge \neg \underline{x} \; ind \; \underline{v}.$$

Proof. Since condition (1) of proposition 3.2 holds trivially, it suffices to show that (3.1) holds, that is $\forall i \in I \; \forall v \in V_\mathcal{V}(i) \; \forall x \in A_i^* : v.x \in \downarrow(V_i^*) \Rightarrow x \in \downarrow(V_i^*)$. But this is the assertion of lemma 3.1.

■

4. A Necessary Condition for Cyclicity.

4.1. Definition. Suppose that $\mathcal{V} = (V_i)_{i \in I}$ is cycle system, then we define

$$W_{\mathcal{V}} = \{\underline{x} \in A_\alpha^* \mid \forall i \in I : \underline{x}(i) \in \downarrow V_i\}.$$

We observe that $\downarrow V_{\mathcal{V}} \subseteq W_{\mathcal{V}} \subseteq L_{\mathcal{V}}$.

Lemma 4.1 Suppose that $\mathcal{V} = (V_i)_{i \in I}$ is a cycle system and suppose that $\underline{x} \in W_{\mathcal{V}}$ and $\underline{v} \in V_{\mathcal{V}}$, such that $\underline{x} \leftrightarrow \underline{v}$, then there exists $\underline{x}_1, \underline{x}_2 \in W_{\mathcal{V}}$ such that

1• $\underline{x}_1 \leq \underline{v}$
2• $\underline{x} = \underline{x}_1 . \underline{x}_2$
3• $\underline{x}_2$ *ind* $\underline{v}$.

Proof. Let $\underline{x} \in W_{\mathcal{V}}$ and that $\underline{v} \in V_{\mathcal{V}}$ such that $\underline{x} \leftrightarrow \underline{v}$. Define $\underline{x}_1 = \underline{x} \sqcap \underline{v}$, so that $\underline{x}_1 \leq \underline{v}$.

If $\Omega < \underline{v}(i) \leq \underline{x}(i)$, then $\underline{v}(i) \in V_i$, and as $\underline{x}(i) \leq w$, some $w \in V_i$, $w = \underline{v}(i)$, by the prefix property, and consequently $\underline{v}(i) = \underline{x}(i)$. Hence, for each i, either $\Omega = \underline{v}(i)$ or $\underline{x}(i) \leq \underline{v}(i)$. Thus, by proposition 2.7:

$$\underline{x}_1(i) = \begin{cases} \Omega \text{ if } \underline{v}(i) = \Omega \\ \underline{x}(i) \text{ otherwise} \end{cases} \tag{4.1}$$

Define $\underline{x}_2 = \underline{x}/\underline{x}_1$ then certainly $\underline{x} = \underline{x}_1 . \underline{x}_2$ and $\underline{x}_1, \underline{x}_2 \in W_{\mathcal{V}}$. If $\underline{v}(i) > \Omega$, then $\underline{x}_1(i) = \underline{x}(i)$, by (4.1), and hence $\underline{x}_2(i) = \Omega$. Thus $\underline{x}_2$ *ind* $\underline{v}$, and we are done.

■

Definition 4.2 An element $\underline{x} \in A_\alpha^*$ will be said to be *connected* $\Leftrightarrow$

$$\forall \underline{u} \leq \underline{x} : \underline{u} \; ind \; \underline{x}/\underline{u} \Rightarrow \underline{u} = \underline{\Omega}_\alpha \vee \underline{u} = \underline{x}.$$

Lemma 4.2 Suppose that $\mathcal{V}$ is a cycle system and suppose that $\underline{w} \in W_{\mathcal{V}}$ is connected and that $\underline{v} \in V_{\mathcal{V}}$ such that $\underline{w} \leftrightarrow \underline{v}$ and $\neg \underline{w}$ *ind* $\underline{v}$, then $\underline{w} \leq \underline{v}$.

Proof. Let $\underline{w} \in W_{\mathcal{V}}$ be connected and $\underline{v} \in V_{\mathcal{V}}$ such that $\underline{w} \leftrightarrow \underline{v}$ and $\neg \underline{w}$ *ind* $\underline{v}$. By lemma 4.1, there exists $\underline{w}_1, \underline{w}_2 \in W_{\mathcal{V}}$ such that $\underline{w}_1 \leq \underline{v}$, $\underline{w} = \underline{w}_1 . \underline{w}_2$ and $\underline{w}_2$ *ind* $\underline{v}$. Since $\underline{w}_1 \leq \underline{v}$ and $\underline{w}_2$ *ind* $\underline{v}$, $\underline{w}_1$ *ind* $\underline{w}_2$. Since $\underline{w}$ is connected, either $\underline{w}_1 = \underline{\Omega}_\alpha$ or $\underline{w}_2 = \underline{\Omega}_\alpha$, by definition 3.5. But, if $\underline{w}_1 = \underline{\Omega}_\alpha$ then $\underline{w} = \underline{w}_2$ *ind* $\underline{v}$, a contradiction. Hence $\underline{w}_2 = \underline{\Omega}_\alpha$, so that $\underline{w} = \underline{w}_1 \leq \underline{v}$ and we are done.

■

Proposition 4.1 Suppose that $\mathcal{V}$ is a Cycle system and suppose that $\underline{x} \in W_{\mathcal{V}}$ is connected and is not an element of $\downarrow V_{\mathcal{V}}$, then $\underline{x} \in L_{\mathcal{V}} - \downarrow(V_{\mathcal{V}}{}^*)$.

Proof. Let $\underline{x} \in W_{\mathcal{V}}$. be connected and not an element of $\downarrow V_{\mathcal{V}}$, then $|\underline{x}| > 0$. If $\underline{x} \in \downarrow(V_{\mathcal{V}}{}^*)$, then $\underline{x} \le \underline{v}_1 \cdots \underline{v}_r$, where $\underline{v}_i \in V_{\mathcal{V}}$, each $i \in I$. Then $\underline{x} \leftrightarrow \underline{v}_1$ and by lemma 2.2, we may assume that $\neg \underline{x}\ ind\ \underline{v}_1$. By lemma 4.2 $\underline{x} \le \underline{v}_1$, a contradiction.

■

Corollary 4.1 If $\mathcal{V}$ is a cyclic cycle system, then every connected element of $W_{\mathcal{V}}$ is an element of $\downarrow V_{\mathcal{V}}$.

■

In order to state our second necessary condition, we need to introduce another notion which plays a central rôle in the subsequent analysis.

Definition 4.3 Suppose that $\mathcal{V}$ is a cycle system and $\underline{x}, \underline{y} \in A_\alpha{}^*$. We define

$$\underline{x} \rhd_{\mathcal{V}} \underline{y} \Leftrightarrow \forall i \in I : \underline{y}(i) > \Omega \Rightarrow \underline{x}(i) \in V_i$$

We establish some important elementary properties of $\rhd_{\mathcal{V}}$.

Lemma 4.3 Suppose that $\mathcal{V}$ is a cycle system. If $\underline{w} \in W_{\mathcal{V}}$ and $\underline{x}, \underline{y} \in A_\alpha{}^*$, then

1• $\underline{w} \rhd_{\mathcal{V}} \underline{y} \Rightarrow (\underline{w}.\underline{y} \in L_{\mathcal{V}} \Leftrightarrow \underline{y} \in L_{\mathcal{V}})$;

2• $\underline{w} \rhd_{\mathcal{V}} \underline{x} \wedge \underline{w} \rhd_{\mathcal{V}} \underline{y} \Rightarrow \underline{w} \rhd_{\mathcal{V}} \underline{x}.\underline{y}$.

Proof. (1) By definitions 3.5 and 3.1, it suffices to show that

$$\underline{w}(i).\underline{y}(i) \in \downarrow(V_i{}^*) \Leftrightarrow \underline{y}(i) \in \downarrow(V_i{}^*)$$

This certainly holds when $\underline{y}(i) = \Omega$, while if $\underline{y}(i) \ne \Omega$, then $\underline{w}(i) \in V_i$ and we may apply lemma 3.1.
(2) Suppose that $\underline{w} \rhd_{\mathcal{V}} \underline{x}$ and $\underline{w} \rhd_{\mathcal{V}} \underline{y}$. If $(\underline{x}.\underline{y})(i) \ne \Omega$, then either $\underline{x}(i) \ne \Omega$ or $\underline{y}(i) \ne \Omega$ and in either case $\underline{w}(i) \in V_i$, so $\underline{w} \rhd_{\mathcal{V}} \underline{x}.\underline{y}$.

■

Lemma 4.4 Suppose that $\mathcal{V}$ is a cycle system. If $\underline{w} \in W_{\mathcal{V}}$ is connected and $a \in A$, such that $\underline{w}.\underline{a} \in \downarrow(V_{\mathcal{V}}{}^*)$ then either $\underline{w}.\underline{a}_\alpha \in W_{\mathcal{V}}$ or $\underline{w} \rhd_{\mathcal{V}} \underline{a}_\alpha$.

Proof. Since $\underline{w}.\underline{a}\in\downarrow(V_\nu{}^*)$, we may find $\underline{v}\in V_\nu$ and $\underline{z}\in V_\nu{}^*$ such that $\underline{w}.\underline{a}_\alpha\leq\underline{v}.\underline{z}$ and by lemma 2.2, we may suppose that $\underline{w}.\underline{a}_\alpha\not\leq\underline{z}$. By the factorisation lemma, we can write $\underline{w}.\underline{a}_\alpha=\underline{u}.\underline{y}$, where $\underline{u}\leq\underline{v}$, $\underline{y}\leq\underline{z}$ and $\underline{v}/\underline{u}\ ind\ \underline{y}$. We consider two cases.

Case 1: $\underline{a}_\alpha\ ind\ \underline{y}$. If $\underline{a}_\alpha(i)>\Omega$, then $\underline{y}(i)=\Omega$ and so $\underline{u}(i)=\underline{w}(i).a$. Hence, for some $\underline{u}'\in M_\alpha$, $\underline{u}=\underline{u}'.\underline{a}_\alpha$. By lemma 2.1, $\underline{u}'\in A_\alpha{}^*$. And now, $\underline{w}.\underline{a}_\alpha=\underline{u}.\underline{y}$ and $\underline{a}_\alpha\ ind\ \underline{y}$, so $\underline{w}.\underline{a}_\alpha=\underline{u}.\underline{y}=\underline{u}'.\underline{a}_\alpha.\underline{y}=\underline{u}'.\underline{y}.\underline{a}_\alpha$ and consequently $\underline{w}=\underline{u}'.\underline{y}$.

If $\neg\underline{w}\ ind\ \underline{u}'$, then $\neg\underline{w}\ ind\ \underline{v}$, and since $\underline{w}\leq\underline{w}.\underline{a}_\alpha\leq\underline{v}.\underline{z}$, $\underline{w}\leftrightarrow\underline{v}$, so that $\underline{w}\leq\underline{v}$, by lemma 4.2. Hence, $\underline{u}'.\underline{y}\leq\underline{v}$ and so $\underline{y}\leq\underline{v}/\underline{u}'$. But, $\underline{a}_\alpha.(\underline{v}/\underline{u})=(\underline{v}/\underline{u}')$ and $\underline{a}_\alpha\ ind\ \underline{y}$ and $\underline{v}/\underline{u}\ ind\ \underline{y}$, so $(\underline{v}/\underline{u}')\ ind\ \underline{y}$, and this, together with $\underline{y}\leq\underline{v}/\underline{u}'$, implies $\underline{y}=\underline{\Omega}_\alpha$. Therefore, $\underline{w}.\underline{a}_\alpha=\underline{u}$ and so $\underline{w}.\underline{a}_\alpha\in\downarrow V_\nu\subseteq W_\nu$.

If $\underline{w}\ ind\ \underline{u}'$, then as $\underline{w}=\underline{u}'.\underline{y}$, $\underline{u}'=\underline{\Omega}_\alpha$. Therefore as $\underline{a}_\alpha=\underline{u}'.\underline{a}_\alpha=\underline{u}\leq\underline{v}$, $\underline{a}_\alpha\in W_\nu$, and also $\underline{w}.\underline{a}_\alpha=\underline{u}.\underline{y}=\underline{a}_\alpha.\underline{y}=\underline{y}.\underline{a}_\alpha$ so that $\underline{w}=\underline{y}$. But, $\underline{a}_\alpha\ ind\ \underline{y}$, so that $\underline{a}_\alpha\ ind\ \underline{w}$, and as $\underline{w},\underline{a}_\alpha\in W_\nu$ and $\underline{a}_\alpha\ ind\ \underline{w}$, $\underline{w}.\underline{a}_\alpha\in W_\nu$.

Case 2: $\neg\underline{a}_\alpha\ ind\ \underline{y}$. There exists $i\in I$ such that $\underline{a}_\alpha(i)>\Omega$ and $\underline{y}(i)>\Omega$, from which it follows that a appears in $\underline{y}$ and so whenever $\underline{a}_\alpha(i)>\Omega$, then $\underline{y}(i)>\Omega$. Hence, when $\underline{a}_\alpha(i)>\Omega$ $\underline{w}(i).a=\underline{u}(i).\underline{y}(i)$ with $\underline{y}(i)>\Omega$, which means that $\underline{y}=\underline{y}'.\underline{a}_\alpha$, some $\underline{y}'\in M_\alpha$, so that $\underline{y}'\in A_\alpha{}^*$ by lemma 2.1. Thus, $\underline{w}=\underline{u}.\underline{y}'$.

If $\neg\underline{w}\ ind\ \underline{u}$, then $\neg\underline{w}\ ind\ \underline{v}$, and since $\underline{w}\leq\underline{w}.\underline{a}_\alpha\leq\underline{v}.\underline{z}$, $\underline{w}\leftrightarrow\underline{v}$, and so $\underline{w}\leq\underline{v}$, by lemma 4.2. Hence, $\underline{u}.\underline{y}'\leq\underline{v}$ and so $\underline{y}'\leq\underline{v}/\underline{u}$. But, $\underline{y}=\underline{y}'.\underline{a}_\alpha$ and $\underline{v}/\underline{u}\ ind\ \underline{y}$, so $\underline{v}/\underline{u}\ ind\ \underline{y}'$ and this, together with $\underline{y}'\leq\underline{v}/\underline{u}$ implies $\underline{y}'=\underline{\Omega}_\alpha$. Thus, $\underline{y}=\underline{a}_\alpha$ and so $\underline{v}/\underline{u}\ ind\ \underline{a}_\alpha$ and also $\underline{w}.\underline{a}_\alpha=\underline{u}.\underline{a}_\alpha$ which means that $\underline{w}=\underline{u}$. And now, if $\underline{a}_\alpha(i)>\Omega$, then $\underline{y}(i)>\Omega$, and as $\underline{v}/\underline{u}\ ind\ \underline{y}$ and $\underline{w}=\underline{u}$, $\underline{w}(i)=\underline{u}(i)=\underline{v}(i)\in V_i$, that is $\underline{w}\rhd_\nu\underline{a}_\alpha$.

If $\underline{w}\ ind\ \underline{u}$, then as $\underline{w}=\underline{u}.\underline{y}'$, it follows that $\underline{u}=\underline{\Omega}_\alpha$. But then, $\underline{w}.\underline{a}_\alpha=\underline{y}'.\underline{a}_\alpha=\underline{y}\leq\underline{z}$, a contradiction to our assumption that $\underline{w}.\underline{a}_\alpha\not\leq\underline{z}$.

■

Proposition 4.2 Suppose that $\mathcal{V}$ is a cycle system and that $\underline{w}\in W_\nu$ is connected, $a\in A$ and $\underline{y}\in A_\alpha{}^*$ such that $\underline{w}.\underline{y}.\underline{a}_\alpha\in\downarrow(V_\nu{}^*)$ and $\underline{w}\rhd_\nu\underline{y}$, then one of the following holds

1• $\underline{y}\ ind\ \underline{a}_\alpha$ and $\underline{w}.\underline{a}_\alpha\in W_\nu$;

2• $\underline{w}\rhd_\nu\underline{y}.\underline{a}_\alpha$.

Proof. If $\underline{y}\ ind\ \underline{a}_\alpha$, then $\underline{w}.\underline{a}_\alpha \le \underline{w}.\underline{a}_\alpha.\underline{y} = \underline{w}.\underline{y}.\underline{a}_\alpha$ and so by lemma 4.4, either $\underline{w}.\underline{a} \in W_\mathcal{V}$, in which case (1) holds, or $\underline{w} \rhd_\mathcal{V} \underline{a}_\alpha$, and since $\underline{w} \rhd_\mathcal{V} \underline{y}$, $\underline{w} \rhd_\mathcal{V} \underline{y}.\underline{a}_\alpha$, by (2) of lemma 4.3, that is (2) holds. So suppose that $\neg \underline{y}\ ind\ \underline{a}_\alpha$.

By hypothesis, there exists $\underline{v}_1, \cdots, \underline{v}_n \in V_\mathcal{V}$ such that $\underline{w}.\underline{y}.\underline{a}_\alpha \le \underline{v}_1 \cdots \underline{v}_n$ and we choose the $\underline{v}_i$ so that n is minimal. Consequently, $\neg \underline{w}.\underline{y}.\underline{a}_\alpha\ ind\ \underline{v}_1$ for otherwise $\underline{w}.\underline{y}.\underline{a}_\alpha \le \underline{v}_2 \cdots \underline{v}_n$, by lemma 2.2. We shall first show that $\underline{w} \le \underline{v}_1$.

If not, then by lemmas 2.2 and 4.2, there exists $1 < m \le n$ such that $\underline{w} \le \underline{v}_m$ and $\underline{w}\ ind\ \underline{v}_r$ for $r < m$. Thus, if $i \in I$ such that $\underline{y}(i) \ne \Omega$, then $\underline{w}(i) \in V_i$ and so $\underline{w}(i) \ne \Omega$, so $\underline{v}_r(i) = \Omega$. Hence, $\underline{y}\ ind\ \underline{v}_r$ for $r < m$. In particular, $\underline{w}.\underline{y}\ ind\ \underline{v}_1$. Now, if $\underline{v}_1(i) \ne \Omega$, then $(\underline{w}.\underline{y})(i) = \Omega$ and so $(\underline{v}_1 \cdots \underline{v}_n)(i) = (\underline{w}.\underline{y}.\underline{a}_\alpha)(i) = \underline{a}_\alpha(i)$ from which it easily follows that $\underline{v}_1 = \underline{a}_\alpha$ and we have a contradiction to $\neg \underline{y}\ ind\ \underline{a}_\alpha$. Thus, $\underline{w} \le \underline{v}_1$, as required.

By the factorisation lemma, 2.8, there exists $\underline{w}_1, \cdots, \underline{w}_n \in A_\alpha{}^*$ such that $\underline{w}.\underline{y}.\underline{a}_\alpha = \underline{w}_1 \cdots \underline{w}_n$ and for each r

(a) $\underline{w}_r \le \underline{v}_r$ and in particular, $\underline{w}_r \in W_\mathcal{V}$;
(b) $\underline{w}_r\ ind\ (\underline{v}_1/\underline{w}_1) \cdots (\underline{v}_{r-1}/\underline{w}_{r-1})$, when $r < n$.

Let m be such that $\underline{w}_m = \underline{w'}_m.\underline{a}_\alpha$, some $\underline{w'} \in A_\alpha{}^*$, and $\underline{w}_r\ ind\ \underline{a}_\alpha$, $r > m$.

If $m = 1$, then $\underline{w}.\underline{y}.\underline{a}_\alpha = \underline{w'}_1.\underline{a}_\alpha.\underline{w}_2 \cdots \underline{w}_n$, $\underline{w}.\underline{y} = \underline{w'}_1.\underline{w}_2 \cdots \underline{w}_n$ and $\underline{a}_\alpha\ ind\ \underline{w}_2 \cdots \underline{w}_n$. As $\neg \underline{y}\ ind\ \underline{a}_\alpha$,t here exists $i \in I$ such that $\underline{y}(i) \ne \Omega$ and $\underline{a}_\alpha(i) \ne \Omega$. Since $\underline{y}(i) \ne \Omega$, $\underline{w}(i) \in V_i$ and as $\underline{w} \le \underline{v}_1$, $\underline{w}(i) = \underline{v}_1(i)$, by the prefix property. But since $\underline{a}_\alpha(i) \ne \Omega$, $(\underline{w}_2 \cdots \underline{w}_n)(i) = \Omega$ and so $\underline{v}_1(i) \le (\underline{w}.\underline{y})(i) = \underline{w'}_1(i) < \underline{w}_1(i) \le \underline{v}_1(i)$, a contradiction.

Thus, $m > 1$, so that $\underline{w}.\underline{y} = \underline{w}_1 \cdots \underline{w'}_m \cdots \underline{w}_n$. If $\underline{a}_\alpha(i) \ne \Omega$, then $\underline{w}_m(i) \ne \Omega$ and so $(\underline{v}_1/\underline{w}_1)(i) = \Omega$, by (b), that is $\underline{w}_1(i) = \underline{v}_1(i)$. Since $\underline{w} \le \underline{v}_1$, either $\underline{w}(i) = \underline{w}_1(i)$ or $\underline{w}(i) < \underline{w}_1(i)$. If $\underline{w}(i) < \underline{w}_1(i)$, then $\underline{y}(i) = (\underline{w}_1(i)/\underline{w}(i)) \cdots \underline{w'}_m(i) \cdots \underline{w}_n(i) > \Omega$ and so $\underline{w}(i) \in V_i$ and we have the contradiction $\underline{w}(i) < \underline{w}_1(i) = \underline{v}_1(i)$ to the prefix property. Hence, when $\underline{a}_\alpha(i) \ne \Omega$, then $\underline{w}(i) = \underline{w}_1(i) = \underline{v}_1(i) \in V_i$ and we have shown that $\underline{w} \rhd_\mathcal{V} \underline{a}_\alpha$, and since $\underline{w} \rhd_\mathcal{V} \underline{y}$, it follows, by (2) of lemma 4.3, that $\underline{w} \rhd_\mathcal{V} \underline{y}.\underline{a}_\alpha$, that is, (2) holds.

■

We name the necessary conditions for a cycle system to be cyclic.

Definition 4.4 If $\mathcal{V}$ is a cycle system, then $\mathcal{V}$ will be said to be *normal* $\Leftrightarrow$ $W_\mathcal{V} \subseteq \downarrow V_\mathcal{V}{}^*$ and for every connected $\underline{w} \in W_\mathcal{V}$:

1• $\underline{w} \in \downarrow V_{\mathcal{V}};$

2• $\forall a \in A\ \forall \underline{y} \in A_\alpha{}^*: \underline{w}.\underline{y}.\underline{a}_\alpha \in L_{\mathcal{V}} \wedge \underline{w} \rhd_{\mathcal{V}} \underline{y} \Rightarrow (\underline{y}\ ind\ \underline{a}_\alpha \wedge \underline{w}.\underline{a}_\alpha \in W_{\mathcal{V}}) \vee \underline{w} \rhd_{\mathcal{V}} \underline{y}.\underline{a}_\alpha$

Proposition 4.3 If $\mathcal{V}$ is a cycle system, then $\mathcal{V}$ is cyclic $\Rightarrow$ $\mathcal{V}$ is normal,

Proof. As $W_{\mathcal{V}} \subseteq L_{\mathcal{V}}$, it is immediate that $L_{\mathcal{V}} = \downarrow(V_{\mathcal{V}}{}^*) \Rightarrow W_{\mathcal{V}} \subseteq \downarrow V_{\mathcal{V}}{}^*$. The other conditions of definition 4.4 follows from corollary 4.1 and proposition 4.2. ■

5. The Two Dimensional Case.

In this section, we examine cycle systems $\mathcal{V}$ having two elements - we shall refer to such cycle systems as two dimensional. We shall suppose that the indexing set $I = \{1,2\}$ and write vectors $\underline{x}$ as pairs $(\underline{x}(1), \underline{x}(2))$. We shall prove that $\mathcal{V}$ is a cyclic if and only if $\mathcal{V}$ is normal.

Let $\underline{x} \in L_{\mathcal{V}}$. We argue by induction on $|\underline{x}|$ that $\underline{x} \in \downarrow(V_{\mathcal{V}}{}^*)$. The case $|\underline{x}| = 0$ is trivial, so let $|\underline{x}| > 0$. If $\underline{v} \leq \underline{x}$, some $\underline{v} \in V_{\mathcal{V}}$, then $\underline{x}/\underline{v} \in L_{\mathcal{V}}$, by (1) of lemma 4.3, and so $\underline{x}/\underline{v} \in \downarrow(V_{\mathcal{V}}{}^*)$, by induction, so $\underline{x} \in \downarrow(V_{\mathcal{V}}{}^*)$. Hence, we may assume:

$$\underline{v} \leq \underline{x}, \text{ for no } \underline{v} \in V_{\mathcal{V}} \qquad (5.1)$$

Let $\underline{w} = \sqcup(\downarrow\underline{x} \cap W_{\mathcal{V}})$. $\underline{w}$ is well defined, by proposition 2.4 since the set $\downarrow\underline{x} \cap W_{\mathcal{V}}$ is bounded above by $\underline{x}$, and by proposition 2.6 and definition 4.1, $\underline{w} \in W_{\mathcal{V}}$. If $\underline{w} = \underline{x}$, then $\underline{x} \in \downarrow(V_{\mathcal{V}}{}^*)$, as $W_{\mathcal{V}} \subseteq \downarrow V_{\mathcal{V}}{}^*$, so we suppose that $\underline{w} \neq \underline{x}$. Hence, there exists $a \in A$ such that $\underline{a}_\alpha \leq \underline{x}/\underline{w}$, that is $\underline{w}.\underline{a}_\alpha \leq \underline{x}$. If $\underline{w}.\underline{a}_\alpha \in W_{\mathcal{V}}$, then $\underline{w}.\underline{a}_\alpha \in \downarrow\underline{x} \cap W_{\mathcal{V}}$, contradicting $\underline{w} = \sqcup(\downarrow\underline{x} \cap W_{\mathcal{V}})$, so we must have $\underline{w}.\underline{a}_\alpha \notin W_{\mathcal{V}}$. Without loss of generality, suppose that $(\underline{w}.\underline{a}_\alpha)(1) \notin V_1$. Since $\underline{w} \in W_{\mathcal{V}}$, $\underline{w}(1) \in \downarrow V_1$, and since $\underline{w}.\underline{a}_\alpha \leq \underline{x}$, $\underline{w}.\underline{a}_\alpha \in L_{\mathcal{V}}$, by proposition 3.1, and so $(\underline{w}.\underline{a}_\alpha)(1) \in \downarrow(V_1{}^*)$. Thus, we must have $\underline{w}(1) \in V_1$ and $a \in \alpha(1)$. If $\underline{w}(2) \in V_2$ or $\underline{w}(2) = \Omega$, then $\underline{w} \in V_{\mathcal{V}}$, contradicting (5.1) and hence we must also have $\underline{w}(2) \in \downarrow V_2 - (V_2 \cup \{\Omega\})$. We next establish that $\underline{w}$ is connected.

5.1. Lemma. If $\mathcal{V}$ is a two dimensional cycle system and $\underline{w} \in A_\alpha{}^*$ is not connected then $(\underline{w}(1), \Omega), (\Omega, \underline{w}(2)) \in A_\alpha{}^*$

Proof. Let $\underline{u} \in A_\alpha{}^*$ such that $\underline{u} \leq \underline{w}$, $\underline{u} \neq \Omega_\alpha$, $\underline{u} \neq \underline{w}$ and $\underline{u}\ ind\ \underline{w}/\underline{u}$. Without loss of generality, assume $\underline{u}(1) \neq \Omega$, so that $(\underline{w}/\underline{u})(1) = \Omega$, since $\underline{u}\ ind\ \underline{w}/\underline{u}$, that is $\underline{u}(1) = \underline{w}(1)$. Since $\underline{u} \neq \underline{w}$ and $\underline{u}(1) = \underline{w}(1)$, $\underline{u}(2) \neq \underline{w}(2)$ and so $(\underline{w}/\underline{u})(2) \neq \Omega$ and so $\underline{u}(2) = \Omega$, as $\underline{u}\ ind\ \underline{w}/\underline{u}$. Thus, $(\underline{w}(1), \Omega) = \underline{u} \in A_\alpha{}^*$ and $(\Omega, \underline{w}(2)) = \underline{w}/\underline{u} \in A_\alpha{}^*$. ■

If $\underline{w}$ is not connected, then $(\underline{w}(1),\Omega) \in V_{\mathcal{V}}$, contradicting (5.1). Hence $\underline{w}$ is connected. We now argue by induction on $|\underline{x}/\underline{w}|$ that $\underline{w} \triangleright_{\mathcal{V}} \underline{x}/\underline{w}$.

Since $\mathcal{V}$ is normal and $\underline{w}.\underline{a}_\alpha \in L_{\mathcal{V}}$ and $\underline{w} \triangleright_{\mathcal{V}} \underline{\Omega}_\alpha$, either $\underline{w}.\underline{a}_\alpha \in W_{\mathcal{V}}$ or $\underline{w} \triangleright_{\mathcal{V}} \underline{a}_\alpha$. But $\underline{w}.\underline{a}_\alpha \notin W_{\mathcal{V}}$, so $\underline{w} \triangleright_{\mathcal{V}} \underline{a}_\alpha$. For the induction step, suppose that $\underline{y} \in A_\alpha{}^*$ and $b \in A$ such that $\underline{y}.\underline{b}_\alpha \leq \underline{x}/\underline{w}$. By induction, $\underline{w} \triangleright_{\mathcal{V}} \underline{y}$. Since $\mathcal{V}$ is normal and $\underline{w}.\underline{y}.\underline{b}_\alpha \in L_{\mathcal{V}}$ and $\underline{w} \triangleright_{\mathcal{V}} \underline{y}$, either $\underline{w}.\underline{b}_\alpha \in W_{\mathcal{V}}$ and $\underline{y}\ ind\ \underline{b}_\alpha$ or $\underline{w} \triangleright_{\mathcal{V}} \underline{y}.\underline{b}_\alpha$. But, in the first case, $\underline{w}.\underline{b}_\alpha \leq \underline{w}.\underline{b}_\alpha.\underline{y} = \underline{w}.\underline{y}.\underline{b}_\alpha \leq \underline{x}$ and so $\underline{w}.\underline{b}_\alpha \in \downarrow\underline{x} \cap W_{\mathcal{V}}$, contradicting $\underline{w} = \sqcup(\downarrow\underline{x} \cap W_{\mathcal{V}})$. So, $\underline{w} \triangleright_{\mathcal{V}} \underline{y}.\underline{b}_\alpha$. By induction, $\underline{w} \triangleright_{\mathcal{V}} \underline{x}/\underline{w}$ and since $\underline{w}(2) \notin V_2$, $\underline{x}(2) = \underline{w}(2)$.

Since $\mathcal{V}$ is normal, there exists $\underline{v} \in V_{\mathcal{V}}$ such that $\underline{w} \leq \underline{v}$. Since $\underline{w}(1) \in V_1$, $\underline{v}(1) = \underline{w}(1)$ by the prefix property, so $\underline{v}(1) \leq \underline{x}(1)$. Also, $\underline{x}(2) = \underline{w}(2) \leq \underline{v}(2)$. We have shown that $\underline{v} \leftrightarrow \underline{x}$. As in the proof of proposition 3.2 we may conclude that $\underline{x} \in \downarrow(V_{\mathcal{V}}{}^*)$. We have proved the following.

Proposition 5.1. A two dimensional cycle system $\mathcal{V}$ is cyclic $\Leftrightarrow$ $\mathcal{V}$ is normal. ■

This result is of little practical use as it stands, because it requires knowledge of all $\underline{w}.\underline{y} \in L_{\mathcal{V}}$ with $\underline{w} \in W_{\mathcal{V}}$ connected. However, in the two dimensional case we can 'localise' normality to give a test for $L_{\mathcal{V}} = \downarrow(V_{\mathcal{V}}{}^*)$.

Definition 5.1 If $\mathcal{V}$ is a cycle system, then $\mathcal{V}$, will be said to be 2-*normal* $\Leftrightarrow$ $W_{\mathcal{V}} \subseteq \downarrow V_{\mathcal{V}}{}^2 = \downarrow\{\underline{v}_1.\underline{v}_2 \mid \underline{v}_1, \underline{v}_2 \in V_{\mathcal{V}}\}$ and for every connected $\underline{w} \in W_{\mathcal{V}}$, $\underline{w} \in \downarrow V_{\mathcal{V}}$; and

$$\forall a \in A\ \forall \underline{u} \in W_{\mathcal{V}}: \underline{w}.\underline{u}.\underline{a}_\alpha \in L_{\mathcal{V}} \wedge \underline{w} \triangleright_{\mathcal{V}} \underline{u} \Rightarrow (\underline{u}\ ind\ \underline{a}_\alpha \wedge \underline{w}.\underline{a}_\alpha \in W_{\mathcal{V}}) \vee \underline{w} \triangleright_{\mathcal{V}} \underline{u}.\underline{a}_\alpha$$

Proposition 5.2 A two dimensional cycle system $\mathcal{V}$ is 2-normal $\Leftrightarrow$ $\mathcal{V}$ is normal.

Proof. Suppose first that $\mathcal{V}$ is 2-normal. As $W_{\mathcal{V}} \subseteq \downarrow V_{\mathcal{V}}{}^2$, certainly $W_{\mathcal{V}} \subseteq \downarrow V_{\mathcal{V}}{}^*$. Condition (1) of definition 4.4 is identical to that of definition 5.1. It remains to be shown that condition (2) of definition 4.4 holds.

Suppose that $\underline{w} \in W_{\mathcal{V}}$ is connected, $\underline{y} \in A_\alpha{}^*$ and $a \in A$. such that $\underline{w}.\underline{y}.\underline{a} \in L_{\mathcal{V}}$ and $\underline{w} \triangleright_{\mathcal{V}} \underline{y}$.

If $\underline{y}(1) \neq \Omega \neq \underline{y}(2)$, then $\underline{w}(1) \in V_1$ and $\underline{w}(2) \in V_2$, because $\underline{w} \triangleright_{\mathcal{V}} \underline{y}$, and certainly $\underline{w} \triangleright_{\mathcal{V}} \underline{y}.\underline{a}_\alpha$ in this case, so suppose, without loss of generality, that $\underline{y}(1) \neq \Omega$ and $\underline{y}(2) = \Omega$.

By definition of $L_{\mathcal{V}}$, there exists $v_1,\cdots,v_n \in V_1$ and $w \in \downarrow V_1$ such that $(\underline{w}.\underline{y}.\underline{a}_\alpha)(1) = v_1\cdots v_n.w$. Since $\underline{w} \rhd_{\mathcal{V}} \underline{y}$ and $\underline{y}(1) \neq \Omega$, $\underline{w}(1) \in V_1$ and so $\underline{w}(1) = v_1$ by the prefix property. Therefore, $\underline{y}(1) = v_2\cdots v_n.w$ and since $\underline{y}(2) = \Omega$, we may conclude that $\underline{w}' = (w,\Omega) \in A_\alpha^*$. and since $\underline{w}(2) \in \downarrow V_2$, $\underline{w}' \in W_{\mathcal{V}}$. And now $\underline{w}(1).w \in \downarrow V_1^*$, so by definition of $L_{\mathcal{V}}$, $\underline{w}.\underline{w}' = (\underline{w}(1).w, \underline{w}(2)) \in L_{\mathcal{V}}$. By the prefix property, $v_1\cdots v_n.w.a \in \downarrow V_1^* \Leftrightarrow w.a \in \downarrow V_1^*$, so $\underline{w}.\underline{w}'.\underline{a}_\alpha \in L_{\mathcal{V}}$. And now, by 2-normality, either $\underline{w}'$ *ind* $\underline{a}_\alpha$ and $\underline{w}.\underline{a} \in W_{\mathcal{V}}$ or $\underline{w} \rhd_{\mathcal{V}} \underline{w}'.\underline{a}_\alpha$. But, since $\underline{y}(2) = \underline{w}'(2) = \Omega$, $\underline{w}'$ *ind* $\underline{a}_\alpha$ implies $\underline{y}$ *ind* $\underline{a}_\alpha$ and $\underline{w} \rhd_{\mathcal{V}} \underline{w}'.\underline{a}_\alpha$ implies $\underline{w} \rhd_{\mathcal{V}} \underline{y}.\underline{a}_\alpha$.

Now, suppose that $\mathcal{V}$ is normal. Condition (1) of definition 5.1 is identical to that of definition 4.4 and clearly condition (2) of definition 5.1 is implied by that of definition 4.4. It remains to be shown that $W_{\mathcal{V}} \subseteq \downarrow V_{\mathcal{V}}^*$ implies $W_{\mathcal{V}} \subseteq \downarrow V_{\mathcal{V}}^2$. Let $\underline{w} \in W_{\mathcal{V}}$. If $\underline{w}$ is connected, then $\underline{w} \in \downarrow V_{\mathcal{V}} \subseteq \downarrow V_{\mathcal{V}}^2$, by condition (1) of definition 5.1. Otherwise $(\underline{w}(1),\Omega),(\Omega,\underline{w}(2)) \in W_{\mathcal{V}}$, by lemma 5.1. If either $\underline{w}(1) = \Omega$ or $\underline{w}(2) = \Omega$, then $\underline{w}$ is connected, a contradiction, so $\underline{w}(1) \neq \Omega$ and $\underline{w}(2) \neq \Omega$. Since $W_{\mathcal{V}} \subseteq \downarrow V_{\mathcal{V}}^*$, there exists $\underline{v}_1,\cdots,\underline{v}_n \in V_{\mathcal{V}}$ such that $\underline{w} \leq \underline{v}_1\cdots\underline{v}_n$. As usual, we may suppose that $\neg\underline{w}$ *ind* $\underline{v}_1$. Without loss of generality, suppose $\underline{v}_1(1) \neq \Omega$, then $(\underline{w}(1),\Omega) \leq \underline{v}_1$, by lemma 4.2. If k is the smallest integer such that $\underline{v}_k(1) \neq \Omega$, then $(\Omega,\underline{w}(2) \leq \underline{v}_k$. We now have $\underline{w} \leq \underline{v}_1.\underline{v}_k$, and so $\underline{w} \in \downarrow V_{\mathcal{V}}^2$, as required.

■

Putting propositions 5.1 and 5.2 together, we obtain:

Proposition 5.3 A two dimensional cycle system $\mathcal{V}$ is cyclic $\Leftrightarrow$ $\mathcal{V}$ is 2-normal.

■

6. A Sufficient Condition for Cyclicity.

Unfortunately, the argument that worked for two dimensional cycle systems breaks down when we go to three dimensions. The problem is that lemma 5.1 does not generalise to three dimensions. However, by strengthening the normality property, we can obtain a necessary condition.

6.1. Definition. A cycle system $\mathcal{V}$ will be said to be *concise* $\Leftrightarrow$ whenever $\underline{w} \in \downarrow V_{\mathcal{V}}$, $\underline{y} \in A_\alpha^*$ and $a \in A$. such that $\underline{w}.\underline{y}.\underline{a}_\alpha \in L_{\mathcal{V}}$ and $\underline{w} \rhd_{\mathcal{V}} \underline{y}$, then one of the following holds

1• $\underline{y}$ *ind* $\underline{a}_\alpha$ and $\underline{w}.\underline{a}_\alpha \in \downarrow V_{\mathcal{V}}$;

2• $\underline{w} \rhd_{\mathcal{V}} \underline{y}.\underline{a}_\alpha$.

Lemma 6.1 If $\mathcal{V}$ is a concise cycle system, and $\underline{x} \in L_\mathcal{V} - \{\underline{\Omega}_\alpha\}$, then there exists $\underline{w} \in \downarrow V_\mathcal{V}$ such that $\underline{w} \neq \underline{\Omega}_\alpha$, $\underline{w} \leq \underline{x}$ and $\underline{w} \rhd_\mathcal{V} \underline{x}/\underline{w}$.

Proof. Let $\underline{x} \in L_\mathcal{V} - \{\underline{\Omega}_\alpha\}$ and define $\underline{w} = \bigsqcup(\downarrow\underline{x} \cap \downarrow V_\mathcal{V})$, then $\underline{w}$ exists because it is bounded above by $\underline{x}$, $\underline{w} \in \downarrow V_\mathcal{V}$ and $\underline{w} \leq \underline{x}$. Also, as $\underline{x} \neq \underline{\Omega}_\alpha$, $\underline{w} \neq \underline{\Omega}_\alpha$. Let $\underline{y} = \underline{x}/\underline{w}$. We argue by induction on $|\underline{y}|$ that $\underline{w} \rhd_\mathcal{V} \underline{y}$.

This is certainly the case when $|\underline{y}| = 0$, so suppose that $\underline{y} = \underline{y}'.\underline{a}_\alpha$, some $a \in A$, then by induction $\underline{w} \rhd_\mathcal{V} \underline{y}'$ and by conciseness, either $\underline{w}.\underline{a}_\alpha \in \downarrow V_\mathcal{V}$ or $\underline{w} \rhd_\mathcal{V} \underline{y}$. But in the first case, we would have $\underline{w}.\underline{a}_\alpha \in \downarrow\underline{x} \cap \downarrow V_\mathcal{V}$ giving a contradiction to $\underline{w} = \bigsqcup(\downarrow\underline{x} \cap \downarrow V_\mathcal{V})$. Hence $\underline{w} \rhd_\mathcal{V} \underline{y}$, as required.

■

Proposition 6.1 If $\mathcal{V}$ is a concise cycle system, then $\mathcal{V}$ is cyclic.

Proof. Let $\underline{x} \in L_\mathcal{V} - \{\underline{\Omega}_\alpha\}$. By lemma 6.1, there exists $\underline{w} \in \downarrow V_\mathcal{V}$ such that $\underline{w} \neq \underline{\Omega}_\alpha$, $\underline{w} \leq \underline{x}$ and $\underline{w} \rhd_\mathcal{V} \underline{x}/\underline{w}$. As $\underline{w} \in \downarrow V_\mathcal{V}$, there exists $\underline{v} \in V_\mathcal{V}$ such that $\underline{w} \leq \underline{v}$. As $\underline{w} \leq \underline{x}$ and $\underline{w} \leq \underline{v}$, $\neg\underline{v}\ \mathit{ind}\ \underline{x}$. We show that $\underline{v} \leftrightarrow \underline{x}$ and apply proposition 3.3.

Let $i \in I$. If $\underline{y}(i)/\underline{w}(i) > \Omega$, then $\underline{w}(i) \in V_i$, because $\underline{w} \rhd_\mathcal{V} \underline{y}/\underline{w}$, and so $\Omega < \underline{w}(i) \leq \underline{v}(i)$, Hence, $\underline{w}(i) = \underline{v}(i)$, by the prefix property and so, $\underline{v}(i) = \underline{w}(i) \leq \underline{x}(i)$. If $\underline{y}(i)/\underline{w}(i) = \Omega$, then $\underline{x}(i) = \underline{w}(i) \leq \underline{v}(i)$.

■

Proposition 6.2 If $\mathcal{V}$ is a cycle system such that every element of $W_\mathcal{V}$ is connected, then $\mathcal{V}$ is cyclic $\Leftrightarrow$ $\mathcal{V}$ is normal.

Proof. If $\mathcal{V}$ is cyclic, then $\mathcal{V}$ is normal, by proposition 4.3. Conversely, suppose that $\mathcal{V}$ is normal, then since every element of $W_\mathcal{V}$ is connected, $\mathcal{V}$ is concise, by (2) of definition 4.4 and definition 6.1. By (1) of definition 4.4, $W_\mathcal{V} \subseteq \downarrow V_\mathcal{V}$, so that $W_\mathcal{V} \subseteq \downarrow(V_\mathcal{V}{}^*)$. By proposition 6.2, $\mathcal{V}$ is cyclic.

■

The conciseness property is not much use in general, since it requires knowledge of all behaviours. However, in certain situations, it may be deduced from local properties.

Definition 6.2 Suppose that $\mathcal{V}$ is a cycle system then $\mathcal{V}$ will be said to be *n-concise* $\Leftrightarrow$ whenever $\underline{w}_1, \cdots, \underline{w}_m \in \downarrow V_\mathcal{V}$. such that $m \leq n$, $\underline{w}_1 \cdots \underline{w}_m.\underline{a}_\alpha \in \downarrow(V_\mathcal{V}{}^*)$ and $\underline{w}_1 \rhd_\mathcal{V} \underline{w}_2 \cdots \underline{w}_m$, then one of the following holds

1• $\underline{w}_2 \cdots \underline{w}_m \; ind \; \underline{a}_\alpha$ and $\underline{w}_1 . \underline{a}_\alpha \in \downarrow V_\mathcal{V}$;
2• $\underline{w}_1 \rhd_\mathcal{V} \underline{w}_2 \cdots \underline{w}_m . \underline{a}_\alpha$.

We observe that if $\mathcal{V}$ is concise then $\mathcal{V}$ is n-concise and that if $\mathcal{V}$ is n-concise and $n > m \geq 2$, then $\mathcal{V}$ is m-concise.

Definition 6.3 If $\mathcal{V}$ is a cycle system then for each, $\underline{w} \in \downarrow V_\mathcal{V}$ we define

1• $\gamma_\mathcal{V}(\underline{w}) = |\{i \in I \mid \underline{w}(i) \in V_i|$
2• $\nu(\underline{w}) = |\{i \in I \mid \underline{w}(i) \neq \Omega\}|$
3• $\chi(\mathcal{V}) = min(\{\nu(\underline{w}) \mid \underline{w} \in \downarrow V_\mathcal{V} \wedge \gamma_\mathcal{V}(\underline{w}) > 0\})$

Obviously, $\nu(\underline{w}) \geq \gamma_\mathcal{V}(\underline{w})$.

Finally, we define the *slack* of $\mathcal{V}$, denoted by $\sigma(\mathcal{V})$, to be $(|\mathcal{V}| - \chi(\mathcal{V})) + 1$. We observe that

$$\nu(\underline{w}) = \gamma_\mathcal{V}(\underline{w}) \Leftrightarrow \underline{w} \in V_\mathcal{V} \tag{6.1}$$

and that if $\underline{w}, \underline{w}' \in \downarrow V_\mathcal{V}$, then

$$\underline{w} \rhd_\mathcal{V} \underline{w}' \Rightarrow \gamma_\mathcal{V}(\underline{w}) \geq \nu(\underline{w}') \tag{6.2}$$

and since $\nu(\underline{w}') \geq \gamma_\mathcal{V}(\underline{w}')$, $\underline{w} \rhd_\mathcal{V} \underline{w}' \Rightarrow \gamma_\mathcal{V}(\underline{w}) \geq \gamma_\mathcal{V}(\underline{w}')$. Also,

$$\forall \underline{w}, \underline{w}' \in \downarrow V_\mathcal{V} : \underline{w} \rhd_\mathcal{V} \underline{w}' \wedge \gamma_\mathcal{V}(\underline{w}) = \gamma_\mathcal{V}(\underline{w}') \Rightarrow \underline{w}' \in V_\mathcal{V} \tag{6.3}$$

for from (6.2), we deduce $\gamma_\mathcal{V}(\underline{w}') \geq \nu(\underline{w}')$ and as $\nu(\underline{w}') \geq \gamma_\mathcal{V}(\underline{w}')$, we may apply (6.1). We now have

Lemma 6.2 Suppose that $\mathcal{V}$ is a cycle system and that $\underline{w}_1, \cdots, \underline{w}_n \in \downarrow V_\mathcal{V}$. such that $\underline{w}_1 \rhd_\mathcal{V} \cdots \rhd_\mathcal{V} \underline{w}_n$, then if $n > \sigma(\mathcal{V})$, then $\underline{w}_r \in V_\mathcal{V}$ for some $1 \leq r \leq n$. Consequently, if $n > \sigma(\mathcal{V}) + 1$, then $\underline{w}_r \in V_\mathcal{V}$ for some $1 < r \leq n$.

Proof. Otherwise, by (6.3), we have $|\mathcal{V}| \geq \gamma(\underline{w}_1) > \cdots > \gamma(\underline{w}_n) \geq \chi(\mathcal{V})$ which entails that $n \leq (|\mathcal{V}| - \chi(\mathcal{V})) + 1$.

■

Lemma 6.3 Let $\mathcal{V}$ be a cycle system and let $\underline{w}_1, \cdots, \underline{w}_n \in \downarrow V_\mathcal{V}$. such that $\underline{w}_1 \rhd_\mathcal{V} \cdots \rhd_\mathcal{V} \underline{w}_n$. If $\underline{y} = \underline{w}_1 \cdots \underline{w}_{r-1} . \underline{w}_{r+1} \cdots \underline{w}_n$, some $1 < r \leq n$, then for all $\underline{u} \in A_\alpha{}^*$:

1• $(\underline{w}_1\cdots\underline{w}_n)(i)>\Omega \Leftrightarrow \underline{y}(i)>\Omega$;

2• If $\underline{w}_r\in V_\nu$, then $\underline{y}.\underline{u}\in L_\nu \Leftrightarrow \underline{w}_1\cdots\underline{w}_n.\underline{u}\in L_\nu$.

Proof. (1) Let $i\in I$. Since $\underline{y}=\underline{w}_1\cdots\underline{w}_{r-1}.\underline{w}_{r+1}\cdots\underline{w}_n$, $(\underline{w}_1\cdots\underline{w}_n)(i)=\Omega\Rightarrow\underline{y}(i)=\Omega$. Conversely, if $\underline{y}(i)=\Omega$, then $\underline{w}_1(i)=\Omega$ and so $\underline{w}_s(i)=\Omega$, all $1\le s\le n$, so $(\underline{w}_1\cdots\underline{w}_n)(i)=\Omega$.

(2) Let $i\in I$. If $\underline{w}_r(i)=\Omega$, then $\underline{y}(i).\underline{u}(i)=\underline{w}_1(i)\cdots\underline{w}_n(i).\underline{u}(i)$, so in this case

$$\underline{y}(i).\underline{u}(i)\in\downarrow(V_i^*)\Leftrightarrow\underline{w}_1(i)\cdots\underline{w}_n(i).\underline{u}(i)\in\downarrow(V_i^*).$$

If $\underline{w}_r(i)\neq\Omega$, then $\underline{w}_1(i),\cdots,\underline{w}_r(i)\in V_\nu$ and so by lemma 3.1:

$$\begin{aligned}\underline{y}(i).\underline{u}(i)\in\downarrow(V_i^*)&\Leftrightarrow\underline{w}_{r+1}(i)\cdots\underline{w}_n(i).\underline{u}(i)\in\downarrow(V_i^*)\\&\Leftrightarrow\underline{w}_1(i)\cdots\underline{w}_n(i).\underline{u}(i)\in\downarrow(V_i^*)\end{aligned}$$

Since $\underline{y}.\underline{u},\underline{w}_1\cdots\underline{w}_n.\underline{u}\in A_\alpha^*$:

$$\begin{aligned}\underline{y}.\underline{u}\in L_\nu&\Leftrightarrow(\forall i\in I:(\underline{y}.\underline{u})(i)\in\downarrow(V_i^*))\\&\Leftrightarrow(\forall i\in I:(\underline{w}_1\cdots\underline{w}_n.\underline{u})(i)\in\downarrow(V_i^*))\Leftrightarrow\underline{w}_1\cdots\underline{w}_n.\underline{u}\in L_\nu\end{aligned}$$

■

Lemma 6.4 If $\mathcal{V}$ is a $\sigma(\mathcal{V})+1$-concise cycle system and $\underline{w}\in\downarrow V_\nu$, $\underline{y}\in A_\alpha^*$ and $a\in A$. such that $\underline{w}.\underline{y}.\underline{a}_\alpha\in L_\nu$ and $\underline{w}\rhd_\nu\underline{y}$, then there exists $n\le\sigma(\mathcal{V})+1$ and $\underline{w}_1,\cdots,\underline{w}_n\in\downarrow V_\nu$ such that $\underline{w}\rhd_\nu\underline{w}_1\rhd_\nu\cdots\rhd_\nu\underline{w}_n$ and

1• $\underline{w}.\underline{w}_1\cdots\underline{w}_n.\underline{a}_\alpha\in L_\nu$;

2• $(\underline{w}_1\cdots\underline{w}_n)(i)=\Omega\Leftrightarrow\underline{y}(i)=\Omega$.

Proof. Let $\underline{w}_1=\sqcup(\downarrow\underline{y}\cap\downarrow V_\nu)$. $\underline{w}_1$ is defined, as $\downarrow\underline{y}\cap\downarrow V_\nu$ is bounded above by $\underline{y}$, and belongs to $\downarrow V_\nu$. As $\underline{w}_1(i)\neq\Omega\Rightarrow\underline{y}(i)\neq\Omega\Rightarrow\underline{w}(i)\in V_i$, $\underline{w}\rhd_\nu\underline{w}_1$. Let $\underline{y}_1=\underline{y}/\underline{w}_1$ and for each $r\ge1$, define $\underline{w}_{r+1}=\sqcup\{\underline{u}\in\downarrow\underline{y}_r\cap\downarrow V_\nu\mid\underline{w}_r\rhd_\nu\underline{u}\}$ and $\underline{y}_{r+1}=\underline{y}_r/\underline{w}_{r+1}$. Again, each $\underline{w}_r$ is defined, as $\{\underline{u}\in\downarrow\underline{y}_r\cap\downarrow V_\nu\mid\underline{w}_r\rhd_\nu\underline{u}\}$ is bounded above by $\underline{y}_r$, and belongs to $\downarrow V_\nu$. If $\underline{w}_{r+1}(i)\neq\Omega$, then $\underline{u}(i)\neq\Omega$, some $\underline{u}\in\downarrow\underline{y}_r\cap\downarrow V_\nu$ with $\underline{w}_r\rhd_\nu\underline{u}$ and so $\underline{w}_r(i)\in V_i$. Thus, $\underline{w}_r\rhd_\nu\underline{w}_{r+1}$, each $r\ge1$.

Suppose that $\underline{w}_n\neq\underline{\Omega}_\alpha$ and $\underline{w}_{n+1}=\underline{\Omega}_\alpha$. By lemmas 6.2 and 6.3, we may assume that $n\le\sigma(\mathcal{V})+1$. We shall prove that $\underline{w}_1\cdots\underline{w}_r=\underline{y}$. Suppose not, then there exists $b \in A$ such that $\underline{b}_\alpha \le \underline{y}/(\underline{w}_1 \cdots \underline{w}_n) = \underline{y}_n / \underline{w}_n$. Thus, $\underline{w}_1 \cdots \underline{w}_n . \underline{b}_\alpha \le \underline{y}$ and so by proposition 3.1 and definition 3.5, $\underline{w}_1 \cdots \underline{w}_n . \underline{b}_\alpha \in L_\mathcal{V}$. As $\underline{w}_1 \rhd_\mathcal{V} \cdots \rhd_\mathcal{V} \underline{w}_n$, $\underline{w}_1 \rhd_\mathcal{V} \underline{w}_2 \cdots \underline{w}_n$ and so as $n \le \sigma(\mathcal{V})+1$ and $\mathcal{V}$ is a $\sigma(\mathcal{V})+1$-concise, either $\underline{w}_1 . \underline{b}_\alpha \in \downarrow V_\mathcal{V}$ and $\underline{b}_\alpha$ *ind* $\underline{w}_2 \cdots \underline{w}_n$ or $\underline{w}_1 \rhd_\mathcal{V} \underline{w}_2 \cdots \underline{w}_n . \underline{b}_\alpha$. But in the first case $\underline{w}_1 . \underline{b}_\alpha \le \underline{w}_1 . \underline{b}_\alpha . \underline{w}_2 \cdots \underline{w}_n = \underline{w}_1 . \underline{w}_2 \cdots \underline{w}_n . \underline{b}_\alpha \le \underline{y}$ and we have a contradiction to $\underline{w}_1 = \sqcup(\downarrow \underline{y} \cap \downarrow V_\mathcal{V})$. Thus, $\underline{w}_1 \rhd_\mathcal{V} \underline{w}_2 \cdots \underline{w}_n . \underline{b}_\alpha$. We prove that whenever $r < n$ and $\underline{w}_r \rhd_\mathcal{V} \underline{w}_{r+1} \cdots \underline{w}_n . \underline{b}_\alpha$, then $\underline{w}_{r+1} \rhd_\mathcal{V} \underline{w}_{r+2} \cdots \underline{w}_n . \underline{b}_\alpha$.

Let $\underline{w}_r \rhd_\mathcal{V} \underline{w}_{r+1} \cdots \underline{w}_n . \underline{b}_\alpha$, then $\underline{w}_{r+1} \cdots \underline{w}_n . \underline{b}_\alpha \in L_\mathcal{V}$, by (1) of lemma 4.3, and as $\underline{w}_{r+1} \rhd_\mathcal{V} \cdots \rhd_\mathcal{V} \underline{w}_n$, $\underline{w}_{r+1} \rhd_\mathcal{V} \underline{w}_{r+2} \cdots \underline{w}_n$. As $n - r \le \sigma(\mathcal{V})+1$ and $\mathcal{V}$ is $\sigma(\mathcal{V})+1$-concise, either $\underline{w}_{r+1} . \underline{b}_\alpha \in \downarrow V_\mathcal{V}$ and $\underline{b}_\alpha$ *ind* $\underline{w}_{r+2} \cdots \underline{w}_n$ or $\underline{w}_{r+1} \rhd_\mathcal{V} \underline{w}_{r+2} \cdots \underline{w}_n . \underline{b}_\alpha$. But, in the first case, $\underline{w}_{r+1} . \underline{b}_\alpha \in \downarrow \underline{y}_r \cap \downarrow V_\mathcal{V}$ and as $\underline{w}_r \rhd_\mathcal{V} \underline{w}_{r+1} \cdots \underline{w}_n . \underline{b}_\alpha$, $\underline{w}_r \rhd_\mathcal{V} \underline{w}_{r+1} . \underline{b}_\alpha$, contradicting $\underline{w}_{r+1} = \sqcup\{\underline{u} \in \downarrow \underline{y}_r \cap \downarrow V_\mathcal{V} \mid \underline{w}_r \rhd_\mathcal{V} \underline{u}\}$.

By induction, $\underline{b}_\alpha \le \underline{y}_n / \underline{w}_n$ and $\underline{w}_n \rhd_\mathcal{V} \underline{b}_\alpha$, contradicting $\underline{w}_{n+1} = \underline{\Omega}_\alpha$.

■

Proposition 6.3 A cycle system $\mathcal{V}$ is $\sigma(\mathcal{V})+1$-concise $\Leftrightarrow$ $\mathcal{V}$ is concise.

Proof. We have already observed that $\mathcal{V}$ is concise $\Rightarrow$ $\mathcal{V}$ is n-concise, all n. Suppose that $\mathcal{V}$ is $\sigma(\mathcal{V})+1$-concise. Let $\underline{w} \in \downarrow V_\mathcal{V}$, $\underline{y} \in A_\alpha^*$ and $a \in A$. such that $\underline{w} . \underline{y} . \underline{a}_\alpha \in L_\mathcal{V}$ and $\underline{w} \rhd_\mathcal{V} \underline{y}$. By lemma 6.4, there exists $n \le \sigma(\mathcal{V})+1$ and $\underline{w}_1, \cdots, \underline{w}_n \in \downarrow V_\mathcal{V}$ such that $\underline{w} \rhd_\mathcal{V} \underline{w}_1 \rhd_\mathcal{V} \cdots \rhd_\mathcal{V} \underline{w}_n$, $\underline{w} . \underline{w}_1 \cdots \underline{w}_n . \underline{a}_\alpha \in L_\mathcal{V}$ and $(\underline{w}_1 \cdots \underline{w}_n)(i) = \Omega \Leftrightarrow \underline{y}(i) = \Omega$.

If $(\underline{w}_1 \cdots \underline{w}_n)(i) \ne \Omega$, then $\underline{y}(i) \ne \Omega$ and so $\underline{w}(i) \in V_i$, as $\underline{w} \rhd_\mathcal{V} \underline{y}$. Hence. $\underline{w} \rhd_\mathcal{V} \underline{w}_1 \cdots \underline{w}_n$. As $\mathcal{V}$ is $\sigma(\mathcal{V})+1$-concise and $n \le \sigma(\mathcal{V})+1$, either $\underline{w} . \underline{a}_\alpha \in \downarrow V_\mathcal{V}$ and $\underline{a}_\alpha$ *ind* $\underline{w}_1 \cdots \underline{w}_n$ or $\underline{w} \rhd_\mathcal{V} \underline{w}_1 \cdots \underline{w}_n . \underline{a}_\alpha$, But, $(\underline{w}_1 \cdots \underline{w}_n)(i) = \Omega \Leftrightarrow \underline{y}(i) = \Omega$ and so $\underline{a}_\alpha$ *ind* $\underline{w}_1 \cdots \underline{w}_n$ implies $\underline{a}_\alpha$ *ind* $\underline{y}$ and $\underline{w}_1 \rhd_\mathcal{V} \underline{w}_2 \cdots \underline{w}_{\sigma(\mathcal{V})} . \underline{a}_\alpha$ implies $\underline{w}_1 \rhd_\mathcal{V} \underline{y} . \underline{a}_\alpha$.

■

6.4 Proposition. If $\mathcal{V}$ is a $\sigma(\mathcal{V})+1$-concise cycle system then $\mathcal{V}$ is cyclic.

Proof. By propositions 6.1 and 6.3.

■

References

[Hoa85] Hoare, C. A.. R: *Communicating Sequential Processes*, Prentice-Hall, 1985

[JaL92] Janicki, R. and Lauer, P. E.: *Specification and Analysis for Concurrent Systems*, Springer Verlag, 1992.

[Maz77] Concurrent Program Schemes and their Interpretations. DAIMI Rep. PB 78, Aarhus University, Aarhus, 1977.

[Maz97] A Prefix Function View of States and Events, Proceedings POMIV'96 Workshop on Partial Order Methods in Verification, Princeton, July 1997.

[Shi82] Shields, M. W.: Non-Sequential Behaviours: 1, Tech. Report CRS-120-82, Department of Computer Science, University of Edinburgh, June 1982.

[Shi97] Shields, M. W.: *Semantics of Parallelism*, Springer Verlag, 1997.

A Product Version of Dynamic Linear Time Temporal Logic

Jesper G. Henriksen[1] and P. S. Thiagarajan[2*]

[1] BRICS**, Department of Computer Science, University of Aarhus, Denmark
[2] SPIC Mathematical Institute, Madras, India

Abstract. We present here a linear time temporal logic which simultaneously extends LTL, the propositional temporal logic of linear time, along two dimensions. Firstly, the until operator is strengthened by indexing it with the regular programs of propositional dynamic logic (PDL). Secondly, the core formulas of the logic are decorated with names of sequential agents drawn from fixed finite set. The resulting logic has a natural semantics in terms of the runs of a distributed program consisting of a finite set of sequential programs that communicate by performing common actions together. We show that our logic, denoted $\mathrm{DLTL}^{\otimes}$, admits an exponential time decision procedure. We also show that $\mathrm{DLTL}^{\otimes}$ is expressively equivalent to the so called regular product languages. Roughly speaking, this class of languages is obtained by starting with synchronized products of (ω-)regular languages and closing under boolean operations. We also sketch how the behaviours captured by our temporal logic fit into the framework of labelled partial orders known as Mazurkiewicz traces.

1 Introduction

We present a linear time temporal logic which extends LTL, the propositional temporal logic of linear time [8,13] along two dimensions. Firstly, we strengthen the until modality by indexing it with the regular programs of PDL, propositional dynamic logic [1,4]. Secondly, we consider networks of sequential agents that communicate by performing common actions together. We then reflect this in the logic by decorating the "core" formulas with the names of the agents. The resulting logic, denoted $\mathrm{DLTL}^{\otimes}$, is a smooth generalization of the logic called product LTL [16] and the logic called dynamic linear time temporal logic [5].

$\mathrm{DLTL}^{\otimes}$ admits a pleasant theory and our technical goal here is to sketch the main results of this theory. We believe that these results provide additional evidence — in a non-sequential setting — suggesting that our technique of combining dynamic and temporal logic as initiated in [5] is a fruitful one.

---

* Part of this work was done while visiting BRICS.
Part of this work has been supported by IFCPAR Project 1502-1.

** Basic Research in Computer Science,
Centre of the Danish National Research Foundation.

In the next section we introduce dynamic linear time temporal logic. We then state two main results concerning this logic. In Section 3 we define regular product languages. These are basically boolean combinations of synchronized products of (ω-)regular languages. We then present a characterization of this class of languages in terms of networks of Büchi automata that coordinate their activities by synchronizing on common letters.

In Section 4 we formulate the temporal logic $\text{DLTL}^{\otimes}$, the main object of study in this paper. In Section 5 we establish an exponential time decision procedure for this logic by exploiting the Büchi automata networks presented in Section 3. In the subsequent section we show that $\text{DLTL}^{\otimes}$ captures exactly the class of regular product languages. It is worth noting that this is the first temporal logical characterization of this important class of distributed behaviours. In the final section we sketch how the behaviours described by our temporal logic (i.e. regular product languages) lie naturally within the domain of regular Mazurkiewicz trace languages.

2 Dynamic Linear Time Temporal Logic

One key feature of the syntax and semantics of our temporal logic is that *actions* will be treated as first class objects. The usual presentation of LTL [8,13] is based on *states*; they are represented as subsets of a finite set of atomic propositions. We wish to bring in actions explicitly because it is awkward, if not difficult, to define synchronized products of sequential components in a purely state-based setting. This method of forming distributed systems is a common and useful one. Moreover, it is the main focus of attention in this paper. Hence it will be handy to work with logics in which both states and actions can be treated on an equal footing. As a vehicle for introducing some terminology we shall first introduce an action-based version of LTL denoted LTL(Σ). We begin with some notations.

Through the rest of the paper we fix a finite non-empty alphabet Σ. We let a, b range over Σ and refer to members of Σ as actions. Σ^* is the set of finite words and Σ^ω is the set of infinite words generated by Σ with $\omega = \{0, 1, \ldots\}$. We set $\Sigma^\infty = \Sigma^* \cup \Sigma^\omega$ and denote the null word by ε. We let σ, σ' range over Σ^∞ and τ, τ', τ'' range over Σ^*. Finally, $\preceq$ is the usual prefix ordering defined over Σ^* and $\mathrm{prf}(\sigma)$ is the set of finite prefixes of σ.

The set of formulas of LTL(Σ) is then given by the syntax:

$$\mathrm{LTL}(\Sigma) ::= \top \mid \sim\alpha \mid \alpha \vee \beta \mid \langle a \rangle \alpha \mid \alpha\, \mathcal{U}\, \beta.$$

For convenience we have avoided introducing atomic propositions and instead just deal with the constant $\top$ and its negation $\sim\top \overset{\Delta}{\Longleftrightarrow} \bot$. Through the rest of this section α, β will range over LTL(Σ). The modality $\langle a \rangle$ is an action-indexed version of the next-state modality of LTL. A model is a ω-sequence $\sigma \in \Sigma^\omega$. For $\tau \in \mathrm{prf}(\sigma)$ we define $\sigma, \tau \models \alpha$ via:

- $\sigma, \tau \models \top$.
- $\sigma, \tau \models \sim\alpha$ iff $\sigma, \tau \not\models \alpha$.

- $\sigma, \tau \models \alpha \vee \beta$ iff $\sigma, \tau \models \alpha$ or $\sigma, \tau \models \beta$.
- $\sigma, \tau \models \langle a \rangle \alpha$ iff $\tau a \in \mathrm{prf}(\sigma)$ and $\sigma, \tau a \models \alpha$.
- $\sigma, \tau \models \alpha \; \mathcal{U} \; \beta$ iff there exists τ' such that $\tau\tau' \in \mathrm{prf}(\sigma)$ and $\sigma, \tau\tau' \models \beta$. Further, for every τ'' such that $\varepsilon \preceq \tau'' \prec \tau'$, it is the case that $\sigma, \tau\tau'' \models \alpha$.

It is well known that LTL(Σ) is equal in expressive power to the first order theory of sequences [2,7]. Consequently this temporal logic is quite limited in in terms of what it can not say. As an example, let $\Sigma = \{a, b\}$. Then the property "at every even position the action b is executed" is not definable in LTL(Σ). This observation, made in a state-based setting by Wolper, is the starting point for the extension of LTL called ETL [20,21]. The route that we have taken to augment the expressive power of LTL(Σ) is similar in spirit but quite different in terms of the structuring mechanisms made available for constructing compound formulas. A more detailed assessment of the similarities and the differences between the two approaches is given in [5].

The extension that we have proposed is called DLTL(Σ). It basically consists of indexing the until operator with the programs of PDL (e.g. [1]). We start by defining the set of regular programs (expressions) generated by Σ. This set is denoted by Prg(Σ) and its syntax is given by:

$$\mathrm{Prg}(\Sigma) ::= a \mid \pi_0 + \pi_1 \mid \pi_0; \pi_1 \mid \pi^*.$$

With each program we associate a set of finite words via the map $|| \cdot || : \mathrm{Prg}(\Sigma) \longrightarrow 2^{\Sigma^*}$. This map is defined in the standard fashion:

- $||a|| = \{a\}$.
- $||\pi_0 + \pi_1|| = ||\pi_0|| \cup ||\pi_1||$.
- $||\pi_0; \pi_1|| = \{\tau_0\tau_1 \mid \tau_0 \in ||\pi_0|| \text{ and } \tau_1 \in ||\pi_1||\}$.
- $||\pi^*|| = \bigcup_{i \in \omega} ||\pi^i||$, where
  - $||\pi^0|| = \{\varepsilon\}$ and
  - $||\pi^{i+1}|| = \{\tau_0\tau_1 \mid \tau_0 \in ||\pi|| \text{ and } \tau_1 \in ||\pi^i||\}$ for every $i \in \omega$.

The set of formulas of DLTL(Σ) is given by the following syntax.

$$\mathrm{DLTL}(\Sigma) ::= \top \mid \sim\alpha \mid \alpha \vee \beta \mid \alpha \, \mathcal{U}^\pi \beta, \quad \pi \in \mathrm{Prg}(\Sigma)$$

A model is a ω-sequence $\sigma \in \Sigma^\omega$. For $\tau \in \mathrm{prf}(\sigma)$ we define $\sigma, \tau \models \alpha$ just as we did for LTL(Σ) in the case of the first three clauses. As for the last one,

- $\sigma, \tau \models \alpha \, \mathcal{U}^\pi \beta$ iff there exists $\tau' \in ||\pi||$ such that $\tau\tau' \in \mathrm{prf}(\sigma)$ and $\sigma, \tau\tau' \models \beta$. Moreover, for every τ'' such that $\varepsilon \preceq \tau'' \prec \tau'$, it is the case that $\sigma, \tau\tau'' \models \alpha$.

Thus DLTL(Σ) adds to LTL(Σ) by strengthening the until operator. To satisfy $\alpha \; \mathcal{U}^\pi \beta$, one must satisfy $\alpha \mathcal{U} \beta$ along some finite stretch of behaviour which is required to be in the (linear time) behaviour of the program π. We now wish to state two of the main results of [5]. To do so, we first say that a formula $\alpha \in \mathrm{DLTL}(\Sigma)$ is *satisfiable* if there exist $\sigma \in \Sigma^\omega$ and $\tau \in \mathrm{prf}(\sigma)$ such that $\sigma, \tau \models \alpha$. Secondly, we associate with a formula α the ω-language L_α via:

$$L_\alpha \stackrel{\text{def}}{=} \{\sigma \in \Sigma^\omega \mid \sigma, \varepsilon \models \alpha\}.$$

A language $L \subseteq \Sigma^\omega$ is said to be DLTL(Σ)-definable if there exists some $\alpha \in$ DLTL(Σ) such that $L = L_\alpha$. Finally, we assume the notions of Büchi and Muller automata and ω-regular languages as formulated in [17].

Theorem 1.

(i) *Given an* $\alpha_0 \in$ DLTL(Σ) *one can effectively construct a Büchi automaton* $\mathcal{B}_{\alpha_0}$ *of size* $2^{O(|\alpha_0|)}$ *such that* $\mathcal{L}(\mathcal{B}_{\alpha_0}) \neq \emptyset$ *iff* α_0 *is satisfiable. Thus the satisfiability problem for* DLTL(Σ) *is decidable in exponential time.*
(ii) $L \subseteq \Sigma^\omega$ *is* ω*-regular iff* L *is* DLTL(Σ)*-definable.*

It is also easy to formulate and solve a natural model checking problem for DLTL(Σ) where finite state programs are modelled as Büchi automata. But we shall not enter into details here.

To close out the section we shall point to two useful derived operators of DLTL(Σ):

- $\langle\pi\rangle\alpha \stackrel{\Delta}{\Longleftrightarrow} \top\, \mathcal{U}^\pi \alpha$.
- $[\pi]\alpha \stackrel{\Delta}{\Longleftrightarrow} \sim\langle\pi\rangle\sim\alpha$.

Suppose $\sigma \in \Sigma^\omega$ is a model and $\tau \in \text{prf}(\sigma)$. It is easy to see that $\sigma, \tau \models \langle\pi\rangle\alpha$ iff there exists $\tau' \in ||\pi||$ such that $\tau\tau' \in \text{prf}(\sigma)$ and $\sigma, \tau\tau' \models \alpha$. It is also easy to see that $\sigma, \tau \models [\pi]\alpha$ iff for every $\tau' \in ||\pi||$, $\tau\tau' \in \text{prf}(\sigma)$ implies $\sigma, \tau\tau' \models \alpha$. In this sense, the program modalities of PDL acquire a linear time semantics in the present setting. As shown in [5] the second part of Theorem 1 goes through even for the the sublogic of DLTL(Σ) obtained by banishing the until operator and instead using $\langle\pi\rangle\alpha$ and the boolean connectives. For an example of what can be said in this sublogic, assume $\Sigma = \{a, b\}$ and define π_{ev} to be the program $((a + b); (a + b))^*$. Then the formula $[\pi_{ev}]\langle b\rangle\top$ says "at every even position the action b is executed".

Next we note that $a \in \Sigma$ is a member of Prg(Σ) and the until operator of LTL(Σ) can be obtained via: $\alpha\mathcal{U}\beta \stackrel{\Delta}{\Longleftrightarrow} \alpha\mathcal{U}^{\Sigma^*}\beta$. Due to second part of Theorem 1 we now have that both syntactically and semantically, LTL(Σ) is a *proper* fragment of DLTL(Σ).

To conclude the section, we note that the material presented here can be easily extended to include finite sequences over Σ as well. We shall assume from now on that this extension has indeed been carried out.

3 Regular Product Languages

A restricted but very useful model of finite state concurrent programs consists of a fixed number of finite state *sequential* programs that coordinate their activities by performing common actions together. A regular product language is an abstract specification of the linear time behaviour of such concurrent programs. The idea is to start with synchronized products of regular languages and close under boolean operations. Formally, we start with a *distributed alphabet* $\widetilde{\Sigma} = \{\Sigma_i\}_{i=1}^K$, a family of alphabets with each Σ_i a non-empty finite set of actions. One key point is that the component alphabets are not necessarily disjoint. Intuitively, $Loc = \{1, \ldots, K\}$ is the set of names of communicating sequential processes synchronizing on common actions, where Σ_i is the set of actions which require the participation of the agent i. Through the rest of the paper we fix a distributed alphabet $\widetilde{\Sigma} = \{\Sigma_i\}_{i=1}^K$ and set $\Sigma = \bigcup_{i=1}^K \Sigma_i$. We carry over the terminology developed in the previous section for dealing with finite and infinite sequences over Σ. In addition, for $\sigma \in \Sigma^\infty$ and $i \in Loc$ we denote by $\sigma \restriction i$ the projection of σ down to Σ_i. In other words, it is the sequence obtained by erasing from σ all occurrences of symbols that are not in Σ_i. We let i, j, k range over $Loc = \{1, \ldots, K\}$ and define $Loc(a) = \{i \mid a \in \Sigma_i\}$. We note that $Loc(a)$ is the set of processes that participate in each occurrence of the action a.

Next we define the K-ary operator $\otimes : 2^{\Sigma_1^\infty} \times \ldots \times 2^{\Sigma_K^\infty} \to 2^{\Sigma^\infty}$ by

$$\otimes(L_1, \ldots, L_K) = \{\sigma \in \Sigma^\infty \mid \sigma \restriction i \in L_i \text{ for each } i \in Loc\}.$$

Usually we will write $\otimes(L_1, \ldots, L_K)$ as $L_1 \otimes L_2 \otimes \ldots \otimes L_K$. Finally, we will say that the language $L \subseteq \Sigma^\infty$ is regular iff $L \cap \Sigma^*$ is a regular subset of Σ^* and $L \cap \Sigma^\omega$ is an ω-regular subset of Σ^ω. Regular product languages can be built up as follows.

Definition 2. $L \subseteq \Sigma^\infty$ is a *direct* regular product language over $\widetilde{\Sigma}$ iff $L = L_1 \otimes \ldots \otimes L_K$ with L_i a regular subset of Σ_i^∞ for each $i \in Loc$.

We let $\mathcal{R}_0^\otimes(\widetilde{\Sigma})$ be the class of direct regular product languages over $\widetilde{\Sigma}$.

Definition 3. The class of regular product languages over $\widetilde{\Sigma}$ is denoted $\mathcal{R}^\otimes(\widetilde{\Sigma})$ and is the least class of languages containing $\mathcal{R}_0^\otimes(\widetilde{\Sigma})$ and satisfying:

- If $L_1, L_2 \in \mathcal{R}^\otimes(\widetilde{\Sigma})$ then $L_1 \cup L_2 \in \mathcal{R}^\otimes(\widetilde{\Sigma})$.

In what follows we will often suppress the mention of the distributed alphabet $\widetilde{\Sigma}$. It is easy to prove that $\mathcal{R}^\otimes$ is closed under boolean operations. The proof of this result as well as other results mentioned in this section can be found in [15]. Just as ω-regular languages are captured by Büchi automata, we can capture regular product languages with the help of networks of Büchi automata. For convenience such automata will be termed product automata.

Definition 4. A *product automaton over* $\widetilde{\Sigma}$ is a structure $\mathcal{A} = (\{\mathcal{A}_i\}_{i \in Loc}, Q_{in})$, where each $\mathcal{A}_i = (Q_i, \longrightarrow_i, F_i, F_i^\omega)$ satisfies:

- Q_i is a non-empty finite set of i-local states.
- $\longrightarrow_i \subseteq Q_i \times \Sigma_i \times Q_i$ is the transition relation of the ith component.
- $F_i \subseteq Q_i$ is a set of finitary accepting states of the ith component.

- $F_i^\omega \subseteq Q_i$ is a set of infinitary accepting states of the ith component.

Moreover, $Q_{in} \subseteq Q_1 \times \ldots \times Q_K$ is a set of global initial states.

Thus, a product automaton is a network of local automata with a global set of initial states. It is necessary to have global initial states in order to obtain the required expressive power. Each local automaton is equipped to cope with both finite and infinite behaviours using the finitary and infinitary accepting states. The infinitary accepting states are to be interpreted as defining a Büchi acceptance condition. This will become clear once we define the language accepted by a product automaton. We choose to deal with both finite and infinite component behaviours because the global behaviour can always induce finite local behaviours. In other words, even if ω-behaviour is the main focus of interest, a global infinite run will consist of one or more components running forever but with some other components, in general, quitting after making a finite number of moves. The notational complications involved in artificially making *all* components to run forever do not seem to be worth the trouble.

Let $\mathcal{A}$ be a product automaton over $\tilde{\Sigma}$. Then $Q_G^{\mathcal{A}} = Q_1 \times \ldots \times Q_K$ is the set of global states of $\mathcal{A}$. The i-local transition relations induce a global transition relation $\longrightarrow_{\mathcal{A}} \subseteq Q_G^{\mathcal{A}} \times \Sigma \times Q_G^{\mathcal{A}}$ as follows:

$$q \xrightarrow{a}_{\mathcal{A}} q' \text{ iff } \begin{array}{l} q[i] \xrightarrow{a}_i q'[i] \text{ for each } i \in Loc(a) \text{ and} \\ q[i] = q'[i] \text{ for each } i \notin Loc(a), \end{array}$$

where $q[i]$ denotes the ith component of $q = (q_1, \ldots, q_K)$. A run of $\mathcal{A}$ over $\sigma \in \Sigma^\infty$ is a mapping $\rho : \text{prf}(\sigma) \to Q_G^{\mathcal{A}}$ satisfying that $\rho(\varepsilon) \in Q_{in}$ and $\rho(\tau) \xrightarrow{a}_{\mathcal{A}} \rho(\tau a)$ for all $\tau a \in \text{prf}(\sigma)$. The run is *accepting* iff the following conditions are satisfied for each i:

- If $\sigma \restriction i$ is finite then $\rho(\tau)[i] \in F_i$ for some $\tau \in \text{prf}(\sigma)$ with $\tau \restriction i = \sigma \restriction i$.
- If $\sigma \restriction i$ is infinite then $\rho(\tau)[i] \in F_i^\omega$ for infinitely many $\tau \in \text{prf}(\sigma)$.

We next define

$$\mathcal{L}(\mathcal{A}) = \{\sigma \in \Sigma^\infty \mid \text{there exists an accepting run of } \mathcal{A} \text{ over } \sigma\}.$$

The next result established relates regular product languages to product automata.

Theorem 5. *$L \in \mathcal{R}^\otimes(\tilde{\Sigma})$ iff $L = \mathcal{L}(\mathcal{A})$ for some product automaton $\mathcal{A}$ over $\tilde{\Sigma}$.*

We will later give solutions to the satisfiability problem for a product version of DLTL with the help of product automata. The following results will be useful in this context. In stating these results we take the *size* of the product automaton $\mathcal{A}$ to be $|Q_G^{\mathcal{A}}|$.

Lemma 6.

- *Let $\mathcal{A}$ be a product automaton. The question $\mathcal{L}(\mathcal{A}) \overset{?}{\neq} \emptyset$ can be effectively decided in time $O(n^2)$, where n is the size of $\mathcal{A}$.*
- *Let $\mathcal{A}_1$ and $\mathcal{A}_2$ be product automata of sizes n_1 and n_2, respectively. Then a product automaton $\mathcal{A}$ of size $O(n_1 n_2)$ with $\mathcal{L}(\mathcal{A}) = \mathcal{L}(\mathcal{A}_1) \cap \mathcal{L}(\mathcal{A}_2)$ can be effectively constructed.*

4 A Product Version of DLTL

We now wish to design a product version of DLTL denoted $\mathrm{DLTL}^{\otimes}(\widetilde{\Sigma})$. It will turn out to have the expressive power of regular product languages over $\widetilde{\Sigma}$. The set of formulas and their *locations* are given by:

- $\top$ is a formula and $\mathrm{loc}(\top) = \emptyset$.
- Suppose α and β are formulas. Then so are $\sim\alpha$ and $\alpha \vee \beta$. Furthermore, $\mathrm{loc}(\sim\alpha) = \mathrm{loc}(\alpha)$ and $\mathrm{loc}(\alpha \vee \beta) = \mathrm{loc}(\alpha) \cup \mathrm{loc}(\beta)$.
- Suppose α and β are formulas such that $\mathrm{loc}(\alpha), \mathrm{loc}(\beta) \subseteq \{i\}$ and suppose $\pi \in \mathrm{Prg}(\Sigma_i)$. Then $\alpha\, \mathcal{U}_i^{\pi} \beta$ is a formula. Moreover, $\mathrm{loc}(\alpha\, \mathcal{U}_i^{\pi} \beta) = \{i\}$.

We note that each formula in $\mathrm{DLTL}^{\otimes}(\widetilde{\Sigma})$ is a boolean combination of formulas taken from the set $\bigcup_{i \in Loc} \mathrm{DLTL}_i^{\otimes}(\widetilde{\Sigma})$ where, for each i,

$$\mathrm{DLTL}_i^{\otimes}(\widetilde{\Sigma}) = \{\alpha \mid \alpha \in \mathrm{DLTL}^{\otimes}(\widetilde{\Sigma}) \text{ and } \mathrm{loc}(\alpha) \subseteq \{i\}\ \}.$$

Once again, we have chosen to avoid dealing with atomic propositions for the sake of convenience. They can be introduced in a local fashion as done in [15]. The decidability result to be presented will go through with minor notational overheads.

As before, we will often suppress the mention of $\widetilde{\Sigma}$. We will also often write τ_i, τ_i' and τ_i'' instead of $\tau \restriction i$, $\tau' \restriction i$ and $\tau'' \restriction i$, respectively with $\tau, \tau', \tau'' \in \Sigma^*$.

A model is a sequence $\sigma \in \Sigma^\infty$ and the semantics of this logic is given as before, with $\tau \in \mathrm{prf}(\sigma)$.

- $\sigma, \tau \models \top$.
- $\sigma, \tau \models \sim\alpha$ iff $\sigma, \tau \not\models \alpha$.
- $\sigma, \tau \models \alpha \vee \beta$ iff $\sigma, \tau \models \alpha$ or $\sigma, \tau \models \beta$.
- $\sigma, \tau \models \alpha\, \mathcal{U}_i^{\pi} \beta$ iff there exists τ' such that $\tau_i' \in ||\pi||$ (recall that $\tau_i' = \tau' \restriction i$) and $\tau\tau' \in \mathrm{prf}(\sigma)$ and $\sigma, \tau\tau' \models \beta$. Further, for every $\tau'' \in \mathrm{prf}(\tau')$, if $\varepsilon \preceq \tau_i'' \prec \tau_i'$ then $\sigma, \tau\tau'' \models \alpha$.

We will say that a formula $\alpha \in \mathrm{DLTL}^{\otimes}(\widetilde{\Sigma})$ is *satisfiable* if there exist $\sigma \in \Sigma^\infty$ and $\tau \in \mathrm{prf}(\sigma)$ such that $\sigma, \tau \models \alpha$. The language defined by α is given by

$$L_\alpha \stackrel{\mathrm{def}}{=} \{\sigma \in \Sigma^\infty \mid \sigma, \varepsilon \models \alpha\}.$$

We say that $L \subseteq \Sigma^\infty$ is $\mathrm{DLTL}^{\otimes}(\widetilde{\Sigma})$-definable if there exists $\alpha \in \mathrm{DLTL}^{\otimes}(\widetilde{\Sigma})$ with $L_\alpha = L$.

5 A Decision Procedure for DLTL$^{\otimes}$

We will show the satisfiability problem for DLTL(Σ) is solvable in deterministic exponential time. This will be achieved by effectively constructing a product automaton $\mathcal{A}_\alpha$ for each $\alpha \in \mathrm{DLTL}^{\otimes}(\tilde{\Sigma})$ such that the language accepted by $\mathcal{A}_\alpha$ is non-empty iff α is satisfiable. Our construction is a common generalization of the one for product LTL in [16] and the one for DLTL(Σ) in [5]. The solution to the satisfiability problem will at once lead to a solution to the model checking problem for programs modelled as synchronizing sequential agents.

Through the rest of the section we fix a formula $\alpha_0 \in \mathrm{DLTL}^{\otimes}$. In order to construct $\mathcal{A}_{\alpha_0}$ we first define the (Fischer-Ladner) closure of α_0. As a first step let $cl(\alpha_0)$ be the least set of formulas satisfying:

- $\alpha_0 \in cl(\alpha_0)$.
- $\sim\alpha \in cl(\alpha_0)$ implies $\alpha \in cl(\alpha_0)$.
- $\alpha \vee \beta \in cl(\alpha_0)$ implies $\alpha, \beta \in cl(\alpha_0)$.
- $\alpha\, \mathcal{U}_i^{\pi} \beta \in cl(\alpha_0)$ implies $\alpha, \beta \in cl(\alpha_0)$.

We will now take the *closure* of α_0 to be $CL(\alpha_0) = cl(\alpha_0) \cup \{\sim\alpha \mid \alpha \in cl(\alpha_0)\}$. From now on we shall identify $\sim\sim\alpha$ with α. Set $CL_i(\alpha_0) = CL(\alpha_0) \cap \mathrm{DLTL}_i^{\otimes}(\tilde{\Sigma})$ for each i. We will often write CL instead of $CL(\alpha_0)$ and CL_i instead of $CL_i(\alpha_0)$. All formulas considered from now on will be assumed to belong to CL_i unless otherwise stated.

An *i-type atom* is a subset $A \subseteq CL_i$ which satisfies:

- $\top \in A$.
- $\alpha \in A$ iff $\sim\alpha \notin A$.
- $\alpha \vee \beta \in A$ iff $\alpha \in A$ or $\beta \in A$.
- $\beta \in A$ and $\varepsilon \in ||\pi||$ implies $\alpha\, \mathcal{U}_i^{\pi} \beta \in A$.

The set of i-type atoms is denoted AT_i. We next define, for each $\alpha \in CL(\alpha_0)$ and $(A_1, \ldots, A_K) \in AT_1 \times \ldots \times AT_K$, the predicate Member$(\alpha, (A_1, \ldots, A_K))$. For convenience this predicate will be denoted as $\alpha \in (A_1, \ldots, A_K)$ and is given inductively by:

- Let $\alpha \in CL_i$. Then $\alpha \in (A_1, \ldots, A_K)$ iff $\alpha \in A_i$.
- Let $\alpha = \sim\beta$. Then $\alpha \in (A_1, \ldots, A_K)$ iff $\beta \notin (A_1, \ldots, A_K)$.
- Let $\alpha = \beta \vee \gamma$. Then $\alpha \in (A_1, \ldots, A_K)$ iff $\beta \in (A_1, \ldots, A_K)$ or $\gamma \in (A_1, \ldots, A_K)$.

The set of *i-type until requirements* is the subset of CL_i given by

$$Req_i = \{\alpha\, \mathcal{U}_i^{\pi} \beta \mid \alpha\, \mathcal{U}_i^{\pi} \beta \in CL_i\}.$$

We shall let ξ, ξ' range over Req_i. For each $\xi = \alpha\, \mathcal{U}_i^{\pi} \beta \in Req_i$ we fix a finite state automaton $\mathcal{A}_\xi$ such that $\mathcal{L}(\mathcal{A}_\xi) = ||\pi||$ where $\mathcal{L}(\mathcal{A}_\xi)$ is the language of finite words accepted by $\mathcal{A}_\xi$. We shall assume each such $\mathcal{A}_\xi$ is of the form $\mathcal{A}_\xi = (Q_\xi, \longrightarrow_\xi, I_\xi, F_\xi)$ where Q_ξ is the set of states, $\longrightarrow_\xi \subseteq Q_\xi \times \Sigma \times Q_\xi$ is the transition relation, $I_\xi \subseteq Q_\xi$ is the set of initial states and $F_\xi \subseteq Q_\xi$ is the set of final states. Without loss of generality, we shall assume that $\xi \neq \xi'$ implies $Q_\xi \cap Q_{\xi'} = \emptyset$ for every $\xi, \xi' \in Req_i$. We set $Q_i = \bigcup_{\xi \in Req_i} Q_\xi$ and $\widehat{Q}_i = Q_i \times \{0,1\}$.

The product automaton $\mathcal{A}_{\alpha_0}$ associated with α_0 is now defined to be $\mathcal{A}_{\alpha_0} = (\{\mathcal{A}_i\}_{i \in Loc}, Q_{in})$ where for each i, $\mathcal{A}_i = (S_i, \Longrightarrow_i, F_i, F_i^\omega)$ is specified as

1. $S_i \subseteq AT_i \times 2^{Q_i} \times 2^{\widehat{Q}_i} \times \{\mathsf{stop}, \mathsf{go}\} \times \{0,1\} \times \{\downarrow, \checkmark\}$ such that

$$(A, X, \widehat{X}, s, x, f) \in S_i$$

   iff the following conditions are satisfied for each $\xi = \alpha\, \mathcal{U}_i^\pi \beta$:
   (i) If $\beta \in A$ then $F_\xi \subseteq X$. (Recall that $\mathcal{A}_\xi = (Q_\xi, \longrightarrow_\xi, I_\xi, F_\xi)$).
   (ii) If $\alpha \in A$ and $q \in X$ for some $q \in I_\xi$ then $\alpha\, \mathcal{U}_i^\pi \beta \in A$.
   (iii) If $\alpha\, \mathcal{U}_i^\pi \beta \in A$ then either $\beta \in A$ and $\varepsilon \in ||\pi||$ or $(q, 1-x) \in \widehat{X}$ for some $q \in I_\xi$. (Note that we are considering the candidate $(A, X, \widehat{X}, s, x, f)$ for membership in S_i).
   (iv) If $(q, z) \in \widehat{X}$ with $q \notin F_\xi$ or $\beta \notin A$ then $\alpha \in A$.
2. The transition relation $\Longrightarrow_i \subseteq S_i \times \Sigma_i \times S_i$ is defined as follows:

$$(A, X, \widehat{X}, s, x, f) \overset{a}{\Longrightarrow}_i (B, Y, \widehat{Y}, t, y, g)$$

   iff the following conditions are satisfied for each $\xi = \alpha\, \mathcal{U}_i^\pi \beta \in Req_i$:
   (i) $s = \mathsf{go}$.
   (ii) Suppose $q' \in Q_\xi \cap Y$ and $q \overset{a}{\longrightarrow}_\xi q'$ and $\alpha \in A$. Then $q \in X$.
   (iii) Suppose $(q, z) \in \widehat{X}$ with $q \in Q_\xi$. Suppose further that $q \notin F_\xi$ or $\beta \notin A$. Then $(q', z) \in \widehat{Y}$ for some q' with $q \overset{a}{\longrightarrow}_\xi q'$.
   (iv) If $f = \checkmark$ then $(y, g) = (1-x, \downarrow)$. If $f = \downarrow$ then,

$$(y,g) = \begin{cases} (x, \downarrow), & \text{if there exists } (q, x) \in \widehat{X} \text{ such that} \\ & q \notin F_\xi \text{ or } \beta \notin A \\ (x, \checkmark), & \text{otherwise.} \end{cases}$$

3. $F_i = \{(A, X, \widehat{X}, s, x, f) \mid s = \mathsf{stop} \text{ and } \widehat{X} = \emptyset\}$.
4. $F_i^\omega = \{(A, X, \widehat{X}, s, x, f) \mid f = \checkmark\}$.

Finally, $Q_{in} \subseteq Q_1 \times \ldots \times Q_K$ is specified as

$$((A_1, X_1, \widehat{X}_1, s_1, x_1, f_1), \ldots, (A_K, X_K, \widehat{X}_K, s_K, x_K, f_K)) \in Q_{in}$$

iff $\alpha_0 \in (A_1, \ldots, A_K)$ and $(x_i, f_i) = (0, \checkmark)$ for every $i \in Loc$.

The main result of this section can now be formulated.

Theorem 7. *$\mathcal{L}(\mathcal{A}_{\alpha_0}) = L_{\alpha_0}$ where $\mathcal{A}_{\alpha_0}$ is as defined above. Hence α_0 is satisfiable iff $\mathcal{L}(\mathcal{A}_{\alpha_0}) \neq \emptyset$. Moreover, the size of $\mathcal{A}_{\alpha_0}$ is $2^{O(|\alpha_0|)}$ and consequently the satisfiability problem for* DLTL$^\otimes(\widetilde{\Sigma})$ *is decidable in exponential time.*

Proof. Let $\sigma \in \mathcal{L}(\mathcal{A}_{\alpha_0})$ by the accepting run $\rho : \mathrm{prf}(\sigma) \to Q_G^{\mathcal{A}}$. For each $\tau \in \mathrm{prf}(\sigma)$ let $\rho(\tau)[i] = (A_{\tau_i}, X_{\tau_i}, \widehat{X}_{\tau_i}, s_{\tau_i}, x_{\tau_i}, f_{\tau_i})$. Then a detailed examination of the above construction reveals that for all $\tau \in \mathrm{prf}(\sigma)$ and $\delta \in CL_i$,

$$\sigma, \tau \models \delta \text{ iff } \delta \in A_{\tau_i}.$$

By definition of Q_{in} we are assured that $\alpha_0 \in (\rho(\varepsilon)[1], \ldots, \rho(\varepsilon)[K])$. Hence a simple induction on the structure of α_0 will show that $\sigma, \varepsilon \models \alpha_0$.

Conversely, if α_0 is satisfiable we may assume that $\sigma, \varepsilon \models \alpha_0$ for some σ. We will construct an accepting run $\rho : \mathrm{prf}(\sigma) \to Q_G^{\mathcal{A}}$. For each $\tau \in \mathrm{prf}(\sigma)$ and each i, we set $\rho(\tau)[i] = (A_{\tau_i}, X_{\tau_i}, \widehat{X}_{\tau_i}, s_{\tau_i}, x_{\tau_i}, f_{\tau_i})$ and define the various components of this tuple as follows. First we define A_{τ_i} by $A_{\tau_i} = \{\alpha \in CL_i \mid \sigma, \tau \models \alpha\}$. Next s_{τ_i} is defined as $s_{\tau_i} = \mathsf{stop}$ iff $\sigma \upharpoonright i = \tau_i$ (recall the convention $\tau \upharpoonright i = \tau_i$). In defining the other components it will be convenient to adopt the following terminology.

Let $\xi = \alpha\, \mathcal{U}_i^{\pi} \beta$ and $q \in Q_\xi$ and $\tau_i \in \Sigma_i^*$. Then an *accepting run of $\mathcal{A}_\xi$ over τ_i starting from* q is a map $R : \mathrm{prf}(\tau_i) \longrightarrow Q_\xi$ such that $R(\varepsilon) = q$, $R(\tau_i) \in F_\xi$ and $R(\tau_i'') \xrightarrow{a}_\xi R(\tau_i''a)$ for every $\tau_i''a \in \mathrm{prf}(\tau_i)$. In case $q \in I_\xi$ we shall just say that R is an *accepting run of $\mathcal{A}_\xi$ over* τ_i.

Let $\xi = \alpha\, \mathcal{U}_i^{\pi} \beta$ and $q \in Q_\xi$. Then $q \in X_{\tau_i}$ iff there exist τ' and R' such that $\tau\tau' \in \mathrm{prf}(\sigma)$, $\sigma, \tau\tau' \models \beta$, and for every $\tau'' \in \mathrm{prf}(\tau')$, if $\varepsilon \preceq \tau_i'' \prec \tau_i'$ then $\sigma, \tau\tau'' \models \alpha$. Furthermore, R' should be an accepting run of $\mathcal{A}_\xi$ over τ_i' starting from q.

To specify the remaining three components we shall make use of a chronicle of obligations.

We'll say that (τ, ξ) is an *obligation* if $\tau \in \mathrm{prf}(\sigma)$ and $\xi = \alpha\, \mathcal{U}_i^{\pi} \beta \in Req_i$ such that $\sigma, \tau \models \alpha\, \mathcal{U}_i^{\pi} \beta$ but $\sigma, \tau \not\models \beta$ or $\varepsilon \notin ||\pi||$. Let (τ, ξ) be an obligation. We shall say that the pair (τ', R') is a *witness* for (τ, ξ) iff $\tau\tau' \in \mathrm{prf}(\sigma)$ and $\sigma, \tau\tau' \models \beta$ and for every $\tau'' \in \mathrm{prf}(\tau')$, if $\varepsilon \preceq \tau_i'' \prec \tau_i'$ then $\sigma, \tau\tau'' \models \alpha$. Furthermore, $\tau_i' \in ||\pi||$ and R' is an accepting run of $\mathcal{A}_\xi$ over τ_i'. A *chronicle set CH* is a set of quadruples satisfying that if $(\tau, \xi, \tau', R') \in CH$ then (τ, ξ) is an obligation and (τ', R') is witness for (τ, ξ). Moreover, for every obligation (τ, ξ) there is a unique element of the form (τ, ξ, τ', R') in CH. We fix such a set CH which clearly exists.

Now x_{τ_i} and f_{τ_i} are defined by mutual induction as follows. For the base case, $(x_\varepsilon, f_\varepsilon) = (0, \checkmark)$. For the induction step, let $\tau = \tau'a$. Suppose $a \notin \Sigma_i$. Then $(x_{\tau_i}, f_{\tau_i}) = (x_{\tau_i'}, f_{\tau_i'})$. So assume that $a \in \Sigma_i$. If $f_{\tau_i'} = \checkmark$ then $(x_{\tau_i}, f_{\tau_i}) = (1 - x_{\tau_i'}, \downarrow)$. Suppose $f_{\tau_i'} = \downarrow$. Then $(x_{\tau_i}, f_{\tau_i}) = (x_{\tau_i'}, \downarrow)$ if there exists $(\tau'', \xi_1, \tau''', R_1') \in CH$ such that $\tau'' \preceq \tau' \prec \tau''\tau'''$ and $x_{\tau_i''} = 1 - x_{\tau_i'}$. Otherwise, $f_{\tau_i} = \checkmark$ and $x_{\tau_i} = x_{\tau_i'}$.

The only remaining component to be dealt with is $\widehat{X}_{\tau_i}$. This is now defined via: $(q, z) \in \widehat{X}_{\tau_i}$ iff there exists $(\tau', \xi, \tau'', R_1') \in CH$ such that for some $\tau''' \in \mathrm{prf}(\tau'')$, $\tau_i' \preceq \tau_i = \tau_i'\tau_i'''$ and furthermore $R_1'(\tau_i''') = q$ and $x_{\tau_i'} = 1 - z$. Using these definitions it is not difficult to show that ρ is an accepting run.

Finally, by Lemma 6 it suffices to show that our construction yields a product automaton of exponential size. Clearly, $CL(\alpha_0)$ is linear in α_0, and surely then

$|AT_1|+\ldots+|AT_K| = 2^{O(|\alpha_0|)}$. Moreover, it is well-known that each $\pi \in \mathrm{Prg}(\Sigma_i)$ in polynomial time can be converted to a finite (non-deterministic) automaton with a linear state space (see [6] for a recent account of such conversions). Then both $Q_1+\ldots+Q_K$ and $\widehat{Q}_1+\ldots+\widehat{Q}_K$ are of size $O(|\alpha_0|)$. Consequently, $|Q^{\mathcal{A}}_G| = 2^{O(|\alpha_0|)}$ as required. □

The procedure outlined above also lends itself to a solution to the *model checking problem*, which is defined as for DLTL except that a finite-state program is now simply a product automaton $\mathcal{P}$. Once again, we do not wish to enter into details.

6 An Expressiveness Result

We now wish to show that our logic is expressively complete with respect to the regular product languages. In fact we will identify a natural sublogic — to be denoted $\mathrm{DLTL}^{\otimes}_{-}$ — which also enjoys this property.

The syntax of the formulas of $\mathrm{DLTL}^{\otimes}_{-}(\widetilde{\Sigma})$ remains as for $\mathrm{DLTL}^{\otimes}(\widetilde{\Sigma})$, but the until modality is to be restricted to the derived operator $\langle\_\rangle_i$. Formally, the set of formulas and locations of this sublogic is obtained via:

- $\top$ is a formula and $\mathrm{loc}(\top) = \emptyset$.
- Suppose α and β are formulas so are $\sim\alpha$ and $\alpha \vee \beta$. Moreover $\mathrm{loc}(\sim\alpha) = \mathrm{loc}(\alpha)$ and $\mathrm{loc}(\alpha \vee \beta) = \mathrm{loc}(\alpha) \cup \mathrm{loc}(\beta)$.
- Suppose α is formula such that $\mathrm{loc}(\alpha) \subseteq \{i\}$ and $\pi \in \mathrm{Prg}(\Sigma_i)$. Then $\langle\pi\rangle_i\alpha$ is formula. Moreover, $\mathrm{loc}(\langle\pi\rangle_i\alpha) = \{i\}$.

Proposition 8. *If $L \in \mathcal{R}^{\otimes}(\widetilde{\Sigma})$ then L is $\mathrm{DLTL}^{\otimes}_{-}(\widetilde{\Sigma})$-definable.*

Proof. It suffices to show that the claim holds for $L \in \mathcal{R}^{\otimes}_0(\widetilde{\Sigma})$ because each member of $\mathcal{R}^{\otimes}(\widetilde{\Sigma})$ is a finite union of languages in $\mathcal{R}^{\otimes}_0(\widetilde{\Sigma})$.

Let $L = L_1 \otimes \ldots \otimes L_K \in \mathcal{R}^{\otimes}_0(\widetilde{\Sigma})$. Then each $L_i \cap \Sigma_i^*$ is regular. Clearly $L_i \cap \Sigma_i^* = ||\pi_i||$ for some $\pi_i \in \mathrm{Prg}(\Sigma_i)$. Now define $\alpha^i_* = \langle\pi_i\rangle_i[\pi'_i]_i\bot$ where $\pi'_i = (a_1 + \ldots + a_n)$ with $\Sigma_i = \{a_1, \ldots, a_n\}$.

Next, $L_i \cap \Sigma_i^\omega$ is ω-regular. Hence it is accepted, due to McNaughton's theorem [10], by a *deterministic* Muller automaton. Choose such an automaton $\mathcal{M} = (Q, q_{in}, \longrightarrow, \mathcal{F})$, which we, without loss of generality, assume to be complete. (See [5] for the formal details). For $q, q' \in Q$ we set $L_{q,q'} = \{\tau \mid q \overset{\tau}{\longrightarrow} q'\}$, which is obviously a regular subset of Σ_i^*. So we can fix $\pi_{q,q'} \in \mathrm{Prg}(\Sigma_i)$ such that $L_{q,q'} = ||\pi_{q,q'}||$. Moreover, by the determinacy of $\mathcal{M}$ it follows that $L_{q,q'} \cap L_{q,q''} \neq \emptyset$ implies $q' = q''$. We now define

$$\alpha^i_\omega = \bigvee_{F\in\mathcal{F}} \bigvee_{q\in F} \langle\pi_{q_{in},q}\rangle_i \left(\bigwedge_{q'\notin F} [\pi_{q,q'}]_i\bot \wedge \bigwedge_{j=0}^{n-1} [\pi_{q,q_j}]_i \langle\pi_{q_j,q_{j\oplus 1}}\rangle_i \top \right)$$

with the assumption $\{q_0, q_1, \ldots, q_{n-1}\}$ is an enumeration of the $F \in \mathcal{F}$ under consideration and "$\oplus$" denotes addition modulo n. It is easy to show that $\sigma \upharpoonright i \in L_i \cap \Sigma_i^\omega$ iff $\sigma, \varepsilon \models \alpha_\omega^i$.

The required formula α is given by $\alpha = \bigwedge_{i \in Loc} \alpha^i$ where $\alpha^i = \alpha_*^i \vee \alpha_\omega^i$ for each i. It is a routine exercise to establish $L_\alpha = L_1 \otimes \ldots \otimes L_K$.

□

On the other hand, Theorem 5 together with Theorem 7 states that L_{α_0} is a product language over $\widetilde{\Sigma}$ for any $\alpha_0 \in \text{DLTL}^\otimes(\widetilde{\Sigma})$. Since $\text{DLTL}_-^\otimes$ is a sublogic of $\text{DLTL}^\otimes$ we have the following expressiveness result.

Corollary 9. *Let $L \subseteq \Sigma^\infty$. Then the following statements are equivalent:*

(i) $L \in \mathcal{R}^\otimes(\widetilde{\Sigma})$.
(ii) *L is $\text{DLTL}_-^\otimes(\widetilde{\Sigma})$-definable.*
(iii) *L is $\text{DLTL}^\otimes(\widetilde{\Sigma})$-definable.*

7 Discussion

We shall conclude this section by placing regular product languages in the broader context of regular Mazurkiewicz trace languages. For an introduction to (Mazurkiewicz) traces related to the concerns of the present paper, we refer the reader to [11]. We shall assume the bare minimum of the background material on traces.

We begin by noting that the distributed alphabet $\widetilde{\Sigma} = \{\Sigma_i\}_{i=1}^K$ induces the trace alphabet $(\Sigma, I_{\widetilde{\Sigma}})$ where the irreflexive and symmetric independence relation $I_{\widetilde{\Sigma}} \subseteq \Sigma \times \Sigma$ is given by:

$$a \; I_{\widetilde{\Sigma}} \; b \;\text{ iff }\; Loc(a) \cap Loc(b) = \emptyset.$$

Recall that $Loc(x) = \{i \mid x \in \Sigma_i\}$ for $x \in \Sigma$. We shall write I instead of $I_{\widetilde{\Sigma}}$ from now on. This independence relation in turn induces the equivalence relation $\approx_I \subseteq \Sigma^\infty \times \Sigma^\infty$ (from now on written as $\approx$) given by:

$$\sigma \approx \sigma' \;\text{ iff }\; \sigma \upharpoonright i = \sigma' \upharpoonright i \;\text{ for every }\; i \in Loc.$$

The $\approx$-equivalence classes of Σ^∞ constitute the set of finite and infinite traces generated by the trace alphabet (Σ, I). Traces can be — upto isomorphisms — uniquely represented as certain Σ-labelled posets where the labelling functions respect I in a natural manner. A trace language is just a subset of $\Sigma^\infty / \approx$.

A language $L \subseteq \Sigma^\infty$ is trace consistent in case $\sigma \in L$ and $\sigma \approx \sigma'$ implies $\sigma' \in L$, for every σ, σ'. The point is, a trace consistent language L canonically represents the trace language $\{[\sigma]_\approx \mid \sigma \in L\}$. We extend this idea to logical formulas by saying that $\alpha \in \text{DLTL}^\otimes(\widetilde{\Sigma})$ is trace consistent iff L_α is trace consistent. It is easy to show that *every* formula of $\text{DLTL}^\otimes(\widetilde{\Sigma})$ is trace consistent. An important feature of properties defined by trace consistent formulas is that they can often be verified efficiently using partial order based reduction techniques [3,12,18]. Consequently, $\text{DLTL}^{\otimes}(\widetilde{\Sigma})$ provides a flexible and powerful means for specifying trace consistent properties of distributed programs. As it turns out, every formula of $\text{DLTL}^{\otimes}(\widetilde{\Sigma})$ defines — via the canonical representation — a regular trace language contained in $\Sigma^{\infty}/\approx$. Hence by Corollary 9, every regular product language corresponds to a regular trace language.

The converse however is not true. To bring this out, consider the distributed alphabet $\widetilde{\Sigma} = \{\{a, a', c\}, \{b, b', c\}\}$ and $L = \{cab, cba, ca'b', cb'a'\}^{\omega}$. Then it is easy to check that L is trace consistent and ω-regular and that it is *not* a regular product language. In a forthcoming paper we shall deal with the problem of extending $\text{DLTL}^{\otimes}(\widetilde{\Sigma})$ so as to capture *all* of the regular trace languages.

References

1. Fischer, M. J., Ladner, R. E.: Propositional dynamic logic of regular programs. Journal of Computer and System Sciences **18**(2) (1979) 194–211
2. Gabbay, A., Pnueli, A., Shelah, S., Stavi, J.: On the temporal analysis of fairness. Proceedings of the 7th Annual Symposium on Principles of Programming Languages, ACM (1980) 163–173
3. Godefroid, P.: Partial-order Methods for the Verification of Concurrent Systems. Lecture Notes in Computer Science 1032, Springer-Verlag (1996)
4. Harel, D.: Dynamic logic. In Gabbay, D., Guenthner, F., eds.: Handbook of Philosophical Logic, Vol. II, Reidel, Dordrecht (1984) 497–604
5. Henriksen, J. G., Thiagarajan, P. S.: Dynamic linear time temporal logic. BRICS technical report RS-97-8, Department of Computer Science, University of Aarhus, Denmark (1997)
6. Hromkovič, J., Seibert, S., Wilke, T.: Translating regular expressions into small ε-free nondeterministic automata. Proceedings of the 12th Annual Symposium on Theoretical Aspects of Computer Science, Lecture Notes in Computer Science 1200, Springer-Verlag (1997) 55–66
7. Kamp, H. R.: Tense Logic and the Theory of Linear Order. Ph.D. thesis, University of California (1968)
8. Manna, Z., Pnueli, A.: The Temporal Logic of Reactive and Concurrent Systems (Specification), Springer-Verlag (1992)
9. Mazurkiewicz, A.: Concurrent program schemes and their interpretations. Technical report DAIMI PB-78, Department of Computer Science, University of Aarhus, Denmark (1977)
10. McNaughton, R.: Testing and generating infinite sequences by a finite automaton. Information and Control **9** (1966) 521–530
11. Mukund, M., Thiagarajan, P. S.: Linear time temporal logics over Mazurkiewicz traces. Proceedings of the 21st Intl. Symposium on Mathematical Foundations of Computer Science, Lecture Notes in Computer Science 1113, Springer-Verlag (1996) pp. 62–92
12. Peled, D.: Partial order reduction: model checking using representatives. Proceedings of the 21st Intl. Symposium on Mathematical Foundations of Computer Science, Lecture Notes in Computer Science 1113, Springer-Verlag (1996) 93–112
13. Pnueli, A.: The temporal logic of programs. Proceedings of the 18th Annual Symposium on Foundations of Computer Science, IEEE (1977) 46–57

14. Thiagarajan, P. S.: A trace based extension of linear time temporal logic. Proceedings of the 9th Annual Symposium on Logic in Computer Science, IEEE (1994) 438–447
15. Thiagarajan, P. S.: PTL over product state spaces. Technical report TCS-95-4, School of Mathematics, SPIC Science Foundation, Madras (1995)
16. Thiagarajan, P. S.: A trace consistent subset of PTL. Proceedings of the 6th Annual Conference on Concurrency Theory, Lecture Notes in Computer Science 962, Springer-Verlag (1995) 438–452
17. Thomas, W.: Automata over infinite objects. In van Leeuwen, J., ed., Handbook of Theoretical Computer Science, Vol. B: Formal Models and Semantics, Elsevier/MIT Press (1990) 133–191
18. Valmari, A.: A stubborn attack on state explosion. Formal Methods in Systems Design **1** (1992) 285–313
19. Vardi, M. Y., Wolper, P.: An automata-theoretic approach to automatic program verification. Proceedings of the 1st Annual Symposium on Logic in Computer Science, IEEE (1986) 332–345
20. Wolper, P.: Temporal logic can be more expressive. Proceedings of the 22nd Annual Symposium on Foundations of Computer Science, IEEE (1981) 340–348
21. Wolper, P., Vardi, M. Y., Sistla, A. P.: Reasoning about infinite computation paths. Proceedings of the 24nd Annual Symposium on Foundations of Computer Science, IEEE (1983) 185–194
22. Zielonka, W.: Notes on finite asynchronous automata. R.A.I.R.O. Informatique Théorique et Applications **21** (1987) 99–135

Reasoning about Cryptographic Protocols in the Spi Calculus

Martín Abadi[1] and Andrew D. Gordon[2]

[1] Digital Equipment Corporation, Systems Research Center
[2] University of Cambridge, Computer Laboratory

Abstract. The spi calculus is an extension of the pi calculus with constructs for encryption and decryption. This paper develops the theory of the spi calculus, focusing on techniques for establishing testing equivalence, and applying these techniques to the proof of authenticity and secrecy properties of cryptographic protocols.

1 From Cryptography to Testing Equivalence

The idea of controlling communication by capabilities underlies both the pi calculus and much of the current work on security in distributed systems (see e.g. [MPW92, Lie93, Sch96b]). In the pi calculus, channel names are capabilities; a process can use a channel only if it has invented or been given the name of the channel, but cannot guess this name. In work on security, on the other hand, the capabilities for communication are often keys, which are used for encrypting and decrypting messages that travel on otherwise unprotected channels.

These observations motivate the definition of the spi calculus, an extension of the pi calculus with constructs for encryption and decryption. In a recent paper [AG97a], we introduced the spi calculus and we showed how it can be used for describing protocols, particularly authentication protocols. This paper develops the theory of the spi calculus, concentrating on results and techniques for verifying security properties of protocols.

As a first, informal example, let us consider a protocol where a user A sends a message M under a shared key K to a user B on a public channel. It is straightforward to write this protocol in the spi calculus. We may want to formalise, and then verify, two important properties of this protocol: (1) if B receives a message, then it is the one that A sent, and (2) no eavesdropper learns M. These properties hold even in the presence of an active attacker, provided the attacker does not have access to K. Taking the point of view of such an attacker, we can rephrase properties (1) and (2) in terms of an informal notion of indistinguishability: (1) the protocol is indistinguishable from one where B discards the message that it receives and acts as though the message was M, and (2) assuming that A and B do not reveal M beforehand or afterwards, the protocol is indistinguishable from one where some other message M' is sent instead of M.

In light of this example, it seems important to find a formal counterpart to the informal notion of indistinguishability. The concurrency literature suggests several candidates. Unfortunately, a straightforward notion of bisimilarity would be too fine-grained (because it would be sensitive to the contents of encrypted messages even if the corresponding keys are never disclosed). A more promising approach is based on testing equivalence. Roughly, two processes P and Q are testing equivalent if, although they may have different internal structure, a third process R cannot differentiate running in parallel with P from running in parallel with Q. We like testing equivalence for the specification of security properties because it is sufficiently coarse-grained, and because a test captures the idea of an observation that another process (such as an attacker) may perform on a process.

Our testing equivalence is a version of De Nicola's and Hennessy's may-testing equivalence [DH84], which essentially relies on tests of safety properties. Our emphasis on safety agrees with that of the security literature, where liveness is often secondary (in part because it is typically hard to guarantee).

While the use of testing equivalence may lead to neat specifications, it also implies serious difficulties in verifications. Naively, in order to prove that two processes P and Q are testing equivalent, one would need to consider an arbitrary attacker R and arbitrary sequences of interactions with R. This paper investigates more sophisticated methods for proving testing equivalence in the spi calculus. Some of these methods are based on earlier work on the pi calculus, with new ingredients motivated by our interest in security and cryptography. While our techniques may not be complete, they constitute a useful set of tools. With these techniques, we can establish security properties of particular cryptographic protocols, for example formal versions of properties (1) and (2) discussed above.

Contents

Section 2 is an informal review of the spi calculus. Section 3 gives two operational semantics of the spi calculus. Section 4 defines testing equivalence precisely and commences its study. Section 5 and 6 study some other equivalences and the new underpinning relation; these are useful in our proofs of testing equivalence. Section 7 discusses how our techniques can be applied, through an example. Finally, Section 8 mentions some related work and some conclusions. Throughout, we restrict attention to shared-key cryptography (where the same key is used for encrypting and decrypting a message); there are variants of the spi calculus for other flavours of cryptography, but we have not yet studied their theory.

This paper is a companion to the paper where we introduced the spi calculus [AG97a]. That paper covers the material of Section 2 at a more leisurely pace, with a gentle introduction to the pi calculus and the spi calculus, and many examples. It also explains the simpler of the operational semantics (the reaction relation), then gives the definition of testing equivalence. It does not contain theorems, proof techniques, or proofs for examples, which are the subject of this paper. Most of the material in the two papers is included in a longer report [AG97b].

2 The Spi Calculus (Informal Summary)

We assume an infinite set of *names* and an infinite set of *variables*. We let m, n, p, q, and r range over names, and let w, x, y, and z range over variables.

The set of *terms* is defined by the grammar:

$L, M, N ::=$	terms
n	name
(M, N)	pair
0	zero
$suc(M)$	successor
$\{M\}_N$	shared-key encryption
x	variable

In the standard pi calculus, names are the only terms. We have added constructs for pairing and numbers, (M, N), 0, and $suc(M)$, so as to permit a direct treatment of protocols that use these constructs. Moreover, we distinguish variables from names; this distinction simplifies the treatment of some equivalences. We have also added a construct for encryption (avoiding the complexity of possible encodings within the pi calculus). Intuitively, $\{M\}_N$ represents the ciphertext obtained by encrypting the term M under the key N using a shared-key cryptosystem such as DES [DES77].

The set of *processes* is defined by the grammar:

$P, Q, R ::=$	processes
$\overline{M}\langle N\rangle.P$	output
$M(x).P$	input
$P \mid Q$	composition
$(\nu n)P$	restriction
$!P$	replication
$[M\ is\ N]\ P$	match
$\mathbf{0}$	nil
$let\ (x, y) = M\ in\ P$	pair splitting
$case\ M\ of\ 0 : P\ suc(x) : Q$	integer case
$case\ L\ of\ \{x\}_N\ in\ P$	shared-key decryption

In $M(x).P$, the variable x is bound in P. In $(\nu n)P$, the name n is bound in P. In $let\ (x, y) = M\ in\ P$, the variables x and y are bound in P. In $case\ M\ of\ 0 : P\ suc(x) : Q$, the variable x is bound in Q. In $case\ L\ of\ \{x\}_N\ in\ P$, the variable x is bound in P. We write $P[M/x]$ for the outcome of replacing each free occurrence of x in process P with the term M, and identify processes up to renaming of bound variables and names. We adopt the abbreviations $\prod_{i \in 1..k} P_i$ for the k-way parallel composition $P_1 \mid \cdots \mid P_k$, and $\overline{M}\langle N\rangle$ for $\overline{M}\langle N\rangle.\mathbf{0}$ and $M(x)$ for $M(x).\mathbf{0}$. We also express the k-fold restriction $(\nu p_1) \cdots (\nu p_k)P$ by $(\nu p_i{}^{i \in 1..k})P$ or, when $\vec{p} = p_1, \ldots, p_k$, by $(\nu \vec{p})P$. Intuitively, processes have the following meanings:

- An *output process* $\overline{m}\langle N\rangle.P$ is ready to output N on m, and then to behave as P. The output happens only when there is a process ready to input from

m. An *input process* $m(x).Q$ is ready to input from m, and then to behave as $Q[N/x]$, where N is the input received.
The general forms $\overline{M}\langle N\rangle.P$ and $M(x).Q$ of output and input allow for the channel to be an arbitrary term M; the only useful cases are for M to be a name, or a variable that gets instantiated to a name.

- A *composition* $P \mid Q$ behaves as P and Q running in parallel.
- A *restriction* $(\nu n)P$ is a process that makes a new, private name n, which may occur in P, and then behaves as P.
- A *replication* $!P$ behaves as infinitely many copies of P running in parallel.
- A *match* $[M\ is\ N]\ P$ behaves as P provided that M and N are the same term; otherwise it is stuck, that is, it does nothing.
- The *nil* process $\mathbf{0}$ does nothing.
- A *pair splitting* process $let\ (x, y) = M\ in\ P$ behaves as $P[N/x][L/y]$ if M is a pair (N, L), and it is stuck if M is not a pair.
- An *integer case* process $case\ M\ of\ 0 : P\ suc(x) : Q$ behaves as P if M is 0, as $Q[N/x]$ if M is $suc(N)$ for some N, and otherwise is stuck.
- A *decryption* process $case\ L\ of\ \{x\}_N\ in\ P$ attempts to decrypt L with the key N. If L has the form $\{M\}_N$, then the process behaves as $P[M/x]$. Otherwise the process is stuck.

For example, $(\nu K)\overline{m}\langle\{0\}_K\rangle$ is a process that creates a name K and then sends the result of encrypting the numeral 0 with K on a channel m. Here we use the letter K for a name because the name plays the role of a key. Since m is not bound, anyone may receive $\{0\}_K$; however, since K is bound, this term cannot be successfully decrypted. In order to illustrate the use of decryption, we add a process that has the necessary key:

$$(\nu K)(\overline{m}\langle\{0\}_K\rangle \mid m(y).case\ y\ of\ \{x\}_K\ in\ \overline{m}\langle x\rangle)$$

The new process (to the right of $\mid$) tries to decrypt the message y that it receives on m using K, and sends the result x on m.

We write $fn(M)$ and $fn(P)$ for the sets of names free in term M and process P respectively, and write $fv(M)$ and $fv(P)$ for the sets of variables free in M and P respectively. A term or process is *closed* if it has no free variables; *Proc* is the set of closed processes.

A context C is a process with a single hole; $C[P]$ is the outcome of filling the hole with P. A congruence is an equivalence relation $\mathcal{R}$ such that if $P\,\mathcal{R}\,Q$ then $C[P]\,\mathcal{R}\,C[Q]$ for any context C. One can restrict attention to closed processes and contexts, but the claims of this paper hold independently of this restriction.

3 Two Operational Semantics

The reaction relation is a concise account of computation in the pi calculus introduced by Milner [Mil92], with ideas from Berry and Boudol [BB92]. In this section we adapt the reaction relation to the spi calculus.

The definition of reaction is rather elegant, but not convenient for proofs (because it relies on an auxiliary notion of structural equivalence). Therefore, we provide an alternative, direct characterisation of reaction. We achieve this by defining a commitment relation, in the style of Milner [Mil95b].

The Reaction Relation

The definition of reaction has several phases. First we define a *reduction relation* $>$ on *Proc*. We require that $!P > (P \mid !P)$, that $[M\ \textit{is}\ M]\ P > P$, and that $\textit{case}\ \{M\}_N\ \textit{of}\ \{x\}_N\ \textit{in}\ P > P[M/x]$; we omit similar conditions for *let* and for the *case* construct for numerals. Then we define a *structural equivalence relation* $\equiv$ on *Proc*. It is the least equivalence relation including $>$ such that $P \equiv P'$ implies $P \mid Q \equiv P' \mid Q$ and $(\nu m)P \equiv (\nu m)P'$, and such that

$$\begin{array}{ccc} P \mid \mathbf{0} \equiv P & P \mid Q \equiv Q \mid P & P \mid (Q \mid R) \equiv (P \mid Q) \mid R \\ (\nu m)(\nu n)P \equiv (\nu n)(\nu m)P & (\nu n)\mathbf{0} \equiv \mathbf{0} & ((\nu n)P) \mid Q \equiv (\nu n)(P \mid Q) \end{array}$$

where, in the last equation, $n \notin \textit{fn}(Q)$. Intuitively, this equivalence relation allows processes to be rearranged so that reaction is possible. Finally, the *reaction relation* $\rightarrow$ is the least relation on *Proc* such that $P \rightarrow P'$ implies $P \mid Q \rightarrow P' \mid Q$ and $(\nu m)P \rightarrow (\nu m)P'$, such that $P \equiv P' \rightarrow Q' \equiv Q$ implies $P \rightarrow Q$, and such that $\overline{m}\langle N\rangle.P \mid m(x).Q \rightarrow P \mid Q[N/x]$.

(The reduction relation, $>$, is not found in previous accounts of the pi calculus. We introduced it in the definition of structural equivalence because it is useful also in the definition of commitment, given next.)

The Commitment Relation

In order to define commitment, we need some new syntactic forms. An *abstraction* is an expression of the form $(x)P$, where x is a bound variable and P is a process. Intuitively, $(x)P$ is like the process $p(x).P$ minus the name p. When F is the abstraction $(x)P$ and M is a term, we write $F(M)$ for $P[M/x]$. A *concretion* is an expression of the form $(\nu m_1, \ldots, m_k)\langle M\rangle P$, where M is a term, P is a process, $k \geq 0$, and the names $m_1, \ldots, m_k$ are bound in M and P. Intuitively, $(\nu m_1, \ldots, m_k)\langle M\rangle P$ is like the process $(\nu m_1) \ldots (\nu m_k)\overline{p}\langle M\rangle P$ minus the name p, provided p is not one of $m_1, \ldots, m_k$. We often write concretions as $(\nu \vec{m})\langle M\rangle P$, where $\vec{m} = m_1, \ldots, m_k$, or simply $(\nu)\langle M\rangle P$ if $k = 0$. Finally, an *agent* is an abstraction, a process, or a concretion. We use the metavariables A and B to stand for arbitrary agents, and let $\textit{fv}(A)$ and $\textit{fn}(A)$ be the sets of free variables and free names of an agent A, respectively.

We extend the restriction and composition operators to arbitrary agents, as follows. For an abstraction $(x)P$, we let $(\nu m)(x)P = (x)(\nu m)P$ and let $R \mid (x)P = (x)(R \mid P)$, assuming that $x \notin \textit{fv}(R)$. For a concretion $(\nu\vec{n})\langle M\rangle Q$, we let $(\nu m)(\nu \vec{n})\langle M\rangle Q = (\nu m, \vec{n})\langle M\rangle Q$ if $m \in \textit{fn}(M)$ and $= (\nu\vec{n})\langle M\rangle(\nu m)Q$ otherwise, and let $R \mid (\nu\vec{n})\langle M\rangle Q = (\nu\vec{n})\langle M\rangle(R \mid Q)$, in all cases assuming that $m \notin \{\vec{n}\}$ and that $\{\vec{n}\} \cap \textit{fn}(R) = \emptyset$. We define the dual composition $A \mid R$ symmetrically. If F

is the abstraction $(x)P$ and C is the concretion $(\nu\vec{n})\langle M\rangle Q$, and $\{\vec{n}\}\cap fn(P)=\emptyset$, we define the *interactions* $F@C$ and $C@F$ to be the processes given by:

$$F@C \triangleq (\nu\vec{n})(P[M/x] \mid Q) \qquad C@F \triangleq (\nu\vec{n})(Q \mid P[M/x])$$

Intuitively, these processes are the possible immediate results of the encounter of F and C. Given a common name p, we have that F is like $p(x).P$ and C is like $(\nu\vec{n})\overline{p}\langle M\rangle P$, so an interaction of F and C is a process obtained when $p(x).P$ and $(\nu\vec{n})\overline{p}\langle M\rangle P$, put in parallel, communicate on p.

An *action* is a name m (representing input), a co-name $\overline{m}$ (representing output), or the distinguished *silent action* τ. The *commitment relation* is written $P \xrightarrow{\alpha} A$, where P is a closed process, α is an action, and A is a closed agent; it is defined inductively by the axioms $m(x).P \xrightarrow{m} (x)P$ and $\overline{m}\langle M\rangle.P \xrightarrow{\overline{m}} (\nu)\langle M\rangle P$, and the rules:

$$\frac{P \xrightarrow{m} F \quad Q \xrightarrow{\overline{m}} C}{P \mid Q \xrightarrow{\tau} F@C} \qquad \frac{P \xrightarrow{\overline{m}} C \quad Q \xrightarrow{m} F}{P \mid Q \xrightarrow{\tau} C@F} \qquad \frac{P > Q \quad Q \xrightarrow{\alpha} A}{P \xrightarrow{\alpha} A}$$

$$\frac{P \xrightarrow{\alpha} A}{P \mid Q \xrightarrow{\alpha} A \mid Q} \qquad \frac{Q \xrightarrow{\alpha} A}{P \mid Q \xrightarrow{\alpha} P \mid A} \qquad \frac{P \xrightarrow{\alpha} A \quad \alpha \notin \{m,\overline{m}\}}{(\nu m)P \xrightarrow{\alpha} (\nu m)A}$$

The commitment relation indexed by τ, $\xrightarrow{\tau}$, is a binary relation on *Proc*. We write $\xrightarrow{\tau}^{*}$ for its reflexive and transitive closure; and we write $P \xrightarrow{\tau}\equiv Q$ when there exists a process R such that $P \xrightarrow{\tau} R$ and $R \equiv Q$.

Proposition 1. *$P \rightarrow Q$ if and only if $P \xrightarrow{\tau}\equiv Q$.*

4 Testing Equivalence

As explained in the introduction, we rely on testing equivalence for the specification of security properties. This section gives the definition of tests and testing equivalence, and some basic results about them.

A *barb* is either a name m or a co-name $\overline{m}$. If P is a closed process, we say that P *exhibits barb* β, and write $P \downarrow \beta$, if P may communicate immediately on β. Similarly, the *convergence* predicate $P \Downarrow \beta$ means that P may communicate on β after some reactions. Formally, these two predicates are defined by the axioms $m(x).P \downarrow m$ and $\overline{m}\langle M\rangle.P \downarrow \overline{m}$, and by the rules:

$$\frac{P \downarrow \beta}{P \mid Q \downarrow \beta} \qquad \frac{P \downarrow \beta \quad \beta \notin \{m,\overline{m}\}}{(\nu m)P \downarrow \beta} \qquad \frac{P \equiv Q \quad Q \downarrow \beta}{P \downarrow \beta}$$

$$\frac{P \downarrow \beta}{P \Downarrow \beta} \qquad \frac{P \rightarrow Q \qquad Q \Downarrow \beta}{P \Downarrow \beta}$$

A *test*, (R, β), consists of a closed process R and a barb β. A closed process P *passes* the test if and only if $(P \mid R) \Downarrow \beta$. The following proposition enables us to use the commitment relation in proofs about tests:

Proposition 2. *$P \downarrow \beta$ if and only if $P \xrightarrow{\beta} A$ for some agent A. Moreover, P passes a test (R, β) if and only if*

$$P \mid R \xrightarrow{\tau}^{*} Q \text{ and } Q \xrightarrow{\beta} A$$

for some agent A and process Q.

The definition of testing induces a testing preorder $\sqsubseteq$ and a testing equivalence $\simeq$ on *Proc*:

$$P \sqsubseteq Q \triangleq \text{for any test } (R, \beta), \text{ if } (P \mid R) \Downarrow \beta \text{ then } (Q \mid R) \Downarrow \beta$$
$$P \simeq Q \triangleq P \sqsubseteq Q \text{ and } Q \sqsubseteq P$$

The following proposition is crucial for proofs of testing equivalence:

Proposition 3. *Testing equivalence is a congruence. Furthermore, structural equivalence implies testing equivalence.*

We have developed a number of auxiliary lemmas about testing equivalence, for use in our verifications. As a sample, we show a proposition that enables us to reduce infinite problems (with replication) to finite but unbounded problems:

Proposition 4. *If $(\nu \vec{p})(P_1 \mid \prod_{i \in 1..n} P_2) \simeq (\nu \vec{p})(Q_1 \mid \prod_{i \in 1..n} Q_2)$ for all $n \geq 0$, then $(\nu \vec{p})(P_1 \mid !P_2) \simeq (\nu \vec{p})(Q_1 \mid !Q_2)$.*

Testing equivalence becomes finer-grained (and perhaps even more compelling) in the presence of a construct $[M \textit{ is not } N]\ P$ for mismatch [BN95]. Our calculus does not include that construct because we have not found a need for it in writing protocols. The same is true for other sensible negative constructs, for example one that checks whether a term is not a pair. We believe that our results remain valid in the presence of such constructs.

5 Other Equivalences Useful in Proofs

In addition to testing equivalence, several other equivalences are useful for reasoning about cryptographic protocols. In particular, barbed congruence is an equivalence with a tractable co-inductive presentation and is stronger than testing equivalence. The definitions of these equivalences are adaptations of corresponding definitions in the pi calculus. However, the presence of encryption affects the use of these equivalences in examples.

Strong Bisimilarity

If $\mathcal{R}$ is a relation on closed processes, we define the relation $\overline{\mathcal{R}}$ on closed agents:

$$\begin{array}{rl} P\, \overline{\mathcal{R}}\, Q & \text{iff } P\, \mathcal{R}\, Q \\ (x)P\, \overline{\mathcal{R}}\, (x)Q & \text{iff } P[M/x]\, \mathcal{R}\, Q[M/x] \text{ for all closed } M \\ (\nu \vec{n})\langle M \rangle P\, \overline{\mathcal{R}}\, (\nu \vec{m})\langle M \rangle Q & \text{iff } \vec{m} \text{ is a permutation of } \vec{n} \text{ and } P\, \mathcal{R}\, Q \end{array}$$

A *strong simulation* is a binary relation $\mathcal{S}$ on *Proc* such that if $P\ \mathcal{S}\ Q$ and $P \xrightarrow{\alpha} A$ then there exists B with $Q \xrightarrow{\alpha} B$ and $A\ \overline{\mathcal{S}}\ B$. A relation $\mathcal{S}$ is a *strong bisimulation* if and only if both $\mathcal{S}$ and its converse $\mathcal{S}^{-1}$ are strong simulations [Mil95b]. *Strong bisimilarity*, written $\sim_s$, is the greatest strong bisimulation, namely the union of all strong bisimulations.

Strong bisimilarity is a rather fine-grained equivalence for the spi calculus. For instance, it discriminates between the processes $(\nu K)\overline{c}\langle\{M\}_K\rangle$ and $(\nu K)\overline{c}\langle\{M'\}_K\rangle$, which we would wish to equate since these processes send encrypted messages under keys that are never disclosed, so their difference should not matter. Still, strong bisimilarity is often useful in justifying particular steps of our proofs.

Barbed Equivalence

Intuitively, one way of weakening strong bisimilarity is to ignore what messages are sent on what channels, and to record only what channels are used. This informal idea leads to the following definition. A *barbed simulation* is a binary relation $\mathcal{S}$ on *Proc* such that $P\ \mathcal{S}\ Q$ implies:

(1) for each barb β, if $P \downarrow \beta$ then $Q \downarrow \beta$, and
(2) if $P \to P'$ then there exists Q' such that $Q \to Q'$ and $P' \equiv\mathcal{S}\equiv Q'$

where $P' \equiv\mathcal{S}\equiv Q'$ means that there exist P'' and Q'' such that $P' \equiv P''$, $P''\ \mathcal{S}\ Q''$, and $Q'' \equiv Q'$. A *barbed bisimulation* is a relation $\mathcal{S}$ such that both $\mathcal{S}$ and $\mathcal{S}^{-1}$ are barbed simulations. *Barbed equivalence*, written $\dot{\sim}$, is the greatest barbed bisimulation.

Proposition 5. *Barbed equivalence is an equivalence relation, and is preserved by restriction. Furthermore, both structural equivalence and strong bisimilarity imply barbed equivalence.*

In order to establish a barbed equivalence, it is often convenient to use Milner's technique of "bisimulation up to" [Mil89, MPW92]. A *barbed simulation up to $\dot{\sim}$ and restriction* is a binary relation $\mathcal{S}$ on *Proc* such that $P\ \mathcal{S}\ Q$ implies:

(1) for each barb β, if $P \downarrow \beta$ then $Q \downarrow \beta$, and
(2) if $P \to P'$ then there exists Q' such that $Q \to Q'$, and there exist P'', Q'', and names $\vec{n}$ such that $P' \dot{\sim} (\nu\vec{n})P''$, $Q' \dot{\sim} (\nu\vec{n})Q''$, and $P''\ \mathcal{S}\ Q''$.

A *barbed bisimulation up to $\dot{\sim}$ and restriction* is a relation $\mathcal{S}$ such that both $\mathcal{S}$ and $\mathcal{S}^{-1}$ are barbed simulations up to $\dot{\sim}$ and restriction.

Proposition 6. *If $\mathcal{S}$ is a barbed bisimulation up to $\dot{\sim}$ and restriction, then $\mathcal{S} \subseteq \dot{\sim}$.*

Barbed equivalence is still only a stepping stone. One reason for this is that there are processes that are barbed equivalent but not strongly bisimilar or testing equivalent, such as $\overline{m}\langle n\rangle.\overline{m}\langle n\rangle$ and $\overline{m}\langle n\rangle$. Moreover, barbed equivalence is far from being a congruence: it is not even closed under composition, as can be seen by comparing $\overline{m}\langle n\rangle.\overline{m}\langle n\rangle \mid m(x)$ and $\overline{m}\langle n\rangle \mid m(x)$.

Barbed Congruence

Barbed congruence, written $\sim$, is the relation on *Proc* obtained by strengthening barbed equivalence as follows:

$$P \sim Q \triangleq \forall R \in Proc(P \mid R \dot{\sim} P \mid R)$$

For example, it is easy to prove that a process that attempts to decrypt "with the wrong key" is barbed congruent to $\mathbf{0}$:

$$case\ M\ of\ \{x\}_K\ in\ P \sim \begin{cases} P[N/x] & \text{if } M = \{N\}_K \text{ for some } N \\ \mathbf{0} & \text{otherwise} \end{cases}$$

This is an example of the fairly obvious fact that barbed congruence does not imply structural equivalence.

As another example, we prove in Section 6 that $(\nu K)\overline{c}\langle\{M\}_K\rangle$ is barbed congruent to $(\nu K)\overline{c}\langle\{M'\}_K\rangle$. This example shows that barbed congruence does not imply strong bisimilarity. It also shows that barbed congruence is not sensitive to the contents of encrypted messages whose keys are not disclosed, suggesting that barbed congruence is coarse-grained enough for interesting cryptographic applications.

Proposition 7. *Barbed congruence is a congruence. Furthermore, both structural equivalence and strong bisimilarity imply barbed congruence, while barbed congruence implies testing equivalence.*

Thus, whenever we wish to prove a testing equivalence, we may try to prove a barbed congruence, as a sufficient condition. However, testing equivalence does not imply barbed congruence, because barbed congruence is more sensitive to τ steps and to branching structure.

6 The Underpinning Relation

This section introduces the *underpinning relation*, which is also useful in proofs. We say that $x_1{:}\{-\}_{p_1}, \ldots, x_n{:}\{-\}_{p_n}$ *underpins* the agent A roughly if A is an agent that may contain occurrences of any of the variables $x_1, \ldots, x_n$, but no occurrences of any of the names $p_1, \ldots, p_n$. We write this:

$$x_1{:}\{-\}_{p_1}, \ldots, x_n{:}\{-\}_{p_n} \vdash A$$

Our intention is that A represents an attacker and that the variables $x_1, \ldots, x_n$ represent ciphertexts that the attacker may have intercepted encrypted under the keys $p_1, \ldots, p_n$, which the attacker does not have. (Here we take all keys to be names as this suffices for our present purposes; but the general case, where a key is an arbitrary term, could also be interesting.)

Next we give a precise definition of the underpinning relation. An *environment* is a finite list of entries of the form $x{:}\{-\}_n$, where x is a variable and n is a name; all the variables must be distinct (but the names need not be). We let $dom(E)$ be the set of variables mentioned in the entries in E, and $keys(E)$ the set of names mentioned in the entries in E. When E is an environment, M a term, and A an agent, we define:

$$E \vdash M \triangleq fv(M) \subseteq dom(E) \text{ and } fn(M) \cap keys(E) = \emptyset$$
$$E \vdash A \triangleq fv(A) \subseteq dom(E) \text{ and } fn(A) \cap keys(E) = \emptyset$$

The relation $\vdash$ is the underpinning relation.

When $x{:}\{-\}_n$ occurs in an environment, we intend that x stands for a ciphertext of the form $\{M\}_n$. An *E-closure* is a substitution that fixes all the variables in E to appropriate ciphertexts; more precisely, an E-closure is a substitution σ of closed ciphertexts for variables such that $E \vdash \sigma$ is derivable from the following rules:

$$\frac{}{\emptyset \vdash \emptyset} \qquad \frac{E \vdash \sigma \quad x \notin dom(E) \quad fv(M) = \emptyset}{E, x{:}\{-\}_n \vdash \sigma, \{M\}_n/x}$$

where $\emptyset$ represents the empty environment, the empty substitution, and the empty set, and $\sigma, \{M\}_n/x$ is the extension of σ that maps x to $\{M\}_n$.

To prove secrecy properties, we would like to show that a process underpinned by an environment acts uniformly no matter which ciphertexts are substituted for the variables in the environment. At first sight one might think that if $E \vdash P$, $E \vdash \sigma$, and $E \vdash \sigma'$, then $P\sigma \sim P\sigma'$ on the reasoning that, since P cannot unwrap the ciphertexts in σ or σ', it will behave the same whether closed by one or the other E-closure. This would hold were it not for the presence of matching in the language. For example, $E = x{:}\{-\}_m, y{:}\{-\}_m$, $P = [x \text{ is } y]\, \overline{p}\langle 0\rangle$, $\sigma = [\{0\}_m/x, \{0\}_m/y]$, and $\sigma' = [\{0\}_m/x, \{suc(0)\}_m/y]$ meet the conditions above, but $P\sigma$ may output 0 whereas $P\sigma'$ is stuck. Thus, P can act contingently on the ciphertexts even though it cannot decrypt them. However, if we insist that σ and σ' be injective (that is, $x = y$ whenever $x\sigma = y\sigma$, and similarly for σ') then we obtain $P\sigma \sim P\sigma'$.

These informal arguments lead to the following results.

Lemma 8. *Suppose that $E \vdash P$ and $E \vdash \sigma$, and that σ is injective. If $P\sigma > Q'$ then there is a process Q with $E \vdash Q$, $fv(Q) \subseteq fv(P)$, $fn(Q) \subseteq fn(P)$, and $Q' = Q\sigma$ such that, whenever $E \vdash \sigma'$ and σ' is injective, $P\sigma' > Q\sigma'$. Similarly, if $P\sigma \xrightarrow{\alpha} A'$ then there is an agent A with $E \vdash A$, $fv(A) \subseteq fv(P)$, $fn(A) \subseteq fn(P)$, and $A' = A\sigma$ such that, whenever $E \vdash \sigma'$ and σ' is injective, $P\sigma' \xrightarrow{\alpha} A\sigma'$.*

Proposition 9. *Suppose that $E \vdash \sigma$ and $E \vdash \sigma'$, and that both σ and σ' are injective. Then $S = \{(P\sigma, P\sigma') \mid E \vdash P\}$ is a barbed bisimulation.*

This last proposition provides an easy way to prove some equivalences, as we now demonstrate with a small proof of a secrecy property. We prove that, for any closed terms M and M':

$$(\nu K)\overline{c}\langle\{M\}_K\rangle \simeq (\nu K)\overline{c}\langle\{M'\}_K\rangle$$

By Proposition 7, we can reduce this testing equivalence to the barbed congruence $(\nu K)\overline{c}\langle\{M\}_K\rangle \sim (\nu K)\overline{c}\langle\{M'\}_K\rangle$. According to the definition of barbed congruence, it suffices to establish the barbed equivalence $((\nu K)\overline{c}\langle\{M\}_K\rangle) \mid R \stackrel{\cdot}{\sim} ((\nu K)\overline{c}\langle\{M'\}_K\rangle) \mid R$ for every closed process R. Since K is bound, we may assume that $K \notin fn(R)$. So we have the structural equivalences $((\nu K)\overline{c}\langle\{M\}_K\rangle) \mid R \equiv (\nu K)(\overline{c}\langle\{M\}_K\rangle \mid R)$ and $((\nu K)\overline{c}\langle\{M'\}_K\rangle) \mid R \equiv (\nu K)(\overline{c}\langle\{M'\}_K\rangle \mid R)$. Since barbed equivalence is an equivalence relation and since it includes structural equivalence (by Proposition 5), it suffices to show that $(\nu K)(\overline{c}\langle\{M\}_K\rangle \mid R) \stackrel{\cdot}{\sim} (\nu K)(\overline{c}\langle\{M'\}_K\rangle \mid R)$. Since restriction preserves barbed equivalence (also by Proposition 5), it suffices to prove that:

$$\overline{c}\langle\{M\}_K\rangle \mid R \stackrel{\cdot}{\sim} \overline{c}\langle\{M'\}_K\rangle \mid R$$

But this follows from Proposition 9 with $E = x{:}\{-\}_K$, $P = \overline{c}\langle x\rangle \mid R$, $\sigma = [\{M\}_K/x]$, and $\sigma' = [\{M'\}_K/x]$.

7 A Simple Example

In this section we describe and verify a two-message protocol. Protocols used in practice generally have more messages, but not many more. We focus on this short protocol in order to allow a concise exposition of our method. We have applied the same method to more complex protocols (in particular, to a seven-message protocol defined in [AG97a]).

The purpose of the protocol is to enable communication between two users or machines A and B. For simplicity, both A and B are fixed, and A sends a finite but unbounded set of messages to B. All the messages are transmitted under the same shared key K_{AB}. The messages are accompanied by nonces, which must be fresh and unpredictable quantities [AN96]; for each message M, A creates a nonce N_A and B creates a nonce N_B. Informally, the protocol is:

$$\begin{array}{lll} \text{Message 1} & B \rightarrow A: & N_B \\ \text{Message 2} & A \rightarrow B: & \{N_A, N_B, M\}_{K_{AB}} \end{array}$$

In Message 1, B challenges A with the nonce N_B. Message 1 may be spontaneous, or it may be triggered by an arbitrary message from A; the details of this do not matter. Message 2 is the transmission of M under K_{AB}. The presence of N_B proves the freshness of Message 2. The presence of N_A guarantees the distinctness of all ciphertexts.

For this example, we encode a triple (L, M, N) by a pair $(L, (M, N))$, and extend pair splitting to triples in the usual way. We also omit the inner brackets from an encrypted triple of the form $\{(N, N', N'')\}_{N'''}$, and simply write $\{N, N', N''\}_{N'''}$.

We express the protocol with the following parameterised definitions:

$$\begin{array}{rcl} A(N_A, M) & \triangleq & c_A(x).\overline{c_B}\langle\{N_A, x, M\}_{K_{AB}}\rangle \\ B(N_B, F) & \triangleq & \overline{c_A}\langle N_B\rangle \mid c_B(x).\mathit{case}\ x\ \mathit{of}\ \{y\}_{K_{AB}}\ \mathit{in} \\ & & \qquad \mathit{let}\ (y_1, y_2, y_3) = y\ \mathit{in} \\ & & \qquad [y_2\ \mathit{is}\ N_B]\ F(y_3) \end{array}$$

$$Sys(M_1, \ldots, M_m, F) \triangleq (\nu K_{AB})((\prod_{k \in 1..m}(\nu N_A)A(N_A, M_k)) \mid !(\nu N_B)B(N_B, F))$$

The channels c_A and c_B represent input channels for A and B, respectively. Parameter F is an abstraction such that $F(M)$ is the behaviour of B when it successfully receives a message M; we assume that the bound parameters of the protocol (including in particular K_{AB}) do not occur free in F. The process $Sys(M_1, \ldots, M_m, F)$ is a description of a complete system where A sends the messages $M_1, \ldots, M_m$ to B, and B applies F to the messages that it receives. The restrictions model the intended scope for the shared key and for the nonces. The replication indicates that B is willing to engage in an arbitrary number of transmissions.

Intuitively, the protocol has an authenticity property: if B accepts a message, then it is one sent by A; moreover, B does not accept message replays. In other words, the property is that if $Sys(M_1, \ldots, M_m, F)$ causes the execution of $F(L_1)$, $\ldots$, $F(L_l)$ then $\{L_1, \ldots, L_l\}$ is a sub-multiset of $\{M_1, \ldots, M_m\}$.

This authenticity property would be fairly obvious if $Sys(M_1, \ldots, M_m, F)$ had the form $(\nu p_k{}^{k \in 1..m})(Q \mid \prod_{k \in 1..m} p_k(x).F(M_k))$, where Q is a process independent of F. The following proposition establishes that $Sys(M_1, \ldots, M_m, F)$ is in fact equivalent to a process of this form:

Proposition 10 (Authenticity). *For any number m and distinct names p_1, $\ldots$, p_m there is a closed process Q with $fn(Q) \subseteq \{p_1, \ldots, p_m, c_A, c_B\}$ such that, for all closed terms M_1, $\ldots$, M_m and all closed abstractions F, if $p_1, \ldots, p_m \notin fn(Sys(M_1, \ldots, M_m, F))$ then:*

$$Sys(M_1, \ldots, M_m, F) \simeq (\nu p_k{}^{k \in 1..m})(Q \mid \prod_{k \in 1..m} p_k(x).F(M_k))$$

Proof. We only sketch the proof, for brevity. It depends on an analysis of the state space of the protocol, and on most of the other propositions presented in this paper. For an arbitrary number m and distinct names p_1, $\ldots$, p_m, we set:

$$Q \triangleq (\nu K_{AB})(\prod_{k \in 1..m}(\nu N_A)A(N_A, p_k) \mid !(\nu N_B)B(N_B, G))$$

where the names K_{AB}, N_A, and N_B are distinct from one another and from p_1, $\ldots$, p_m, c_A, c_B, and where G is the abstraction $(x)\overline{x}\langle 0\rangle$. (The choice of 0 is somewhat arbitrary; any term with no free names or variables would do instead.) It follows that $fn(Q) = \{p_1, \ldots, p_m, c_A, c_B\}$. Consider any closed terms M_1, $\ldots$, M_m, and any closed abstraction F such that none of the names p_1, $\ldots$, p_m occurs free in $Sys(M_1, \ldots, M_m, F)$. We may assume that the bound name K_{AB} does not occur free in M_1, $\ldots$, M_m, or F. The right-hand side of the proposition is structurally equivalent to:

$$(\nu K_{AB})(\prod_{k \in 1..m}(\nu p_k)((\nu N_A)A(N_A, p_k) \mid p_k(x).F(M_k)) \mid !(\nu N_B)B(N_B, G)) \tag{1}$$

Therefore, by Proposition 4, it suffices to show that

$$(\nu K_{AB})(\prod_{k \in 1..m}(\nu N_A)A(N_A, M_k) \mid \prod_{s \in 1..r}(\nu N_B)B(N_B, F)) \tag{2}$$

and

$$(\nu K_{AB})(\prod_{k\in 1..m}(\nu p_k)((\nu N_A)A(N_A, p_k) \mid p_k(x).F(M_k)) \mid \prod_{s\in 1..r}(\nu N_B)B(N_B, G)) \tag{3}$$

are testing equivalent for all $r \geq 0$. By Propositions 5 and 7 (and via several small formal manipulations), it suffices to prove that the following two processes are barbed equivalent:

$$\prod_{k\in 1..m} A(N_{Ak}, M_k) \mid \prod_{s\in 1..r} B(N_{Bs}, \tau.F) \mid R \tag{4}$$

$$(\nu p_k{}^{k\in 1..m})(\prod_{k\in 1..m}(A(N_{Ak}, p_k) \mid p_k(x).F(M_k)) \mid \prod_{s\in 1..r} B(N_{Bs}, G) \mid R) \tag{5}$$

where N_{A1}, ..., N_{Am}, N_{B1}, ..., N_{Br} are distinct, fresh names, and R is an arbitrary closed process such that none of the names K_{AB}, N_{A1}, ..., N_{Am}, N_{B1}, ..., N_{Br}, p_1, ..., p_m occurs free in R; and where $\tau.F$ is defined by $(\tau.F)(M) = (\nu m)(\overline{m}\langle 0\rangle \mid m(x).F(M))$ with m a fresh name and x a fresh variable.

The remainder of the proof consists in constructing a relation $\mathcal{S}$ such that $\equiv\mathcal{S}\equiv$ relates processes (4) and (5), and establishing that $\mathcal{S}$ is a barbed bisimulation up to $\dot{\sim}$ and restriction. It then follows that processes (4) and (5) are barbed equivalent by Proposition 6. We omit the definition of $\mathcal{S}$ and its study, which relies on Proposition 1. □

Intuitively, the protocol has a secrecy property too: if no information about the messages is given away as they are accepted, then no external observer can identify the messages. However, the observer may be able to tell how many messages are transmitted. This secrecy property is captured in the following proposition:

Proposition 11 (Secrecy). *For any pairs of closed terms* (M_1, M_1'), ..., (M_m, M_m') *and any closed abstraction* F, *if* $F(M_i) \simeq F(M_i')$ *for each* $i \in 1..m$ *then:*

$$Sys(M_1, \ldots, M_m, F) \simeq Sys(M_1', \ldots, M_m', F)$$

Proof. Proposition 10 implies that

$$Sys(M_1, \ldots, M_m, F) \simeq (\nu p_k{}^{k\in 1..m})(Q \mid \prod_{k\in 1..m} p_k(x).F(M_k))$$

and

$$Sys(M_1', \ldots, M_m', F) \simeq (\nu p_k{}^{k\in 1..m})(Q \mid \prod_{k\in 1..m} p_k(x).F(M_k'))$$

for some process Q and some names p_1, ..., p_m. Since testing equivalence is a congruence (by Proposition 3), if $F(M_i) \simeq F(M_i')$ for each $i \in 1..m$ then:

$$(\nu p_k{}^{k\in 1..m})(Q \mid \prod_{k\in 1..m} p_k(x).F(M_k)) \simeq (\nu p_k{}^{k\in 1..m})(Q \mid \prod_{k\in 1..m} p_k(x).F(M_k'))$$

The claim follows by transitivity. □

8 Conclusions

In the last few years, the importance of reasoning about cryptographic protocols has been widely recognised, and several methods have been used for this task. Those methods are based on a large variety of formal frameworks: temporal logics, modal logics, state-transition models, CSP (see e.g. [MCF87, BAN89, Kem89, Mil95a, Mea92, GM95, Low96, Sch96a]). The main emphasis of that work has been on authenticity properties.

Proofs in the spi calculus are sometimes more difficult than proofs in those earlier frameworks. The sources of this difficulty are in part the novelties and advantages of the spi-calculus approach: the expressive scoping mechanisms of the pi calculus; the treatment of secrecy properties; the view of attacks as tests, and the focus on testing equivalence. We hope that, through techniques such as ours, proofs in the spi calculus will become easier, even routine.

Acknowledgements

Paola Quaglia, Steve Schneider, and Peter Sewell suggested improvements to a draft of this paper.

References

[AG97a] M. Abadi and A. D. Gordon. A calculus for cryptographic protocols: The spi calculus. To appear in the Proceedings of the Fourth ACM Conference on Computer and Communications Security, 1997.

[AG97b] M. Abadi and A. D. Gordon. A calculus for cryptographic protocols: The spi calculus. Technical Report 414, University of Cambridge Computer Laboratory, January 1997.

[AN96] M. Abadi and R. Needham. Prudent engineering practice for cryptographic protocols. *IEEE Transactions on Software Engineering*, 22(1):6–15, January 1996.

[BAN89] M. Burrows, M. Abadi, and R. M. Needham. A logic of authentication. *Proceedings of the Royal Society of London A*, 426:233–271, 1989. A preliminary version appeared as Digital Equipment Corporation Systems Research Center report No. 39, February 1989.

[BB92] G. Berry and G. Boudol. The chemical abstract machine. *Theoretical Computer Science*, 96(1):217–248, April 1992.

[BN95] M. Boreale and R. De Nicola. Testing equivalence for mobile processes. *Information and Computation*, 120(2):279–303, August 1995.

[DES77] Data encryption standard. Fed. Inform. Processing Standards Pub. 46, National Bureau of Standards, Washington DC, January 1977.

[DH84] R. De Nicola and M. C. B. Hennessy. Testing equivalences for processes. *Theoretical Computer Science*, 34:83–133, 1984.

[GM95] J. Gray and J. McLean. Using temporal logic to specify and verify cryptographic protocols (progress report). In *Proceedings of the 8th IEEE Computer Security Foundations Workshop*, pages 108–116, 1995.

[Kem89] R. A. Kemmerer. Analyzing encryption protocols using formal verification techniques. *IEEE Journal on Selected Areas in Communications*, 7, 1989.

[Lie93] A. Liebl. Authentication in distributed systems: A bibliography. *ACM Operating Systems Review*, 27(4):31–41, 1993.

[Low96] G. Lowe. Breaking and fixing the Needham-Schroeder public-key protocol using FDR. In *Tools and Algorithms for the Construction and Analysis of Systems*, volume 1055 of *Lecture Notes in Computer Science*, pages 147–166. Springer Verlag, 1996.

[MCF87] J. K. Millen, S. C. Clark, and S. B. Freedman. The Interrogator: Protocol security analysis. *IEEE Transactions on Software Engineering*, SE-13(2):274–288, February 1987.

[Mea92] C. Meadows. Applying formal methods to the analysis of a key management protocol. *Journal of Computer Security*, 1(1):5–36, 1992.

[Mil89] R. Milner. *Communication and Concurrency*. Prentice-Hall International, 1989.

[Mil92] R. Milner. Functions as processes. *Mathematical Structures in Computer Science*, 2:119–141, 1992.

[Mil95a] J. K. Millen. The Interrogator model. In *IEEE Symposium on Security and Privacy*, pages 251–260, 1995.

[Mil95b] R. Milner. The π-calculus. Undergraduate lecture notes, Cambridge University, 1995.

[MPW92] R. Milner, J. Parrow, and D. Walker. A calculus of mobile processes, parts I and II. *Information and Computation*, pages 1–40 and 41–77, September 1992.

[Sch96a] S. Schneider. Security properties and CSP. In *IEEE Symposium on Security and Privacy*, pages 174–187, 1996.

[Sch96b] B. Schneier. *Applied Cryptography: Protocols, Algorithms, and Source Code in C*. John Wiley & Sons, Inc., second edition, 1996.

Modularity for Timed and Hybrid Systems*

Rajeev Alur Thomas A. Henzinger

EECS Department, University of California, Berkeley, CA 94720-1770, U.S.A.
Email: {alur,tah}@eecs.berkeley.edu

Abstract. In a trace-based world, the modular specification, verification, and control of live systems require each module to be *receptive*; that is, each module must be able to meet its liveness assumptions no matter how the other modules behave. In a real-time world, liveness is automatically present in the form of *diverging time*. The receptiveness condition, then, translates to the requirement that a module must be able to let time diverge no matter how the environment behaves. We study the receptiveness condition for real-time systems by extending the model of *reactive modules* to timed and hybrid modules. We define the receptiveness of such a module as the existence of a winning strategy in a game of the module against its environment. By solving the game on region graphs, we present an (optimal) EXPTIME algorithm for checking the receptiveness of propositional timed modules. By giving a fixpoint characterization of the game, we present a symbolic procedure for checking the receptiveness of linear hybrid modules. Finally, we present an assume-guarantee principle for reasoning about timed and hybrid modules, and a method for synthesizing receptive controllers of timed and hybrid modules.

1 Introduction

Over the past decade, much research has focused on the modeling and verification of *timed* systems [12], which have hard real-time constraints, and *hybrid* systems [16, 11, 7], which contain both discrete and continuous components. Most of this research[2] has emphasized *closed* systems, which can be considered in isolation, and neglected *open* systems, whose behavior is influenced by the behavior of an external environment.[3] For example, the ubiquitous train-gate system from the real-time literature is usually studied as a compound closed system, and no properties are proved about how the train behaves relative to *any* gate, or about how the gate behaves relative to any train. This is because if the components of a system interact with each other, then each component by itself must be treated as an open system.

One reason for the lack of emphasis on open real-time systems may be that a proper formalization is far from "obvious." When time is of the essence, a liveness assumption enters automatically, namely, the assumption that no system should be able to prevent time from diverging. A physical discrete system may "stop" time finitely often within any finite time span, to perform its actions, but it may not perform infinitely many actions within a finite amount of time. Consider, for example, the classical zeno paradox: a discrete observer that looks at a runner at times 1/2, 3/4, 7/8, etc., will never observe the runner cross the finishing line. Indeed, applied to a timed system that represents the runner and to a control objective that the state *finished* is never entered, classical

* This research was supported in part by the ONR YIP award N00014-95-1-0520, by the NSF CAREER award CCR-9501708, by the NSF grant CCR-9504469, by the AFOSR contract F49620-93-1-0056, by the ARO MURI grant DAAH-04-96-1-0341, by the ARPA grant NAG2-892, and by the SRC contract 95-DC-324.036.

[2] Including most previous work by the authors.

[3] A notable exception is the work on timed and hybrid I/O automata [17, 23].

control methods yield a controller that "prevents" the runner from finishing by issuing infinitely many control actions [22, 24]. Such a controller, of course, cannot be realized physically.[4]

For *live closed* systems, the appropriate condition is *machine closure* [3]: every finite run can be extended to an infinite live run. In the case of real-time systems, the machine-closure condition is usually called *nonzenoness* [9, 18]: every finite trajectory can be extended to a divergent trajectory; that is, no matter what the system does, there is always a possibility for time to diverge. Since machine closure is not closed under parallel composition, for *live open* systems, the appropriate condition becomes trickier. To see this, consider a module P that issues an output at time 0, then waits for an input; if the input arrives at time δ_1, the module issues the next output at time $\delta_1 + 1/2$ and waits for another input; if the second input arrives at time δ_2, the next output is issued at time $\delta_2 + 1/4$; etc. Second, consider a module Q that waits for an input and once the input arrives at time ϵ_1, the module issues an output at time $\epsilon_1 + 1/2$; then the module waits for another input, and if the second input arrives at time ϵ_2, the next output is issued at time $\epsilon_2 + 1/4$; etc. While each module, P and Q, by itself is nonzeno (there is always a possibility for time to diverge), the composition $P||Q$ generates events at times 0, 1/2, 1, 5/4, 3/2, 13/8, etc., and thus prevents time from progressing past 2.

A proper condition for live open systems, therefore, must take into account adversarial, rather than cooperative, environments. Such a condition, called *receptiveness*, is best formulated as a game [13, 8, 17]: a module is receptive iff in a two-player game against the environment, the module has a strategy to generate an infinite live run. Then, the composition of two receptive modules is again receptive (and machine-closed). In the case of real-time systems, a receptiveness game was first defined for I/O automata [17]. Here, we define and algorithmically analyze a receptiveness game for timed systems that are modeled as discrete systems with clock variables, à la *timed automata* [2], and for hybrid systems that are modeled as discrete systems with continuous variables, à la *hybrid automata* [1].

In each move of our receptiveness game for timed systems, the module proposes to let time $\delta \geq 0$ pass, and the environment proposes to let time $\delta' \geq 0$ pass (if the module wants to update the discrete state, then $\delta = 0$, and the same is true for the environment). If either $\delta = 0$ or $\delta' = 0$, then the module and the environment update the discrete state, according to a protocol for discrete systems, and no time elapses. If both $\delta > 0$ and $\delta' > 0$, then time $min(\delta, \delta')$ elapses, and the discrete state stays unchanged. If $\delta \leq \delta'$, the move is charged to the module; otherwise, the move is charged to the environment. The module is called *receptive* iff in this game, it has a strategy that will never generate a convergent trajectory unless all but finitely many moves are charged to the environment.

Since timed and hybrid automata are models for closed systems, we extend the open-system model of *reactive modules* [5] with clock variables, to obtain *timed modules*, and with continuous variables, to obtain *hybrid modules*. The formalism of reactive modules was developed for specifying highly heterogeneous systems, with mixed hardware and software components, and mixed synchronous and asynchronous interactions between components. We continue this theme of heterogeneity by providing reactive modules with mechanisms for specifying mixed timing, as well as mixed discrete-continuous behavior.

By defining and studying the receptiveness game for timed and hybrid modules, we accomplish four results. First, we extend the assume-guarantee principle for modular reasoning from reactive

[4] To circumvent such absurdities, [10] introduce an "anti-Zeno" constant δ for controllers, which ensures that a controller cannot act more than once every δ time units. This requirement, of course, may cause us to fail finding a controller for a perfectly controllable situation.

modules to timed and hybrid modules; the soundness of the principle depends on the receptiveness of all participating modules.[5] Second, by giving a fixpoint characterization of the receptiveness game, we develop a symbolic procedure for checking the receptiveness of timed and linear hybrid modules (which are closely related to linear hybrid automata [6]); this procedure can be easily implemented in existing tools such as KRONOS [14] and HYTECH [19]. Third, by reducing the receptiveness game to a coBüchi game on finite region graphs, we give an exponential algorithm for checking the receptiveness of propositional timed modules (which are timed modules with finitely many discrete states); the algorithm is optimal, as we show the problem to be complete for EXPTIME. Fourth, we address the controller-synthesis problem for timed and hybrid modules, and show how classical methods (both symbolic and enumerative) can be used for synthesizing controllers that are guaranteed to be receptive (provided such a controller exists).

As is to be expected, "open" problems about timed systems (receptiveness checking, control) are theoretically harder than the corresponding "closed" problems (nonzenoness checking, verification); while the latter are generally complete for PSPACE, the former are complete for EXPTIME. In practice, both open and closed problems can be solved using symbolic fixpoint computations. It should also be noted that while throughout, we consider the dense time domain of the nonnegative reals, our motivation and our conclusions apply equally to the digital-clock model, where all timestamps are truncated to integer values, and a system may prevent time from diverging by insisting on infinitely many moves of delay 0.

2 Timed Modules

We extend the model of *reactive modules* [5] to allow for the specification of real-time behavior.

Discrete variables vs. clock variables. A timed module P has a finite set of typed variables, denoted X_P. Some of the variables are updated in a discrete fashion, and the other variables change continuously when time elapses. Accordingly, the set X_P of module variables is partitioned into two sets, the set $discX_P$ of *discrete variables*, and the set $clkX_P$ of *clock variables*. The type of all clock variables is $\mathbb{R}$. A *state* of P is a valuation for the variables in X_P. Events, such as the sending of messages, are modeled by toggling discrete variables of type $\mathbb{B}$.

System vs. environment. The module P represents a system that interacts with an environment. Some of the variables in X_P are updated by the module, and the other variables in X_P are updated by the environment. Accordingly, the set X_P is partitioned into two sets, the set $ctrX_P$ of *controlled variables*, and the set $extlX_P$ of *external variables*. A controlled variable may be either discrete or a clock, and an external variable may be either discrete or a clock.

States vs. observations. Not all controlled variables of the module P are visible to the environment. Accordingly, the set $ctrX_P$ is partitioned further into two sets, the set $privX_P$ of *private variables*, and the set $intfX_P$ of *interface variables*. The interface variables and the external variables are *observable*, denoted $obsX_P$. An *observation* of P is a valuation for the variables in $obsX_P$. The observation of a state s, then, is the projection $s[obsX_P]$ of s to the observable variables.

Update rounds vs. time rounds. The module P proceeds in a sequence of rounds. The first round is an *initialization round*, during which the variables in X_P are initialized. Each subsequent round is either an update round or a time round. During each *update round*, the variables in X_P are updated, by the module and the environment, in zero time. During each *time round*, the values of

[5] A more specialized assume-guarantee principle for timed systems was presented in [27]. Its soundness follows from syntactic restrictions that ensure receptiveness.

all discrete variables in $discX_P$ remain unchanged, and the values of all clock variables in $clkX_P$ increase continuously and uniformly, at the rate 1, as time advances. For a variable x, we use the unprimed symbol x to refer to the value of x at the beginning of a round, and the primed symbol x' to refer to the value of x at the end of a round. If s is a valuation for a set X of variables, by X' we denote the corresponding set $\{x' \mid x \in X\}$ of primed variables, and by s' we denote the valuation for X' that assigns the value $s[x]$ to each variable x'.

Update rounds. As in synchronous languages such as ESTEREL, each update round consists of several subrounds. Unlike in ESTEREL, however, every variable is updated in exactly one subround of each update round. The controlled variables are partitioned into groups called atoms, and the variables within a group are updated simultaneously, in the same subround of each round. The atoms are partially ordered. If atom A precedes atom B in the partial ordering, then in each round, the A-subround must precede the B-subround, and the updated values of the variables controlled by B may depend on the updated values of the variables controlled by A. The updates that are permitted by an atom are specified using executable actions. For two sets X and Y of variables, an *action* from X to Y is a binary relation between the valuations for X and the valuations for Y. The action α from X to Y is *executable* if for every valuation s for X, the number of valuations t for Y with $(s,t) \in \alpha$ is nonzero and finite. Executable actions are nonblocking (always enabled) and ensure finite control branching.

Time rounds. Each time round has a positive real-valued *duration* (update rounds are defined to have duration 0). For a state s, and a real $\delta \in \mathbb{R}_{\geq 0}$, we write $s+\delta$ for the state that assigns the value $x[s]$ to each discrete variable x and the value $x[s]+\delta$ to each clock variable x. Thus, if the state at the beginning of a time round with duration δ is s, then the state at the end of the round is $s+\delta$. The durations that are permitted by an atom are specified using executable delays. A *delay* over a set X of variables is a binary relation between the valuations for X and the valuations for X'. The delay β over X is *executable* if the following two conditions are met. First, $(s,s') \in \beta$ for every valuation s for X. Second, for every valuation s for X and every real $\delta \in \mathbb{R}_{\geq 0}$, if $(s, s'+\delta) \in \beta$, then for all nonnegative reals $\epsilon < \delta$, both $(s, s'+\epsilon) \in \beta$ and $(s+\epsilon, s'+\delta) \in \beta$. An executable delay specifies for every state a maximal (possibly 0 or infinite) duration that may elapse (possibly in several steps) without violating the delay.

Definition 1. *[Timed atom]* Let X be a finite set of typed variables. A (*timed*) X-*atom* A consists of a declaration and a body. The atom declaration consists of a set $ctrX_A \subseteq X$ of *controlled variables* and a set $waitX_A \subseteq X \backslash ctrX_A$ of *awaited variables*. The atom body consists of an executable *initial action* $Init_A$ from $waitX'_A$ to $ctrX'_A$, an executable *update action* $Update_A$ from $X \cup waitX'_A$ to $ctrX'_A$, and an executable delay $Delay_A$ over $ctrX_A \cup waitX_A$. We require the update action $Update_A$ to be *round-insensitive*; that is, $(s \cup s'[waitX'_A], s'[ctrX'_A]) \in Update_A$ for every valuation s for X. ■

During the initialization round, the atom A waits for the initial values of the variables in $waitX_A$ before initializing the variables in $ctrX_A$. During each subsequent round, the X-atom A reads the values of the variables in X at the beginning of the round and decides which duration (possibly 0) it is prepared to let elapse. We say that in state s, the atom A *permits* the duration $\delta \in \mathbb{R}_{\geq 0}$ if $(s, s'+\delta) \in Delay_A$. If the duration of the round is decided to be 0, then the round is an update round, and the atom waits for the updated values of the variables in $waitX_A$ before updating the variables in $ctrX_A$. We say that the variable x *awaits* the variable y, and write $x \succ_A y$, if $x \in ctrX_A$ and $y \in waitX_A$. Round-insensitivity ensures that whenever the values of the awaited variables do not change, then the values of the controlled variables may remain unchanged.[6]

[6] Round-insensitivity is not required for discrete modules [5], but allows the treatment of degenerate, zero-duration time rounds as update rounds.

Definition 2. *[Timed module]* A (*timed*) *module* P consists of a declaration and a body. The module declaration is a finite set X_P of typed variables that is partitioned into private variables $privX_P$, interface variables $intfX_P$, and external variables $extlX_P$. The module body is a set $\mathcal{A}_P$ of X_P-atoms such that (1) $(\bigcup_{A \in \mathcal{A}_P} ctrX_A) = ctrX_P$, (2) $ctrX_A \cap ctrX_B = \emptyset$ for all atoms A and B in $\mathcal{A}_P$, and (3) the transitive closure $\succ_P = (\bigcup_{A \in \mathcal{A}_P} \succ_A)^+$ is asymmetric. ■

The first two conditions ensure that the atoms of P control precisely the variables in $ctrX_P$, and that each variable in $ctrX_P$ is controlled by precisely one atom. The third condition ensures that the await dependencies among the variables in X_P are acyclic. A linear ordering $A_0, \ldots, A_k$ of the atoms in $\mathcal{A}_P$ is *consistent* if for all $0 \leq i < j \leq k$, the awaited variables of A_i are disjoint from the controlled variables of A_j. The asymmetry of $\succ_P$ ensures that there exists a consistent ordering.

Module execution. During the initialization round, first the external variables are assigned arbitrary values of the appropriate types, and then the atoms in $\mathcal{A}_P$ are executed in a consistent order. Each subsequent round is either an update round or a time round whose duration is permitted by all atoms. During an update round, first the external variables are assigned arbitrary values of the appropriate types, and then the update actions of the atoms are executed in a consistent order.

Module syntax. Variable declarations are indicated by keywords such as **awaits**, for the awaited variables of an atom, and **private**, for the private variables of a module. Clock variables have the type $\mathbb{C}$. Initial and update actions are specified by the keywords **init** and **update**, followed by guarded assignments. Delays are specified by the keyword **delay** followed by guarded invariants, where the guard constrains unprimed variables and the invariant constrains primed clock variables. An invariant permits all durations that do not invalidate the invariant. If several guards are true, then one of the corresponding assignments or invariants is chosen nondeterministically. If none of the guards are true, then all controlled variables stay unchanged and no positive duration is permitted.

Example: timed circuits. The module *Delay* of Figure 1 specifies a delay element that copies the boolean input *in* to the boolean output *out* after a delay between 1 to 2 time units. Initially, the module is stable with the output equal to the input. In each update round, if the input changes, the module becomes unstable. Once it becomes unstable, within 1 to 2 time units, it toggles the output and returns to a stable state. To enforce the time bounds, a clock x is started whenever the module becomes unstable. Then, the guard $x \geq 1$ enforces the lower time bound, and the invariant $x' \leq 2$ enforces the upper time bound. If the input changes while the module is unstable, a hazard occurs, and the output may change arbitrarily, independently of the input. Note that if the module is stable or hazardous, any amount of time may elapse. It is easy to describe synchronous gates and latches as modules [5]. Asynchronous circuits, then, can be described by combining gates, latches, and delay elements [13]. ■

Propositional timed modules. A timed module P is *propositional* if all discrete variables of P have finite types (boolean or enumerated), and if the initial actions, the update actions, and the delays of P constrain the clock variables in very restricted ways: in guards and invariants, clocks are compared to rational constants, and in assignments, clocks are either left unchanged or assigned rational constants. For example, the delay element *Delay* is a propositional timed module. In a technical sense, propositional timed modules are open versions of timed automata [2].

Transition graph of a module. Every module P defines an edge-labeled transition graph whose vertices are the states of P, and whose labels are nonnegative reals that represent the durations of

module *Delay*
  interface $out : \mathbb{B}$
  external $in : \mathbb{B}$
  private $state : \{stable, unstable, hazard\};\ x : \mathbb{C}$
  atom $state, out, x$ **awaits** in'
    init $state' := stable;\ out' := in'$
    update
    $[]\ state = stable \wedge in' \neq in \ \rightarrow\ state' := unstable;\ x' := 0$
    $[]\ state = unstable \wedge x \geq 1 \ \rightarrow\ state' := stable;\ out' := in'$
    $[]\ state = unstable \wedge x < 1 \wedge in' \neq in \ \rightarrow\ state' := hazard$
    $[]\ state = hazard \ \rightarrow\ out' := 0$
    $[]\ state = hazard \ \rightarrow\ out' := 1$
    delay
    $[]\ state = stable \ \rightarrow\ true$
    $[]\ state = unstable \wedge x \leq 2 \ \rightarrow\ x' \leq 2$
    $[]\ state = hazard \ \rightarrow\ true$

Fig. 1. Delay element

transitions. A state s is *initial* if $(s'[waitX'_A], s'[ctrX'_A]) \in Init_A$ for each atom A of P. For two states s and t, define $s \xrightarrow{0} t$ if $(s \cup t'[waitX'_A], t'[ctrX'_A]) \in Update_A$ for each atom A of P, and define $s \xrightarrow{\delta} t$, for a positive duration $\delta \in \mathbb{R}_{>0}$, if $t = s + \delta$ and $(s, t') \in Delay_A$ for each atom A of P.

Trajectories of a module. A *trajectory* of the module P is a finite sequence of states and durations of the form $s_0 \xrightarrow{\delta_1} s_1 \xrightarrow{\delta_2} \cdots \xrightarrow{\delta_n} s_n$. We denote this trajectory by the pair $(\overline{s}_{0..n}, \overline{\delta}_{1..n})$. The *length* of the trajectory $(\overline{s}_{0..n}, \overline{\delta}_{1..n})$ is n, and its *accumulated duration* is the sum $\Sigma_{1 \leq i \leq n} \delta_i$ of all transition durations. The trajectory $(\overline{s}_{0..n}, \overline{\delta}_{1..n})$ is a *source-s* trajectory if $s_0 = s$, and an *initialized* trajectory if s_0 is an initial state of P. If $(\overline{s}_{0..n}, \overline{\delta}_{1..n})$ is an initialized trajectory, then s_n is a *reachable* state of P. If the module P contains a single atom A only, we sometimes refer to the trajectories and reachable states of P as trajectories and reachable states of A.

Traces of a module. If $(\overline{s}_{0..n}, \overline{\delta}_{1..n})$ is an (initialized) trajectory of the module P, then the corresponding sequence $s_0[obsX_P] \xrightarrow{\delta_1} \cdots \xrightarrow{\delta_n} s_n[obsX_P]$ of observations and durations is an (initialized) *trace* of P. Thus, a trace retains information about changes to observations and the corresponding times. We write $(\overline{a}_{0..n}, \overline{\delta}_{1..n})$ for the trace $a_0 \xrightarrow{\delta_1} \cdots \xrightarrow{\delta_n} a_n$. To obtain the trace language of a module, we close the set of initialized traces under stuttering. Closure under stuttering combines consecutive transitions that do not change the values of observable discrete variables and produce no discontinuity in the evolution of observable clock variables.

Definition 3. *[Trace language]* The *(timed) trace language* L_P of a module P is the least set such that (1) every initialized trace of P belongs to L_P, and (2) if $(\overline{a}_{0..n}, \overline{\delta}_{1..n})$ belongs to L_P, and for some $0 < i \leq n$, both $a_i[discX_P] = a_{i-1}[discX_P]$ and $a_{i+1}[clkX_P] = a_{i-1}[clkX_P] + \delta_i + \delta_{i+1}$, then $a_0 \xrightarrow{\delta_1} \cdots \xrightarrow{\delta_{i-1}} a_{i-1} \xrightarrow{\delta_i + \delta_{i+1}} a_{i+1} \xrightarrow{\delta_{i+2}} \cdots \xrightarrow{\delta_n} s_n$ also belongs to L_P. ■

For every module P, the trace language L_P is prefix-closed. Since all update actions are nonblocking, every trace in L_P is a proper prefix of some other trace in L_P.

Implementation preorder. The trace semantics of a module P consists of the trace language L_P, together with all information that is necessary for describing the possible interactions of P with the environment: the set $intfX_P$ of interface variables, the set $extlX_P$ of external variables, and the await dependencies $\succ_P \cap (intfX_P \times obsX_P)$ between interface variables and observable variables.

Definition 4. *[Implementation]* The module P *implements* the module Q, written $P \preceq Q$, if (1) every interface variable of Q is an interface variable of P, (2) every external variable of Q is an observable variable of P, (3) for all variables x in $obsX_Q$ and all variables y in $intfX_Q$, if $y \succ_Q x$ then $y \succ_P x$, and (4) if $(\overline{a}_{0..n}, \overline{\delta}_{1..n})$ belongs to L_P, then the projection $(\overline{a}[obsX_Q]_{0...n}, \overline{\delta}_{1...n})$ belongs to L_Q. ■

The first three conditions ensure that the compatibility constraints imposed by P on its environment are stronger than those imposed by Q. The fourth condition is conventional trace inclusion. It is easy to check that the implementation relation $\preceq$ is a preorder (i.e., reflexive and transitive).

Parallel composition. Modules can be combined using the three operations of variable renaming, variable hiding, and parallel composition [5]. Here, we focus on parallel composition only. The two modules P and Q are *compatible* if (1) the interface variables of P and Q are disjoint, and (2) the await dependencies among the observable variables of P and Q are acyclic —that is, the transitive closure $(\succ_P \cup \succ_Q)^+$ is asymmetric. It follows that if P and R are compatible modules, and $P \preceq Q$, then Q and R are also compatible.

Definition 5. *[Composition]* If P and Q are two compatible modules, then the *composition* $P \| Q$ is the module with the set $privX_{P\|Q} = privX_P \cup privX_Q$ of private variables, the set $intfX_{P\|Q} = intfX_P \cup intfX_Q$ of interface variables, the set $extlX_{P\|Q} = (extlX_P \cup extlX_Q) \backslash intfX_{P\|Q}$ of external variables, and the set $\mathcal{A}_{P\|Q} = \mathcal{A}_P \cup \mathcal{A}_Q$ of atoms. ■

It is easy to check that for two compatible modules P and Q, the composition $P\|Q$ is again a module. Henceforth, whenever we write $P\|Q$, we assume that P and Q are compatible.

Proposition 6. *The composition operator has the following properties.*

(1) A trace $(\overline{a}_{0..n}, \overline{\delta}_{1..n})$ belongs to $L_{P\|Q}$ iff the projection $(\overline{a}[obsX_P]_{0..n}, \overline{\delta}_{1..n})$ belongs to L_P and the projection $(\overline{a}[obsX_Q]_{0..n}, \overline{\delta}_{1..n})$ belongs to L_Q.
(2) $P\|Q \preceq P$.
(3) If $P \preceq Q$, then $P\|R \preceq Q\|R$.

Thus, parallel composition behaves like logical conjunction. Property (3) asserts that the implementation preorder is a congruence with respect to composition.

3 Nonzenoness and Receptiveness

It is easy to specify modules that prevent time from diverging. We now rule out such modules, which cannot be realized physically.

Nonzeno modules. Consider the module *Zeno* of Figure 2. While every trajectory of *Zeno* can be extended to a trajectory of arbitrary length, not every trajectory can be extended to a trajectory of arbitrary accumulated duration: by choosing the update $a' := 1$, the module *Zeno* can prevent the divergence of time.

Definition 7. *[Nonzenoness]* A module P is *nonzeno* if for every reachable state s of P, there exists a source-s trajectory of accumulated duration 1. ■

```
module Zeno
  private a: 𝔹; x: ℂ
  atom a, x
    init a' := 0; x' := 0
    update
    [] a = 0 → x' := 0
    [] a = 0 → a' := 1
    delay
    [] x < 2 → x' < 2
```

```
module Nonreceptive
  external a: 𝔹
  private x: ℂ
  atom x
    init x' := 0
    update
    [] a = 0 → x' := 0
    delay
    [] x < 2 → x' < 2
```

Fig. 2. Zeno and nonreceptive modules

Since trajectories of accumulated duration 1 can be concatenated to a trajectory of arbitrary accumulated duration, nonzeno modules cannot prevent time from diverging.

Proposition 8. *For every nonzeno module P, every trace in L_P can be extended to a trace of arbitrary accumulated duration.*

The symbolic fixpoint-computation procedure of [21] for checking if a given timed automaton is nonzeno can be used for timed modules also. Furthermore, it follows that for propositional timed modules, the problem of checking nonzenoness is complete for PSPACE.

Receptive modules. Nonzenoness is an existential property of a module, and hence, it is not preserved under composition [9, 17]. A simple case in point is the module *Nonreceptive* of Figure 2. While the module *Nonreceptive* is nonzeno, its ability to let time diverge depends on the cooperation of the environment. In particular, if the environment keeps the value of the external variable a always 1, then time cannot progress beyond 2. Consequently, we want to consider only those modules that cannot prevent time from diverging no matter what a "reasonable" environment does. In particular, a nonzeno environment would not be considered reasonable, because it may be the source of the trouble. For compound modules that prevent time from diverging, we must therefore assign the "blame" to one or both components. This assignment of blame is best formalized as a game.

We formalize the receptiveness game for atoms. To define receptiveness we need to consider infinite trajectories: an *ω-trajectory* of the atom A is an infinite sequence $(\overline{s}_{0..}, \overline{\delta}_{1..}) = s_0 \xrightarrow{\delta_1} s_1 \xrightarrow{\delta_2} \cdots$ of states and durations such that every finite prefix of $(\overline{s}_{0..}, \overline{\delta}_{1..})$ is a trajectory of A. The accumulated duration $\Sigma_{i \geq 1} \delta_i$ of the ω-trajectory $(\overline{s}_{0..}, \overline{\delta}_{1..})$ may be finite or infinite.

Consider an X-atom A, and for simplicity, assume that A has no awaited variables. The receptiveness game starts in a reachable state of A. The two players, the protagonist representing the atom, and the adversary representing the environment, take turns to incrementally produce an ω-trajectory of A. Following [17], each round is charged to one of the two players depending on which player blocks the passage of time. Suppose that the current state of the game is s. In each round, first, the protagonist either chooses, in conformance with the update action of A, a new valuation t for the controlled variables in $ctrX_A$, or it proposes a positive duration $\delta \in \mathbb{R}_{>0}$ that is permitted by the delay of A.

- If the protagonist chooses new values for the controlled variables, then the adversary chooses a new valuation u for the remaining variables in $X \backslash ctrX_A$, and the state of the game changes to $t \cup u$. In this case, the round is charged to the protagonist.

- If the protagonist proposes a duration $\delta > 0$, then the adversary either chooses a new valuation u for the variables in $X \backslash ctrX_A$, or it also proposes a positive duration $\delta' \in \mathbb{R}_{>0}$. In the former case, no time elapses, the state of the game changes to $s[ctrX_A] \cup u$, and the round is charged to the adversary. In the latter case, a time round of duration equal to the minimum of δ and δ' is executed. If $\delta < \delta'$, then the state of the game changes to $s + \delta$ and the round is charged to the adversary. If $\delta \geq \delta'$, then the state of the game changes to $s + \delta'$ and the round is charged to the protagonist.

At any round, if the accumulated duration of the trajectory produced so far reaches (or exceeds) 1, the protagonist wins. If the game continues at infinitum, an ω-trajectory with duration less than 1 is produced. In this case, the protagonist wins the game iff only finitely many rounds are charged to the protagonist. Observe that the charging of rounds is asymmetric: when both the players propose an update round, or both propose a time round of the same duration, the round is charged to the protagonist. This, together with the requirement that only finitely many rounds can be charged to a winning protagonist, ensures that the atom does not collaborate with the environment to block the passage of time. If the protagonist has a strategy to win the game, the atom A is called receptive.

In general, when the atom A has awaited variables, each round consists of three steps: first, the adversary either chooses to update the awaited variables or it proposes a positive duration, followed by the two steps described above. We formalize the moves of the protagonist by defining a pair of strategies: a delay strategy to propose the duration of the next round, and an update strategy to choose the new values of the controlled variables. For a set Y of variables, let Σ_Y be the set of valuations for Y. A *delay strategy* for the X-atom A is a function $F_d \colon \Sigma_X \rightarrow \mathbb{R}_{\geq 0}$ such that if $t = s + F_d(s)$, then $(s, t') \in Delay_A$. An *update strategy* for A is a function $F_u : \Sigma_X \times \Sigma_{waitX_A} \rightarrow \Sigma_{ctrX_A}$ such that if $F_u(s, t) = u$, then $(s \cup t', u') \in Update_A$. The update strategy F_u *matches* the delay strategy F_d if for every valuation s for X, if $F_d(s) > 0$ then $F_u(s, s[waitX_A]) = s[ctrX_A]$. For a delay strategy F_d and a matching update strategy F_u, the ω-trajectory $(\overline{s}_{0..}, \overline{\delta}_{1..})$ of A is a (F_d, F_u)-*outcome* if for all $i \geq 0$, (1) the duration of each round is bounded by the duration selected by the delay strategy: $\delta_{i+1} \leq F_d(s_i)$; and (2) in each round of duration 0, the controlled part of the new state is selected by the update strategy: if $\delta_{i+1} = 0$, then $s_{i+1}[ctrX_A] = F_u(s_i, s_{i+1}[waitX_A])$.

Definition 9. *[***Receptiveness***]* An atom A is *receptive* if there exist a delay strategy F_d and a matching update strategy F_u for A such that there is no ω-trajectory $(\overline{s}_{0..}, \overline{\delta}_{1..})$ of A satisfying (1) s_0 is a reachable state of A, (2) $(\overline{s}_{0..}, \overline{\delta}_{1..})$ is an (F_d, F_u)-outcome, (3) the accumulated duration of $(\overline{s}_{0..}, \overline{\delta}_{1..})$ is less than 1, and (4) there are infinitely many positions i with $F_d(s_i) = \delta_{i+1}$. A module P is *receptive* if all atoms of P are receptive. ■

Update and delay strategies have been defined history-free (i.e., they depend only on the current state of the game). It is easy to check that the availability of more powerful, history-dependent strategies would not alter the definition of receptiveness. Since the atoms of a compound module are the atoms of the component modules, receptiveness is closed under parallel composition.

Proposition 10. *If two modules P and Q are receptive, then the module $P||Q$ is also receptive.*

The following theorem identifies receptiveness is a sufficient condition for nonzenoness that is closed under parallel composition.

Theorem 11. *Every receptive module is nonzeno.*

3.1 Assume-Guarantee Reasoning for Timed Modules

Consider the problem of verifying that the (complex) module $P_1||P_2$ implements the (simpler) module $Q_1||Q_2$. Since the implementation preorder is a congruence with respect to parallel composition, it suffices to prove the desired refinement for each component separately: (a) $P_1 \preceq Q_1$, and (b) $P_2 \preceq Q_2$. These proof obligations, however, are rarely satisfied if the components interact. An assume-guarantee principle allows us to replace (a) and (b) by two weaker obligations, namely, (a') $P_1||Q_2 \preceq Q_1$ and (b') $Q_1||P_2 \preceq Q_2$ [25, 8, 4]. Obligation (a') asserts that P_1 implements Q_1, under the hypothesis that its environment behaves like Q_2, and obligation (b') asserts that P_2 implements Q_2, under the hypothesis that its environment behaves like Q_1. Despite the apparent circularity, the assume-guarantee principle is valid if all involved modules are receptive.

Theorem 12. *For receptive modules P_1, P_2, Q_1, and Q_2, if $P_1||Q_2 \preceq Q_1$ and $Q_1||P_2 \preceq Q_2$, then $P_1||P_2 \preceq Q_1||Q_2$.*

3.2 Deciding the Receptiveness of Propositional Timed Atoms

We now address the problem of checking automatically if a given atom A is receptive. For this purpose, we view the receptiveness game as a two-player infinite game on an extended state space with a coBüchi winning condition. First, we introduce a new clock variable now, which is 0 at the beginning of the game, and changes value only by advancing with time. Second, we introduce a binary variable $blame$, whose type is the set $\{atom, env\}$. The value of $blame$ is set to $atom$ during each round that is charged to the atom, and it is set to env during each round that is charged to the environment. Then, the *positions* of the game are the triples (s, ϵ, b), where s is a state of A, the nonnegative real $\epsilon \in \mathbb{R}_{\geq 0}$ gives a value to the clock variable now, and the bit b gives a value to the variable $blame$. The *winning condition* for the protagonist is the temporal-logic formula

$$\varphi_{win}: \ \Diamond(now = 1) \lor \Diamond\Box(blame = env)$$

("eventually $now = 1$, or only finitely often $blame = atom$"). It follows that the atom A is receptive iff for all reachable states s of A, the protagonist has a winning strategy in the position $(s, 0, atom)$.

Symbolic strategy checking. We give a symbolic algorithm for computing the set of positions in which the protagonist has a winning strategy. To simplify the presentation, we assume that the atom A has no awaited variables. A *region* σ of A is a set of game positions. We define an operator Pre on regions such that a position belongs to $Pre(\sigma)$ iff the atom A has a way of choosing new values for the controlled variables or of proposing a positive duration so that, irrespective of what the environment does, the position after the next move will be in σ.

Definition 13. *[Pre]* For a region σ of the atom A, the region $Pre(\sigma)$ is the set of positions (s, ϵ, b) that satisfy one of the following two conditions: (1) there exists a valuation t for the controlled variables $ctrX_A$ such that $(s, t) \in Update_A$ and for every valuation u for $X \backslash ctrX_A$, the position $(t \cup u, \epsilon, atom)$ is in σ; or (2) there exists a positive duration $\delta \in \mathbb{R}_{>0}$ such that (i) for every valuation u for $X \backslash ctrX_A$, the position $(s[ctrX_A] \cup u, \epsilon, env)$ is in σ, (ii) the position $(s + \delta, \epsilon + \delta, atom)$ is in σ, and (iii) for every positive duration $\delta' < \delta$, the position $(s + \delta', \epsilon + \delta', env)$ is in σ. ■

Observe that Pre is a monotonic operator on regions. The positions in which the protagonist has a winning strategy can be characterized using Pre, boolean operators on regions, and fixpoints.

Theorem 14. *The atom A is receptive iff for every reachable state s of A, the position* $(s, 0, atom)$ *belongs to the set* $\nu X. \mu Y. Pre((now \geq 1 \vee blame = env \vee Y) \wedge X)$.

This theorem immediately suggests a symbolic fixpoint-computation procedure for checking receptiveness. The procedure is effective as long as we know how to compute the operator *Pre*. This is the case, for example, for propositional timed modules, where the procedure can be implemented using existing symbolic model checkers such as KRONOS [14].

Enumerative strategy checking. For every timed automaton, there exists a finite partitioning of the state space called *region equivalence* [2]. The definition of region equivalence carries over straightforwardly to the states and the positions of the atoms of propositional timed modules. For an atom A of a propositional timed module, we write $\cong_A^R$ for the region equivalence of A. The number of equivalence classes of $\cong_A^R$ is finite, exponential in the size of the description of A. A *block* of $\cong_A^R$ is a union of $\cong_A^R$-equivalence classes.

Proposition 15. *If A is an atom of a propositional timed module, and the region* σ *is a block of the region equivalence* $\cong_A^R$, *then the region* $Pre(\sigma)$ *is also a block of* $\cong_A^R$.

This implies that all regions generated during the symbolic fixpoint-computation procedure are blocks of $\cong_A^R$, and therefore, for propositional timed modules, the termination of the procedure is guaranteed. Alternatively, one can construct the $\cong_A^R$-quotient graph of the infinite graph for the receptiveness game, and solve the coBüchi game on the resulting finite graph. Since the number of positions of the $\cong_A^R$-quotient graph is exponential in the description of A, and the complexity of solving a coBüchi game on a finite graph is quadratic in the number of vertices, we have an exponential decision procedure for checking receptiveness. The procedure is optimal, because already solving finite reachability games on timed automata is EXPTIME-hard [20].

Theorem 16. *Given an atom A of a propositional timed module, the problem of checking if A is receptive is complete for* EXPTIME.

It should be noted that, since receptiveness is closed under parallel composition, it suffices to check atoms for receptiveness in isolation.

3.3 Controller Synthesis for Propositional Timed Modules

The supervisory-control problem for modules asks, given a module P (the "plant") and a set *safe* of observations of P, construct a module Q (the "supervisor" or "controller") such that the observations of all reachable states of $P||Q$ are contained in *safe* [26]. This problem, and more general control problems, can be solved using fixpoint computation [24]: first, compute the set *controllable* of states of the module P in which the environment has a winning strategy for the winning condition $\Box safe$; then, construct a module Q that, when composed with P, prevents P from leaving the set *controllable*. In this formulation of the problem, however, the synthesized controller Q may achieve its goal by stopping time (an example of this is given at the end of Section 4). Such a controller cannot be realized physically. Hence, we reformulate the problem, and solve the reformulated problem.

Definition 17. *[**Control**]* The *supervisory-control problem* for modules asks, given a receptive module P and a set *safe* of observations of P, construct a receptive module Q such that the observations of all reachable states of $P||Q$ are contained in *safe* (or indicate that no such module Q exists). ■

If the module P contains k atoms, then the ω-trajectories of P can be considered possible outcomes of a $(k+1)$-player infinite game between the atoms and the environment. Each round of the game is charged to one of the atoms or to the environment, depending which player proposes the minimal duration (in the case of ties, the environment —that is, the controller— is charged). We extend the state space of P by introducing a new clock variable T and a binary variable *blame*, whose type is $\{module, env\}$. The initial value of T is 0, and T is reset to 0 whenever its value reaches 1. The value of *blame* is set to *module* during each round that is charged to some atom of P, and to *env* during each round that is charged to the environment. Then, the initial state s of the module P is controllable iff the environment has a winning strategy in the position $(s, 0, module)$ for the winning condition

$$\psi_{win}: \Box safe \wedge (\Box\Diamond(blame = env) \Rightarrow \Box\Diamond(T = 0) \wedge \Box\Diamond(T = 1))$$

("always *safe*, and if infinitely often $blame = env$, then infinitely often T is reset"). Since the winning condition ψ_{win} is a single-pair Streett condition, it suffices to consider memory-free strategies, and the winning positions can be characterized using a symbolic fixpoint expression. This gives a symbolic procedure for solving the supervisory-control problem. Since the complexity of solving a single-pair Streett game on a finite graph is cubic in the number of vertices [15], we have an exponential decision procedure for the supervisory control of propositional timed modules.

Theorem 18. *Given a receptive propositional timed module P and a set* safe *of observations of P, the supervisory-control problem (P, safe) is complete for* EXPTIME.

It should be noted that, since receptiveness enters into ψ_{win} as a Streett condition, the supervisory-control problem can be solved at no extra cost for more complex control requirements than $\Box safe$.

4 Hybrid Modules

We generalize timed modules to hybrid modules. All continuous variables of a timed module are clocks. Hybrid modules admit more general continuous variables such as temperature or pressure. Hence, for a hybrid module P, the set X_P of module variables is partitioned into two disjoint sets, the set $discX_P$ of discrete variables and the set $contX_P$ of continuous variables. The type of all continuous variables is $\mathbb{R}$. During each update round, the variables in X_P are updated, as before, in zero time. During each time round, the values of all discrete variables in $discX_P$ remain unchanged, and the values of all continuous variables in $contX_P$ evolve continuously for the duration of the round (which is positive).

Formally, during each time round, the trajectory of a hybrid module follows a flow. A *flow* for X is a continuous and piecewise-smooth function f from the nonnegative reals $\mathbb{R}_{\geq 0}$ to the set Σ_X of valuations for X such that $f(\delta)[x] = f(0)[x]$ for every discrete variable x and every nonnegative real $\delta \in \mathbb{R}_{\geq 0}$. By *piecewise-smooth* we mean that the nonnegative real line $\mathbb{R}_{\geq 0}$ can be partitioned into finitely many intervals such that the function f is in C^∞ on each interval. The flow f is a *source-s* flow if $f(0) = s$. We write $\dot{f}$ for the first derivative of the flow f. Notice that the function $\dot{f}$ is again piecewise-smooth but not necessarily continuous.

The flows that are permitted by a hybrid atom are specified using executable activities. Consider three sets X, Y, and Z of variables with $Y \subseteq X$ and $Z \subseteq X \backslash Y$. An *activity* γ from X to Z, given Y, is a ternary relation between the valuations for X, the flows for Y, and the flows for Z such that $(s, g, h) \in \gamma$ implies that g is a source-$s[Y]$ flow and h is a source-$s[Z]$ flow. The activity γ is *executable* if the following two conditions are met. First, for every valuation s for X and every flow g for Y, there is a flow h for Z such that $(s, g, h) \in \gamma$. Second, for every real $\delta \in \mathbb{R}_{\geq 0}$, if

$(s, g, h) \in \gamma$ and $g'(\epsilon) = g(\epsilon)$ for all $\epsilon \leq \delta$, then there is a flow h' such that $(s, g', h') \in \gamma$ and $h'(\epsilon) = h(\epsilon)$ for all $\epsilon \leq \delta$. The first condition is a nonblocking condition; the second condition ensures that the value $h(\delta)$ of the chosen flow h at time δ depends only on the values $g(\epsilon)$ of the given flow g at times $\epsilon \leq \delta$.

We use differential equations and differential inequalities to specify activities. As examples, consider the following activities from $\{y, z\}$ to $\{z\}$, given $\{y\}$. For an initial value z_0 of z and a flow g for y, the differential constraint $\dot{z} := 1$ specifies the flow $f(\delta)[z] = z_0 + \delta$; that is, z is a clock variable. The differential constraint $\dot{z} := z$ specifies the flow $f(\delta)[z] = e^{\ln z_0 + \delta}$; that is, z increases exponentially independent of y. The differential constraint $\dot{z} := \dot{y}$ specifies the flow $f(\delta)[z] = z_0 + (g(\delta)[y] - g(0)[y])$; that is, z copies the rate of y. The differential constraint $0.9 \leq \dot{z} \leq 1.1$ specifies the infinite set of flows f with $f(0)[z] = z_0$ and $0.9 \leq \dot{f}(\delta) \leq 1.1$ for all $\delta \in \mathbb{R}_{\geq 0}$; that is, z behaves like a clock with a drift of at most 10%.

The durations that are permitted by a hybrid atom are specified using executable delays. For an activity γ from X to Z, given Y, a delay β over $Y \cup Z$ is *γ-executable* if for every valuation s for $Y \cup Z$ and every real $\delta \in \mathbb{R}_{\geq 0}$, (1) $(s, s') \in \beta$ and (2) if $(s, g, h) \in \gamma$ and $(s, g(\delta)' \cup h(\delta)') \in \beta$, then $(s, g(\epsilon)' \cup h(\epsilon)') \in \beta$ and $(g(\epsilon) \cup h(\epsilon), g(\delta)' \cup h(\delta)') \in \beta$ for all nonnegative reals $\epsilon < \delta$. A γ-executable delay specifies for every state and every flow that is possible according to γ a maximal (possibly 0 or infinite) permissible duration.

Definition 19. *[Hybrid atoms and modules]* Let X be a finite set of typed variables. A *hybrid X-atom* A consists of a declaration and a body. The atom declaration is the same as for a timed atom. The atom body consists of an executable *initial action* $Init_A$ from $waitX'_A$ to $ctrX'_A$, an executable *update action* $Update_A$ from $X \cup waitX'_A$ to $ctrX'_A$, an executable activity $Flow_A$ from X to $ctrX_A$, given $waitX_A$, and a $Flow_A$-executable delay $Delay_A$ over $ctrX_A \cup waitX_A$. A *hybrid module* is the same as a timed module except that its atoms are hybrid. The *composition* of hybrid modules is defined as for timed modules. ■

Linear hybrid modules. Particularly suitable for analysis is a subclass of hybrid modules called linear hybrid modules. Essentially, a hybrid module P is *linear* if all discrete variables of P have finite types, and the continuous variables X of P occur in the guards, assignments, invariants, and differential constraints of P only within linear expressions over X or over $\dot{X} = \{\dot{x} \mid x \in X\}$. In a technical sense, linear hybrid modules are open versions of linear hybrid automata [6].

Trace semantics. An X-atom A *permits* the flow f for X if $(f(0), f[waitX_A], f[ctrX_A]) \in Flow_A$. The transition graph of a hybrid module P is best defined as an edge-labeled graph whose vertices are the flows over X_P that are permitted by all atoms of P, and whose labels are nonnegative reals that represent the duration of flows: if a flow f has an outgoing edge labeled δ, then on all trajectories through that edge the flow f contributes duration δ. Formally, a flow f of P is *initial* if $(f(0)'[waitX'_A], f(0)'[ctrX'_A]) \in Init_A$ for each atom A of P. For two flows f and g of P and a nonnegative duration $\delta \in \mathbb{R}_{\geq 0}$, we define $f \xrightarrow{\delta} g$ if $(f(0), f(\delta)') \in Delay_A$ and $(f(\delta) \cup g(0)'[waitX'_A], g(0)'[ctrX'_A]) \in Update_A$ for each atom A of P. Trajectories, then, are sequences of flows and durations, and traces are projections of trajectories to the observable variables. The trace-language of a hybrid module is obtained by closing its traces under stuttering. Nonzenoness for hybrid modules is defined as for timed modules.

Receptiveness. Consider a hybrid atom without awaited variables. A round of the receptiveness game proceeds as follows: first, the atom proposes a duration δ and chooses either a new valuation (if $\delta = 0$) or a flow (if $\delta > 0$) for the controlled variables; then, the environment proposes a duration $\delta' \leq \delta$ and chooses either a new valuation (if $\delta' = 0$) or a flow (if $\delta' > 0$) for the

module *TwoTanks*
  interface $w_L, w_R : \mathbb{R}$
  external *pipe*: {*left*, *right*}
  atom w_L, w_R
    init $w'_L := 5;\ w'_R := 10$
    flow
    $[\!]$ $pipe = left \ \rightarrow\ \dot{w}_L := 1;\ \dot{w}_R := -2 \cdot \mathrm{sign}(w_R)$
    $[\!]$ $pipe = right \ \rightarrow\ \dot{w}_L := -2 \cdot \mathrm{sign}(w_L);\ \dot{w}_R := 1$
    delay
    $[\!]$ *true* $\rightarrow$ *true*

Fig. 3. Two tanks running out of water

uncontrolled variables. The round is resolved as before: if $\delta = \delta' = 0$, then both the controlled and the uncontrolled variables are updated according to the chosen valuations, and the round is charged to the atom; if $\delta > \delta' = 0$, then the controlled variables stay unchanged, the uncontrolled variables are updated, and the round is charged to the environment; if $\delta = \delta' > 0$, then both the controlled and the uncontrolled variables evolve according to the chosen flows for duration δ, and the round is charged to the atom; if $\delta > \delta' > 0$, then both the controlled and the uncontrolled variables evolve according to the chosen flows for duration δ', and the round is charged to the environment. The atom is *receptive* if it has a strategy such that starting from any reachable state, the strategy either produces a trajectory of accumulated duration 1, or it results in an infinite sequence of rounds of which only finitely many are charged to the atom. As before, a hybrid module is receptive if all its atoms are receptive.

Similar to Section 3, it can be shown that the receptive hybrid modules are closed under parallel composition, that every receptive hybrid module is nonzeno, and that the assume-guarantee principle holds for receptive hybrid modules.[7] Furthermore, the fixpoint expression from Theorem 16 provides a symbolic procedure for checking the receptiveness of linear hybrid modules, for which the *Pre* operator can be computed. Similarly, the fixpoint characterization of the winning condition for the game from Section 3.3 suggests a symbolic procedure for synthesizing receptive controllers for linear hybrid automata. Both procedures, while not guaranteed to terminate, can be implemented using the primitives supplied by the symbolic model checker HyTech [19] for linear hybrid automata.

Example: water tanks. The hybrid module *TwoTanks* of Figure 3 models two water tanks and a common water source that provides water at the rate of 3 units per second. Through a pipe, the water source can be directed either to the left tank or to the right tank. Both tanks have openings at the bottom, and from each tank, water drains at the rate of 2 units per second. Initially, the left tank contains $w_L = 5$ units of water, and the right tank contains $w_R = 10$ units of water. This system is of interest, because by ignoring the receptiveness condition, one can devise a controller that keeps both water levels at no less than 2 units (i.e., the condition *safe* is $w_L \geq 2 \wedge w_R \geq 2$): whenever w_L falls to 2, direct the pipe to the left tank, and whenever w_R falls to 2, direct the pipe to the right tank. Such a controller, of course, cannot be realized physically, because it would cause the pipe to switch back and forth infinitely often within a finite amount of time. Indeed, according to our definitions, there is no receptive controller that keeps both water levels positive forever. ■

[7] If the implementation preorder considers ω-trace inclusion, rather than the inclusion of finite traces, then finite interface branching is required for the soundness of the assume-guarantee principle.

References

[1] R. Alur, C. Courcoubetis, N. Halbwachs, T.A. Henzinger, P.-H. Ho, X. Nicollin, A. Olivero, J. Sifakis, S. Yovine. The algorithmic analysis of hybrid systems. *Theoretical Computer Science*, 138:3–34, 1995.

[2] R. Alur, D.L. Dill. A theory of timed automata. *Theoretical Computer Science*, 126:183–235, 1994.

[3] K.R. Apt, N. Francez, S. Katz. Appraising fairness in languages for distributed programming. *Distributed Computing*, 2:226–241, 1988.

[4] R. Alur, T.A. Henzinger. Local liveness for compositional modeling of fair reactive systems. In *Computer-aided Verification*, Springer LNCS 939, pp. 166-179, 1995.

[5] R. Alur, T.A. Henzinger. Reactive modules. In *Proc. IEEE Symp. Logic in Computer Science*, pp. 207–218, 1996.

[6] R. Alur, T.A. Henzinger, P.-H. Ho. Automatic symbolic verification of embedded systems. *IEEE Trans. Software Engineering*, 22:181–201, 1996.

[7] R. Alur, T.A. Henzinger, E.D. Sontag, eds. *Hybrid Systems III: Verification and Control*. Springer LNCS 1066, 1996.

[8] M. Abadi, L. Lamport. Composing specifications. *ACM Trans. Programming Languages and Systems*, 15:73–132, 1993.

[9] M. Abadi, L. Lamport. An old-fashioned recipe for real time. In *Real Time: Theory in Practice*, Springer LNCS 600, pp. 1–27, 1992.

[10] E. Asarin, O. Maler, A. Pnueli. Symbolic controller synthesis for discrete and timed systems. In *Hybrid Systems II*, Springer LNCS 999, pp. 1–20, 1995.

[11] P. Antsaklis, A. Nerode, W. Kohn, S. Sastry, eds. *Hybrid Systems II*. Springer LNCS 999, 1995.

[12] J.W. de Bakker, K. Huizing, W.-P. de Roever, G. Rozenberg, eds. *Real Time: Theory in Practice*. Springer LNCS 600, 1992.

[13] D.L. Dill. *Trace Theory for Automatic Hierarchical Verification of Speed-independent Circuits*. MIT Press, 1989.

[14] C. Daws, A. Olivero, S. Tripakis, S. Yovine. The tool KRONOS. In *Hybrid Systems III*, Springer LNCS 1066, pp. 208–219, 1996.

[15] E.A. Emerson, C. Jutla. The complexity of tree automata and logics of programs. In *Proc. IEEE Symp. Foundations of Computer Science*, pp. 328–337, 1988.

[16] R.L. Grossman, A. Nerode, A.P. Ravn, H. Rischel, eds. *Hybrid Systems*. Springer LNCS 736, 1993.

[17] R. Gawlick, R. Segala, J.F. Sogaard-Andersen, N.A. Lynch. Liveness in timed and untimed systems. In *Automata, Languages, and Programming*, Springer LNCS 820, pp. 166-177, 1994.

[18] T.A. Henzinger. Sooner is safer than later. *Information Processing Letters*, 43:135–141, 1992.

[19] T.A. Henzinger, P.-H. Ho, H. Wong-Toi. HYTECH: the next generation. In *Proc. IEEE Real-time Systems Symp.*, pp. 56–65, 1995.

[20] T.A. Henzinger, P.W. Kopke. Discrete-time control for rectangular hybrid automata. In *Automata, Languages, and Programming*, Springer LNCS, 1997.

[21] T.A. Henzinger, X. Nicollin, J. Sifakis, S. Yovine. Symbolic model checking for real-time systems. *Information and Computation*, 111:193–244, 1994.

[22] G. Hoffmann, H. Wong-Toi. The input-output control of real-time discrete-event systems. In *Proc. IEEE Real-time Systems Symp.*, pp. 256–265, 1992.

[23] N.A. Lynch, R. Segala, F. Vaandrager, H.B. Weinberg. Hybrid I/O Automata. In *Hybrid Systems III*, Springer LNCS 1066, pp. 496–510, 1996.

[24] O. Maler, A. Pnueli, J. Sifakis. On the synthesis of discrete controllers for timed systems. In *Theoretical Aspects of Computer Science*, Springer LNCS 900, pp. 229–242, 1995.

[25] A. Pnueli. In transition from global to modular temporal reasoning about programs. In *Logics and Models of Concurrent Systems*, Springer LNCS, pp. 123–144, 1984.

[26] P.J. Ramadge, W.M. Wonham. Supervisory control of a class of discrete-event processes. *SIAM J. Control and Optimization*, 25:206–230, 1987.

[27] S. Tasiran, R. Alur, R.P. Kurshan, R.K. Brayton. Verifying abstractions of timed systems. In *Concurrency Theory*, Springer LNCS 1119, pp. 546–562, 1996.

A Universal Reactive Machine*

Henrik Reif Andersen Simon Mørk Morten Ulrik Sørensen

Department of Information Technology, Building 344,
Technical University of Denmark, DK–2800 Lyngby, Denmark.

Abstract. Turing showed the existence of a model universal for the set of Turing machines in the sense that given an encoding of any Turing machine as input the universal Turing machine simulates it. We introduce the concept of universality for reactive systems and construct a CCS process universal in the sense that, given an encoding of *any* CCS process, it behaves like this process up to weak bisimulation. This construction has a rather non-constructive use of silent actions and we argue that this would be the case for any universal CCS process.

1 Introduction

Turing proposed in 1937 a model of sequential computation, now known as Turing machines [4]. He showed, by construction, that among Turing machines, there exists one which is universal in the sense that it can realize *any* Turing machine (including itself) when given an encoding of it. Turing used the universal Turing machine to give a negative answer to Hilbert's Entscheidungsproblem for mathematics. Apart from showing the limits of mathematics, the universal Turing machine has another more constructive use: If Turing is right in his thesis that Turing machines capture everything that is computable, a universal Turing machine can compute everything computable. In fact, the success of modern general-purpose computers can be seen as a consequence of this: they implement a universal Turing machine. They can solve any computable task by providing them with the right encoding of an algorithm for it. It is an analogy of this more constructive view we investigate.

Turing machines compute partial functions: given some input they either diverge or terminate with a computed output. *Reactive systems* are different. They are characterized by the fact that they continue to interact with their environment, and termination is typically not a desired property. Many models of reactive systems have been proposed. The quality of these models are often measured in terms of their algebraic properties, the extent to which they capture concurrency, and the ease of which they allow formal verification.

In the light of Turing's results, another reasonable requirement is that a reactive model should also contain a *Universal Reactive Machine* (URM).

* Work supported by the Danish Technical Research Council, project CoDesign.
E-mail and WWW addresses of the first two authors: {hra,sm}@it.dtu.dk, http://www.it.dtu.dk/{~hra,~sm}

The URM should be capable of simulating *any* reactive process within the model. The question here, which is rather more involved than that for Turing machines, is that of what simulation means. This boils down to a discussion on what equivalence of reactive systems is. Equivalence of Turing programs simply means that they should terminate on the same inputs with the same results. For reactive systems it seems that there is no obvious best choice. (See, for instance, the list of proposed equivalences in [1].) Hence, any model of reactive systems must come equipped with a notion of equivalence. So "simulating" should mean that the behavior of the reactive system being realized is equivalent to the URM simulation.

In this paper we shall investigate to what extent CCS [2] is universal.[1] CCS is a model for a class of concurrent, reactive systems that has a fixed set of channels on which interaction can take place. Typical examples are found among embedded systems, for instance, vending machines and airbag controllers. We propose a URM for CCS, which has a rather non-constructive use of silent actions. We show that the process is indeed universal using weak bisimulation as the equivalence. However, we also argue that without a non-constructive use of silent actions, no universal process can be constructed.

2 CCS

We assume given a countable set of (channel) *names* $\mathcal{N}$ ranged over by $a, b, c, \ldots$. Each name a has an associated *co-name* $\overline{a}$. We use $\overline{\mathcal{N}}$ to denote the set of co-names $\{\overline{a} \mid a \in \mathcal{N}\}$, assumed disjoint from $\mathcal{N}$. For any name a we let $\overline{\overline{a}} = a$. Processes will be characterized by their ability to perform *actions*, modeled by the set $Act = \mathcal{N} \cup \overline{\mathcal{N}} \cup \{\tau\}$, where τ denotes a distinguished *internal* (or *silent*) action. We use $\alpha, \beta, \ldots$ to range over the set of actions Act.

The syntax of *process expressions* is given by the grammar:

$$E ::= \mathbf{0} \mid \alpha.E \mid E+E \mid E|E \mid E\setminus L \mid E[f] \mid X \mid \mathbf{rec}\, X.E$$

The constructions are as follows: *Nil*: $\mathbf{0}$ is the process which can perform no action. *Prefix*: $\alpha.P$ can perform action α and then behave as P. *Sum*: $P+Q$ behaves as either of P or Q, the choice being made with the first action. For a finite set $\{P_1, \ldots, P_n\}$ of processes we write $\sum_{i=1}^{n} P_i$ for $P_1 + \ldots + P_n$. *Composition*: $P \mid Q$ represents P and Q executing concurrently with possible two-party synchronization. *Restriction*: $P\setminus L$ behaves as P except that actions in L, a finite subset of $\mathcal{N} \cup \overline{\mathcal{N}}$, are restricted to take place within P. *Relabeling*: $P[f]$ behaves as P except that actions α are relabeled with respect to the partial function $f : \mathcal{N} \rightharpoonup \mathcal{N}$ with finite domain. The function f is extended to a total function on Act by taking $f(\overline{a}) = \overline{f(a)}$ for any a within the domain

[1] Of course, the question only makes sense for finitary CCS, i.e., the version of CCS where sums, relabelings, and restrictions are finite. Notice, that even with this restriction processes can still have infinitely many states.

$$\alpha.P \stackrel{\alpha}{\to} P \qquad \frac{P_1 \stackrel{\alpha}{\to} P_1'}{P_1 + P_2 \stackrel{\alpha}{\to} P_1'} \qquad \frac{P_2 \stackrel{\alpha}{\to} P_2'}{P_1 + P_2 \stackrel{\alpha}{\to} P_2'}$$

$$\frac{P_1 \stackrel{\alpha}{\to} P_1'}{P_1 \,|\, P_2 \stackrel{\alpha}{\to} P_1' \,|\, P_2} \qquad \frac{P_2 \stackrel{\alpha}{\to} P_2'}{P_1 \,|\, P_2 \stackrel{\alpha}{\to} P_1 \,|\, P_2'} \qquad \frac{P_1 \stackrel{\alpha}{\to} P_1' \quad P_2 \stackrel{\bar{\alpha}}{\to} P_2'}{P_1 \,|\, P_2 \stackrel{\tau}{\to} P_1' \,|\, P_2'}$$

$$\frac{P \stackrel{\alpha}{\to} P'}{P \setminus L \stackrel{\alpha}{\to} P' \setminus L}(\alpha \notin L) \qquad \frac{P \stackrel{\alpha}{\to} P'}{P[f] \stackrel{f(\alpha)}{\to} P'[f]} \qquad \frac{E[\mathbf{rec}\, X.E/X] \stackrel{\alpha}{\to} P'}{\mathbf{rec}\, X.E \stackrel{\alpha}{\to} P'}$$

Fig. 1. The operational semantics of CCS processes

of f, and $f(\alpha) = \alpha$ for any other action. *Recursion*: $\mathbf{rec}\, X.E$ behaves as the infinite unfolding of $\mathbf{rec}\, X.E$ for X in E. In $\mathbf{rec}\, X.E$ the process variable X is *bound* by the recursion operator. If a process variable X is not bound by a recursion operator, it is *free*. A *process* P is a process expression with no free process variables. We use $P, Q, R, \ldots$ to range over processes.

Instead of using only simple recursion, $\mathbf{rec}\, X.E$, we will allow ourselves to define mutually recursive processes by means of process equations: $A_1 = P_1, \cdots, A_n = P_n$. This can be seen merely as an abbreviation for nested applications of simple recursion and does not add expressive power [2, p.165].

The semantics of processes is a labeled transition system $\mathcal{T} = (\mathcal{P}, \to)$, where $\mathcal{P}$ is the set of *all processes* and $\to \subseteq \mathcal{P} \times Act \times \mathcal{P}$ is the *transition relation*, defined inductively by the rules of figure 1. Let $\stackrel{\tau^*}{\to}$ be the transitive, reflexive closure of $\stackrel{\tau}{\to}$. We define a notion of *weak transitions* by taking for any $t = \alpha_1\alpha_2\ldots\alpha_n \in Act^*$, $P \stackrel{t}{\Rightarrow} P'$ to hold when $P \stackrel{\tau^*}{\to}\stackrel{\alpha_1}{\to}\stackrel{\tau^*}{\to}\stackrel{\alpha_2}{\to}\stackrel{\tau^*}{\to}\cdots\stackrel{\alpha_n}{\to}\stackrel{\tau^*}{\to} P'$. Furthermore, for any sequence $s \in Act^*$, let $\hat{t}$ denote the sub-sequence of t in which all occurrences of τ has been removed.

The notion of observation equivalence for CCS processes put forward by Milner is that of being (weakly) bisimilar. A *weak bisimulation* $\mathcal{S}$ is a relation over processes, such that for all $(P, Q) \in \mathcal{S}$:

(i) whenever $P \stackrel{\alpha}{\to} P'$ then, for some Q', $Q \stackrel{\hat{\alpha}}{\Rightarrow} Q'$ and $(P', Q') \in \mathcal{S}$,

(ii) whenever $Q \stackrel{\alpha}{\to} Q'$ then, for some P', $P \stackrel{\hat{\alpha}}{\Rightarrow} P'$ and $(P', Q') \in \mathcal{S}$.

Two processes P and Q are said to be *(weakly) bisimilar* if there exists a weak bisimulation $\mathcal{S}$ containing (P, Q). We write this as $P \approx Q$. If $\mathcal{S}$ satisfies the above conditions with $\stackrel{\alpha}{\to}$ in place of $\stackrel{\hat{\alpha}}{\Rightarrow}$, $\mathcal{S}$ is a *strong bisimulation*. We write $P \sim Q$ if P and Q belongs to some strong bisimulation and say that P and Q are *strongly bisimilar*.

In the sequel we use a few auxiliary notions for processes. The *successors of* P is the set $succ(P) = \{(\alpha, P') \mid P \stackrel{\alpha}{\to} P'\}$. A pair (α, P') in $succ(P)$ will be called a *choice for* P. The *sort* of a process P is the set of actions which occur on some transition of P, i.e., the set $sort(P) = \{\alpha \in Act \mid \exists t \in Act^*. \exists P'.\ P \stackrel{t}{\to}\stackrel{\alpha}{\to} P'\}$. A process that can be reached from P by a sequence of transitions is called a *descendant* of P. Finally, a process P is *guarded* if in all recursions $\mathbf{rec}\, X.E$ in P, X appears only in subexpressions of prefixes.

3 Turing Machines

Despite its apparent simplicity, CCS is at least as expressive as Turing machines. We show this by giving a construction that for any Turing machine gives a CCS process that computes the same function.

Formally, a *deterministic Turing machine* over the alphabet $\{0, 1, \#\}$ is a quadruple $M = (V, \delta, s, h)$ where V is a set of *states*, $s \in V$ the *start state*, $h \in V$ the *halting state*, and $\delta : V \setminus \{h\} \times \{0, 1, \#\} \to V \times \{0, 1, \#\} \times \{l, r\}$ the *transition function*. If $\delta(v, e) = (v', e', d')$, the Turing machine moves from state v to state v' if the contents of the tape-cell under the head is e, overwrites the cell with e' and moves the head either left ($d' = l$) or right ($d' = r$). The moves of a Turing machine M can be formalized as a relation $\Longrightarrow_M$ on configurations $\langle v, (\sigma_l, e, \sigma_r) \rangle$ consisting of a state of the machine v, the contents of the tape to the left of the head σ_l, the contents under the head e, and the contents to the right of the head σ_r which has a rightmost, infinite sequence of *blanks*, $\#$. The relation $\Longrightarrow_M$ is defined for all v by $\langle v, (\sigma_l, e, \sigma_r) \rangle \Longrightarrow_M \langle v', (\sigma_l', e', \sigma_r') \rangle$, if

$$\delta(v, e) = (v', e'', l), \sigma_l = \sigma_l' e', \sigma_r' = e'' \sigma_r, \text{ or}$$
$$\delta(v, e) = (v', e'', r), \sigma_l' = \sigma_l e'', \sigma_r = e' \sigma_r'.$$

If σ_l is empty and $\delta(v, e) = (v', e', l)$, i.e. the head should move left, the machine "hangs." There is no possible move. Similarly, if v is the halting state h, no move is possible. Otherwise, there is exactly one possible move, since the Turing machine is deterministic.

Any Turing machine M with its infinite tape, can be modeled by a CCS process. The tape communicates via the actions $R = \{rd_e, wr_e \mid e \in \{0, 1, \#\}\} \cup \{mv_l, mv_r\}$ that reads a symbol from the head, writes a new symbol to the head, or asks the head to move left or right. For each state v of M, that is not the halting state h, we shall define a CCS-process M_v:

$$M_v = \sum_{e \in \{0, 1, \#\}} rd_e.\overline{wr}_{e'}.\overline{mv}_{d'}.M_{v'}$$

where in each summand, $(v', e', d') = \delta(v, e)$. In order to make re-execution of the Turing machine possible, we use two special names, $\checkmark_{in}$ and $\checkmark_{out}$, to start the Turing machine and to signal termination.

The Turing machine M will be modeled by the process $\widetilde{M} = \checkmark_{in}.M_s$ composed with a tape, T_σ:

$$(T_\sigma \mid \widetilde{M}) \setminus R.$$

For the halting state we take $M_h = \overline{\checkmark_{out}}.\checkmark_{in}.M_s$. In general, we use the symbol $\checkmark$ with various subscripts for actions that transfer control between processes.

A any point during the run of a Turing machine, the part of the tape to the left of the head will be finite, while the part to the right will be infinite. Nevertheless, only a finite, leftmost part of the tape to the right will contain symbols from $\{0, 1\}$. The remaining part of the tape will contain blanks ($\#$)

only. A tape can therefore be modeled using two stacks, each of which models a part of the tape. The stack modeling the right (infinite) part of the tape pops blanks when it becomes empty. Hence, using the stacks of section 6, we can construct a tape such that that the following lemma holds:

Lemma 1 (Turing Machine Encoding). *Assume M is a deterministic Turing machine with initial state s and halting state h. If $\langle s, \sigma \rangle \Longrightarrow_M^* \langle h, \sigma' \rangle$, where $*$ denotes transitive, reflexive closure, then*

$$(1)\quad (T_\sigma \mid \widetilde{M}) \setminus R \xrightarrow{\surd_{in}} \xrightarrow{\tau}{}^{*} \xrightarrow{\overline{\surd_{out}}} (T_{\sigma'} \mid \widetilde{M}) \setminus R$$

$$(2)\quad (T_\sigma \mid \widetilde{M}) \setminus R \xrightarrow{\surd_{in}} \xrightarrow{\tau}{}^{*} P \text{ and } (T_\sigma \mid \widetilde{M}) \setminus R \xrightarrow{\surd_{in}} \xrightarrow{\tau}{}^{*} P' \text{ implies } P \approx P'$$

In order to make the URM construction more intuitive, we shall in some cases use Turing machines with *two* tapes. As it is well-known an extra tape does not increase the computational power.

4 Reactive Universality

For the class of systems we consider, and for which CCS is a model, it is a distinct feature that there is only a finite set of channel names on which the system can communicate. In terms of CCS, this is the fact that all processes have a *finite* sort. This gives rise to a problem. We are searching for a URM to which we can send an encoding of any process P, and upon receiving it, the URM should behave like P. However, such a URM does not exist since it would need to have an infinite sort, namely the sort of all channel names.

What we can hope for instead is the existence of a URM universal for processes with sorts taken from some given, finite set of channel names, A. Or, even better, a URM general in the sense that it can be *instantiated* with any finite set of channel names, thereby simulating processes with channels from this set. To emphasize the universal nature the URM is split into two parts. One part, $\mathcal{U}$, which initially receives the encoding of a process P and performs the computations needed for the simulation, and a second part, $\mathcal{I}_A$, which translates the internal encoding of action names into real, un-encoded names in the alphabet A. In this way, the dependency upon the alphabet A can be localized to the *interface*, $\mathcal{I}_A$, but $\mathcal{U}$ should be the same for all alphabets.The communication with $\mathcal{I}_A$ should take place through a fixed, finite set of actions, I, independent of A.

Assuming that $\widehat{P}$ is some encoding of processes P in terms of $0'$ and $1'$, we write $\widehat{P}.\mathbf{0}$ to mean a sequence of prefixes $\alpha_1.\alpha_2.\cdots.\alpha_n.\mathbf{0}$ where $\alpha_1\alpha_2\cdots\alpha_n = \widehat{P} \in \{0', 1'\}^*$. This leads us to require the following property of a *universal reactive machine*, $\mathcal{U}$:

> *For all finite alphabets A not containing the names $I \cup \{0', 1'\}$, there exists an interface process $\mathcal{I}_A$, such that for all guarded processes P with $sort(P) \subseteq A$:*
>
> $$P \approx (\widehat{P}.\mathbf{0} \mid (\mathcal{U} \mid \mathcal{I}_A) \setminus I) \setminus \{0', 1'\}.$$

The order of quantification is essential. The interface should depend *only* on the alphabet, *not* of the process to be simulated.

Using CCS terms, there is, obviously, no hope of achieving strong bisimilarity, since the universal machine must make some internal computation not present in P. It is also impossible to achieve observational congruence, since the process on the right will always have some initial τ's due to the loading of P. The closest we can get, in general, is that $\tau.P$ is observational congruent to the simulation of P.

Even for weak bisimulation we can expect problems. These problems arise from the fact that even though the alphabet of names is finite, there is no upper bound on the number of different successors in the processes to be simulated, i.e., the number of choices is unbounded. We discuss this below.

Within the universal machine we shall need to manipulate values such as process terms and sets of actions. This can be done by Turing machines using any reasonable encoding, such as a Gödel encoding. We are not concerned with the details of these encodings.

5 Implementing Choices

We now turn to the construction of a URM in CCS. As it will turn out the difficult part will be in the construction of the interface $\mathcal{I}_A$.

Initially, $\mathcal{U}$ loads the encoding $\widehat{P}$ of the process P to be simulated. At any point in the simulation $\mathcal{U}$ maintains a current state of P and computes its successors according to the inference rules of figure 1. It is in order to ensure termination of this computation that we restrict attention to guarded processes.

The URM will repeatedly go through the following steps:

1. $\mathcal{U}$ computes the set of successors, $succ(P) = \{(\alpha_1, P_1), \ldots, (\alpha_n, P_n)\}$.
2. The actions of this set are computed.
3. These actions are sent to $\mathcal{I}_A$.
4. $\mathcal{I}_A$ selects one of the successors, for instance the i'th, possibly synchronizing with the environment.
5. The selection, i, is sent back to $\mathcal{U}$.
6. $\mathcal{U}$ computes the descendent P_i which becomes the new current state.

As can be seen from figure 2, $\mathcal{U}$ is comprised by: Three Turing machines TM_1, TM_2, and TM_3 for carrying out the calculations in step 1, 2, and 6; two Turing tapes TP_1 and TP_2 for storing the results; a process *Port* taking care of the communication between $\mathcal{U}$ and $\mathcal{I}_A$ in step 3 and 5; and a process *Load* for loading the initial process onto tape TP_1. The process expression for $\mathcal{U}$ is:

$$\mathcal{U} = (\mathit{Load} \,|\, \text{TM}_1 \,|\, \text{TM}_2 \,|\, \text{TM}_3 \,|\, \text{TP}_1 \,|\, \text{TP}_2 \,|\, \mathit{Port}) \\ \setminus \{\surd_1, \surd_2, \surd_3, \surd_{port}\} \cup \{rd_e^i, wr_e^i, mv_l^i, mv_r^i \mid e \in \{0, 1, \#\}, i \in \{1, 2\}\}$$

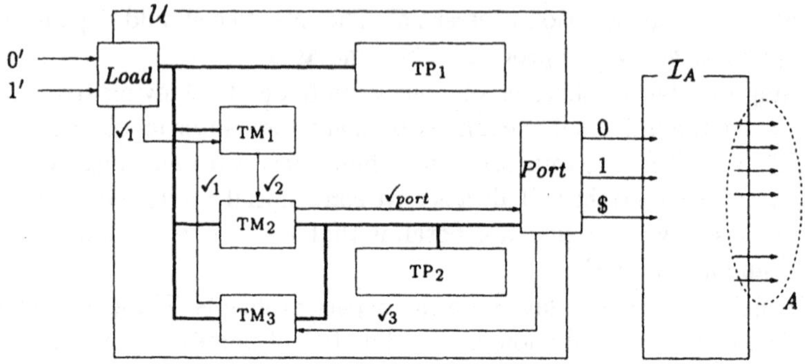

Fig. 2. Structure of the URM. The fat lines denote collections of channels.

5.1 Distribution of Choices

An interface should be as simple as possible. Given a set of successors, it should offer the enabled channels to the environment and upon selection send the representation back to $\mathcal{U}$. As a special case, one of the enabled actions may be τ, the silent action. This way of letting the interface select one of the choices, is made possible by the following lemma:

Lemma 2 (Choice Distribution). *Assume P, Q, and R are defined by:*

$$P = \sum_{i=1}^{n} \beta_i.P_i \qquad Q = \sum_{i=1}^{n} \beta_i.\bar{c}_i.\mathbf{0} \qquad R = \sum_{i=1}^{n} c_i.P_i,$$

where $c_1, \ldots, c_n$ are n different actions not in the sort of P. Then,

$$P \approx (Q \,|\, R) \setminus \{c_1, c_2, \ldots, c_n\}.$$

The choices in P are distributed among Q and R such that Q *selects* a β_i and sends the selection to R, which proceeds as P_i. This allows $\mathcal{U}$ to compute on encodings of actions and let the interface translate them into names in the alphabet A. The problem remaining is to implement a process which can be *sent* the choices of a process P and then behave like Q in the lemma.

5.2 Unbounded Choices

Constructing an interface process that can receive (an encoding of) a set of choices and behave like these is a bit tricky. As an example, consider a process Q with $succ(Q) = \{(\tau, Q_1), (a, Q_2), (a, Q_3), (b, Q_4)\}$, shown in figure 3. How is the choices of Q to be provided by the interface?

Since the τ action concerns no interaction with the environment, one might decide *inside* $\mathcal{U}$ whether to ask $\mathcal{I}_A$ to synchronize with the environment on either of a and b, or whether to do the τ action without involving $\mathcal{I}_A$. This corresponds to the situation illustrated by R_1 in figure 3. Unfortunately, R_1 and Q are not bisimilar: R_1 can make an internal move, thereby reaching a state in which a and b are enabled, but Q_1 can no longer be reached. There is no such state in Q. We conclude that τ actions must be enabled in the interface just like other actions.

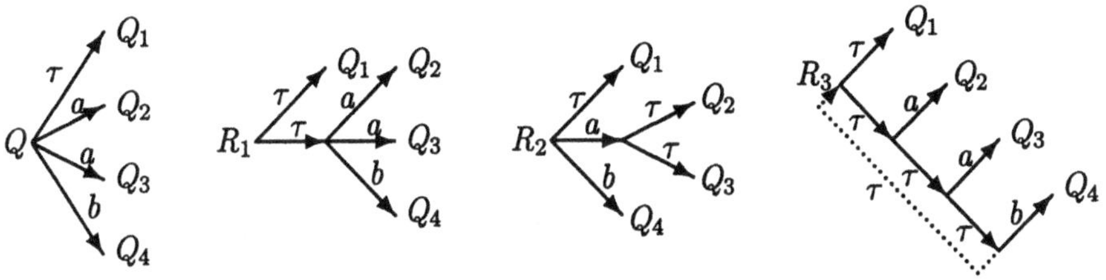

Fig. 3. Different attempts to simulate Q. Note that $R_1 \not\approx Q$, $R_2 \not\approx Q$, and $R_3 \not\approx Q$, but that $R_3 \approx Q$ if the dashed τ transition is added.

The next suggestion to solve the problem is therefore to send the set $\{\tau, a, b\}$ of enabled actions to $\mathcal{I}_A$ and let it either decide that the τ action must be taken, or synchronize with the environment on a or b. In case the action a is received, $\mathcal{U}$ will then choose between the a-descendents. This is illustrated by R_2 in the figure. But R_2 is not bisimilar to Q, since R_2 can perform an a action, thereby reaching a state in which both Q_2 and Q_3 can be reached by internal moves, which is not possible for Q. This is an example of the in-equivalence

$$\alpha.P + \alpha.Q \not\approx \alpha.(\tau.P + \tau.Q),$$

which holds for any action $\alpha \in Act \setminus \{\tau\}$ and processes P and Q satisfying $P \not\approx Q$. So, we must be able to distinguish between instances of the same action when a choice is sent from $\mathcal{U}$ to $\mathcal{I}_A$.

This leads us to the final suggestion of building up the choices gradually. This corresponds to the process R_3 in figure 3 (without the dashed τ transition). The flat collection of alternatives which constitute Q has been turned into a sequence of nested, binary alternatives, each of them determining whether a certain instance of an action should be chosen or not. But R_3 is not bisimilar to Q either. For example, R_3 can reach a state (by τ actions) in which no a action is enabled, which Q cannot. However, by adding a τ transition from the rightmost branch and back to the root (shown as a dashed line in the figure), we can make it bisimilar to Q. In other words, we are never pre-empting choices. By making more τ-moves we can get back to any of the choices. This idea is captured by the following lemma for *gluing* states together:

Lemma 3 (Gluing). *If P is a process with $P = \sum_{i=1}^{n} \beta_i.P_i$ and $Q_i, 1 \leq i \leq n$ are processes defined by $Q_i = \beta_i.P_i + \tau.Q_{(i \bmod n)+1}$, then for all $i, 1 \leq i \leq n$:*

$$P \approx Q_i$$

Proof. Take $S = \{(P, Q_i) \mid 1 \leq i \leq n\} \cup \{(U, U) \mid U \in \mathcal{P}\}$.
If $P \xrightarrow{\beta} P'$ then clearly $\beta = \beta_j$ and $P' = P_j$ for some i. To match this Q_i can make a number of τ-transitions to get to Q_j, and then, since we have $Q_j \xrightarrow{\beta_j} P_j$, we get the matching pair $(P_j, P_j) \in S$. Conversely, if $Q_i \xrightarrow{\beta} Q'$,

then either $\beta = \beta_i, Q' = P_i$, or $\beta = \tau, Q = Q_{(i \bmod n)+1}$. In the first case, this can be matched by the move $P \xrightarrow{\beta_i} P_i$, and in the second by the empty move, resulting in the pair $(P, Q_{(i \bmod n)+1})$ which belongs to S.

The choice distribution lemma and the gluing lemma allow us to implement an interface capable of presenting unbounded choices of a finite alphabet to the environment.

6 A Universal Reactive Machine

In section 5 we described the overall structure of the URM. We now first briefly define the stacks, used for implementation of tapes and for counters in the interface. We then focus on the details of the interface, since this is the most challenging part of the construction.

6.1 Stacks

Stacks are used in forming Turing tapes and for storing intermediate values during computations in the interface. A stack which can contain elements from the (finite) set Λ has sort $sort(Stack_\Lambda) = \{emp, nemp, res\} \cup \{pop_e, push_e \mid e \in \Lambda\}$ modeling the following operations on stacks: check for emptiness, non-emptiness, resetting (emptying the stack), pushing and popping of elements. $Stack_\Lambda$ is equal to the process C_{emp}:

$$\begin{aligned} C_{emp} &= res.C_{emp} + emp.C_{emp} + \sum_{e\in\Lambda} push_e.(C_e \mid C_{emp}[f]) \setminus R \\ e \in \Lambda,\ C_e &= res.C_{emp} + nemp.C_e + \sum_{e'\in\Lambda} push_{e'}.\overline{rpush_e}.C_{e'} \\ &\quad + pop_e.(\overline{remp}.C_{emp} + \sum_{e'\in\Lambda} \overline{rpop_{e'}}.C_{e'}), \end{aligned}$$

where $R = \{rpush_e, rpop_e \mid e \in \Lambda\} \cup \{remp, x\}$ and $f = \bigcup_{e\in\Lambda}[push_e \mapsto rpush_e, pop_e \mapsto rpop_e] \cup [emp \mapsto remp, res \mapsto x, nemp \mapsto x]$.

A stack consists of a collection of *cells*. Each cell is either empty (and denotes the end of the stack) or contains an element from Λ and channels to the rest of the stack (channels $remp$, $rpush_e$ and $rpop_e$). When an element is pushed onto a stack, either the stack is empty (C_{emp}), or the top cell contains some element e'. In the first case, the empty cell will turn into two cells, a cell containing e followed by an empty cell. In the other case, the top cell will contain the element e and re-push (by $rpush_{e'}$) its old element e' onto the rest of the stack. In this fashion, elements ripple down the stack, and new cells are produced at the bottom. Note that when elements are popped or the stack is reset, cells at the bottom of the stack are cut off as garbage.

A counter that can be in- and decreased, reset (to zero) and tested for zero-ness is defined as a stack over a singleton set:

$$Counter = Stack_{\{\bot\}}[emp \mapsto zero, nemp \mapsto nzero, pop_\bot \mapsto decr, push_\bot \mapsto incr]$$

$$\begin{array}{lcl} St(\vec{n},\vec{n}') & \stackrel{res}{\Longrightarrow} & St(\vec{0},\vec{0}) \\ St(\vec{n},\vec{n}') & \stackrel{copy}{\Longrightarrow} & St(\vec{n},\vec{n}) \\ St(\langle\cdots n_i \cdots\rangle,\vec{n}') & \stackrel{inc_i}{\Longrightarrow} & St(\langle\cdots n_i+1\cdots\rangle,\vec{n}') \\ St(\vec{n},\langle\cdots n'_i \cdots\rangle) & \stackrel{dec'_i}{\Longrightarrow} & St(\vec{n},\langle\cdots n'_i-1\cdots\rangle) \\ St(\vec{n},\vec{n}'), n'_i = 0 & \stackrel{\overline{zero'_i}}{\Longrightarrow} & St(\vec{n},\vec{n}') \\ St(\vec{n},\vec{n}'), n'_i > 0 & \stackrel{\overline{nzero'_i}}{\Longrightarrow} & St(\vec{n},\vec{n}') \end{array}$$

Table 1. The transitions of the store, *St*.

6.2 The Interface

Recall, we are assuming that *Act* is countable. Let therefore $\iota : Act \rightarrow I\!N$ be a bijection between *Act* and the natural numbers $I\!N$, such that $\iota(\tau) = 0$. For any finite alphabet $A \subseteq Act$ there exists a least k such that all actions α in A have $\iota(\alpha) \leq k$. Therefore, we can assume that the elements of *Act* are numbered such that $A \subseteq \{\alpha_0, \ldots, \alpha_k\}$ where α_i is the action with index i, i.e. $\iota(\alpha_i) = i$. We can use these indices to partition any set of successors, $succ(P)$, with a maximal index of actions $l \leq k$, as follows:

$$succ(P) = \bigcup_{i=0}^{l} \{(\alpha_i, P_i^1), \ldots, (\alpha_i, P_i^{n_i})\}$$

where $0 \leq n_i$ for $0 \leq i \leq l$ is the number of α_i-successors. We use the notation $\vec{n} = \langle n_0, \ldots, n_l\rangle$ to denote an l-vector consisting of such numbers.

From the discussion in section 5.2 we know that it is not enough to send the set of enabled actions to the interface. The different occurrences must be distinguishable. We achieve this by using pairs (α_i, j) for some j with $1 \leq j \leq n_i$ to represent that the j'th α_i-successors was chosen. The order of the choices is irrelevant, so we only send the n_i's to the interface, which in turn generates n_i different α_i choices. We represent $\vec{n}$ by the sequence of actions

$$1^{n_0}01^{n_1}01^{n_2}0\ldots01^{n_l}\$,$$

where a^i denotes i consecutive a actions.

The interface receives such a vector $\vec{n}$ and stores it. In fact, we shall need to store two vectors of numbers $\vec{n}$ and $\vec{n}'$. We write $St(\vec{n},\vec{n}')$ for a store containing the two vectors $\vec{n}$ and $\vec{n}'$. Using $2k$ counters, and at least one extra counter, it is not difficult to define a store as a CCS process with the behaviour, at least up to strong bisimulation, shown in table 1. The sort of the store is

$$R_k = \{inc_i, dec'_i, zero'_i, nzero'_i \mid 1 \leq i \leq k\} \cup \{copy, res\}.$$

Apart from the store, which initially contains two k-vectors of zeros, $St(\vec{0},\vec{0})$, the interface consists of a control process, P_0:

$$\mathcal{I}_A \;=\; (P_0 \mid St(\vec{0},\vec{0})) \setminus R_k$$

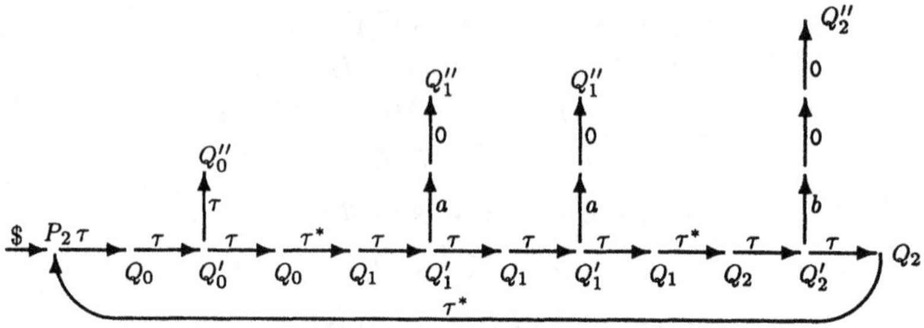

Fig. 4. The transitions of the interface after receiving the encoding 101101 of the vector $\langle 1,2,1\rangle$ which represents the set of choices $(\tau,1),(a,2),(1,b)$ when $\iota(\tau)=0,\iota(a)=1,\iota(b)=2$.

The control part initially receives an $\vec{n}$ and then proceed to offer the choices encoded in $\vec{n}$. In order to define it, we use processes $P_0,\ldots,P_k$, such that in state P_i, $n_0,\ldots,n_{i-1}$ has been received and n_i is being received. We take $P_{k+1}=\mathbf{0}$, which will be reached, deadlocking the system, if a vector larger than k is sent. For $i\in\{0,1,\ldots,k\}$ define:

$$\begin{aligned}
P_i &= 1.\overline{inc_i}.P_i + 0.P_{i+1} + \$.\overline{copy}.Q_0\\
Q_i &= \begin{cases} nzero'_i.Q'_i + zero'_i.Q_{(i+1)} & \text{if } i<k\\ nzero'_i.Q'_i + zero'_i.\overline{copy}.Q_0 & \text{if } i=k\end{cases}\\
Q'_i &= \alpha_i.Q''_i + \overline{dec'_i}.Q_i\\
Q''_i &= \overline{0}^i.Q'''_i\\
Q'''_i &= nzero'_i.1.\overline{dec'_i}.Q'''_i + zero'_i.res.\$.P_0
\end{aligned}$$

The states Q_i, Q'_i, Q''_i, Q'''_i implements, by gluing and by use of the store, the choice represented by $\vec{n}$. The process Q_i tests whether n'_i is zero. If so, it moves on to Q_{i+1} (to Q_0, re-initializing $\vec{n}'$ to $\vec{n}$, if $i=k$), and if not, it continues as Q'_i. The process Q'_i offers α_i if $n'_i>0$, and if not, continues as Q_i, decrementing n'_i. In this manner all the choices are offered in a cyclic manner: From any Q_i with any value of $n'_i\le n_i$ in the store, it is possible to reach by synchronizing on *dec*, *nzero*, and *zero*, any other $Q_{i'}$ with any value of $n'_{i'}\le n_{i'}$ in the store. Q''_i is the state where α_i has been selected and the vector $0^i1^{n'_i}$ representing the choice (α_i,n'_i) must be sent to $\mathcal{U}$. Finally, state Q'''_i transmits the selection back to $\mathcal{U}$. Figure 4 shows an example. The behaviour of the interface is captured by the following lemma:

Lemma 4 (Interface). *Assume A is some finite alphabet. Let $k=\max(\iota(A))$ be the maximal index of an action in A. For all l-vectors, $\vec{n}$, of numbers with $l\le k$ the following holds:*

$$\mathcal{I}_A \stackrel{s}{\Longrightarrow} (Q_0 \mid St(\vec{n},\vec{0}))\setminus R_k,$$

where $s=1^{n_0}0\cdots01^{n_l}\$$. Moreover,

$$(Q_0 \mid St(\vec{n},\vec{0}))\setminus R_k \approx \sum_{i=0}^{k}\sum_{j=1}^{n_i}\alpha_i.0^i.1^j.\$.\mathcal{I}_A.$$

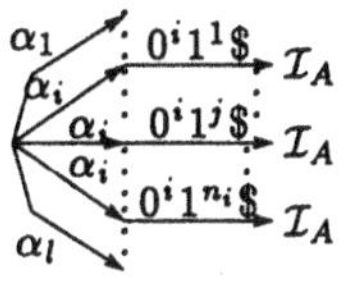

Fig. 5. The choices $\sum_{i=0}^{k} \sum_{j=1}^{n_i} \alpha_i.0^i.1^j.\$.\mathcal{I}_A$ implemented by $\mathcal{I}_A$.

Figure 5 illustrates the choices as implemented by $\mathcal{I}_A$.

7 Technical Results

In proving that the constructed process is universal in the sense described in section 4, we make use of the notion of being τ-determinate:

Definition 5. A process P is *τ-determinate on $\mathcal{Q}$* if whenever $P \xrightarrow{\tau^*} P'$ and $P' \in \mathcal{Q}$ then $P \approx P'$. If P is τ-determinate on all processes $\mathcal{P}$, we shall simply say that P is *τ-determinate.*

Processes that are τ-determinate arise naturally when constructing processes that implements functions. In fact, from lemma 1 (property 2) it follows immediately, that encodings of Turing machines are τ-determinate. Moreover, the transmission of successor sets from $\mathcal{U}$ to $\mathcal{I}_A$ and the transmission of a selection back from $\mathcal{I}_A$ to $\mathcal{U}$ are both simple sequential protocols, from which no further progress can be made before the transmission has terminated. They are also both τ-determinate on the intermediate states. In general, the universal machine has a very deterministic behaviour. The only source of observable non-determinism, is the selections of choices in the interface. This localization of non-determinism greatly simplifies the proof.

In order to make the discussion more precise, we shall need to introduce notation for some of the intermediate states in $\mathcal{U}$. We use U_P to denote the state where the encoding of P is stored on tape TP_1. In fact, there is a set of states, all weakly bisimilar, which represent the situation where P is stored on the tape. This is due to the fact that elements may ripple down (or up) the stack after the synchronization performing a push (or a pop). We let U_P represent this equivalence class of states, by taking it to be the state where the stacks have stabilized. Similarly, U_σ is the state where the set of choices σ is stored on tape TP_1 and the stacks have stabilized. Finally, $U_{\sigma,i}$ is the state where the set of choices σ is still stored on tape TP_1 and the encoding of i, the index of the selected choice, is stored on tape TP_2.

As described in section 5 the universal machine goes through six stages:

$$
\begin{array}{ll}
(U_P \,|\, \mathcal{I}_A) \setminus L & \\
\quad \xrightarrow{\tau^*} (U_{succ(P)} \,|\, \mathcal{I}_A) \setminus L & \text{(1: successors computation by TM}_1\text{)} \\
\quad \xrightarrow{\tau^*} (U_{succ(P)} \,|\, \mathcal{I}_A) \setminus L & \text{(2: computation of the actions)} \\
\quad \xrightarrow{\tau^*} (U_{succ(P)} \,|\, Q_0 \,|\, St(\vec{n}, \vec{n}')) \setminus L & \text{(3: successors transmission by } Port\text{)} \\
\quad \xrightarrow{\tau^*} (U_{succ(P)} \,|\, Q_i' \,|\, St(\vec{n}, \vec{n}'')) \setminus L & \text{(4a: gluing: initial } \tau\text{'s)}
\end{array}
$$

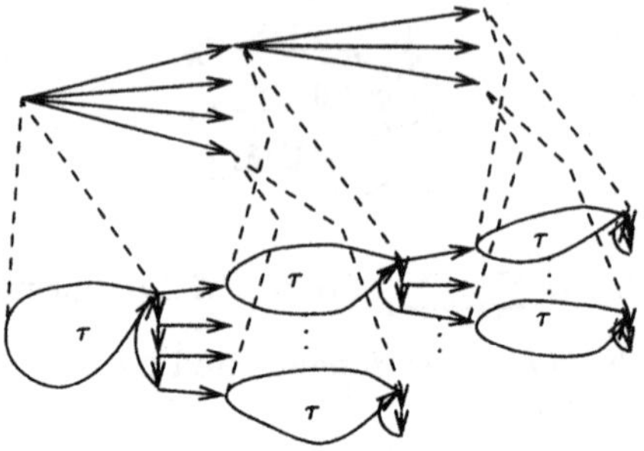

Fig. 6. The stages of $\mathcal{U}$. The big areas of τ's covers stages 5, 6, 1, 2, and 3. The relation S, used in the proof of correctness of $\mathcal{U}$, is shown with dashed lines.

$$\stackrel{\alpha_i}{\rightarrow} (U_{succ(P)} \mid Q_i'' \mid St(\vec{n}, \vec{n}''')) \setminus L \qquad \text{(4b: gluing: selection)}$$
$$\stackrel{\tau^*}{\rightarrow} (U_{succ(P),i} \mid \mathcal{I}_A) \setminus L \qquad \text{(5: selection transmission)}$$
$$\stackrel{\tau^*}{\rightarrow} (U_{P_i} \mid \mathcal{I}_A) \setminus L \qquad \text{(6: computation of selected process)}$$

Stages 1, 2, 3, 5, and 6 are τ-determinate, in the sense, that any intermediate process within these stages are bisimilar to the starting state. The non-deterministic choices are made in stage 4a and 4b. Figure 6 illustrates the stages. The overall working of $\mathcal{U}$ can be seen as changes between equivalence classes of states. Each equivalence class corresponds to (i.e. is weakly bisimilar to) a state of the simulated process.

Theorem 6 (Universality of $\mathcal{U}$). *Assume A is a finite alphabet not containing* 0,1,\$,0′, *and* 1′. *For all guarded processes P, satisfying $sort(P) \subseteq A$ we have:*

$$P \approx (\widehat{P}.\mathbf{0} \mid (\mathcal{U} \mid \mathcal{I}_A) \setminus \{0,1,\$\}) \setminus \{0',1'\}$$

Proof. (Sketch) From the definition of $\mathcal{U}$ it is clear that initially the only possible transitions will load the encoding of P and store it on the tape TP_1, i.e.

$$(\widehat{P}.\mathbf{0} \mid (\mathcal{U} \mid \mathcal{I}_A) \setminus \{0,1,\$\}) \setminus \{0',1'\} \stackrel{\tau^*}{\rightarrow} (U_P \mid \mathcal{I}_A) \setminus \{0,1,\$\}.$$

Clearly, all the intermediate states are weakly bisimilar. Hence, from the transitivity of $\approx$ it suffices to prove

$$P \approx (U_P \mid \mathcal{I}_A) \setminus \{0,1,\$\}.$$

We shall do this by defining a relation S, containing the pair $((U_P \mid \mathcal{I}_A) \setminus \{0,1,\$\}, P)$, and show that it is a weak bisimulation. Define S by

$$S = \{(P,Q) \mid P \in \mathcal{P} \text{ and } Q \text{ is any intermediate state in stage } 1, 2, 3, \text{4a from } (U_P \mid \mathcal{I}_A) \setminus L, \text{ or in stage 5 or 6 leading to } (U_P \mid \mathcal{I}_A) \setminus L\}$$

In order to show that S is a weak bisimulation we must check the two conditions (i) and (ii). For condition (i) we proceed as follows. If $P \stackrel{\alpha}{\rightarrow} P'$ then

$(\alpha, P') \in succ(P)$ and $\alpha = \alpha_i, P' = P_i$ for some i. Going through a proper subset of the stages 5, 6, 1, 2, 3, and 4a we arrive at the state where the interface can perform α_i:

$$Q \overset{\tau^*}{\to} (U_{succ(P)} \,|\, Q_i') \setminus L \overset{\alpha_i}{\to} (U_{succ(P)} \,|\, Q_i'') \setminus L$$

Since this last process will lead to $(U_{P_i} \,|\, \mathcal{I}_A) \setminus L$, we have

$$(P', (U_{succ(P)} \,|\, Q_i'') \setminus L) \in S.$$

For condition (*ii*) there are two cases two consider. First, if Q can make a transition $Q \overset{\tau}{\to} Q'$ to another intermediate state in stage 5, 6, 1, 2, 3, or 4a, then by definition of S also $(Q', P) \in S$. Secondly, if Q makes a transition performing a selection $Q \overset{\alpha_i}{\to} Q'$ this can be matched by a move of P leading to (Q', P') which also must be in S.

8 The Necessity of Gluing

From an implementational point of view, the gluing is somewhat counterintuitive, since it exploits the inability of weak bisimulation to distinguish between divergent processes (i.e. processes containing infinite sequences of τ's) and convergent processes. (See for instance the discussion in [2, p.148+249].) However, without the use of τ loops to construct unbounded choices, there seems to be *no way* of constructing a machine that is universal for CCS.[2]

From the discussion in section 5.2 it follows that we cannot implement the choices by gradually determining whether a given instance of an action should be chosen or not. Apart from gluing, this leaves us with the only possibility of directly having the flat choice. We now argue that this is not really a possibility. In order to be more precise, we introduce a notion of strongly matching:

Definition 7. A process P is said to *strongly match* Q when, for any successor (α, Q') of Q, there is a P successor (α, P') such that $P' \approx Q'$

Furthermore, recall from section 6.2, that α_i is the action in *Act* with $\iota(\alpha_i) = i$. What is required is that the interface should be able to reach a state *strongly matching* $\sum_{i=0}^{l} \sum_{j=1}^{n_i} \alpha_i.1^j.P_{ij}$ upon receiving any l vector $\vec{n}$ of numbers $\langle n_1, \ldots, n_l \rangle$. Such an interface would, in particular, need to have descendants strongly matching *any* process in the set

$$\mathcal{Q}_A = \{\sum_{i=1}^{n} \beta_i.1^i.0 \mid \beta_i \in A, n \in I\!N\}.$$

Since $\mathcal{Q}_A$ contains infinitely many non-bisimilar processes, all the sums could not be directly present in the interface. They would have to be constructed

[2] This is the case even if we only simulate processes originally without τ loops.

by computation. The only way to achieve infinitely many non-bisimilar descendants is by recursion over parallel composition. However, if β_i and β_j were generated by two different parallel processes Q_i and Q_j, they could not be *preemptive*. No matter how Q_i and Q_j are composed with other processes, it will be the case that if $Q_i \xrightarrow{\beta_i} Q_i'$ and $Q_j \xrightarrow{\beta_j} Q_j'$ then no matter which of the two choices were made, we would still have the opportunity of performing the other. Therefore, there are no alternatives to gluing.

9 Conclusion

We have introduced the concept of universality for reactive systems and raised the question whether a universal reactive machine exists for CCS. We pointed out the difficulties with choices, and showed how to solve them by a rather non-constructive use of τ's, called gluing. We argued that gluing is necessary for achieving a URM for CCS under weak bisimulation.

An obvious question for future work would be whether using a weaker equivalence makes possible a more natural interface. Another would be to keep the equivalence but reconsider the semantics of CCS, such that processes as $a.P + a.Q$ and $a.(\tau.P + \tau.Q)$ become equivalent. From an implementational point of view, a two-level semantics, computing firstly the enabled actions, and then secondly choosing non-deterministically among the descendants of the selected action, is appealing. It suggests an immediate way of implementing it. Instead of changing the equivalence or the semantics, one could try to identify an interesting subset of CCS for which a universal reactive machine can be constructed without gluing. We have found no such subset.

Finally, the answers to the question of universality for other models of reactive systems are interesting. In particular, for models capturing other classes of systems than CCS, e.g., the π-calculus [3], this seems like a challenge.

References

1. R.J. van Glabbeek. *Comparative Concurrency Semantics and Refinement of Actions.* PhD thesis, Free University, Amsterdam, 1990.
2. Robin Milner. *Communication and Concurrency.* Prentice Hall, 1989.
3. Robin Milner, Joachim Parrow, and David Walker. A calculus of mobile processes (Parts I and II). *Information and Computation*, 100:1–77, 1992.
4. Alan M. Turing. On computable numbers, with an application to the Entscheidungsproblem. *Proc. London Math. Soc. (Ser. 2)*, 42:230–265, 1937. A correction in volume 43 pp. 544–546.

Bounded Stacks, Bags and Queues

J.C.M. Baeten[1] and J.A. Bergstra[2,3]

[1] Department of Mathematics and Computing Science,
Eindhoven University of Technology,
P.O. Box 513, NL-5600 MB Eindhoven, The Netherlands,
josb@win.tue.nl, http://www.win.tue.nl/cs/fm/josb/
[2] Programming Research Group, University of Amsterdam,
Kruislaan 403, NL-1098 SJ Amsterdam, The Netherlands
[3] Department of Philosophy, Utrecht University,
Heidelberglaan 8, NL-3584 CS Utrecht, The Netherlands,
janb@phil.ruu.nl, http://www.wins.uva.nl/research/prog/people/janb/

Abstract. We prove that a bounded stack can be specified in process algebra with just the operators alternative and sequential composition and iteration. The bounded bag cannot be specified with these operators, but can be specified if we add the parallel composition operator without communication (free merge). The bounded queue cannot even be specified in this signature; we need a form of variable binding such as given by general communication and encapsulation, the state operator, or abstraction.

1 Introduction

We investigate the definability of bounded bags, stacks and queues in process algebras with iteration. In particular, it is shown that a bounded stack can be specified in process algebra with just the operators alternative and sequential composition and iteration. The bounded bag cannot be specified with these operators, but can be specified if we add the parallel composition operator without communication (free merge). The bounded queue cannot even be specified in this signature; we need a form of variable binding such as given by general communication and encapsulation, the state operator, or abstraction.

This situation is remarkably similar to the situation we have with the specification of the unbounded versions with recursion instead of iteration. There, we have that the unbounded stack is not a regular process, but is finitely definable using alternative and sequential composition and recursion (see [4]). The unbounded bag cannot be finitely specified using alternative, sequential composition and recursion, but can be so specified if we use the free merge in addition (see [3]). The unbounded queue cannot be finitely specified using the signature including free merge (see [5]), but can be specified if we add an operator that features some form of variable binding, such as general communication with encapsulation, renaming or abstraction (see [1]).

From [2] we know that in process algebra with alternative, sequential and parallel composition (with communication) and iteration, not all regular processes can be defined. That paper also shows that we gain expressivity, each time we add one of these operators. The present paper shows that some well-known processes, namely bounded buffers, can serve to show the difference in expressivity.

2 Process Algebra with Iteration

The simplest process algebra is BPA, Basic Process Algebra. Its signature just contains a number of constants, called *atomic actions*, and two binary operators, $+$ which is *alternative composition* and $\cdot$ which is *sequential composition*. The axioms of BPA are the five axioms A1-5 in Table 1 below.

We extend BPA to BPA_δ by adding the constant δ denoting *inaction* with axioms A6,7 in Table 1. We extend BPA to PA by adding the parallel composition operator $\|$, *free merge* (merge without communication) with axioms M1-4. These axioms make use of the auxiliary operator $\lfloor\!\lfloor$, *left merge*. The combination of BPA_δ and PA is PA_δ. A denotes the set of atomic actions, $A_\delta = A \cup \{\delta\}$.

$x + y = y + x$	A1	$x \parallel y = x \lfloor\!\lfloor y + y \lfloor\!\lfloor x$	M1
$(x + y) + z = x + (y + z)$	A2	$a \lfloor\!\lfloor x = a \cdot x$	M2
$x + x = x$	A3	$a \cdot x \lfloor\!\lfloor y = a \cdot (x \parallel y)$	M3
$(x + y) \cdot z = x \cdot z + y \cdot z$	A4	$(x + y) \lfloor\!\lfloor z = x \lfloor\!\lfloor z + y \lfloor\!\lfloor z$	M4
$(x \cdot y) \cdot z = x \cdot (y \cdot z)$	A5		
$x + \delta = x$	A6	$x^* y = x \cdot (x^* y) + y$	BKS
$\delta \cdot x = \delta$	A7		

Table 1. Axioms of PA_δ^* $(a \in A_\delta)$.

Finally, we have in Table 1 the iteration operator * or *binary Kleene star* with defining equation BKS. In x^*y, we can iterate x and terminate by executing y. Much more about iteration can be found in [2]. Iteration gives a limited form of recursion, since p^*q is the solution of the recursive equation

$$X = p \cdot X + q.$$

BPA_δ^* is BPA_δ plus iteration.

Below we will occasionally use recursive equations. They will always be *linear*, i.e. of the form

$$X = \sum_{i=1}^{n} a_i \cdot X_i + \sum_{j=1}^{m} b_j$$

for variables X, X_i and $a_i, b_j \in A_\delta$. The key assumption we will need concerning linear recursive equations is that they have a unique solution.

We can use the axioms above and the assumption about unique solutions in order to prove that two process expressions denote the same process. Conversely, we will also need a way to tell when two process expressions cannot denote the same process. Certainly, two processes that are equal must be able to perform the same sequences of actions (must have the same *traces*. Even more, any state of one process must have a corresponding similar state in the other process. This equality is captured by the well-known notion of *bisimulation* (see [6]).

First, we describe which actions a process expression can perform. We do this by defining an operational semantics for process expressions. This semantics is given by means of Plotkin style *action rules* (see [7]).

For each atomic action a we have two predicates on process expressions: a binary relation $\xrightarrow{a}$ and a unary relation $\xrightarrow{a} \surd$. Intuitively, they have the following meaning:

- $p \xrightarrow{a} q$ means that p can perform an a-step and evolve into q
- $p \xrightarrow{a} \surd$ means that p can perform an a-step and terminate successfully

The action rules defining these predicates by structural induction are given in Table 2 (x, y range over process expressions). In the following sections, we will use this operational semantics in a rather informal way: when we say that process expression p can do an a-step to process expression q, we mean $p \xrightarrow{a} q$.

$$a \xrightarrow{a} \surd$$

$$\frac{x \xrightarrow{a} x'}{x \cdot y \xrightarrow{a} x' \cdot y} \qquad \frac{x \xrightarrow{a} \surd}{x \cdot y \xrightarrow{a} y}$$

$$\frac{x \xrightarrow{a} x'}{x + y \xrightarrow{a} x', y + x \xrightarrow{a} x'} \qquad \frac{x \xrightarrow{a} \surd}{x + y \xrightarrow{a} \surd, y + x \xrightarrow{a} \surd}$$

$$\frac{x \xrightarrow{a} x'}{x \parallel y \xrightarrow{a} x' \parallel y, y \parallel x \xrightarrow{a} y \parallel x', x \mathbin{⌊\!⌊} y \xrightarrow{a} x' \parallel y} \qquad \frac{x \xrightarrow{a} \surd}{x \parallel y \xrightarrow{a} y, y \parallel x \xrightarrow{a} y, x \mathbin{⌊\!⌊} y \xrightarrow{a} y}$$

$$\frac{x \xrightarrow{a} x'}{x^* y \xrightarrow{a} x' \cdot (x^* y)} \qquad \frac{x \xrightarrow{a} \surd}{x^* y \xrightarrow{a} x^* y}$$

$$\frac{y \xrightarrow{a} y'}{x^* y \xrightarrow{a} y'} \qquad \frac{y \xrightarrow{a} \surd}{x^* y \xrightarrow{a} \surd}$$

Table 2. Operational rules for PA^*_δ $(a \in A)$.

On the basis of these action rules, we define the notion of bisimulation: we say a symmetric binary relation R on process expressions is a *bisimulation* iff the following holds for all process expressions p, p', q and all actions $a \in A$:

- if $p \xrightarrow{a} p'$ and $R(p, q)$, then there is a process expression q' such that $q \xrightarrow{a} q'$ and $R(p', q')$
- if $p \xrightarrow{a} \sqrt{}$ and $R(p, q)$, then $q \xrightarrow{a} \sqrt{}$

Then, we say that process expressions p and q are bisimilar, $p \underline{\leftrightarrow} q$, iff there exists a bisimulation R with $R(p, q)$. From [2] we know that bisimulation is a congruence relation on process expressions, and that the set of process expressions modulo bisimulation constitutes a model for PA_{δ}^{*}.

3 Stack

We first give a system of linear equations for the stack. We have given a finite data type D. We use bounded sequences over D to parametrize the process variables. We use the following notations for such sequences:

- $[\,]$ denotes the empty sequence
- $[d]$ denotes the singleton sequence, for each $d \in D$
- $\frown$ denotes concatenation of sequences
- $|\sigma|$ denotes the length of sequence σ

The n-bounded stack ($n \geq 1$) has a specification with variables $S^n(\sigma)$, for each sequence σ with $|\sigma| \leq n$. The input of an element d is denoted by action $r(d)$ (*read d*), the output of d by $s(d)$ (*send d*). An alternative composition with one summand for each element of D is abbreviated by sum notation.

$$S^n([\,]) = \sum_{d \in D} r(d) \cdot S^n([d])$$

$$S^n([d] \frown \sigma) = s(d) \cdot S^n(\sigma) + \sum_{e \in D} r(e) \cdot S^n([e] \frown [d] \frown \sigma)$$

(for each $d \in D$ and sequence σ, if $|\sigma| < n - 1$)

$$S^n([d] \frown \sigma) = s(d) \cdot S^n(\sigma)$$

(for each $d \in D$ and sequence σ, if $|\sigma| = n - 1$).

It can be noted that this case distinction can be avoided, if we specify operators *head, tail* on sequences, and use a conditional operator that allows one or both summands depending on the length of the sequence. We refrain from doing this here, since we do not want to deal with the relationship between error handling in data type specifications and process algebra.

Theorem 1 *The bounded stack can be specified in BPA_{δ}^{*}.*

Proof Consider the following specification.

$$Stack(n) =$$

$$\left(\sum_{d_1\in D} r(d_1)\cdot\left(\sum_{d_2\in D} r(d_2)\cdot\left(\dots\left(\sum_{d_n\in D} r(d_n)\cdot s(d_n)\right)^{*}\dots\right)^{*} s(d_2)\right)^{*} s(d_1)\right)^{*}\delta$$

Inductively, we can define these processes as follows.

$$Elt(1) = \sum_{d\in D} r(d)\cdot s(d)$$

$$Elt(n+1) = \sum_{e\in D} r(e)\cdot Elt(n)^{*}s(e)$$

$$Stack(n) = Elt(n)^{*}\delta.$$

Now we have to prove that $Stack(n) = S^n([\,])$ holds for each n. In order to do this, we have to provide an expression for each state of the stack in terms of the variables $Stack(n), Elt(n)$. We define these expressions $T^n(\sigma)$ inductively:

$$T^n([\,]) = Stack(n)$$

$$T^n([d]^\frown\sigma) = (Elt(n-k-1)^{*}s(d))\cdot T^n(\sigma)$$

(for each $d \in D$ and sequence σ with $|\sigma| = k < n-1$)

$$T^n([d]^\frown\sigma) = s(d)\cdot T^n(\sigma)$$

(for each $d \in D$ and sequence σ with $|\sigma| = n-1$).

Now it is straightforward to show that the set of variables $T^n(\sigma)$ form a solution for the linear equations $S^n(\sigma)$. By uniqueness of solutions, we obtain $T^n(\sigma) = S^n(\sigma)$, so in particular $Stack(n) = S^n([\,])$. □

4 Bag

We proceed to give a system of linear equations for the bag. We now use bounded bags or multi-sets over data set D to parametrize the process variables. We use the following notations for such bags:

- $\emptyset$ denotes the empty bag
- $\{d\}$ denotes the singleton bag, for each $d \in D$
- $\cup$ denotes bag union, $-$ bag difference
- $|\beta|$ denotes the size of bag β

The n-bounded bag ($n \geq 1$) has a specification with variables $B^n(\beta)$, for each multi-set β with $|\beta| \leq n$. As before, the input of d is denoted $r(d)$, the output of d by $s(d)$.

$$B^n(\emptyset) = \sum_{d \in D} r(d) \cdot B^n(\{d\})$$

$$B^n(\beta) = \sum_{d \in \beta} s(d) \cdot B^n(\beta - \{d\}) + \sum_{e \in D} r(e) \cdot B^n(\{e\} \cup \beta)$$

(for each multi-set β with $0 < |\beta| < n$)

$$B^n(\beta) = \sum_{d \in \beta} s(d) \cdot B^n(\beta - \{d\})$$

(for each multi-set β with $|\beta| = n$)

Theorem 2 *The bounded bag can be specified in PA^*_δ.*

Proof Consider the following specification.

$$Bag(n) = \mathop{\|}_{i=1}^{n} \left(\sum_{d \in D} r(d) \cdot s(d) \right)^* \delta$$

Or, defined by induction:

$$Bag(1) = Elt(1)^* \delta$$

$$Bag(n+1) = Bag(n) \parallel Bag(1)$$

Now we have to prove that $Bag(n) = B^n(\emptyset)$ holds for each n. In order to do this, we will provide an expression for each state of the bag in terms of the variables $Bag(n)$. We define these expressions $C^n(\beta)$ as follows:

$$C^n(\emptyset) = Bag(n)$$

$$C^n(\beta) = Bag(n-k) \parallel \mathop{\|}_{d \in \beta} (s(d) \cdot Bag(1))$$

(for each multi-set β with $0 < |\beta| = k < n$)

$$C^n(\beta) = \mathop{\|}_{d \in \beta} (s(d) \cdot Bag(1))$$

(for each multi-set β with $|\beta| = n$).

Now it is straightforward to show that the set of variables $C^n(\beta)$ form a solution for the linear equations $B^n(\beta)$. By uniqueness of solutions, we obtain $C^n(\beta) = B^n(\beta)$, so in particular $Bag(n) = B^n(\emptyset)$. □

Next, we want to prove the following theorem.

Theorem 3 *Bag(n) cannot be specified in* BPA^*_δ, *if* $n \geq 2$ *and* $|D| \geq 2$.

The proof of this theorem is quite involved. We first make a number of definitions and prove some propositions.

We consider the set of finite transition systems over the set of atomic actions A that contain no deadlock nodes. Let G be such a transition system, then $|G|$ denotes the set of states of G. G has a root $r \in |G|$ and a transition relation $\rightarrow \subseteq |G| \times A \times |G|$. The domain of $\rightarrow$ is $dom(\rightarrow) = \{s \in |G| | \exists t \in |G| \exists a \in A s \xrightarrow{a} t\}$, the codomain is $codom(\rightarrow) = \{t \in |G| \mid \exists s \in |G| \; \exists a \in A \; s \xrightarrow{a} t\}$.

For $p \in dom(\rightarrow)$, $G(p)$ is the process (modulo bisimulation) represented by the graph G with p serving as the root. We notice that states in G are not labeled.

Example 4 Let $|G| = \{0, 1, 2, 3, 4\}, A = \{a, b, c, d\}, \rightarrow = \{0 \xrightarrow{a} 1, 1 \xrightarrow{b} 2, 2 \xrightarrow{c} 1, 1 \xrightarrow{d} 3, 3 \xrightarrow{a} 4\}$ with root 0, then $G(0) = a \cdot ((b \cdot c)^*(d \cdot a)), G(1) = (b \cdot c)^*(d \cdot a), G(2) = c \cdot G(1), G(3) = a$. Note $4 \notin dom(\rightarrow)$.

We will use the following definitions, where X, Y range over processes and p, q range over $dom(\rightarrow)$.

- $X \sqsubseteq Y$ iff $X + Y = Y$
- $I(X) \subseteq A$ is the set of initial actions of X
- $X \in K_G(p, q)$ iff $X \cdot G(q) \sqsubseteq G(p)$
- $X \in K^+_G(p, q)$ iff $X \cdot G(q) = G(p)$
- $X \in K^\infty_G(p, q)$ iff $X \in K_G(p, q)$ and X has an infinite trace
- $X \in K^f_G(p, q)$ iff $X \in K_G(p, q)$ and X has only finite traces
- $K^{+,f}_G(p, q) = K^+_G(p, q) \cap K^f_G(p, q)$, and similarly for other double superscripts

We notice that $\delta \in K_G(p, q)$ but no $X \in K_G(p, q)$ has a proper state equal to δ and $\delta \notin K^+_G(p, q)$.

Further, we call G *deterministic* if $p \xrightarrow{a} q$ and $p \xrightarrow{a} q'$ imply $q = q'$, and we call G *invertible* if $p \xrightarrow{a} q$ and $p' \xrightarrow{a} q$ imply $p = p'$. Next, we call G *fully abstract* if $G(p) = G(q)$ implies that $p = q$. We call G *non-stuttering* if for no state p and action a we have $p \xrightarrow{a} p$.

We extend $\rightarrow$ to $\rightarrow^* \subseteq |G| \times A^* \times |G|$ in the usual way. If G is deterministic and $s \xrightarrow{\sigma}{}^* t$ we will also denote t with $\sigma(s)$. Similarly, if G is invertible we will denote s with $\sigma^{-1}(t)$. We write $\sigma(p) \downarrow$ if $\sigma(p)$ is defined, $\sigma(p) \uparrow$ if $\sigma(p)$ is not defined.

Lemma 5 (Representation Lemma) Let G be deterministic, then for $p \in dom(\rightarrow)$ we have

$$G(p) = \sum_{a \in A, a(p)\downarrow, a(p) \in dom(\rightarrow)} a \cdot G(a(p)) + \sum_{a \in A, a(p)\downarrow, a(p) \notin dom(\rightarrow)} a$$

Proof The proof follows straightforwardly from the definitions. □

Next, we prove a series of propositions about the sets $K_G(p,q)$.

Proposition 6 Let G be deterministic and fully abstract. If $X \in K_G(p,q)$ and $X \xrightarrow{\sigma}^* \surd$ then $\sigma(p) = q$.

Proof $X \cdot G(q) \xrightarrow{\sigma}^* G(q)$ and $G(p) \xrightarrow{\sigma}^* G(\sigma(p))$, so by determinism $G(q) = G(\sigma(p))$ whence using full abstraction $q = \sigma(p)$. □

Proposition 7 If $X + Y \in K_G^\infty(p,q)$ then $X, Y \in K_G(p,q)$ and $X \in K_G^\infty(p,q)$ or $Y \in K_G^\infty(p,q)$.

Proof If $X+Y \in K_G^\infty(p,q)$ then $(X+Y)\cdot G(q) = X\cdot G(q) + Y\cdot G(q) \sqsubseteq G(p)$. Thus $X \cdot G(q) \sqsubseteq G(p)$ and $Y \cdot G(q) \sqsubseteq G(p)$, so $X, Y \in K_G(p,q)$. Further, if $X + Y$ has an infinite trace then either X or Y has an infinite trace. □

Proposition 8 Let G be deterministic. Let $X \in K_G(p,q), |\sigma| > 0$. If $X \xrightarrow{\sigma}^* Y$ then $Y \in K_G^+(\sigma(p), q)$.

Proof We use induction on the length of σ. If $|\sigma| = 1$, let $\sigma = a$. Using the representation lemma for p and $X \cdot G(q) \sqsubseteq G(p)$, we find $a \cdot Y \cdot G(q) = a \cdot G(a(p))$ and $Y \cdot G(q) = G(a(p))$ which yield $Y \in K_G^+(a(p), q)$.

If $|\sigma| = n+1$, put $\sigma = a \cdot \tau$. We have $X \xrightarrow{a} Y \xrightarrow{\tau}^* Z$. Using the same argument as above we find $Y \in K_G^+(a(p), q)$, so certainly $Y \in K_G(a(p), q)$. Then using the induction hypothesis: $Z \in K_G(\sigma(a(p)), q) = K_G(a\sigma(p), q)$. □

Proposition 9 Let $X \cdot Y \in K_G^\infty(p,q)$. If X does not terminate then $X \in K_G^\infty(p,q)$.

Proof As X does not terminate, $X = X \cdot Y$. □

Proposition 10 Let G be deterministic and let $X \cdot Y \in K_G(p,q)$. If $X \xrightarrow{\sigma}^* \surd$ then $X \in K_G(p, \sigma(p))$ and $Y \in K_G(\sigma(p), q)$. If moreover $X \cdot Y$ has an infinite trace, then at least one of X, Y has an infinite trace.

Proof If $X \xrightarrow{\sigma}^* \surd$ then $X \cdot Y \xrightarrow{\sigma}^* Y$. Using Proposition 8, we find $Y \in K_G^+(\sigma(p), q)$, so certainly $Y \in K_G(\sigma(p), q)$. Moreover, it follows that $Y \cdot G(q) = G(\sigma(p))$. Since $X \cdot Y \cdot G(q) \sqsubseteq G(p)$, we get $X \cdot G(\sigma(p)) \sqsubseteq G(p)$. This means $X \in K_G(p, \sigma(p))$. The last remark is immediate. □

Proposition 11 Let G be deterministic, invertible and fully abstract. If $X^*Y \in K_G(p,q)$, then $X \in K_G(p,p)$ and $Y \in K_G(p,q)$.

Proof $Y \cdot G(q) \sqsubseteq (X \cdot (X^*Y) + Y) \cdot G(q) = (X^*Y) \cdot G(q) \sqsubseteq G(p)$, so $Y \in K_G(p,q)$.

For X, we distinguish two cases. If X does not terminate, then $X \cdot G(p) = X = X \cdot G(q) \sqsubseteq (X+Y) \cdot G(q) = (X^*Y) \cdot G(q) \sqsubseteq G(p)$, so $X \in K_G(p,p)$.

Otherwise, there is a trace σ with $X \xrightarrow{\sigma}{}^{*} \surd$. This implies $X^*Y \xrightarrow{\sigma} X^*Y$. It follows by Proposition 8 that $X^*Y \in K_G^+(\sigma(p),q)$. Applying the same argument once more we obtain $X^*Y \in K_G^+(\sigma(\sigma(p)),q)$. This means $G(\sigma(p)) = (X^*Y) \cdot G(q) = G(\sigma(\sigma(p)))$. Using full abstraction $\sigma(p) = \sigma(\sigma(p))$. Using invertibility $p = \sigma(p)$ and so $X^*Y \in K_G^+(p,q)$. This means $(X^*Y) \cdot G(q) = G(p)$.

Now $X \cdot G(p) = X \cdot (X^*Y) \cdot G(q) \sqsubseteq (X^*Y) \cdot G(q) \sqsubseteq G(p)$, which means $X \in K_G(p,p)$. □

Proposition 12 Let G be deterministic and fully abstract. If there is an infinite path in G from p that avoids q then $K_G^{+,f}(p,q) = \emptyset$.

Proof Suppose $X \in K_G^+(p,q)$. Let $p \xrightarrow{a_0} p_1 \xrightarrow{a_1} p_2 \ldots$ be an infinite path avoiding q. Thus $\sigma = a_0 a_1 a_2 \ldots$ is a trace of $G(p) = X \cdot G(q)$. Since $G(p)$ does not deadlock, X does not deadlock either. Let τ be a finite initial segment of σ.

Suppose that $X \xrightarrow{\tau} \surd$, then by Proposition 6 $q = \tau(p)$ which contradicts the assumption on σ. We see that after no finite initial trace of σ X terminates, whence it has an infinite trace. Hence $K_G^{+,f}(p,q) = \emptyset$. □

Proposition 13 Let G be deterministic, non-stuttering and fully abstract. Let $X \in K_G^f(p,p)$. If $a \in I(X)$, then it is not the case that $X \xrightarrow{a} \surd$. Whenever $X \xrightarrow{\sigma}{}^{*} Y$, we have $Y \in K_G^{+,f}(\sigma(p),p)$.

Proof Suppose $X \xrightarrow{a} \surd$. Using $X \cdot G(p) \sqsubseteq G(p)$ and determinism, we find $G(p) = G(a(p))$. Full abstraction yields $p = a(p)$ which contradicts the non-stuttering property.

Next, let $X \xrightarrow{\sigma}{}^{*} Y$ then $Y \in K_G^+(\sigma(p),p)$ (by Proposition 8). As an infinite trace for Y implies an infinite trace for X, we obtain finiteness as well. □

Now we need one more definition for the last, highly technical proposition. Let $W_G(p,a,b)$ be the property of graph G, state p and actions a,b that holds if for each state q there is an infinite path in G from p which avoids q and that either starts with a step a or with a step b.

Proposition 14 Let $X \in K_G(p,q)$, suppose $a,b \in I(X)$ such that $W_G(p,a,b)$ holds. Then $X \in K_G^{\infty}(p,q)$.

Proof Let σ be an infinite path starting from p avoiding q. Assume, without loss of generality, that σ starts with a. Arguing as in Proposition 12, we find $X \in K_G^{\infty}(p,q)$. However, instead of $X \in K_G^+(p,q)$, we now use $a \in I(X)$ to see that X allows the initial a step. □

Now we have collected all ingredients necessary to start the proof for the bag.

Theorem 3 *Bag(n) cannot be specified in* BPA^*_δ*, if* $n \geq 2$ *and* $|D| \geq 2$.

Proof Take $n = 2$ and $|D| = 2$, say $D = \{0, 1\}$. The argument for larger n, D is not more complicated. Let G be the graph of $Bag(2)$. The states are multi-sets of data elements of size 0,1 or 2, denoting the contents of the bag, so $\emptyset, 0, 1, 00, 01$ and 11. The graph of $Bag(2)$ is shown in Fig. 1.

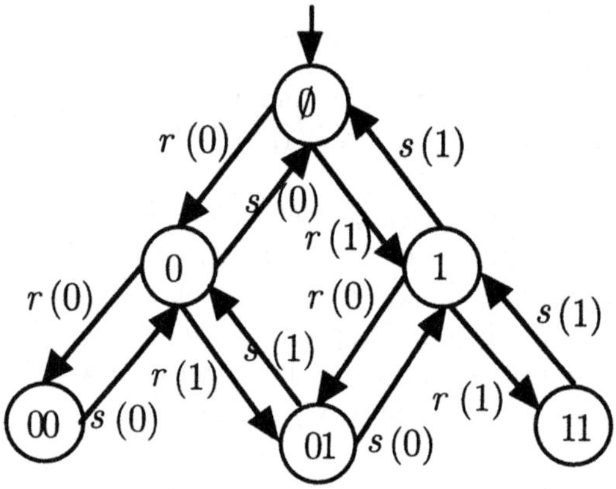

Fig. 1. The graph of $Bag(2)$.

Notice that G is deterministic, invertible and fully abstract. We see $B^2(\emptyset) \in K^\infty_G(\emptyset, \emptyset)$.

We will prove that for all states p, q, no element of $K^\infty_G(p, q)$ can be defined by an expression over BPA^*_δ. Since $B^2(\emptyset) \in K^\infty_G(\emptyset, \emptyset)$, this suffices to prove the theorem. Suppose, for a contradiction, that P is a minimal expression over BPA^*_δ defining some element of a $K^\infty_G(p, q)$ for certain states p, q. We use a case distinction on the form of P.

- P is an atomic action, then P has no infinite trace. This is a contradiction.
- P is a sum, so $P = Q + R$. Since $P \in K^\infty(p, q)$, at least one of Q and R is in $K^\infty(p, q)$ by Proposition 7. This contradicts the minimality of P.
- P is a product, so $P = Q \cdot R$. Using Proposition 9, either $X \in K^\infty_G(p, q)$ of for some r we have $R \in K^\infty_G(r, q)$, again contradicting the minimality of P.
- Otherwise, P is an iteration, so $P = Q^* R$. By Proposition 11, $Q \in K_G(p, p)$, $R \in K_G(p, q)$. From minimality of P we conclude $Q \in K^f_G(p, p)$.
  We claim now that either $p = 0$ and $Q = r(0) \cdot s(0)$, or $p = 1$ and $Q = r(1) \cdot s(1)$. In order to prove this claim, we first make the following observation.

The only states m, n of the bag for which $K_G^{+,f}(m,n) \neq \emptyset$ are either $m = 00, n = 0$ (e.g., process $s(0) \in K_G^{+,f}(m,n)$) or $m = 11, n = 1$ (e.g., process $s(1) \in K_G^{+,f}(m,n)$). For, for all other pairs m, n there is, by inspection of the graph, an infinite path from m avoiding n, and by Proposition 12 this gives $K_G^{+,f}(m,n) = \emptyset$.
Now, to prove the claim, an initial action a of $Q \in K_G^f(p,p)$ cannot lead to termination, by Proposition 13. So action a leads to $Y \in K_G^{+,f}(a(p),p)$. By the previous observation, we must have either $a(p) = 00, p = 0$ and $a = r(0)$, or $a(p) = 11, p = 1$ and $a = r(1)$. By inspection of the graph, we see that in the one case Y must start with $s(0)$ and in the other case with $s(1)$.
Consider the first case and let $Y \in K_G^f(0,0)$. Due to Proposition 8, if σ is a non-terminating trace of Y (say $Y \xrightarrow{\sigma}{}^* Z$), we have that $Z \in K_G^{+,f}(\sigma(0),0)$, and hence by the observation above $\sigma(0) = 00$. Now look at a trace τ of Y. For a trace of length 1 this is fine. The first action is $r(0)$ and it leads to state 00. As 00 differs from 0, $r(0)$ is not a terminating trace for Y. Now consider a larger trace. Inspection of the graph G shows that the second action in a trace of Y must be $s(0)$. After this second step, termination is necessary. Otherwise (with $\sigma = r(0)s(0)$), $\sigma(0) = 00$ must hold which is false. So $r(0)s(0)$ is the one and only completed trace of the finite process Y. It follows that $Y = r(0) \cdot s(0)$.
In the following, we again concentrate on the first case. We have $(r(0) \cdot s(0))^*R \in K_G^\infty(0,q)$. As $(r(0) \cdot s(0))^*R \xrightarrow{r(0)s(0)}{}^* (r(0) \cdot s(0))^*R$, by Proposition 8 in fact $(r(0) \cdot s(0))^*R \in K_G^{+,\infty}(0,q)$. This means $r(1), s(0) \in I(R)$ since both $r(1)$ and $s(0)$ are in $I(G(0))$. Inspection of G (slightly cumbersome) yields that $W_G(0, r(1), s(0))$ holds. Thus by Proposition 14 $R \in K_G^\infty(0,q)$ which contradicts the minimality of P.

□

5 Queue

We give a system of linear equations for the (first in first out) queue. We use the notation for sequences we also used in the case of the stack.

The n-bounded queue ($n \geq 1$) has a specification with variables $Q^n(\sigma)$, for each sequence σ with $|\sigma| \leq n$.

$$Q^n([\,]) = \sum_{d \in D} r(d) \cdot Q^n([d])$$

$$Q^n(\sigma^\frown[d]) = s(d) \cdot Q^n(\sigma) + \sum_{e \in D} r(e) \cdot Q^n([e]^\frown\sigma^\frown[d])$$

(for each $d \in D$ and sequence σ, if $|\sigma| < n - 1$)

$$Q^n(\sigma^\frown[d]) = s(d) \cdot Q^n(\sigma)$$

(for each $d \in D$ and sequence σ, if $|\sigma| = n-1$).

Theorem 15 *$Q^n(\emptyset)$ cannot be specified in PA^*_δ, if $n \geq 2$ and $|D| \geq 2$.*

Proof The proof is similar to the proof for the bag. Again take $n = 2$ and $D = \{0,1\}$. Let G be the graph of *Queue*(2). The states are sequences of data elements of size 0,1 or 2, denoting the contents of the queue. See Fig. 2.

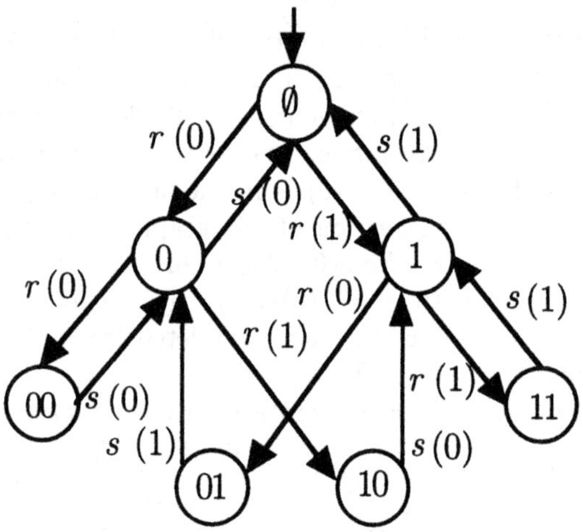

Fig. 2. The graph of *Queue*(2).

Notice that G is deterministic, invertible and fully abstract. We use the same induction as in the case of the bag. The cases for atomic action, sum and product go the same as for the bag. We have two cases left.

- Let $P \in K^\infty_G(p,q)$ be of the form $Q \cdot R$. We find that $Q \in K_G(p,p), R \in K_G(p,q)$. We may assume $Q \in K^+_G(p,p)$. As in the case of the bag, we can show that either $p = 0$ and $Q = r(0) \cdot s(0)$ or $p = 1$ and $Q = r(1) \cdot s(1)$. The proof of the claim involves more case distinction than in the case of the bag, but is straightforward. The proof is finished in a similar way.
- The remaining case is $P = Q \parallel R$. Since P has an infinite trace, at least one of Q, R has an infinite trace. Without loss of generality, assume this is Q. Suppose R has a terminating trace, $R \xrightarrow{\sigma}{}^* \surd$. Then $Q \parallel R \xrightarrow{\sigma}{}^* Q$ and so $Q \in K^+_G(\sigma(p), q)$. Since Q has an infinite trace, this contradicts the minimality of P. It follows that R has no finite terminating traces. If R deadlocks, say $R \xrightarrow{\sigma}{}^* \delta$, then $Q \parallel R \xrightarrow{\sigma}{}^* Q \parallel \delta = Q \cdot \delta$. Then $Q \cdot \delta \in K^+_G(\sigma(p), q)$,

so $Q \cdot \delta = G(\sigma(p))$. As $G(\sigma(p))$ cannot deadlock, Q cannot terminate, so $Q \cdot \delta = Q$ and $Q \in K_G^+(\sigma(p), q)$. This contradicts the minimality of P so R cannot deadlock either.
Thus R has no deadlocks and cannot terminate. Symmetrically, the same holds for Q. Now take a step from Q, say $Q \xrightarrow{a} Q'$. By Proposition 8 $Q' \parallel R \in K_G^{+,\infty}(a(p), q)$, in fact due to nontermination $Q' \parallel R = G(a(p))$. Observe that both actions $s(0), s(1)$ must occur in the alphabet of $Q' \parallel R$.
Suppose Q' has a trace containing $s(0)$, say $Q' \xrightarrow{\sigma}{}^* Q'' \xrightarrow{s(0)} Q'''$, and R has a trace containing $s(1)$, say $R \xrightarrow{\rho}{}^* R' \xrightarrow{s(1)} R''$. Then $Q' \parallel R \xrightarrow{\sigma\rho}{}^* Q''' \parallel R''$ and both $s(0), s(1)$ are possible from this state. This is impossible, since a queue can only output one action at a time. It follows that R has no traces containing $s(1)$. As we have a bounded queue, its traces must have some output, so this must be $s(0)$. The same argument shows that Q' must show output $s(0)$ only, but then $Q' \parallel R$ never allows $s(1)$, which is a contradiction.

□

If we go beyond the signature of PA_δ^*, then finite specifications for a bounded queue without recursion (but with iteration) can be given. A well-known one is that an n-bounded queue can be given as a parallel composition of n coupled one-place buffers. In order to specify this, we need parallel composition with communication, encapsulation and abstraction. In terms of the chaining operator of Vaandrager (see [8]), we can give a definition as follows:

$$Queue(1) = Elt(1)^*\delta$$

$$Queue(n+1) = Queue(n) \gg Queue(1)$$

For more details, we refer to [8].
Here, we give a different finite specification for the queue, in the signature obtained by adding the state operator of [1] to BPA_δ^*. The state operator is indexed by a finite data type S, and comes with two functions:

- *action* : $A \times S \rightarrow A_\delta$, giving the action that is executed when an action is tried in a certain state (the result is δ if the intended action is blocked in this state)
- *effect* : $A \times S \rightarrow S$, giving the resulting state when the action is executed in a certain state

Then, we have the equations for the state operator given in Table 3.
Now, to define the n-bounded queue, we use as state space the set of sequences of data elements of length $\leq n$. We use actions $r(d), s(d)$ as before and the extra action *out*. The action and effect functions are trivial (i.e. $action(a, s) = a$, $effect(a, s) = s$) except in the following cases:

$\lambda_s(\delta) = \delta$
$\lambda_s(a) = action(a, s)$
$\lambda_s(a \cdot x) = a(s) \cdot \lambda_{effect(a,s)}(x)$
$\lambda_s(x + y) = \lambda_s(x) + \lambda_s(y)$

Table 3. Axioms for the State Operator ($a \in A$).

- $effect(out, \sigma^\frown[d]) = \sigma$ (for $d \in D$, $|\sigma| < n$)
- $effect(r(d), \sigma) = [d]^\frown\sigma$ (for $d \in D$, $|\sigma| < n$)
- $action(out, [\,]) = \delta$
- $action(out, \sigma^\frown[d]) = s(d)$ (for $d \in D$, $|\sigma| < n$)
- $action(r(d), \sigma) = \delta$ (for $d \in D$, $|\sigma| = n$)

Now, the definition of the n-bounded queue is as follows:

$$Queue(n) = \lambda_{[\,]}((out + \sum_{d \in D} r(d))^* \delta)$$

Then it is not difficult to show that $Queue(n) = Q^n([\,])$ holds for each n, by showing that $Q^n(\sigma) = \lambda_\sigma((out + \sum_{d \in D} r(d))^* \delta)$, for each sequence σ of length $\leq n$.

6 Conclusion

We find a remarkable similarity between the definability issues for bounded and unbounded bags, stacks and queues, when using iteration in the bounded cases and recursion in the unbounded cases.

References

1. J.C.M. Baeten and J.A. Bergstra. Global renaming operators in concrete process algebra. *Information and Computation*, 78:205–245, 1988.
2. J.A. Bergstra, I. Bethke, and A. Ponse. Process algebra with iteration and nesting. *The Computer Journal*, 37(4):243–258, 1994.
3. J.A. Bergstra and J.W. Klop. The algebra of recursively defined processes and the algebra of regular processes. In J. Paredaens, editor, *Proceedings 11th ICALP*, number 172 in LNCS, pages 82–95. Springer Verlag, 1984.
4. J.A. Bergstra and J.W. Klop. Algebra of communicating processes. In J.W. de Bakker, M. Hazewinkel, and J.K. Lenstra, editors, *Mathematics and Computer Science I*, volume 1 of *CWI Monograph*, pages 89–138. North-Holland, Amsterdam, 1986.
5. J.A. Bergstra and J. Tiuryn. Process algebra semantics for queues. *Fundamenta Informaticae*, X:213–224, 1987.

6. D.M.R. Park. Concurrency and automata on infinite sequences. In P. Deussen, editor, *Proceedings 5th GI Conference*, number 104 in LNCS, pages 167–183. Springer Verlag, 1981.
7. G.D. Plotkin. An operational semantics for CSP. In D. Bjørner, editor, *Proceedings Conference on Formal Description of Programming Concepts II*, pages 199–225. North-Holland, Amsterdam, 1983.
8. F.W. Vaandrager. Process algebra semantics of POOL. In J.C.M. Baeten, editor, *Applications of Process Algebra*, number 17 in Cambridge Tracts in Theoretical Computer Science, pages 173–236. Cambridge University Press, 1990.

Adding Partial Orders to Linear Temporal Logic

Girish Bhat[1] and Doron Peled[2]

[1] Department of Computer Science, North Carolina State University, Raleigh, NC 27606, USA
email: gsbhat1@eos.ncsu.edu
[2] Bell Laboratories, 700 Mountain Ave., Murray Hill, NJ, 07974, USA
email: doron@research.bell-labs.com

Abstract. Modeling execution as partial orders increases the flexibility in reasoning about concurrent programs by allowing the use of alternative, equivalent execution sequences. This is a desirable feature in specifying concurrent systems which allows formalizing frequently used arguments such as 'in an equivalent execution sequence', or 'in a consistent global state, not necessarily on the execution sequence' to be formalized. However, due to the addition of structure to the model, verification of partial order properties is non-trivial and sparse. We present here a new approach which allows expressing and verifying partial order properties. It is based on modeling an execution as a linear sequence of global states, where each state is equipped with its past partial-order history. The temporal logic BPLTL (for Branching Past Linear Temporal Logic) is introduced. We provide a sound and relatively complete proof system for the logic BPLTL over transitions programs. Our proof system augments an existing proof system for LTL.

1 Introduction

Modeling concurrent systems is a challenging effort. It involves representing the activity of multiple co-existing agents which interact or interfere with each other. The wealth of models for distributed systems stem from the sometimes conflicting effort to maintain on one hand abstraction and simplicity, and on the other hand to capture intricate features. Thus, various different dichotomies were developed, aimed at describing concurrent systems at different levels of abstraction. This includes issues such as discrete vs. real-time models, synchronous (with simultaneous actions) vs. asynchronous (interleaved actions) models, instantaneous actions vs. actions with duration, and linearly ordered (interleaving) vs. partially ordered (causal) executions.

The main focus of this work is on the latter pair of dichotomies. One advantage of the linear model is that it forms a simpler mathematical structure than the partial order. On the other hand, the partial order model exercises a more flexible definition of global states, corresponding to consistent sets of executed events, termed *cuts* or *slices* [15]. As a result, instead of having a single predecessor, each global state may have multiple predecessor states. This reflects the observation that in a distributed system, different global views of the system can co-exist, and furthermore, there are several equivalent ways to reach a state corresponding to the possible linearizations of a partially ordered set of events. Thus, the past of a global state can be viewed as a branching structure. Many algorithms are based on this view, e.g., for finding a global balance of a distributed financial system [2], obtaining database consistency or computer bus cache coherence.

In this paper, we suggest a combined model of execution, which inherits from both the linear and partial order models. We view an execution as a distinguished *linear structure* such that for each state in this structure, we include its *branching past*. Thus, the global states occurring on the linear execution before some state s can be a strict subset of the history of s. In other words, looking backwards from a given state, one may observe several alternative sequences, grouped into a branching structure; looking forward, there is only a distinguished one.

For example, suppose a process P_1 can execute the atomic actions a and then b, while P_2 can independently do c, as in the lefthand side of Figure 1. Thus, the partial order between the events resulted in from executing these actions is as follows: a precedes b, while c is unordered (concurrent) with both of them. Assume a distinguished interleaving sequence with the order *acb*. We will identify a state with the set of actions executed. Notice that the sequences *abc* and *cab* are alternative linearizations of the partial order. Looking back from the state that corresponds to executing *acb*, there are two predecessors: one corresponding to executing *ac*, and one corresponding to the execution of *ab*, as in the righthand side of Figure 1. The latter state is not a global state of the sequence *acb*, but in its alternative equivalent one *abc*.

This way of modeling concurrent systems, where for each execution there is a distinguished future and a multiple, equivalent past, can be shown to be convenient for specifying and reasoning about concurrent and distributed systems. In particular this is useful for algorithms that take advantage of the disability of a distributed observer of a concurrent system to distinguish whether one history reflects better the execution than another.

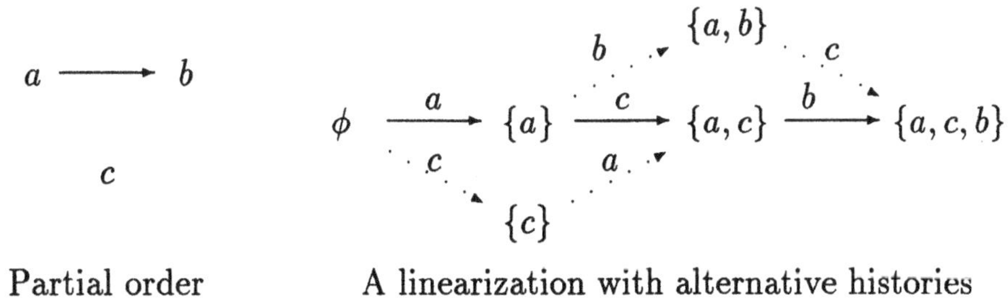

Fig. 1. A partial order with a distinguish linearlization

We define a new temporal logic, called BPLTL (Branching Past Linear Temporal Logic), for reasoning about such combined models. This logic allows using linear past or future temporal logic operators interpreted over a distinguished interleaving sequence. It uses past CTL-like branching time operators to reason about the branching past, interpreted over structures obtained from partial order executions. This logic inherits properties from both LTL (Linear Temporal Logic) and the past version of ISTL (Interleaving Set Temporal Logic) where the branching structure reflects the different linearizations of a partial order execution [4, 9]. The logic exploits the simplicity of using linear structures for modeling concurrent executions, yet enhanced by the ability to express properties about alternative global states.

We provide a sound and relatively complete proof system for BPLTL over transition programs. This proof system extends the Manna-Pnueli proof system for LTL [6], with partial order backward proof rules in the style of [9].

One advantage of our approach, is that it allows exploiting an existing proof system over transitions programs for the logic LTL. New proof rules, for handling the branching past, are added on top of existing LTL proof rules, obtaining a relatively complete proof system. Thus, one can augment an existing implementation of the LTL proof system using mechanical verifiers, to include the capability of reasoning over partial order properties. For comparison, the proof system for ISTL in [9] includes only a subset of the ISTL properties. The examples provided for BPLTL, show that many interesting properties, e.g., those that where used for the logic ISTL [9], are expressible in BPLTL.

Other temporal logics interpreted over partial order executions include, e.g., POTL [13], ISTL [4, 9], CTL_P [11], TrPTL [17] and TLC [1]. Among the above, only the logics ISTL and CTL_P are interpreted over linearizations of partial order executions, or traces, while the rest reason directly over the partially ordered set of events of each execution. The logic CTL_P [11] and ISTL [4, 9] are closely related to BPLTL. ISTL has the capability of reasoning about multiple equivalent futures, and CTL_P has the capability of reasoning about different branching futures (even non-equivalent ones). A survey paper on logics for partial orders appears in [12]. In the examples given here, we hope to demonstrate that in many cases, limiting the expressiveness to alternative pasts is sufficient.

2 Programs and Traces

2.1 Programs

A program will be defined over a first order signature $\mathcal{L}$, with relation and function symbols interpreted over a first order structure $\mathcal{A}$. An *assignment* J over a tuple of variables $\mathbf{y}$ is a mapping, associating with each variable z in $\mathbf{y}$ a value $J(z)$ from its associated domain. If t is a term, denote by $J(t)$ the interpretation of the term t under the assignment J and the structure $\mathcal{A}$. Similarly, when $\mathbf{t}$ is a tuple of terms, $J(\mathbf{t})$ is a tuple of values, where $J(\mathbf{t})_i$ is $J(t_i)$.

For an assignment J and a first order formula φ, denote the fact that φ holds over $\mathcal{A}$ and J by the standard notation $J \models^{\mathcal{A}} \varphi$. If φ is a sentence, i.e., it has no free variables, we write the fact that φ holds in $\mathcal{A}$ by $\models^{\mathcal{A}} \varphi$. We omit the structure $\mathcal{A}$ when it is understood from the context.

A *program* P is a quadruple $\langle T, D, \mathbf{y}, \Theta \rangle$ where T is a set of operations, $D \subseteq T \times T$ is a dependency relation between operations, satisfying the conditions given below, $\mathbf{y} = \langle y_1, y_2, \ldots, y_m \rangle$ is a tuple of variables, and the *initial condition*

$\Theta \in \mathcal{L}$ is a satisfiable predicate with free variables from $\mathbf{y}$. In addition, the program associates with each operation $\tau \in T$, a pair $\langle en_\tau^P(\mathbf{y}),\ f_\tau^P(\mathbf{y})\rangle$ where en_τ^P is a predicate over $\mathcal{L}$ (the *enabling condition*) and f_τ^P (the *transformation function*) is a tuple of $|\,\mathbf{y}\,|$ terms over $\mathcal{L}$. All the variables of f_τ^P and the free variables of en_τ^P are from $\mathbf{y}$. The enabling condition controls when the operation can execute, while the transformation dictates the new values of the program variables, calculated using the expressions in f_τ^P from the old values.

We will denote by $\mathbf{z} \subseteq \mathbf{y}$ the fact that the variables in $\mathbf{z}$ are included in the variables of $\mathbf{y}$. Let $I \subseteq \{1 \ldots |\mathbf{r}|\}$, where $\mathbf{r}$ is a tuple. If $I = \{j_1, j_2, \ldots, j_k\}$, with $j_1 < j_2 < \ldots < j_k$, then denote by $\mathbf{r} \downarrow I$ the tuple $\langle r_{j_1}, r_{j_2}, \ldots, r_{j_k}\rangle$. That is, the projection of $\mathbf{r}$ over the indices in I. If $\mathbf{z} \subseteq \mathbf{y}$, then $I_\mathbf{z}^\mathbf{y}$ are the indices of the variables in $\mathbf{y}$ that are also in $\mathbf{z}$.

The relation $comm(\alpha, \beta, \bar{z})$ defined below represent the *commutativity* between operations α and β with respect to the variables $\mathbf{z} \subseteq \mathbf{y}$.

Definition 1. $comm(\alpha, \beta, \mathbf{z})$ holds iff $(en_\alpha^P(\mathbf{y}) \wedge en_\beta^P(\mathbf{y})) \rightarrow f_\alpha^P(f_\beta^P(\mathbf{y})) \downarrow I_\mathbf{z}^\mathbf{y} = f_\beta^P(f_\alpha^P(\mathbf{y})) \downarrow I_\mathbf{z}^\mathbf{y}$.

The following conditions are required for each pair of operations α, β such that $(\alpha, \beta) \notin D$:

- $en_\alpha^P(\mathbf{y}) \rightarrow (en_\beta^P(\mathbf{y}) \leftrightarrow en_\beta^P(f_\alpha^P(\mathbf{y})))$ [independent operations can neither disable nor enable each other.]
- $comm(\alpha, \beta, \mathbf{y})$ holds. [commutativity of independent operations w.r.t. *all* the variables.]

An operation τ can be written as the guarded command $\langle en_\tau(\mathbf{y}) \longrightarrow \mathbf{y} := f_\tau^P(\mathbf{y})\rangle$. The intended meaning is that the condition before the arrow controls when the operation may execute and the effect of the operation is to simultaneously assign the $|\mathbf{y}|$ expressions $f_\tau^P(\mathbf{y})$ into the set of variables $\mathbf{y}$. For example, $\langle y_1 < y_2 \longrightarrow (y_2, y_1, y_3) := (y_1, y_2, y_3)\rangle$ is an operation that switches between the values of the variables y_1 and y_2, if y_1 is smaller than y_2. The value of y_3 is unaltered. Since a typical operation changes only a subset of the program variables, we will usually denote explicitly only the expressions assigned to the variables that may be changed (e.g., $\langle y_1 < y_2 \longrightarrow (y_2, y_1) := (y_1, y_2)\rangle$).

A *history* of a program P is a pair $h = \langle J, v\rangle$ where J is an assignment, called the *initial assignment of* h, and $v \in T^*$. Furthermore, the following condition is satisfied: Let $n = |\,v\,|$, $v = \alpha_1\alpha_2 \ldots \alpha_n$. There exists a sequencc of assignments $J_0, J_1, \ldots, J_n$ with $J_0 = J$ such that for each $0 < i \leq n$,

1. $J_{i-1} \models en_{\alpha_i}(\mathbf{y})$ [α_i is enabled in J_{i-1}], and
2. for each $0 \leq k < |\,\mathbf{y}\,|$, $J_i(y_k) = f_{\alpha_i}^P(J_{i-1}(\mathbf{y}))_k$ [i.e., $J_i(y_k)$ is the kth component in the tuple obtained when applying the transformation $f_{\alpha_i}^P$ to the values assigned by J_{i-1}].

For each history $h = \langle J, v\rangle$, let $J_{|v|}$ be denoted by fin_h. This is called the *final assignment* of h. We use h, h', $h_i, \ldots$ for histories.

2.2 Augmented Programs

For purposes of verification, and in particular the proof system of [6], it is typical that one needs to transform a program.

Definition 2. An augmentation $P' = \langle \Theta', T, D, \mathbf{z} \rangle$ of a program $P = \langle \Theta, T, D, \mathbf{y} \rangle$, denoted $P \angle P'$ satisfies the following conditions:

1. $\mathbf{z} \supset \mathbf{y}$, where $\mathbf{z} \setminus \mathbf{y} = \{z_1', z_2', \ldots, z_m'\}$ are called *auxiliary variable.*
2. $\Theta' = \Theta \wedge \theta$ where $\Theta \rightarrow \exists z_1' \exists z_2' \ldots \exists z_m' \ \theta$.
3. For each $\tau \in T$,
   - $en_\tau^{P'} = en_\tau^{P}$.
   - $f_\tau^{P'}$ is a tuple of $|\mathbf{z}|$ terms, where $f_\tau^{P'}(\mathbf{z}) \downarrow I_{\mathbf{y}}^{\mathbf{z}} = f_\tau^{P}(\mathbf{y})$

We will use two types of auxiliary variables, *trace variables* and *sequence variables.* An auxiliary trace variable x must satisfy that for each $(\alpha, \beta) \notin D$, $comm(\alpha, \beta, \{x\})$ holds. Trace variables are used to record the history of traces, hence their value should not depend on the order in which independent operations are executed. Sequence variables are used to record the history of sequences.

Programs obtained as augmentation of other programs inherit many but not all of their properties. In the sequel, it would be noted when an augmented program is treated differently.

2.3 Traces

Definition 3. Two strings $v, w \in T^*$ are *equivalent* iff there exists a sequence of strings $v_1, v_2, \ldots, v_n$ with $v_1 = v$ and $v_n = w$, and for each $1 \leq i < n$ there exist $u, \bar{u} \in T^*$, $(\alpha, \beta) \notin D$ such that $v_i = u\alpha\beta\bar{u}$, $v_{i+1} = u\beta\alpha\bar{u}$. This is denoted $v \equiv w$.

For example, let $T = \{\alpha, \beta, \gamma\}$, $D = Id_T \cup \{(\alpha, \gamma), (\gamma, \alpha)\}$. Then, $\alpha\alpha\beta\beta\gamma\gamma \equiv \alpha\beta\alpha\gamma\beta\gamma \equiv \beta\alpha\alpha\gamma\gamma\beta$, but $\alpha\alpha\beta\gamma\gamma \not\equiv \gamma\gamma\beta\alpha\alpha$ (because the α's and the γ's cannot be interchanged).

A *trace* is an equivalence class of strings [7]. We denote a trace σ also as $[w]$, with w any element of σ. Traces will be denoted using σ, σ', σ_i, $\rho, \ldots$. Concatenation between two traces $\sigma_1 = [v]$ and $\sigma_2 = [w]$, denoted $\sigma_1\sigma_2$, is defined to be $[vw]$.

The prefix relation '$\sqsubseteq$' between traces is defined as $\sigma_1 \sqsubseteq \sigma_2$ iff there exists some σ_3 such that $\sigma_1\sigma_3 = \sigma_2$. It is said that σ_1 is *subsumed* by σ_2. If in addition, the length of σ_1 is shorter than the length of σ_2 by exactly one operation, it is said that σ_2 is a *successor* of σ_1. We denote this by $\sigma_1 \rhd \sigma_2$. If $\sigma' \sqsubseteq \sigma$, denote by σ/σ' the trace ρ such that $\sigma'\rho = \sigma$. It is said that ρ is a *suffix* of σ.

It is easy to see that because of the conditions on independence, for a program P, if $h = \langle J, u \rangle$ is a history of P, and $u \equiv w$, then $h' = \langle J, w \rangle$ is also a history of P. Since the enabledness conditions in an augmented program are the same as the original program, this also holds for an augmented program. For a program it holds that, $fin_h = fin_{h'}$, but this does not have to hold for an augmented program, as the sequence auxiliary variables can distinguish between the execution order of independent operations.

We thus assume that each trace contains a distinguished sequence $\delta(\sigma) \in \sigma$. Then $fin_{\langle J,\, \sigma\rangle} = fin_{\langle J,\, \delta(\sigma)\rangle}$. For programs, the function $\delta(\sigma)$ is defined arbitrarily, since equivalent sequences result in the same final assignment. We will discuss a specific distinguishing function δ for augmented programs in the sequel.

An *accessible pair* of a program P is a pair $\langle J,\, \sigma\rangle$, where J is an initial assignment, which satisfies the initial condition Θ, and σ is a trace such that $\langle J,\, h\rangle$ is a history of P, and $h \in \sigma$. We extend the relation $\rhd$ to accessible pairs such that $\langle J,\, \sigma\rangle \rhd \langle J',\, \rho\rangle$ exactly when $J = J'$ and $\sigma \rhd \rho$.

We will denote $\langle J,\, \sigma\rangle \models \varphi$ iff $fin_{\langle J,\, \sigma\rangle} \models \varphi$. Denote by $\Delta(\sigma)$ the set of operations that occur in (any string that is a member of) the trace σ. An *accessible sequence* of P is a sequence of accessible pairs of the form $\langle J,\, \sigma_0\rangle, \langle J,\, \sigma_1\rangle, ...$ such that $J \models \Theta$, $\sigma_0 = [\varepsilon]$, and for every i, $\sigma_i \rhd \sigma_{i+1}$. If an accessible sequence cannot be extended, then we refer to it as an *execution* of P. Let $Exec(P)$ be the set of all executions. Fairness is orthogonal to the definition of an execution, and limits the sequences that are considered to be executions. If a fairness assumption is used, $FairExec(P)$ is the set of fair executions.

Let R be a binary relation between elements of a countable set S. Let R^* represent the reflexive and transitive closure of R. R is *reduced* if for each $(s,t) \in R, (s,t) \notin (R \setminus (s,t))^*$. Finally, R is said to be *acyclic* if R^* is acyclic, i.e., for s,t such that $s \neq t$ if $(s,t) \in R^*$ then $(t,s) \notin R^*$. For a finite or infinite sequence ξ let $\xi(i)$ represent the ith element of ξ. If ξ is a finite sequence, then $last(\xi)$ represents the last element in ξ.

3 Syntax and Semantics of BPLTL

We now introduce a new temporal logic, titled *Branching Past Linear Temporal Logic* (BPLTL). In each model for this logic, the future is linear, but the past has a mixed interpretation, i.e., some past formulas have branching time interpretation and some have linear time interpretation. We show later how this enables us to specify many interesting properties not expressible in LTL. In fact, it is sufficient to restrict to a linear future and branching past; linear past was added for the benefit of the proof system. The syntax of our logic is given below.

3.1 Syntax

We assume the existence of a first-order structure $\mathcal{L}$, containing variables, relations and function symbols, over which first order predicates are defined. We use $\varphi, \varphi_1, \varphi_2, ...$ to denote first order predicates over $\mathcal{L}$. Now, to define the syntax of BPLTL we define two kinds of formulas, *path* formulas denoted by $\kappa, \gamma ...$ and *state* formulas denoted by $p, q ....$ We use $\mathcal{K}$ and Γ to represent sets of path and state formulas respectively. BPLTL formulas are essentially the set of path formulas.

Path Formulas ($\mathcal{K}$)
- if $\kappa \in \Gamma$ then $\kappa \in \mathcal{K}$.
- if $\kappa,\ \gamma \in \mathcal{K}$ then $\kappa \vee \gamma$, $\neg\kappa \in \mathcal{K}$.
- if $\kappa,\ \gamma \in \mathcal{K}$ then $(\kappa \mathcal{U} \gamma)$, $(\kappa \mathcal{S} \gamma)$, $\bigcirc\kappa$, $\ominus\kappa \in \mathcal{K}$.

State Formulas (Γ) $\begin{cases} \bullet \text{ for every first order predicate } \varphi \text{ over } \mathcal{L}, \varphi \in \Gamma. \\ \bullet \text{ if } p, q \in \Gamma \text{ then } p \vee q, \neg p \in \Gamma. \\ \bullet \text{ for state formulas } p \text{ and } q, \mathsf{E}(p\mathsf{S}q), \mathsf{EY}p, \\ \quad \mathsf{A}(p\mathsf{S}q) \in \Gamma. \end{cases}$

For technical convenience we introduce the following dual operators: $\mathbf{T} = \varphi \vee \neg\varphi$, $\mathbf{F} = \neg\mathbf{T}$, $\mathsf{AY}p = \neg(\mathsf{EY}\neg p)$, $\kappa\mathcal{Z}\gamma = \neg(\neg\kappa\mathcal{S}\neg\gamma)$, $\mathsf{E}(p\mathsf{Z}q) = \neg\mathsf{A}(\neg p\mathsf{S}\neg q)$ and $\mathsf{A}(p\mathsf{Z}q) = \neg\mathsf{E}(\neg p\mathsf{S}\neg q)$. Additional temporal operators are as follows: $\Diamond\kappa = \mathbf{T}\mathcal{U}\kappa$, $\Box\kappa = \neg\Diamond\neg\kappa$, $\diamondminus\kappa = \mathbf{T}\mathcal{S}\kappa$, $\boxminus\kappa = \neg\diamondminus\neg\kappa$, $\mathsf{EH}p = \mathsf{E}(p\mathsf{S}start)$ where $start = \mathsf{AY}\mathbf{F}$ is a formula representing the initial state in the sequence, $\mathsf{EP}p = \mathsf{E}(\mathbf{T}\mathsf{S}p)$, for ψ and η either path or state formulas we have, $\psi \wedge \eta = \neg(\neg\psi \vee \neg\eta)$, $\psi \rightarrow \eta = \neg\psi \vee \eta$, $\psi \leftrightarrow \eta = (\psi \rightarrow \eta)\wedge(\eta \rightarrow \psi)$, and finally, $\kappa \Rightarrow \gamma = \Box(\kappa \rightarrow \gamma)$, $\kappa \Leftrightarrow \gamma = \Box(\kappa \leftrightarrow \gamma)$.

We use E() to represent state formulas of the form $\mathsf{EY}p, \mathsf{E}(p_1\mathsf{S}p_2)$ and $\mathsf{E}(p_1\mathsf{Z}p_2)$. A() is used to represent state formulas of the form $\mathsf{AY}p, \mathsf{A}(p_1\mathsf{S}p_2)$ and $\mathsf{A}(p_1\mathsf{Z}p_2)$.

3.2 Semantics

The semantics of BPLTL is given with respect to abstract structures called *BPLTL structures.*

Definition 4. A BPLTL structure $\mathcal{M}$ is of the form $\langle S, s_0, \prec, \xi, \Xi\rangle$ where S is a set of states, $s_0 \in S$ is some distinguished state, $\prec$ is a reduced acyclic relation between states, $\xi \in S^\omega$ is a distinguished sequence of states , $\Xi \subseteq S^*$ is set of finite sequences of states. In addition $\mathcal{M}$ satisfies the following constraints:

- For every $s \in S$, $s_0 \prec s$.
- For every $\rho \in \Xi \cup \{\xi\}$, $\rho(i) \prec \rho(i+1)$ and $\rho(0) = s_0$.

For a structure $\mathcal{M}$, we associate a first-order structure $\mathcal{A}$ and a labeling function L over the domain S such that $L(s)$ is an assignment for the variables in the first order signature $\mathcal{L}$. The semantics of a BPLTL formula is given with respect to a $\langle\mathcal{M}, \mathcal{A}, L\rangle$ as follows:

- $(\xi, i) \models p$ iff $\xi(i) \models p$.
- $(\xi, i) \models \kappa \vee \gamma$ iff $(\xi, i) \models \kappa$ or $(\xi, i) \models \gamma$.
- $(\xi, i) \models \neg\kappa$ iff $(\xi, i) \not\models \kappa$.
- $(\xi, i) \models \bigcirc\kappa$ iff $(\xi, i+1) \models \kappa$.
- $(\xi, i) \models \ominus\kappa$ iff $i > 0$ and $(\xi, i-1) \models \kappa$.
- $(\xi, i) \models \kappa\mathcal{U}\gamma$ iff there exist $j \geq i$ such that $(\xi, j) \models \gamma$ and for each l such that $i \leq l < j$, $(\xi, l) \models \kappa$.
- $(\xi, i) \models \kappa\mathcal{S}\gamma$ iff there exists j such that $0 \leq j \leq i$ $(\xi, j) \models \gamma$ and for each l such that $j < l \leq i$, $(\xi, l) \models \kappa$.

The satisfaction of a state formula at a state $s \in S$ is now defined as follows:

- $s \models \varphi$ iff $L(s) \models^{\mathcal{A}} \varphi$.
- $s \models p \vee q$ iff $s \models p$ or $s \models q$.
- $s \models \neg p$ iff $s \not\models p$.
- $s \models \mathsf{EY}p$ iff there exists a $\rho \in \Xi$ such that $last(\rho) = s$ and $\rho(|\rho| - 1) \models p$

- $s \models \mathsf{E}(p\mathsf{S}q)$ iff there exists a $\rho \in \Xi$ such that $last(\rho) = s$ and there exists j such that $0 \leq j \leq |\rho|$, $\rho(j) \models q$ and for all k such that $j < k \leq |\rho|$, $\rho(k) \models p$.
- $s \models \mathsf{A}(p\mathsf{S}q)$ iff for every $\rho \in \Xi$ such that $last(\rho) = s$, there exists j such that $0 \leq j \leq |\rho|$ and $\rho(j) \models q$ and for all k such that $j < k \leq |\rho|$, $\rho(k) \models p$.

Definition 5. For every BPLTL formula κ, a structure $\mathcal{M} = \langle S, q_0, \prec, \xi, \Xi \rangle$, a first-order structure $\mathcal{A}$, a labeling function L, $\langle \mathcal{M}, \mathcal{A}, L \rangle \models \kappa$ iff $(\xi, 0) \models \kappa$.

3.3 Special Subsets of BPLTL and Normal Forms

We distinguish three classes of BPLTL formulas:

Pure LTL formulas consist of formulas that do not contain any branching past formula of the form E() or A().

General path formulas consist of formulas which contain LTL modalities like $\mathcal{U}$ and $\mathcal{S}$ and also subformulas of the form E() and A().

State formulas consist of elements of Γ (defined in the previous section).

For a BPLTL formula κ a state formula p is a *top-level state subformula* of κ if p is a strict subformula of the form E() or A() and there is no other strict state subformula of the form E() or A() that contains p.

Next we consider two normal forms for BPLTL formulas. The first normal form is *positive normal form* (PNF). A BPLTL formula κ is in *positive normal form* if the only negated subformulas are first-order predicates.

The second normal form, which we refer to as *MP-normal form*, is inspired by the normal form given by Manna and Pnueli [6] for LTL. They have shown that every LTL formula is equivalent to a formula of the form $\bigwedge_i^n (\Box\Diamond\kappa_i \vee \Diamond\Box\gamma_i)$ where κ_i and γ_i are *strict past formulas*, i.e., formulas that do not contain any future operators. The same result holds for BPLTL too. This is a consequence of following lemma:

Lemma 6. *If all the occurrences of a set of propositions appearing in a valid LTL formula are respectively replaced by BPLTL state formulas, the resulting formula is a valid BPLTL formula.*

Therefore, to transform an arbitrary BPLTL formula into the MP-normal form, first replace the top-level state formulas by distinct propositions. The resulting LTL formula can then be transformed into the MP-normal form. Finally, replacing the propositions by the original BPLTL formulas, we get a BPLTL formula in the MP-normal form.

If a formula is in both MP-normal and positive normal form then it is said to be in *MP-positive normal form.*

Lemma 7. *Every BPLTL formula can be transformed into a formula in MP-positive normal form.*

Proof. Given an arbitrary BPLTL formula, first reduce it into MP-normal form. The transformed formula is of the form $\bigwedge_{i=1}^n (\Box\Diamond\kappa_i \vee \Diamond\Box\gamma_i)$. To reduce this formula to PNF we need to reduce the formulas κ_i and γ_i to PNF. This can be done by pushing the negations inwards using dual temporal operators. For example, $\neg(\kappa\mathcal{S}\gamma)$ can be transformed into $\neg\kappa\mathcal{Z}\neg\gamma$. Similarly, $\neg\mathsf{EY}p$ and $\neg\mathsf{E}(p\mathsf{S}q)$ can be transformed into $\mathsf{AY}\neg p$ and $\mathsf{A}(\neg p\mathsf{Z}\neg q)$ respectively.

We use $\mathsf{T}(\kappa)$ to denote the list of top-level state subformulas of κ. We also define the *depth* of an BPLTL formula. Intuitively, this is the nesting of branching modalities in a formula. A formal definition of this concept is as follows.

Definition 8. The depth of a path or state formula η is inductively defined as follows.

- If κ contains no subformulas of the form $\mathsf{E}()$ or $\mathsf{A}()$, $depth(\eta) = 0$.
- For any other formula η, $depth(\eta) = 1 + max\{\, depth(p_i) \mid p_i \in \mathsf{T}(\eta)\,\}$.

Let $\mathsf{T}(\eta) = \langle p_1, \ldots, p_n \rangle$ and $\Phi = \langle \varphi_1, \ldots, \varphi_n \rangle$, i.e., a tuple of state formulas. Define $stat_\Phi(\eta)$ to be the formula obtained by replacing every p_i by φ_i. Note that if η is a path formula then $stat_\Phi(\eta)$ is an LTL formula. If η is a state formula of then $stat_\Phi(\eta)$ is a state formula of depth 1.

We will say that a subformula p of ψ is *negated*, if $\neg p$ is a subformula of ψ. Another important lemma which is needed for the soundness of the proof system is as follows.

Lemma 9 Monotonicity. *Let κ be a BPLTL formula in positive normal form. Let $\kappa[p_1/q_1, \ldots p_n/q_n]$ be the formula obtained by replacing each occurrence of a top-level state formula q_i with state formula p_i. Then $\kappa[p_1/q_1 \ldots p_n/q_n] \Rightarrow \kappa$ if $\forall 1 \leq i \leq n$, $p_i \Rightarrow q_i$.*

3.4 Program Interpretation

We now show how to interpret a concurrent program P as a BPLTL model.

Let $\xi = \langle J, \sigma_0 \rangle, \langle J, \sigma_1 \rangle, \langle J, \sigma_2 \rangle \ldots$ be an execution (fair execution, respectively) sequence of P. We will construct a BPLTL structure $\mathcal{M}_{(\xi,P)}$ for it.

Let $past(\xi) = \{\langle J, \sigma \rangle | \exists \rho \exists i\, \sigma \sqsubseteq \rho \wedge \xi(i) = \langle J, \rho \rangle\}$, and $\prec_\xi = \rhd \cap (past(\xi) \times past(\xi))$. Let Ξ_ξ be the set of finite accessible sequences of the form $s_0 \rhd s_1 \rhd s_2 \rhd \ldots \prec_\xi s_n$ such that $s_0 = \langle J, [\varepsilon] \rangle$, and s_n is in ξ.

For each element ξ of $Exec(P)$ ($FairExec(P)$, respectively), we define the BPLTL structure $\mathcal{M}_{(\xi,P)}$ to be $\langle past(\xi), \langle J, [\varepsilon] \rangle, \prec_\xi, \xi, \Xi_\xi \rangle$. Define the labeling function L_ξ for this structure such that for $\langle J, \sigma \rangle \in past(\xi)$, $L_\xi(\langle J, \sigma \rangle) = fin_{\langle J,\, \sigma \rangle}$. Now, P satisfies a formula κ iff for every $\xi \in Exec(P)$, $\langle \mathcal{M}_{(\xi,P)}, \mathcal{A}, L_\xi \rangle \models \kappa$. The above interpretation gives the semantics when there is no fairness.

Recall that for an augmented program which does not satisfy both the independence conditions, one should provide a specific distinguishing function δ in order to give interpretation for $fin_{\langle J,\, \sigma \rangle}$. For the proof system that follows, it is important that the interpretation would be consistent with the sequence of executed operations forming ξ. This sequence can be defined as $seq(\xi) = x_0\, x_1\, x_2 \ldots$, where for each $i > 0$, $\sigma_i = \sigma_{i-1}[x_i]$. Hence, one can define δ as follows: when $w \in \sigma$ such that w is a prefix of $seq(\xi)$, then $\delta(\sigma) = w$. Otherwise, δ can be defined arbitrarily.

4 A Sound and Complete Proof System

In this section we present a sound and complete proof system for proving BPLTL formulas. The proof rules will be presented separately for the different classes of formulas described in section 3.3.

We first give a brief sketch of how the proof system is used for proving formulas. Given an arbitrary BPLTL formula κ, first transform the formula into the MP-positive normal form (see Section 3.2). If κ is a general path formula then find predicates that *characterize* the formulas in $\top(\kappa)$. That is, if $p_i \in \top(\kappa)$ then find a first order predicate φ_i such that $\varphi_i \Rightarrow p_i$. Moreover, it must hold that P satisfies $stat_{\Phi}(\kappa)$ (thus that φ_i are not 'too strong'). This may require a transformation of the program by augmenting it with history variables. Note that in this case the auxiliary variables used are trace variables. Then replace each p_i in κ by φ_i and prove the resulting LTL formula $stat_{\Phi}(\kappa)$ using a sound and complete proof system for LTL, e.g., [6]. The proof of this formula may again need the use of auxiliary variables, but the auxiliary variables used in this case are sequence variables. Thus, proof of a general path formula is reduced to the proofs of pure LTL formulas and state formulas. A proof rule (STAT) encodes this procedure. Soundness of this rule is a direct consequence of the monotonicity Lemma 9.

We now need to prove that $\varphi_p \Rightarrow p$. The state subformula p itself may contain subformulas of the form E() or A() . Like in the general path formulas case, this can be handled by finding predicates that characterize these formulas. In this case the proof of state formulas of depth d is reduced to the proofs of state formulas of depth $d-1$ and 1. Note that when all the top-level state subformulas of a state formula are replaced by first-order predicates, the resulting formula is of depth 1, i.e., formulas of the form E() and A() such that all the state subformulas are first-order predicates. We give explicit proof rules for such formulas in the sequel.

4.1 Proof Rules for LTL Formulas

For proving pure LTL formulas we use the Manna-Pnueli proof system [6] for LTL. Although the LTL formulas we consider are slightly different from the formulas in their logic (namely, our logic has $\mathcal{Z}$ operator which is absent from their logic), their proof system can be easily adapted.

An interesting feature of the Manna-Pnueli proof system is that it does not have any explicit rules for proving past formulas. Past formulas are eliminated altogether by program transformation. The key idea is to introduce a boolean variable for each past subformula and update it in such a way that the variable is *true* at a particular state iff the corresponding formula holds in that state. For instance, consider the subformula $\kappa = \ominus\varphi$. A corresponding boolean variable b_κ is added to the set of program variables. Now, the transitions of the program are modified in such a way that if at any state φ holds, then every transition taken from that state updates b_κ to true. Note that this kind of transformation works here because the pure past LTL formulas refer to a single distinguished past. When the past is branching, simple boolean variables do not suffice since we would need to keep track of information about all paths that could lead to that state.

4.2 Proof Rules for State Formulas and General Path Formulas

Our proof system includes, as in [6] all the first order tautologies.

Rule 1 EPREV: This is the proof rule for proving properties of the form $\varphi \Rightarrow \mathsf{EY}\psi$. This rule assumes that we are given a certain action τ.

$$\begin{array}{l} \text{C1 } \varphi \Rightarrow \eta \\ \text{C2 } \Theta \Rightarrow \neg\eta \\ \text{C3 } wp_\alpha(\eta) \Rightarrow \text{F for every } \alpha \text{ such that } \alpha \neq \tau \text{ and } (\alpha,\tau) \in D \\ \text{C4 } wp_\alpha(\eta) \Rightarrow \eta \text{ for every } \alpha \text{ such that } (\alpha,\tau) \notin D \\ \text{C5 } wp_\tau(\varphi) \Rightarrow \psi \\ \hline \quad \varphi \Rightarrow \mathsf{EY}\psi \end{array}$$

Rule 2 APREV: This is the proof rule for proving properties of the form $\varphi \Rightarrow \mathsf{AY}\psi$.

$$\frac{\forall \tau \in T\,(wp_\tau(\varphi) \Rightarrow \psi)}{\varphi \Rightarrow \mathsf{AY}\psi}$$

Rule 3 ESINCE: The rule **ESINCE** is used to prove formulas of the form $\varphi \Rightarrow \mathsf{E}(\varphi_1 \mathsf{S} \varphi_2)$.

$$\begin{array}{l} \text{C1 } \varphi \Rightarrow \eta \\ \text{C2 } \eta \Rightarrow \varphi_2 \vee (\varphi_1 \wedge \varphi_3) \\ \text{C3 } \varphi_3 \Rightarrow \mathsf{EY}\eta \\ \hline \quad \varphi \Rightarrow \mathsf{E}(\varphi_1 \mathsf{S} \varphi_2) \end{array}$$

Rule 4 ASINCE: The rule **ASINCE** is used to prove formulas of the form $\varphi \Rightarrow \mathsf{A}(\varphi_1 \mathsf{S} \varphi_2)$

$$\begin{array}{l} \text{C1 } \varphi \Rightarrow \eta \\ \text{C2 } \eta \Rightarrow \varphi_2 \vee (\varphi_1 \wedge \varphi_3) \\ \text{C3 } \varphi_3 \Rightarrow \mathsf{AY}\eta \\ \text{C4 } \varphi_3 \Rightarrow \mathsf{EY}\text{T} \\ \hline \quad \varphi \Rightarrow \mathsf{A}(\varphi_1 \mathsf{S} \varphi_2) \end{array}$$

Rule 5 EREL: The rule **EREL** is used to prove formulas of the form $\varphi \Rightarrow \mathsf{E}(\varphi_1 \mathsf{Z} \varphi_2)$.

$$\begin{array}{l} \text{C1 } \varphi \Rightarrow \eta \\ \text{C2 } \eta \Rightarrow \varphi_2 \wedge (\varphi_1 \vee \varphi_3 \vee \varphi_4) \\ \text{C3 } \varphi_3 \Rightarrow \mathsf{EY}\eta \\ \text{C4 } \varphi_4 \Rightarrow \mathsf{AY}\text{F} \\ \hline \quad \varphi \Rightarrow \mathsf{E}(\varphi_1 \mathsf{Z} \varphi_2) \end{array}$$

Rule 6 AREL: The rule **AREL** is used to prove formulas of the form $\varphi \Rightarrow \mathsf{A}(\varphi_1 \mathsf{Z} \varphi_2)$.

$$\frac{\begin{array}{l}\text{C1 } \varphi \Rightarrow \eta \\ \text{C2 } \eta \Rightarrow \varphi_2 \wedge (\varphi_1 \vee \varphi_3) \\ \text{C3 } \varphi_3 \Rightarrow \mathsf{AY}\eta\end{array}}{\varphi \Rightarrow \mathsf{A}(\varphi_1 \mathsf{Z} \varphi_2)}$$

Rule 7 SPLIT:

$$\frac{\begin{array}{l}\text{C1 } p_1 \Rightarrow p \\ \text{C2 } p_2 \Rightarrow p\end{array}}{p_1 \vee p_2 \Rightarrow p}$$

Rule 8 TRANS:

$$\frac{\begin{array}{l}\text{C1 } p_1 \Rightarrow p_2 \\ \text{C2 } p_2 \Rightarrow p_3\end{array}}{p_1 \Rightarrow p_3}$$

Rule 9 STAT: This proof rule is used for proving general path formulas or state formulas η of arbitrary depth *in positive normal form*. In the former case the application of this rule reduces the proof to the proof of pure LTL formulas and state formulas. In the latter case it reduces the depth of the formula to be proved. Note that this proof rule is sound only if the formula η is in positive normal form.

$$\frac{\begin{array}{l}\forall i\, \varphi_i \Rightarrow p_i \text{ for } \Phi = \langle \varphi_1, \ldots, \varphi_n \rangle \text{ and } \mathsf{T}(\eta) = \langle p_1, \ldots, p_n \rangle \\ \varphi \Rightarrow stat_\Phi(\eta)\end{array}}{\varphi \Rightarrow \eta}$$

Rule 10 TR: This proof rule handles program transformations. Here κ does not refer to any of the auxiliary variables.

$$\frac{\begin{array}{l}P \angle P' \\ P' \models \kappa\end{array}}{P \models \kappa}$$

Due to space limitations, the proofs of soundness and relative completeness of our proof system will appear in the full version.

5 Examples

5.1 Specifying Serializability

Concurrency control of database systems involves executing the user requests in such a way that there is no interference among them. Such requests should behave as if each transaction was executed atomically. Another way of viewing this requirement is that the requests should behave as if they were executed in some serial order. This behavior is commonly referred to as *serializability*. We now show how this property can be specified in BPLTL.

Let $\{T_1, \ldots, T_n\}$ be a set of transactions, where each transaction is a set of atomic transitions. For each transaction T_i we have predicates $start_i$, $active_i$

and $terminated_i$, which are true when the transaction has started, is active, or has terminated, respectively. For each transaction, at any time, exactly one of these predicates is true. Assume each transaction executes once and terminates. The predicate *start* denote $\bigwedge_i start_i$ and *terminated* denote $\bigwedge_i(terminated_i)$. Also let *atomic* denote $\bigwedge_i(active_i \rightarrow \bigwedge_{j \neq i}(\neg active_j))$. Then serializability is specified by the following BPLTL formula.

$$terminated \Rightarrow (\mathsf{E}(atomic\ \mathsf{S}\ start))$$

5.2 Correctness of the Snapshot Algorithm

Another property which can be specified very naturally in BPLTL is the correctness of the Chandy-Lamport snapshot algorithm [2]. This algorithm is superposed on some basic distributed algorithm. The objective is to record a global state of the underlying algorithm. The correctness requirement is that the recorded global state must occur on some path which is equivalent to this path (but not necessarily on the current distinguished path). This can be written in BPLTL as follows:

"the global state recorded is s" $\Rightarrow$ EP "the global state is s"

5.3 A Sample Proof

We now present a small example illustrating how our proof system can be used. It consists of a finite state system, taken from [9]. Notice that albeit the use of a finite state example, the proof system can and is primarily intended to be used for infinite state systems. However, variations of this example have become yardsticks for demonstrating partial order verification methods [9, 12, 16].

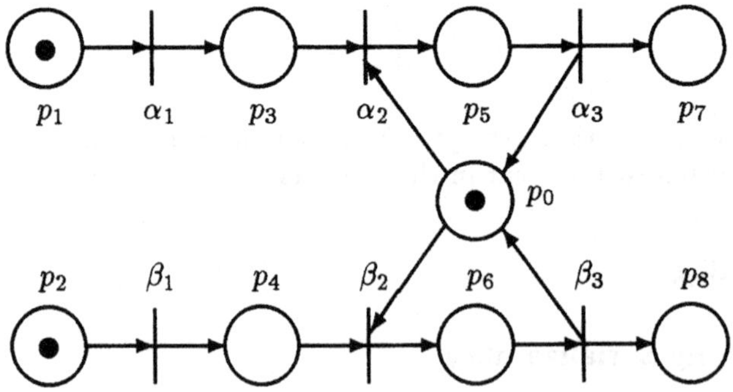

Fig. 2. Net A.

Consider the Net A (understanding Petri-Net notation is not necessary for this example), depicted in Figure 2. Then,

$$T = \{\alpha_1, \alpha_2, \alpha_3, \beta_1, \beta_2, \beta_3\}$$

$$D = Id_T \cup \{(\alpha_i,\ \beta_j) \mid 2 \le i,\ j \le 3\} \cup \{(\beta_i,\ \alpha_j) \mid 2 \le i,\ j \le 3\}$$
$$\cup\{(\alpha_i,\ \alpha_j) \mid i+j \in \{3,\ 5\}\} \cup \{(\beta_i,\ \beta_j) \mid i+j \in \{3,\ 5\}\}$$

The variables associated with the net are $\{p_i \mid 0 \le i \le 8\}$. We use $\{p_{i_1}, \ldots, p_{i_j}\}$ to denote the states where only variables $p_{i_1}, \ldots, p_{i_j}$ are true (viewed in terms of the net, it means that only locations $p_1, \ldots, p_i$ have tokens). The initial condition Θ is $\{p_0, p_1, p_2\}$. The pairs of enabling conditions and transformation functions for each operation are listed below.

$$\alpha_1 : \langle p_1 = 1 \wedge p_3 = 0 \longrightarrow (p_1, p_3) := (0, 1)\rangle$$
$$\beta_1 : \langle p_2 = 1 \wedge p_4 = 0 \longrightarrow (p_2, p_4) := (0, 1)\rangle$$
$$\alpha_2 : \langle p_0 = p_3 = 1 \wedge p_5 = 0 \longrightarrow (p_0, p_3, p_5) := (0, 0, 1)\rangle$$
$$\beta_2 : \langle p_0 = p_4 = 1 \wedge p_6 = 0 \longrightarrow (p_0, p_4, p_6) := (0, 0, 1)\rangle$$
$$\alpha_3 : \langle p_5 = 1 \wedge p_0 = p_7 = 0 \longrightarrow (p_0, p_5, p_7) := (1, 0, 1)\rangle$$
$$\beta_3 : \langle p_6 = 1 \wedge p_0 = p_8 = 0 \longrightarrow (p_0, p_6, p_8) := (1, 0, 1)\rangle$$

This net can be viewed as the concurrency control algorithm for a database. The transactions are $T_1 = \{\alpha_1, \alpha_2, \alpha_3\}$ and $T_2 = \{\beta_1, \beta_2, \beta_3\}$. Dependency between operations α and β means that either both operations belong to the same transaction or they constitute conflicting reads and writes. We want to verify that serializability holds for this system, i.e., the system should behave *as if* each transaction was executed atomically.

Let $start_1 = p_1$, $start_2 = p_2$, $terminated_1 = p_7$, $terminated_2 = p_8$, $active_1 = p_3 \vee p_5$, $active_2 = p_4 \vee p_6$. For simplicity, we use $start = \{p_1, p_2\}$ and $atomic = (\neg active_1 \vee \neg active_2) = \{p_1 \vee p_2 \vee p_7 \vee p_8\}$. It can be easily verified that these predicates are invariantly equivalent to the ones defined in Section 5.1. We need to prove $terminated \Rightarrow \mathsf{E}(atomic\ \mathsf{S}\ start)$.

Finally, let *serial* denote $\{p_1, p_0, p_4\} \vee \{p_1, p_6\} \vee \{p_1, p_0, p_8\} \vee \{p_3, p_0, p_8\} \vee \{p_5, p_8\} \vee \{p_2, p_3, p_0\} \vee \{p_2, p_5\} \vee \{p_2, p_0, p_7\} \vee \{p_4, p_0, p_7\} \vee \{p_6, p_7\} \vee \{p_0, p_7, p_8\}$.

We also need to introduce an auxiliary variable *aux* to distinguish the cases where the program terminates after executing traces $[\alpha_1\alpha_2\alpha_3\beta_2\beta_2\beta_3]$ and $[\beta_2\beta_2\beta_3\alpha_1\alpha_2\alpha_3]$. *aux* is a string and it is initialized to the empty string ϵ. It is updated when either α_2 or β_2 is executed. The transformed operations α_2 and β_2 appear as follows.

$$\alpha_2 : \langle p_0 = p_3 = 1 \wedge p_5 = 0 \longrightarrow (p_0, p_3, p_5, aux) := (0, 0, 1, aux\alpha_2)\rangle$$
$$\beta_2 : \langle p_0 = p_4 = 1 \wedge p_6 = 0 \longrightarrow (p_0, p_4, p_6, aux) := (0, 0, 1, aux\beta_2)\rangle$$

The following table summarizes the proof.

1. $\{p_1, p_0, p_4\} \Rightarrow \mathsf{EY}\ atomic$ [**EPREV**; $\eta = \{p_1, p_0, p_4\}$; $\tau = \beta_1$]
2. $\{p_1, p_6\} \Rightarrow \mathsf{EY}\ atomic$ [**EPREV**; $\eta = \{p_1, p_6\}$;$\tau = \beta_2$]
3. $\{p_1, p_0, p_8\} \Rightarrow \mathsf{EY}\ atomic$ [**EPREV**; $\eta = \{p_1, p_0, p_8\}$; $\tau = \beta_3$]
4. $\{p_3, p_0, p_8\} \Rightarrow \mathsf{EY}\ atomic$ [**EPREV**; $\eta = p_3$; $\tau = \alpha_1$]
5. $\{p_5, p_8\} \Rightarrow \mathsf{EY}\ atomic$ [**EPREV**; $\eta = \{p_5, p_8\}$; $\tau = \alpha_2$]
6. $\{p_2, p_3, p_0\} \Rightarrow \mathsf{EY}\ atomic$ [**EPREV**; $\eta = \{p_2, p_3, p_0\}$; $\tau = \alpha_1$]
7. $\{p_2, p_5\} \Rightarrow \mathsf{EY}\ atomic$ [**EPREV**; $\eta = \{p_2, p_5\}$; $\tau = \alpha_2$]
8. $\{p_2, p_0, p_7\} \Rightarrow \mathsf{EY}\ atomic$ [**EPREV**; $\eta = \{p_2, p_0, p_7\}$; $\tau = \alpha_3$]
9. $\{p_4, p_0, p_7\} \Rightarrow \mathsf{EY}\ atomic$[**EPREV**; $\eta = p_4$; $\tau = \beta_1$]
10. $\{p_6, p_7\} \Rightarrow \mathsf{EY}\ atomic$ [**EPREV**; $\eta = \{p_6, p_7\}$; $\tau = \beta_2$]

11. $(\{p_0, p_7, p_8\} \wedge aux = \alpha_2\beta_2) \Rightarrow \mathsf{EY}\, atomic$ [**EPREV**; $\eta = \{p_0, p_7, p_8\} \wedge aux = \alpha_2\beta_2$; $\tau = \beta_3$]
12. $(\{p_0, p_7, p_8\} \wedge aux = \beta_2\alpha_2) \Rightarrow \mathsf{EY}\, atomic$ [**EPREV**; $\eta = \{p_0, p_7, p_8\} \wedge aux = \beta_2\alpha_2$; $\tau = \alpha_3$]
13. $(\{p_0, p_7, p_8\} \wedge aux = \alpha_2\beta_2) \vee (\{p_0, p_7, p_8\} \wedge aux = \beta_2\alpha_2) \Rightarrow \mathsf{EY} atomic$ [**SPLIT**]
14. $\{p_0, p_7, p_8\} \Rightarrow (\{p_0, p_7, p_8\} \wedge aux = \alpha_2\beta_2) \vee (\{p_0, p_7, p_8\} \wedge aux = \beta_2\alpha_2)$ [LTL proof rules]
15. $\{p_0, p_7, p_8\} \Rightarrow \mathsf{EY}\, atomic$ [**TRANS**]
16. $serial \Rightarrow \mathsf{EY}\, atomic$ [**SPLIT**]
17. $(atomic \wedge \neg start) \Rightarrow serial$ [LTL proof system]
18. $atomic \Rightarrow start \vee (atomic \wedge \neg start)$ [LTL proof system]
19. $atomic \Rightarrow atomic$ [Tautology]
20. $atomic \Rightarrow \mathsf{E}(atomic\ \mathsf{S}\ start)$ [**ESINCE**; $\eta = atomic$; $\varphi_3 = (atomic \wedge \neg start)$]
21. $terminated \Rightarrow atomic$ [LTL proof system]
22. $terminated \Rightarrow \mathsf{E}(atomic\ \mathsf{S}\ start)$ [**TRANS**]

The above proof was for the transformed program. Using the **TR** proof rule it can be shown that the property holds for the original program as well.

6 Conclusions

In this paper, a new approach for modeling and reasoning about concurrent systems was presented. Executions are described using a distinguished linear execution sequence, where each state on this sequence is equipped with a branching past, representing all the alternative equivalent ways to reach it. This approach is best suited for cases where some states that do not appear on the main linear execution are important. The logic BPLTL was presented for reasoning about such structures. We presented a sound and relatively complete proof system for transition programs, in the style of Manna and Pnueli [6].

The proof system provided here avoids some difficulties of the ISTL approach; whereas the ISTL proof system in [9] uses forward-backward reasoning for future ISTL properties, the logic BPLTL forces properties that explicitly express the forward-backward character of the property. Moreover, limiting the logic to linear future and branching past was useful in obtaining a relatively complete proof system for the *entire logic* (which is not the case in [9], where the proof system includes only a part of the ISTL properties).

One advantage of the ISTL approach is however that it allows verifying properties of interleaving sequences using convenient sequences (when the property does not distinguish between equivalent sequences but the proof over some sequences is simpler than over others) [5]. This approach can be combined with the BPLTL proof system, by allowing ISTL proof rules for the future part of BPLTL for properties that do not distinguish between equivalent sequences. Identifying such properties can be done using a new PSPACE decision procedure [10].

It is not difficult to construct, along the same lines of our work, a sound and relatively complete proof system for a subset of the logic CTL_P. However, for the full CTL_P, which allows *future* branching subformulas to be nested within *past* subformulas this is still an open problem.

Acknowledgement

The authors wish to thank Amir Pnueli for insightful comments he has made during a previous joint work ([9]), which have inspired this work.

References

1. R. Alur W. Penczek, D. Peled, Model-Checking of Causality Properties, *10th Symposium on Logic in Computer Science*, IEEE, 1995, 90–100, San Diego, California, USA.
2. K. M. Chandy, L. Lamport, Distributed Snapshots: determining the global state of distributed systems, *ACM Transactions on Computer Systems* 3 (1985), 63–75.
3. D. Harel, *First order Dynamic Logic*, Lecture Notes in Computer Science 68, Springer, 1979.
4. S. Katz, D. Peled, Interleaving Set Temporal Logic, Theoretical Computer Science, Vol. 75, Number 3, 21–43
5. S. Katz, D. Peled, Verification of Distributed Programs using Representative Interleaving Sequences, *Distributed Computing* 6 (1992) 107–120.
6. Z. Manna, A. Pnueli, Completing the Temporal Picture, *Proceedings 16th International Colloquium on Automata, Languages and Programming*, Lecture Notes in Computer Science 372, Springer, 1989, 534–558.
7. A. Mazurkiewicz, Trace semantics, in: W. Brauer, W. Reisig, G. Rozenberg (eds.) *Proceedings of Advances in Petri Nets* 1986, Bad Honnef, Lecture Notes in Computer Science 255, Springer, 1987, 279–324.
8. D. Peled, S. Katz, A. Pnueli, Specifying and Proving Serializability in Temporal Logic, *6th IEEE annual symposium on Logic in Computer Science*, Amsterdam, The Netherlands, July 1991, 232–245.
9. D. Peled, A. Pnueli, Proving partial order properties. *Theoretical Computer Science* 126, 143–182, 1994.
10. D. Peled, Th. Wilke, P. Wolper, An Algorithmic Approach for Checking Closure Properties of ω-Regular Languages, CONCUR'96, *7th International Conference on Concurrency Theory*, Pisa, Italy, 1996.
11. W. Penczek, Temporal Logics for Trace Systems: On Automated Verification, *International Journal of Foundations of Computer Science*, 4 (1993), 31-67.
12. W. Penczek, R. Kuiper, Traces and Logic, in V. Diekert, G. Rozenberg (eds.) *The Book of Traces*, World Scientific, 1995, 307–390.
13. S. Pinter, P. Wolper, A temporal logic for reasoning about partially ordered computations, *3rd ACM Symposium on Principles of Distributed Computing*, Vancouver, B. C., Canada, August 1984, 23–27.
14. V. Pratt, Modeling concurrency with partial orders, *International Journal of Parallel Programming*, 15 (1986), 33–71.
15. W. Reisig, Partial order semantics versus interleaving semantics for CSP like languages and its impact on fairness. *Proc. 11th International Colloquium on Automata, Languages and Programming*, Lecture Notes in Computer Science 172, 1984, Springer, 403–413.
16. W. Reisig, Interleaved Progress, Concurrent Progress and Local Progress, in D. Peled, V. Pratt, G. Holzmann (eds.), *Partial Order Methods in Verification*, AMS, to appear, 1997.
17. P.S. Thiagarajan, A Trace Based Extension of Linear Time Temporal Logic. *Proceedings of 10th IEEE Logic in Computer Science*, 1994.

Reachability Analysis of Pushdown Automata: Application to Model-Checking

Ahmed Bouajjani[1] Javier Esparza[2*] Oded Maler[1]

[1] VERIMAG, Centre Equation, 2 av. de Vignate, 38610 Gières, France.
email: Ahmed.Bouajjani@imag.fr, Oded.Maler@imag.fr
[2] Inst. für Informatik, Tech. Univ. München, Arcisstr. 21, 81539 München, Germany.
email: esparza@informatik.tu-muenchen.de

Abstract. We apply the *symbolic* analysis principle to pushdown systems. We represent (possibly infinite) sets of configurations of such systems by means of finite-state automata. In order to reason in a uniform way about analysis problems involving both existential and universal path quantification (such as model-checking for branching-time logics), we consider the more general class of *alternating* pushdown systems and use *alternating* finite-state automata as a representation structure for sets of their configurations. We give a simple and natural procedure to compute sets of predecessors using this representation structure. We incorporate this procedure into the automata-theoretic approach to model-checking to define new model-checking algorithms for pushdown systems against both linear and branching-time properties. From these results we derive upper bounds for several model-checking problems as well as matching lower bounds.

1 Introduction

Systems are commonly modeled by various types of transition systems, including finite automata, pushdown automata, Petri nets, timed or hybrid automata, etc. In this framework, most of the system analysis problems (model-checking, synthesis) reduce to various kinds of "reachability problems" on these models. It is therefore fundamental for system analysis to develop algorithms that compute the set of *all predecessors* of a given set of states S, i.e., the set of states from which it is possible to reach S.

Let $pre(S)$ denote the set of immediate predecessors (via a single transition) of the set S, and let $pre^*(S)$ denote the set of all its predecessors. Clearly, $pre^*(S)$ is the limit of the *infinite* increasing sequence $\{X_i\}_{i\geq 0}$ given by $X_0 = S$ and $X_{i+1} = X_i \cup pre(X_i)$ for every $i \geq 0$.

In the case of finite-state systems, the sets X_i are all finite, and the sequence $\{X_i\}_{i\geq 0}$ is guaranteed to reach a fixpoint, which immediately provides an algorithm to compute $pre^*(S)$. Unfortunately, these properties no longer hold for any non-trivial class of infinite-state systems. For such systems, the first task is then to find a class of *finite* structures that can represent the infinite sets of states we are

* Supported by the University Joseph Fourier (Grenoble I) and by Teilprojekt A3 of the Sonderforschungsbereich 342.

interested in. Since boolean combinations of sets of states are usually interesting, the class should be closed under boolean operations. Moreover, since we wish to check if a given state (for instance the initial state) belongs to an infinite set, the membership problem of the class should be decidable. Once such a class has been found, it remains to show that it is (effectively) closed under the pre^* function.

Several instances of systems and their corresponding representation structures have been considered in the literature. For example, in the case of timed automata, special kinds of polyhedra (regions) are used to represent infinite sets of states (vectors of reals corresponding to clock valuations) [3]. Polyhedra are also used for linear hybrid systems. However, in this case, there is no algorithm for computing a finite representation of the *exact* set of predecessors (the reachability problem is undecidable), but upper approximations of this set can be calculated [2]. In [5], representation structures called QDD's are introduced for FIFO-channel systems. These structures are finite-state automata representing sets of queue contents. As in the case of linear hybrid systems, the procedure for calculating the set of predecessors for these structures is not guaranteed to terminate. Finally, notice that symbolic representations (e.g. BDD's [10]) are also used in the finite-state case in order to overcome the state-explosion problem [17].

In this paper we consider pushdown systems,as well as the more general class of *alternating pushdown systems*, i.e., pushdown systems with both existential and universal nondeterminism (see [20] for a survey on alternating automata). This general setting allows to reason in a uniform way about *analysis* problems where existential and universal path quantification must be considered, like model-checking for branching-time temporal logics (see Section 5) and also about *synthesis* problems, such as finding winning strategies for 2-player games (see [4]).

A state (we use rather the word "configuration") of a pushdown system is a pair $\langle p, w \rangle$ where p is control location and w is a sequence of stack symbols (the stack contents). As a representation structure for sets of configurations, we propose the *alternating multi-automaton* (AMA), an alternating finite-state automaton with one initial state for each control location. The automaton recognizes the configuration $\langle p, w \rangle$ if it accepts the word w from the initial state corresponding to p. It is important to remember that an AMA is just a tool to represent a set of configurations, and not to confuse its "behaviour" with that of the pushdown system.

It is easy to show that AMA's are closed under boolean operations, and that its membership problem is decidable. Our main result is a simple and natural algorithm for computing the pre^* function. As an application, we construct elegant model-checking algorithms for pushdown systems w.r.t. both linear and branching-time temporal logics. More precisely, we show how to construct AMA's accepting the set of *all* configurations satisfying ω-regular properties of linear-time temporal logics (including all properties expressible in LTL [18] or the linear-time μ-calculus [19]), or properties expressed as formulas of the alternation-free modal μ-calculus. A first version of these results appeared in [8] (where the logic CTL [13] is considered instead of the more expressive alternation-free modal μ-calculus).

Moreover, our approach allows us to obtain a number of complexity results: we show that the model-checking problems mentioned above are in DEXPTIME, and that the model-checking problem for pushdown systems and a subset of CTL can be solved in PSPACE. Using a technique due to Walukiewicz [22], we complement these results with matching lower bounds, i.e., we show that all these problems are complete for their corresponding complexity classes.

The paper is structured as follows. In Section 2, we give an algorithm which computes the *pre** function for pushdown systems. In this case, the representation structure is a simple nondeterministic multi-automaton (i.e., without alternation). We apply this algorithm in Section 3 to the model-checking problem for linear-time logics. In Section 4, we generalize the algorithm given in Section 2 to alternating pushdown systems. In Section 5, we apply the new algorithm to the model-checking problem for branching-time logics. Proofs of the theorems can be found in the full paper [7].

2 Reachability in pushdown systems

2.1 Pushdown Systems

A pushdown system (PDS for short) is a triplet $\mathcal{P} = (P, \Gamma, \Delta)$ where P is a finite set of *control locations*, Γ is a finite *stack alphabet*, and $\Delta \subseteq (P \times \Gamma) \times (P \times \Gamma^*)$ is a finite set of *transition rules*. If $((q,\gamma),(q',w)) \in \Delta$ then we write $(q,\gamma) \hookrightarrow (q',w)$ (we reserve $\rightarrow$ to denote the transition relations of finite automata).

Notice that PDS's have no input alphabet. We do not use them as language acceptors but are rather interested in the behaviours they generate.

A *configuration* of $\mathcal{P}$ is a pair $\langle p, w\rangle$ where $p \in P$ is a control location and $w \in \Gamma^*$ is a *stack content*.

If $(q,\gamma) \hookrightarrow (q',w)$, then for every $w' \in \Gamma^*$ the configuration $\langle q, \gamma w'\rangle$ is an *immediate predecessor* of $\langle q', ww'\rangle$, and $\langle q', ww'\rangle$ is an *immediate successor* of $\langle q, \gamma w'\rangle$. The *reachability relation* $\Rightarrow$ is the reflexive and transitive closure of the immediate successor relation. A *run* of $\mathcal{P}$ is a maximal sequence of configurations such that for each two consecutive configurations c_i and c_{i+1}, c_{i+1} is an immediate successor of c_i. The set of all runs of $\mathcal{P}$ is denoted by $Runs_{\mathcal{P}}$.

The predecessor function $pre_{\mathcal{P}} : 2^{P\times\Gamma^*} \rightarrow 2^{P\times\Gamma^*}$ is defined as follows: c belongs to $pre_{\mathcal{P}}(C)$ if some immediate successor of c belongs to C. The reflexive and transitive closure of $pre_{\mathcal{P}}$ is denoted by $pre^*_{\mathcal{P}}$. Clearly, $pre^*_{\mathcal{P}}(C) = \{c \in P \times \Gamma^* \mid \exists c' \in C.\, c \Rightarrow c'\}$. We denote by $pre^+_{\mathcal{P}}$ the function $pre_{\mathcal{P}} \circ pre^*_{\mathcal{P}}$. We will omit the subscript $\mathcal{P}$ and write simply *pre*, *pre**, and *pre*$^+$ when it is clear from the context which system is under consideration.

2.2 Multi-automata

Let $\mathcal{P} = (P, \Gamma, \Delta)$ be a pushdown system where $P = \{p^1, \ldots p^m\}$. A $\mathcal{P}$-*multi-automaton* ($\mathcal{P}$-MA for short, or just MA when $\mathcal{P}$ is clear from the context) is a tuple $\mathcal{A} = (\Gamma, Q, \delta, I, F)$ where Q is a finite set of *states*, $\delta \subseteq Q \times \Gamma \times Q$ is a set of *transitions*, $I = \{s^1, \ldots s^m\} \subseteq Q$ is a set of *initial states* and $F \subseteq Q$ is a set of *final states*.

We define the *transition relation* $\longrightarrow \subseteq Q \times \Gamma^* \times Q$ as the smallest relation satisfying:

- if $(q,\gamma,q') \in \delta$ then $q \xrightarrow{\gamma} q'$,

- $q \xrightarrow{\varepsilon} q$ for every $q \in Q$, and
- if $q \xrightarrow{w} q''$ and $q'' \xrightarrow{\gamma} q'$ then $q \xrightarrow{w\gamma} q'$.

$\mathcal{A}$ *accepts* or *recognizes* a configuration $\langle p^i, w\rangle$ if $s^i \xrightarrow{w} q$ for some $q \in F$. The set of configurations recognized by $\mathcal{A}$ is denoted by $Conf(\mathcal{A})$. A set of configurations is *regular* if it is recognized by some MA.

A w-*run* of $\mathcal{A}$, where $w = \gamma_1 \ldots \gamma_n \in \Gamma^*$, is a sequence $s^i \xrightarrow{\gamma_1} q_1 \ldots \xrightarrow{\gamma_n} q_n$.

2.3 Calculating pre^*

Fix a pushdown system $\mathcal{P} = (P, \Gamma, \Delta)$ where $P = \{p^1, \ldots, p^m\}$. We show in this section that given a regular set of configurations C of $\mathcal{P}$ recognized by a MA $\mathcal{A}$, we can construct another MA $\mathcal{A}_{pre^*}$ recognizing $pre^*(C)$.

By definition, $pre^*(C) = \bigcup_{i \geq 0} X_i$ with $X_0 = C$ and $X_{i+1} = X_i \cup pre(X_i)$ for every $i \geq 0$. Therefore, one may try to calculate $pre^*(C)$ by iteratively constructing the increasing sequence $X_0, X_1, \ldots$. If $X_{i+1} = X_i$ holds for some $i \geq 0$, then it is clear that $X_i = pre^*(C)$.

However, the existence of such a fixed point is not guaranteed in general, and we may never reach the limit of the X_i sequence. Consider for instance the PDS with one state p, one stack symbol γ, and one transition rule $(p, \gamma) \hookrightarrow (p, \varepsilon)$, and take $C = \{\langle p, \varepsilon\rangle\}$. Clearly, we have $X_i = \{\langle p, \varepsilon\rangle, \langle p, \gamma\rangle, \ldots, \langle p, \gamma^i\rangle\}$ and so $X_{i+1} \neq X_i$ for every $i \geq 0$.

To overcome this problem, we calculate $pre^*(C)$ differently, as the limit of another increasing sequence of sets of configurations $Y_0, Y_1, \ldots$ for which we can prove the following properties:

P1. $\exists i \geq 0.\ Y_{i+1} = Y_i$,
P2. $\forall i \geq 0.\ X_i \subseteq Y_i$,
P3. $\forall i \geq 0.\ Y_i \subseteq \bigcup_{j \geq 0} X_j \ = pre^*(C)$.

Property (P1) ensures termination of the procedure that computes the sequence of Y_i's. Property (P2) ensures that, by calculating the limit of the Y_i's, we capture (at least) the whole set $pre^*(C)$, and property (P3) ensures that only elements of $pre^*(C)$ are captured.

The Y_i's are formally defined as the sets of configurations recognized by a sequence $\mathcal{A}_0, \mathcal{A}_1 \ldots$ of MA's satisfying for every $i \geq 0$ the following property: $\mathcal{A}_{i+1}$ has *the same states* as $\mathcal{A}_i$, and possibly a superset of its transitions. Since a MA with n states and m input symbols can have at most $n^2 \cdot m$ transitions, the Y_i's must converge to a fixpoint.[3]

We start with a MA $\mathcal{A}$ recognizing the regular set of configurations C. We assume without loss of generality that $\mathcal{A}$ has no transition leading to an initial state (every MA can be converted to one having this property). We take $\mathcal{A}_0 = \mathcal{A}$. We denote by $\rightarrow_i$ the transition relation of $\mathcal{A}_i$. For every $i \geq 0$, $\mathcal{A}_{i+1}$ is obtained from $\mathcal{A}_i$ by conserving the same states and transitions, and adding for every transition rule

[3] The idea is inspired by the construction given in [6], pages 91-93, of a finite-state automaton recognizing the closure of a regular language under the rewriting relation induced by a *monadic string-rewriting system*.

$(p^j, \gamma) \hookrightarrow (p^k, w)$ and every state q such that $s^k \xrightarrow{w}_i q$ a new transition $s^j \xrightarrow{\gamma}_{i+1} q$. Then, for every $i \geq 0$ we define $Y_i = Conf(\mathcal{A}_i)$. Note that the new transitions added to $\mathcal{A}_i$ in order to construct $\mathcal{A}_{i+1}$ start at initial states.

To understand the idea behind this construction, observe that $\langle p^k, \gamma w' \rangle$ is an immediate predecessor of $\langle p^j, ww' \rangle$ by the rule $(p^j, \gamma) \hookrightarrow (p^k, w)$. So, if the word ww' is accepted starting from s^k by $\mathcal{A}_i$ ($s^k \xrightarrow{w}_i q \xrightarrow{w'}_i q' \in F$), then the new transition in $\mathcal{A}_{i+1}$ allows to accept $\gamma w'$ starting from s^j ($s^j \xrightarrow{\gamma}_{i+1} q \xrightarrow{w'}_i q' \in F$). Let us illustrate the construction by means of an example.

Let $\mathcal{P}$ be the PDS such that $P = \{p^1, p^2\}$, $\Gamma = \{\gamma_1, \ldots, \gamma_6\}$, and Δ contains the rules

$$(p^2, \gamma_4) \hookrightarrow (p^2, \gamma_1\gamma_2) \quad (p^1, \gamma_5) \hookrightarrow (p^2, \gamma_4\gamma_3) \quad (p^1, \gamma_6) \hookrightarrow (p^1, \varepsilon)$$

Consider the set of configurations $C = \{\langle p^2, \gamma_1\gamma_2\gamma_3 \rangle\}$. It can be represented by a MA $\mathcal{A}$ such that $Q = \{s^1, s^2, q_1, q_2, q_3\}$, $I = \{s^1, s^2\}$, $F = \{q_3\}$, and δ contains the transitions $s^2 \xrightarrow{\gamma_1} q_1$, $q_1 \xrightarrow{\gamma_2} q_2$, and $q_2 \xrightarrow{\gamma_3} q_3$.

The picture below shows the automaton $\mathcal{A}_{pre^*}$ obtained at the end of the construction.

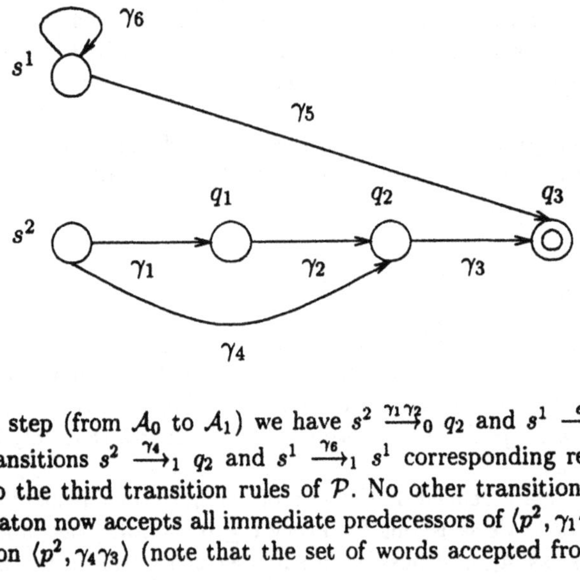

In the first step (from $\mathcal{A}_0$ to $\mathcal{A}_1$) we have $s^2 \xrightarrow{\gamma_1\gamma_2}_0 q_2$ and $s^1 \xrightarrow{\epsilon}_0 s^1$, and so we add the transitions $s^2 \xrightarrow{\gamma_4}_1 q_2$ and $s^1 \xrightarrow{\gamma_6}_1 s^1$ corresponding respectively to the first and to the third transition rules of $\mathcal{P}$. No other transitions are added. The new automaton now accepts all immediate predecessors of $\langle p^2, \gamma_1\gamma_2\gamma_3 \rangle$, namely the configuration $\langle p^2, \gamma_4\gamma_3 \rangle$ (note that the set of words accepted from s^1 is empty at this step).

In the second step, we add the transition $s^1 \xrightarrow{\gamma_5}_2 q_3$, corresponding to the second transition rule of $\mathcal{P}$. At this point the construction stops since no further transition must be added. So, we have $\mathcal{A}_{pre^*} = \mathcal{A}_2$, and

$$pre^*(C) = (\{p^1\} \times \gamma_6^*\gamma_5) \cup (\{p^2\} \times \{\gamma_1\gamma_2\gamma_3, \gamma_4\gamma_3\})$$

Observe that in this example we have $X_1 = Y_1$ but $X_2 \subset Y_2$. Indeed, in the second step of the construction, after adding $s^1 \xrightarrow{\gamma_5}_2 q_3$, $\mathcal{A}_2$ accepts all the configurations of the form $\langle p^1, \gamma_6^k\gamma_5 \rangle$ for every $k \geq 0$, whereas only $\langle p^1, \gamma_5 \rangle$ belongs to X_2. However, despite the fact that these configurations are not immediate predecessors of X_1 configurations, they are all in $pre^*(C)$ because $\langle p^1, \gamma_6^k \gamma_5 \rangle \in X_{k+2}$ for every $k \geq 0$.

The proofs of the properties (P1), (P2), and (P3) are given in the full paper. We deduce from these properties the following theorem.

Theorem 2.1 *Given a PDS $\mathcal{P}$ and a regular set of configurations recognized by a $\mathcal{P}$-MA $\mathcal{A}$, we can construct a $\mathcal{P}$-MA $\mathcal{A}_{pre^*}$ recognizing $pre^*(Conf(\mathcal{A}))$.*

We conclude the section with a remark on complexity. In order to construct $\mathcal{A}_{i+1}$ from $\mathcal{A}_i$, we compute for each transition rule $\langle p, \gamma \rangle \hookrightarrow \langle p', w \rangle$ of the PDS $\mathcal{P}$ the set of states q such that $s' \xrightarrow{w}_i q$, and then add the transition $s \xrightarrow{\gamma}_{i+1} q$ to $\mathcal{A}_{i+1}$. The computation time of the set is quadratic in the number of states of $\mathcal{A}_i$ (which is equal to the number of states of $\mathcal{A}$) and linear in the length of w ([1], Theorem 9.5). Thus, the construction of $\mathcal{A}_{i+1}$ from $\mathcal{A}_i$ takes time $O(|\mathcal{A}|^2 \cdot |\mathcal{P}|^2)$.

Now, the sequence $\mathcal{A}_0, \mathcal{A}_1, \ldots$ must reach the fixpoint $\mathcal{A}_{pre^*}$ after at most $O(|\mathcal{A}|^2 \cdot |\mathcal{P}|)$ steps, because this is an upper bound on the number of transitions of any $\mathcal{P}$-MA having the same states as $\mathcal{A}$. So the computation of $\mathcal{A}_{pre^*}$ takes $O(|\mathcal{A}|^4 \cdot |\mathcal{P}|^3)$ time.

3 Model-Checking Linear-Time Temporal Logics

Let *Prop* be a finite set of atomic propositions, and let $\Sigma = 2^{Prop}$. It is well known that the semantics of properties expressed in linear time temporal logics like LTL or the linear-time μ-calculus are ω-regular sets over the alphabet Σ. Moreover, there exist algorithms which construct Büchi automata to recognize these sets [21, 20]. This is all we need to know about these logics in this paper in order to give model checking algorithms for PDS's.

Let $\mathcal{P} = (P, \Gamma, \Delta)$ be a PDS, and let $\Lambda: P \to \Sigma$ be a labelling function, which associates a set of true propositions with every control location p. Given a formula φ of such an ω-regular logic we wish to solve the following problem:

> Compute the set of *all* configurations c of $\mathcal{P}$ such that every run starting from c satisfies φ (via the labelling function Λ).

Then, the model checking problem consists in checking whether a given initial configuration belongs to this set of configurations.

We start by constructing a Büchi automaton $\mathcal{B}$ corresponding to the negation of φ. The product of the PDS $\mathcal{P}$ and this Büchi automaton yields a Büchi PDS $\mathcal{BP}$ with a set of *repeating control locations* $G \subseteq P$. Then, the original problem reduces straightforwardly to the following *accepting run problem*:

> Compute the set C of configurations c of $\mathcal{BP}$ such that $\mathcal{BP}$ has an accepting run starting from c (i.e., a run which visits infinitely often configurations with control locations in G).

(Notice that the emptiness problem of Büchi PDS's - whether the initial configuration has an accepting run - reduces to the accepting run problem via the membership problem of MA).

The following proposition shows that the accepting run problem of Büchi PDS's can be reduced to a reachability problem:

Proposition 3.1 *Let c be a configuration of a Büchi PDS $\mathcal{BP}$. $\mathcal{BP}$ has an accepting run starting from c if and only if there exist configurations $\langle p, \gamma \rangle$, $\langle g, u \rangle$, and $\langle p, \gamma v \rangle$, not all three equal, such that $g \in G$ and:*

(1) $c \Rightarrow \langle p, \gamma w \rangle$ for some $w \in \Gamma^*$, and
(2) $\langle p, \gamma \rangle \Rightarrow \langle g, u \rangle \Rightarrow \langle p, \gamma v \rangle$.

We can reformulate conditions (1) and (2) of Proposition 3.1 as follows:

(1′) $c \in pre^*(\{p\} \times \gamma\Gamma^*)$, and
(2′) $\langle p, \gamma \rangle \in pre^+((G \times \Gamma^*) \cap pre^*(\{p\} \times \gamma\Gamma^*))$.

Since $G \times \Gamma^*$ and $\{p\} \times \gamma\Gamma^*$ are regular sets, we can use Theorem 2.1 to construct MA's recognizing the sets $pre^*(\{p\} \times \gamma\Gamma^*)$ and $pre^+((G \times \Gamma^*) \cap pre^*(\{p\} \times \gamma\Gamma^*))$ (for pre^+ we need to define for a MA $\mathcal{A}$ another MA recognizing $pre(Conf(\mathcal{A}))$, which is a simple exercise). Therefore, by Proposition 3.1, we can construct a MA which recognizes the set of all configurations having an accepting run: First, we determine all the configurations $\langle p, \gamma \rangle$ (there are finitely many of them) for which (2′) holds, and then we construct a MA recognizing the union of the sets $pre^*(\{p\} \times \gamma\Gamma^*)$ for all such pairs.

The sizes of the MA's for the sets $G \times \Gamma^*$ and $\{p\} \times \gamma\Gamma^*$ are polynomial in the size of the Büchi PDS. Hence, since the computation of $pre^*_{\mathcal{P}}(Conf(\mathcal{A}))$ for a MA $\mathcal{A}$ takes polynomial time in the size of $\mathcal{P}$ and the number of states of $\mathcal{A}$, we deduce the following result:

Theorem 3.1 *The accepting run problem of Büchi PDS's can be solved in polynomial time.*

Since the membership problem of MA's can be solved in linear time, a consequence of Theorem 3.1 is that the emptiness problem of Büchi PDS's can also be solved in polynomial time.

Theorem 3.2 *The model checking problems for LTL and the linear-time μ-calculus and PDS's are DEXPTIME-complete. The model checking problem for a fixed formula is polynomial in the size of the PDS.*

Proof. Let us first prove membership in DEXPTIME. Let $\mathcal{P}$ be a PDS of size $n_{\mathcal{P}}$ and φ a formula of length n_φ. It is well known that it is possible to construct a Büchi automaton $\mathcal{B}$ for the negation of φ having exponential size in n_φ, and this construction can be done in exponential time [21, 19]. Hence, the product of $\mathcal{P}$ and $\mathcal{B}$ has polynomial size in $n_{\mathcal{P}}$ and exponential size on n_φ. Applying Theorem 3.1 we obtain an exponential time bound. If the formula φ is fixed, then we have an algorithm polynomial in $n_{\mathcal{P}}$.

To prove hardness, we use a reduction from the problem of deciding whether a given linearly bounded alternating Turing machine accepts a given input or not. The details of the reduction are given in the full paper. □

The model-checking problem for LTL or the linear-time μ-calculus and finite-state systems is known to be PSPACE-complete, but polynomial in the size of the system. Since the properties of systems one wishes to check can be usually encoded into short formulas, model-checkers based on linear-time logics, like SPIN [16], have proved to be useful in practice. Theorem 3.2 shows that the complexity of model-checking for PDS's is worse than the complexity for finite-state systems, but not much worse: it remains polynomial in the size of the system.

4 Reachability in Alternating Pushdown Systems

4.1 Alternating Pushdown Systems

We consider now the problem of computing the set of predecessors of a regular set of configurations of an *alternating* pushdown system. We show that this set is also regular, and we give a procedure for constructing its representation by means of *alternating* finite-state multi-automata. To this end, we generalize the technique described in the Section 2. The construction we give is used in the model checking algorithms for branching-time logics given in the next section.

An *alternating pushdown system* (APDS for short) is a triplet $\mathcal{P} = (P, \Gamma, \Delta)$, where P and Γ are as for PDSs, and Δ is a function that assigns to each element of $P \times \Gamma$ a negation-free boolean formula over elements of $P \times \Gamma^*$. We assume that boolean formulae are always in disjunctive normal form, which allows us to equivalently define Δ as a subset of the set $(P \times \Gamma) \times 2^{P \times \Gamma^*}$ of *transition rules*: for example, instead of writing

$$\Delta(p, \gamma) = ((p_1, w_1) \vee (p_2, w_2)) \wedge (p_3, w_3)$$

we write

$$\{ ((p, \gamma), \{(p_1, w_1), (p_3, w_3)\}) \, , \; ((p, \gamma), \{(p_2, w_2), (p_3, w_3)\}) \} \subseteq \Delta$$

or just

$$(p, \gamma) \hookrightarrow \{(p_1, w_1), (p_3, w_3)\} \, , \; (p, \gamma) \hookrightarrow \{(p_2, w_2), (p_3, w_3)\}$$

If $(p, \gamma) \hookrightarrow \{(p_1, w_1), \ldots, (p_n, w_n)\}$, then for every $w \in \Gamma^*$ the configuration $\langle p, \gamma w \rangle$ is an *immediate predecessor* of the set $\{\langle p_1, w_1 w \rangle, \ldots, \langle p_n, w_n w \rangle\}$, and this set is an *immediate successor* of $\langle p, \gamma w \rangle$. Intuitively, at the configuration $\langle p, \gamma w \rangle$ the APDS selects nondeterministically a transition rule of the form

$$(p, \gamma) \hookrightarrow \{(p_1, w_1), \ldots, (p_n, w_n)\}$$

and forks into n copies in the configurations $\langle p_1, w_1 w \rangle, \ldots, \langle p_n, w_n w \rangle$.

A *run* of $\mathcal{P}$ for an initial configuration c is a tree of configurations with root c, such that the children of a node c' are the configurations that belong to one of its immediate successors (nodes of the form $\langle p, \varepsilon \rangle$ have no successors).

We define the *reachability relation* $\Rightarrow \subseteq (P \times \Gamma^*) \times 2^{P \times \Gamma^*}$ between configurations and sets of configurations. Informally, $c \Rightarrow C$ if and only if C is a finite frontier (finite maximal set of incomparable nodes) of a run of $\mathcal{P}$ starting from c. Formally, $\Rightarrow$ is the smallest subset of $(P \times \Gamma^*) \times 2^{P \times \Gamma^*}$ such that:

1. $c \Rightarrow \{c\}$ for every $c \in P \times \Gamma^*$,
2. if c is an immediate predecessor of C, then $c \Rightarrow C$,

3. if $c \Rightarrow \{c_1, \ldots, c_n\}$ and $c_i \Rightarrow C_i$ for each $1 \leq i \leq n$, then $c \Rightarrow (C_1 \cup \ldots \cup C_n)$.

The function $pre_\mathcal{P}: 2^{P\times\Gamma^*} \to 2^{P\times\Gamma^*}$ is now defined as follows: c belongs to $pre_\mathcal{P}(C)$ if some immediate successor of c is contained in C (observe that the immediate successor of c is now a set). We denote by $pre^*_\mathcal{P}$ the transitive closure of $\lambda C. (C \cup pre_\mathcal{P}(C))$, i.e., given a set of configurations C, $pre^*_\mathcal{P}(C) = \bigcup_{i\geq 0} X_i$, where $X_0 = C$ and $X_{i+1} = X_i \cup pre_\mathcal{P}(X_i)$, for every $i \geq 0$. As in the case of PDS's, $pre^*_\mathcal{P}(C) = \{c \in P \times \Gamma^* \mid \exists C' \subseteq C. \, c \Rightarrow C'\}$.

4.2 Alternating multi-automata

Fix an APDS $\mathcal{P} = (P, \Gamma, \Delta)$. An *alternating $\mathcal{P}$-multi-automaton* ($\mathcal{P}$-AMA for short, or just AMA when $\mathcal{P}$ is clear from the context) is a tuple $\mathcal{A} = (\Gamma, Q, \delta, I, F)$ which differs from an MA only in the nature of δ. δ is now a function that assigns to every pair of $Q \times \Gamma$ a positive boolean formula with Q as set of variables. As in the case of APDSs, we can equivalently represent δ as a set of transitions, which are elements of $(Q \times \Gamma) \times 2^Q$.

The *transition relation* $\rightarrow \subseteq Q \times \Gamma^* \times 2^Q$ is the smallest relation satisfying

- if $(q, \gamma, Q') \in \delta$ then $q \xrightarrow{\gamma} Q'$,
- $q \xrightarrow{\varepsilon} \{q\}$ for every $q \in Q$,
- if $q \xrightarrow{w} \{q_1, \ldots, q_n\}$ and $q_i \xrightarrow{\gamma} Q_i$ for each $1 \leq i \leq n$, then $q \xrightarrow{w\gamma} (Q_1 \cup \ldots \cup Q_n)$.

A configuration $\langle p^i, w\rangle$ is *recognized* by $\mathcal{A}$ if $s^i \xrightarrow{w} Q'$ for some $Q' \subseteq F$. Given a finite sequence $w \in \Gamma^*$ and a state $q \in Q$, a *run* of $\mathcal{A}$ over w starting from q is a finite tree whose nodes are labelled by states in Q and whose edges are labelled by symbols in Γ, such that the root is labelled by q, and the labelling of the other nodes is consistent with δ. Notice that in such a tree each sequence of edges going from the root to the leaves is labelled by w, and hence, all the edges starting at the same level of the tree have the same label, and all the leaves of the tree are at the same height.

It is immediate to show that AMA's are closed under boolean operations. We mention also that the membership problem for AMA's can be solved in polynomial time.

4.3 Calculating pre^*

Let $\mathcal{P} = (P, \Gamma, \Delta)$ be an alternating pushdown system. We show in this section that given a regular set of configurations C of $\mathcal{P}$, recognized by an *alternating*-multi-automaton $\mathcal{A}$, we can construct another AMA $\mathcal{A}_{pre^*}$ such that $Conf(\mathcal{A}_{pre^*}) = pre^*(C)$.

The construction is very similar to that of the non-alternating case. We assume without loss of generality that no transition of $\mathcal{A}$ leads to a set of states containing an initial state. We define a sequence of AMA's $\mathcal{A}_0, \mathcal{A}_1, \ldots$ such that $\mathcal{A}_0 = \mathcal{A}$. For every $i \geq 0$, $\mathcal{A}_{i+1}$ is obtained from $\mathcal{A}_i$ by conserving the same states and transitions, and adding for every transition rule

$$\langle p^j, \gamma\rangle \hookrightarrow \{\langle p^{k_1}, w_1\rangle, \ldots, \langle p^{k_m}, w_m\rangle\}$$

and every set

$$s^{k_1} \xrightarrow{w_1}_i P_1 \;,\; \ldots \;,\; s^{k_m} \xrightarrow{w_m}_i P_m$$

a new transition

$$s^j \xrightarrow{\gamma}_{i+1} (P_1 \cup \ldots \cup P_m)$$

Then, define $Y_i = Conf(\mathcal{A}_i)$ for every $i \geq 0$.

The intuitive justification of the construction is that we add the configuration $\langle p^j, \gamma w\rangle$ to the set of predecessors of C whenever all the configurations $\langle p^{k_1}, w_1 w\rangle$, ..., $\langle p^{k_m}, w_m w\rangle$ are already in this set. So, if for every $\ell \in \{1, \ldots, m\}$, the word $w_\ell w$ is accepted by $\mathcal{A}_i$ starting from s^{k_ℓ}, which means that $s^{k_\ell} \xrightarrow{w_\ell}_i P_\ell$ and $\forall p \in P_\ell .\, p \xrightarrow{w}_i Q_i \subseteq F$, then, due to the new transition, the word γw is accepted by $\mathcal{A}_{i+1}$ starting from s^j. Notice that the new transition imposes that only words w that are accepted starting from all the states in the P_ℓ's can be considered (w is in the intersection of the languages of all these states). The use of alternating automata allows to represent this intersection without modification of the number of states of the original automaton $\mathcal{A}$. This is crucial for the termination argument of the construction.

The following theorem, which shows the correcteness of the construction of $\mathcal{A}_{pre^*}$, is proved in the full paper:

Theorem 4.1 *Given an APDS $\mathcal{P}$ and a regular set of configurations recognized by a $\mathcal{P}$-AMA $\mathcal{A}$, we can construct a $\mathcal{P}$-AMA $\mathcal{A}_{pre^*}$ recognizing $pre^*(Conf(\mathcal{A}))$.*

It follows easily from the facts below that the algorithm is polynomial on the size of $\mathcal{P}$ and (singly) exponential in the size of $\mathcal{A}$:

- $\mathcal{A}_{pre^*}$ has the same states as $\mathcal{A}$,
- a $\mathcal{P}$-AMA with k states has $O(n_\mathcal{P} \cdot k \cdot 2^k)$ transitions, where $n_\mathcal{P}$ is the size of $\mathcal{P}$, and
- during the construction of the sequence $\mathcal{A}_0, \mathcal{A}_1, \ldots$, polynomial time suffices to decide if a new transition can be added to the current automaton.

5 Model-Checking Branching-Time Temporal Logics

5.1 The alternation-free (propositional) μ-calculus

Let *Prop* be a set of atomic propositions and $\mathcal{X}$ a finite set of variables. The set of formulas of the (propositional) μ-calculus is defined by the following grammar:

$$\varphi ::= \pi \in Prop \mid X \in \mathcal{X} \mid \neg\varphi \mid \varphi \vee \varphi \mid \exists\bigcirc\varphi \mid \mu X.\, \varphi$$

where in formulas of the form $\mu X.\, \varphi$, the variable X must occur in φ under an even number of negations. In addition, we consider the usual abbreviations: the boolean connectives $\wedge$ and $\Rightarrow$, $\forall\bigcirc\varphi = \neg\exists\bigcirc\neg\varphi$, and $\nu X.\, \varphi(X) = \neg\mu X.\, \neg\varphi(\neg X)$. We write $\sigma X.\, \varphi(X)$ for either $\mu X.\, \varphi(X)$ or $\nu X.\, \varphi(X)$.

The notion of free occurrence of a variable in a formula is defined as usual by considering μ and ν as quantifiers. We suppose without loss of generality that in every formula each variable is bound at most once. We write $\varphi(X)$ to indicate that

X occurs free in φ. A formula φ is *closed* if no variable occurs free in it, otherwise it is *open*.

We interpret formulas on the set of configurations of a PDS $\mathcal{P} = (P, \Gamma, \Delta)$. We use a labelling function $\Lambda : P \to 2^{Prop}$, and a valuation $\mathcal{V}$ which assigns to each variable a set of configurations. The set of configurations of $\mathcal{P}$ satisfying a formula φ is denoted by $[\![\varphi]\!]_{\mathcal{P}}(\mathcal{V})$ and is defined by the following rules:

$$\begin{aligned}
[\![\pi]\!]_{\mathcal{P}}(\mathcal{V}) &= \Lambda^{-1}(\pi) \times \Gamma^* \\
[\![X]\!]_{\mathcal{P}}(\mathcal{V}) &= \mathcal{V}(X) \\
[\![\neg\phi]\!]_{\mathcal{P}}(\mathcal{V}) &= (P \times \Gamma^*) \setminus [\![\phi]\!]_{\mathcal{P}}(\mathcal{V}) \\
[\![\phi_1 \vee \phi_2]\!]_{\mathcal{P}}(\mathcal{V}) &= [\![\phi_1]\!]_{\mathcal{P}}(\mathcal{V}) \cup [\![\phi_2]\!]_{\mathcal{P}}(\mathcal{V}) \\
[\![\exists\bigcirc\varphi]\!]_{\mathcal{P}}(\mathcal{V}) &= pre([\![\varphi]\!]_{\mathcal{P}}(\mathcal{V})) \\
[\![\nu X.\phi]\!]_{\mathcal{P}}(\mathcal{V}) &= \bigcup\{C \subseteq P \times \Gamma^* \mid C \subseteq [\![\phi]\!]_{\mathcal{P}}(\mathcal{V}[C/X])\}
\end{aligned}$$

where $\mathcal{V}[C/X]$ is the valuation which coincides with $\mathcal{V}$ for all variables but X, where it takes the value C.

The set of formulas in *positive normal form* is defined by the following syntax:

$$\varphi ::= \pi \mid \neg\pi \mid X \mid \varphi \vee \varphi \mid \varphi \wedge \varphi \mid \exists\bigcirc\varphi \mid \forall\bigcirc\varphi \mid \mu X.\varphi \mid \nu X.\varphi$$

It is easy to show that every formula is equivalent to a formula in positive normal form (push negations inside).

A σ-subformula of a formula $\sigma X.\ \phi(X)$ is *proper* if it does not contain any occurrence of X. The alternation-free μ-calculus is the set of formulas φ in positive normal form such that for every σ-subformula ϕ of φ the following holds:

- if ϕ is a μ-formula, then all its ν-subformulas are proper, and
- if ϕ is a ν-formula, then all its μ-subformulas are proper.

Given a formula φ, we define its *closure* $cl(\varphi)$ as the smallest set of formulas containing φ and such that

- if $\phi_1 \vee \phi_2 \in cl(\varphi)$ or $\phi_1 \wedge \phi_2 \in cl(\varphi)$ then $\phi_1 \in cl(\varphi)$ and $\phi_2 \in cl(\varphi)$,
- if $\exists\bigcirc\phi \in cl(\varphi)$ or $\forall\bigcirc\phi \in cl(\varphi)$ then $\phi \in cl(\varphi)$,
- if $\sigma X.\ \phi(X) \in cl(\varphi)$ then $\phi(\sigma X.\ \phi(X)) \in cl(\varphi)$.

It is easy to see that the closure of a formula is always a finite set, and that its cardinality is bounded by the length of the formula.

The Model-Checker Consider a PDS $\mathcal{P} = (P, \Gamma, \Delta)$ and a labelling function $\Lambda : P \to 2^{Prop}$. Let φ be a formula of the alternation-free μ-calculus, and let $\mathcal{V}$ be a valuation of the free variables in φ.

We show how to construct an AMA $\mathcal{A}_\varphi$ recognizing $[\![\varphi]\!]_{\mathcal{P}}(\mathcal{V})$. From now on we drop the indices and write just $[\![\varphi]\!]$.

We start by considering the case where all the σ-subformulas of φ are μ-formulas. We construct an APDS $\mathcal{AP}$ which is, roughly speaking, the product of $\mathcal{P}$ and the alternating automaton corresponding to φ [14]; we then reduce the problem of computing $[\![\varphi]\!]$ to computing the value of $pre^*_{\mathcal{AP}}$ for a certain regular set of configurations. Intuitively, a configuration $\langle [p, \phi], w\rangle$ belongs to this set if ϕ is a basic formula of the form π, $\neg\pi$, or X, for X free in ϕ, and the configuration $\langle p, w\rangle$ of $\mathcal{P}$ satisfies ϕ. Observe that whether $\langle p, w\rangle$ satisfies ϕ or not can be decided by direct inspection of the labelling function Λ and the valuation $\mathcal{V}$. The AND-branching in the transition rules of $\mathcal{AP}$ is due to conjunctions and universal path quantifications (in $\forall\bigcirc$ operators) occurring in the formula φ.

Formally, we define the APDS $\mathcal{AP} = (P^{\varphi}_{\mathcal{P}}, \Gamma, \Delta^{\varphi}_{\mathcal{P}})$ where

- $P^{\varphi}_{\mathcal{P}} = P \times cl(\varphi)$,
- $\Delta^{\varphi}_{\mathcal{P}}$ is the smallest set of transition rules satisfying the following conditions for every control location $[p, \phi]$ and every stack symbol γ:
  - if $\phi = \phi_1 \vee \phi_2$, then $([p,\phi],\gamma) \hookrightarrow ([p,\phi_1],\gamma)$ and $([p,\phi],\gamma) \hookrightarrow ([p,\phi_2],\gamma)$,
  - if $\phi = \phi_1 \wedge \phi_2$, then $([p,\phi],\gamma) \hookrightarrow \{\ ([p,\phi_1],\gamma), ([p,\phi_2],\gamma)\ \}$,
  - if $\phi = \mu X.\ \psi(X)$, then $([p,\phi],\gamma) \hookrightarrow ([p,\psi(\phi)],\gamma)$,
  - if $\phi = \exists\bigcirc\psi$ and $(p,\gamma) \hookrightarrow (q,w)$ is a transition rule of $\mathcal{P}$, then $([p,\phi],\gamma) \hookrightarrow ([q,\psi],w)$,
  - if $\phi = \forall\bigcirc\psi$ then $([p,\phi],\gamma) \hookrightarrow \{([q,\psi],w) \mid (p,\gamma) \hookrightarrow (q,w)\}$.

Let C_t (where the index t stands for true) be the subset of configurations of $\mathcal{AP}$ containing all configurations of the form

- $\langle [p,\pi], w\rangle$, where $\pi \in \Lambda(p)$,
- $\langle [p,\neg\pi], w\rangle$, where $\pi \notin \Lambda(p)$,
- $\langle [p,X], w\rangle$, where X is free in φ and $\langle p, w\rangle \in \mathcal{V}(X)$.

Clearly, if $\mathcal{V}(X)$ is a regular set of configurations for every variable X free in φ, then C_t is also a regular set of configurations.

The following result can be easily proved using standard techniques based on the notion of signature [9]:

Proposition 5.1 *Let $\mathcal{AP}$ be the APDS obtained from $\mathcal{P}$ and φ using the construction above. A configuration $\langle p, w\rangle$ of $\mathcal{P}$ belongs to $[\![\varphi]\!]$ iff the configuration $\langle [p,\varphi], w\rangle$ of $\mathcal{AP}$ belongs to $pre^*_{\mathcal{AP}}(C_t)$.*

Applying Theorem 2.1 we obtain a procedure to compute an AMA $\mathcal{A}_\varphi$ which accepts exactly the configurations of $\mathcal{P}$ that satisfy φ.

The case in which all the σ-subformulas of φ are ν-subformulas is now easy to solve: the negation of φ is equivalent to a formula φ' in positive normal form whose σ-subformulas are all μ-subformulas. Applying Theorem 2.1 we construct an AMA which accepts the configurations of $\mathcal{P}$ that satisfy φ'. We then just use the fact that AMA's are closed under complementation.

Let us now consider the general case of in which φ is an arbitrary formula of the alternation-free μ-calculus. We can assume without loss of generality that φ is a σ-formula (otherwise a "dummy" fixpoint can be added). The following property (which does *not* hold for the full μ-calculus) follows easily from the definitions, and allows us to construct the AMA $\mathcal{A}_\varphi$. We use the following notation: given a family $\Phi = \{\phi_i\}_{i=1}^n$ of subformulae of φ, which are pairwise incomparable with respect to the subformula relation, and a family $U = \{U_i\}_{i=1}^n$ of fresh variables, $\varphi[U/\Phi]$ denotes the result of simultaneously substituting U_i for ϕ_i in φ.

Proposition 5.2 *Let φ be a μ-formula (ν-formula) of the alternation-free μ-calculus, and let $\Phi = \{\phi_i\}_{i=1}^n$ be the family of maximal ν-subformulas (μ-subformulas) of ϕ with respect to the subformula relation. Then*

$$[\![\varphi]\!] = [\![\varphi[U/\Phi]]\!](\mathcal{V}')$$

where $U = \{U_i\}_{i=1}^n$ is a suitable family of fresh variables, and $\mathcal{V}'$ is the valuation which extends $\mathcal{V}$ by assigning to each U_i the set $[\![\phi_i]\!]$.

Observe that if φ is a μ-formula (ν-formula), then all the σ-subformulas of $\varphi[U/\Phi]$ are also μ-formulas (ν-formulas). Together with Proposition 5.1, this leads immediately to a recursive algorithm for computing $\mathcal{A}_\varphi$: for every $\phi \in \Phi$, compute recursively AMA's $\mathcal{A}_\phi$ recognizing $[\![\phi]\!]$, and then use them and Proposition 5.2 to compute $\mathcal{A}_\varphi$. Consequently we have:

Theorem 5.1 *Let $\mathcal{P}$ be a PDS, let φ a formula of the alternation-free μ-calculus, and let $\mathcal{V}$ be a valuation of the free variables of φ. We can construct an AMA $\mathcal{A}_\varphi$ such that $Conf(\mathcal{A}_\varphi) = [\![\varphi]\!]_{\mathcal{P}}(\mathcal{V})$.*

Complexity Walukiewicz has shown in [22] that there exists a formula of the alternation-free μ-calculus such that the model checking problem for PDS's and this formula is DEXPTIME-complete. This implies that all model-checking algorithms must have exponential complexity in the size of the system. We show that the algorithm we have obtained (which is very different from the one presented in [22]) has this complexity.

Let $n_{\mathcal{P}}$ be the size of $\mathcal{P}$ and let n_φ be the length of φ. We define a tree of σ-subformulas of φ: the root of the tree is φ; the children of a μ-subformula (ν-subformula) ϕ are the maximal ν-subformulas (μ-subformulas) of ϕ. Clearly, the number of nodes of the tree does not exceed n_φ.

Let ϕ be a leaf of the tree. The AMA $\mathcal{A}_\phi$ recognizing $[\![\phi]\!]$ is obtained by applying the pre^* construction to the AMA recognizing the set C_t. Since the latter has $O(n_{\mathcal{P}} \cdot n_\varphi)$ states, $\mathcal{A}_\phi$ has also $O(n_{\mathcal{P}} \cdot n_\varphi)$ states.

Now, let ϕ be an internal node of the tree with children $\phi_1, \ldots, \phi_k$. If the AMA recognizing $[\![\phi_i]\!]$ has n_i states, then the AMA recognizing $[\![\phi]\!]$ has $O(\Sigma_{i=1}^n n_i + n_{\mathcal{P}} \cdot n_\varphi)$. Since the number of nodes of the tree does not exceed n_φ, the AMA $\mathcal{A}_\varphi$ recognizing $[\![\varphi]\!]$ has $O(n_{\mathcal{P}} \cdot n_\varphi^2)$ states. Since each AMA can be constructed in exponential time in the number of states, the algorithm is singly exponential in $n_{\mathcal{P}}$ and n_φ.

5.2 The logic EF

The alternation-free μ-calculus is a rather powerful logic. Proper sublogics, like CTL, are considered to be sufficiently expressive for many applications. This raises the question whether the model-checking problem for PDS's and some interesting fragment of the alternation-free μ-calculus may lie in some complexity class below DEXPTIME. In this section we show that this is the case: we prove that the model-checking problem for the logic EF (propositional logic plus the temporal operator EF) is in PSPACE.[4] However, the problem turns out to be PSPACE-complete,

[4] We assume $PSPACE \neq DEXPTIME$

even PSPACE-complete in the size of the system. Therefore, the complexity gap between the alternation-free μ-calculus and its sublogics is rather small.

Given a set *Prop* of atomic propositions, the set of formulas of EF is defined by the following grammar:

$$\varphi ::= \pi \in Prop \mid \neg\varphi \mid \varphi \vee \varphi \mid \exists\bigcirc\varphi \mid EF\varphi$$

The semantics of formulas of the form π, $\neg\varphi$, $\varphi_1 \vee \varphi_2$, and $\exists\bigcirc\varphi$ is defined as for the alternation-free μ-calculus. A configuration c satisfies a formula $EF\varphi$ if there exists a configuration c' reachable from c that satisfies φ.

We consider the proof of membership in PSPACE first, since this is the part that makes use of our reachability analysis. The hardness part is a standard reduction from the acceptance problem for linearly bounded Turing machines.

Fix a PDS $\mathcal{P}(P, \Gamma, \Delta)$ and a configuration c of $\mathcal{P}$. Denote by $R(c)$ the set of words $pw \in P\Gamma^*$ such that $\langle p, w\rangle$ is reachable from c. We have the following result (the proof is in the full paper):

Theorem 5.2 *The set $R(c)$ is regular. Moreover, $R(c)$ is recognized by a finite multi automaton having polynomially many states in the sum of the sizes of c and $\mathcal{P}$.*

Given a formula φ of the alternation-free μ-calculus, denote by $R(c, \varphi)$ the set of words $pw \in P\Gamma^*$ such that $\langle p, w\rangle$ is reachable from c *and* satisfies φ. By Theorem 5.2 and Theorem 5.1, we have:

Corollary 5.1 *Let φ be a formula of the alternation-free μ-calculus. The set $R(c, \varphi)$ is regular, and is recognized by an alternating finite automaton having polynomially many states in the sum of the sizes of c, $\mathcal{P}$ and φ.*

We can now obtain our first result concerning the logic EF:

Theorem 5.3 *The model checking problem for the logic EF and pushdown automata is in PSPACE.*

Proof. Let $\mathcal{P}$ be a PDS and let φ be a formula of EF. We show by induction on the structure of φ that the problem of deciding if a given configuration c of $\mathcal{P}$ satisfies ϕ can be solved in nondeterministic polynomial space in the size of c, $\mathcal{P}$ and φ.

The cases $\varphi = \pi, \varphi_1 \vee \varphi_2, \neg\varphi_1$ are trivial. So let $\varphi = EF\varphi_1$, and assume that we can decide whether a configuration c satisfies φ_1 using nondeterministic polynomial space in the size of c, $\mathcal{P}$ and φ_1.

By the definition of the semantics of EF, $\mathcal{P}$ satisfies φ iff there exists a configuration c_1 reachable from c which satisfies φ_1.

If an AMA with n states recognizes a nonempty set, then it recognizes some word of length at most n. Therefore, by Corollary 5.1, we can assume that c_1 has polynomial size in $\mathcal{P}$ and φ_1. The following nondeterministic algorithm decides in polynomial space if $\mathcal{P}$ satisfies φ:

- Guess a configuration c_1 of polynomial size in $\mathcal{P}$ and φ;
- Check in polynomial time in the size of c_1 and $\mathcal{P}$ that c_1 is reachable from c;

– Check in polynomial space in the size of c_1, $\mathcal{P}$ and φ_1 that c_1 satisfies φ_1.

The membership of the model checking in PSPACE follows now from NPSPACE = PSPACE. □

In the full paper, we give the proof of the following hardness result:

Theorem 5.4 *The model checking problem for the logic EF and pushdown systems is PSPACE-hard.*

Finally, from the proof of Theorem 5.4, we can deduce that the following stronger result also holds:

Corollary 5.2 *There is a formula φ of EF such that the problem of deciding if a PDS satisfies φ is PSPACE-complete.*

6 Conclusion

We have applied the "*symbolic*" analysis principle to a class of infinite state systems, namely pushdown systems. We have represented (possibly infinite) sets of configurations using finite-state automata, and have proposed a simple procedure to compute sets of predecessors. Using this procedure and the automata-theoretic approach to model-checking, we have obtained model-checking algorithms for both linear and branching-time properties. From these results we have derived upper bounds for several model-checking problems. We have also provided matching lower bounds by means of some reductions based on Walukiewicz's ideas [22].

The model-checking problem for pushdown systems and the modal μ-calculus (or its alternation-free fragment) has been studied in several papers [11, 12, 22]. The main advantage of our approach (apart from an homogeneous treatment of both branching-time and linear-time logics) is the simplicity of our algorithms: only well known concepts from automata theory are needed to understand them. They constitute smooth generalizations of global model-checking algorithms for branching-time logics and finite-state systems.

An approach similar to ours, based on automata representation of the stack contents, has been adopted in [15]. However, the techniques used there are different from ours, and the branching-time properties are expressed there in a logic (CTL*) which is incomparable with the alternation-free modal μ-calculus.

We do not know whether our approach can be extended to the full modal μ-calculus. The exact complexity of the model-checking problem for pushdown systems and CTL is also open: it lies somewhere between PSPACE and DEXPTIME. These questions, and the extension of the symbolic analysis principle to other classes of systems with infinite state spaces, are left for future investigations.

References

1. A.V. Aho, J.E. Hopcroft, and J.D. Ullman. *The Design and Analysis of Computer Algorithms*. Addison-Wesley, 1976.

2. R. Alur, C. Courcoubetis, N. Halbwachs, T. Henzinger, P. Ho, X. Nicollin, A. Olivero, J. Sifakis, and S. Yovine. The Algorithmic Analysis of Hybrid Systems. *TCS*, 138, 1995.
3. R. Alur and D. Dill. A Theory of Timed Automata. *TCS*, 126, 1994.
4. E. Asarin, O. Maler, and A. Pnueli. Symbolic Controller Synthesis for Discrete and Timed Systems. In *Hybrid Systems II*. LNCS 999, 1995.
5. B. Boigelot and P. Godefroid. Symbolic Verification of Communication Protocols with Infinite State Spaces using QDDs. In *CAV'96*. LNCS 1102, 1996.
6. R.V. Book and F. Otto. *String-Rewriting Systems*. Springer-Verlag, 1993.
7. A. Bouajjani, J. Esparza, and O. Maler. Reachability Analysis of Pushdown Automata: Application to Model Checking. Tech. Rep. VERIMAG, 1997. ftp://ftp.imag.fr/imag/SPECTRE/ODED/pda.ps.gz, http://papa.informatik.tu-muenchen.de/forschung/sfb342_a3/refs.html.
8. A. Bouajjani and O. Maler. Reachability Analysis of Pushdown Automata. In *Infinity'96*. tech. rep. MIP-9614, Univ. Passau, 1996.
9. J.C. Bradfield. *Verifying Temporal Properties of Systems*. Birkhauser, 1992.
10. R. Bryant. Symbolic Boolean Manipulation with Ordered Binary-Decision Diagrams. *ACM Computing Surveys*, 24, 1992.
11. O. Burkart and B. Steffen. Model Checking for Context-Free Processes. In *CONCUR'92*, 1992. LNCS 630.
12. O. Burkart and B. Steffen. Composition, Decomposition and Model-Checking of Pushdown Processes. *Nordic Journal of Computing*, 2, 1995.
13. E.M. Clarke, E.A. Emerson, and E. Sistla. Automatic Verification of Finite State Concurrent Systems using Temporal Logic Specifications: A Practical Approach. In *POPL'83*. ACM, 1983.
14. E.A. Emerson. Automated Temporal Reasoning about Reactive Systems. In *Logics for Concurrency*. LNCS 1043, 1996.
15. A. Finkel, B. Willems, and P. Wolper. A Direct Symbolic Approach to Model Checking Pushdown Systems. In *Personal communication*, 1997.
16. G. Holzmann. Basic SPIN manual. Technical report, Bell Laboratories, 1994.
17. K.L. McMillan. *Symbolic Model-Checking: an Approach to the State-Explosion Problem*. Kluwer, 1993.
18. A. Pnueli. The Temporal Logic of Programs. In *FOCS'77*. IEEE, 1977.
19. M.Y. Vardi. A Temporal Fixpoint Calculus. In *POPL'88*. ACM, 1988.
20. M.Y. Vardi. Alternating Automata and Program Verification. In *Computer Science Today*. LNCS 1000, 1995.
21. M.Y. Vardi and P. Wolper. An Automata-Theoretic Approach to Automatic Program Verification. In *LICS'86*. IEEE, 1986.
22. I. Walukiewicz. Pushdown Processes: Games and Model Checking. In *CAV'96*. LNCS 1102, 1996.

Synthesis of Nets with Inhibitor Arcs *

Nadia Busi and G. Michele Pinna

Dipartimento di Matematica, Università di Siena,
Via del Capitano 15, I-53100 Siena, Italy
e-mail: busi@cs.unibo.it, pinna@di.unipi.it

Abstract. The synthesis problem for Petri nets consists in the construction of a net system whose behaviour is specified by a given transition system. In this paper we deal with the synthesis of elementary net systems extended with inhibitor arcs, i.e. arcs that test for absence of tokens in a place. We characterize the class of transitions systems corresponding to the sequential execution of these nets, which is a proper extension of the one obtained by the execution of nets without inhibitor arcs. Finally, we try to minimize the number of inhibitor arcs; we look for conditions guaranteeing that an inhibitor arc is really used, i.e. its presence influences the behaviour of the net.

1 Introduction

In recent years there has been a growing interest in *contextual nets.* Besides the ordinary arcs, in contextual nets also some other arcs types are considered: arcs that just *test* for presence of tokens (Montanari and Rossi [9] argue that in this way the potential concurrency of a net is reflected, whereas Vogler goes a step further, showing that already on the level of sequential behaviour the introduction of these arcs[2] can be traced [13]), and arcs that test for absence of tokens (hence introducing sequentializations that are history dependent, indeed inhibitor arcs are strictly connected with priorities and non monotonic enabling). The reasons of the interest are mainly due to the possibility of using contextual Petri nets as a faithful model for, among others, *concurrent constraint programming* ([9]), the π-calculus ([5]) or to prove correctness of protocols ([13]).
Another line of research has focussed on the synthesis of nets from the sequential (concurrent) behaviour represented via transition systems (possibly enriched). This whole line of research has been originated by the papers [8] where the notion of *region* was introduced. A region is a good candidate for representing a condition that must hold for an event to happen. One of the basic questions was: how it is possible to synthesize a net from the sequential observations of its behaviour (usually represented as a transition system), and which properties characterize such sequential observations (see also [2, 3, 1, 11] and [14, 10] among others, also for the synthesis of nets from non sequential observation).

* Research partially supported by MURST, quota 60%.

[2] These arcs are called *contextual arcs* in [9] and *read arcs* in [13].

In this paper we consider the problem of synthesizing an elementary net system with inhibitor arcs from the sequential observation given in form of a transition system. Inhibitor arcs forbid some event to happen because of the presence of some condition that should be absent, hence they basically cut down the behaviour, i.e. some execution sequences are not any longer observable. The main consequence is that now some *edges* are missing in the transition system. Let us consider the simple situation when considering two events a and b such that the happening of b inhibits the happening of a. The resulting rooted transition system is the following one:

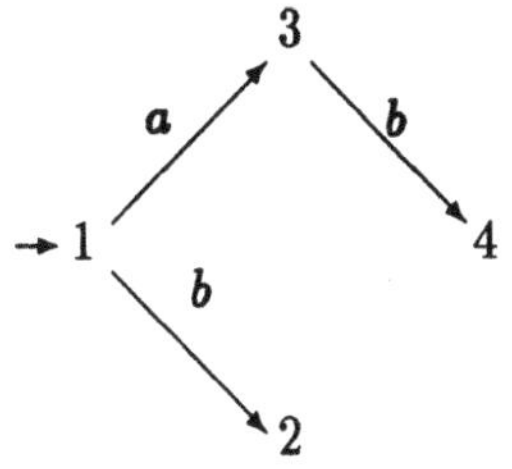

which is, as already noticed in [7], not isomorphic to a state graph of any elementary net system: the synthesized net is a net where the event b doesn't inhibit a. The reason is that the regions characterize the events entering or leaving the regions, and the fact that a sequence is ruled out because of an inhibition is not captured by any region. As we said, the notion of region capture essentially the fact that a certain condition must hold when a certain event happens (and doesn't hold after the execution of this event). Hence the regions representing conditions that do not hold when an event happens are good candidates for representing *inhibiting conditions*. Among these only few are really interesting, namely the ones that should contain an event but they doesn't: in the transition system above the region $\{2, 4\}$ has this characteristic.

It this paper we will show how to synthesize an elementary net system with inhibitor arcs from a transition system, and we will state the conditions under which a transition system is isomorphic to the state graph of such a system. It will turn out that inhibitor arcs that are really used, i.e. they have an influence on the behaviour of the elementary net without them, connect sequential components of the net, reflecting the intuition that an inhibitor arc (or, otherwise stated, an inhibiting condition) shouldn't appear *inside* a sequential component. This fact shed some light on the real usage of inhibitor arcs.

Note that the synthesis problem for nets with inhibitor arcs can be solved also within the general framework of [3], however we look for a more direct characterization of transition systems.

The paper is organized as follows: in Sections 2, 3 and 4 we recall some basic notions about transition systems, elementary net systems and regions respectively. In Section 5 we face with the synthesis problem of elementary net systems with inhibitor arcs and we propose techniques to minimize the number of inhibitor arcs we need to use to get the required behaviour. Finally, in Section 6 we outline some topics for future research.

2 Transition Systems

We assume that a finite set of *action* Act is given.

Definition 1. A *(finite) labelled graph* over an alphabet Act is the triple $G = (V, Act, \rightarrow)$ where V is a (finite) set of *vertices* and $\rightarrow \subseteq V \times Act \times V$ is a (finite) set of *labelled edges*.
A *rooted* labelled graph is a labelled graph with a distinguished initial state v_0. □

In the following we use $v \xrightarrow{a} v'$ to denote $(v, a, v') \in \rightarrow$.
A path between two vertices v and v' is a sequence of vertices $v_0, v_1, \ldots, v_n$ such that $n \geq 0$, $v = v_0$, $v' = v_n$ and $v_i \xrightarrow{a_i} v_{i+1}$ for each $0 \leq i < n$; if the graph is rooted we say that a vertex v is reachable if and only if there exists a path from the initial vertex to v. With $Act_{\rightarrow}$ we denote the actions appearing in $\rightarrow$ i.e. $Act_{\rightarrow} = \{a \in Act \mid \exists v, v' \in V \text{ and } v \xrightarrow{a} v'\}$.

Definition 2. Given a graph $G = (V, Act, \rightarrow)$, then $G' = (V', Act, \rightarrow')$ is a *subgraph* of G iff $V' \subseteq V$ and $\rightarrow' \subseteq \rightarrow \cap (V' \times Act \times V')$. If $\rightarrow' = \rightarrow \cap (V' \times Act \times V')$ we say that G' is the *subgraph induced by* V'. □

Definition 3. A *morphism* f between two graphs $G = (V, Act, \rightarrow)$ and $G' = (V', Act, \rightarrow')$ is a mapping $f : V \rightarrow V'$ such that $[v \xrightarrow{a} v'] \Rightarrow [f(v) = f(v') \vee f(v) \xrightarrow{a}{}' f(v')]$. If the graphs are rooted, then $f(v_0) = v'_0$. □

Note that the definition of subgraph can be easily characterized in term of a morphism which is an embedding on vertices. Two graphs are *isomorphic* iff the morphism f is an isomorphism and $v \xrightarrow{a} v' \Leftrightarrow f(v) \xrightarrow{a}{}' f(v')$.
We consider labelled graphs which satisfy some additional constraints.

Definition 4. A *transition system* is the triple $A = (St, E, \rightarrow)$, where St is a set of *states*, E is a nonempty set of *events* and $\rightarrow \subseteq St \times E \times St$ is a *transition relation* such that

1. $\forall s \xrightarrow{e} s', s \neq s'$,
2. $\forall e \in E\ \exists s \xrightarrow{e} s'$.

A *rooted* transition system is a tuple $A = (St, E, \rightarrow, s_0)$, where $(St, E, \rightarrow)$ is a transition system and $s_0 \in St$ is a distinguished *initial* state. Moreover, each state is reachable from the initial one, i.e. for all $s \in St$ there exists a path from s_0 to s. □

The first condition says that the transition system is *self loop free* and the second that each event determines at least a change of state.
We omit the word rooted when it is clear from the context. Given a transition system $A = (St, E, \rightarrow)$, then $A' = (St', E', \rightarrow')$ where $St' \subseteq St$, $E' \subseteq E$ and $\rightarrow' \subseteq \rightarrow$ is a *subtransition system*. A' is the *subtransition system induced by* St' if $\rightarrow' = \rightarrow \cap (St' \times E \times St')$ and $E' = E_{\rightarrow'}$.
We end this part specializing the notion of morphism to transition systems.

Definition 5. Let $A = (St, E, \rightarrow, s_0)$ and $A' = (St', E, \rightarrow', s'_0)$ be two transition systems. Then $f : St \rightarrow St'$ is a *G-morphism* iff

- it is a graph morphism
- $f(s_0) = s'_0$
- if $s \xrightarrow{e} s'$ and $f(s) \xrightarrow{e}' f(s')$ then $f(s_1) \xrightarrow{e}' f(s'_1)$ for every $s_1 \xrightarrow{e} s'_1$.

If f is a bijection and $s \xrightarrow{e} s' \Leftrightarrow f(s) \xrightarrow{e}' f(s')$, A and A' are isomorphic ($A \cong A'$). □

A G-morphism represents the fact that A' can *partially* simulate A, i.e. whenever A can evolve also A' can, provided that the move is defined (and if it is not then the two states become indistinguishable). The third requirement is to assure that the simulation is uniform on an event.

3 Elementary net systems

We recall some basic notions on elementary nets [12], extending them with inhibitor arcs (for this notion see [9] and [6]).

Definition 6. A *net* is a tuple (B, E, F) such that $B \cup E \neq \emptyset$, $B \cap E = \emptyset$, $F \subseteq (B \times E) \cup (E \times B)$ and $dom(F) \cup ran(F) = B \cup E$[3]. □

The elements of B are called *conditions* and the elements of E are called *events.* F is the *flow relation*. For $x \in B \cup E$, we define ${}^\bullet x = \{y \in B \cup E \mid (y, x) \in F\}$ and $x^\bullet = \{y \in B \cup E \mid (x, y) \in F\}$. A net is *simple* iff $\forall x, y \in B \cup E$ ${}^\bullet x = {}^\bullet y$ and $x^\bullet = y^\bullet$ implies that $x = y$, it is *condition simple* if it is simple only $\forall x, y \in B$, it is pure if $\forall x \in B \cup E$ ${}^\bullet x \cap x^\bullet = \emptyset$ (i.e. the net doesn't contain self loops), and it is connected iff $\forall x, y \in B \cup E$ $(x, y) \in (F \cup F^{-1})^*$.
A subset of B is called a *case*. We say that a condition b holds in the case c if $b \in c$. An event e is *enabled* at c if ${}^\bullet e \subseteq c$ and $e^\bullet \cap c = \emptyset$. The execution of an enabled event e at c produces the case $c' = (c \setminus {}^\bullet e) \cup e^\bullet$. This is written as $c[e\rangle c'$. Note that if ${}^\bullet e \cap e^\bullet \neq \emptyset$ then e can never fire.

Definition 7. An *elementary net system* (ens) is a tuple $N = (B, E, F, c_0)$ such that (B, E, F) is a net and $c_0 \subseteq B$ is the *initial case*. □

The set of *reachable cases*, denoted by $[c_0\rangle$, is defined inductively as follows:

- $c_0 \in [c_0\rangle$
- if $c \in [c_0\rangle$ and $c[e\rangle c'$, then $c' \in [c_0\rangle$.

Definition 8. Let $N = (B, E, F, c_0)$ be an elementary net system.
Then $sg(N) = ([c_0\rangle, E, \rightarrow, c_0)$ where $c \xrightarrow{e} c'$ iff $c \in [c_0\rangle$ and $c[e\rangle c'$, is the *case graph* of N. □

We introduce now the notion of elementary net system with inhibitor arcs.

[3] $dom(F) = \{x \mid (x, y) \in F\}$ and $ran(F) = \{y \mid (x, y) \in F\}$.

Definition 9. An elementary net system with *inhibitor* arcs (ensi) is a tuple $N = (B, E, F, I, c_0)$ where (B, E, F, c_0) is an elementary net system and $I \subseteq B \times E$ is a set of *inhibitor* arcs. □

Given a net with inhibitor arcs, we define $^\circ e = \{b \in B \mid (b, e) \in I\}$. An event e is enabled at a case c iff $^\bullet e \subseteq c$, $e^\bullet \cap c = \emptyset$ and $^\circ e \cap c = \emptyset$. The execution of the event e in an elementary net system with inhibitor arcs is defined in the same way as the execution of the event in the net *without* inhibitor arcs, only the conditions under which an event can execute are changed. Hence the notations for the execution of an event as well for the reachable cases are not changed. Given a net $N = (B, E, F, I, c_0)$, then with $\tilde{N} = (B, E, F, c_0)$ we denote the net obtained by N deleting the inhibitor arcs.
A simple but useful consequence of the fact that the evolution of a system with inhibitor arcs depends uniquely on the evolution of the system without the inhibitor arcs, provided that events can happen, is summarized by the following proposition.

Proposition 10. *Let $N = (B, E, F, I, c_0)$ be an elementary net with inhibitor arcs. Then $sg(N)$ is a subgraph of $sg(\tilde{N})$.* □

Given an elementary net system (with inhibitor arcs) $N = (B, E, F, I, c_0)$, we say that $e \in E$ is *useful* iff exists $c \in [c_0\rangle$ such that e is enabled at c; otherwise e is *useless*. N is *reduced* iff each $e \in E$ is useful. Along the same line of [7] it is easy to say that

Proposition 11. *Given an elementary net system N, there exists a reduced elementary net system N' such that $sg(N)$ and $sg(N')$ are isomorphic.* □

We finally recall the notion of state-machine net, adapting it to the fact that now we consider nets with inhibitor arcs. As a state-machine net represents a *sequential* net, quite clearly there is no inhibitor arc.

Definition 12. An elementary net system $N = (B, E, F, I, c_0)$ is a state-machine iff $\forall e \in E$, $|^\bullet e| = 1 = |e^\bullet|$, $I = \emptyset$ and $|c_0| = 1$. □

Definition 13. Let $N = (B, E, F, I, c_0)$ be an elementary net system with inhibitor arcs. N is decomposable into state-machine components iff there exists a set $N_i = (B_i, E_i, F_i, \emptyset, c_{0i})$, $i \in \{1, \ldots, m\}$ such that $\forall i$ N_i is a state-machine net, $B = \bigcup B_i$, $E = \bigcup E_i$, $F_i = F \cap ((B_i \times E_i) \cup (E_i \times B_i))$, $c_{0i} = c_0 \cap B_i$ and $(b, e) \in I$ implies that $e \in E_j$ and $b \in B_k$ and $j \neq k$. □

Differently from the usual definition of decomposition, where the set of components alone is able to determine the composed elementary net system, here the inhibitor arcs should be given “separately”.

4 Regions

Regions are the basic tool to split the monolithic states of the transition system into a distributed state. As the state in an elementary net system is represented by a subset of conditions, we look for a set of conditions whose subsets correspond to states in the transition system. We group together a subset of states in which a given condition b holds; subsets of that type will be called regions. Let r be such a subset. Suppose condition b is necessary for an event e to happen, i.e. the condition is in the preset of the event: after the occurrence of that event, the condition no longer holds. Let $s \in r$; then, the condition b holds in s; if the event e happens, then we have a transition $s \xrightarrow{e} s'$; moreover, the condition b no longer holds in state s', so $s' \notin r$. So, for each state in r, if an e-labelled transition exits from it then that transition enters a state that is not in r. Moreover, if a state s is outside r, then e cannot happen in s, because the necessary condition b does not hold; so we do not have e labelled transitions exiting from s. To summarize, if b is a necessary condition for e, then each e-labelled transition of the graph starts inside r and ends outside r. Analogously, if an event e makes the condition b true, i.e. b is in the postset of e, we can see that each e-labelled transition has source outside r and target inside r. Suppose now that condition b is unrelated to event e, i.e. b is neither in the preset nor in the postset of e. If the event e happens in a state where b holds, then the condition continues to be true also in the state reached after the occurrence of e; that is, if an e-labelled transition starts inside r, then it also ends inside r. Analogously, if e happens in a state where b is false, b continues to be false also after the execution of e; so, e-labelled transitions starting outside r also end outside r.
By definition of evolution of an elementary net, we have that an event with a condition b in both its preset and its postset can never happen. From the above discussion we deduce that e-labelled transitions have an uniform behaviour w.r.t. r: either all of them cross r exiting, or all of them cross r entering, or none of them cross r.
We recall here the notion of region and some relevant results that will be used later (see [8, 4, 11] among others).

Definition 14. Let $A = (St, E, \rightarrow)$ be a transition system, a set $r \subseteq St$ is said to be a *region* if and only if $\forall s_1 \xrightarrow{e} s'_1, s_2 \xrightarrow{e} s'_2$ ($s_1 \in r$ and $s'_1 \notin r \Leftrightarrow s_2 \in r$ and $s'_2 \notin r$) and ($s_1 \notin r$ and $s'_1 \in r \Leftrightarrow s_2 \notin r$ and $s'_2 \in r$). □

It is easy to see that both St and $\emptyset$ are regions, and they are called the *trivial* regions. The set of *non-trivial* regions of a transition system A will be denoted with R_A, and for each $s \in St$ with R_s we denote the set of non-trivial regions containing s.

Definition 15. Let r be a region of the transition system $A = (St, E, \rightarrow)$, we define:

- ${}^\bullet r = \{e \in E \mid \exists s \xrightarrow{e} s' \text{ such that } s \in r \text{ and } s' \notin r\}$ (pre-set of r),
- $r^\bullet = \{e \in E \mid \exists s \xrightarrow{e} s' \text{ such that } s \notin r \text{ and } s' \in r\}$ (post-set of r),

- ${}^\bullet e = \{r \in R_A \mid \exists s \xrightarrow{e} s'$ such that $s \in r$ and $s' \notin r\}$ (pre-regions of e), and
- $e^\bullet = \{r \in R_A \mid \exists s \xrightarrow{e} s'$ such that $s \notin r$ and $s' \in r\}$ (post-regions of e). □

We say that an event e *crosses the border* of a region r iff $e \in r^\bullet \cup {}^\bullet r$.
Following [4], we list some properties of the regions of a transition system A. With $Min(R_A)$ we denote the set of *minimal* regions with respect to set inclusion, i.e. the set $\{r \mid r \in R_A$ and $\forall r' \in R_A, r \neq r' \Rightarrow r' \not\subseteq r\}$.

1. let r be a region, then $St \setminus r$ is a region,
2. let r and r' be two disjoint regions, then $r \cup r'$ is a region,
3. let r and r' be two regions such that $r \subseteq r'$, then $r' \setminus r$ is a region,
4. let r be a region and e be an event that doesn't cross the border of r. Let r' be a minimal region such that $r' \subseteq r$ and $r' \in {}^\bullet e$. Then $(r \setminus r') \in e^\bullet$,
5. let $s \in St$ be a state of A and r a region containing s. Then there is a minimal region r' such that $s \in r'$ and $r' \subseteq r$,
6. let r be a region of A and $e \in E$ be an event such that $e \in {}^\bullet r$. Then there is $r' \in Min(R_A)$ such that $r' \subseteq r$ and $e \in {}^\bullet r'$, and symmetrically if $e \in r^\bullet$.

As already stated in [4], a consequence of these properties is that each region can be seen as the union of a set of mutually disjoint minimal regions, i.e. $r = \bigcup_{i \in I} r_i$ where, for each $i \in I$, $r_i \in Min(R_A)$ and for each $i \neq j$ $r_i \cap r_j = \emptyset$.
We finally relate the regions of two transitions system in the following sense:

Proposition 16. *Let $A = (St, E, \rightarrow, s_0)$ and $A' = (St', E', \rightarrow', s'_0)$ be two transition systems and f be a G-morphism between them. Suppose that r is a region of A', then $f^{-1}(r)$ is a region of A.* □

5 Synthesis of nets with inhibitor arcs

The problem of the synthesis of nets from a transition system can be stated as follows: *given a transition system A, there exists an elementary net system N such that A and $sg(N)$ are isomorphic?*. We are interested in solving the same problem for the nets with inhibitor arcs, i.e. given a transition system enjoying some properties, is it isomorphic to the state graph of an elementary net system with inhibitor arcs?
We need to understand what regions are candidates to represent inhibiting conditions, i.e. conditions that must be false for an event to happen. Suppose b is an inhibiting condition for e (i.e. b is in the inhibiting set of e); let r be the set of states where b holds. We have that no e-labelled transition starts from states inside r, because in those states the inhibiting condition b holds. So, the pair (b, e) is a good candidate to be an inhibiting arc in the net iff no e-labelled transition is inside r or crosses r exiting.
Suppose now that e-labelled transitions cross r entering; though being allowable, the inhibiting arc (b, e) is completely useless, because in this case the condition b is already in the postset of e, and for an event to happen we require its postset not to hold. Then, for a pair (b, e) to be a possible inhibitor arc, we require that each e-labelled transition neither lies inside r nor crosses r in any direction.

Definition 17. Let $A = (S, E, \rightarrow)$ be a transition system. The set of potential inhibiting arcs is the set of pairs of regions and events of E defined as follows: $(r, e) \in PI(A)$ iff $s \xrightarrow{e} s'$ implies $s, s' \notin r$. □

Starting from a transition system, we show how to construct a tuple, that turns out to be an elementary net system with inhibitor arcs provided that a condition is fulfilled. The net we construct is called *saturated*, because it contains all the nontrivial regions as conditions, and all potential inhibitor arcs. Then, we show under which conditions the saturated net is an elementary net system and its sequential case graph is isomorphic to the TS.

Definition 18. Let $A = (St, E, \rightarrow, s_0)$ be a transition system[4]. We define the tuple $sat(A) = (R_A, E, F, PI(A), c_0)$, where

- $(r, e) \in F$ iff $r \in {}^\bullet e$;
- $(e, r) \in F$ iff $r \in e^\bullet$;
- $r \in c_0$ iff $s_0 \in r$. □

In general, $sat(A)$ is not an ensi, because of the possible presence of isolated events. Consider the following transition system:

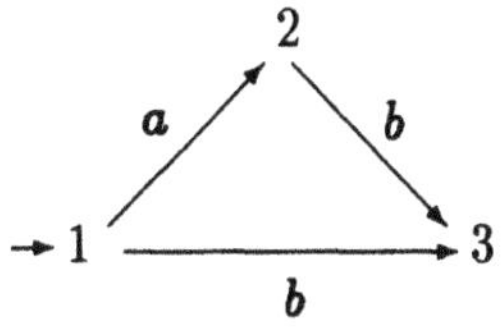

Its nontrivial regions are $\{1, 2\}$ and $\{3\}$; it's easy to see that ${}^\bullet a = \emptyset = a^\bullet$; thus, a is an isolated event. The problem arises from the fact that the states 1 and 2 cannot be "separated" using regions, i.e. there is no region such that $1 \in r$ iff $2 \notin r$.

If a transition system represents the state graph of a net, its states correspond to cases of the net; as a case is a subset of conditions, for two cases to be different there must exist a condition belonging to one case and not to the other. Regions are used as conditions in the synthesized net; moreover, if a state belongs to a region, then that region belongs to the case corresponding to that state. So, the fact that two states cannot be separated by any region means that they will be identified in the case graph of the synthesized net; in other words, the net cannot generate all the states of the transition system.

For this reason, we require a transition system to satisfy the following *state separation property* (see e.g.[7]).

Definition 19. Let $A = (St, E, \rightarrow, s_0)$ be a transition system and $R \subseteq R_A$. We say that R satisfies the state separation property (SSP) in A iff
for all $s, s' \in St$, if $s \neq s'$ then there exists a region $r \in R$ such that $(s \in r \Leftrightarrow s' \notin r)$.

[4] the construction could be carried out also if A is a rooted graph.

We say that A satisfies the state separation property iff R_A satisfies the state separation property in A. □

Proposition 20. *Let A be a transition system. If A satisfies SSP then $\mathbf{sat}(A)$ is an elementary net system with inhibitor arcs.* □

To show that A is isomorphic to the case graph of $\mathbf{sat}(A)$, we need a further condition, that we explain below. We recall that conditions of the net $\mathbf{sat}(A)$ are the nontrivial regions of A; given a state s and a region r, $s \in r$ means that the condition r holds at state s. Thus, the isomorphism maps a state s to the case formed by the conditions holding in s; this case turns out to be the set R_s of regions containing s.
Suppose that the graph doesn't contain an e-labelled arc exiting from s. Then we need that e is not enabled in the case corresponding to s. For e not to be enabled at R_s, one of the following must hold:

- ${}^\bullet e \not\subseteq R_s$; this means that there exists a region r such that $r \in {}^\bullet e$ and $r \notin R_s$, or, equivalently, $r \in {}^\bullet e$ and $s \notin r$
- $e^\bullet \cap R_s \neq \emptyset$; this means that there exists a region r such that $r \in e^\bullet$ and $r \in R_s$
- ${}^\circ e \cap R_s \neq \emptyset$; this means that there exists a region r such that $(r, e) \in PI(A)$ and $r \in R_s$

The properties listed above give rise to a property that regions and potential inhibitor arcs of A must satisfy if we want that $sg(\mathbf{sat}(A))$ is isomorphic to A. This property is an extension of the event state separation property ([7]) that deals with potential inhibiting arcs.

Definition 21. Let $A = (St, E, \rightarrow, s_0)$ be a transition system, $R \subseteq R_A$ and $I \subseteq PI(A)$. We say that R, I satisfy the extended event state separation property (EESSP) in A iff
for all $s \in St$, $e \in E$, if $s \overset{e}{\not\rightarrow}$ then at least one of the following conditions holds:

- there exists a region $r \in R$ such that $r \in {}^\bullet e$ and $s \notin r$
- there exists a region $r \in R$ such that $r \in e^\bullet$ and $s \in r$
- there exists a region $r \in R$ and an inhibiting arc $(r, e) \in I$ such that $s \in r$

We say that A satisfies the EESSP iff $R_A, PI(A)$ satisfy the EESSP in A. □

If a transition system A satisfies SSP and EESSP then it is isomorphic to the state graph of the saturated net generated from A. To prove this fact we need the following lemma, stating a correspondence between arcs in the transition system and firings in the saturated net.

Lemma 22. *Let $A = (St, E, \rightarrow, s_0)$ be a transition system satisfying SSP and EESSP.*
If $s \overset{e}{\rightarrow} s'$ then $R_s[e\rangle R_{s'}$.
If $R_s[e\rangle c$ then there exists $s' \in St$ such that $s \overset{e}{\rightarrow} s'$ and $c = R_{s'}$. □

Theorem 23. *Let A be a transition system. If A satisfies SSP and EESSP then A is isomorphic to $sg(\mathbf{sat}(A))$.* □

We show that the case graph of an ensi is a transition system and satisfies SSP and EESSP.

Theorem 24. *Let N be a reduced*[5] *ensi. Then the graph $sg(N)$ is a transition system and satisfies SSP and EESSP.* □

Note that the requirement for the net to be reduced is not restrictive; in fact, Proposition 11 ensures that for each ensi there exists a reduced ensi whose case graphs are isomorphic. We have the following

Proposition 25. *Let A be a transition system. If $A \cong sg(sat(A))$ then $sat(A)$ is condition simple and reduced.* □

Summarizing the two theorems above, we have that being transition system and satisfying SSP and EESSP is a necessary and sufficient condition for a graph to be (isomorphic to) the case graph of an ensi.
As we said before, regions are the candidates to represent conditions of the net we are synthesizing; however, maybe that not all those conditions are necessary to construct a net with the given behaviour. For example, we have immediately seen that it's useless to put in the net the conditions corresponding to the trivial regions. Similarly, also some potential inhibiting arc could be useless. For this reason, we show how to construct a net from a arbitrary sets of regions and potential inhibiting arcs.

Definition 26. Let $A = (S, E, \rightarrow, s_0)$ be a transition system, $R \subseteq R_A$ and $I \subseteq PI(A) \cap R$. We define $gen_A(R, I) = (R, E, F, I, c_0)$, where:

- $(r, e) \in F$ iff $r \in {}^\bullet e$;
- $(e, r) \in F$ iff $r \in e^\bullet$;
- $r \in c_0$ iff $s_0 \in r$ □

As for the saturated version, we have the following results:

Theorem 27. *Let A be a transition system, $R \subseteq R_A$ and $I \subseteq PI(A)$.*
If R satisfies SSP in A then $gen_A(R, I)$ is an elementary net system with inhibitor arcs.
If R, I satisfy SSP and EESSP in A then A is isomorphic to $sg(gen_A(R, I))$ (the isomorphism maps a state s to the set of regions $R_s \cap R$).
If A is isomorphic to $sg(gen_A(R, I))$ then R, I satisfy SSP and EESSP in A. □

[5] The above restriction to reduced ensi, as well as the requirement on graphs of the existence of an e-labelled arc for each event e, are introduced to keep the definitions of $sg(N)$ and $sat(A)$ as simple as possible. Using the current constructions, if a net contains useless events, we obtain a case graph not satisfying EESSP. On the other side, if an event of a graph is not used to label an arc, we obtain a net with isolated events. The two restrictions can be dropped if in the construction of sg we restrict the events of $sg(N)$ to the useful events of N; similarly we take as events of $sat(A)$ the set of events of the graph that label some arc.

Note that SSP and EESSP are monotonic on sets of regions and inhibitor arcs in the following sense:

Proposition 28. *Let A be a transition system, $R, R' \subseteq R_A$ and $I, I' \subseteq PI(A)$. If R satisfies SSP in A then also $R \cup R'$ satisfies SSP in A. If R, I satisfy EESSP in A then also $R \cup R', I \cup I'$ satisfy EESSP in A.* □

From this proposition and the theorem above it easily follows that:

Corollary 29. *Let A be a transition system, $R, R' \subseteq R_A$ and $I, I' \subseteq PI(A)$. If A is isomorphic to $sg(gen_A(R, I))$, then A is also isomorphic to $sg(gen_A(R \cup R', I \cup I'))$.* □

This means that, once the net generated by a subset of regions and inhibitor arcs has a state graph isomorphic to the given transition system, the addition of other conditions (regions) and/or inhibitor arcs does not alterate the behaviour of the net. Clearly, we have that $sat(A) = gen_A(R_A, PI(A))$; thus we have

Corollary 30. *A transition system A satisfies SSP and EESSP iff there exist $R \subseteq R_A$ and $I \subseteq PI(A)$ such that A is isomorphic to $sg(gen_A(R, I))$.* □

Now we present a technique to add the least number of inhibitor arcs, once we have fixed the set R of regions we use: for each event e, construct the set $S_e = \{s \mid s \not\xrightarrow{e} \wedge \forall r \in R((r \in {}^\bullet e \Rightarrow s \in r) \wedge (r \in e^\bullet \Rightarrow s \notin r))\}$. If this set is empty, then we do not need to add inhibitor arcs on event e; otherwise, we look for a small set of regions, that can be used as inhibiting places of e, covering S_e. In other words, we look for a set R' such that: $R' \subseteq R$, $\forall r \in R'((r, e) \in PI(A))$ and $S_e \subseteq \bigcup_{r \in R'} r$. Moreover, we require that the cardinality of R' is the minimum among the sets satisfying the above requirements. Then, we add the inhibitor arcs $\{(r, e) \mid r \in R'\}$. It may happen that we cannot find such a set; in that case, we have to change the set of regions R.

If A is (isomorphic to) the case graph of an ensi, and we take the whole R_A as set of regions, then clearly we can always find (one of) the smallest set of inhibitor arcs we have to use; moreover, if A is isomorphic to the case graph of an ens (without inhibitor arcs), then all the sets S_e turn out to be empty, and we obtain a net without inhibitor arcs.

The interesting thing is that we can say the same if we take the set of minimal regions. We need the following:

Proposition 31. *Let A be a transition system, $r, r' \in R_A$. If $(r, e) \in PI(A)$ and $r' \subseteq r$ then $(r', e) \in PI(A)$.* □

Corollary 32. *Let A be a transition system. If A satisfies SSP and EESSP then there exists $I \subseteq PI(A)$ such that $sg(gen_A(Min(R_A), I)) \cong A$.* □

Now we show a construction of an ensi, whose conditions are the minimal regions, based on the following intuition: the case graph of an ensi N is a subgraph of the case graph of the ens $\tilde{N}$ (obtained from N by deleting the inhibitor arcs), and the lacking arcs in $sg(N)$ give information on the inhibitor arcs.

We recall from [4] some basic properties, characterizing the transition systems that are isomorphic to the case graph of an ens: A transition system A satisfies the *event separation property* (ESP) iff $\forall e \in E$ there exist regions r, r' such that $e \in {}^\bullet r$ and $e \in r'^\bullet$. A satisfies the *forward closure property* iff $\forall s \in St, \forall e \in E$ if ${}^\bullet e \subseteq R_s$ then there exists $s' \in St$ and $s \xrightarrow{e} s'$.
We look for a characterization of the case graphs of nets with inhibitor arcs, based on following observation: the transition systems we consider do not satisfy the forward closure property, but a weaker version of it, that corresponds to say that when a diamond is not accomplished because an edge is missing, then there is a region containing exactly these four vertices. This takes into account the fact that an inhibitor arc forbids the happening of an event which otherwise is enabled, hence there are *missing* transitions. To be able to formulate this property, that we will call *weak forward closure property*, we need some auxiliary notions.
We say that a minimal region r *contains* an event e iff there exists $s, s' \in r$ such that $s \xrightarrow{e} s'$. We are interested here in finding a relationship between a region that contains a certain event e and one that doesn't. More precisely we look for those regions that are *good* candidates to be an inhibiting place.

Definition 33. Let $A = (St, E, \rightarrow)$ be a transition system and r, r' be two minimal regions of A such that r contains an event e and r' doesn't, and $r \cap r' = \emptyset$. We say that r and r' are *compatible* with respect to e (denoted with $r \overset{e}{\leftrightarrow} r'$) if there exist two other minimal regions $\hat{r}$ and $\hat{r}'$ such that following conditions are satisfied:

- $(r \cup r') \subseteq (\hat{r} \cup \hat{r}')$,
- $\hat{r} \cap r \neq \emptyset$ and $\hat{r}' \cap r' \neq \emptyset$, and
- $e \in {}^\bullet\hat{r}'$ and $e \in \hat{r}^\bullet$. □

We illustrate the intuition behind this definition. Consider two disjoint minimal regions such that one contains an event e and the other doesn't. If they can be covered by two other minimal regions in the way described above, then quite clearly the region that doesn't contain e represents a condition that inhibits e. With the aid of this notion, we can now state the desired property.

Definition 34. A transition system $A = (St, E, \rightarrow)$ satisfies the *weak forward closure property* iff whenever there exists a state $s \in St$ and an event $e \in E$ such that ${}^\bullet e \subseteq R_s$ and $s \overset{e}{\not\rightarrow}$, then there exists a state s' such that $e^\bullet \subseteq R_{s'}$, $\{s, s'\}$ is included in a minimal region r and there exists a region $r' \overset{e}{\leftrightarrow} r$ such that $r' \cap (\cup_{\hat{r} \in R_s} \hat{r}) \neq \emptyset$. □

We show now that the state graph of a net with inhibitor arcs satisfies the state separation property, the event separation property and the weak forward closure.

Proposition 35. *Let $N = (B, E, F, I, c_0)$ be an elementary net with inhibitor arcs. Then $f : sg(N) \rightarrow sg(N)$, defined as the identity on the states of $sg(N)$ is a G-morphism.* □

Using this proposition it is easy to show that:

Proposition 36. *Let $N = (B, E, F, I, c_0)$ be an elementary net with inhibitor arcs. Then $sg(N)$ is a state separated, event separated and weakly closed transition system.* □

With the help of the definition of compatibility, we can specialize the definition 26 as follows.

Definition 37. Let $A = (S, E, \rightarrow, s_0)$ be a rooted labelled transition system, $Min(R_A)$ be the set of its minimal regions and I a subset of $PI(A)$ such that $(r, e) \in I$ iff $r \overset{e}{\leftrightarrow} r'$ for some $r' \in Min(A)$ such that r' contains e. We define $min(A) = gen_A(Min(R_A), I)$. □

The morphism defined as $s \mapsto \{r \in R_s | r \in Min(A)\}$ is an isomorphism between A and $sg(min(A))$.

Theorem 38. *Let A be a transition system that satisfies the state separation property, the event separation property and the weak forward closure property. Then $A \cong sg(min(A))$.* □

If we consider all the potential inhibitor arcs, it is easy to see that many of them are superfluous, where superfluous means the behavior of net is not influenced by the presence of the arc. Indeed many of these arcs connect conditions that never holds when the "potentially" inhibited event happen. In the following we try to understand the conditions that make an inhibitor arc a *used* one. It will turn out that inhibitor arcs connect different state-machine components of a net. In [4] it is shown that the transition system isomorphic to the state graph of an elementary net carries enough information to identify the state-machine components of the net. We specialize this result showing that an inhibitor arc is generated only between state-machine components, that accounts to say that if an inhibitor arc is present *inside* a state-machine component, then it is superfluous.

We start recalling how it is possible to construct the state-machine components of a net. We identify the set of conditions of a component with the aid of the following proposition (fact 4.3 in [4]).

Proposition 39. *Let $Z = \{r_1, \ldots, r_k\}$ be a family of regions of a transition system $A = (S, E, \rightarrow, s_0)$ such that $\forall i, j \in \{1, \ldots, k\}$ $r_i \cap r_j = \emptyset$ and $\forall r \in R_A$ $r \notin Z$ implies that $\exists r_i \in Z$ such that $r \cap r_i \neq \emptyset$. Then*

1. $\bigcup r_i = S$,
2. $\forall e \in E$ $|{}^{\bullet}e \cap Z| \leq 1$ *and* $|e^{\bullet} \cap Z| \leq 1$, *and*
3. $\forall e \in E$ $e \in {}^{\bullet}r_i$ *iff* $\exists j$ $e \in r_j^{\bullet}$. □

In [4] it is proved that the states of A can be decomposed into disjoint minimal regions, and any such decomposition form a sequential component. Moreover the set of all the possible decomposition determines the sequential components that cover the corresponding net.

We prove that in the net generated by a decomposition there is no inhibitor arc. Let Z be a set of regions of a transition system A, we denote with In_Z the subset of events of A which are internal in the regions of Z. Notice that if Z meets the requirements of proposition 39, then for each $e \in In_Z$, $\forall i \in \{1, \ldots, k\}$ $e \notin ({}^\bullet r_i \cup r_i^\bullet)$.

Proposition 40. *Let* $Z = \{r_1, \ldots, r_k\}$ *be a family of regions of a transition system* $A = (S, E, \rightarrow, s_0)$ *such that* $\forall i, j \in \{1, \ldots, k\}$ $r_i \cap r_j = \emptyset$ *and* $\forall r \in R_A$ $r \notin Z$ *implies that* $\exists r_i \in Z$ *such that* $r \cap r_i \neq \emptyset$. *Then* $(Z, E \setminus In_Z, F_Z, \emptyset, c_Z)$ *where* $(r, e) \in F_Z$ *iff* $e \in r^\bullet$, $(e, r) \in F_Z$ *iff* $e \in {}^\bullet r$ *and* $r \in c_Z$ *iff* $s_0 \in r$ *is a state machine component of the net and it doesn't contain any inhibitor arc.* □

The net is clearly a state-machine component. In order to establish that it doesn't have inhibitor arcs it is enough to consider the set of inhibitor arcs of the net generated as in definition 37: consider an event e such that (r, e) is an inhibitor arc and $e \in E \setminus In_Z$, and take r_i such that $e \in r_i^\bullet$, clearly $r_i \cap r \neq \emptyset$, hence $r \notin Z$. We can then use the results in [4], that can be summarized as follows.

Theorem 41. *Let* A *be a transition systems. Then the* $(Min(A), I)$*-generated net can be decomposed in state-machine components* $(B_i, E_i, F_i, \emptyset, c_i)$ *and if* $(r, e) \in I$ *then* $r \in B_i$, $e \in E_j$ *and* $i \neq j$. □

Considering again the transition system depicted in the introduction, we synthesize two state-machine components (one performing a and the other b) connected via an inhibitor arc forbidding the happening of a once that b has happend.

6 Future work

In this paper we tackled the synthesis problem for elementary net systems with inhibitor arcs. It could be interesting to extend this study to contextual nets; the introduction of positive contextual arcs and the interplay of these with the inhibiting ones could give rise to results about the minimum number of places and contextual arcs the synthesized net must contain to produce a given behaviour. By the introduction of inhibitor arcs, we have extended the class of transition systems that are isomorphic to the case graph of a net. Another step in that direction should be to weaken the requirement for the case graph of the synthesized net to be isomorphic to the given transition system. For example, bisimulation is a widely accepted equivalence, relating transition systems that are intended to exhibit the same behaviour. Consider e.g. the two figures in Introduction and in Section 5: the two transitions systems are bisimilar, but only for the one in the Introduction there exists a net with an isomorphic case graph. We think it may be interesting to find bisimulation-preserving rules that transform a transition system in a form to which we can apply the construction in Definition 26 to produce a net. We are also looking for a direct characterization of transition systems representing the behaviour of a net up to bisimulation.

Acknowledgements. We thank the anonymous referees for their helpful suggestions.

References

1. E. Badouel, L. Bernardinello, and P. Darondeau. The synthesis problem for elementary net systems is NP-complete. Inria Research Report 2558, 1995. to appear in Theoretical Computer Science.
2. E. Badouel and P. Darondeau. Trace nets and process automata. *Acta Informatica*, 32:647–679, 1995.
3. E. Badouel and P. Darondeau. On the synthesis of general Petri nets. Inria Research Report 3025, 1996.
4. L. Bernardinello. Synthesis of net systems. In *Application and Theory of Petri Nets 1993*, Lecture Notes in Computer Science 691, pages 89–105, 1993.
5. N. Busi and R. Gorrieri. A Petri net semantics for π-calculus. In *Proceeding of CONCUR'95*, Lecture Notes in Computer Science 962, pages 145–159, 1995.
6. N. Busi and G. M. Pinna. Nonsequential semantics for contextual P/T nets. In *Application and Theory of Petri Nets 1996*, Lecture Notes in Computer Science 1091, pages 113–132, 1996.
7. J. Desel and W. Reisig. The synthesis problem of Petri nets. *Acta Informatica*, 33:296–315, 1996.
8. A. Ehrenfeucht and G. Rozenberg. Partial (set) 2-structures; I and II. *Acta Informatica*, 27:315–368, 1990.
9. U. Montanari and F. Rossi. Contextual nets. *Acta Informatica*, 32:545–596, 1995.
10. M. Mukund. Petri nets and step transition systems. *International Journal of Foundations of Computer Sciences*, 3:443–478, 1992.
11. M. Nielsen, G. Rozenberg, and P. S. Thiagarajan. Elementary transition systems. *Theoretical Computer Science*, 96:3–33, 1992.
12. P. S. Thiagarajan. Elementary net system. In *Advances in Petri Nets 1986: Part I*, Lecture Notes in Computer Science 254, pages 26–59, 1987.
13. W. Vogler. Efficiency of asynchronous systems and read arcs in Petri nets. Univerität Augsburg, Institut für Mathematik, Report 352, 1996.
14. P. W. Hoogers, H. C.M. Kleijn, and P. S. Thiagarajan. An event structure semantics for general Petri nets. *Theoretical Computer Science*, 153:129–170, 1996.

An Algebraic Theory of Multiple Clocks

Rance Cleaveland[1,*], Gerald Lüttgen[2,**], and Michael Mendler[3,***]

[1] Department of Computer Science, North Carolina State University, Raleigh, NC 27695-8206, USA, e-mail: rance@eos.ncsu.edu
[2] Fakultät für Mathematik und Informatik, Universität Passau, D-94030 Passau, Germany, e-mail: {luettgen,mendler}@fmi.uni-passau.de

Abstract. This paper develops a temporal process algebra, CSA, for reasoning about *distributed* systems that involve *qualitative* timing constraints. It is a conservative extension of Milner's CCS that combines the idea of *multiple clocks* from the algebra PMC with the assumption of *maximal progress* familiar from timed process algebras such as TPL. Using a typical class of examples drawn from hardware design, we motivate why these features are useful and in some cases necessary for modeling and verifying distributed systems. We also present fully-abstract behavioral congruences based on the notion of strong bisimulation and observational equivalence, respectively. For temporal strong bisimulation we give sound and complete axiomatizations for several classes of processes.

1 Introduction

Process algebras [10,12] provide a well-studied framework for modeling and verifying concurrent systems [6,8]. These theories typically consist of a simple language with a rigorously defined semantics mapping terms to labeled transition systems. They also usually support equational reasoning as a basis for system verification: an equivalence on processes is defined that equates systems on the basis of their observable behavior, and this relation is used to relate specifications, which describe desired system behavior, and implementations. In order to support *compositional reasoning*, researchers have typically concentrated on equivalences that are also congruences for the given languages.

Traditionally, process algebras have been developed with a view toward modeling the nondeterministic behavior of concurrent and distributed systems. More recent work has incorporated other aspects of system behavior, including real time [1,9,13,14,16]. Most of this later work, however, has been devoted to modeling centralized, as opposed to distributed systems; the real-time work, in particular, has (implicitly or explicitly) focused on systems with a single clock. In this

* Research supported by NSF/DARPA grant CCR-9014775, NSF grant CCR-9120995, ONR Young Investigator Award N00014-92-J-1582, NSF Young Investigator Award CCR-9257963, NSF grant CCR-9402807, and AFOSR grant F49620-95-1-0508.

** Research support partly provided by the German Academic Exchange Service under grant D/95/09026 (Doktorandenstipendium HSP II / AUFE).

*** Author supported by the *Deutsche Forschungsgemeinschaft*.

paper we present a temporal process algebra, called CSA (Calculus for Synchrony and Asynchrony), which is aimed at modeling distributed, timed systems that contain a number of independent clocks. Technically, CSA extends Hennessy and Regan's TPL [9] with constructs from PMC [1] that enable the management of multiple clocks. In doing so we replace the global notion of ***maximal progress*** found in TPL with a local one that is more appropriate for distributed systems. This combination of features yields a convenient formalism for modeling distributed timed systems; it also introduces semantic subtleties the solutions to which constitute the body of this paper.

It should be noted that clocks in CSA are intended to capture qualitative timing constraints, in which it is not the absolute occurrence time or duration of actions that is constrained but their relative ordering and sequencing with respect to clocks. This contrasts with other theories of real-time, which typically focus on precisely measuring the time that elapses between different system events. In this respect CSA follows the philosophy advocated by Nicollin and Sifakis [14] and others, as well as synchronous languages such as ESTEREL [3].

2 Motivation

One standard hardware architecture consists of a number of cooperating synchronous systems which are distributed over different modules, e.g. chips or boards. Typically, each module possesses its own central clock to update all of its registers in a synchronous fashion. The clocks of different modules are independent, so that the modules change their states asynchronously with respect to each other. Such architectures are also called ***globally-asynchronous, locally-synchronous*** [4]. They not only arise through physical distribution, e.g. in computer networks where different sites cannot be synchronized by the same clock, but are also typical for heterogeneous real-time applications. A concrete example is the Brüel & Kjær 2145 Vehicle Signal Analyzer reported in [2].

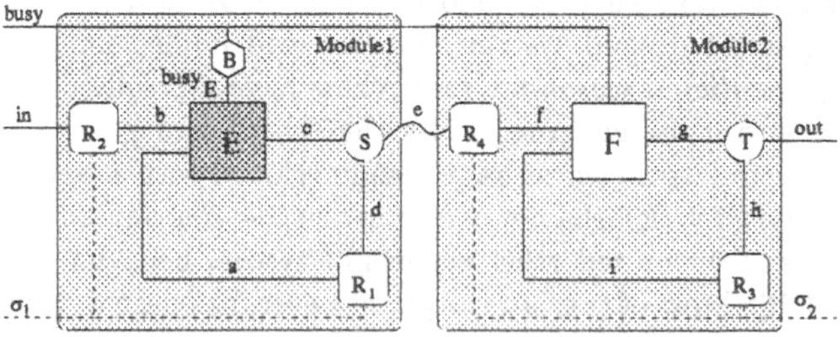

Fig. 1. A globally-asynchronous, locally-synchronous system

A generic example for a globally-asynchronous, locally-synchronous system is depicted in Fig. 1, where solid lines represent communication channels and dashed lines symbolize channels of clocks. Both modules, `Module1` and `Module2`, have their own local clocks σ_1 and σ_2, respectively, and their own function blocks, registers, and buffers. In every clock cycle, the function block E computes a new value from the current values of the state registers R_1 and R_2, obtained through channels a and b, and outputs it on channel c to be propagated further through S to register R_1 via channel d and to the environment via channel e. External input enters the computation through channel *in*. Register R_2 stores the most recent input value from the environment and, thus, ensures that E never has to wait for the environment. Component S and busy buffer B are explained later. Module2 operates in a similar fashion, with its external input being fed by the output of Module1.

The example clearly suggests how we can benefit from a concept of multiple clocks to model real-world distributed systems. The question of what is an adequate notion of clock leads us to the second characteristic of our process algebra: the maximal progress assumption. The fundamental feature of the clock σ_1 is that it must tick only after the previous clock cycle has been completed, i.e. after the function block E has finished its internal computations and the new value has arrived at register R_1. Otherwise, the value stored into R_1 upon the tick of σ_1 is undefined. If Module1 has more than one register reading d they may all take different values, and an inconsistent state may arise. The maximal progress assumption guarantees that a clock tick is delayed until all internal computations or communications have come to an end.

To take account of distribution, the maximal progress property must be "localized" and imposed on every module independently. For instance, the clock σ_1 of Module1 must be able to tick as soon as the previous cycle of σ_1 has been completed, regardless of the state of Module2, which operates asynchronously with respect to Module1. In contrast, the traditional global version of maximal progress would imply that *all* clocks have to wait for *all* computations to complete, whence the system would be globally synchronous.

The combined concept of multiple clocks and local maximal progress is quite powerful. It supports *horizontal* and *vertical* forms of synchronous decomposition that correspond to temporal abstractions with synchronized and nested scales of time. The horizontal form has already been made explicit above. The vertical form arises when we implement, say, the function E of Module1 as a whole synchronous system in itself, with its own local clock (see Sect. 4).

3 Syntax and Semantics

In this section we define the syntax and semantics of our language CSA, which is inspired by the process algebras TPL [9] and PMC [1], which both descend from ATP [14]. The syntax of CSA is essentially the same as in PMC; it extends Milner's CCS [12] with a *timeout operator* and a clock *ignore operator*. The timeout operator occurs in other real-time process algebras [1,9] and was originally introduced in ATP, where it is called *unit-delay*. The ignore operator originates with PMC, though here it is a primitive operation, not derivable as in PMC.

The semantical framework of CSA is based on a notion of transition system that involves two kinds of transitions, *action* transitions and *clock* transitions, modeling two different mechanisms of synchronization and communication in distributed systems. Action transitions, like in CCS, are local handshake communications in which two processes synchronize to take a joint state change together. A clock represents the progress of time, which manifests itself in a recurrent global synchronization event, the clock transition, in which all process components that are in the regime, or in the scope, of this clock are forced to take part.

In CSA action and clock transitions are not orthogonal concepts that can be specified independently from each other, but are connected in line with the following intuitions: (1) A clock records the *progress* of time, with two successive clock events marking an interval of time. (2) The *passage* of time is determined by internal computations that are within the regime of the clock. This yields the very specific semantic connection between actions and clocks, known as the *maximal progress assumption* [9,16]. Maximal progress usually is read as the condition that "communications must occur whenever they are possible," i.e. a process cannot be intercepted by a clock as long as it is able to perform internal computations.

The last feature of CSA is *clock scoping.* Since we are dealing with distributed systems and multiple clocks, it is natural to localize the maximal progress assumption with respect to clocks and to limit the scope of clocks. A communication that reaches outside the scope is an external computation that must be considered asynchronous with respect to the clock. Different clocks, which represent different local views of time, may have disjoint, overlapping, or nested scopes, and amount to different abstractions of time.

Note that clocks in our setting are abstract in the sense that we do not prejudice any particular way to interpret them. We are free to think of a clock as the ticking of a global real-time watch measuring off absolute process time in constant or non-constant intervals, as the system clock of a synchronous processor, as a recurrent external interrupt, or as the completion signal of a distributed synchronization protocol. Thus, clocks can be used as a general and flexible means for bundling asynchronous behavior into sequenced intervals, and to give local meaning to the notions of "before," "after," and "state."

3.1 Syntax of CSA

Formally, let Λ be a countable set of action labels, not including the so-called *silent* or *internal* action τ. With every $a \in \Lambda$ we associate a *complementary action* $\overline{a}$. We define $\overline{\Lambda} \stackrel{\mathrm{df}}{=} \{\overline{a} \mid a \in \Lambda\}$ and take $\mathcal{A}$ to denote the set of all actions $\Lambda \cup \overline{\Lambda} \cup \{\tau\}$, where $\tau \notin \Lambda \cup \overline{\Lambda}$. Complementation is lifted to $\Lambda \cup \overline{\Lambda}$ by defining $\overline{\overline{a}} = a$. As in CCS [12] an action a communicates with its complement $\overline{a}$ to produce the internal action τ. We let $a, b, \ldots$ range over $\Lambda \cup \overline{\Lambda}$ and $\alpha, \beta, \ldots$ over $\mathcal{A}$. Besides the set $\mathcal{A}$ of actions, CSA is parameterized in a set $\mathcal{T} = \{\sigma, \sigma', \rho, \ldots\}$

of *clocks*. The syntax of our language is defined by the following BNF

$$P ::= \mathbf{0} \mid x \mid \alpha.P \mid P+P \mid P|P \mid P[f] \mid P\setminus L \mid P\uparrow\sigma \mid \lfloor P\rfloor\sigma(P) \mid \mu x.P$$

where x is a *variable* taken from a countably infinite set of variables $\mathcal{V}$, $f : \mathcal{A} \to \mathcal{A}$ is a *finite relabeling*, and $L \subseteq \mathcal{A} \setminus \{\tau\}$ is a *restriction set*. For convenience, we define $\overline{L} \stackrel{\text{df}}{=} \{\overline{a} \mid a \in L\}$. A finite relabeling satisfies the properties $f(\tau) = \tau$, $f(\overline{a}) = \overline{f(a)}$, and $|\{\alpha \mid f(\alpha) \neq \alpha\}| < \infty$. Moreover, $\uparrow$ is called the (static) *ignore operator* and $\lfloor\cdot\rfloor\sigma(\cdot)$ the *timeout operator*. Further, we use the standard definitions for the *sort* of a term P, $\mathsf{sort}(P) \subseteq \Lambda \cup \overline{\Lambda}$, *static* and *dynamic* operators, *free* and *bound* variables, *open* and *closed* terms, and *contexts*. A process variable is called *guarded* in a process term if each occurrence of the variable is in the scope of a prefix or of the second argument of a timeout (see below). We refer to closed and guarded terms as *processes*. Let $\mathcal{P}$ be the set of all processes, ranged over by P, Q, R, and denote syntactic equality on $\mathcal{P}$ by $\equiv$. We extend the timeout operator to sequences of clocks by defining $\lfloor P\rfloor \stackrel{\text{df}}{=} P$ and $\lfloor P\rfloor\sigma_1(Q_1)\dots\sigma_n(Q_n) \stackrel{\text{df}}{=} \lfloor\lfloor P\rfloor\sigma_1(Q_1)\dots\sigma_{n-1}(Q_{n-1})\rfloor\sigma_n(Q_n)$. We often further abbreviate sequences $\sigma_1\dots\sigma_n$ of clocks by $\boldsymbol{\sigma}$ and sequences $Q_1\dots Q_n$ of processes by $\mathbf{Q}$. In this vein, $\lfloor P\rfloor\boldsymbol{\sigma}(\mathbf{Q})$ is a shorthand for $\lfloor P\rfloor\sigma_1(Q_1)\dots\sigma_n(Q_n)$.

Table 1. Clock scoping

$\mathrm{I}_\sigma(\alpha.P) \stackrel{\text{df}}{=} \{\alpha\}$	$\mathrm{I}_\sigma(\mu x.P) \stackrel{\text{df}}{=} \mathrm{I}_\sigma(P[\mu x.P/x])$
$\mathrm{I}_\sigma(P+Q) \stackrel{\text{df}}{=} \mathrm{I}_\sigma(P) \cup \mathrm{I}_\sigma(Q)$	$\mathrm{I}_\sigma(P\|Q) \stackrel{\text{df}}{=} \mathrm{I}_\sigma(P) \cup \mathrm{I}_\sigma(Q) \cup \{\tau \mid \mathrm{I}_\sigma(P) \cap \overline{\mathrm{I}_\sigma(Q)} \neq \emptyset\}$
$\mathrm{I}_\sigma(P[f]) \stackrel{\text{df}}{=} \{f(\alpha) \mid \alpha \in \mathrm{I}_\sigma(P)\}$	$\mathrm{I}_\sigma(P\setminus L) \stackrel{\text{df}}{=} \mathrm{I}_\sigma(P) \setminus (L \cup \overline{L})$
$\mathrm{I}_\sigma(\lfloor P\rfloor\sigma'(Q)) \stackrel{\text{df}}{=} \mathrm{I}_\sigma(P)$	$\mathrm{I}_\sigma(P\uparrow\sigma') \stackrel{\text{df}}{=} \mathrm{I}_\sigma(P)$ if $\sigma \neq \sigma'$

3.2 Semantics of CSA

The *operational semantics* of a CSA process $P \in \mathcal{P}$ is given by a labeled transition system $\langle \mathcal{P}, \mathcal{A} \cup \mathcal{T}, \longrightarrow, P\rangle$ where $\mathcal{P}$ is the set of states, $\mathcal{A} \cup \mathcal{T}$ the alphabet, $\longrightarrow$ the transition relation, and P the start state. We refer to transitions with labels in $\mathcal{A}$ as *action transitions*, and to those with labels in $\mathcal{T}$ as *clock transitions*. The transition relation $\longrightarrow \subseteq \mathcal{P} \times (\mathcal{A} \cup \mathcal{T}) \times \mathcal{P}$ for CSA is defined in Table 2 using operational rules. For the sake of simplicity, let us use γ for a representative of $\mathcal{A} \cup \mathcal{T}$, and write $P \stackrel{\gamma}{\to} P'$ instead of $\langle P, \gamma, P'\rangle \in \longrightarrow$ and $P \stackrel{\gamma}{\to}$ for $\exists P' \in \mathcal{P}. P \stackrel{\gamma}{\to} P'$.

To ensure maximal progress the operational rules involve side conditions on *initial action sets*. Beside the usual definition of $\mathrm{I}(P)$ for the initial action set of a process P – where $\mathrm{I}(P\uparrow\sigma)$ and $\mathrm{I}(\lfloor P\rfloor\sigma(Q))$ are given by $\mathrm{I}(P)$ – we define the set $\mathrm{I}_\sigma(P) \subseteq \mathrm{I}(P)$ of all initial actions of P *within the scope* of the clock σ

as the smallest set satisfying the equations in Table 1. Note that the sets $\mathrm{I}(P)$ and $\mathrm{I}_\sigma(P)$ are well-defined since all processes are closed and guarded. Moreover, $\mathrm{I}_\sigma(P) = \mathrm{I}(P)$ whenever P does not contain any ignore operator. Finally, we define initial visible action sets by $\mathbb{I}(P) \stackrel{\mathrm{df}}{=} \mathrm{I}(P) \setminus \{\tau\}$ and $\mathbb{I}_\sigma(P) \stackrel{\mathrm{df}}{=} \mathrm{I}_\sigma(P) \setminus \{\tau\}$.

Table 2. Operational semantics for CSA

Act	$\dfrac{-}{\alpha.P \stackrel{\alpha}{\to} P}$	tAct	$\dfrac{-}{a.P \stackrel{\sigma}{\to} a.P}\ \sigma \in \mathcal{T}$
Sum1	$\dfrac{P \stackrel{\alpha}{\to} P'}{P + Q \stackrel{\alpha}{\to} P'}$	tNil	$\dfrac{-}{\mathbf{0} \stackrel{\sigma}{\to} \mathbf{0}}\ \sigma \in \mathcal{T}$
Sum2	$\dfrac{Q \stackrel{\alpha}{\to} Q'}{P + Q \stackrel{\alpha}{\to} Q'}$	tSum	$\dfrac{P \stackrel{\sigma}{\to} P' \quad Q \stackrel{\sigma}{\to} Q'}{P + Q \stackrel{\sigma}{\to} P' + Q'}$
Rel	$\dfrac{P \stackrel{\alpha}{\to} P'}{P[f] \stackrel{f(\alpha)}{\to} P'[f]}$	tRel	$\dfrac{P \stackrel{\sigma}{\to} P'}{P[f] \stackrel{\sigma}{\to} P'[f]}$
Res	$\dfrac{P \stackrel{\alpha}{\to} P'}{P \setminus L \stackrel{\alpha}{\to} P' \setminus L}\ \alpha \notin L \cup \overline{L}$	tRes	$\dfrac{P \stackrel{\sigma}{\to} P'}{P \setminus L \stackrel{\sigma}{\to} P' \setminus L}$
Com1	$\dfrac{P \stackrel{\alpha}{\to} P'}{P\|Q \stackrel{\alpha}{\to} P'\|Q}$	tCom	$\dfrac{P \stackrel{\sigma}{\to} P' \quad Q \stackrel{\sigma}{\to} Q'}{P\|Q \stackrel{\sigma}{\to} P'\|Q'}\ \tau \notin \mathrm{I}_\sigma(P\|Q)$
Com2	$\dfrac{Q \stackrel{\alpha}{\to} Q'}{P\|Q \stackrel{\alpha}{\to} P\|Q'}$	tIgn1	$\dfrac{-}{P{\uparrow}\sigma \stackrel{\sigma}{\to} P{\uparrow}\sigma}$
Com3	$\dfrac{P \stackrel{a}{\to} P' \quad Q \stackrel{\overline{a}}{\to} Q'}{P\|Q \stackrel{\tau}{\to} P'\|Q'}$	tIgn2	$\dfrac{P \stackrel{\sigma'}{\to} P'}{P{\uparrow}\sigma \stackrel{\sigma'}{\to} P'{\uparrow}\sigma}\ \sigma \neq \sigma'$
Ign	$\dfrac{P \stackrel{\alpha}{\to} P'}{P{\uparrow}\sigma \stackrel{\alpha}{\to} P'{\uparrow}\sigma}$	tTO1	$\dfrac{-}{\lfloor P \rfloor \sigma(Q) \stackrel{\sigma}{\to} Q}\ \tau \notin \mathrm{I}_\sigma(P)$
TO	$\dfrac{P \stackrel{\alpha}{\to} P'}{\lfloor P \rfloor \sigma(Q) \stackrel{\alpha}{\to} P'}$	tTO2	$\dfrac{P \stackrel{\sigma'}{\to} P'}{\lfloor P \rfloor \sigma(Q) \stackrel{\sigma'}{\to} P'}\ \sigma \neq \sigma'$
Rec	$\dfrac{P[\mu x.P/x] \stackrel{\alpha}{\to} P'}{\mu x.P \stackrel{\alpha}{\to} P'}$	tRec	$\dfrac{P[\mu x.P/x] \stackrel{\sigma}{\to} P'}{\mu x.P \stackrel{\sigma}{\to} P'}$

The operational semantics for action transitions extends the one of CCS by rules dealing with the ignore and the timeout operator. More precisely, the process $\alpha.P$ may engage in action α and then behave like P. The *summation operator* $+$ denotes nondeterministic choice, i.e. the process $P + Q$ may either behave like P or Q. The *restriction operator* $\setminus L$ prohibits the execution of actions in $L \cup \overline{L}$ and thus permits the scoping of actions. $P[f]$ behaves exactly as P where ordinary actions are renamed by the *relabeling* f. The process $P|Q$ stands for the *parallel composition* of P and Q according to an interleaving semantics with synchronized communication on complementary actions resulting in the internal action τ. The processes $P{\uparrow}\sigma$ and $\lfloor P \rfloor \sigma(Q)$ behave like P for action transitions. The timeout operator disappears as soon as P engages in an action transition, thereby observably changing its state. Finally, $\mu x.P$ denotes *recursion*, i.e. $\mu x.P$ is a process which behaves as a distinguished solution of the equation $x = P$.

With respect to clock transitions the operational semantics is set up such that if $\tau \in \mathrm{I}_\sigma(P)$ then the clock σ is inhibited. We refer to this kind of pre-emption as *local maximal progress*. Its local nature lies in the facts that, in general, $\mathrm{I}_\sigma(P) \neq \mathrm{I}(P)$ and that the sets $\mathrm{I}_\sigma(P)$ may be different for different clocks. Accordingly, the process $\alpha.P$ may idle for each clock σ whenever $\alpha \neq \tau$. Time has to proceed equally on both sides of summation, i.e. $P+Q$ can engage in a clock transition and, thus, delay the nondeterministic choice if and only if both P and Q can engage in the clock tick. Also both argument processes of a parallel composition have to synchronize on clock transitions according to Rule tCom. Its side condition implements local maximal progress and can alternatively be written as $\mathbb{I}_\sigma(P) \cap \overline{\mathbb{I}_\sigma(Q)} = \emptyset$, i.e. there is no pending communication between P and Q on an action that lies in the scope of σ. Regarding the ignore operator, the process $P\uparrow\sigma$ is capable of performing a σ-loop, i.e. P *ignores* σ, regardless if $\tau \in \mathrm{I}_\sigma(P)$ or not. This is consistent with our definition $\mathrm{I}_\sigma(P\uparrow\sigma) \stackrel{\mathrm{df}}{=} \emptyset$, which means that none of the initial actions of P is in the scope of clock σ. Thus, $\uparrow$ is actually not a *scoping* but a *co-scoping* operator, i.e. all processes are assumed to be within the scope of all clocks unless explicitly excluded using an ignore. Using co-scoping instead of scoping simplifies the operational rules when dealing with multiple local clocks, since the traditional rules for summation and parallel composition with respect to timed transitions need not be changed. Moreover, the process $\lfloor P \rfloor \sigma(Q)$ can perform a σ-transition to Q provided P cannot engage in an internal action which is in the scope of clock σ. Since a clock transition too represents an observable change of state, the timeout operator disappears as soon as P engages in such a transition. This intuition is the same as for the corresponding unit-delay operator in ATP [14]. For multiple clocks this leads to rule tTO2 in which the timeout for σ is dropped when a different σ' ticks. The idea is that the ordering of the σ and σ' ticks is observable and the first one determines the state change. Note, however, that by using recursion to insert explicit clock idling persistent versions of the timeout can be obtained.

The operational semantics for CSA possesses several important properties. First, the summation and the parallel operator of CSA are associative and commutative. Second, a process can always engage in a clock transition provided it cannot perform an internal action which is in the scope of this clock. Formally, $\tau \notin \mathrm{I}_\sigma(P)$ implies $P \stackrel{\sigma}{\rightarrow}$. Third, the semantics satisfies the *local maximal progress* and the *local time determinacy* property. Both are generalizations of the well-known maximal progress and time determinacy properties, for global time, to a local notion of time in terms of multiple local clocks. Local maximal progress states that $P \stackrel{\sigma}{\rightarrow}$ implies $\tau \notin \mathrm{I}_\sigma(P)$. Time determinacy, which is a common feature of all real-time process algebras, states that processes react in a deterministic way to clock ticks, reflecting the intuition that mere progress of time does not resolve choices. Formally, $P \stackrel{\sigma}{\rightarrow} P'$ and $P \stackrel{\sigma}{\rightarrow} P''$ implies $P' \equiv P''$.

It is not difficult to see that CSA is a conservative extension of TPL if we drop TPL's *undefined* process Ω, which has been introduced to define a semantics based on *testing* [7]. Restricting $\mathcal{T}$ to a single clock, say $\mathcal{T} = \{\sigma\}$, and dropping the ignore operator, gives us precisely the syntax and operational semantics of TPL. Note that in this single-clock version of CSA the timed prefixing of TPL can be derived as $\sigma.P \stackrel{\text{df}}{=} \lfloor 0 \rfloor \sigma(P)$. Moreover, CCS [12] can be identified as the subcalculus of CSA which is obtained by defining $\mathcal{T} = \emptyset$.

Finally, it is worth mentioning that CSA allows us to express *clock constraints* by processes. For example, if we want to relate the speeds of clocks we can do so by composing the system under consideration in parallel with a process expressing the corresponding constraint. As this issue is not central to this paper, however, we do not address it further.

4 Example (revisited)

Now we formally describe the example presented in Sect. 2 in our algebra CSA. We refer to Fig. 1 and assume that we refine the function module E by a complete synchronous subsystem with its own local clock $\rho \in \mathcal{T} \stackrel{\text{df}}{=} \{\sigma_1, \sigma_2, \rho\}$, as depicted in Fig. 2. At top level the structure of the overall system `System` is $(\texttt{Module1} \uparrow \sigma_2 \mid \texttt{Module2} \uparrow \sigma_1 \uparrow \rho) \setminus \{e\}$. This captures the asynchronous parallel composition of `Module1` and `Module2`. The ignore operators $\uparrow \sigma_1$ and $\uparrow \sigma_2$ are introduced so as to make both modules ignore each other's clocks. The clock ρ is internal to `Module1`, whence `Module2` ignores it with $\uparrow \rho$. The channel e connecting both modules is internal to `System`, and thus restricted by $\setminus\{e\}$.

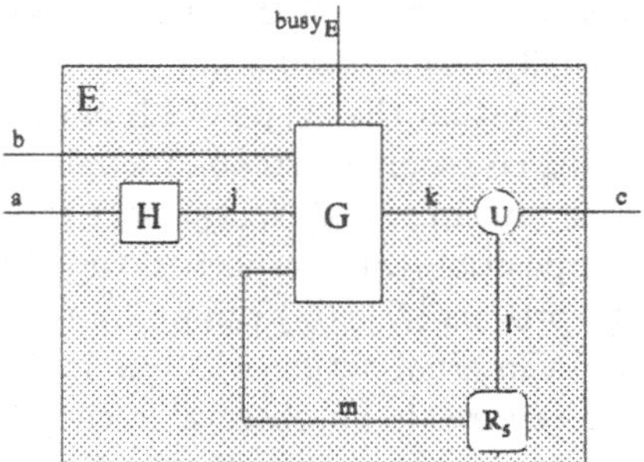

Fig. 2. Component E (refined)

At the next structural level we break up the two asynchronous modules, each of which is a synchronous subsystem. Let us look at the internals of `Module1`, which is $(\texttt{E} \mid (\texttt{R}_1 \mid \texttt{R}_2 \mid \texttt{S} \mid \texttt{B}) \uparrow \rho) \setminus \{a, b, c, d, \texttt{busy}_\texttt{E}\}$. It is a parallel composition of a function block `E`, state registers $\texttt{R}_1$ and $\texttt{R}_2$, a busy buffer `B`, and a special fork component `S`. These components communicate via the channels $\{a, b, c, d, \texttt{busy}_\texttt{E}\}$ which are internal to `Module1` and hence are restricted away. The parallel subsystem $(\texttt{R}_1 \mid \texttt{R}_2 \mid \texttt{S} \mid \texttt{B}) \uparrow \rho$ ignores the clock ρ, making ρ local to the function block `E`. This function block finally is decomposed to the synchronous system $\texttt{E} \stackrel{\text{df}}{=} (\texttt{H} \mid \texttt{G} \mid \texttt{R}_5 \mid \texttt{U}) \setminus \{j, k, l, m\}$.

Now let us turn our attention to the synchronous subsystem `E` (cf. Fig. 2). Block `E` should read its inputs from channels a and b, take an arbitrary number of cycles of clock ρ to compute a result that is then passed over to the environment on output channel c. The algorithm for this computation is contained in function block `G`. The register $\texttt{R}_5$ stores the intermediate values, i.e. represents the local state on which the algorithm works. The function block `H` may be a preprocessing stage, and the component U is assumed to be a fork process that distributes the data on its input k to outputs c and l, i.e. $\mathtt{U} \stackrel{\text{df}}{=} \mu x_0 . k.\bar{l}.(\mu x_1 . \bar{c}.x_0 + \tau.x_1)$. The τ-loop indicates waiting for external output through channel c, which will inhibit the local clock ρ as long as the output has not been delivered.

In CSA the register might be specified as $\mathtt{R}_5 \stackrel{\text{df}}{=} \mu x.\ \lfloor l.x \rfloor \rho(\mu y.\overline{m}.x + l.y)$. It continuously accepts an updating input on channel l, and when the clock ρ ticks it changes its state to $\mu y.\overline{m}.\mathtt{R}_5 + l.y$. In this state the output action $\overline{m}$ starts the next computation cycle, while the l-loop makes sure that the register is always input enabled. If our channels would carry real data then the new value injected into the next cycle with $\overline{m}$ would be the last value read in from input l *before* the clock tick. This means that the l-loop *after* the clock must not change the registered value. From the value supplied by $\overline{m}$ after each clock tick, the function blocks compute a next state value that eventually ends up being latched into $\mathtt{R}_5$ again through l. Then the cycle is completed and ρ may tick again. To indicate the simplest case of a function block let H be the trivial iteration $\mathtt{H} \stackrel{\text{df}}{=} \mu x.\, a.\tau.\bar{j}.x$. Accordingly, H first reads an external input from a, then performs an internal computation represented by τ, and finally outputs on j, whereupon it returns to the initial state. For a function block with more than one input more complicated input-output pattern are possible. For instance, we want G to implement an algorithm that reads its inputs b and j and initial state m and then computes its function in a number of steps, storing intermediate results in register $\mathtt{R}_5$. The following CSA process specifies such a behavior:

$$\mathtt{G} \stackrel{\text{df}}{=} \mu x_0 . m.j.b.\mathtt{G}_1 \qquad \mathtt{G}_1 \stackrel{\text{df}}{=} \mu x_1 . \tau.(\bar{k}.x_0 + \bar{k}.\mathtt{G}_2) \qquad \mathtt{G}_2 \stackrel{\text{df}}{=} \mu x_2 . m.x_1 + \overline{\mathtt{busy}_\mathtt{E}}.x_2\ .$$

G consumes the register value on m and the result of function H on j, reads an input from the environment through channel b, and then passes to $\mathtt{G}_1$, which is the actual computation state. After a finite amount of internal computation, indicated by the leading τ, a result is computed that may be output with action $\bar{k}$. Now two possibilities arise: either the algorithm is completed, in which case we pass back to the initial state G (variable x_0), or we carry on with another clock cycle, in which case we move to state $\mathtt{G}_2$. This decision, of course, depends on the data, but since we do not consider values, we model this as a nondeterministic choice. In $\mathtt{G}_2$ we have reached a final state of a single ρ clock cycle, but only an intermediate state of the algorithm implemented by E. The $\overline{\mathtt{busy}_\mathtt{E}}$-loop signals this to the environment of E in order to inhibit the outer clock σ_1. In the intermediate state $\mathtt{G}_2$ of the algorithm we do not need to read new input data, but only get the next state by m and continue with $\mathtt{G}_1$.

The above specification example shows how the ignore operator can be used to localize clocks, and the timeout operator to model the synchronized updating of registers. Maximal progress controls when a clock tick is possible and when it is delayed. The only way to stop a clock is by internal divergence, e.g. arising from a feed-back loop that does not contain any clocked register. In this case of a violated design rule, the functional blocks produce divergence and the local clock of that module is never able to tick. This relationship between design error, internal divergence, and conceptual time stop is very natural for synchronous hardware, which stresses the adequacy of the maximal progress model.

5 Temporal Strong Bisimulation

The transition systems produced by the operational semantics are a rather fine-grained semantic view of processes. Therefore, we develop a semantic theory based on bisimulation [12]. Our aim in this section is to characterize the largest congruence contained in the "naive" strong bisimulation [12] where we treat clocks as actions.

Definition 1. A symmetric relation $\mathcal{R} \subseteq \mathcal{P} \times \mathcal{P}$ is called ***naive strong bisimulation*** if for every $\langle P, Q\rangle \in \mathcal{R}$, $\gamma \in \mathcal{A} \cup \mathcal{T}$, the following condition holds: $P \xrightarrow{\gamma} P'$ implies $\exists Q'.\, Q \xrightarrow{\gamma} Q'$ and $\langle P', Q'\rangle \in \mathcal{R}$. We write $P \sim_{\mathrm{n}} Q$ if there exists a naive strong bisimulation $\mathcal{R}$ such that $\langle P, Q\rangle \in \mathcal{R}$.

It is straightforward to establish that $\sim_{\mathrm{n}}$ is the *largest* naive strong bisimulation and that $\sim_{\mathrm{n}}$ is an equivalence relation. Unfortunately, $\sim_{\mathrm{n}}$ is *not* a congruence. The reason is that the transition system of a process P does not contain the clock scoping information $\mathrm{I}_\sigma(P)$ needed to determine the transition system of $C[P]$ for all contexts $C[X]$. For instance, $a.\mathbf{0} \sim_{\mathrm{n}} a.\mathbf{0}\uparrow\sigma$ but $a.\mathbf{0} \,|\, \overline{a}.\mathbf{0} \not\sim_{\mathrm{n}} (a.\mathbf{0}\uparrow\sigma) \,|\, \overline{a}.\mathbf{0}$ since the right-hand process can do a σ-transition while the corresponding σ-transition of the left-hand process is pre-empted due to maximal progress. In this example $a.\mathbf{0}$ and $a.\mathbf{0}\uparrow\sigma$ have identical transition systems but different clock scoping, effecting different pre-emption of clock transitions in parallel contexts. In order to find the largest congruence contained in $\sim_{\mathrm{n}}$ we have to take into account the scope of clocks.

Definition 2. A symmetric relation $\mathcal{R} \subseteq \mathcal{P} \times \mathcal{P}$ is a ***temporal strong bisimulation*** if for every $\langle P, Q\rangle \in \mathcal{R}$, $\alpha \in \mathcal{A}$, and $\sigma \in \mathcal{T}$ the following conditions hold.

1. $P \xrightarrow{\alpha} P'$ implies $\exists Q'.\, Q \xrightarrow{\alpha} Q'$ and $\langle P', Q'\rangle \in \mathcal{R}$.
2. $P \xrightarrow{\sigma} P'$ implies $\mathbb{I}_\sigma(Q) \subseteq \mathbb{I}_\sigma(P)$ and $\exists Q'.\, Q \xrightarrow{\sigma} Q'$ and $\langle P', Q'\rangle \in \mathcal{R}$.

We write $P \simeq Q$ if $\langle P, Q\rangle \in \mathcal{R}$ for some temporal strong bisimulation $\mathcal{R}$.

The definition of $P \simeq Q$ requires not only that all clock transitions in P and Q must match each other, but also that with respect to all these clocks σ the pre-emption potential of both P and Q must be identical, i.e. $\mathbb{I}_\sigma(P) = \mathbb{I}_\sigma(Q)$.

Theorem 3. *The relation $\simeq$ is the* largest congruence *contained in $\sim_{\mathrm{n}}$.*

Axiomatic Characterization

In this section, we provide an axiomatization of $\simeq$ for *regular* processes, i.e. a class of finite-state processes that do not contain static operators inside recursion. In order to develop the axiomatization, it is convenient to add a new ignore operator $\downarrow$ to CSA, called *dynamic ignore*, which is compositional with respect to temporal strong bisimulation. Its semantics is defined by the following operational rules.

$$\text{DIgn}\ \frac{P \stackrel{\alpha}{\rightarrow} P'}{P\downarrow\sigma \stackrel{\alpha}{\rightarrow} P'} \qquad \text{tDIgn1}\ \frac{-}{P\downarrow\sigma \stackrel{\sigma}{\rightarrow} P\downarrow\sigma} \qquad \text{tDIgn2}\ \frac{P \stackrel{\sigma'}{\rightarrow} P'}{P\downarrow\sigma \stackrel{\sigma'}{\rightarrow} P'\downarrow\sigma}\ \sigma \neq \sigma'$$

Moreover, we extend the definition of $\text{I}_\sigma(\cdot)$ by $\text{I}_\sigma(P\downarrow\rho) \stackrel{\text{df}}{=} \text{I}_\sigma(P\uparrow\rho)$.

A process $P \in \mathcal{P}$ is called *regular* if it is built from nil, prefix, summation, timeout, dynamic ignore, variables, and recursion. We say that P is *rs-free*, where *rs* abbreviates *recursion through static operators*, if every subterm $\mu x.\, Q$ of P is regular. Finally, a process P is *finite* if it does not contain the recursion operator.

Table 3. Axiomatization of $\simeq$ (Part I)

(A1)	$t+u=u+t$	(B1)	$\lfloor\lfloor t\rfloor\sigma(u)\rfloor\sigma(v)=\lfloor t\rfloor\sigma(v)$	
(A2)	$t+(u+v)=(t+u)+v$	(B2)	$\lfloor\lfloor t\rfloor\sigma(u)\rfloor\sigma'(v)=\lfloor\lfloor t\rfloor\sigma'(v)\rfloor\sigma(u)$	$\sigma\neq\sigma'$
(A3)	$t+t=t$	(B3)	$\lfloor t\rfloor\sigma(u)+\lfloor v\rfloor\sigma(w)=\lfloor t+v\rfloor\sigma(u+w)$	
(A4)	$t+0=t$			
(D1)	$0[f]=0$	(C1)	$0\setminus L=0$	
(D2)	$(\alpha.t)[f]=f(\alpha).(t[f])$	(C2)	$(\alpha.t)\setminus L=0$	$\alpha\in L\cup\overline{L}$
(D3)	$(t+u)[f]=t[f]+u[f]$	(C3)	$(\alpha.t)\setminus L=\alpha.(t\setminus L)$	$\alpha\notin L\cup\overline{L}$
(D4)	$(\lfloor t\rfloor\sigma(u))[f]=\lfloor t[f]\rfloor\sigma(u[f])$	(C4)	$(t+u)\setminus L=t\setminus L+u\setminus L$	
		(C5)	$(\lfloor t\rfloor\sigma(u))\setminus L=\lfloor t\setminus L\rfloor\sigma(u\setminus L)$	

Now, we turn to the axioms for temporal strong bisimulation. We write $\vdash P = Q$ if P can be rewritten to Q by using the axioms in the Tables 3, 4, and 5 which are sound for arbitrary CSA processes. Many axioms are identical to the ones presented in [1] for PMC. Axioms (L1)–(L8) and (I8) deal with the new dynamic ignore operator, where Axiom (I8) captures the relationship between the static and the dynamic ignore operator. Moreover, the expansion axiom, Axiom (E), has been adapted for our algebra. The new semantic extension compared to PMC is reflected by Axioms (P1), (P2), (S1), and (S2). Equations (P1) and (P2) deal with the (local) pre-emptive power of τ, and Equations (S1) and (S2) make the implicit idling of clocks explicit.

Axioms (L5) and (L6) allow us to introduce $P\downarrow T$, where $T = \{\sigma_1, \dots \sigma_n\}$ is a finite set of clocks, as a shorthand for $P\downarrow\sigma_1 \dots \downarrow\sigma_n$. The same is true if we replace the dynamic ignore operator by the static one (cf. Axioms (I5) and (I6)). Thus, the simplifying notation in Axioms (L8), (P1), (P2), and (E) is justified.

In order to prove the completeness of our axiomatization with respect to temporal strong bisimulation we introduce a notion of *normal form* that is based on the following definition. A term t is called *in summation form* if it is of the shape $t \equiv \lfloor\sum_{i\in I}(\sum_{j\in J_i} \alpha_i.x_{ij})\downarrow T_i\rfloor\sigma(\mathbf{y})$, where $\sum$ is the indexed version of $+$,

Table 4. Axiomatization of $\simeq$ (Part II)

(I1)	$\mathbf{0}\uparrow\sigma=\mathbf{0}$	(I5)	$(t\uparrow\sigma)\uparrow\sigma=t\uparrow\sigma$
(I2)	$(t+u)\uparrow\sigma=t\uparrow\sigma+u\uparrow\sigma$	(I6)	$(t\uparrow\sigma)\uparrow\rho=(t\uparrow\rho)\uparrow\sigma$
(I3)	$(t\setminus L)\uparrow\sigma=(t\uparrow\sigma)\setminus L$	(I7)	$(\lfloor t\rfloor\rho(u))\uparrow\sigma=\lfloor t\uparrow\sigma\rfloor\rho(u\uparrow\sigma)\sigma((\lfloor t\rfloor\rho(u))\uparrow\sigma)$
(I4)	$(t[f])\uparrow\sigma=(t\uparrow\sigma)[f]$	(I8)	$(\alpha.t)\uparrow\sigma=(\alpha.(t\uparrow\sigma))\downarrow\sigma$
(L1)	$\mathbf{0}\downarrow\sigma=\mathbf{0}$	(L5)	$(t\downarrow\sigma)\downarrow\sigma=t\downarrow\sigma$
(L2)	$(t+u)\downarrow\sigma=t\downarrow\sigma+u\downarrow\sigma$	(L6)	$(t\downarrow\sigma)\downarrow\rho=(t\downarrow\rho)\downarrow\sigma$
(L3)	$(t\setminus L)\downarrow\sigma=(t\downarrow\sigma)\setminus L$	(L7)	$(\lfloor t\rfloor\rho(u))\downarrow\sigma=\lfloor t\downarrow\sigma\rfloor\rho(u\downarrow\sigma)\sigma((\lfloor t\rfloor\rho(u))\downarrow\sigma)$
(L4)	$(t[f])\downarrow\sigma=(t\downarrow\sigma)[f]$	(L8)	$(\alpha.t)\downarrow T+(\alpha.u)\downarrow T'=(\alpha.t+\alpha.u)\downarrow(T\cap T')$
(S1)	$\mathbf{0}=\lfloor\mathbf{0}\rfloor\sigma(\mathbf{0})$	(P1)	$(\tau.t)\downarrow T+u\downarrow\sigma=(\tau.t)\downarrow T+u \quad \sigma\notin T$
(S2)	$\alpha.t=\lfloor\alpha.t\rfloor\sigma(\alpha.t)$	(P2)	$\lfloor(\tau.t)\downarrow T+u\rfloor\sigma(v)=(\tau.t)\downarrow T+u \quad \sigma\notin T$

the x_{ij} and $\mathbf{y} = y_1, y_2, \ldots, y_n$ are process variables, $\boldsymbol{\sigma} = \sigma_1, \sigma_2, \ldots, \sigma_n$ clocks, and $\alpha_i \in \mathcal{A}$. The index sets I and J_i, $i \in I$, are assumed to be finite, possibly empty, initial intervals of the natural numbers. By definition, $\sum_{i\in\emptyset} t_i \equiv \mathbf{0}$ is in summation form.

Table 5. Axiomatization of $\simeq$ (Part III)

(E) Let $t \equiv \lfloor\sum_{i\in I}(\sum_{j\in J_i} \alpha_i.t_{ij})\downarrow T_i\rfloor\boldsymbol{\sigma}(\mathbf{v})$, $u \equiv \lfloor\sum_{i\in I}(\sum_{k\in K_i} \alpha_i.u_{ik})\downarrow U_i\rfloor\boldsymbol{\sigma}(\mathbf{w})$ and $\boldsymbol{\sigma} \equiv \sigma_1, \ldots, \sigma_n$ .Then $t\,|\,u = \lfloor r\rfloor\sigma_1(v_1\,|\,w_1)\ldots\sigma_n(v_n\,|\,w_n)$ where
$$r \equiv \textstyle\sum_{i\in I}((\sum_{j\in J_i} \alpha_i.(t_{ij}\,|\,u))\downarrow T_i + (\sum_{k\in K_i} \alpha_i.(t\,|\,u_{ik}))\downarrow U_i) + \sum_{i,i'\in I}\{\sum_{j\in J_i}\sum_{k\in K_i}(\tau.(t_{ij}\,|\,u_{i'k}))\downarrow(T_i\cup U_{i'}) \mid \alpha_i = \overline{\alpha}_{i'}\}$$

(R0)	$\mu x.t = \mu y.(t[y/x])$	y does not occur in t
(R1)	$\mu x.t = t[\mu x.t/x]$	
(R2)	$\vdash u = t[u/x]$ implies $\vdash u = \mu x.t$	x guarded in t

The Expansion Axiom (E) in Table 5 shows how we can eliminate the parallel composition operator. The timeout part of $t|u$ is defined componentwise for each clock. The summation part r splits up into two summands. The summand in the first line considers action transitions performed by one side alone, while the summand in the second line deals with the communication case. The dynamic ignore operators are determined naturally by our clock-scoping semantics. Specifically, the dynamic ignore set $\downarrow T_i \cup U_{i'}$ leaves the internal action τ in the scope of a clock σ if and only if $\sigma \notin T_i$ and $\sigma \notin U_{i'}$, i.e. σ is connected to each of the communicating actions α_i and $\overline{\alpha}_{i'}$.

Definition 4. The term $t \equiv \lfloor\sum_{i\in I}(\sum_{j\in J_i} \alpha_i.x_{ij})\downarrow T_i\rfloor\boldsymbol{\sigma}(\mathbf{y})$ in summation form is in *normal form* if it satisfies the following: (1) $\forall i \in I.\ \alpha_i = \tau$ iff $i = 0$,

(2) $\forall i, i' \in I.\ i \neq i'$ implies $\alpha_i \neq \alpha_{i'}$, and (3) $\forall \sigma \in \mathcal{T}.\ J_0 \neq \emptyset \wedge \sigma \notin T_0$ implies $\sigma \notin \sigma \wedge \forall i \in I. \sigma \notin T_i$.

The completeness proof adapts Milner's technique [11] in characterizing recursive processes uniquely by systems of equations in normal form. A ***normal form equation system***, into which every regular process can be unrolled, is a sequence $\langle y_i = t_i \mid i < n \rangle$ $(n \geq 1)$ of equations such that all t_i are in normal form and the free variables of all t_i are among $\mathbf{y}$.

Theorem 5. *For regular processes P and Q we have:* $\vdash P = Q$ *iff* $P \simeq Q$.

The completeness result can be extended to the class of rs-free processes by eliminating the static operators, using the Expansion Axiom (E) to get rid of parallel composition, eliminating restriction by Axioms (C1)–(C5), (L3), and (I3), and renaming by Axioms (D1)–(D4), (L4), and (I4). Finally, leaving out Axioms (R0)–(R2) for recursion, we obtain a complete axiomatization for *finite* processes. The corresponding completeness proof follows the standard lines (cf. [12]). It is based on a notion of normal form for terms, which corresponds to the one in Definition 4 where we substitute the variables x_{ij} and y_k by terms that are again in normal form.

6 Temporal Observational Congruence

The semantic congruence developed in the previous section is too fine for verifying systems in practice since it requires that two equivalent systems must match each other's internal transitions exactly. Consequently, we want to abstract from internal actions and develop a semantic congruence from the point of view of an external observer.

Observational equivalence is a notion of bisimulation in which any sequence of internal τ's may be skipped. For $\gamma \in \mathcal{A} \cup \mathcal{T}$ we define $\hat{\gamma} \stackrel{\text{df}}{=} \epsilon$ if $\gamma = \tau$ and $\hat{\gamma} \stackrel{\text{df}}{=} \gamma$, otherwise. Further, let $\stackrel{\epsilon}{\Rightarrow} \stackrel{\text{df}}{=} \stackrel{\tau}{\rightarrow}^*$ and $P \stackrel{\gamma}{\Rightarrow} Q$ iff there exist processes R and S such that $P \stackrel{\epsilon}{\Rightarrow} R \stackrel{\gamma}{\rightarrow} S \stackrel{\epsilon}{\Rightarrow} Q$. Carrying over Milner's weak bisimulation [12] to CSA naively would suggest the following definition.

Definition 6. A symmetric relation $\mathcal{R} \subseteq \mathcal{P} \times \mathcal{P}$ is a ***naive temporal weak bisimulation*** if for every $\langle P, Q \rangle \in \mathcal{R}$, $\gamma \in \mathcal{A} \cup \mathcal{T}$, the following condition holds: $P \stackrel{\gamma}{\rightarrow} P'$ implies $\exists Q'. Q \stackrel{\hat{\gamma}}{\Rightarrow} Q'$ and $\langle P', Q' \rangle \in \mathcal{R}$. We write $P \approx_{\mathrm{n}} Q$ if there exists a naive temporal weak bisimulation $\mathcal{R}$ such that $\langle P, Q \rangle \in \mathcal{R}$.

It is not surprising that $\approx_{\mathrm{n}}$ is not a congruence, for the same reason that weak bisimulation equivalence is not a congruence for CCS. In contrast to CCS, however, $\approx_{\mathrm{n}}$ is not even a congruence for parallel composition. The problem is that, again, the relation fails to account for clock scoping. The following refinement of the above definition is needed for the static contexts.

Definition 7. A symmetric relation $\mathcal{R} \subseteq \mathcal{P} \times \mathcal{P}$ is a *temporal weak bisimulation* if for every $\langle P, Q \rangle \in \mathcal{R}$, $\alpha \in \mathcal{A}$, and $\sigma \in \mathcal{T}$ the following conditions hold.

1. $P \stackrel{\alpha}{\rightarrow} P'$ implies $\exists Q'. Q \stackrel{\hat{\alpha}}{\Rightarrow} Q'$ and $\langle P', Q' \rangle \in \mathcal{R}$.
2. $P \stackrel{\sigma}{\rightarrow} P'$ implies
   $\exists Q', Q'', Q'''. Q \stackrel{\epsilon}{\Rightarrow} Q'' \stackrel{\sigma}{\rightarrow} Q''' \stackrel{\epsilon}{\Rightarrow} Q'$, $\mathbb{I}_\sigma(Q'') \subseteq \mathbb{I}_\sigma(P)$, and $\langle P', Q' \rangle \in \mathcal{R}$.

We write $P \approx Q$ if $\langle P, Q \rangle \in \mathcal{R}$ for some temporal weak bisimulation $\mathcal{R}$.

Proposition 8. *The relation $\approx$ is a congruence with respect to prefixing and the static CSA operators. It is characterized as the largest congruence contained in $\approx_{\mathrm{n}}$, in the subalgebra of CSA induced by these operators.*

In order to identify the largest equivalence contained in $\approx_{\mathrm{n}}$ that is also a congruence for the other dynamic operators, the summation fix of CCS is not sufficient due to the special nature of clock transitions.

Definition 9. A symmetric relation $\mathcal{R} \subseteq \mathcal{P} \times \mathcal{P}$ is a *temporal observational congruence* if for every $\langle P, Q \rangle \in \mathcal{R}$, $\alpha \in \mathcal{A}$, and $\sigma \in \mathcal{T}$ the following conditions hold:

1. $P \stackrel{\alpha}{\rightarrow} P'$ implies $\exists Q'. Q \stackrel{\alpha}{\Rightarrow} Q'$ and $P' \approx Q'$.
2. $P \stackrel{\sigma}{\rightarrow} P'$ implies $\mathbb{I}_\sigma(Q) \subseteq \mathbb{I}_\sigma(P)$ and $\exists Q'. Q \stackrel{\sigma}{\rightarrow} Q'$ and $\langle P', Q' \rangle \in \mathcal{R}$.

We write $P \underline{\approx} Q$ if $\langle P, Q \rangle \in \mathcal{R}$ for some temporal observational congruence $\mathcal{R}$.

Theorem 10. *The relation $\underline{\approx}$ is the* largest congruence *contained in $\approx_{\mathrm{n}}$.*

For details as well as the proofs of our results we refer the reader to [5].

7 Conclusions

We have presented the temporal process algebra CSA with multiple clocks and a local maximal progress assumption. CSA is closely related to the process algebras TPL and PMC which both are inspired by ATP. Whereas TPL does not deal with multiple clocks, and the semantics of PMC does not ensure maximal progress, CSA combines both features under the special consideration of the distribution of systems. By means of a generic example we have demonstrated the utility of CSA as a semantic framework for dealing with synchrony and asynchrony in which we can express various levels of time and synchronization. We have developed a fully-abstract semantic theory based on the notion of bisimulation. Alternative characterizations of our behavioral relations (see [5]) allow us to adapt standard partition refinement algorithms [15] for their computation.

Moreover, our results show that CSA is a conservative extension of TPL not only in terms of operational semantics but also in terms of strong and weak bisimulation. This means that our main theorems also apply to TPL. In particular, specializing Theorem 10 to the TPL fragment yields a characterization of observational congruence for TPL.

Future work will especially focus on two aspects. On the one hand, CSA should be implemented in the Concurrency Workbench of North Carolina [6], an automatic verification tool. On the other hand, an axiomatic characterization of temporal observational congruence may be interesting since it would support a better understanding of the underlying semantic theory and simplify a comparison with other temporal process algebras.

References

1. H.R. Andersen and M. Mendler. An asynchronous process algebra with multiple clocks. In D. Sannella, editor, *European Symposium on Programming*, volume 788 of *Lecture Notes in Computer Science*, pages 58–73. Springer-Verlag, 1994.
2. H.R. Andersen and M. Mendler. Describing a signal analyzer in the process algebra PMC — A case study. In P. D. Mosses, M. Nielsen, and M. I. Schwartzbach, editors, *Theory and Practice of Software Development, TAPSOFT'95*, volume 915 of *Lecture Notes in Computer Science*, pages 620–635. Springer-Verlag, 1995.
3. G. Berry and G. Gonthier. The ESTEREL synchronous programming language: Design, semantics, implementation. *Science of Computer Programming*, 19:87–152, 1992.
4. D.M. Chapiro. Reliable high-speed arbitration and synchronization. *IEEE Transaction on Computers*, C-36(10):1251–1255, October 1987.
5. R. Cleaveland, G. Lüttgen, and M. Mendler. An algebraic theory of multiple clocks. Technical report, North Carolina State University, Raleigh, NC, USA, 1997. To appear.
6. R. Cleaveland and S. Sims. The NCSU Concurrency Workbench. In R. Alur and T. Henzinger, editors, *Computer Aided Verification (CAV '96)*, volume 1102 of *Lecture Notes in Computer Science*, pages 394–397, New Brunswick, New Jersey, July 1996. Springer-Verlag.
7. R. De Nicola and M.C.B. Hennessy. Testing equivalences for processes. *Theoretical Computer Science*, 34:83–133, 1983.
8. W. Elseaidy, J. Baugh, and R. Cleaveland. Verification of an active control system using temporal process algebra. *Engineering with Computers*, 12:46–61, 1996.
9. M. Hennessy and T. Regan. A process algebra for timed systems. *Information and Computation*, 117:221–239, 1995.
10. C.A.R. Hoare. *Communicating Sequential Processes*. Prentice-Hall, London, 1985.
11. R. Milner. A complete inference system for a class of regular behaviours. *Journal of Computer and System Sciences*, 28:439–466, 1984.
12. R. Milner. *Communication and Concurrency*. Prentice-Hall, London, 1989.
13. F. Moller and C. Tofts. A temporal calculus of communicating systems. In J.C.M. Baeten and J.W. Klop, editors, *CONCUR '90*, volume 458 of *Lecture Notes in Computer Science*, pages 401–415, Amsterdam, August 1990. Springer-Verlag.
14. X. Nicollin and J. Sifakis. The algebra of timed processes, ATP: Theory and application. *Information and Computation*, 114:131–178, 1994.
15. R. Paige and R.E. Tarjan. Three partition refinement algorithms. *SIAM Journal of Computing*, 16(6):973–989, December 1987.
16. W. Yi. CCS + time = an interleaving model for real time systems. In J. Leach Albert, B. Monien, and M. Rodríguez Artalejo, editors, *Automata, Languages and Programming (ICALP '91)*, volume 510 of *Lecture Notes in Computer Science*, pages 217–228, Madrid, July 1991. Springer-Verlag.

Horizontal and Vertical Structuring Techniques for Statecharts [a]

Hartmut Ehrig*, Robert Geisler*, Marcus Klar**, Julia Padberg*
* Technische Universität Berlin, FB Informatik
Sekr. 6-1, Franklinstr. 28/29, D-10587 Berlin.

** Fraunhofer-Institut für Software- und Systemtechnik ISST
Kurstr. 33, D-10117 Berlin.

E-mail: {ehrig,geislerr,mklar,padberg}@cs.tu-berlin.de

Abstract

In this paper we present an algebraic approach to statecharts as they are used in the STATEMATE tool in the style of "Petri-Nets are Monoids" for place-transition nets developed by Meseguer and Montanari. We apply the framework of high-level-replacement systems, a categorical generalization of graph transformation systems, in order to define union as horizontal as well as transformation and refinement as vertical structuring techniques for statecharts. The first main result shows compatibility of union and transformation in a suitable category of statecharts. We present an algorithm for the computation of all transitions enabled within one step. The second main result shows the correctness of this algorithm. We define refinement morphisms for statecharts, which allow refinement of arbitrary states, in contrast to concepts in the literature where only basic and root states are subject of refinement. The third main result shows that refinement morphisms are compatible with the behavior of statecharts as defined in the formal semantics.

1 Introduction

The great success of statecharts [5,10] as a visual specification technique for concurrent and reactive systems is mainly due to its compact representation of concurrency and hierarchy. The existing STATEMATE tool [7] is offering sophisticated simulation and prototyping facilities and has thus led to a broad acceptance of this formalism. Similar to other specification techniques for concurrent systems horizontal and vertical structuring techniques are most important for the development of large and complex systems, but the theory of statecharts offers only little support for this problem. In this paper we present horizontal and vertical structuring techniques and results for statecharts from two points of view: On one hand we study union and transformation in analogy to approaches for graph transformation systems and Petri nets recently developed in the literature [2,13,4]. On the other hand we present a formal semantics of (a subset of) STATEMATE statecharts [8] and a new notion of refinement, which is compatible with this formal semantics and allows refinement of arbitrary states in contrast to some other concepts of refinement for statecharts.

As pointed out horizontal and vertical structuring techniques have been studied for various kinds of specification techniques in the literature. They are

[a] This work is part of the German BMBF-project ESPRESS and of the joint research project "DFG-Forschergruppe PETRINETZ-TECHNOLOGIE", supported by the German Research Council (DFG).

new for statecharts. Other notions for formal semantics of statecharts are given in [9,11,12,14], but they are not conform with the STATEMATE semantics [8]. An overview of several statechart variants is given in [17]. For different kinds of object oriented statecharts [1,6,15,16] refinement techniques have been studied allowing root and basic state refinement, but not refinement of general states as in our case. Moreover no formal semantics has been presented for these approaches.

In section 2 we present the basic notions of abstract statecharts and statecharts. Union and transformation of abstract statecharts and the first main result are presented in section 3. The behavior of statecharts in the sense of STATEMATE is given in section 4. The correctness of the presented algorithm is the second main result. The definition of a behavior compatible refinement of statecharts in section 5 is the third main result. Because of space restrictions we are only able to present short proof ideas. A more detailed version is available from the authors.

2 Statecharts

Statecharts are automata equipped with hierarchy and concurrency. Hierarchy is achieved by embedding one statechart in a state of another one. Concurrency is expressed by the parallel composition of two statecharts. These structuring mechanisms are described by the notion of *hierarchical state space*.

Definition 2.1 (Hierarchical State Space) *Given a set of states* $\mathcal{S}$, *a distinguished state* root$\in \mathcal{S}$, *a function*[b] $\mathsf{substates} : \mathcal{S} \rightarrow \mathbb{F}\mathcal{S}$, *a function* $\mathsf{decomp} : \mathcal{S} \rightarrow \{and, xor, basic\}$, *applying to each state its decomposition type, such that*[c] substates *forms a tree structure with* root *as the root of the tree, the basic states are the leaves, and all and states must have xor states as substates, i.e.* $\forall\, s \in \mathcal{S}, s' \in \mathsf{substates}(s) \bullet \mathsf{decomp}(s) = and \Rightarrow \mathsf{decomp}(s') = xor$. *We call* $\mathcal{HS} = (\mathcal{S}, \mathsf{root}, \mathsf{substates}, \mathsf{decomp})$ *a hierarchical state space.*

A *configuration* contains all states a statechart resides in at a moment.

Definition 2.2 (Configuration) *Given a hierarchical state space* $\mathcal{HS}$. *We call a set of states* $C \subseteq \mathcal{S}$ *a partial configuration w.r.t. a state s if the following holds:*

- $s \in C \wedge \forall\, s' \in C \bullet s' \preceq s$
- $\forall\, s' \in \mathcal{S} \bullet s' \notin C \Rightarrow C \cap \mathsf{substates}^+(s') = \emptyset$
- $\forall\, s' \in C \bullet \mathsf{decomp}(s') = and \Rightarrow \mathsf{substates}(s') \subset C$
- $\forall\, s' \in C \bullet \mathsf{decomp}(s') = xor \Rightarrow \exists_1\, s'' \in \mathsf{substates}(s') \bullet s'' \in C \vee \mathsf{substates}^+(s') \cap C = \emptyset$

A partial configuration C w.r.t. s is called total, if $\forall\, s' \in C \bullet \mathsf{decomp}(s') = xor \Rightarrow \exists_1\, s'' \in \mathsf{substates}(s') \bullet s'' \in C$. *For a state s the set of all total resp. partial configurations w.r.t. s is denoted by* $\mathcal{C}(s)$ *resp.* $\mathcal{C}_p(s)$. *We write* $\mathcal{C}$ *for* $\mathcal{C}(\mathsf{root})$ *resp.* $\mathcal{C}_p$ *for* $\mathcal{C}_p(\mathsf{root})$.

---

[b] $\mathbb{F}_1$ resp. $\mathbb{F}$ stand for (nonempty) finite powerset.

[c] $\mathsf{substates}^+$ and $\mathsf{substates}^*$ denote the irreflexive, resp. the reflexive and transitive closure of substates

If the system can be simultaneously in two states s, s' that are not ancestrally related via substates, then we say the two states are parallel, written $s \parallel s'$. We call a set S of states parallel, if all states are pairwise parallel.

A hierarchical state space equipped with a set of labeled transitions is called an *abstract statechart*. The transitions are labeled by an *event expression*, its triggering condition, and a set of events that are generated when the transition is taken. This set is called the *action* of the transition.

For a set of events $\mathcal{E}$ we define the set of event expressions $T_{\mathbb{B}}(\mathcal{E})$ inductively as follows (for $E \in T_{\mathbb{B}}(\mathcal{E}), e \in \mathcal{E}$): $E ::= \text{true} \mid \text{false} \mid e \mid \textit{not } E \mid E_1 \textit{ and } E_2 \mid E_1 \textit{ or } E_2$

A statechart consists of a *hierarchical state space* together with transitions between these states that have labels of the form *condition/action*.

Definition 2.3 (Abstract Statechart) *An abstract statechart* $\mathcal{ASC} = (\mathcal{HS}, \mathcal{T}, \mathcal{E}, \textsf{source}, \textsf{dest}, \textsf{cond}, \textsf{action})$ *consists of a hierarchical state space* $\mathcal{HS}$, *a set of transitions* $\mathcal{T}$, *a set of events* $\mathcal{E}$, *and two functions* source, dest*:* $\mathcal{T} \rightarrow \mathbb{F}_1\, \mathcal{S}$, *denoting the source and destination states for every transition, with the property that the source- resp. destination states of each transition are parallel. The function* cond*:* $\mathcal{T} \rightarrow T_{\mathbb{B}}(\mathcal{E})$ *describes for each transition its trigger condition, and the function* action*:* $\mathcal{T} \rightarrow \mathbb{F}\,\mathcal{E}$ *assigns to each transition the set of events generated, when the transition is taken. In the following, the function* arena : $\mathcal{T} \rightarrow \mathcal{S}$ *will denote the context of a transition, i.e. the xor state enclosing all sources and destinations of the transition.*

The *system state* of a statechart consists of a partial configuration and a set of events that are valid at one point in time. From a system state, we can determine the set of enabled transitions that can be taken in the next step.

Definition 2.4 (System State) *Given an abstract statechart* $\mathcal{ASC}$, *the set of system states is given by* $\Sigma = \mathcal{C}_p \times \mathbb{F}\,\mathcal{E}$.

In statecharts for the substates of an *xor* state a *default transition* is given. This default transition is targeting into the state that is entered, when a transition is taken that ends in the *xor* state. For an example, see the default transition into state *Working* in Figure 2 below. These default transitions can be resolved by extending the outer transitions into the corresponding default state. In the example the transition labeled *repair* in the second statechart in Figure 2 would be extended into the the state *Init*.

The *initial system state* of a statechart is determined by taking the default transitions at the beginning of the statecharts run, possibly generating some events. For the second statechart in Figure 2, the initial system state is {root, *Working*, *Init*} with an empty set of events.

Definition 2.5 (Statechart) *A statechart* $\mathcal{SC} = (\mathcal{ASC}, \Theta)$ *is a pair of an an abstract statechart* $\mathcal{ASC}$ *and an initial system state* $\Theta = (C, E) \in \Sigma$ *such that* $C \in \mathcal{C}$. $\mathcal{ASC}$ *has the property that all its transitions are complete in the sense that*[d] $\forall\, t \in \mathcal{T} \bullet \textsf{dest}^{\dagger}(t) \in \mathcal{C}(\textsf{arena}(t))$

[d] $\textsf{dest}^{\dagger}(t) = \{s \in \mathcal{S} \mid \exists\, s' \in \textsf{dest}(t) \bullet s' \preceq s \preceq \textsf{arena}(t)\}$, where $\prec$ denotes the ordering induced by substates.

3 Union and Transformation

In this section we transfer well-known concepts horizontal and vertical structuring from Petri nets to statecharts. Especially, the construction of *union* is an important horizontal structuring technique for Petri nets, whereas *transformations* are used as rule-based refinement and abstraction. The construction of unions and transformations is based on *high-level replacement systems*, a categorical generalization of graph grammars and a general categorical description for high-level structures as structures, algebraic specifications, graph grammars, hypergraph grammars, low- and high-level Petri nets among others [3]. The category of abstract statecharts, does not have pushouts in general, but only for specific morphisms. This is sufficient to define unions and transformations and to consider this category as an instance of high-level replacement systems.

We want to illustrate the concepts of union and transformation by an example depicted in Figure 1. The left and the right hand squares are both unions. A union merges two statecharts via some common interface. In this example the interface is a statechart consisting only of state K. In Figure 1 the statecharts A and B are the unions of A and C via K, and R and C via K respectively. Combining two unions it is possible to build a transformation. A rule $p = (L \overset{l}{\leftarrow} K \overset{r}{\rightarrow} R)$ with three statecharts L, K, and R, called the left hand side, the interface, and the right hand side respectively, is shown in the upper row of figure 1. The application of rule p to the statechart A leads to a transformation $A \overset{p}{\Longrightarrow} B$, where B is the transformed statechart.

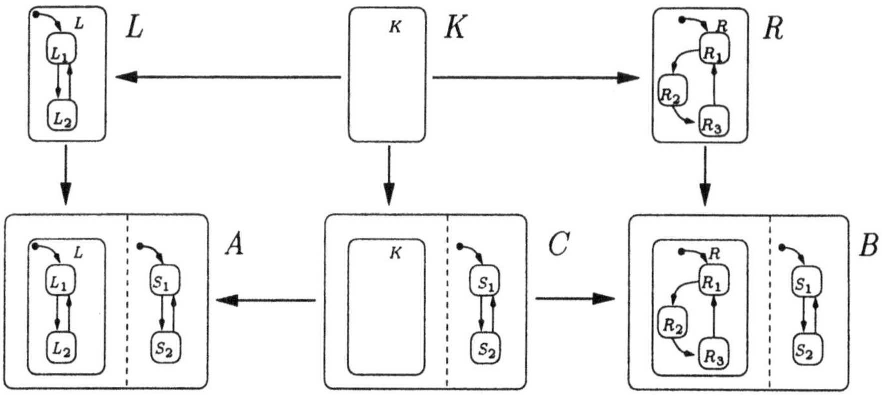

Figure 1: Transformation

In order to define union and transformation we introduce morphisms for abstract statecharts, which are mappings of the underlying components with additional conditions concerning the hierarchical state space. This leads to the category of abstract statecharts.

Definition 3.1 (Category ASC) *The category* **ASC** *of abstract statecharts consists of abstract statecharts (see Def. 2.3)* $ASC = (\mathcal{HS}, \mathcal{T}, \mathcal{E},$ source, dest, cond, action) *and of abstract statechart morphisms that are given by the mor-*

phisms of the components[e] $f_{ASC} : \mathcal{ASC}_1 \to \mathcal{ASC}_2$ *with* $f_{ASC} = (f_S, f_T, f_E)$ *where we have* $f_S : \mathcal{S}_1 \to \mathcal{S}_2$, $f_T : \mathcal{T}_1 \to \mathcal{T}_2$, *and* $f_E : \mathcal{E}_1 \to \mathcal{E}_2$ *such that*

1. $f_S(\mathsf{substates}_1(s_1)) \subseteq \mathsf{substates}_2(f_S(s_2))$,
   that is f_S *corresponds to graph homomorphisms*
2. $f_S \circ \mathsf{source}_1 = \mathsf{source}_2 \circ f_T$ *and* $f_S \circ \mathsf{dest}_1 = \mathsf{dest}_2 \circ f_T$,
   that is (f_S, f_T) *is compatible with* source *and* dest,
3. $f_E \circ \mathsf{action}_1 = \mathsf{action}_2 \circ f_T$ *and* $f_E \circ \mathsf{cond}_1 = \mathsf{cond}_2 \circ f_T$,
   that is (f_T, f_E) *is compatible with* cond *and* action,
4. $\mathsf{decomp}_1(s_1) \neq basic \Rightarrow \mathsf{decomp}_1(s_1) = \mathsf{decomp}_2(f_S(s_1))$
   that is and as well as xor states are preserved.

The following fact presents the technical basis for transformation and union.

Fact 3.1 (Pushouts in ASC) *In the category* **ASC** *the pushout of two morphisms exists, if one morphism is* root *preserving, the other is basic state preserving, and both are componentwise injective.*

Proof Idea: Pushouts in **ASC** are constructed componentswise in the category **SETS**. In the state component we have to construct a pushout in the category **HS** of hierachical state spaces, where the pushout construction corresponds to the gluing of trees via shared subtrees. In order to make sure that the gluing becomes a tree (and not only a graph) we require that one morphism is root preserving and the other one basic state (leaf) preserving and both of them are injective. It is important to note that in the pushout diagram the morphism opposite to the root preserving morphism becomes root preserving (defining the root of the pushout object), and that the one opposite to the leaf preserving morphism becomes leaf preserving. An additional problem is to show that in the pushout object we keep the property of abstract statecharts that the source (resp. destination) states of each transition are parallel.

Union of abstract statecharts can be considered as union with respect to a common interface in each of the components, mainly the state space, the set of transitions and the set of events.

Definition 3.2 (Union in ASC) *The union* A *of two abstract statecharts* A_1 *and* A_2 *via some interface* I, *denoted by* $(A_1, A_2) \overset{I}{\Longrightarrow} A$, *is given by the following pushout in the category* **ASC**

$$\begin{array}{ccc} I & \xrightarrow{in_1} & A_1 \\ {\scriptstyle in_2}\downarrow & = & \downarrow \\ A_2 & \longrightarrow & A \end{array}$$

where the morphism in_1 *is* root *preserving and* in_2 *is basic state preserving and both are injective.*

According to figure 1 a transformation $A \overset{p}{\Longrightarrow} B$ is defined using two pushout squares **(1)** and **(2)** in the category **ASC** of abstract statecharts.

Definition 3.3 (Rules and Transformations in ASC) *A rule* $p = (L \overset{l}{\leftarrow} K \overset{r}{\rightarrow} R)$ *in* **ASC** *consists of the abstract statecharts* L, K *and* R, *called the left hand side, the interface and the right hand side respectively, and two morphisms*

[e] We use the same presentation also for extensions of the morphisms.

$K \xrightarrow{l} L$ and $K \xrightarrow{r} R$ where both morphisms are root preserving and injective.
A (direct) transformation of an abstract statechart $A \overset{p}{\Longrightarrow} B$ applying the rule $p = (L \overset{l}{\leftarrow} K \overset{r}{\rightarrow} R)$ to an abstract statechart A leading to a transformed abstract statechart B is given by:

$$\begin{array}{ccccc} L & \xleftarrow{\;l\;} & K & \xrightarrow{\;r\;} & R \\ {\scriptstyle g_1}\downarrow & (1) & {\scriptstyle g_2}\downarrow & (2) & \downarrow{\scriptstyle g_3} \\ A & \xleftarrow[c_1]{} & C & \xrightarrow[c_2]{} & B \end{array}$$

where the morphisms l, r, c_1 and c_2 are root preserving and g_1, g_2 and g_3 are basic state preserving, all are injective, and **(1)** *and* **(2)** *are pushouts in* **ASC**.

To achieve compatibility between horizontal and vertical structuring, we must have suitable independence conditions which intuitively means that the interface I for the union is not changed by the transformations.

Now we show our main compatibility result between horizontal and vertical structuring, in our case between union and transformation of abstract statecharts.

Theorem 3.1 (Compatibility of Union and Transformation)
Given a union $(A_1, A_2) \overset{I}{\rightarrowtail\!\!\Rightarrow} A$ independent from the transformations $A_i \overset{p_i}{\Longrightarrow} B_i$ for $i = 1, 2$, then there is an abstract statechart B obtained by the union $(B_1, B_2) \overset{I}{\rightarrowtail\!\!\Rightarrow} B$ and by the transformation $A \overset{p_1+p_2}{\Longrightarrow} B$ via the parallel rule $p_1 + p_2$, such that we have

$$(A_1, A_2) \overset{I}{\rightarrowtail\!\!\Rightarrow} A \overset{p_1+p_2}{\Longrightarrow} B = (A_1, A_2) \overset{(p_1,p_2)}{\Longrightarrow} (B_1, B_2) \overset{I}{\rightarrowtail\!\!\Rightarrow} B$$

Remarks: *(1) $(A_1, A_2) \overset{(p_1,p_2)}{\Longrightarrow} (B_1, B_2)$ denotes the tupling of the separate transformations of $A_1 \overset{p_1}{\Longrightarrow} B_1$ and $A_2 \overset{p_2}{\Longrightarrow} B_2$. (2) Independence of union $(A_1, A_2) \overset{I}{\Longrightarrow} A$ and transformation $A_i \overset{p_i}{\Longrightarrow} B_i$ with morphisms $in_i : A_i \to A$ and $(A_i \overset{c_{i1}}{\leftarrow} C_i \overset{c_{i2}}{\rightarrow} B_i)$ is defined by the existence of morphisms $f_i : I \to C_i$ $(i = 1, 2)$, such that $c_{i1} \circ f_i = in_i$, f_1 is* root *preserving, and $f_1, f_2, c_{i2} \circ f_2$ are basic state preserving.*

Proof Idea: First of all note, that the parallel rule $p_1 + p_2$ is given by $p_1 + p_2 = (L_1 + L_2 \overset{l_1+l_2}{\leftarrow} K_1 + K_2 \overset{r_1+r_2}{\rightarrow} R_1 + R_2)$, where $A_1 + A_2$ is the disjoint union of abstract statecharts A_1 and A_2. Formally spoken, $A_1 + A_2$ is no longer an abstract statechart, because we have two roots, but it can be considered as a coproduct in a suitable category **AN** of action nets.[f] In fact, pushouts in **ASC** can be first constructed in **AN** and then the pushout object in **AN** can be enriched to become a pushout in **ASC**. The compatibility theorem for union and transformation is known for high-level-replacement systems (see [13]) and can be applied directly to the category **AN**, where independence of union and transformation means only the existence of morphisms $f_i : I \to C_i, (i = 1, 2)$ without root and *basic* state preservation properties. In order to make sure that all objects constructed in **AN** become objects in **ASC**, i.e. abstract statecharts, we have additional assumptions concerning root and *basic* state preservation as given in remark (2).

[f] The category **AN** of action nets is only used in this proof and will be studied elsewhere in more detail.

Since this general notion of transformation should be used in the requirements phase of system development similar to the transformation of Petri nets in the requirement analysis of a medical information system [4], it is most important to have compatibility of union and tranformation. But transformations in these kinds of applications do not preserve the behavior of systems in general.

4 Behavior of Statecharts

As pointed out in [8] the STATEMATE semantics of statecharts is different from most of the semantics defined for statecharts in the literature. Roughly spoken, in the STATEMATE semantics changes made in a step do not take effect in the current, but only in the next step. In this section we define the behavior of abstract statecharts that corresponds to the semantics of a subset of STATEMATE statecharts. We present an algorithm for the computation of all transitions enabled within one step and a corresponding correctness result (theorem 4.1). Note that the concepts in this section can be applied to statecharts and to abstract statecharts.[g]

In every system state, the set of *consistently enabled transitions* has to be considered for the execution of steps.

Definition 4.1 (Enabled Transitions) *Given an abstract statechart $\mathcal{ASC}$ and a system state $\sigma = (C, E) \in \Sigma$ we define the set of (potentially) enabled transitions*[h] $\mathsf{enabled}_\sigma = \{t \in \mathcal{T} \mid \sigma \models \mathsf{cond}(t) \wedge \forall s \in \mathsf{source}(t) \bullet s \in C\}$.
A set T is called set of enabled transitions if we have

1. $\| (T)$ [i], *i.e. T is consistent (the transitions in T are parallel).*
2. $\forall t \in T \bullet t \in \mathsf{enabled}_\sigma$, *i.e. all $t \in T$ are triggered.*
3. $\forall t \in T \bullet \neg \exists t' \in \mathsf{enabled}_\sigma \bullet \mathsf{arena}(t) \prec \mathsf{arena}(t')$, *i.e. T is relevant (the hierarchy is preserved).*
4. $\forall t \in \mathsf{enabled}_\sigma \setminus T \bullet \neg \| (T \cup \{t\})$, *i.e. T is maximal.*

The set of all sets of consistently enabled transition is denoted by En_σ.

The following algorithm delivers a set of consistently enabled transitions for a system state $\sigma = (C, E)$.

Definition 4.2 (Computation of Enabled Transitions) *Given a system state $\sigma = (C, E)$ we use the notation of appendix A (including the corresponding preconditions) to define the following algorithm for the computation of consistently enabled transitions. Starting with the root-state the set En is determined using the subsequent rules. After applying these rules, the variable En will contain a set of consistently enabled transitions.*

1. *Init:*

$\square$

(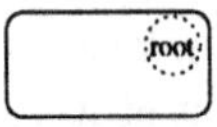 , σ, En)

The algorithm starts with the root-state.

[g]With the exception of Definition 4.4 that is applicable only to statecharts.

[h]the validity of an event expression w.r.t. a system state (C, E) is defined over the set E, i.e. $(C, E) \models e \Leftrightarrow e \in E$ for an event $e \in \mathcal{E}$.

[i]We call two transitions t_1 and t_2 parallel ($t_1 \| t_2$) if $\mathsf{arena}(t_1) \| \mathsf{arena}(t_2)$. Again we extend this definition of sets of transitions T, written $\| (T)$, if all transitions are pairwise parallel.

2. Execution:

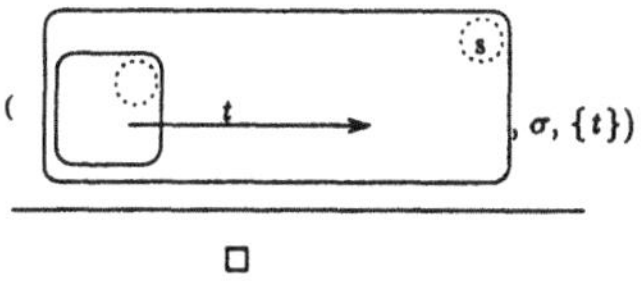

if the condition of t is valid in σ, i.e. σ ⊨ cond(t)

If an enabled transition is found, the current set of enabled transitions is bound with {t} and the algorithm terminates for the actual branch.

3. Recursion xor Decomposition:

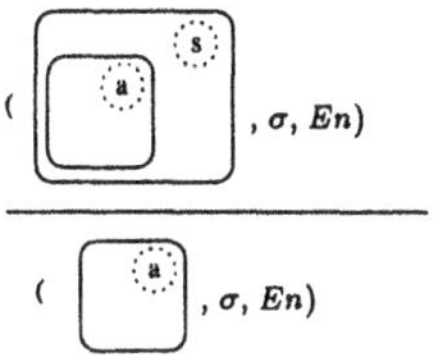

provided that rule 2 is not applicable in state s

If an xor state does not comprise an enabled transition, the search is continued in the substate of the state that is an element of the actual configuration. The set En is bound with the value of its substate.

4. Recursion and Decomposition:

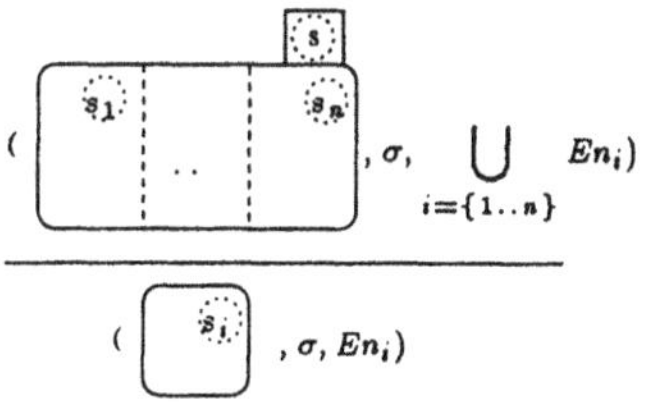

for all i ∈ {1,...,n}, provided that rule 2 is not applicable in state s

If an and state does not comprise an enabled transition, the search is continued in all of its substates. The set En is bound with the union of the results of these substates.

5. End:

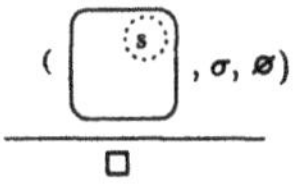

if decomp*(s) = basic or if* decomp*(s)= xor and there is no substate of s in C, i.e.* substates$(s) \cap C = \emptyset$

If either a basic state or an xor state without descendants in the actual configuration was reached, no enabled transitions were found in this branch of the search tree and the algorithm terminates.

Note that there is a nondeterministic choice in rule 2, when there is more than one enabled transition in the context of the state. This means that there might be different results for the variable *En*.

Theorem 4.1 (Correctness of the Algorithm) *Given a system state* $\sigma = (C, E) \in \Sigma$. *The set of all possible executions of the algorithm yields exactly the set* En_σ.

Proof Idea: According to the structure of statecharts it is possible to show that the result of the algorithm fulfills the conditions of definition 4.1, i.e. the negative application conditions of rules 3 and 4 ensure the fourth condition that is the resulting set of transitions is indeed maximal parallel.

In the following, we define how to compute for a given system state its successor state by explicitly constructing the successor configuration and the set of events that is generated in a step.

Definition 4.3 (Execution of a Step) *From a system state $\sigma = (C, E)$ and a set of consistently enabled transitions $T \in \mathsf{En}_\sigma$ we can compute the next (possibly partial) configuration by executing the enabled transitions:*
$\mathsf{Conf}_\sigma(T) = (C \setminus \bigcup_{t \in T} \mathsf{substates}^+(\mathsf{arena}(t))) \cup \bigcup_{t \in T} \mathsf{dest}^\dagger(t)$.
We can compute the events generated by the system in the next step as follows:
$\mathsf{generated}_\sigma(T) = \bigcup_{t \in T} \mathsf{action}(t)$.
A step is performed by executing all enabled transitions: $\mathsf{step} : \Sigma \times \mathsf{En}_\sigma \to \Sigma$ *is defined as follows:* $\forall \sigma = (C, E) \in \Sigma, T \in \mathsf{En}_\sigma \bullet \mathsf{step}((C, E), T) = (\mathsf{Conf}_\sigma(T), \mathsf{generated}_\sigma(T))$

Now we define the dynamic behavior of a statechart by describing what a *run* of a statechart is.

Definition 4.4 (Behavior of Statecharts) *The behavior of a statechart is the set of all runs the statechart can perform. We define a semantic relation* $\_ \triangleright \_ : \Sigma \leftrightarrow \Sigma$ *with* $\forall \sigma, \sigma' \in \Sigma \bullet \sigma \triangleright \sigma' \Leftrightarrow \exists T \in \mathsf{En}_\sigma \bullet \mathsf{step}(\sigma, T) = \sigma'$.
A run of a statechart $\mathcal{SC}=(\mathcal{AN}, \Theta)$ *is a sequence of system states* $\rho = \sigma_0, \sigma_1, \ldots$ *, such that* $\sigma_0 = \Theta \wedge \forall i \in 1, \ldots, \#\rho \bullet \sigma_{i-1} \triangleright \sigma_i$. *A state* $\sigma \in \Sigma$ *is called accessible, if there is a run* $\sigma_0, \ldots, \sigma$. *We define the set of all accessible system states:* $\Sigma^{acc} = \{\sigma \in \Sigma \mid \sigma \text{ is accessible}\}$.

Note that due to the transition completeness condition in the definition of statecharts, all accessible system states have total configurations.

5 Refinement of Statecharts

We are considering three types of state refinement according to the structure of statecharts (see figure 2). The first one allows to add behavior to a *basic* state (*Working*). The second form refines an *xor* state *Working* to the parallel states *Watch* and *Working* which are contained in an additional *and* state *Operating*. The third form allows to add parallel behavior, the state *Watch*2 to an *and* state (*Operating*). These forms of refinement generalize the notion of subtyping provided by several object-oriented methods for statecharts.

Definition 5.1 (Statechart Morphism) *Given two statecharts* $\mathcal{SC}_i = ((\mathcal{S}_i, \mathcal{T}_i, \mathcal{E}_i, \mathsf{source}_i, \mathsf{dest}_i, \mathsf{decomp}_i, \mathsf{substates}_i, \mathsf{root}_i, \mathsf{cond}_i, \mathsf{action}_i), \Theta_i)$*, for* $i = 1, 2$. *A statechart morphism* $f : \mathcal{SC}_1 \to \mathcal{SC}_2$ *is a family of mappings* $f_\mathcal{S} : \mathcal{S}_1 \to \mathcal{S}_2, f_\mathcal{T} : \mathcal{T}_1 \to \mathcal{T}_2$ *and* $f_\mathcal{E} : \mathcal{E}_1 \to \mathcal{E}_2$*, that assigns the states, transitions and events of the first statechart to those of the second one in a structure compatible way:*

1. $\tau_f(\Theta_2) = \Theta_1$, *i.e. the initial system state is preserved*[j]
2. $\forall t_1 \in \mathcal{T}_1 \bullet f_\mathcal{S}(\mathsf{source}_1(t_1)) = \mathsf{source}_2(f_\mathcal{T}(t_1))$, *i.e. transition sources are preserved.*
3. $\forall t_1 \in \mathcal{T}_1, s_1 \in \mathsf{dest}_1(t_1) \bullet \exists s_2 \in \mathcal{S}_2 \bullet \mathsf{dest}_2(f_\mathcal{T}(t_1)) \wedge s_2 \preceq_2 f_\mathcal{S}(s_1)$, *i.e. transitions might be extended into substates of their original destinations.*

[j] with τ_f as given in Definition 5.2

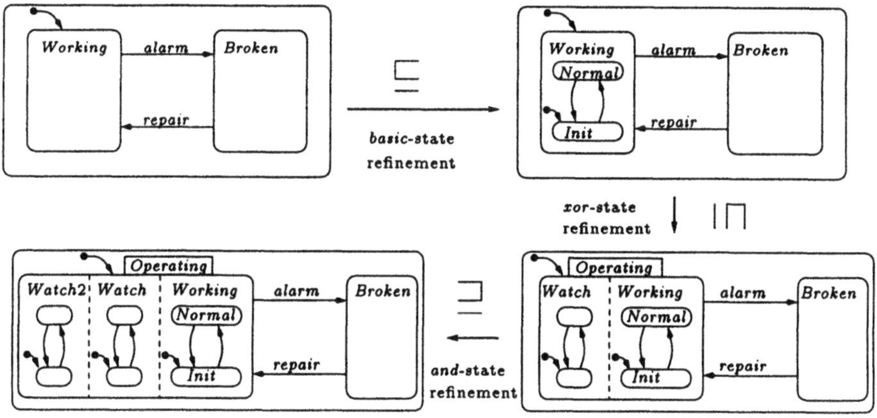

Figure 2: Refinement of Statecharts

4. $\forall\, s_1 \in \mathcal{S}_1 \bullet \mathsf{decomp}_1(s_1) \neq basic \Rightarrow \mathsf{decomp}_1(s_1) = \mathsf{decomp}_2(f_\mathcal{S}(s_1))$, *i.e. xor and and states are preserved.*

5. $\forall\, s_1 \in \mathcal{S}_1 \bullet f_\mathcal{S}(\mathsf{substates}_1(s_1)) \subseteq \mathsf{substates}_2^+(f_\mathcal{S}(s1))$, *i.e. $\prec$ is preserved.*

6. $\forall\, t_1 \in \mathcal{T}_1, E_2 \subseteq \mathcal{E}_2 \bullet \tau_f(E_2) \models_1 \mathsf{cond}_1(t_1) \Leftrightarrow E_2 \models_2 \mathsf{cond}_2(f_\mathcal{T}(t_1))$, *i.e. the condition under which a transition is enabled is preserved.*

7. $\forall\, t_2 \in f_\mathcal{T}(\mathcal{T}_1) \bullet f_\mathcal{E}(\mathsf{action}_1(\tau_f(t_2))) \subseteq \mathsf{action}_2(f_\mathcal{T}(t_2))$, *i.e. all events that are generated by a transition in the original statechart are also generated by the corresponding transition in the refined statechart.*

In order to define behavior compatibility we need to construct for every system state of the refined statechart the corresponding system state of the original statechart. We will prove that this construction indeed yields a system state if the underlying morphism is behavior preserving (see Lemma 5.2).

Definition 5.2 (Preimage of a State) *Given a statechart morphism $f : SC_1 \to SC_2$, we can define a function $\tau_f : \Sigma_2 \to (\mathcal{S}_1 \times \mathcal{E}_1)$ that assigns to every state its preimage as follows: $\forall (C, E) \in \Sigma_2 \bullet \tau_f(C, E) = (f_\mathcal{S}^{-1}(C), f_\mathcal{E}^{-1}(E))$. In the same way, we define $\tau_f : \mathbb{F}\mathcal{T}_2 \to \mathbb{F}\mathcal{T}_1$ as $\forall\, T_2 \in \mathbb{F}\mathcal{T}_2 \bullet \tau_f(T_2) = f_\mathcal{T}^{-1}(T_2)$.*

Now we present a concept of behavior compatibility for statechart morphisms. The idea is that a system state of the original statechart is always reflected in one or more corresponding system states of the refined statechart. We require, that the execution of corresponding steps on both levels lead again to corresponding system states.

Definition 5.3 (Behavior Compatible Statechart Morphism)

A statechart morphism $f : SC_1 \to SC_2$ is behavior compatible, if the behavior of the first statechart is preserved by the morphism in the following way: $\forall\, \sigma_2 \in \Sigma_2^{acc}, T \in \mathsf{En}_{\sigma_2} \bullet$ $\mathsf{step}_1(\tau_f(\sigma_2), \tau_f(T)) = \tau_f(\mathsf{step}_2(\sigma_2, T))$, i.e. the diagram on the right commutes.

$$
\begin{array}{ccc}
\sigma_1 & \xrightarrow{\ \tau_f(T)\ } & \sigma_1' \\
\uparrow{\scriptstyle \tau_f} & = & \uparrow{\scriptstyle \tau_f} \\
\sigma_2 & \xrightarrow[\ T\ ]{} & \sigma_2'
\end{array}
$$

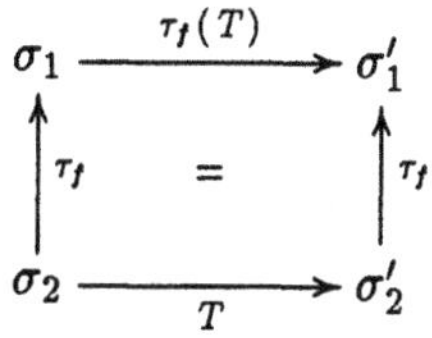

In Definition 5.4 we give conditions under which a statechart morphism $f : \mathcal{SC}_1 \rightarrow \mathcal{SC}_2$ is behavior compatible. These rather technical conditions are justified by the requirement that we want to allow refinement of all kinds of states. We call these behavior compatible morphisms *refinement morphisms.*

Definition 5.4 (Refinement Morphism) *A statechart morphism $f : \mathcal{SC}_1 \rightarrow \mathcal{SC}_2$ is called a refinement morphism, if it fulfills the following conditions:* [k]

1. f_S *is injective*
2. $\forall\, s_1 \in \mathcal{S}_1 \bullet \mathsf{decomp}_1(s_1) \neq xor \;\Rightarrow f_S(\mathsf{substates}_1(s_1)) \subseteq \mathsf{substates}_2(f_S(s_1))$
3. $\forall\, s_1, s_1' \in \mathcal{S}_1, s_2 \in \mathcal{S}_2 \setminus f_S(\mathcal{S}_1) \bullet f_S(s_1) \prec_2 s_2 \prec_2 f_S(s_1') \Rightarrow \mathsf{decomp}_2(s_2) = and$
4. $\forall\, s_2 \in \mathcal{S}_2 \bullet f_S(\mathsf{root}_1) \prec_2 s_2 \Rightarrow \mathsf{decomp}_2(s_2) = and$
5. $\forall\, t_1 \in \mathcal{T}_1 \bullet f_S(\mathsf{arena}_1(t_1)) = \mathsf{arena}_2(f_{\mathcal{T}}(t_1))$
6. $\forall\, t_2 \in \mathcal{T}_2 \setminus f_{\mathcal{T}}(\mathcal{T}_1) \bullet (\exists\, s_1 \in \mathcal{S}_1 \bullet \mathsf{decomp}_1(s_1) = basic \;\wedge \mathsf{arena}_2(t_2) \preceq f_S(s_1)) \vee$
   $(\mathsf{arena}_2(t_2) \in \mathcal{S}_2 \setminus f_S(\mathcal{S}_1))$
7. $\forall\, t_2 \in \mathcal{T}_2 \setminus f_{\mathcal{T}}(\mathcal{T}_1) \bullet \neg\, \mathsf{occurs}(\mathsf{action}_2(t_2), f_{\mathcal{E}}^{\#}(ran\, \mathsf{cond}_1))$
8. $\forall\, t_2 \in f_{\mathcal{T}}(\mathcal{T}_1), e_2 \in \mathsf{action}_2(t_2) \setminus f_{\mathcal{E}}(\mathsf{action}_1(\tau_f(t_2)) \bullet \neg\, \mathsf{occurs}(e_2, f_{\mathcal{E}}(ran\, \mathsf{cond}_1))$

These conditions look rather complicated. Nevertheless, they are necessary to achieve general state refinement as we demonstrate in the subsequent examples. We present only those parts of the mapped statecharts that are of interest for our purpose. If no translation for an element is given, we assume the identity mapping.

In Figure 3, we have a non-injective morphism which violates condition 1. It is not behavior preserving, because when being in state $(\{A, B\}, \{e_1, e_2\})$, the transition labeled e_1 is taken, while in state $(\{f_S(A), f_S(B)\}, \{e_1, e_2\})$ transition labelled e_2 is taken because $\mathsf{arena}(e_1) \prec \mathsf{arena}(e_2)$.

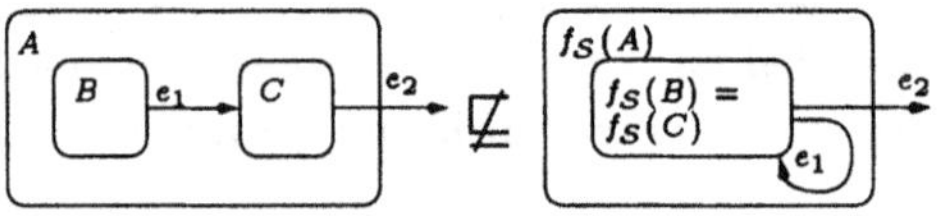

Figure 3: Violation of condition 1

The conditions 2 and 3 require a structure preservation in the sense that between two *xor* states an *and* state can be inserted. This can be interpreted as the refinement of the second *xor* state by adding parallel behavior to it. However, the $\prec$-relation must be preserved by the morphism. An example for this kind of refinement, called the *xor* refinement is given in Figure 2.

In the situation depicted in Figure 4, the root state is embedded into an *xor* state which violates condition 4. This makes it impossible, to determine the abstract state for the concrete state $(\{\mathsf{root}_2, A_2\}, \emptyset)$.

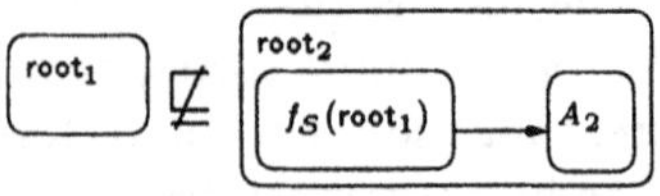

Figure 4: Violation of condition 4

[k] $f_{\mathcal{E}}^{\#}$ is the extension of $f_{\mathcal{E}}$ to event expressions. ran denotes the range of a function. The predicate occurs describes the subterm property of event expressions.

An example of violation of condition 5 is given on Figure 5. Executing a step in system state $(\{fs(A), fs(C)\}, \{e_1\})$ leads to $(\{fs(B), fs(D)\}, \{e_2\})$, and this state does not correspond to the state obtained by executing the step on the abstract level, i.e. $(\{A, D\}, \{e_2\})$.

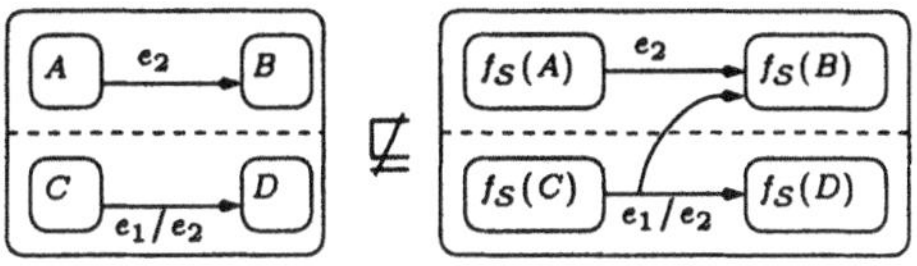

Figure 5: Violation of condition 5

A transition was added where not allowed on Figure 6 which violates condition 6. Consider being in state $fs(C)$. Then the transition into state $fs(B)$ would be taken in the concrete level, while on the abstract level nothing would happen and thus the resulting states would not match according to definition 5.3.

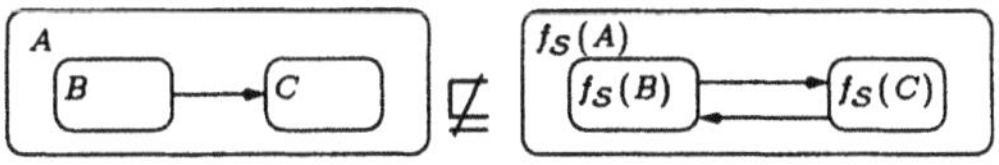

Figure 6: Violation of condition 6

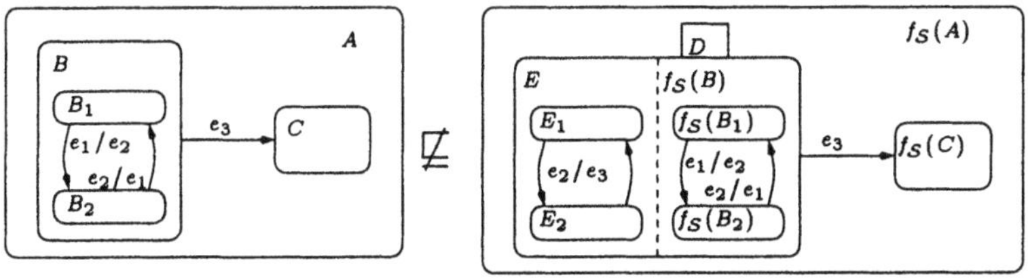

Figure 7: Violation of condition 7

We consider Figure 7 for violation of condition 7. In the additional parallel state E of the new statechart the event e_3 is generated, leading to the exit of state D in the following step. This is not compatible with the behavior of the original statechart.

Finally, for violation of condition 8 consider Figure 8. The event e_3 is additionally generated when the transition from $fs(B)$ to $fs(C)$ is taken with the consequence that in the next step the state $fs(A)$ is left, while this is not the case in the original statechart.

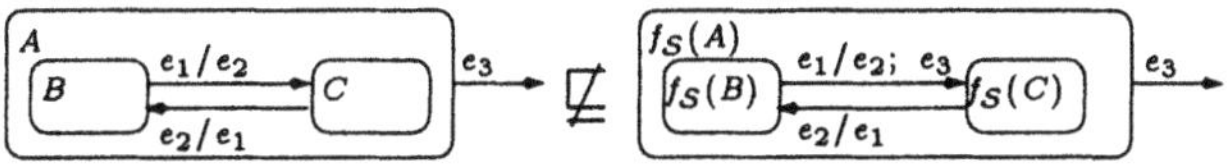

Figure 8: Violation of condition 8

Our notion of refinement requires, that every configuration of the refined statechart can be "restricted" to a configuration of the original statechart, omitting the additional behavior of the refined statechart. In order to do so, we prove, that the root state of the first statechart is included in every configuration of the refined statechart.

Lemma 5.1 (Image of the Root State) *Given a refinement morphism $f : SC_1 \rightarrow SC_2$. Then the root state of the first statechart is included in every configuration of the second one, i.e. $\forall\, C \in \mathcal{C}_2 \bullet f_S(\mathsf{root}_1) \in C$.*

Proof Idea: this follows directly from condition 4 of definition 5.4.

Now we can give a construction, that transforms every "concrete" state into its "abstract" counterpart.

Lemma 5.2 (Constructing the Preimage of a State) *Given a refinement morphism $f : SC_1 \rightarrow SC_2$. Then the function τ_f is mapping every accessible (concrete) state in Σ_2^{acc} to an (abstract) state in Σ_1, i.e. $\forall\, \sigma_2 \in \Sigma_2^{acc} \bullet \tau_f(\sigma_2) \in \Sigma_1$.*

Proof Idea: We show that the first component of $\tau_f(\sigma_2) = (C_2, E_2)$ is indeed a (total) configuration, i.e. it fulfills the conditions of definition 2.2. For this proof we use the refinement morphism properties and lemma 5.1.

Finally, we can prove, that the refinement morphisms are indeed behavior compatible, that is the diagram in definition 5.3 commutes for arbitrary refinement morphisms.

Theorem 5.1 (Refinement Morphisms are Behavior Compatible) *Every refinement morphism $f : SC_1 \rightarrow SC_2$ is behavior compatible in the sense of definition 5.3.*

Proof Idea: According to lemma 5.2 we have for each $\sigma_2 \in \Sigma_2^{acc}$ and each consistently enabled set T of SC_2 a preimage state $\tau_f(\sigma_2) \in \Sigma_1^{acc}$. Following the rules 1-5 of the algorithm in definition 4.2 for the computation of enabled transitions in the case of $T \in \Sigma_2^{acc}$ we show that $\tau_f(T)$ is a consistently enabled set of SC_1. Following the construction of T anf $\tau_f(T)$ we compute $\sigma_2' = \mathsf{step}_2(\sigma_2, T)$ in SC_2 and $\sigma_1' = \mathsf{step}_1(\tau_f(\sigma_2), \tau_f(T))$ in SC_1 according to definition 4.3 and show $\sigma_1' = \tau_f(\sigma_2')$.

6 Conclusion

We have introduced new formal concepts and results for union, transformation, behavior and refinement of statecharts, which are suitable for horizontal and vertical structuring of concurrent systems. The concepts of union and transformation have been defined by pushout constructions for abstract statecharts as an instantiation of corresponding constructions and results for high-level-replacement systems. Behavior and refinement have been formally defined for statecharts as used in the STATEMATE system. However, we have only considered statecharts without history symbols and data variables and some "syntactic sugar". It is an interesting open problem to extend our constructions and results to the general case of STATEMATE statecharts and also to object oriented statecharts in the sense of [6].

A Graphical Notation

One of the most striking features of the statecharts formalism is its graphical representation. Exploiting this, we will give also a graphical definition for some of the semantical key concepts. For this purpose, we will use the following notation, assuming a given system state $\sigma = (C, E) \in \Sigma$ of a statechart $SC = ((\mathcal{S}, \mathsf{root}, \mathsf{substates}, \mathsf{decomp}, \mathcal{T}, \mathcal{E}, \mathsf{source}, \mathsf{dest}, \mathsf{cond}, \mathsf{action}), \Theta)$ (see defintion 2.5):

1. 

s is a state, i.e. $s \in \mathcal{S}$

2. 

s is in the actual configuration, i.e. $s \in C$

3. 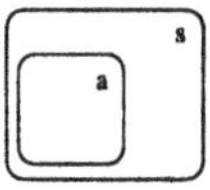

s contains a substate a, i.e. $\mathsf{decomp}(s) = xor \wedge a \in \mathsf{substates}(s)$

4. 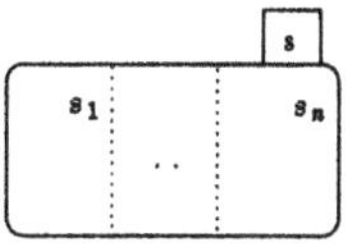

s contains the parallel substates $s_1, .., s_n$, i.e. $\mathsf{decomp}(s) = and \wedge \mathsf{substates}(s) = \{s_1, .., s_n\}$

5. 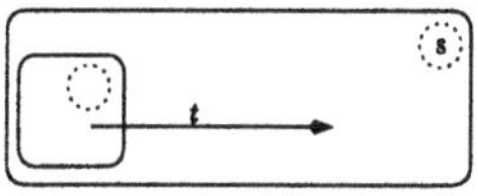

s contains a transition which sources are active, i.e. $t \in \mathcal{T} \wedge \mathsf{arena}(t) = s \wedge \mathsf{source}(t) \subset C$

References

[1] S. Cook and J. Daniels. *Designing Object Systems - Object-Oriented Modelling with Syntropy.* Prentice Hall, 1994.

[2] H. Ehrig, A. Habel, H.-J. Kreowski, and F. Parisi-Presicce. From graph grammars to High Level Replacement Systems. pages 269–291. Springer-Verlag, 1991. Lecture Notes in Computer Science 532.

[3] H. Ehrig, A. Habel, H.-J. Kreowski, and F. Parisi-Presicce. Parallelism and concurrency in high-level replacement systems. *Math. Struct. in Comp. Science*, 1:361–404, 1991.

[4] C. Ermel, J. Padberg, and H. Ehrig. Requirements Engineering of a Medical Information System Using Rule-Based Refinement of Petri Nets. In *Proc. Integrated Design and Process Technology*, 1996.

[5] D. Harel. Statecharts: A visual formalism for complex systems. *Science of Computer Programming*, 8(3):231–274, June 1987.

[6] D. Harel and E. Gery. Executable object modeling with statecharts. In *Proc. of 18th ICSE, Berlin*, March 1996.

[7] D. Harel, H. Lachover, A. Naamad, A. Pnueli, M. Politi, R. Sherman, A. Shtull-Trauring, and M. Trakhtenbrot. Statemate: A working environment for the development of complex reactive systems. *IEEE Transactions on Software Engineering*, 16 No. 4, Apr. 1990.

[8] D. Harel and A. Naamad. The STATEMATE semantics of statecharts. *ACM Trans. Soft. Eng. Method.*, Oct. 1996.

[9] D. Harel, A. Pnueli, J. P. Schmidt, and R. Sherman. On the formal semantics of statecharts. In *Symposium on Logic in Computer Science*, pages 54–64, New York, 1987. IEEE Computer Society Press.

[10] D. Harel and M. Politi. Modeling reactive systems with statecharts: The statemate approach. i-Logix Inc, Three Riverside Drive, Andover, MA 01810, USA, June 1996. Part No. D-1100-43, 6/96.

[11] C. Huizing, R. Gerth, and W. P. de Roever. Modelling statecharts behaviour in a fully abstract way. In *Proc. 13th CAAP*, volume 299 of *Lecture Notes in Computer Science*. Springer-Verlag, 1988.

[12] F. Maraninchi. Operational and compositional semantics of synchronous automaton composition. In *Proc. CONCUR'92 - Third International Conference on Concurrency Theory*, volume 630 of *Lecture Notes in Computer Science*, pages 530 – 564, 1992.

[13] J. Padberg, H. Ehrig, and L. Ribeiro. Algebraic high-level net transformation systems. *Mathematical Structures in Computer Science*, 5:217–256, 1995.

[14] A. Pnueli and M. Shalev. What is in a step: On the semantics of statecharts. In T. Ito and A. R. Meyer, editors, *Theoretical Aspects of Computer Software*, pages 244–264, New York, Sept. 1991. Springer-Verlag. Lecture Notes in Computer Science 526.

[15] J. Rumbaugh, M. Blaha, W. Premerlani, F. Eddy, and W. Lorensen. *Object-Oriented Modeling and Design.* Prentice Hall, 1991.

[16] B. Selic, G. Gullekson, and P. Ward. *Real-Time Object-Oriented Modeling.* Wiley, 1994.

[17] M. von der Beeck. A comparison of statecharts variants. In Langmaak, de Roever, and Vytopil, editors, *Formal Techniques in Real-Time and Fault-Tolerant Systems*, volume 863 of *Lecture Notes in Computer Science*, pages 128–148, 1994.

Implicit Typing à la ML for the Join-Calculus *

Cédric Fournet † Cosimo Laneve ‡
Luc Maranget† Didier Rémy†

Abstract

We adapt the Damas-Milner typing discipline to the join-calculus. The main result is a new generalization criterion that extends the polymorphism of ML to join-definitions. We prove the correctness of our typing rules with regard to a chemical semantics. We also relate typed extensions of the core join-calculus to functional languages.

1 Introduction

The distributed implementation of concurrent calculi with message passing raises the problem of implementing communication channels, which finally reduces to the specification of channel managers. In order to reflect this need in the language itself, a new formalism has been recently introduced : the *join-calculus* [2]. This calculus is similar to Milner's asynchronous π-calculus, except that the operations of restriction, reception and replication are all combined into a single receptor definition. Such a combination yields better control over communication. In [2, 3], we relied on this locality property to model realistic distributed systems. In this paper, we propose a type system for the join-calculus whose simplicity owes much to locality.

The join-calculus is quite expressive (a lot of examples may be found in [2, 3]) and has been turned into a programming language. A convenient syntax has been provided for sequential composition, process migration and failure detection. A distributed implementation is under way and would benefit from static analyses of programs. A good static semantics should of course rely on a type system. The types we need should be expressive enough for most useful programs and easy to understand for programmers.

This goal is achieved by adapting the Damas-Milner typing discipline developed for ML [1] to the join calculus. From the typing point of view, definitions in the join-calculus are a generalized form of let expressions in ML and polymorphism can be introduced right after typechecking the clauses of a join-definition.

*This work is partly supported by the ESPRIT CONFER-2 WG-21836

†INRIA Rocquencourt, BP 105, 78153 Le Chesnay Cedex France.

‡Dipartimento di Scienze dell'Informazione, University of Bologna, Mura Anteo Zamboni 7, 40127 Bologna, Italy

However, synchronization on channels is more demanding than plain function calls, as it interacts with polymorphism. Our main result is a generalization criterion for the join-calculus that addresses this issue. We prove the correctness of the resulting typing rules with regard to our concurrent semantics by adapting standard techniques to the chemical framework. Thus, without any change, the join calculus becomes a typed process calculus with implicit parametric polymorphism.

1.1 Polymorphism in the join-calculus

The join-calculus is essentially a name-passing calculus: port names are defined, then used as addresses in messages that convey other names. These messages are polyadic; the type of a name carrying n objects of type $\tau_1, \ldots, \tau_n$ is written $\langle \tau_1, \ldots, \tau_n \rangle$. Traditional languages come with system-supplied primitives, which can be used in the programming practice. Similarly, we could assume system-supplied primitive names for a language based on the join-calculus, such as `print_int` that outputs its integer argument on the console. Then,

def `print_two_ints`⟨`x`,`y`⟩ ▷ `print_int`⟨`x`⟩ | `print_int`⟨`y`⟩

defines a new name `print_two_ints` that prints two integers; more precisely, when the name `print_two_ints` receives a couple of arguments ⟨`x`,`y`⟩, it activates two processes `print_int`⟨`x`⟩ and `print_int`⟨`y`⟩ running concurrently. The type of the primitive `print_int` is ⟨`int`⟩ (i.e., a name that carries one integer) and the type of the new name `print_two_ints` is ⟨`int`, `int`⟩ (i.e., a name that carries two integers).

In this context, a name with a polymorphic type in the join-calculus is reminiscent of a polymorphic function in ML: both don't need to perform fully type-specific operations on their arguments. Thus, the types of the arguments are not completely specified and unspecified parts are represented by type variables that stand for just any type. This framework is known as *parametric* polymorphism. For instance, consider the following definition:

def `apply`⟨`k`,`x`⟩ ▷ `k`⟨`x`⟩

The name `apply` takes two arguments `k` and `x` and activates the process `k`⟨`x`⟩. Thus, if `x` is of type τ, then `k` must carry names of type τ, i.e. be of type $\langle \tau \rangle$. The name `apply` can be given type $\langle \langle \tau \rangle, \tau \rangle$ for any type τ. As in ML, this is emphasized by giving `apply` the type scheme $\forall \alpha. \langle \langle \alpha \rangle, \alpha \rangle$. Therefore `apply` can take arguments as `print_int` and `4`, by the call `apply`⟨`print_int`,`4`⟩, thereby instantiating α with the type `int`. Given another primitive `print_string`, another legitimate invocation `apply`⟨`print_string`,`'foo'`⟩ would instantiate α with the type `string`.

The join-calculus improves on ML by providing synchronization between join patterns (several messages in parallel). Consider, for instance, a variant of `apply` that receives `k` and `x` from different sources.

def `port`⟨`k`⟩ | `arg`⟨`x`⟩ ▷ `k`⟨`x`⟩

The concurrent activation of the co-defined names **port** and **arg** fires $\mathtt{k}\langle\mathtt{x}\rangle$. The names **port** and **arg** can be typed with $\langle\langle\alpha\rangle\rangle$ and $\langle\alpha\rangle$, respectively. Observe, however, that names **port** and **arg** are correlated, which is reflected by the use of the same type variable α in their types. This forbids to give **port** and **arg** the type schemes $\forall\alpha.\langle\alpha\rangle$ and $\forall\alpha.\langle\langle\alpha\rangle\rangle$. Otherwise, their types schemes could be instantiated independently, loosing their correlation. Clearly, sending the primitive `print_string` on **port** and an integer on **arg** would result in a run-time type error: attempting to print an integer as a string.

As a consequence, our generalization rule copes with synchronization in an abstract way: a type variable cannot be generalized if it appears free in the type of *several* co-defined names.

1.2 Overview

In section 2, we recall the syntax and semantics of the join-calculus and we present the type system. The original RCHAM used in [3] has a defect as regards typing; we introduce a variant and we relate it to the original. In section 3, we establish the main result: we prove subject reduction in a chemical setting and we show that well-typed programs cannot go wrong at run-time. In section 4, we briefly discuss type inference, as implemented in our prototype compiler. In section 5, we extend the join-calculus with support for functions and expressions, an useful step towards an effective programming language. We generalize the type system accordingly. This extension provides a good basis for a detailed comparison with type systems for functional languages. In section 6, we compare our work with other type systems that have been proposed for concurrent calculi.

2 The typed join-calculus

2.1 Syntax

While names already provide enough expressiveness [2], it is convenient here to supplement names with constants that represent basic values 1, 2... ,'foo'... and primitives add, `string_of_int`, `print`, along with their basic types such as `int`, `string`.

For names, we assume given a set of port names $x \in \mathcal{N}$ and a set of constants $k \in \mathcal{K}$. We use $u \in \mathcal{N} \cup \mathcal{K}$ to denote a name in general. For types, we assume given a set of basic types $b \in \mathcal{T}$ and a set of type variables α.

$$
\begin{aligned}
P &::= u\langle u_i^{\ i\in 1..p}\rangle \mid \mathbf{def}\ D\ \mathbf{in}\ P \mid P \mid P \\
D &::= J \triangleright P \mid D \wedge D \\
J &::= x\langle x_i^{\ i\in 1..p}\rangle \mid J \mid J
\end{aligned}
\qquad
\begin{aligned}
\tau &::= b \mid \alpha \mid \langle \tau_i^{\ i\in 1..p}\rangle \\
\sigma &::= \tau \mid \forall\alpha.\sigma \\
A &::= \emptyset \mid A + (u:\sigma) \\
B &::= \emptyset \mid B + (u:\tau)
\end{aligned}
$$

A process P is either a message, a defining process, or a parallel composition of processes; a definition D consists of one or several clauses $J \triangleright P$ that associate a guarded process P to a specific message pattern J; a join-pattern J consists of one or several messages in parallel. We say that the pattern $J = \ldots x\langle z_i \ ^{i\in 1..p}\rangle \ldots$ defines the name x. We note $dv(D)$ for the set of all names that are defined in D.

Processes and definitions are known modulo renaming of bound variables, as substitution performs α-conversion to avoid captures.

A type τ is either a basic type, a type variable, or a message type conveying a fixed number of types; a type scheme σ may quantify over type variables; a typing environment A associates type schemes to names, while a simple environment B associates types to names. Given an environment A that already associates a type scheme to a name u, the new environment $A + (u : \sigma)$ is well formed and associates σ to u.

Primitive names $\mathcal{K}$ are given with a primitive typing environment $A_{\mathcal{K}}$ of domain $\mathcal{K}$.

2.2 Typing rules

There are three kinds of typing judgments:

$A \vdash u : \tau$	the name u has type τ in A;
$A \vdash P$	the process P is well-typed in A;
$A \vdash D :: B$	the definition D is well-typed in A with types B for its defined names.

The following rules describe valid proofs for our judgments. They are much inspired by the typing rules for the (polyadic) λ-calculus plus `let rec`, the real innovation being the generalization in DEF.

(Inst)
$$\frac{u : \forall \alpha_i \ ^{i\in 1..n}. \tau \in A}{A \vdash u : \tau[\tau_i/\alpha_i \ ^{i\in 1..n}]}$$

(Par)
$$\frac{A \vdash P \qquad A \vdash Q}{A \vdash P \mid Q}$$

(Message)
$$\frac{A \vdash u : \langle \tau_i \ ^{i\in 1..n}\rangle \qquad (A \vdash u_i : \tau_i) \ ^{i\in 1..n}}{A \vdash u\langle u_i \ ^{i\in 1..n}\rangle}$$

(Rule)
$$\frac{A + u_{ij} : \tau_{ij} \ ^{i\in 1..n, j\in 1..m_i} \vdash P}{A \vdash x_1\langle u_{1j} \ ^{j\in 1..m_1}\rangle \mid \ldots x_n\langle u_{nj} \ ^{j\in 1..m_n}\rangle \triangleright P :: (x_i : \langle \tau_{ij} \ ^{j\in 1..m_i}\rangle) \ ^{i\in 1..n}}$$

(And)
$$\frac{A \vdash D_1 :: B_1 \qquad A \vdash D_2 :: B_2}{A \vdash D_1 \wedge D_2 :: B_1 \oplus B_2}$$

(Def)
$$\frac{A + B \vdash D :: B \qquad A + \mathrm{Gen}(B, A) \vdash P}{A \vdash \mathbf{def}\ D \ \mathbf{in}\ P}$$

The rules use the following definitions:

- $B_1 \oplus B_2$ is $B_1 + B_2$, and requires B_1 and B_2 to be equal on $dv(B_1) \cap dv(B_2)$.
- $\mathrm{Gen}(B, A)$ is the generalization of the simple environment B of the form $(x_i : \tau_i)^{\,i \in 1..n}$ with respect to A: let $fv(A)$ be the set $\bigcup_{(x:\sigma) \in A} fv(\sigma)$ where $fv(\sigma)$ contains the free variables of σ; let $B \backslash x$ be the environment B without the binding for x. Then $\mathrm{Gen}(B, A)$ is $(x_i : \forall (fv(\tau_i) - fv(A + B \backslash x_i)) . \tau_i)^{\,i \in 1..n}$.

2.3 Chemical Semantics

For our type system to be of some use, we must show its consistency with respect to the semantics of the join-calculus.

This semantics is specified as a reflexive chemical abstract machine (RCHAM), as in [2]. The state of the computation is a *chemical soup* $\mathcal{D} \Vdash \mathcal{P}$ that consists of two multisets: active definitions $\mathcal{D}$ and running processes $\mathcal{P}$.

The chemical soup evolves according to two families of rules: *Structural rules* $\rightleftharpoons$ are reversible ($\rightharpoonup$ is heating, $\leftharpoondown$ is cooling); they represent the syntactical rearrangement of terms (heating breaks terms into smaller ones, cooling builds larger terms from their components). *Reduction rules* $\longrightarrow$ consume specific processes present in the soup, replacing them by some others; they are the basic computation steps. In the following, a generic rule will be denoted by the symbol $\rightleftharpoons\!\!\!\!\rightarrow$, and we will write $dv(\mathcal{D})$ for the union $\bigcup_{D \in \mathcal{D}} dv(D)$.

Every rule applies on any matching subpart of the soup. More explicitly, for every rule $\rightleftharpoons\!\!\!\!\rightarrow$, we also have a context rule:

(Context)

$$\frac{\mathcal{D}_1 \Vdash \mathcal{P}_1 \rightleftharpoons\!\!\!\!\rightarrow \mathcal{D}_2 \Vdash \mathcal{P}_2 \qquad (fv(\mathcal{D}) \cup fv(\mathcal{P})) \cap dv(\mathcal{D}_1 \backslash \mathcal{D}_2 \cup \mathcal{D}_2 \backslash \mathcal{D}_1) = \emptyset}{\mathcal{D} \cup \mathcal{D}_1 \Vdash \mathcal{P}_1 \cup \mathcal{P} \rightleftharpoons\!\!\!\!\rightarrow \mathcal{D} \cup \mathcal{D}_2 \Vdash \mathcal{P}_2 \cup \mathcal{P}}$$

A chemical semantics naturally induces a structural equivalence $\equiv$ on terms, defined as the smallest structural congruence that contains $\rightleftharpoons$; this leads to a more classical presentation of the semantics as term rewriting modulo equivalence.

The original machine

In [2, 3], the chemical rules are:

$$\begin{array}{rclr}
\Vdash P_1 \mid P_2 & \rightleftharpoons & \Vdash P_1, P_2 & \text{S-PAR} \\
D_1 \wedge D_2 \Vdash & \rightleftharpoons & D_1, D_2 \Vdash & \text{S-AND} \\
\Vdash \mathbf{def}\ D\ \mathbf{in}\ P & \rightleftharpoons & D \Vdash P & \text{S-DEF} \\
& & & \\
J \triangleright P \Vdash \varphi(J) & \longrightarrow & J \triangleright P \Vdash \varphi(P) & \text{R-}\beta \\
\Vdash k\langle u_i^{\ i \in 1..p} \rangle & \longrightarrow & \Vdash P & \text{R-}\delta
\end{array}$$

with the side-conditions:

- (S-DEF) the names defined in D must not appear anywhere in solution but in the reacting process and definition D and P. This condition is global; in combination with α-renaming it enforces lexical scoping.
- (R-β) $\varphi(\cdot)$ substitute actual names for the received variables in J and P.
- (R-δ) $(u_i\ ^{i\in 1..p}, P) \in \delta_k$, where $\{\delta_k, k \in \mathcal{K}\}$ is a family of primitive relations that map names $u_i\ ^{i\in 1..p}$ to processes P.

We would expect every typing property to be preserved by the structural equivalence, but this is not the case here. The trouble lies in the grouping of definitions that changes outer bound occurrences into recursive ones. Given two definitions D_1 and D_2 such that some names defined by D_1 occur free in D_2, but not the converse, we have

$$\texttt{def } D_1 \texttt{ in def } D_2 \texttt{ in } P \equiv \texttt{def } D_1 \wedge D_2 \texttt{ in } P$$

Unfortunately, the valid typing judgments for the names defined in D_1 and used in D_2 are not the same on each side of the equivalence. Polymorphic typing can be used in the left program and not in the right program. In fact, we run across the classical limitation of typing for mutually-recursive functions.

The restricted machine

To solve this problem, we introduce a variant of the RCHAM that is better suited to our typing purposes. In the new machine, definitions with several clauses are not heated; more specifically, the structural rule S-AND disappears and the reduction rule R-β is generalized:

$$
\begin{array}{rclr}
\Vdash P_1 \mid P_2 & \rightleftharpoons' & \Vdash P_1, P_2 & \text{S-PAR} \\
\Vdash \texttt{def } D \texttt{ in } P & \rightleftharpoons' & D \Vdash P & \text{S-DEF} \\
\\
\cdots \wedge J \rhd P \wedge \cdots \Vdash \varphi(J) & \longrightarrow' & \cdots \wedge J \rhd P \wedge \cdots \Vdash \varphi(P) & \text{R-}\beta\text{'} \\
\Vdash k\langle u\ ^{i\in 1..p}\rangle & \longrightarrow' & \Vdash P & \text{R-}\delta
\end{array}
$$

In the rule R-β' above, $\cdots \wedge J \rhd P \wedge \cdots$ stands for an active definition that contains the clause $J \rhd P$. This notation now expresses the commutativity and the associativity of $\wedge$, which were conveyed more explicitly by the structural rule S-AND.

In addition, and for every chemical soup $\mathcal{D} \Vdash \mathcal{P}$, we require every name to be defined in exactly one definition of $\mathcal{D}$:

$$\forall D, D' \in \mathcal{D}, dv(D) \cap dv(D') = \emptyset$$

We now relate this restricted machine to the original one. Let us first consider machines that operate on completely diluted solutions (i.e., heating rules cannot apply anymore). There is a straightforward correspondence between chemical solutions of the two formalisms: processes are the same atoms; definitions are equivalent to the clauses that enter into it. Given this equivalence, β-reduction is the same relation in both frameworks. In the general case, structural cooling in the first machine may lead to more programs. However, we still have:

$$(\longrightarrow) \subset (\longrightarrow') \subset (\overset{\text{S-And}}{\rightharpoonup})^* \circ (\longrightarrow) \circ (\overset{\text{S-And}}{\leftharpoondown})^*$$

In the following, we use the restricted chemical machine without further discussion. We drop the $'$ notation and write $\longrightarrow$ and $\rightleftharpoons$ for the restricted chemical rules.

2.4 Type-checking solutions

Typing of programs easily extends to chemical solutions. First, we introduce a judgment $A \vdash D$ to state that the assumptions made in A on the names defined in D are the same as if those names had been added in A after typing the definition D. Precisely, we type D in the environment A extended (actually overridden) with new assumptions B that must be exactly the typing environment produced by D as in rule DEF; then, we check that the generalization of B in A is equal to A restricted to $dv(B)$, i.e. $\text{Gen}(B, A)$ is a subset of A. Observe that $A + B$ is also $(A \setminus dv(B)) + B$.

We introduce a new typing judgment $A \vdash \mathcal{D} \Vdash \mathcal{P}$ to state that the chemical solution $\mathcal{D} \Vdash \mathcal{P}$ is well-typed in environment A. This happens when all definitions and all processes are independently well typed in the same environment A:

(Multi)
$$\frac{A + B \vdash D :: B \qquad \text{Gen}(B, A) \subset A}{A \vdash D}$$

(Soup)
$$\frac{\forall P \in \mathcal{P}, A \vdash P \qquad \forall D \in \mathcal{D}, A \vdash D}{A \vdash \mathcal{D} \Vdash \mathcal{P}}$$

Typing chemical solutions simplifies our proofs by avoiding some of the technicalities introduced by the more common formalism of term-rewriting modulo structural equivalence. In particular, the chemistry treats structural rearrangements and proper reductions in the same way. This simplification has already been profitably used in untyped concurrency theory.

3 Correctness of the evaluation

From a quite abstract point of view, let us assume that some evaluation steps of a program P yields a new program P'. Typing and evaluation agree when two facts hold: first, a typing derivation of P' can be constructed from a typing derivation of P. Second, messages present in P' cannot cause "run-time type errors" such as the addition of a string or sending one argument only on a binary name (no type mismatch for primitives, no wrong arity for defined names).

3.1 Assumptions on primitives

For the reduction to be sound, we assume that the primitive reduction relations are consistent with the primitive typing environment $A_{\mathcal{K}}$ introduced in section 2.1. That is, for every typing environment A and for every $k \in \mathcal{K}$, we have:

$$A + A_{\mathcal{K}} \vdash k\langle u_i \,^{i\in 1..p}\rangle \text{ and } (u_i \,^{i\in 1..p}, P) \in \delta_k \Rightarrow A + A_{\mathcal{K}} \vdash P$$

In particular, the free names of P are either primitives or among the u_i.

3.2 Basic properties for the typing

Lemma 1 (Useless variable) *Let u be a name that is not free in P or D, nor defined in D. Then we have:*

$$\begin{array}{rcl} A \vdash P & \Leftrightarrow & A + (u : \sigma) \vdash P \\ A \vdash D :: B & \Leftrightarrow & A + (u : \sigma) \vdash D :: B \end{array}$$

Lemma 2 (Renaming of type variables) *Let φ be a substitution on type variables. We have:*

$$\begin{array}{rcl} A \vdash P & \Rightarrow & \varphi(A) \vdash P \\ A \vdash D :: B & \Rightarrow & \varphi(A) \vdash D :: \varphi(B) \end{array}$$

We say that a type $\forall \bar{\alpha}. \tau$ is *more general* than $\forall \bar{\alpha}'. \tau'$ if τ' is of the form $\tau[\bar{\tau''}/\bar{\alpha}]$. This notion lifts to set of assumptions as follows: A' is more general than A if A and A' have the same domain and for each u in their domain, $A'(u)$ is more general than $A(u)$.

Lemma 3 (Generalization) *If $A \vdash P$ and A' is more general than A, then $A' \vdash P$.*

Lemma 4 (Substitution of a name in a term) *If $A + (u : \tau) \vdash P$ and $A \vdash v : \tau$ then $A \vdash P[v/u]$.*

3.3 Subject reduction

Two environments A and A' *agree* when their restrictions to primitive names are equal. We define the relation $\subset$ between RCHAMs as the preservation of typings, that is, $\mathcal{D} \Vdash \mathcal{P} \subset \mathcal{D}' \Vdash \mathcal{P}'$ if for any typing environment A such that $A \vdash \mathcal{D} \Vdash \mathcal{P}$, there exists a typing environment A' such the $A' \vdash \mathcal{D}' \Vdash \mathcal{P}'$ and A and A' agree.

Theorem 1 (subject-reduction) *One-step chemical reductions preserve typings*

Proof: In fact, we prove the stronger property that typing environments also agree on variable names, except maybe on variable names that are defined in either chemical soup but not in both.

That is, for every $\rightleftharpoons$, let $\mathcal{D} \Vdash \mathcal{P} \rightleftharpoons \mathcal{D}' \Vdash \mathcal{P}'$ and $A \vdash \mathcal{D} \Vdash \mathcal{P}$. We show that $\mathcal{D}' \Vdash \mathcal{P}'$ is well-typed in an environment A' that possibly differ from A only on $dv((\mathcal{D} \setminus \mathcal{D}') \cup (\mathcal{D}' \setminus \mathcal{D}))$. We prove this property by induction on the number of applications of rule CONTEXT in the derivation of the one-step reduction.

Basic case: We first consider the basic case for every reaction rule.

Subcase S-Par: The reduction is $\Vdash P_1 \mid P_2 \rightleftharpoons \Vdash P_1, P_2$.
Heating: Clearly, if $A \vdash P_1 \mid P_2$ then $A \vdash P_1, P_2$ by rules PAR and DEF.
Cooling: is as easy.

Subcase S-Def: The reduction is $\Vdash \mathbf{def}\ D \ \mathbf{in}\ P \rightleftharpoons D \Vdash P$.
Heating: Let us assume that $A \vdash \mathbf{def}\ D\ \mathbf{in}\ P$, that is, there is a derivation ending with:

$$\frac{A + B \vdash D :: B \qquad A + \mathrm{Gen}(B, A) \vdash P}{A \vdash \mathbf{def}\ D\ \mathbf{in}\ P}\ (\text{DEF})$$

Clearly, DEF and SOUP give $A + \mathrm{Gen}(B, A) \vdash D \Vdash P$.
Cooling: Let $A \vdash D \Vdash P$. Then A is of the form $A' + \mathrm{Gen}(B, A')$ and we have both $A' + B \vdash D :: B$ and $A' + \mathrm{Gen}(B, A') \vdash P$. Thus, by DEF, $A' \vdash \mathbf{def}\ D\ \mathbf{in}\ P$.

In both cases, the two typing environments agree on primitive names and on names defined both in the solution to the left and to the right of the structural rule.

Subcase R-β: We first assume that D is $J \triangleright Q$. Therefore let $A \vdash J \triangleright Q \Vdash \varphi(J)$, where J is of the form $x_1\langle\tilde{u}_1\rangle \mid \ldots x_n\langle\tilde{u}_n\rangle$. By the rules DEF, SOUP and RULE, the hypothesis $A \vdash J \triangleright Q \Vdash \varphi(J)$ reduces to assume $A = A' + \mathrm{Gen}(B, A')$ and

$$A \vdash \varphi(J) \tag{1}$$
$$A' + B + (\tilde{u}_i : \tilde{\tau}_i)^{\,i\in 1..n} \vdash P \tag{2}$$

where B is $(x_i : \langle\tilde{\tau}_i\rangle)^{\,i\in 1..n}$ and $\mathrm{Gen}(B, A')$ is $(x_i : \forall \tilde{\alpha}_i.\, \tilde{\tau}_i)^{\,i\in 1..n}$, where $\tilde{\alpha}_i$ is equal to $fv(\tilde{\tau}_i) \setminus (fv(A') \cup fv(\tilde{\tau}_j)^{\,j\neq i})$.

Observe that the derivation of the judgment (1) must have the shape:

$$\frac{\dfrac{A \vdash x_i : \langle\tilde{\tau}'_i\rangle \qquad A \vdash \varphi(\tilde{u}_i) : \tilde{\tau}'_i}{A \vdash x_i\langle\varphi(\tilde{u}_i)\rangle}\ (\text{MESSAGE}) \qquad i \in 1..n}{A \vdash \varphi(J)}\ (\text{PAR}) \tag{3}$$

where types $\tilde{\tau}'_i$ are type instances $\theta_i(\tilde{\tau}_i)$ of $\forall \tilde{\alpha}_i.\, \tau_i$, where θ_i ranges in $\tilde{\alpha}_i$. Since generalizable variables never occur in two different bindings, the domains of θ_i's are disjoint and we can define the sum θ of θ_i's for i in $1..n$.

Now, applying the substitution φ, which leaves A' unchanged, to the judgment (2), we get:

$$A' + (x_i : \langle\theta(\tilde{\tau}_i)\rangle)^{\,i\in 1..n} + (\tilde{u}_i : \theta(\tilde{\tau}_i))^{\,i\in 1..n} \vdash P$$

By lemma 3, we can generalize the assumptions of the above judgment as follows:

$$A + (\tilde{u}_i : \theta(\tilde{\tau}_j))^{\,i\in 1..n} \vdash P$$

This judgment and the hypothesis $A \vdash \varphi(\tilde{u}_i) : \tilde{\tau}'_i$ of (3) allow to derive, by the name substitution lemma 4, $A \vdash P[\varphi(\tilde{u}_j)/\tilde{u}_j]$, i.e. $A \vdash \varphi(P)$.

We now consider the general case of a definition $J \rhd P \wedge D$. By the rules DEF and SOUP, the hypothesis $A \vdash J \rhd P \wedge D \Vdash \varphi(J)$ reduces to assuming $A = A' + \mathrm{Gen}(B, A')$ and

$$A' + B \vdash J \rhd P \wedge D :: B \qquad A \vdash \varphi(J)$$

By the leftmost judgment and the rule AND it follows that $B = B' \oplus B''$ and $A' + B' \vdash J \rhd P :: B'$ and $A' + B'' \vdash D :: B''$. By lemma 1 applied to $A' + B' \vdash J \rhd P :: B'$ it follows $A' + B \vdash J \rhd P :: B'$. We reduce to the basic case above by instantiating RULE with this last judgment.

Subcase R-δ: By hypothesis.

Inductive case: We now prove the inductive step uniformly for the context rules. We assume $A \vdash \mathcal{D} \cup \mathcal{D}_1 \Vdash \mathcal{P} \cup \mathcal{P}_1$ and $\mathcal{D}_1 \Vdash \mathcal{P}_1 \rightleftharpoons \mathcal{D}_2 \Vdash \mathcal{P}_2$. By rule DEF and SOUP, we know that $\mathcal{D}$, $\mathcal{D}_1$, $\mathcal{P}$, and $\mathcal{P}_1$ are all well-typed in A. In particular, $A \vdash \mathcal{D}_1 \Vdash \mathcal{P}_1$. Therefore, by inductive hypothesis, there exists A' such that $A' \vdash \mathcal{D}_2 \Vdash \mathcal{P}_2$, i.e. $A' \vdash \mathcal{D}_2$ and $A' \vdash \mathcal{P}_2$. By inductive hypothesis A and A' agrees modulo names that are defined in $\mathcal{D}_1$ and $\mathcal{D}_2$ but not in both. Let X be such set of names. Then names defined in $\mathcal{D}$ are disjoint from X, by the condition in the premise of the rule (CONTEXT). Therefore $A' \vdash \mathcal{D}$ by lemma 1 applied to $A \vdash \mathcal{D}$. Furthermore, the side condition of the rule S-DEF also forces $fv(\mathcal{P})$ to be disjoint from $dv((\mathcal{D}_1 \setminus \mathcal{D}_2) \cup (\mathcal{D}_2 \setminus \mathcal{D}_2))$. Thus, we also have $A' \vdash \mathcal{P}$, by lemma 1 applied to $A \vdash \mathcal{P}$. Finally, $A' \vdash \mathcal{D} \cup \mathcal{D}_2 \Vdash \mathcal{P} \cup \mathcal{P}_2$ follows by SOUP. ■

3.4 No run-time errors

We state the correctness of a computation from what can be observed from running chemical machines. When ill-formed messages are released in a solution with a consistent set of primitives (see 3.1), there is no reduction that would consume them, so they remain visible, exactly as barbs on free names in an untyped setting. In this case the computation has failed.

Definition 1 A chemical solution $\mathcal{D} \Vdash \mathcal{P}$ has failed when $\mathcal{P}$ contains either:

- A message $k\langle u_i \; ^{i \in 1..n} \rangle$ when no δ-rule applies;
- A message $x\langle u_i \; ^{i \in 1..n} \rangle$ when x is not defined in $\mathcal{D}$, or defined with arity $m \neq n$.

Theorem 2 (Correct computation) *A well-typed chemical machine cannot fail through chemical reduction or equivalence. In particular, a typed program cannot fail.*

Proof: Neither kind of messages of the previous definition can appear in a well-typed chemical soup; chemical typing is preserved by chemical rewriting. ■

4 Type inference

Since types and typing rules are in essence those of ML, our type system also allows for type inference. Precisely, there exists an algorithm that given a soup $\mathcal{D} \Vdash \mathcal{P}$ and a typing environment A_0 that binds the free names of $\mathcal{D}$ and $\mathcal{P}$ with the exception of the active names $dv(\mathcal{D})$, returns a typing environment A of domains $dv(\mathcal{D})$ such that $A_0 \oplus A \vdash \mathcal{D} \Vdash \mathcal{P}$, or fails if no such typing environment exists. Morever, if the algorithms succeeds, then A is principal, that is, for any other typing environment A' of domain $dv(\mathcal{D})$ such that $A_0 \oplus A' \vdash \mathcal{D} \Vdash \mathcal{P}$, then A is more general than A'.

The complete formalization is a straightforward adaptation of the one for ML [1].

5 Functional constructs

In this section, we extend the join-calculus with functions and expressions and we refine the type system accordingly. Such extensions turn the join-calculus into a practical core language that can be seen as a concurrent extension of a small call-by-value functional language with concurrent evaluation and join-call synchronization.

5.1 Programming in the join-calculus

In practice, programmers feel uncomfortable with the non-deterministic behavior of the "print two integer" example of the introduction; they would often prefer to print `x`, then `y`. The standard trick for enforcing sequential control is to use continuation passing style. Indeed, our implementation provides a synchronous `print_int` primitive that takes two arguments: an integer to be output, and a continuation to be triggered thereafter. This continuation is used for synchronization only; it carries no argument, and has type $\langle\rangle$. Thus, the type of the synchronous `print_int` is $\langle$`int`$, \langle\rangle\rangle$. The synchronous version of `print_two_ints` also takes an extra continuation argument, and has type $\langle$`int`$,$ `int`$, \langle\rangle\rangle$:

```
def print_two_ints⟨x,y,k⟩ ▷
  def ky⟨⟩ ▷ k⟨⟩ in
  def kx⟨⟩ ▷ print_int⟨y,ky⟩ in
  print_int⟨x,kx⟩
```

The continuation passing style idiom is so common in process calculi that it deserves a convenient syntax that avoids writing explicit continuations (see also [8]). In our setting, continuation arguments are implicit in both primitive names and user-defined names. The synchronous version of "print two integers" becomes:

```
def print_two_ints⟨x,y⟩ ▷
  print_int⟨x⟩ ; print_int⟨y⟩ ; reply to print_two_ints
```

The sequencing operator ";" avoids the definition of explicit continuations inside the body of `print_two_ints`. The final call to continuation is left explicit. This keeps the introduction of synchronous names simple and general, since a join-calculus definition may introduce several synchronous names (and thus several continuations) simultaneously. We write **reply** $u_1, ...u_p$ **to** x by analogy to the C **return** instruction. We also provide a sequencing binding **let** $x_1, ...x_p = e$ **in** P, where e is an expression, i.e. some kind of process with a continuation. More generally, we do not refrain from the temptation of using $\langle \tau_1, \ldots, \tau_q \rangle \rightarrow \langle \tau'_1, \ldots, \tau'_p \rangle$ as a convenient synonym for $\langle \tau_1, \ldots, \tau_q, \langle \tau'_1, \ldots, \tau'_p \rangle \rangle$. Hence, the type of `print_two_ints` can be written $\langle \mathtt{int}, \mathtt{int} \rangle \rightarrow \langle \rangle$.

5.2 Functions as names

Port names can now be used in two different manners: either asynchronously or synchronously. The synchronous invocation of a name u is performed by the new **let** $x_i{}^{i \in 1..p} = u\langle u_j{}^{j \in 1..q} \rangle$ **in** P construct. The other new construct **reply** $u_i{}^{i \in 1..p}$ **to** x is the asynchronous invocation of the continuation of x. At run-time, it will fire the pending P of a matching **let** $x_i{}^{i \in 1..p} = x\langle u_j{}^{j \in 1..q} \rangle$ **in** P construct.

$$
\begin{aligned}
P ::= {} & u\langle u_i{}^{i \in 1..p} \rangle \\
| {} & \mathbf{def}\ D\ \mathbf{in}\ P \\
| {} & P \mid P \\
| {} & \mathbf{let}\ x_i{}^{i \in 1..p} = u\langle u_j{}^{j \in 1..q} \rangle\ \mathbf{in}\ P \\
| {} & \mathbf{reply}\ u_i{}^{i \in 1..p}\ \mathbf{to}\ x
\end{aligned}
\qquad
\begin{aligned}
\tau ::= {} & b \mid \alpha \mid \langle \tau_i{}^{i \in 1..p} \rangle \\
| {} & \langle \tau_j{}^{j \in 1..q} \rangle \rightarrow \langle \tau'_i{}^{i \in 1..p} \rangle \\
\sigma ::= {} & \tau \mid \forall \alpha . \sigma
\end{aligned}
$$

Patterns, clauses and typing environments are as before. The sequencing operator ";" corresponds to the **let** construct with $p = 0$. There are two additional typing rules for the new constructs:

(Let-Val)

$$
\frac{A \vdash u : \langle \tau_j{}^{j \in 1..q} \rangle \rightarrow \langle \tau'_i{}^{i \in 1..p} \rangle \qquad (A \vdash u_j : \tau_j)^{j \in 1..q} \qquad A + (x_i : \tau'_i)^{i \in 1..p} \vdash P}{A \vdash \mathbf{let}\ x_i{}^{i \in 1..p} = u\langle u_j{}^{j \in 1..q} \rangle\ \mathbf{in}\ P}
$$

(Reply)

$$
\frac{A \vdash x : \langle \tau_j{}^{j \in 1..q} \rangle \rightarrow \langle \tau'_i{}^{i \in 1..p} \rangle \qquad (A \vdash u_i : \tau'_i)^{i \in 1..p}}{A \vdash \mathbf{reply}\ u_i{}^{i \in 1..p}\ \mathbf{to}\ x}
$$

The typing rules guarantee that synchronous and asynchronous invocations on the same name do not mix. Moreover, an user-defined name x must be invoked synchronously when its definition includes type consistent occurrences of the **reply** $u_i{}^{i \in 1..p}$ **to** x construct.

Therefore, we give names an asynchronous or synchronous status. Name status may be determined by typing, provided the following agreement: every name whose synchronous usage is not detected by the type inference system is considered asynchronous. In the following, we simply write f, instead of x, for synchronous names.

5.3 A typed CPS encoding

As usual for process calculi, we translate functional names back to the initial join-calculus. The translation applies to type correct programs and once synchronous names have been identified. Given a synchronous name f, we introduce the fresh name κ_f for its continuation; we also use the reserved name κ for intermediate continuations generated while translating **lets**. The call-by-value translation is:

$$\begin{array}{rcll} f\langle u_i \,^{i\in 1..p}\rangle & \stackrel{def}{=} & f\langle u_i \,^{i\in 1..p}, \kappa_f\rangle & \text{(in join-patterns } J) \\ \texttt{reply}\ u_i \,^{i\in 1..p}\ \texttt{to}\ f & \stackrel{def}{=} & \kappa_f\langle u_i \,^{i\in 1..p}\rangle & \text{(in guarded processes } P) \\ \texttt{let}\ x_i \,^{i\in 1..p} = f\langle u_j \,^{j\in 1..q}\rangle\ \texttt{in}\ P & \stackrel{def}{=} & \texttt{def}\ \kappa\langle x_i \,^{i\in 1..p}\rangle \triangleright P\ \texttt{in}\ f\langle u_j \,^{j\in 1..q}, \kappa\rangle & \end{array}$$

$$\langle \tau_j \,^{j\in 1..q}\rangle \rightarrow \langle \tau'_i \,^{i\in 1..p}\rangle \stackrel{def}{=} \langle \tau_j \,^{j\in 1..q}, \langle \tau'_i \,^{i\in 1..p}\rangle\rangle$$

The two additional typing rules, once their operands have been translated, are derived from the type system of section 2:

(translated Let-Val)

$$\frac{A \vdash f : \langle \tau_j \,^{j\in 1..q}, \langle \tau'_i \,^{i\in 1..p}\rangle\rangle \qquad (A \vdash u_j : \tau_j)\,^{j\in 1..q} \qquad A + (x_i : \tau'_i)\,^{i\in 1..p} \vdash P}{A \vdash \texttt{def}\ \kappa\langle x_i \,^{i\in 1..p}\rangle \triangleright P\ \texttt{in}\ f\langle u_j \,^{j\in 1..q}, \kappa\rangle}$$

(translated Reply)

$$\frac{A \vdash f : \langle \tau_j \,^{j\in 1..q}, \langle \tau'_i \,^{i\in 1..p}\rangle\rangle \qquad (A \vdash u_i : \tau'_i)\,^{i\in 1..p}}{A \vdash \kappa_f\langle u_i \,^{i\in 1..p}\rangle}$$

5.4 A join-calculus-based language

A complete syntax for processes and expressions is:

$$\begin{array}{rll} P ::= & u\langle E_i \,^{i\in 1..p}\rangle \\ & \mid \texttt{def}\ D\ \texttt{in}\ P \\ & \mid P \mid P \\ & \mid \texttt{let}\ x_i \,^{i\in 1..p} = E\ \texttt{in}\ P \\ & \mid \texttt{reply}\ E_i \,^{i\in 1..p}\ \texttt{to}\ x \end{array} \qquad \begin{array}{rll} E ::= & u \\ & \mid u\langle E_i \,^{i\in 1..p}\rangle \\ & \mid \texttt{def}\ D\ \texttt{in}\ E \\ & \mid \texttt{let}\ x_i \,^{i\in 1..p} \triangleright E\ \texttt{in}\ E \end{array}$$

Clauses and definitions are as before.

Again, expressions are only a convenient syntactic sugar, which can be removed. This new translation amounts to introducing explicit bindings of the kind of the previous section for all subexpressions, nested calls being translated top-down, left-to-right.

$$\begin{array}{rcl} \texttt{reply}\ E_i \,^{i\in 1..p}\ \texttt{to}\ f & \stackrel{def}{=} & \kappa_f\langle E_i \,^{i\in 1..p}\rangle \text{ (in guarded processes } P) \\ u\langle E_i \,^{i\in 1..p}\rangle & \stackrel{def}{=} & (\texttt{let}\ x_i = E_i\ \texttt{in})\,^{i\in 1..p} u\langle x_i \,^{i\in 1..p}\rangle \\ \texttt{let}\ x = u\ \texttt{in}\ P & \stackrel{def}{=} & P\{x/u\} \\ \texttt{let}\ x_i \,^{i\in 1..p} = f\langle E_j \,^{j\in 1..q}\rangle\ \texttt{in}\ P & \stackrel{def}{=} & \texttt{def}\ \kappa\langle x_i \,^{i\in 1..p}\rangle = P\ \texttt{in}\ f\langle E_j \,^{j\in 1..q}, \kappa\rangle \end{array}$$

In practice, we introduce new typing judgments for expressions ($A \vdash E : \tau_i\ ^{i \in 1..p}$), along with new typing rules. The typing rules for expressions are derived from the previous ones and are omitted.

5.5 A comparison with functional types

If we remove join-composition in patterns and parallel-composition in processes from our language, we get a polyadic functional kernel similar to core-ML : both the reductions and the typing rules do correspond. Let us consider in detail how we would translate the `let` binder of ML. According to the `let`-bound expression, there are two cases with distinct typing properties. When the syntax suffices to identify functions either directly or as aliases, we use a generalizing definition :

$$\begin{array}{rcl} [\![\mathtt{let}\ f(x) = e_1\ \mathtt{in}\ e_2]\!] & = & \mathtt{def}\ f\langle x\rangle \triangleright \mathtt{reply}\ e_1\ \mathtt{to}\ f\ \mathtt{in}\ e_2 \\ [\![\mathtt{let}\ g = \mathtt{let}\ f(x) = e_1\ \mathtt{in}\ f\ \mathtt{in}\ e_2]\!] & = & \mathtt{def}\ f\langle x\rangle \triangleright \mathtt{reply}\ x\ \mathtt{to}\ f\ \mathtt{in}\ e_2[f/g] \end{array}$$

For other values (e.g. function calls), we use a continuation message to convey the result, which forces this result to be monomorphic. This restricts polymorphism to syntactic values and is thus equivalent to Wright's proposal for ML [13] :

$$[\![\mathtt{let}\ x = f(u)\ \mathtt{in}\ e_2]\!] \quad = \quad \mathtt{def}\ \kappa\langle x\rangle \triangleright e_2\ \mathtt{in}\ f\langle u, \kappa\rangle$$

Typing side-effects

The language as a whole is more expressive than ML ; it provides support for general, concurrent programming, including imperative constructs and side-effects as messages. For instance, reference cells need not be taken as primitives ; they are programmable in the join-calculus using the following definition :

```
def ref⟨x⟩ ▷
  def get ⟨⟩ | state⟨x⟩ ▷ state⟨x⟩ | reply x to get
  and set⟨y⟩ | state⟨x⟩ ▷ state⟨y⟩ | reply to set
  in  state⟨x⟩ | reply get,set to ref in ...
```

Here, the `state` is kept local and, more importantly, both methods `get` and `set` are returned in the same message. Since only one name `ref` has been defined, its type $\langle\alpha \rightarrow \langle\langle\rangle \rightarrow \langle\alpha\rangle, \langle\alpha\rangle \rightarrow \langle\rangle\rangle\rangle$, can obviously be generalized. And `ref` can be used polymorphically :

```
let g1,s1 = ref⟨'hello'⟩ in
let g2,s2 = ref⟨3⟩ in ...
```

More generally, join-calculus definitions may describe protocols that involve sophisticated synchronization of numerous methods and/or partial states, but this is largely independent of the typing, as long as side-effects are tracked using the sharing of type variables.

This is in contrast with the classical approach in ML, where references are introduced in a "pure" language as dangerous black boxes that cannot be given polymorphic types, and that communicate with a global store by magic. In [14], references are introduced as local stores that can be extruded. This is slightly closer to the join-calculus, but again references are a new special construct. If required, the store can still be identified as some part of the chemical machine, that consists of the instances of cell definitions on the left-hand-side, and of their state messages on the right-hand-side. The approach taken in the join-calculus is uniform and, by the way, it allows to type at least as much as ML with references.

6 Related works for concurrent languages

In the area of name-passing process calculi, the first step was taken by Milner in 1991 [6]. Milner introduced an improvement of the π-calculus, called *polyadic π-calculus*, where channels are allowed to carry tuples of messages. Polyadicity naturally supports a concept of "sorting", which is in our view a humble word for typing. In the context of polyadic π-calculus, maintaining the type discipline enforces channels to always carry tuples of the same length and nature.

The first extension of Milner's system has been undertaken by Pierce and Sangiorgi. They distinguish between input-only, output-only, and input-output channels. This extension naturally leads to recursive types with subtyping [7]. Since then more and more elaborate extensions have then been proposed and experimented, mostly around the `Pict` language, a strongly-typed implementation of the π-calculus with support for functions and objects [8, 11]. Recently, a further extension captures linearity information in channel types [4]. This provides a finer account on communication patterns, and static type inference leads to a more efficient compilation.

The type systems of all these authors are usually more sophisticated than ours. Some of this sophistication is due to the complexity of the π-calculus semantics and is thus irrelevant in our case. Nevertheless, sophisticated static analysis such as deadlock or linearity analysis would be useful in an optimizing join-calculus compiler. We chose not to integrate such high-level analyses in the basic type system.

The basic theory of polymorphic extensions of Milner's sort discipline for π-calculus has been developed by Turner in his PhD thesis [11]. We recall that Turner's polymorphism is *explicit*: inputs and outputs are always annotated with sorts. For example, the π-calculus process $\overline{x}[y,z] \mid x[u,w].\,\overline{u}[w]$ is tagged as follows:

$$\overline{x}[\mathtt{int}; y, z] \mid x[\alpha; u :\uparrow \alpha, w : \alpha].\,\overline{u}[\alpha; w] \ .$$

Consequently, explicit abstraction and application of types are interleaved with communication: in the above example the sort α in the output $\overline{u}[\alpha; w]$ depends on the message received on the channel x. This commitment to explicit polymorphism in π-calculus follows from the absence of a place where sort generalization may occur.

Typing à la ML for concurrent languages is not new. Proposals have been defined for languages which combine functional and concurrent primitives (among the others, Concurrent ML [9] and Facile [10]). An analogous approach has recently been taken by Vasconcelos for an extension of π-calculus with agent names [12]. In these languages channels are always monomorphic, and polymorphism is only allowed under functional abstractions. This enables to parameterize processes by arguments of different types. However, two processes can never communicate values of different types on the same channel, which restricts the expressiveness of the language. In particular, it is impossible to implement polymorphic services. As a simplified example, consider a computing server:

```
def run⟨f,x,r⟩ ▷ f⟨x,r⟩ in ...
```

This defines a channel run of type $\langle\langle\alpha,\langle\beta\rangle\rangle,\alpha,\langle\beta\rangle\rangle$ to which expensive requests can be sent together with a channel to receive the result (in the distributed join calculus, the location of the server would also be passed to f so that f can choose to migrate to the server before intensive computing.)

There is apparently no way to define such a service in CML, Facile, or the language proposed in [12]. In fact, this limitation has been known in CML. The solution would be to use first-order, explicit existential types such as in [5]. Then, the channel run could be given the monomorphic type $\exists\alpha,\beta.\langle\langle\alpha,\langle\beta\rangle\rangle,\alpha,\langle\beta\rangle\rangle$. Unsurprisingly, the translation of the example in PICT would give run a similar type.

7 Conclusion

We have typed the join-calculus using traditional parametric polymorphism. Thereby, we demonstrate that successful concepts and techniques now familiar in functional programming carries over to concurrent programming.

This experience strengthens our confidence both in the join-calculus and in parametric polymorphism. The join-calculus is a practical concurrent programming language because it support a simple, convenient and well established typing paradigm. ML polymorphism is not bound to ML; it can sustain significant changes in the language semantics, provided lexical scoping is maintained and generalization points are clearly identified.

References

[1] L. Damas and R. Milner. Principal type schemes for functional programs. In *Proceedings on Principles of Programmining Languages*, pages 207 – 212, 1982.

[2] C. Fournet and G. Gonthier. The reflexive chemical abstract machine and the join-calculus. In *23rd ACM Symposium on Principles of Programming Languages (POPL'96)*, 1996.

[3] C. Fournet, G. Gonthier, J.-J. Lévy, L. Maranget, and D. Rémy. A calculus of mobile agents. In *7th International Conference on Concurrency Theory (CONCUR'96)*, 1996. LNCS 1119.

[4] N. Kobayashi, B. C. Pierce, and D. N. Turner. Linear types and pi-calculus. In *23rd ACM Symposium on Principles of Programming Languages (POPL'96)*, 1996.

[5] K. Läufer and M. Odersky. An extension of ML with first-class abstract types. In *Proceedings of the ACM SIGPLAN Workshop on ML and its Applications*, 1992.

[6] R. Milner. The polyadic π-calculus: a tutorial. In Bauer, Brawer, and Schwichtenberg, editors, *Logic and Algebra of Specification*. Springer Verlag, 1993.

[7] B. Pierce and D. Sangiorgi. Typing and subtyping for mobile processes. In *Logic in Computer Science*, pages 187 – 215, 1993.

[8] B. Pierce and D. Turner. Pict: a programming language based on the pi-calculus, 1995. To appear.

[9] J. H. Reppy. Concurrent ML: Design, application and semantics. In *Programming, Concurrency, Simulation and Automated Reasoning*, pages 165 – 198, 1992. LNCS 693.

[10] B. Thomsen. Polymorphic sorts and types for concurrent functional programs. Technical Report ECRC-93-10, European Computer-Industry Research Center, Munich, Germany, 1993.

[11] D. N. Turner. *The π-calculus: Types, polymorphism and implementation.* PhD thesis, LFCS, University of Edinburgh, 1995.

[12] V. T. Vasconcelos. Predicative polymorphism in the π-calculus. In *Proceedings of 5th Conference on Parallel Architectures and Languages (PARLE 94)*, 1994. LNCS.

[13] A. K. Wright. Polymorphism for imperative languages without imperative types. Technical Report 93-200, Rice University, February 1993.

[14] A. K. Wright and M. Felleisen. A syntactic approach to type soundness. *Information and Computation*, 115(1):38–94, 1994.

Proving Safety Properties of Infinite State Systems by Compilation into Presburger Arithmetic

Laurent Fribourg *

Hans Olsén

LSV, E.N.S. Cachan & CNRS
61 av. Wilson, 94235 Cachan-France
fribourg@lsv.ens-cachan.fr

IDA, Linköping University
S-58183 Linköping-Sweden
hanol@ida.liu.se

Abstract. We present in this paper a method combining path decomposition and bottom-up computation features for characterizing the reachability sets of Petri nets within Presburger arithmetic. An application of our method is the automatic verification of safety properties of Petri nets with infinite reachability sets. Our implementation is made of a decomposition module and an arithmetic module, the latter being built upon Boudet-Comon's algorithm for solving the decision problem for Presburger arithmetic. Our approach will be illustrated on three nontrivial examples of Petri nets with unbounded places and parametric initial markings.

1 Introduction

We are interested in this paper in proving safety properties of infinite state systems. We will focus on Petri nets although our approach is applicable to other discrete models of concurrent systems such as automata with counters (see, e.g., [10]). There will be two sources of infinity for the state space of Petri nets that we will consider: the first one is the unboundedness of some places of the net; the second one comes from the fact that the initial marking of the net may contain parameters, thus representing an infinite family of markings. The safety properties that we will consider, will be merely of the form $\overline{x} \in lfp \Rightarrow I(\overline{x})$, where $\overline{x}$ represents a marking, lfp represents the set of reachable markings of the Petri net, and $I(\overline{x})$ a simple arithmetic relation characteristic of the safety property to be proved. Our method consists in characterizing the reachability relation $\overline{x} \in lfp$ as a formula $\xi(\overline{x})$ belonging to Presburger arithmetic (i.e., arithmetic without $\times$), then to prove $\xi(\overline{x}) \Rightarrow I(\overline{x})$ using a decision procedure for Presburger arithmetic [16]. The objective of our work is similar to the one of Hiraishi [11]. However Hiraishi constructs the arithmetic characterization of the set of reachable markings in a bottom-up manner by refining Karp-Miller's method for constructing coverability trees [14]. In contrast, our arithmetic characterization $\xi(\overline{x})$ is constructed using basically a structural method of path decomposition

* Part of this work was done while the author was visiting IASI-CNR (Roma), supported by HCM-Network CHRX.CT.930414 and IASI-CNR.

[18, 8]. Nevertheless, as explained hereafter in the paper, we will also integrate into the procedure some forward (bottom-up) computation routines that will speed up the arithmetic construction by propagating the initial marking values and testing the invariance of the intermediate constructed formulas.

2 Preliminaries

It is convenient to see the reachability problem for Petri nets as a least fixed-point problem for a certain class of logic programs with constraints over the integers domain $\mathcal{Z}$ [12]. These programs are of the form:

$$\begin{array}{lll} & p(\overline{x}) & \leftarrow B(\overline{x}). \\ r_1: & p(\overline{x}+\overline{t}_{r_1}) & \leftarrow \overline{x} > \overline{a}_{r_1},\ p(\overline{x}). \\ & \vdots & \\ r_m: & p(\overline{x}+\overline{t}_{r_m}) & \leftarrow \overline{x} > \overline{a}_{r_m},\ p(\overline{x}). \end{array}$$

where $\overline{x}$ is a vector of variables ranging over $\mathcal{Z}^n$, for some n, $B(\overline{x})$ a linear integer relation (relation defined by a Presburger formula), $\overline{t}_{r_i} \in \mathcal{Z}^n$ is a vector of constants, and $\overline{a}_{r_i}$ is a vector of constants belonging to $(\mathcal{Z}\cup\{-\infty\})^n$. As usual, $z > -\infty$, $z \neq -\infty$ and $-\infty \pm z = z \pm (-\infty) = -\infty$ for any integer $z \in \mathcal{Z}$, and $-\infty \geq -\infty$. For any vectors $\overline{x}_1$ and $\overline{x}_2$, we define $\overline{x}_1 > \overline{x}_2$ (resp. $\overline{x}_1 \geq \overline{x}_2$) to hold, if and only if the inequalities hold componentwise. The expression $max(\overline{x}_1, \overline{x}_2)$ denotes the vector obtained by taking the maximum of $\overline{x}_1$ and $\overline{x}_2$ componentwise. Since $z > -\infty$ holds for any $z \in \mathcal{Z}$, any constraint of the form $x > -\infty$, is simply considered as *true*.

One can see these programs as classical programs with counters expressed under a logic programming form. These programs have thus the power of expressivity of Turing machines. Henceforth we will refer to this class of programs as *programs with $\mathcal{Z}$-counters*. In the next section, we will see how these programs naturally encode the *reachability problem* for Petri nets (with inhibitors).

We now introduce a convenient description of the forward (or bottom-up) execution of programs with $\mathcal{Z}$-counters. A clause r of the form: $p(\overline{x}+\overline{t}_r) \leftarrow \overline{x} > \overline{a}_r, p(\overline{x})$ will be characterized by a couple $\langle \overline{t}_r, \overline{a}_r \rangle$. We say that $\overline{x}'$ is reachable from $\overline{x}$ via a clause $r : \langle \overline{t}_r, \overline{a}_r \rangle$, and denote $\overline{x} \xrightarrow{r} \overline{x}'$, if: $\overline{x}' = \overline{x} + \overline{t}_r \ \wedge \ \overline{x} > \overline{a}_r$. More generally, let $\Sigma = \{r_1, \ldots, r_m\}$. A sequence $w \in \Sigma^*$ is called a *path*. A path w is characterized by a couple $\langle \overline{t}_w, \overline{a}_w \rangle$ where $\overline{t}_w$ and $\overline{a}_w$ are recursively defined by respectively:

$$\begin{aligned} \overline{t}_\epsilon &= \overline{0} \\ \overline{t}_{rw} &= \overline{t}_r + \overline{t}_w \end{aligned}$$

$$\begin{aligned} \overline{a}_\epsilon &= -\overline{\infty} \\ \overline{a}_{rw} &= max(\overline{a}_r, \overline{a}_w - \overline{t}_r) \end{aligned}$$

We say that $\overline{x}'$ is reachable from $\overline{x}$ via a path $w : \langle \overline{t}_w, \overline{a}_w \rangle$, and denote $\overline{x} \xrightarrow{w} \overline{x}'$, if: $\overline{x}' = \overline{x} + \overline{t}_w \ \wedge \ \overline{x} > \overline{a}_w$. Given two paths w_1 and w_2, it follows from the above definition that: $\overline{x} \xrightarrow{w_1 w_2} \overline{x}'$ iff $\exists \overline{x}'' : \ \overline{x} \xrightarrow{w_1} \overline{x}'' \wedge \overline{x}'' \xrightarrow{w_2} \overline{x}'$. Given a language $L \subseteq \Sigma^*$, we say that $\bar{x}'$ is reachable from $\bar{x}$ via L, and denote $\bar{x} \xrightarrow{L} \bar{x}'$, if $\exists w \in L : \bar{x} \xrightarrow{w} \bar{x}'$. As usual, the reflexive-transitive closure of relation $\xrightarrow{L}$ is denoted $\xrightarrow{L^*}$. We also write $\bar{x} \xrightarrow{L_1} \bar{x}'' \xrightarrow{L_2} \bar{x}'$, instead of $\bar{x} \xrightarrow{L_1} \bar{x}'' \wedge \bar{x}'' \xrightarrow{L_2} \bar{x}'$. From the definitions above, we immediately get:

Proposition 1. *For any path $w \in \Sigma^*$ and any languages $L_1, L_2 \subseteq \Sigma^*$. We have:*

1. $\bar{x} \xrightarrow{L_1 L_2} \bar{x}' \Leftrightarrow \exists\, \bar{x}'' : \bar{x} \xrightarrow{L_1} \bar{x}'' \xrightarrow{L_2} \bar{x}'$
2. $\bar{x} \xrightarrow{w^*} \bar{x}' \Leftrightarrow \exists\, k \geq 0 : \bar{x}' = \bar{x} + k \cdot \bar{t}_w \wedge \forall\, 0 \leq k' < k : \bar{x} + k' \cdot \bar{t}_w > \bar{a}_w$

Note, in the last equivalence, that if $k = 0$, then $\bar{x} = \bar{x}'$ and $\forall\, 0 \leq k' < k$: $\bar{x} + k' \cdot \bar{t}_w > \bar{a}_w$ is vacuously true. It is easy to see that, for $k > 0$, the universally quantified subexpression is equivalent to $\bar{x} + (k-1) \cdot \bar{t}_w^- > \bar{a}_w$ where $\bar{t}_w^-$ is the vector obtained from $\bar{t}_w$ by letting all nonnegative components be set to zero. Therefore, the whole equivalence becomes:

2'. $\bar{x} \xrightarrow{w^*} \bar{x}' \Leftrightarrow \bar{x}' = \bar{x} \vee \exists\, k > 0 : \bar{x}' = \bar{x} + k \cdot \bar{t}_w \wedge \bar{x} + (k-1) \cdot \bar{t}_w^- > \bar{a}_w$

As a consequence, given a path w, the relation $\bar{x} \xrightarrow{w^*} \bar{x}'$ is actually an *existentially* quantified formula of Presburger arithmetic having $\bar{x}$ and $\bar{x}'$ as free variables. More generally, define a *flat* language as a language of the form $w_1^* \ldots. w_c^*$ where each w_i $(1 \leq i \leq c)$ is a path [2]. By proposition 1 it follows that the relation $\bar{x} \xrightarrow{L} \bar{x}'$ for a flat language L, can be expressed as an existentially quantified formula of Presburger arithmetic, having $\bar{x}$ and $\bar{x}'$ as free variables. More precisely, the reachability relation $\bar{x} \xrightarrow{L} \bar{x}'$ is expressed as a disjunction of a number of matrix expressions of the form: $\exists\, \bar{k}_i : \bar{x}' = \bar{x} + C_i \bar{k}_i \wedge \bar{x} + D_i \bar{k}_i > \bar{e}_i$ where C_i and D_i are matrices, and $\bar{e}_i$ some vector of constants. Such a formula can be simplified as a quantifier-free formula, say $\zeta_L(\bar{x}, \bar{x}')$, by elimination of the existentially quantified variables $\bar{k}_i$ through a Presburger decision procedure (see [16]).
Given a program with $B(\bar{x})$ as a base case and recursive clauses Σ, the least fixed-point of its immediate consequence operator (see [12][13]), which is also the least $\mathcal{Z}$-model, may be expressed as: $lfp = \{\, \bar{x}' \mid \exists \bar{x} : B(\bar{x}) \wedge \bar{x} \xrightarrow{\Sigma^*} \bar{x}' \,\}$. Our aim is to characterize the membership relation $\bar{y} \in lfp$ as a quantifier-free formula having $\bar{y}$ as free variables. In order to achieve this, our approach here is to find a flat language $L \subseteq \Sigma^*$, such that the following equivalence holds: $\bar{x} \xrightarrow{\Sigma^*} \bar{x}' \Leftrightarrow \bar{x} \xrightarrow{L} \bar{x}'$. An arithmetic characterization of $\bar{y} \in lfp$ is then: $\exists \bar{x}\, B(\bar{x}) \wedge \zeta_L(\bar{x}, \bar{y})$. Such a formula can be in turn simplified as, say $\xi_{B,L}(\bar{y})$, by elimination of $\bar{x}$ again through a Presburger decision procedure.
Given a formula $\xi(\bar{x})$ and a path w, we call *w-closure* of $\xi(\bar{x})$, a quantifier-free formula $\xi'(\bar{x})$ obtained from $\exists \bar{z} : \xi(\bar{z}) \wedge \bar{z} \xrightarrow{w^*} \bar{x}$ by elimination of all the existential variables (*viz.*, $\bar{z}$ and variable k implicit in $\bar{z} \xrightarrow{w^*} \bar{x}$). We say that *a path w lets invariant* a formula ξ if $\xi(\bar{x}) \wedge \bar{x} \xrightarrow{w} \bar{x}'$ implies $\xi(\bar{x}')$, for all $\bar{x}, \bar{x}'$. We say that *a set Σ lets invariant* ξ, and write 'invariant(ξ,Σ)', if every element

[2] A close (but slightly different) notion has been introduced by Ginsburg [9] under the name of 'bounded language'.

of Σ lets invariant ξ. In the following, given a formula ξ and a language L, we will often abbreviate an expression of the form $\xi(\overline{x}) \wedge \overline{x} \xrightarrow{L} \overline{x}'$ as $\xi(\overline{x}) \xrightarrow{L} \overline{x}'$. The w-closure of a formula ξ will be accordingly denoted as $\xi \xrightarrow{w^*}$. Note that ξ always implies $\xi \xrightarrow{w^*}$, and that the converse holds iff w lets invariant ξ.

3 Encoding of the reachability problem of Petri Nets

Consider a Petri net with n places and m transitions. In this section, we sketch out how to encode the reachability problem for Petri nets, via an n-ary predicate p defined by a program with $\mathcal{Z}$-counters. Each place j $(1 \leq j \leq n)$ of the Petri net will be encoded as an arithmetic variable x_j. A marking is encoded as a tuple $\langle b_1, ..., b_n \rangle$ of n nonnegative integers. (The value b_j represents the number of tokens contained in place j.) Each transition i $(1 \leq i \leq m)$ will be encoded as a recursive clause r_i. An atom of the form $p(b_1, ..., b_n)$ means that a marking $\langle b_1, ..., b_n \rangle$ is reachable from the initial marking. The predicate p is defined as follows:

- The base clause r_0 is of the form:
  $p(x_1, ..., x_n) \leftarrow x_1 = b_1^0, ..., x_n = b_n^0.$
  where $\langle b_1^0, ..., b_n^0 \rangle$ denotes the initial marking.
- The clause r_i $(1 \leq i \leq m)$, coding for the i-th transition, is of the form:
  $p(x_1 + t_{i,1}, ..., x_n + t_{i,n}) \leftarrow \phi_i(x_1, ..., x_n), p(x_1, ..., x_n).$
  Here $t_{i,j}$ is the sum of the weights of the output arrows from transition i to place j, minus the sum of the weights of the input arrows from place j to transition i. The expression $\phi_i(x_1, ..., x_n)$ is of the form: $x_{j_1} > a_{j_1} - 1 \wedge ... \wedge x_{j_{c_i}} > a_{j_{c_i}} - 1 \wedge x_{k_1} = 0 \wedge \ldots \wedge x_{k_{d_i}} = 0$, where $j_1, ..., j_{c_i}$ are the input places of transition i, a_{j_α} is the weight of the arc going from place j_α to transition i $(1 \leq \alpha \leq c_i)$, and $k_1, ..., k_{d_i}$ are the inhibitors places of transition i. (The condition ϕ_i expresses that the i-th transition is enabled.)

A priori such a program does not belong to the class we consider due to the constraints of the form $x_{k_\alpha} = 0$ $(1 \leq \alpha \leq d_i)$. However by adding extra arguments, say x'_{k_α} $(1 \leq \alpha \leq d_i)$, which are initialized with 1 minus the initial value of x_{k_α}, and are incremented (resp. decremented) when x_{k_α} is decremented (resp. incremented), one can replace the constraint $x_{k_\alpha} = 0$ with $x'_{k_\alpha} > 0$. [3]
The least fixed-point *lfp* associated with the program corresponds to the *reachability set* associated with the Petri net, i.e. the set of all the markings reachable from the initial marking.
Sometimes it is interesting to reason generically with some *parametric initial markings*, i.e., initial markings where certain places are assigned parameters instead of constant values. This defines a family of Petri nets, which are obtained by replacing successively the parameters with all the possible nonnegative values. One can easily encode the reachability relation for a Petri net with a parametric initial marking via a program with $\mathcal{Z}$-counter by adding the initial marking

[3] By construction, x'_{k_α} is always equal to $1 - x_{k_\alpha}$, and may thus take negative values.

parameters as extra arguments of the encoding predicate. In the case of a Petri net with an initial marking containing a tuple of parameters, say $\overline{q}$, our aim is to characterize the relation $\overline{y} \in lfp$ as an arithmetical formula $\xi(\overline{q}, \overline{y})$ having $\overline{q}$ and $\overline{y}$ as free variables. This will allow us to determine all the values of the parameters $\overline{q}$ for which a given safety property holds (see sections 7.1, 7.2).

Example 1. Consider the Petri net in figure 1. (This example is the "swimming-pool" net from M. Latteux, see [3, 6].) With the initial marking $x_1 = x_2 = x_3 =$

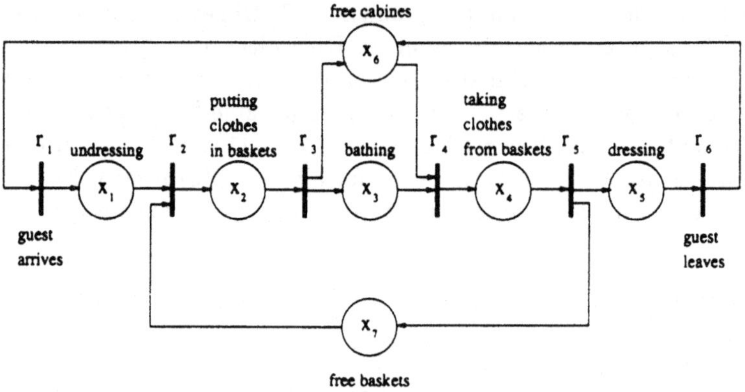

Figure 1

$x_4 = x_5 = 0$, $x_6 = q_1$ and $x_7 = q_2$ for some nonnegative parameters q_1 and q_2, the task is to show that there exists a deadlock regardless of what q_1 and q_2 are. The program encoding the reachability problem for this net is the following:

$$r_0: \; p(q_1, q_2, x_1, x_2, x_3, x_4, x_5, x_6, x_7) \leftarrow x_1 = 0, x_2 = 0, x_3 = 0, x_4 = 0, x_5 = 0, x_6 = q_1, x_7 = q_2.$$

$$r_1: \; p(q_1, q_2, x_1 + 1, x_2, x_3, x_4, x_5, x_6 - 1, x_7) \leftarrow x_6 > 0, p(q_1, q_2, x_1, x_2, x_3, x_4, x_5, x_6, x_7).$$

$$r_2: \; p(q_1, q_2, x_1 - 1, x_2 + 1, x_3, x_4, x_5, x_6, x_7 - 1) \leftarrow x_1 > 0, x_7 > 0, p(q_1, q_2, x_1, x_2, x_3, x_4, x_5, x_6, x_7).$$

$$r_3: \; p(q_1, q_2, x_1, x_2 - 1, x_3 + 1, x_4, x_5, x_6 + 1, x_7) \leftarrow x_2 > 0, p(q_1, q_2, x_1, x_2, x_3, x_4, x_5, x_6, x_7).$$

$$r_4: \; p(q_1, q_2, x_1, x_2, x_3 - 1, x_4 + 1, x_5, x_6 - 1, x_7) \leftarrow x_3 > 0, x_6 > 0, p(q_1, q_2, x_1, x_2, x_3, x_4, x_5, x_6, x_7).$$

$$r_5: \; p(q_1, q_2, x_1, x_2, x_3, x_4 - 1, x_5 + 1, x_6, x_7 + 1) \leftarrow x_4 > 0, p(q_1, q_2, x_1, x_2, x_3, x_4, x_5, x_6, x_7).$$

$$r_6: \; p(q_1, q_2, x_1, x_2, x_3, x_4, x_5 - 1, x_6 + 1, x_7) \leftarrow x_5 > 0, p(q_1, q_2, x_1, x_2, x_3, x_4, x_5, x_6, x_7).$$

4 Construction of Reachability Sets

Let us consider a program defined by a set of transitions $\Sigma_{original} : \{r_1, ..., r_m\}$. In order to characterize the relation $\overline{x} \xrightarrow{\{r_1, \cdots, r_m\}^*} \overline{x}'$, we will construct a sequence

$\{L_i\}_i$ of subsets of $\{r_1, ..., r_m\}^*$ which are "reachably-equivalent" to $\{r_1, ..., r_m\}^*$ in the sense that, for any $\overline{x}$ and $\overline{x}'$: $\overline{x} \xrightarrow{\{r_1,...,r_m\}^*} \overline{x}' \Leftrightarrow \overline{x} \xrightarrow{L} \overline{x}'$, and such that the last language in the sequence is flat. Such a flat language $L \subseteq \{r_1, ..., r_m\}^*$ will be generated by applying repeatedly a set of *decomposition* rules. Schematically, each decomposition rule, when applied to a set Σ, transforms it into a list Δ of sets of the form $[\Sigma_1, \Sigma_2, \ldots, \Sigma_c]$ such that Σ^* is reachably-equivalent to the language $\Sigma_1^* \Sigma_2^* \ldots \Sigma_c^*$. Every element of Σ_i $(1 \leq i \leq c)$ is either an element r of Σ, or is a path w obtained by composition of several elements of Σ. The process of decomposition is iterated on the list Δ: one set Σ_j of Δ is selected, and the list resulting from its decomposition is inserted in place of it within Δ, thus generating a new sequence Δ'. The process is iterated until either:

- all the sets $\Sigma_1, ..., \Sigma_c$ of the current list Δ are singletons of the form $\{w_1\}, \{w_2\}, \cdots, \{w_c\}$. This means that the language $\Sigma_1^* \Sigma_2^* ... \Sigma_c^*$ associated with Δ is flat (*termination with success*), or
- no decomposition rule applies onto the selected set Σ_j of list Δ (*termination with failure*).

Note that the process cannot loop forever because each decomposition rule transforms a set Σ into a sequence of sets of "lower dimension" [8]. The number of rules of decomposition is 5. They are: stratification, monotonic transition, monotonic guard, cyclic post-fusion and cyclic pre-fusion (see [8] for details). They are tried in this order, and the first that succeeds is applied. When a flat language $L : w_1^* \ldots w_c^*$ has been generated, a decision procedure for Presburger arithmetic is invoked in order to construct the formula $\xi_{B,L}$ (see section 2). Starting from the base case relation B, the arithmetic decision procedure computes $\xi_{B,L}$ by extending B with the successive w_i-closures $(1 \leq i \leq c)$. Formally, $\xi_{B,L}(\overline{x}')$ is defined to be $\xi_c(\overline{x}')$ where $\xi_0(\overline{x}')$ is $B(\overline{x}')$, and $\xi_{i+1}(\overline{x}')$ is a quantifier-free formula obtained from $\exists \overline{x} : \xi_i(\overline{x}) \wedge \overline{x} \xrightarrow{w_{i+1}^*} \overline{x}'$ by elimination of the existential variables $\overline{x}$ and k_{i+1} (implicit in $\overline{x} \xrightarrow{w_{i+1}^*} \overline{x}'$). Actually a more efficient system is implemented by invoking earlier the arithmetic decision procedure, and starting to construct $\xi_{B,L}$ during the decomposition process, without waiting for the flat language L to be fully generated. This is explained in the next section. Sometimes, it is interesting to keep track of the number of times k_i each w_i is repeated inside sequences of the form $w_1^* \ldots w_c^*$. In such cases one may construct a formula $\xi_c(\overline{x}', k_1, ..., k_c)$ where $\xi_0(\overline{x}')$ is $B(\overline{x}')$, and $\xi_{i+1}(\overline{x}', \overline{k}_i, k_{i+1})$ is a quantifier-free formula equivalent to $\exists \overline{x} : \xi_i(\overline{x}, \overline{k}_i) \wedge \overline{x} \xrightarrow{w_{i+1}^{k_{i+1}}} \overline{x}'$. This is useful when one wishes to exhibit some "counter-example" path $w_1^{k_1} \cdots w_c^{k_c}$ which ends at a marking that violates the safety property under study (see 7.1).

5 General Description of the System

Our system consists of a decomposition procedure and a decision procedure for Presburger arithmetic. We will represent the sequence Δ of decomposed languages as a list. Initially, Δ contains a single element: $\Sigma_{original}$. At each step, the *leftmost element* (head) of Δ is selected for further decomposition. The system builds up a formula ξ, which will eventually characterize the least fixed-point. This formula is initialized with the base case relation B, and is extended by Σ-closure whenever the head Σ of Δ is a singleton. Before attempting any decomposition onto Σ, one checks whether it lets invariant ξ (because there is no point in decomposing a set of transitions that will not yield anything new). The top loop of our procedure is thus as follows:

```
ξ := B;  Δ := [Σ_original];
while not empty(Δ) do
    Σ := head(Δ);  Δ := tail(Δ);
    if not invariant(ξ, Σ) then
        if singleton(Σ) then  ξ := ξ −Σ*→
        else  Δ := decompose(Σ) ⊗ Δ
        fi
    fi
od
```

where Δ is a list of sets of transitions, ξ is a Presburger formula, and $\otimes$ is append. The arithmetic form $\xi_{B,L}$ of the least fixed-point is given by the exit value of ξ when executing the program. Henceforth, we will denote this exit formula by ξ_{final}. The associated flat language L is the composed sequence $\Sigma_1^* ... \Sigma_c^*$ where the Σ_is are the successive singletons used during the program execution for extending ξ by closure (step: $\xi := \xi \xrightarrow{\Sigma^*}$). The language L "covers" all the reachable markings of the net in the sense that: $B(\overline{x}) \wedge \overline{x} \xrightarrow{L} \overline{x}' \Leftrightarrow B(\overline{x}) \wedge \overline{x} \xrightarrow{\Sigma^*_{original}} \overline{x}'$. The invariance check before attempting decomposition is important since it allows to discard a lot of sets Σ of transitions, and shortens considerably the length of the computed flat language.

5.1 Invariance check

As mentioned, before attempting to decompose a set of transitions, we first check whether all the transitions in the head language Σ let the current arithmetic formula ξ computed so far, invariant. If this is the case, the set is simply dropped and attention is moved to the next set. That is, before decomposing Σ, we check whether $\xi(\overline{x}) \xrightarrow{\Sigma} \overline{x}' \Rightarrow \xi(\overline{x}')$ holds (see section 2). This is *a priori* a computationally expensive (space-exponential) test. However, by storing in a set $\Im$ those transitions that have been discovered to keep ξ invariant, a lot of redundant computations are avoided. Consider for example a list Δ made of the set $\{w_1, w_2, w_3\}$. Before trying to decompose $\{w_1, w_2, w_3\}$ we test the invariance of ξ for each of the transitions w_1, w_2, w_3. Assume that at least one of the three fails to let $\xi(\overline{x})$ invariant and that the decomposition rule of "monotonic transition" (see [8]) applies to w_2, say. At the next step we have to consider the list $\Delta' : [\{w_1, w_3\}, \{w_2\}, \{w_1, w_3\}]$, and have to test ξ for invariance through the head language $\{w_1, w_3\}$. But invariance of ξ through w_1 and w_3 has already been tested, so the invariance check consists at this point in a simple table look up.

When computing a w-closure of ξ, the information in $\Im$ is *a priori* lost, and the new formula ξ' has a new set $\Im'$ of invariant transitions, which should be constructed. Here again, a lot of costly invariance tests can be saved by observing that a transition, say v, of $\Im$, which commutes with w is guaranteed to be still in $\Im'$. This is formally justified by the following (easily provable):

Proposition 2. *Suppose:*

1. $\xi(\overline{x}) \xrightarrow{v} \overline{x}' \;\Rightarrow\; \xi(\overline{x}')$	invariance of v
2. $\xi'(\overline{x}') \;\equiv\; \exists \overline{x} :\; \xi(\overline{x}) \xrightarrow{w^{*}} \overline{x}'$	w-closure
3. $\overline{x} \xrightarrow{wv} \overline{x}' \;\Rightarrow\; \overline{x} \xrightarrow{vw} \overline{x}'$	commutation

Then invariance of v is preserved by ξ', i.e.: $\quad \xi'(\overline{x}) \xrightarrow{v} \overline{x}' \;\Rightarrow\; \xi'(\overline{x}')$.

By inspecting the definition of $\overline{x} \xrightarrow{wv} \overline{x}'$, and $\overline{x} \xrightarrow{vw} \overline{x}'$, one can see that the commutation check 3 of proposition 2 reduces to verifying a number inequalities among constants, which is computationally cheap. Transitions of $\Im$ that fail the commutation check usually turn out to have lost their invariance.

5.2 Failure of decomposition

So far in this section, we have assumed that the procedure of decomposition always succeeds. This may not be the case. In case of failure (i.e., when no rule of decomposition applies to the current set Σ), our strategy consists to remove some transitions from Σ according to some heuristics (essentially, random choice) until some decomposition rule applies or Σ becomes a singleton. This removal endangers the completeness of the finally generated formula ξ_{final} in the sense that it may not correspond any longer to a fixed-point. In such a case (i.e., when a transition of the original language $\Sigma_{original}$ does not let invariant ξ_{final}) the system detects it, and the whole procedure of fixed-point computation restarts with ξ_{final} taken as a new base case formula (in place of B). This process is iterated until a fixed-point is actually reached. (There is no guarantee that such a fixed-point will be reached as the process may now loop forever.) An example of such a process with transition removal and restarting, is given in section 7.3.

5.3 Space Explosion

Our underlying decomposition strategy allows to alleviate the problem of space explosion that immediately occurs with naive methods based on exhaustive state exploration (in the case of finite state systems). This is because, among all the paths that go from a generic marking to another one, only a reduced number of "representative" paths is retained when applying the decomposition strategy (see [18]). This path selectivity is reinforced through interaction with the arithmetic module because quantities of (invariant) transitions are discarded. Naturally, even if our method allows us to treat automatically some examples that are usually done by hand (see section 7), we also have to face quickly with a space explosion problem. From a theoretical point of view, this may be explained by the worst-case complexity of our procedure, which is space-superexponential due to the exponential space-complexity of the operation of w-closure (quantifier elimination) and the fact that the size of the language (number of w-closures) grows itself exponentially during the process of decomposition. This space explosion phenomenon is particularly sensitive when one deals with Petri nets having more than one parameter in their initial markings. A solution for overcoming the problem is sometimes to reduce the original Petri net into a simpler net through transformation rules, as those of Berthelot [1], which preserve basic safety properties (e.g., deadlock-freeness, boundedness). An example of such a preliminary net transformation is given in section 7.1.

6 Arithmetic Module

The decision procedure for Presburger arithmetic that we have implemented is Boudet-Comon's algorithm [2]. It has turned out to be very well suited for our needs. Given a system of equations and inequations, the Boudet-Comon algorithm generates a finite state automaton recognising the language of all solutions written as strings of binary digits. This algorithm has nearly optimal worst case complexity and behaves according to our experience very well in practice. One of the advantages is its simplicity. Variable elimination, conjunction, disjunction, negation and inclusion are all achieved by standard automata theoretic methods such as projection, intersection, union, complement and emptiness testing. Another advantage of Boudet-Comon method is that, due to its simplicity and generality, it is easy to construct specialized programs for computing specific relations on its top, or to store information during its execution. We have exploited this feature for making easier the proof of general safety properties such as boundedness and detection of deadlock, as explained hereafter.
Detecting unboundedness is achieved by investigating wether the reachability set is finite or infinite which is done efficiently by investigating the loops in Boudet-Comon's automaton. A deadlock in a Petri net may defined by:

$$\text{deadlock}(\overline{q},\overline{x}) \;\equiv\; \xi_{final}(\overline{q},\overline{x}) \;\wedge\; \text{no\_transition\_enabled}(\overline{x})$$

where no_transition_enabled is specified as:

$$\text{no\_transition\_enabled}(\overline{x}) \;\equiv\; \forall r_i \in \Sigma_{original} : \;\neg\phi_i(\overline{x})$$

Explicitly defining no_transition_enabled($\overline{x}$) as above and then computing the automaton and intersecting with the fixed-point ξ_{final}, is not so efficient. We have therefore implemented a simple deadlock detector that directly computes ("on the fly") the automaton defining the relation deadlock($\overline{q},\overline{x}$) according to the definition above throughout the construction of ξ_{final}.
A drawback of Boudet-Comon's method is that, from the automaton, there is no known way to derive an explicit expression (like, e.g., a quantifier-free formula) of the characterized arithmetic relation. It is however possible to *enumerate* the set of solutions of the arithmetic relation. This set is usually infinite, but

sometimes one is just interested by knowing the existence and/or the form of one solution (e.g., a path leading to a deadlock marking). Besides, by projection on to an appropriate subset of variables, it is often possible to reduce the infinite space of solutions to a finite one, thus extracting some useful information (e.g., boundedness of some places). See, e.g., section 7.2.

7 Experimental Results

In this section we present some experimental data from three Petri nets having infinite reachability sets: the two first ones have parametrized initial markings while the third one has some unbounded places. We generate for each of them the reachability sets under the form of a Boudet-Comon automaton, and are then able to prove for them various properties. The implementation has been written in SICSTUS-Prolog by the second author. It is around 4000 lines long, and runs on SPARC-10. With each example, we give two tables. The columns of the first table are to be interpreted as: S for 'Stratification', MT for 'Monotonic Transition', MG for 'Monotonic Guard', PoF for 'Cyclic Post-Fusion', PrF for 'Cyclic Pre-Fusion' and ND for 'No Decomposition applies'. The number in each column is the number of times the corresponding decomposition rule was applied. The second table IT (Invariant Transition set) has two rows: The top row is the number of transitions in the set, and the bottom row is the number of times a set of this size was discarded. The explicit form of the flat computed language L will be also given. (Recall that the paths belonging to L "cover" all the reachable markings of the net.)

7.1 Swimming Pool

This example comes from M. Latteux (see, e.g.,[6]). Consider the Petri net in figure 1. With the initial marking $x_1 = x_2 = x_3 = x_4 = x_5 = 0$, $x_6 = q_1$ and $x_7 = q_2$ for some parameters q_1 and q_2, the task is to show that there exists a deadlock whatever the values of q_1 and q_2 are. (The proof is done by hand in [6].) Our implementation does not succeed in computing the fixpoint since the automaton representing the reachability set grows too large (SICSTUS aborts after having generated 2500 states when determinizing an automaton having 386 states with 252 transitions leaving each state). So we apply our method not on the original net, but on a reduced version obtained by applying manually Berthelot's postfusion rule (fusing r_2 and r_3, and *eliminating* x_2) [1]. The reduced net is represented at figure 2. For any values of q_1 and q_2, the reduced net is guaranteed to be deadlock-free iff the original one is.
Computing the parametric reachability set we have the following statistics:

S	MT	MG	PoF	PrF	tot	ND
3	0	2	4	1	10	0

IT:

no. transitions	1	2	3	tot
no. disposals	8	1	3	12

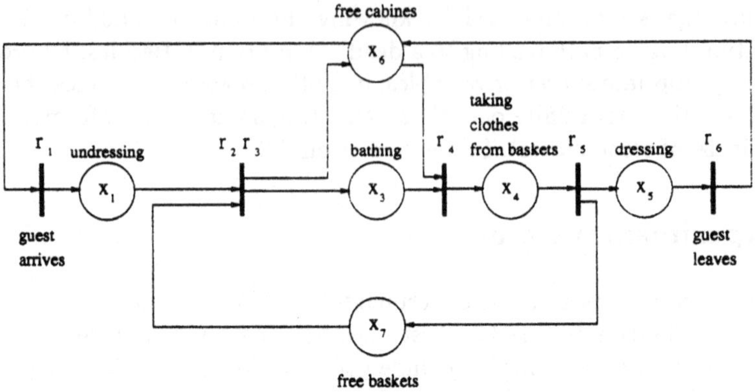

Figure 2

The flat language is computed in 10422 seconds (3.9 hours), and is:
$r_1^*(r_2r_3r_1)^*(r_2r_3)^*r_4^*r_5^*(r_2r_3)^*(r_4r_5r_2r_3)^*(r_4r_5)^*r_1^*r_4^*$
For the reduced swimming pool net of figure 2 the relation deadlock$(q_1, q_2, \overline{x})$ is computed in 12.27 seconds, and: $\forall q_1, q_2\ \exists \overline{x}:$ deadlock$(q_1, q_2, \overline{x})$ (that is, for any q_1 and q_2 there is a deadlock) is verified in 0.02 seconds. For every couple of values c_1 and c_2 for q_1 and q_2, the system can compute path vectors in order to characterize the paths leading to a deadlock. This yields paths of the form $r_1^{c_1}(r_2r_3r_1)^{c_2}$.

7.2 Manufacturing System

This example is taken from [5] (cf. [19]). Consider the Petri net of figure 3. It

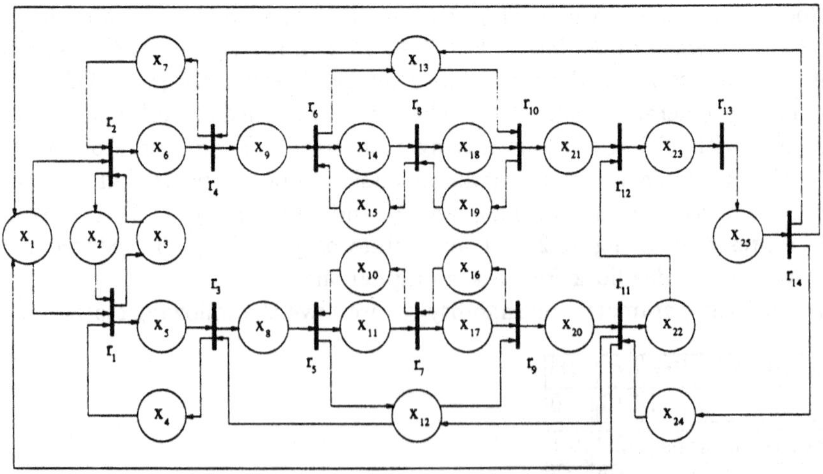
Figure 3

models an automated manufacturing system with four machines, two robots, two buffers (x_{10} and x_{15}) and an assembly cell. The initial marking is: $x_1 = q$ for some nonnegative parameter q, $x_2 = x_4 = x_7 = x_{12} = x_{13} = x_{16} = x_{19} = x_{24} = 1$, $x_{10} = x_{15} = 3$ (thus, the buffers have capacity 3). All other places are empty (that is, all other variables are 0). The task is to discover for which values of q the system may end up in deadlock. (In [19], deadlock-freeness is shown only for $1 \leq q \leq 4$. In [5], deadlock-freeness is proved using some mixed integer programming techniques for $1 \leq q \leq 8$; A path leading to a deadlock is then generated for $q = 9$.) Computing the reachability set, we get the following statistics:

S	MT	MG	PoF	PrF	tot	ND
0	2	61	37	14	114	0

IT:

no. transitions	1	2	3	4	5	6	7	8	9	10	11	12	tot
no. disposals	42	24	18	24	19	13	8	17	2	1	2	1	171

The flat language is computed in 23396 seconds (6.5 hours). It is
$r_1^* r_2^* r_4^* r_6^* r_8^* r_{10}^* r_3^* r_1^* r_2^* r_4^* r_6^* r_{10}^* r_8^* r_5^* (r_3 r_5)^* (r_1 r_3 r_5)^* \; r_2^* r_4^* r_6^* r_{10}^* r_8^* r_1^* r_2^* r_4^* r_6^* r_{10}^* r_8^*$
$r_3^* r_1^* r_2^* r_4^* r_6^* r_{10}^* r_8^* r_7^* r_5^* r_3^* r_1^* r_2^* (r_9 r_7)^* r_9^* r_{11}^* r_3^* r_5^* r_2^* \; r_1^* r_3^* r_5^* r_7^* (r_2 r_1)^* r_2^* r_4^* r_6^* r_{10}^* r_8^*$
$r_{10}^* r_9^* r_7^* r_{12}^* r_{13}^*$.
The relation deadlock$(q, \overline{x})$ is computed in 11.9 seconds. Define the relation:

$$\text{live}(q) \;\equiv\; \neg \exists \overline{x} : \; \text{deadlock}(q, \overline{x})$$

Thus live(q) is the set of parameters for which there is no deadlock in the system. It is computed in 0.09 seconds, and found to be finite in 0.01 seconds. Its enumeration then gives: $\{1, 2, 3, 4, 5, 6, 7, 8\}$. We have therefore a fully automated proof that the system is deadlock free for all the initial markings (of the form given above) for which $1 \leq q \leq 8$, and that for all other value of q, a deadlock exists (note that from deadlock$(q, \overline{x})$, all the deadlock markings for any q may be retrieved, as well as a path to any of them). To prove that the net is bounded for any q amounts to verifying: $\forall q \; \exists \overline{b} \; \forall \overline{x} : \; \xi_{final}(q, \overline{x}) \; \Rightarrow \; \overline{x} \leq \overline{b}$. Our system is too naively implemented to prove this formula as stated, so instead we verify something stronger. We eliminate by projection parameter q and variable x_1 into ξ_{final}, thus getting:

$$\text{subsystem}_1(x_2, x_3, \ldots, x_{25}) \;\equiv\; \exists q, x_1 : \; \xi_{final}(q, x_1, x_2, \ldots, x_{25})$$

The relation subsystem$_1(x_2, x_3, \ldots, x_{25})$ is computed in 38.74 seconds and is shown to be finite (it has 2144 elements) in 1.22 seconds. This shows that all the places but x_1 are bounded. Secondly we compute

$$\text{subsystem}_2(q, x_1) \;\equiv\; \exists x_2, x_3, \ldots, x_{25} : \; \xi_{final}(q, x_1, x_2, \ldots, x_{25})$$

in 7.89 seconds and prove: $\text{subsystem}_2(x_1, q) \;\Rightarrow\; x_1 \leq q$ in 0.03 seconds. Therefore the system is bounded for all values of q.

7.3 Alternating Bit Protocol

This example is taken from [4] where all the correctness proofs are done by hand. Consider the alternating bit protocol of figure 4. The initial marking is:

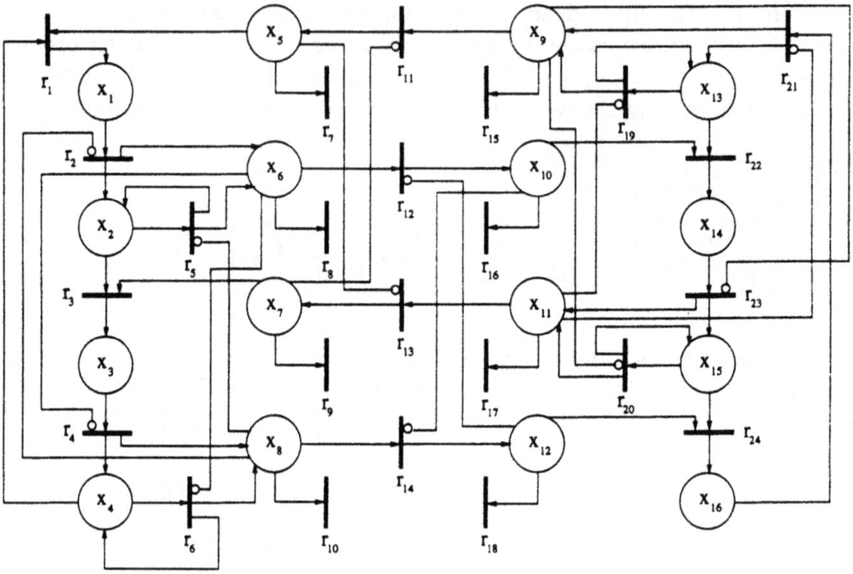

Figure 4

$x_1 = 1, x_{13} = 1$ and $x_i = 0$ for $1 \leq i \leq 14, i \neq 1, i \neq 13$. Note that the system has 8 inhibitor places (which are are the places linked to inhibitor arcs, represented as circle-headed arrows, on the figure). These places are simulated with 8 extra variables. Since there are 16 places in the net, we get a problem with 24 variables. In this example, when computing the reachability set, the decomposition process fails several times. So the system drops some transition chosen according to a simple heuristic (basically random choice). It may then happen that the decomposition process ends without having reached the least fixed-point, in which case the process is restarted with the formula ξ lastly generated as a new base case (see section 5.2). We have conducted the experiment many times with this example, and always eventually reached the least fixed-point. We give below statistics for a a typical computation (which succeeded after three rounds of decomposition).

S	MT	MG	PoF	PrF	tot	ND
12	24	48	26	0	110	6

IT:

no. transitions	1	2	4	5	6	7	8	9	10	11	12	13
no. disposals	23	7	3	4	6	4	9	7	6	3	6	3

The first decomposition round ends after 33 seconds, and yields language

$$L_1 = r_2^* r_8^* r_{12}^* r_{22}^* r_{23}^* r_{20}^* r_{17}^* r_{19}^* r_{22}^* r_{13}^* r_3^* r_4^* r_6^* r_{14}^* r_{10}^* r_{24}^* r_{21}^* r_{19}^* r_{15}^* \ .$$

At the second round, the decomposition ends after 48 seconds, yielding:
$L_2 = r_{11}^* r_{23}^* r_{20}^* r_{17}^* r_1^* r_2^* r_5^* r_3^* r_8^*$.
At the third round, the decomposition ends after 47 seconds, yielding:
$L_3 = r_{12}^* r_4^* r_6^* r_{10}^*$.
for which the least fixed-point is reached. The flat language for this example is therefore $L_1 L_2 L_3$.
The correctness of the protocol is expressed as follows (see [4]):

i. $\xi_{final}(\overline{x}) \ \wedge \ x_1 = 1 \ \Rightarrow \ x_{13} = 1 \ \wedge \ x_6 = x_{10} = x_{11} = x_7 = 0$
ii. $\xi_{final}(\overline{x}) \ \wedge \ x_3 = 1 \ \Rightarrow \ x_{15} = 1 \ \wedge \ x_8 = x_{12} = x_9 = x_5 = 0$
iii. $\xi_{final}(\overline{x}) \ \wedge \ x_{14} = 1 \ \Rightarrow \ x_2 = 1 \ \wedge \ x_{11} = x_7 = x_8 = x_{12} = 0$
iv. $\xi_{final}(\overline{x}) \ \wedge \ x_{16} = 1 \ \Rightarrow \ x_4 = 1 \ \wedge \ x_9 = x_5 = x_6 = x_{10} = 0$

These four implications were proved in 1.52 seconds each. In 8 seconds, the unbounded places x_5, x_6, x_7, x_8, x_9, x_{10}, x_{11} and x_{12} were found. (Note that they coincide exactly with the inhibitor places.)

8 Final Remarks

We have illustrated on three nontrivial examples of Petri nets how our top-down method of decomposition enhanced by forward propagation of the initial values and invariance checks, allows us to characterize arithmetically infinite reachability sets and (dis)prove automatically various safety properties. We have also successfully applied our procedure to examples of automata with counters taken from [10], and on classical examples with finite reachability sets such as dining-philosophers or Peterson's mutual exclusion algorithm. As observed by Hiraishi [11], such a kind of method is not universal because it is known that there exist Petri nets whose reachability sets are not characterizable in Presburger arithmetic. However in practice, the main problem that we have to deal with is the state explosion problem, which prevents the construction of Boudet-Comon's automaton. We have indicated one way to alleviate this problem by reducing the original net to a simpler one that retains its main safety properties (through Berthelot's transformations). Another way that we would like to explore is to use a *compositional* approach, in order to reduce the verification of a global safety property to the verification of several local ones (see, e.g., [7, 15, 17]).

References

1. G. Berthelot. "Transformations and Decompositions of Nets". *Advances in Petri Nets*, LNCS 254, Springer-Verlag, 1986, pp. 359-376.
2. A. Boudet and H. Comon, "Diophantine Equations, Presburger Arithmetic and Finite Automata", *Proc. CAAP*, LNCS 1059, Springer-Verlag, 1996, pp. 30–43.
3. G.W. Brams. *Réseaux de Petri: Théorie et Pratique*, Masson, Paris, 1983.
4. J.M. Couvreur and E. Paviot-Adet. "New Structural Invariants for Petri Nets Analysis". *Proc. Application and Theory of Petri Nets*, LNCS 815, Springer-Verlag, 1994.

5. F. Chu and X. Xie. *Deadlock Analysis of Petri Nets Using Siphons and Mathematical Programming.* Submitted to *IEEE Trans. on Robotics and Automation*, 1996, 29 pages.
6. R. David and H. Alla. *Du Grafcet aux Réseaux de Petri*, Hermès, Paris, 1989.
7. A. Finkel and L. Petrucci. "Composition/Décomposition de Réseaux de Petri et de leurs Graphes de Couverture". *Informatique Théorique et Applications 28:2*, 1994, pp. 73-124.
8. L. Fribourg and H. Olsén. *A Decompositional Approach for Computing the Least Fixed-points of Datalog Programs with Z-counters.* Technical Report LIENS-96-12, Ecole Normale Supérieure, Paris, July 1996. (Available on http://www.dmi.ens.fr/dmi/preprints)
9. S. Ginsburg. *The Mathematical Theory of Context-Free Languages.* McGraw-Hill, 1966.
10. N. Halbwachs. "Delay Analysis in Synchronous Programs", *Proc. Computer Aided Verification*, LNCS 697, Springer-Verlag, 1993, pp. 333-346.
11. K. Hiraishi. "Reduced State Space Representation for Unbounded Vector State Spaces", *Proc. Application and Theory of Petri Nets*, LNCS 1091, Springer-Verlag, 1996, pp. 230-248.
12. J. Jaffar and J.L. Lassez. "Constraint Logic Programming", *Proc. 14th ACM Symp. on Principles of Programming Languages*, 1987, pp. 111-119.
13. P. Kanellakis, G. Kuper and P. Revesz. "Constraint Query Languages". Internal Report, November 1990. (Short version in *Proc. 9th ACM Symp. on Principles of Database Systems*, Nashville, 1990, pp. 299-313).
14. R.M. Karp and R.E. Miller. "Parallel Program Schemata". *J. Computer and System Sciences: 3*, 1969, pp. 147-195.
15. F. Laroussinie and K. Larsen. "Compositional Model Checking of Real Time Systems". *Proc. CONCUR*, LNCS 962, Springer-Verlag, 1995, pp. 27–41.
16. M. Presburger. "Uber die Vollstandingen einer gewissen Systems der Arithmetik ganzer Zahlen, in welchem die Addition als einzige Operation hervotritt", *Comptes Rendus du premier Congrès des Mathématiciens des Pays Slaves*, Varszawa, 1929.
17. A. Valmari. "Compositional State Space Generation", *Advances in Petri Nets*, LNCS 674, Springer-Verlag, 1993, pp. 427-457.
18. H-C. Yen. "On the Regularity of Petri Net Languages". *Information and Computation 124*, 1996, pp. 168-181.
19. M.C. Zhou, F. Dicesare and A.A. Desrochers. "A Hybrid Methodology for Synthesis of Petri Net Models for Manufacturing Systems", *IEEE Trans. on Robotics and Automation*, vol. 8:3, 1992, pp. 350-361.

Axiomatizing Flat Iteration

R.J. van Glabbeek*
Computer Science Department, Stanford University
Stanford, CA 94305-9045, USA.
rvg@cs.stanford.edu

Flat iteration is a variation on the original binary version of the Kleene star operation P^*Q, obtained by restricting the first argument to be a sum of atomic actions. It generalizes prefix iteration, in which the first argument is a single action. Complete finite equational axiomatizations are given for five notions of bisimulation congruence over basic CCS with flat iteration, viz. strong congruence, branching congruence, η-congruence, delay congruence and weak congruence. Such axiomatizations were already known for prefix iteration and are known not to exist for general iteration. The use of flat iteration has two main advantages over prefix iteration:

1. The current axiomatizations generalize to full CCS, whereas the prefix iteration approach does not allow an elimination theorem for an asynchronous parallel composition operator.
2. The greater expressiveness of flat iteration allows for much shorter completeness proofs.

In the setting of prefix iteration, the most convenient way to obtain the completeness theorems for η-, delay, and weak congruence was by reduction to the completeness theorem for branching congruence. In the case of weak congruence this turned out to be much simpler than the only direct proof found. In the setting of flat iteration on the other hand, the completeness theorems for delay and weak (but not η-) congruence can equally well be obtained by reduction to the one for strong congruence, without using branching congruence as an intermediate step. Moreover, the completeness results for prefix iteration can be retrieved from those for flat iteration, thus obtaining a second indirect approach for proving completeness for delay and weak congruence in the setting of prefix iteration.

1 Introduction

The research literature on process theory has recently witnessed a resurgence of interest in Kleene star-like operations [6, 11, 9, 19, 8, 3, 10, 1, 2]. In [8] tree-based models for theories involving Kleene's star operation * [15] are studied. [6] investigates the expressive power of variations on standard process description languages in which infinite behaviours are defined by means of * rather than by means of systems of recursion equations. The papers [11, 19, 9, 3, 10, 1, 2] study

*This work was supported by ONR under grant number N00014-92-J-1974.

the possibility of giving finite equational axiomatizations of bisimulation-like equivalences over fragments of such languages. This study is continued here.

In [11] a complete finite equational axiomatization of strong bisimulation equivalence was given for a process algebra featuring choice, sequential composition, and the original binary version of the Kleene star operation P^*Q [15]. [19] shows that such an axiomatization does not exists in the presence of the process 0 denoting inaction, or a process denoting successful termination. The same proof strategy can be adopted to conclude that there is no finite equational axiomatization for weak or branching bisimulation over an enrichment of this basic process algebra with an internal action.

For this reason restrictions of the Kleene star have been investigated. [9] presents a finite, complete equational axiomatization of strong bisimulation equivalence for Basic CCS (the fragment of Milner's CCS [16] containing the operations needed to express finite synchronization trees) with *prefix iteration*. Prefix iteration is a variation on the binary Kleene star operation P^*Q, obtained by restricting the first argument to be an atomic action. The same is done in [1] for *string iteration*. The work of [9] has been extended in [2] and its predecessors [3, 10, 12] to cope with *weak*, *delay*, *eta-* and *branching bisimulation congruence* in a setting with the unobservable action τ. Motivation and background material on these behavioural congruences can be found, e.g., in [16] and [13]. The strategy adopted in [2] in establishing the completeness results is based upon the use of branching equivalence in the analysis of weak, delay and η-equivalence, advocated in [12]. Following [12], complete axiomatizations for weak, delay and η-congruence were obtained from one for branching congruence by:

1. identifying a collection of process terms on which branching congruence coincides with the congruence one aims at axiomatizing, and

2. finding an axiom system that allows for the reduction of every process term to one of the required form.

Perhaps surprisingly, the proof for weak congruence so obtained is simpler than the one given in [3] which only uses properties of weak congruence. The direct proof method employed in [3] yields a long proof with many case distinctions, while the indirect proof via branching congruence in [2] is considerably shorter, and relies on a general relationship between the two congruences. Moreover, attempts to obtain a direct proof of the completeness theorem for weak congruence which is simpler than the one presented in [3] have been to no avail.

Results The present paper extends the results from [9] and [2] from prefix iteration to *flat iteration*. Flat iteration was first mentioned in the technical report version of [6]; it allows the first argument P of P^*Q to be a (possibly empty) sum of actions. For convenience, the CCS operator of action-prefixing is also generalized to prefixing with sums of actions.

My completeness proofs are considerably shorter than the ones in [2]. This is mostly a result of the presence of expressions of the form 0^*P in the language, which allows a collapse of several cases in the case distinction in [2]. In addition, the results for weak and delay congruence can be obtained without using branching congruence as an intermediate step. Thanks to the greater expressiveness of flat iteration, these results can be reduced to the one for strong congruence, using the same proof strategy as outlined above. However, the proposed reduction to strong congruence does not work for η- and branching congruence.

In addition I derive the existing axiomatizations for prefix iteration from the ones for flat iteration. In the case of weak congruence one finds therefore that although a direct proof is cumbersome, there is a choice between two attractive indirect proofs. One of them involves first establishing the result for branching congruence; the other involves first establishing the result for a richer language.

Finally, extending a result from [6], I derive an expansion theorem for the CCS parallel composition operator in the setting of flat iteration. This is the key to extending the complete axiomatizations of this paper to full CCS. I show that such a theorem does not exist in the setting of prefix iteration.

As in [2], my completeness proofs apply to open terms directly, and thus yield the ω-completeness of the axiomatizations as well as their completeness for closed terms. However, the generalization to full CCS applies to closed terms only.

Outline of the paper Section 2 introduces the language of basic CCS with flat iteration, BCCS^{f*}, and its operational semantics. It also recalls the definitions of strong, branching, η-, delay and weak congruence. The axiom systems that will be shown to completely characterize the aforementioned congruences over BCCS^{f*} are presented in Section 3, and Section 4 contains the proofs of their completeness. In Section 5 the existing axiomatizations for prefix iteration are derived from the ones for flat iteration. Finally, Section 6 indicates how the completeness results of this paper, unlike the ones for prefix iteration, can, at least for closed terms, be extended to full CCS.

2 Basic CCS with Flat Iteration

Assume a set A of observable *actions*. Let $\tau \notin A$ denote a special *invisible action* and write $A_\tau := A \cup \{\tau\}$. Also assume an infinite set Var of *variables*, disjoint with A_τ. Let $x, y, ...$ range over Var, $a, b, ...$ over A, $\alpha, \beta, \gamma, ...$ over A_τ and ξ over $A_\tau \cup \mathsf{Var}$.

The two-sorted language BCCS^{f*} of basic CCS with flat iteration is given by the BNF grammar:

$$S ::= 0 \mid \alpha \mid S + S$$

$$P ::= x \mid 0 \mid S.P \mid P + P \mid S^*P$$

Terms of sort S are called *sumforms*, whereas terms of sort P are called *process expressions*. The set of sumforms is denoted by SF and the set of (open) process expressions by $\mathbb{T}$. Let s, t, u range over SF and P, Q, R, S, T over $\mathbb{T}$. In writing terms over the above syntax one may leave out redundant brackets, assuming that $+$ binds weaker than . and *. For $I = \{i_1, \ldots, i_n\}$ a finite index set, $\sum_{i \in I} P_i$ or $\sum \{P_i \mid i \in I\}$ denotes $P_{i_1} + \cdots + P_{i_n}$. By convention, $\sum_{i \in \emptyset} P_i$ stands for 0.

The transition relations $\xrightarrow{\xi}$ are the least subsets of $(\mathbb{T} \times \mathbb{T}) \cup \mathrm{SF}$ satisfying the rules in Fig. 1. These determine the operational semantics of BCCS^{f*}. A transition $P \xrightarrow{\alpha} Q$ ($\alpha \in A_\tau$) indicates that the system represented by the term P can perform the action α, thereby evolving into Q, whereas $P \xrightarrow{x} P'$ means that the initial behaviour of P may depend on the term that is substituted for the process variable x. It is not hard to see that if $P \xrightarrow{x} P'$ then $P' = x$. A transition $s \xrightarrow{\alpha}$ just says that α is one of the actions in the sumform s.

$$\frac{}{\alpha \xrightarrow{\alpha}} \qquad \frac{s \xrightarrow{\alpha}}{s+t \xrightarrow{\alpha}} \qquad \frac{t \xrightarrow{\alpha}}{s+t \xrightarrow{\alpha}}$$

$$\frac{}{x \xrightarrow{x} x} \qquad \frac{s \xrightarrow{\alpha}}{s.P \xrightarrow{\alpha} P} \qquad \frac{P \xrightarrow{\xi} P'}{P+Q \xrightarrow{\xi} P'} \qquad \frac{Q \xrightarrow{\xi} Q'}{P+Q \xrightarrow{\xi} Q'}$$

$$\frac{s \xrightarrow{\alpha}}{s^*P \xrightarrow{\alpha} s^*P} \qquad \frac{P \xrightarrow{\xi} P'}{s^*P \xrightarrow{\xi} P'}$$

Fig. 1: Transition rules for BCCS^{f*}

The set $\mathsf{der}(P)$ of *derivatives* of P is the least set containing P that is closed under action-transitions. Formally, $\mathsf{pder}(P)$ is the least set satisfying:

if $Q \in \{P\} \cup \mathsf{pder}(P)$ and $Q \xrightarrow{\alpha} Q'$ for some $\alpha \in A_\tau$, then $Q' \in \mathsf{pder}(P)$,

and $\mathsf{der}(P) = \{P\} \cup \mathsf{pder}(P)$. Members of $\mathsf{pder}(P)$ are called *proper* derivatives.

Definition 2.1 Write $p \Rightarrow q$ for $\exists n \geq 0 : \exists p_0, \ldots, p_n : p = p_0 \xrightarrow{\tau} p_1 \xrightarrow{\tau} \ldots \xrightarrow{\tau} p_n = q$, i.e. a (possibly empty) path of τ-steps from p to q. Furthermore, for $\xi \in A_\tau \cup \mathsf{Var}$, write $p \xrightarrow{(\xi)} q$ for $p \xrightarrow{\xi} q \vee (\xi = \tau \wedge p = q)$. Thus $\xrightarrow{(\xi)}$ is the same as $\xrightarrow{\xi}$ for $\xi \in A \cup \mathsf{Var}$, and $\xrightarrow{(\tau)}$ denotes zero or one τ-steps.

A *weak bisimulation* is a symmetric binary relation $\mathcal{R}$ on $\mathbb{T}$, such that

$$s\mathcal{R}t \wedge s \xrightarrow{\xi} s' \text{ implies } \exists t_1, t_2, t' : t \Rightarrow t_1 \xrightarrow{(\xi)} t_2 \Rightarrow t' \wedge s'\mathcal{R}t'. \tag{1}$$

A weak bisimulation is a *delay bisimulation* if in the conclusion of (1) one has $t_2 = t'$. It is an *η-bisimulation* if one has $s\mathcal{R}t_1$, and it is a *branching bisimulation* if one has both $t_2 = t'$ and $s\mathcal{R}t_1$. Finally, it is a *strong bisimulation* if one has

$$s\mathcal{R}t \wedge s \xrightarrow{\xi} s' \text{ implies } \exists t' : t \xrightarrow{\xi} t' \wedge s'\mathcal{R}t'.$$

Let s, w, d, b be abbreviations for *strong*, *weak*, *delay* and *branching*, and let $\aleph$ range over $\{s, w, d, \eta, b\}$. Then two processes $P, Q \in \mathbb{T}$ are $\aleph$*(-bisimulation) equivalent*—notation $P \leftrightarrow_\aleph Q$—if there is a $\aleph$-bisimulation $\mathcal{R}$ with $P\mathcal{R}Q$.

Following [17, 2], the above definitions depart from the standard approach followed in, e.g., [16] in that notions of bisimulation equivalence are defined that apply to open terms directly. Usually, bisimulation equivalences like those presented in Def. 2.1 are defined explicitly for closed process expressions only. Open process expressions are then regarded equivalent iff they are equivalent under any closed substitution of their (free) variables. In [2] it has been shown, for the language BCCS with prefix iteration, that both approaches yield the same equivalence relation over open terms. The same proof applies to $BCCS^{f*}$. For this result it is essential that the set A of observable actions is nonempty.

The following lemma will be of use in the completeness proof for branching congruence (cf. the proof of Propn. 4.2). It is a standard result for branching bisimulation equivalence.

Lemma 2.2 (Stuttering Lemma [13]) *If $P_0 \overset{\tau}{\to} \cdots \overset{\tau}{\to} P_n$ and $P_n \underline{\leftrightarrow}_b P_0$, then $P_i \underline{\leftrightarrow}_b P_0$ for $i = 1, ..., n-1$.*

The definition of $\underline{\leftrightarrow}_b$ is equivalent to the one in [13], as follows immediately from the proof of the stuttering lemma in [13]. However, what is here introduced as a branching bisimulation was there called a *semi branching bisimulation*, whereas "branching bisimulation" was the name of a slightly more restrictive type of relation. The advantages of the current setup have been pointed out in [5].

Proposition 2.3 *Each of the relations $\underline{\leftrightarrow}_\aleph$ ($\aleph \in \{s, b, \eta, d, w\}$) is an equivalence relation and the largest $\aleph$-bisimulation. Furthermore, for all P, Q,*

$$P \underline{\leftrightarrow}_s Q \;\Rightarrow\; P \underline{\leftrightarrow}_b Q \;\Rightarrow\; P \underline{\leftrightarrow}_d Q$$
$$\Downarrow \qquad\qquad \Downarrow$$
$$P \underline{\leftrightarrow}_\eta Q \;\Rightarrow\; P \underline{\leftrightarrow}_w Q.$$

Proof: For $\aleph \in \{s, b, \eta, d, w\}$, the identity relation, the converse of a $\aleph$-bisimulation and the symmetric closure of the composition of two $\aleph$-bisimulations are all $\aleph$-bisimulations. Hence $\underline{\leftrightarrow}_\aleph$ is an equivalence relation. As pointed out in [5], for this argument to apply to branching bisimulations it is essential that the definition of a branching bisimulation is relaxed to that of a semi branching bisimulation.

That $\underline{\leftrightarrow}_\aleph$ is the largest $\aleph$-bisimulation follows immediately from the observation that the set of $\aleph$-bisimulations is closed under arbitrary unions. The implications hold by definition. $\square$

For $s, t \in$ SF write $s \leq t$ if $\forall \alpha (s \overset{\alpha}{\to} \;\Rightarrow t \overset{\alpha}{\to})$, and $s \underline{\leftrightarrow} t$ if $s \leq t$ and $t \leq s$. It is easily checked that $\underline{\leftrightarrow}$ is a congruence on sumforms in the sense that

if $s \underline{\leftrightarrow} t$ then $s + u \underline{\leftrightarrow} t + u$, $u + s \underline{\leftrightarrow} u + t$, $s.P \underline{\leftrightarrow}_s t.P$, and $s^* P \underline{\leftrightarrow}_s t^* P$.

Likewise, $\underline{\leftrightarrow}_s$ turns out to be a congruence on $\mathbb{T}$ in the sense that

if $P \underline{\leftrightarrow}_s Q$ then $P + R \underline{\leftrightarrow}_s Q + R$, $R + P \underline{\leftrightarrow}_s R + Q$, $s.P \underline{\leftrightarrow}_s s.Q$ and $s^* P \underline{\leftrightarrow}_s s^* Q$.

However, for the standard reasons explained in, e.g., [16], none of the equivalences $\underline{\leftrightarrow}_w$, $\underline{\leftrightarrow}_d$, $\underline{\leftrightarrow}_\eta$ and $\underline{\leftrightarrow}_b$ is a congruence with respect to $+$. In fact, also none of these equivalences is preserved by $*$ [2]. Following Milner [16], the solution to these congruence problems is by now standard; it is sufficient to consider, for each equivalence $\underline{\leftrightarrow}_\aleph$, the largest congruence over $\mathbb{T}$ contained in it. These largest congruences can be explicitly characterized as follows.

Definition 2.4

- P and Q are *branching congruent*, written $P \mathrel{\underline{\leftrightarrow}}_b^c Q$, iff for all $\xi \in A_\tau \cup \mathsf{Var}$,

  1. if $P \overset{\xi}{\to} P'$, then $Q \overset{\xi}{\to} Q'$ for some Q' such that $P' \mathrel{\underline{\leftrightarrow}}_b Q'$;

  2. if $Q \overset{\xi}{\to} Q'$, then $P \overset{\xi}{\to} P'$ for some P' such that $P' \mathrel{\underline{\leftrightarrow}}_b Q'$.

- P and Q are *η-congruent*, written $P \mathrel{\underline{\leftrightarrow}}_\eta^c Q$, iff for all $\xi \in A_\tau \cup \mathsf{Var}$,

  1. if $P \overset{\xi}{\to} P'$, then $Q \overset{\xi}{\to} Q_1 \Rightarrow Q'$ for some Q_1, Q' such that $P' \mathrel{\underline{\leftrightarrow}}_\eta Q'$;

  2. if $Q \overset{\xi}{\to} Q'$, then $P \overset{\xi}{\to} P_1 \Rightarrow P'$ for some P_1, P' such that $P' \mathrel{\underline{\leftrightarrow}}_\eta Q'$.

- P and Q are *delay congruent*, written $P \mathrel{\underline{\leftrightarrow}}_d^c Q$, iff for all $\xi \in A_\tau \cup \mathsf{Var}$,

  1. if $P \overset{\xi}{\to} P'$, then $Q \Rightarrow Q_1 \overset{\xi}{\to} Q'$ for some Q_1, Q' such that $P' \mathrel{\underline{\leftrightarrow}}_d Q'$;

  2. if $Q \overset{\xi}{\to} Q'$, then $P \Rightarrow P_1 \overset{\xi}{\to} P'$ for some P_1, P' such that $P' \mathrel{\underline{\leftrightarrow}}_d Q'$.

- P and Q are *weakly congruent*, written $P \mathrel{\underline{\leftrightarrow}}_w^c Q$, iff for all $\xi \in A_\tau \cup \mathsf{Var}$,

  1. if $P \overset{\xi}{\to} P'$, then $Q \Rightarrow\overset{\xi}{\to}\Rightarrow Q'$ for some Q' such that $P' \mathrel{\underline{\leftrightarrow}}_w Q'$;

  2. if $Q \overset{\xi}{\to} Q'$, then $P \Rightarrow\overset{\xi}{\to}\Rightarrow P'$ for some P' such that $P' \mathrel{\underline{\leftrightarrow}}_w Q'$.

- Finally, *strong congruence*, denoted $\mathrel{\underline{\leftrightarrow}}_s^c$, is the same as $\mathrel{\underline{\leftrightarrow}}_s$.

Proposition 2.5 *For every $\aleph \in \{s, b, \eta, d, w\}$, the relation $\mathrel{\underline{\leftrightarrow}}_\aleph^c$ is the largest congruence over $\mathbb{T}$ contained in $\mathrel{\underline{\leftrightarrow}}_\aleph$.*

Proof: Exactly as in [2]. □

3   Axiom Systems

Table 1 presents the axiom system $\mathcal{E}_s$, which will be shown to completely characterize strong congruence over BCCS^{f*}. The entries in this table are axiom schemes in the sense that there is one axiom for every choice of the sumforms s, t, u. For an axiom system $\mathcal{T}$, one writes $\mathcal{T} \vdash P = Q$ iff the equation $P = Q$ is provable from the axiom system $\mathcal{T}$ using the rules of equational logic. For a collection of equations X over the signature of BCCS^{f*}, $P \overset{X}{=} Q$ is used as a short-hand for A1–A4,$X \vdash P = Q$. The axioms A1–4 are known to completely characterize the operator $+$ of CCS. As this operator occurs both in sumforms and in process expressions, these axioms appear for each of the two sorts. It is easily checked that they are sound and complete for $\mathrel{\underline{\leftrightarrow}}$ on sumforms:

Proposition 3.1 $s \mathrel{\underline{\leftrightarrow}} t \Leftrightarrow \text{A1–4} \vdash s = t$. *Moreover,* $s \le t \Leftrightarrow \text{A1–4} \vdash t = t + s$.

The axioms A5 and A6 are inspired by the ACP axioms for sequential composition [7], and the axiom FA1 stems from [10], where a form of iteration P^*Q was used in which P had to be either an action, or a process (like 0) that cannot perform any actions. In [6] three axioms for general iteration in a process

A1	$x+y$	$=$	$y+x$	$s+t$	$=$	$t+s$
A2	$(x+y)+z$	$=$	$x+(y+z)$	$(s+t)+u$	$=$	$s+(t+u)$
A3	$x+x$	$=$	x	$s+s$	$=$	s
A4	$x+0$	$=$	x	$s+0$	$=$	s
A5	$(s+t).x$	$=$	$s.x+t.x$			
A6	$0.x$	$=$	0			
FA1	0^*x	$=$	x			
FA2	$s^*(t.(s+t)^*x+x)$	$=$	$(s+t)^*x$			

Table 1: The axiom system $\mathcal{E}_s$

algebra without 0 where proposed, called BKS1–3. These axioms where shown to be complete in [11]. The axiom BKS2 deals with the interaction between iteration and general sequential composition, and therefore has no counterpart in BCCS^{f*}. My axiom FA2 is obtained from BKS3 by requiring the first argument in an expression P^*Q to be a sumform. In the same spirit, the axiom BKS1 could be modified to $t.(t^*x)+x=t^*x$. This law is derivable from $\mathcal{E}_s$ by setting $s=0$ in FA2. The remaining axiom $a^*(a^*x)=a^*x$ of [9] is derivable as well: take $s=t$ in FA2 and apply BKS1 to the left-hand side.

In addition to the axioms in $\mathcal{E}_s$, the axiom systems $\mathcal{E}_\aleph$ ($\aleph \in \{b,\eta,d,w\}$) include equations describing the various ways in which the congruences $\underline{\leftrightarrow}_\aleph^c$ abstract away from internal actions τ. These equations are presented in Table 2. The axiom system $\mathcal{E}_b$ is obtained by adding the axioms FT1–2 to $\mathcal{E}_s$, and $\mathcal{E}_\eta$ extends $\mathcal{E}_b$ with the equations T3 and FT3. The set of axioms $\mathcal{E}_d$ consists of the axioms of $\mathcal{E}_s$ together with T1 and FFIR. Finally, $\mathcal{E}_w$ extends $\mathcal{E}_d$ with T3 and FT3.

The equations T1 and T3 are standard laws for the silent action τ in weak congruence. Together with T2: $\tau.x=\tau.x+x$ and the laws for strong congruence,

$\mathcal{E}_\eta$	$\mathcal{E}_b$	FT1	$(s+\tau)^*x$	$=$	$\tau.(s^*x)+(s^*x)$
$\mathcal{E}_\eta$	$\mathcal{E}_b$	FT2	$\alpha.s^*(\tau.s^*(x+y)+x)$	$=$	$\alpha.s^*(x+y)$
$\mathcal{E}_\eta$	$\mathcal{E}_w$	T3	$\alpha.(x+\tau.y)$	$=$	$\alpha.(x+\tau.y)+\alpha.y$
$\mathcal{E}_\eta$	$\mathcal{E}_w$	FT3	$s^*(x+\tau.y)$	$=$	$s^*(x+\tau.y+s.y)$
$\mathcal{E}_w$	$\mathcal{E}_d$	T1	$\alpha.\tau.x$	$=$	$\alpha.x$
$\mathcal{E}_w$	$\mathcal{E}_d$	FFIR	$(s+\tau)^*x$	$=$	$\tau.(s^*x)$

Table 2: Extra axioms for $\mathcal{E}_\eta$, $\mathcal{E}_b$, $\mathcal{E}_d$ and $\mathcal{E}_w$

they are known to completely characterize weak congruence in the absence of iteration. Here T2 is derivable from $\mathcal{E}_s$ and FFIR (set $s = 0$ in FFIR and apply BKS1 on τ^*x). Also the law $\alpha.(\tau.(x+y)+x) = \alpha.(x+y)$, which together with the laws for strong congruence characterizes branching bisimulation for BCCS without iteration, is derivable: just take $s = 0$ in FT2.

The four remaining axioms, which describe the interplay between τ and prefix iteration, are new here. The law FFIR is a generalization of the ***Fair Iteration Rule*** $\tau^*x = \tau.x$ (FIR$_1$) of [6], which is an equational formulation of *Koomen's Fair Abstraction Rule* [4]. Like FIR, FFIR expresses that modulo weak (or delay) congruence a process remains the same if τ-loops are added (or deleted) in (or from) its proper derivatives. The law FT1 has the same function in branching (or η-)bisimulation semantics, but has to be formulated more carefully because T2 is not valid there. Note that FT1 can be reformulated as $\alpha.(s+\tau)^*x = \alpha.s^*x$. The laws FT2 and FT3 are straightforward generalizations of the laws PB2 and PT3 of [2]. The remaining law PT2 of [2] is (by the forthcoming completeness theorem for $\leftrightarrow_d^c$) derivable from the ones given here.

Note that even over a finite alphabet A there exist infinitely many sumforms. Hence the axiomatizations as given here are infinite. However, for each axiom scheme only the instantiations are needed in which the sumforms have the form $\sum_{i=1}^{n} \alpha_i$ in which all the α_i's are different. With this modification each of the axiom systems $\mathcal{E}_\aleph$ ($\aleph \in \{s, b, \eta, d, w\}$) is finite if so is the set of actions A. If A is not finite, the axiomatizations can still be interpreted as finite ones, namely by replacing the actions α in FT2 and T2,3 by sumforms t, introducing variables that range over sumforms, and interpreting each entry in the resulting Tables 1–4 as a single axiom in which s, t and u are such variables.

The following states the soundness of the axiom systems.

Proposition 3.2 *Let* $\aleph \in \{s, b, \eta, d, w\}$. *If* $\mathcal{E}_\aleph \vdash P = Q$, *then* $P \leftrightarrow_\aleph^c Q$.

Proof: As $\leftrightarrow_\aleph^c$ is a congruence, it is sufficient to show that each equation in $\mathcal{E}_\aleph$ is sound with respect to it. This is rather straightforward and left to the reader. □

As in [2], it can be shown that $\mathcal{E}_w \vdash \mathcal{E}_d \vdash \mathcal{E}_b \vdash \mathcal{E}_s$ and $\mathcal{E}_w \vdash \mathcal{E}_\eta \vdash \mathcal{E}_b$, where $\mathcal{T} \vdash \mathcal{T}'$ denotes that $\mathcal{T} \vdash P = Q$ for every equation $(P = Q) \in \mathcal{T}'$.

4 Completeness

This section is entirely devoted to detailed proofs of the completeness of the axiom systems $\mathcal{E}_\aleph$ ($\aleph \in \{s, b, \eta, d, w\}$) with respect to $\leftrightarrow_\aleph^c$ over the language of open terms $\mathbb{T}$. The first subsection contains the completeness proof for branching congruence. Its contents also apply to strong congruence if you read $\mathcal{E}_s$ for $\mathcal{E}_b$, $\leftrightarrow_s$ for $\leftrightarrow_b$, α for a, and α for (α) and skip the underlined and sidelined parts.

4.1 Completeness for strong and branching congruence

First I identify a subset of process expressions of a special form, which will be convenient in the proof of the completeness result. Following a long-established tradition in the literature on process theory, these terms are referred to as *normal forms*. The set of normal forms is the smallest set of process expressions of the form

$$s^*(\sum_{i \in I} \alpha_i.P_i + \sum_{j \in J} x_j),$$

where $s \overset{\tau}{\nrightarrow}$, the terms P_i are themselves normal forms, and I, J are finite index sets. (Recall that the empty sum represents 0.)

Lemma 4.1 *Each term in* $\mathbb{T}$ *can be proven equal to a normal form using equations A1–6, FA1,2 and* FT1.

Proof: A straightforward induction on the structure of process expressions. The expressions x and 0 can be brought in the required form by a single application of FA1. Now suppose P and Q have the required form. Then $s.P$ can be brought in normal form using A5 or A6 (possibly after applying A4 on s), followed by FA1. $P+Q$ can be brought in normal form by first applying the derivable law $t^*x = t.(t^*x) + x$ (BKS1) on each of P and Q, then A4–6 to rewrite the subterms $t.(t^*x)$, and concluding with FA1. Finally s^*P is dealt with by applying BKS1 on P, again followed by A4–6. In case $s \overset{\tau}{\rightarrow}$, apply FT1, followed by another round of BKS1, A4–6 and FA1. □

Note that this is the only place in the completeness proof where the axioms FA1 and FT1 are used. The following result is the key to the completeness theorem.

Proposition 4.2 *For all* $P, Q \in \mathbb{T}$, *if* $P \underline{\leftrightarrow}_b Q$, *then,* $\forall \gamma \in A_\tau : \mathcal{E}_b \vdash \underline{\gamma.P} = \underline{\gamma.Q}$.

Proof: First of all, note that, as the equations in $\mathcal{E}_b$ are sound with respect to $\underline{\leftrightarrow}_b^c$, and, *a fortiori*, with respect to $\underline{\leftrightarrow}_b$, by Lem. 4.1 it is sufficient to prove that the statement of the proposition holds for branching equivalent normal forms P and Q. I do so by complete induction on the sum of the sizes of P and Q.

Let $P = s^*(\sum_i \alpha_i.P_i + \sum_k x_k)$ and $Q = t^*(\sum_j \beta_j.Q_j + \sum_l y_l)$. Write P' for $\sum_i \alpha_i.P_i + \sum_k x_k$ and Q' for $\sum_j \beta_j.Q_j + \sum_l y_l$. Consider the following two conditions:

A. $P_i \underline{\leftrightarrow}_b Q$ for some i;

B. $Q_j \underline{\leftrightarrow}_b P$ for some j.

I distinguish two cases in the proof, depending on which of these conditions hold.

I Suppose that both of A and B hold. In this case, there exist i and j such that $P_i \underline{\leftrightarrow}_b Q \underline{\leftrightarrow}_b P \underline{\leftrightarrow}_b Q_j$. Applying the inductive hypothesis to the equivalences $P \underline{\leftrightarrow}_b Q_j$, $Q_j \underline{\leftrightarrow}_b P_i$ and $P_i \underline{\leftrightarrow}_b Q$, one infers that, for all $\gamma \in A_\tau$,

$$\mathcal{E}_b \vdash \underline{\gamma.P} = \underline{\gamma.Q_j} = \underline{\gamma.P_i} = \underline{\gamma.Q}$$

II Suppose that at most one of A and B holds. Assume, without loss of generality, that B does not hold.

Suppose $s \overset{a}{\rightarrow}$. As $P \underline{\leftrightarrow}_b Q$, the transition $P \overset{a}{\rightarrow} P$ must be matched by a sequence of transitions $Q = Q_0 \overset{\tau}{\rightarrow} Q_1 \overset{\tau}{\rightarrow} \cdots \overset{\tau}{\rightarrow} Q_n \overset{a}{\rightarrow} Q''$ with $P \underline{\leftrightarrow}_b Q_n$ and $P \underline{\leftrightarrow}_b Q''$. As condition B does *not* hold, using Lem. 2.2 it follows that $n = 0$, $Q'' = Q$ and $t \overset{a}{\rightarrow}$. Hence $\mathcal{E}_b \vdash t = t + s$ by Prop. 3.1.

Let $u = \sum\left\{\alpha_i \mid P_i \leftrightarrow_b Q \wedge (t \xrightarrow{\alpha_i} \vee \alpha_i = \tau)\right\}$ and $v = \sum\left\{\alpha_i \mid P_i \leftrightarrow_b Q \wedge t \xrightarrow{\alpha_i}\right\}$.
Then $\mathcal{E}_b \vdash t = t + v = t + s + v$.
For every summand $\alpha_i.P_i$ of P' with $P_i \leftrightarrow_b Q$, induction yields $\mathcal{E}_b \vdash \alpha_i.P_i = \alpha_i.Q$. Hence, using axiom A5 to assemble all such summands with $u \xrightarrow{\alpha_i}$, and possibly using A4 and/or A6 if there are no or only such summands, one infers that

$$\mathcal{E}_b \vdash P = s^*(u.Q + S)$$

where $S = \sum\left\{\alpha_i.P_i \mid P_i \not\leftrightarrow_b Q \vee (t \overset{\alpha_i}{\not\rightarrow} \wedge \alpha_i \neq \tau)\right\} + \sum_k x_k$.

Consider now a summand $\alpha_i.P_i$ of S. As $P \leftrightarrow_b Q$, the transition $P \xrightarrow{\alpha_i} P_i$ must be matched by a sequence $Q = Q_0 \xrightarrow{\tau} Q_1 \xrightarrow{\tau} \cdots \xrightarrow{\tau} Q_n \xrightarrow{(\alpha_i)} Q''$ with $P \leftrightarrow_b Q_n$ and $P_i \leftrightarrow_b Q''$. As condition B does not hold, using Lem. 2.2 it follows that $n = 0$.
Furthermore, the possibility $Q \xrightarrow{(\alpha_i)} Q \leftrightarrow_b P_i$ is ruled out by the construction of S. Hence, each summand $\alpha_i.P_i$ of S matches with a summand $\beta_j.Q_j$ of Q', in the sense that $\alpha_i = \beta_j$ and $P_i \leftrightarrow_b Q_j$. For each such pair of related summands, induction yields

$$\mathcal{E}_b \vdash \alpha_i.P_i = \alpha_i.Q_j = \beta_j.Q_j \ .$$

Moreover, each summand x_k of S must be a summand of Q'. Hence, possibly using axiom A3, it follows that $\mathcal{E}_b \vdash Q' = Q' + S$. Now I distinguish two sub-cases.

IIa Suppose that A does not hold for an index i with $\alpha_i = \tau$. Again using Lem. 2.2, it follows that every summand $\beta_j.Q_j$ of Q' matches with a summand $\alpha_i.P_i$ of S (since also B does not hold, the cases $Q_j \leftrightarrow_b P$ and $Q_j \leftrightarrow_b Q \leftrightarrow_b P$ do not apply), and every y_l is equal to an x_k. Possibly using axiom A3, it follows that $\mathcal{E}_b \vdash S = Q' + S = Q'$. Moreover, whenever $t \xrightarrow{a}$ then $Q \xrightarrow{a} Q$, so $P \xrightarrow{a} P'' \leftrightarrow_b Q$ and hence either $s \xrightarrow{a}$ or $v \xrightarrow{a}$. It follows that $\mathcal{E}_b \vdash t = s + v$. Finally $u = v$, so

$$\gamma.P = \gamma.s^*(v.Q + S) = \gamma.s^*(v.(s+v)^*S + S) \overset{\text{FA2}}{=} \gamma.(s+v)^*S = \gamma.Q.$$

IIb Suppose that A holds for an index i with $\alpha_i = \tau$. Then $\mathcal{E}_b \vdash u = \tau + v$, so

$$\begin{aligned}
\gamma.P &\overset{\text{A5}}{=} \gamma.s^*(\tau.Q + v.Q + S) \\
&= \gamma.s^*\Big(\tau.t^*\big(Q' + S\big) + v.t^*\big(Q' + S\big) + S\Big) \\
&\overset{\text{FA2}}{=} \gamma.s^*\left(\tau.s^*\Big(t.(s+t)^*\big(Q' + S\big) + Q' + S\Big) + v.t^*\big(Q' + S\big) + S\right) \\
&= \gamma.s^*\left(\tau.s^*\Big(Q' + (t+v).t^*\big(Q' + S\big) + S\Big) + v.t^*\big(Q' + S\big) + S\right) \\
&\overset{\text{FT2, A5}}{=} \gamma.s^*\Big(Q' + (t+v).t^*\big(Q' + S\big) + S\Big) \\
&\overset{\text{FA2}}{=} \gamma.t^*(Q' + S) \ = \ \gamma.Q.
\end{aligned}$$

The proof of the inductive step is now complete. □

Theorem 4.3 *Let $P, Q \in \mathbb{T}$. If $P \leftrightarrow_b^c Q$, then $\mathcal{E}_b \vdash P = Q$.*

Proof: Consider two process expressions P and Q that are branching congruent. Using the same technique as in the proof of Lem. 4.1, one may derive that

$$\mathcal{E}_b \vdash P = \sum\{\alpha_i.P_i \mid i \in I\} + \sum\{x_j \mid j \in J\} \quad \text{and}$$
$$\mathcal{E}_b \vdash Q = \sum\{\beta_k.Q_k \mid k \in K\} + \sum\{y_l \mid l \in L\}$$

for some finite index sets I, J, K, L. As $P \leftrightarrow_b^c Q$, it follows that

1. for every $i \in I$ there exists an index $k_i \in K$ such that $\alpha_i = \beta_{k_i}$ and $P_i \leftrightarrow_b Q_{k_i}$,
2. and for every $j \in J$ there exists an index $l_j \in L$ such that $x_j = y_{l_j}$.

By Propn. 4.2, for every $i \in I$ one may infer that

$$\mathcal{E}_b \vdash \alpha_i.P_i = \alpha_i.Q_{k_i} = \beta_{k_i}.Q_{k_i} \ .$$

Using A3 it follows immediately that $\mathcal{E}_b \vdash Q = P + Q$. By symmetry one obtains $\mathcal{E}_b \vdash P = P + Q = Q$. □

4.2 Completeness for η-, delay, and weak congruence

I now proceed to derive completeness results for η-, delay, and weak congruence from the ones for strong and branching congruence. The key to this derivation is the observation that, for certain classes of process expressions, these congruence relations coincide with $\leftrightarrow_s$ or $\leftrightarrow_b^c$. These classes of process expressions are defined below.

Definition 4.4 A term P is:

- *η-saturated* iff for each of its derivatives Q, R and S and $\xi \in A_\tau \cup \mathsf{Var}$ one has that:
$$Q \xrightarrow{\xi} R \xrightarrow{\tau} S \text{ implies } Q \xrightarrow{\xi} S.$$
- *d-saturated* iff for each of its derivatives Q, R and S and $\xi \in A_\tau \cup \mathsf{Var}$ one has that:
$$Q \xrightarrow{\tau} R \xrightarrow{\xi} S \text{ implies } Q \xrightarrow{\xi} S.$$
- *w-saturated* iff it is both η- and d-saturated.
- *strongly $\aleph$-saturated* (for $\aleph \in \{\eta, d, w\}$) if it is $\aleph$-saturated and for each of its proper derivatives $Q \in \mathsf{pder}(P)$ there is a *τ-loop* $Q \xrightarrow{\tau} Q$.

The following was first observed in [13] for process graphs.

Theorem 4.5

1. *If P and Q are $\aleph$-saturated, $\aleph \in \{\eta, d, w\}$, and $P \leftrightarrow_\aleph^c Q$, then $P \leftrightarrow_b^c Q$.*
2. *If P and Q are strongly $\aleph$-saturated, $\aleph \in \{d, w\}$, and $P \leftrightarrow_\aleph^c Q$, then $P \leftrightarrow_s Q$.*

Proof: In case 1, the relation

$$\mathcal{B} \stackrel{\text{def}}{=} \{(S,T) \mid S \leftrightarrow_\aleph T, \ \ S,T \ \aleph\text{-saturated}\}$$

is a branching bisimulation. From this it follows easily (as shown in [2]) that $P \leftrightarrow_\aleph^c Q$ implies $P \leftrightarrow_b^c Q$. In case 2, $\mathcal{B}$ is a strong bisimulation. □

Note that the second statement does not apply to $\leftrightarrow_\eta^c$. A counterexample concerns the terms $P = a.\tau^*\tau.\tau^*b.\tau^*0 + a.\tau^*b.\tau^*0$ and $Q = a.\tau^*b.\tau^*0$. These terms are strongly η-saturated and $P \leftrightarrow_\eta^c Q$, but $P \not\leftrightarrow_s Q$.

Theorem 4.6 *Let $\aleph \in \{\eta, d, w\}$.*

1. *For each term P, $\mathcal{E}_\aleph \vdash P = P'$ for some $\aleph$-saturated term P'.*
2. *For each term P, $\mathcal{E}_\aleph \vdash P = P''$ for some strongly $\aleph$-saturated term P''.*

Proof: The first statement has been shown in [2] for the language BCCS^{p*}. The resulting term P' has the form $P' = \sum_{i \in I} \alpha_i.P_i + \sum_{j \in J} x_j$. The same proof applies here.

For the second result, first prove P equal to a term P' as above, and bring the subterms P_i for $i \in I$ in normal form, using Lem. 4.1. Now each proper derivative of the resulting term has the form s^*Q, and appears in a subterm of the form $\alpha.s^*Q$. In combination with T1, the axiom FFIR derives $\alpha.s^*x = \alpha.(s+\tau)^*x$. As mentioned before, this law is also derivable from $\mathcal{E}_b$. Applying this law to all subterms of the form $\alpha.s^*Q$ results in a term P'' that is still $\aleph$-saturated, and for which each proper derivative Q has a τ-loop $Q \xrightarrow{\tau} Q$. □

The results in Thms. 4.5.1 and 4.6.1 effectively reduce the completeness problem for η-, delay, and weak congruence over $\mathbb{T}$ to that for branching congruence.

Corollary 4.7 *Let $\aleph \in \{\eta, d, w\}$. If $P \,\underline{\leftrightarrow}^c_\aleph\, Q$, then $\mathcal{E}_\aleph \vdash P = Q$.*

Proof (for the case $\aleph = \eta$): Suppose that $P \,\underline{\leftrightarrow}^c_\aleph\, Q$. Prove P and Q equal to $\aleph$-saturated processes P' and Q', respectively (Thm. 4.6.1). By the soundness of the axiom system $\mathcal{E}_\aleph$ (Propn. 3.2), P' and Q' are $\aleph$-congruent. It follows that P' and Q' are branching congruent (Thm. 4.5.1). Hence, by Thm. 4.3, $\mathcal{E}_b \vdash P' = Q'$. The claim now follows because $\mathcal{E}_b \subset \mathcal{E}_\eta$. □

The cases $\aleph = d$ and $\aleph = w$ can be proved in the same way, using in the last step that $\mathcal{E}_w \vdash \mathcal{E}_d \vdash \mathcal{E}_b \vdash P = Q$ (cf. the last sentence of Section 3). However, Thms. 4.5.2 and 4.6.2 allow a simpler proof that doesn't need the completeness result for branching bisimulation as an intermediate step, but instead reduces the problem to the completeness for strong congruence.

Proof of Corollary 4.7 (for the cases $\aleph \in \{d, w\}$): Suppose that $P \,\underline{\leftrightarrow}^c_\aleph\, Q$. Prove P and Q equal to strongly $\aleph$-saturated processes P' and Q', respectively (Thm. 4.6.2). By the soundness of the axiom system $\mathcal{E}_\aleph$ (Propn. 3.2), P' and Q' are $\aleph$-congruent. It follows that P' and Q' are strong congruent (Thm. 4.5.2). Hence, by Prop. 4.2 for strong congruence, $\mathcal{E}_s \vdash P' = Q'$. The claim now follows because $\mathcal{E}_s \subset \mathcal{E}_\aleph$. □

5 Prefix Iteration

In this section I derive complete axiomatizations for prefix iteration from the ones for flat iteration. A BCCS^{f*} process expression is a BCCS^{p*} expression iff in each subexpression $s.P$ or s^*P, the sumform s consists of a single action $\alpha \in A_\tau$. The following result about the expressiveness of BCCS^{p*} stems from [3].

Lemma 5.1 *If P_0 is a* BCCS^{p*} *expression and $P_n \Rightarrow\xrightarrow{a_n} P_{n+1}$ for $n = 0, 1, 2, ...$, then there is an N such that $a_n = a_N$ for $n > N$.*

Definition 5.2 A BCCS^{f*} expression P_0 is a *potential* BCCS^{p*} *expression* if every sequence $P_n \Rightarrow\xrightarrow{a_n} P_{n+1}$ $(n = 0, 1, 2, ...)$ has the property of Lem. 5.1.

It is easy to see that a potential BCCS^{p*} expression can not be weakly equivalent to an expression that is not so. Hence, using Propn. 3.2 (soundness):

Lemma 5.3 *Let $\aleph \in \{s, b, \eta, d, w\}$. If $\mathcal{E}_\aleph \vdash P = Q$ then either both P and Q are potential* BCCS^{p*} *expressions, or neither of them is.*

Using structural induction, the following Lemma is straightforward:

Lemma 5.4 *If s^*P is a subterm of a potential* BCCS^{p*} *expression, then either* A1–4 $\vdash s = 0$ *or* A1–4 $\vdash s = \alpha \in A_\tau$ *or* A1–4 $\vdash s = a + \tau$ *with $a \in A$. Moreover, these alternatives are mutually exclusive.*

Let R be the rewrite system consisting of the axioms A5, A6, FA1 and FT1, read from left to right. As these rewrite rules have no overlapping redexes, R is confluent, and it is equally straightforward to see that it is terminating. Now let φ be the operator on potential BCCS^{p*} expressions P that first converts any sumform s in a subterm s^*Q of P into one of the forms 0, α or $a + \tau$ (using A1–4 and Lem. 5.4), and subsequently brings the resulting term in normal form w.r.t. R. Note that the resulting term $\varphi(P)$ is a BCCS^{p*} expression.

Theorem 5.5 *Let $\aleph \in \{b, \eta, d, w\}$. The theory*

$$\varphi(\mathcal{E}_\aleph) = \{\varphi(P) = \varphi(Q) \mid (P = Q) \in \mathcal{E}_\aleph\}$$

is a complete axiomatization of $\underline{\leftrightarrow}^c_\aleph$ over the language BCCS^{p*}.

Proof: An equation $P = Q$ is provable in equational logic iff there exists a sequence $T_0, ..., T_n$ with $P = T_0$, $Q = T_n$, and the equation $T_{i-1} = T_i$ is obtained from one axiom by means of substitution, placement in a context and (possibly) symmetry $(i = 1, ..., n)$. Suppose that $P \underline{\leftrightarrow}^c_\aleph Q$ for certain BCCS^{p*} expressions P and Q. As P and Q are also BCCS^{f*} expressions, this implies $\mathcal{E}_\aleph \vdash P = Q$. Thus, by Lem. 5.3, there exists a proof-sequence as mentioned above in which all the T_i are potential BCCS^{p*} expressions. Now, for $i = 1, ..., n$, the equation $\varphi(T_{i-1}) = \varphi(T_i)$ can be obtained from an axiom in $\varphi(\mathcal{E}_\aleph)$ by means of substitution, placement in a context and symmetry. This yields a proof-sequence for the equation $\varphi(P) = \varphi(Q)$. However, since P and Q are BCCS^{p*} expressions, $\varphi(P) = P$ and $\varphi(Q) = Q$. Hence $\varphi(\mathcal{E}_\aleph) \vdash P = Q$. □

In the axiom systems $\varphi(\mathcal{E}_\aleph)$, the axioms A5, A6 and FA1 evaluate to identities, whereas the axioms A1–4, T1 and T3 remain unchanged. Furthermore, there are three axioms corresponding to each of FT1–3 and FFIR, depending on whether s evaluates to 0, α, or $a + \tau$, and nine corresponding to FA2, depending on how s and t evaluate. All resulting axiomatizations turn out to be derivable from the corresponding axiomatizations in [2] and vice versa. Hence the above constitutes an alternative proof of the completeness results in [2].

A similar result can be obtained for $\aleph = s$, but in that case τ should be treated as a normal action, and FT1 should be omitted from the rewrite system.

6 Parallelism

Complete axiomatizations of strong and weak bisimulation congruence over full CCS without recursion or iteration were given in [14]. The strategy, in both cases, was to prove every such CCS expression strongly equivalent to a BCCS expression, using the well known *expansion theorem*, and then apply the relevant completeness theorem for BCCS expressions. This method does not work in the setting of prefix iteration, as the parallel composition of two BCCS^{p*} expressions need not be (weakly) equivalent to a BCCS^{p*} expression. A simple counterexample concerns the expression $a^*0 \mid b^*0$, which is not a potential BCCS^{p*} expression in the sense of Def. 5.2. However, an expansion theorem for CCS^{f*} poses no problem: let $P = s^* \sum_{i\in I} \alpha_i.P_i$ and $Q = t^* \sum_{j\in J} \beta_j.Q_j$, then

$$P \mid Q \leftrightarrow_s (s+t+\gamma)^* \left(\sum_{i\in I} \alpha_i.(P_i \mid Q) + \sum_{j\in J} \beta_j.(P \mid Q_j) + C \right)$$

with

$$C = \sum_{\alpha_i = \overline{\beta_j}} \tau.(P_i \mid Q_j) + \sum_{i\in I,\ t \overset{\overline{\alpha_i}}{\rightarrow}} \tau.(P_i \mid Q) + \sum_{j\in J,\ s \overset{\overline{\beta_j}}{\rightarrow}} \tau.(P \mid Q_j)$$

and $\gamma = \begin{cases} \tau & \text{if there is an } a \in A \text{ with } s \overset{a}{\rightarrow} \text{ and } t \overset{\bar{a}}{\rightarrow} \\ 0 & \text{otherwise.} \end{cases}$

For a parallel composition without communication just leave out γ and C; in this shape the theorem was first found in [6].

In the presence of a CSP-style parallel composition in which processes are forced to synchronize over a shared alphabet [18], closed expressions with flat iteration can be expressed in terms of prefix iteration. An expression

$$(a+b)^*(c.P + d.Q)$$

for instance, in which c and d do not occur in P and Q, is strongly equivalent to

$$a^*(c.0 + d.0) \|_{\{c,d\}} b^*(c.P + d.Q)$$

where synchronization over c and d is enforced. In the general case renaming operators are needed as well.

Acknowledgment The inspiration to write this paper originated from the fruitful collaboration with Luca Aceto, Wan Fokkink and Anna Ingólfsdóttir in [2]. The referees are thanked for careful proofreading, and correcting the expansion theorem above.

References

[1] L. Aceto and J.F. Groote (1995), *A complete equational axiomatization for MPA with string iteration*, BRICS Research Report RS-95-28, Department of Mathematics and Computer Science, Aalborg University. Available by anonymous ftp from `ftp.daimi.aau.dk` in the directory `pub/BRICS/RS/95/28`.

[2] L. ACETO, W. FOKKINK, R. VAN GLABBEEK AND A. INGÓLFSDÓTTIR (1996), *Axiomatizing prefix iteration with silent steps*, I&C 127(1), pp. 26–40.

[3] L. ACETO AND A. INGÓLFSDÓTTIR (1996), *An equational axiomatization of observation congruence for prefix iteration*, in Proc. AMAST '96, Munich, Germany, M. Wirsing and M. Nivat, eds., LNCS 1101, Springer-Verlag, pp. 195–209.

[4] J. BAETEN, J. BERGSTRA AND J. KLOP (1987), *On the consistency of Koomen's fair abstraction rule*, TCS 51, pp. 129–176.

[5] T. BASTEN (1996), *Branching bisimilarity is an equivalence indeed!*, IPL 58(3), pp. 141–147.

[6] J. BERGSTRA, I. BETHKE AND A. PONSE (1994), *Process algebra with iteration and nesting*, Computer Journal 37, pp. 243–258. Originally appeared as report P9314, Programming Research Group, University of Amsterdam, 1993.

[7] J. BERGSTRA AND J. KLOP (1984), *The algebra of recursively defined processes and the algebra of regular processes*, in Proceedings 11th ICALP, Antwerpen, J. Paredaens, ed., LNCS 172, Springer-Verlag, pp. 82–95.

[8] F. CORRADINI, R. DE NICOLA AND A. LABELLA (1995), *Fully abstract models for nondeterministic Kleene algebras (extended abstract)*, in Proc. CONCUR 95, Philadelphia, I. Lee and S. Smolka, eds., LNCS 962, Springer-Verlag, pp. 130–144.

[9] W. FOKKINK (1994), *A complete equational axiomatization for prefix iteration*, IPL 52, pp. 333–337.

[10] W. FOKKINK (1996), *A complete axiomatization for prefix iteration in branching bisimulation*, Fundamenta Informaticae 26, pp. 103–113.

[11] W. FOKKINK AND H. ZANTEMA (1994), *Basic process algebra with iteration: Completeness of its equational axioms*, Computer Journal 37, pp. 259–267.

[12] R. V. GLABBEEK (1995), *Branching bisimulation as a tool in the analysis of weak bisimulation*. Available at `ftp://boole.stanford.edu/pub/DVI/tool.dvi.gz`.

[13] R. V. GLABBEEK AND W. WEIJLAND (1996), *Branching time and abstraction in bisimulation semantics*, JACM 43(3), pp. 555–600.

[14] M. HENNESSY AND R. MILNER (1985), *Algebraic laws for nondeterminism and concurrency*, JACM 32, pp. 137–161.

[15] S. KLEENE (1956), *Representation of events in nerve nets and finite automata*, in Automata Studies, C. Shannon and J. McCarthy, eds., Princeton University Press, pp. 3–41.

[16] R. MILNER (1989), *Communication and Concurrency*, Prentice-Hall.

[17] R. MILNER (1989), *A complete axiomatisation for observational congruence of finite-state behaviours*, I&C 81, pp. 227–247.

[18] E.-R. OLDEROG AND C.A.R. HOARE (1986), *Specification-oriented semantics for communicating processes*, Acta Informatica 23, pp. 9–66.

[19] P. SEWELL (1994), *Bisimulation is not finitely (first order) equationally axiomatisable*, in Proc. 9th LICS, Paris, IEEE Computer Society Press, pp. 62–70.

Probabilistic Concurrent Constraint Programming

Vineet Gupta * Radha Jagadeesan ** Vijay Saraswat ***

Abstract. We extend cc to allow the specification of a discrete probability distribution for random variables. We demonstrate the expressiveness of pcc by synthesizing combinators for default reasoning. We extend pcc uniformly over time, to get a synchronous reactive probabilistic programming language, Timed pcc. We describe operational and denotational models for pcc (and Timed pcc). The key feature of the denotational model(s) is that parallel composition is essentially set intersection. We show that the denotational model of pcc (resp. Timed pcc) is conservative over cc (resp. tcc). We also show that the denotational models are fully abstract for an operational semantics that records probability information.

1 Introduction

Concurrent constraint programming (CCP, [Sar93]) is an approach to computation which uses constraints for the compositional specification of concurrent systems. It replaces the traditional notion of a store as a valuation of variables with the notion of a store as a constraint on the possible values of variables. Computation progresses by accumulating constraints in the store, and by checking whether the store entails constraints. A salient aspect of the cc computation model is that programs may be thought of as imposing constraints on the evolution of the system. cc provides four basic constructs: (tell) a (for a a primitive constraint), parallel composition (A, B), positive ask (**if** a **then** A) and hiding (**new** X **in** A). The program a imposes the constraint a. The program (A, B) imposes the constraints of both A and B — logically, this is the conjunction of A and B. **new** X **in** A imposes the constraints of A, but hides the variable X from the other programs — logically, this can be thought of as a form of existential quantification. The program **if** a **then** A reduces to A as and when the store entails a — logically, this is an (intuitionistic) implication.

A primary domain of applicability for CCP ideas is the compositional modeling of physical systems [FBB+94, FS95, GSS95]. To handle reactive systems, such as controllers for reprographics system components such as paper-feed mechanisms, CCP was extended in [SJG94] to handle discrete time. The basic idea was to adapt to CCP the Synchrony Hypothesis of Berry et al: Time is measured by the sequence of instantaneous interactions that the program has with its environment. The need to handle interrupts instantaneously (e.g., a paper jam causing power to be interrupted) rather than at the next occasion when the environment interacts with the system was handled by introducing a

* Xerox PARC, 3333 Coyote Hill Road, Palo Alto Ca 94304; vgupta@parc.xerox.com
** Department of Mathematics, Loyola University-Lake Shore Campus, Chicago IL 60626. radha@math.luc.edu
*** AT & T Research, 180 Park Avenue, Florham Park, NJ 07932; vj@research.att.com

new idea [SJG]: a combinator (**if** a **else** A) which triggers A on the *absence* of e, that is under the assumption that e has not been produced in the store, and will not be produced throughout system execution at the present time instant. This causes the input-output relation of processes to be possibly non-monotonic but [SJG] presents a simple denotational model. The resulting theory is considerably smoother and enables the extension to hybrid systems in [GJS], which is necessary to handle continuously varying components such as variable-speed motors.

This entire conceptual framework is based, however, on the assumption that enough information will be available to model a given physical system in as accurate detail as is needed so that appropriate causal, determinate constraint-based models can be constructed. However, this assumption is violated in many physical situations — it becomes necessary to work with approximate, incomplete or uncertain information. We consider three paradigmatic examples. Consider first a telephony system that has to respond to alarms being generated from another complicated system that may only be available as a black-box. A natural model to consider for the black-box is a stochastic one, which represents the timing and duration of the alarm by random variables with some given probability distribution. Consider next situations in which it becomes necessary to model the system stochastically: for instance, not enough may be known about the mechanisms controlling wear-and-tear of rollers so that the actual departure time of a sheet of paper from a worn roller may have to be approximated by a suitably chosen distribution of a random variable. It becomes necessary then to compute system response in a setting in which system models and inputs may behave stochastically. Third, consider model-based diagnosis settings. Often information is available about *failure models* and their associated probabilities, for instance from field studies and studies of manufacturing practices. Failure models can be incorporated by assigning a variable, typically called the *mode* of the component to represent the physical state of the component, and associating a failure model with each value of the mode variable. Probabilistic information can be incorporated by letting the mode vary according to the given probability distribution [dKW89]. The computational task at hand becomes the calculation of the most probable diagnostic hypothesis, given observations about the current state of the system.

In this paper we develop the underlying theory for (timed) *probabilistic* cc — (timed) cc augmented with the ability to describe stochastic inputs and system components - thereby making it possible to address the phenomena above within CCP. Our basic move is to allow the introduction of (discrete) random variables (RVs) with a given probability distribution. A run of the system will choose a value for an RV, with the given probability; these probability values accumulate as more and more choices are made in the course of the run. Alternate choices lead to alternate runs, with their own accumulated probability values. Inconsistencies between chosen values of RVs and constraints in the store lead to some runs being dropped. Now the possibly multiple consistent (normalized) outcomes of the various runs can be declared as the probabilistic outputs of the program. The extension to timed pcc is done in exactly the same way as the extension of cc to `tcc` [SJG94], using the Synchrony Hypothesis.

Probabilistic cc. In more detail we proceed as follows. We add a single combinator **new** (r, f) **in** A where r is a variable, f is its probability mass function, and A is an agent. Intuitively, such an expression is executed by making a choice for the r according to the mass function f.

Example 1. Consider the program:

$$\textbf{new}\ (r, f : f(0) = f(1) = f(2) = f(3) = 0.25)\ \textbf{in}\ [\textbf{if}\ r = 0\ \textbf{then}\ a, \textbf{if}\ r = 1\ \textbf{then}\ b]$$

On input `true`, this program can produce outputs a, b or `true`. The probability of a being the output is .25; similarly for b. The probability of the output `true` is .5.

Random variables, like any other variables, may be constrained. These constraints may cause portions of the space of the joint probability distribution to be eliminated due to inconsistency.

Example 2. Consider the program below, with the same f as before, and with the constraint $r \in \{0, 1\}$ interpreted as " r is 0 or 1" [HSD92].

$$\textbf{new}\ (r, f)\ \textbf{in}\ [\textbf{if}\ r = 0\ \textbf{then}\ a, \textbf{if}\ r = 1\ \textbf{then}\ b, r \in \{0, 1\}]$$

On input `true`, this program will produce outputs a or b; `true` is not a valid output, because of the constraint $r \in \{0, 1\}$. Each of the two execution paths are associated with the number 0.25 because of f; however to compute the probability of each path, we must normalize these numbers with the sum of the numbers associated with all successful execution paths. This yields the probability $0.5 = (0.25/(0.25+0.25))$ for each path.

We make the following further assumptions on RVs (such as r in the above program)

1. RVs are uniquely associated with probability distributions — this is achieved syntactically by requiring that the probability distribution be imposed when the variable is declared.
2. Distinct RVs are assumed to be independent — correlations between RVs, *i.e.* joint probability distributions, are achieved by constraints.

Example 3. Consider the program (with f as before):

$$[\textbf{new}\ (r, f)\ \textbf{in}\ x = r], [\textbf{new}\ (r', f)\ \textbf{in}\ [\textbf{if}\ r' \in \{0, 1\}\ \textbf{then}\ x = r']]$$

The first agent causes the generation of four execution paths, each with associated number 0.25. For each of these, the second generates four more; however paths corresponding to six choices for $r \times r'$ are ruled out. Consequently the following results (with associated probabilities) are obtained: $x = 0(0.3), x = 1(0.3), x = 2(0.2), x = 3(0.2)$.

The presence of RVs such as above allows us to construct program combinators reminiscent of combinators that detect "negative information" in synchronous programming languages [Hal93, BB91, Har87, SJG].

Example 4. Consider the program

$$\textbf{new}\ (r, g : g(0) = \epsilon, g(1) = (1-\epsilon))\ \textbf{in}\ [\textbf{if}\ a\ \textbf{then}\ r = 0, \textbf{if}\ r = 1\ \textbf{then}\ b]$$

This program on input `true` produces constraint b with probability $(1-\epsilon)$ and `true` with probability ϵ. On input a the program results in a with probability 1. Thus, this program can be thought of as **if** a **else** $_{(1-\epsilon)}$ b *i.e.* if a is not present, produce b with probability $(1-\epsilon)$. Note however that if a is present, b is *not* produced. Note that the same result can be obtained by running n-fold parallel composition of $\epsilon = 0.5$ components, for arbitrarily large n.

In essence, we have used the RV to set up a very high expectation that b will be produced; however, this expectation can be categorically denied on the production of a since the entire probability mass is shifted to the hitherto low end possibility. The construct can be generalized to arbitrary agents A by:

$$\textbf{if}\ a\ \textbf{else}\ _{(1-\epsilon)}A \stackrel{d}{=} \textbf{new}\ X\ \textbf{in}\ [\textbf{if}\ a\ \textbf{else}\ _{(1-\epsilon)}\ X, \textbf{if}\ X\ \textbf{then}\ A]$$

Note however, that the program **if** a **else** $_{1-\epsilon}b$, **if** b **else** $_{1-\epsilon}a$ is determinately probabilistic [MMS96] rather than *indeterminate*: assuming ϵ is very small, it produces on input `true` the distribution $(a, 0.5), (b, 0.5)$, rather than producing either a or b indeterminately.

Example 5 Probabilistic Or. The probabilistic choice operator of [JP89], $P +_r Q$, can be defined as follows:

$$\textbf{new}\ (X, f : (f(0) = r, f(1) = (1-r)))\ \textbf{in}\ (\textbf{if}\ X = 0\ \textbf{then}\ P, \textbf{if}\ X = 1\ \textbf{then}\ Q)$$

$P +_r Q$ reduces to P with probability r and to Q with probability $(1-r)$. [JP89] require that this operator satisfies the laws of commutativity, associativity and absorption ($P +_r P = P$); this will be the case in the model we now develop.

What is a model for pcc*?* We briefly review the model for cc programs, referring the reader to [SRP91] for details. An observation of a cc program A is a store u in which it is quiescent, i.e. running A in the store u adds no further information to the store. Formally we define the relation $A \downarrow^u$, read as *A converges on u* or *A is quiescent on u*, with the evident axioms:

$$\frac{a \in u}{a \downarrow^u} \quad \frac{A_1 \downarrow^u \quad A_2 \downarrow^u}{(A_1, A_2) \downarrow^u} \quad \frac{c \notin u}{(\textbf{if}\ c\ \textbf{then}\ A) \downarrow^u} \quad \frac{A \downarrow^u}{(\textbf{if}\ c\ \textbf{then}\ A) \downarrow^u} \quad \frac{A \downarrow^v \quad \exists_X u = \exists_X v}{(\textbf{new}\ X\ \textbf{in}\ A) \downarrow^u}$$

The denotation of a program A can be taken to be the set of all u such that $A \downarrow^u$. The semantics is compositional since the axioms above are compositional, i.e. the convergence of A on u depends only upon the convergence of the sub-programs of A on u. The output of A on any given input a is now the least u containing a on which A converges. This immediately tells us that the set denoting A must be closed under $\sqcap$. Such a set is called a *closure operator*. It is easy to adjust this view in the presence of divergence, where divergence may arise because of infinite execution sequences or inconsistency of generated constraints [SRP91]. In essence, the denotation becomes a *partial* closure operator, characterized by sets of constraints closed under *non-empty* glbs.

We turn now to pcc. We make two crucial observations. First, note that an RV-valuation (i.e., an assignment of values to hidden RVs) reduces a pcc program to a cc program, which can be represented as a set of its quiescent points. Consider Example 4. The choice of r as 0 yields the fixed-point set $\{\mathtt{true}, a, b, a \wedge b\}$. Similarly the choice of r as 1 yields $\{b\}$ — this is the fixed-point set of a partial closure operator undefined on a.

One might consider, then, the denotation of a pcc process to be a set of pairs (c, p) where c is a fixed-point, and p is the sum of the probabilities associated with the RV-valuations which realize c, that is, for which c is a fixed-point. However, from just this information it is not possible to recover the fixed-point *set* generated by an RV-valuation; hence it is necessary to record correlations explicitly. That is, for an arbitrary set of fixed-points X, record (the sum of the probabilities associated with) those valuations on RVs for which all elements of X are fixed-points. Technically, this is best done by associating with the set S of fixed-points a probability lattice, defined formally in Section 2.2, which associates a probability with each element in the freely-generated complete and completely distributive lattice (= free profinite lattice, [Joh82]) on S. A process P can then be taken to be a pair (P_A, P_C) where P_A is a set of constraints, and P_C a probability lattice on P_A; P must satisfy conditions that ensure that it is "generable" from a program, intuitively, that it is possible to recover from it a (finite) set of (partial) closure operators, namely those generated by the reduction of the given program under different RV-valuations.

Thus for instance the program in Example 4 has the fixed-point set $\{\mathtt{true}, a, b, a \wedge b\}$. The probability lattice associated with this process yields 0.5 for $\mathtt{true}$, a, $a \wedge b$ and 1 for b; 0.5 for the collection $\{\mathtt{true}, a, a \wedge b, b\}$ (since each element in this set is a fixed-point for the RV-valuation $X = 0$, which has probability 0.5); 0.5 for the collection $\{a, b\}$ etc.

The resulting model has the following key properties: (1) parallel composition is essentially set intersection (Section 2.3); (2) there is a natural embedding of the space of cc processes into the space of pcc processes (Section 2.3); (3) it is fully abstract with respect to a notion of observation that includes probabilities (Section 2.5).

Timed pcc arises from pcc by the integration of a notion of time. This allows the representation of (possibly probabilistic) timed reactive systems. We use the same mechanism to extend pcc that was used to extend Default cc to Default tcc in [SJG]. At each time step the computation executed is a pcc program. Computation progresses in cycles: input a constraint from the environment, compute to quiescence and compute the program to be executed at subsequent time instants.

As for Default tcc we add to the untimed pcc a single temporal control construct: **hence** A. Declaratively, **hence** A imposes the "constraints" of A at every time instant after the current one. Operationally, if **hence** A is invoked at time t, a new copy of A is invoked at each instant in $t' > t$. As shown in [SJG] **hence** can combine with ask operations to yield rich patterns of temporal evolution. In particular, Timed pcc satisfies probabilistic variants of following key features of synchronous programming languages: (1) The notion of time is *multiform* — any signal can serve as the notion of time. (2) All the ESTEREL-style combinators, including (the probabilistic versions of) the strong preemption combinators such as "`do A watching a`", are expressible.

The construction of the denotational model of Timed pcc from pcc follows the idea that "processes are relations extended over time" ([Abr93, Abr94]). Formally, the construction follows the definition of the Default tcc model from the Default cc model described in [SJG]. Consequently, the model for Timed pcc "inherits" the good formal properties of pcc (Section 3): (1) Parallel composition is essentially set intersection in this model; (2) The Timed pcc model is conservative over the `tcc` model of [SJG94]; (3) The Timed pcc model is fully abstract.

Related work The role of probability has been extensively studied in the context of several models of concurrency. Typically, these studies have involved a marriage of a concurrent computation model with a model of probability. For example, stochastic Petri nets [Mar89, VN92] add Markov chains to the underlying Petri net model. Similarly probabilistic process algebras add a notion of randomness to the underlying process algebra model. This theory is well developed and is primarily about the interaction between probability and non-determinism, see for example [HJ90, vGSST90, JY95, LS91, HS86, CSZ92]. These studies have been carried out in the traditional framework of semantic theories of process algebras, *e.g.* theories of (probabilistic) testing, relationship with (probabilistic) temporal logics etc.

We start with the underlying concurrent model being cc. Inspired by [BLFG95], we build an integrated treatment of probability and the underlying concurrent programming paradigm. This is revealed in the dual roles played by the underlying cc paradigm. In addition to being utilized in the specification of system (this is similar to the use of the Petri nets/process algebras in the above approaches), the cc paradigm is exploited to build and specify joint probability distributions of several variables (as illustrated in earlier examples). Furthermore, our model remains determinately probablistic.

The development of probabilistic frameworks in knowledge representation has been extensive [Pea88]. It is easy to see how to express the joint probability distributions of Bayesian networks within pcc, e.g. by associating a random variable for each row in the joint conditional dependence matrix for each node in the network. In this sense, pcc provides a simple but powerful notation for Bayesian networks. It also seems feasible to represent probabilistic Dempster-Shafer rules of the form "If it is Sunday, John will go to the baseball game" with a given strength (say 0.8) as the agent:

$$\textbf{if } \mathit{sunday}(\mathit{today}) \textbf{ then new } (x, f : f(1) = 0.8, f(0) = 0.2) \textbf{ in}$$
$$\textbf{if } x = 1 \textbf{ then } \mathit{will\_go}(\mathit{john}, \mathit{bgame})$$

However, pcc does not allow the direct manipulation of conditional probability assertions e.g. `p(fly(tweety) | bird(tweety)) = 0.9` as in the logics of [Nil86, FJM90].

2 Model for Probabilistic cc

2.1 Constraint systems with discrete random variables

A constraint system with discrete random variables extends the usual notion of constraint systems with special variables called random variables, that can take values from non-negative integers $\mathbb{N}$. Such constraint systems have an explicit notion of inconsistencies of random variables.

Such a constraint system $\mathcal{D}$ is a system of partial information, consisting of a set of primitive constraints (first-order formulas) or *tokens* D, closed under conjunction and existential quantification, and an inference relation (logical entailment) $\vdash$ that relates tokens to tokens. We use $a, b, \ldots$ to range over tokens. The entailment relation induces through symmetric closure the logical equivalence relation, $\approx$.

Definition 1. A *constraint system with random variables* is a structure $\langle D, \vdash, \mathbf{Var}, \mathbf{RandVar} \subseteq \mathbf{Var}, \{\exists_X \mid X \in \mathbf{Var}\}, \mathtt{false} \in D\rangle$ such that:

1. D is closed under conjunction($\wedge$); $\vdash \subseteq D \times D$ satisfies:
   (a) $(\forall a)\,[\mathtt{false} \vdash a]$
   (b) Identity: $a \vdash a$, $\quad a \vdash a'$ and $a' \wedge a'' \vdash b$ imply that $a \wedge a'' \vdash b$.
   (c) Conjunction: $a \wedge b \vdash a$, $a \wedge b \vdash b$, $a \vdash b_1$ and $a \vdash b_2$ implies that $a \vdash b_1 \wedge b_2$.
2. $\mathbf{Var}$ is an infinite set of *variables*, such that for each variable $X \in \mathbf{Var}$, $\exists_X : D \to D$ is an operation satisfying usual laws on existentials:

$$a \vdash \exists_X a,\ \exists_X(a \wedge \exists_X b) \approx \exists_X a \wedge \exists_X b,\ \exists_X \exists_Y a \approx \exists_Y \exists_X a,\ a \vdash b \Rightarrow \exists_X a \vdash \exists_X b.$$

3. $\mathbf{RandVar}$ is a set of *random variables* satisfying:
   (a) $(\forall r \in \mathbf{RandVar})\ (\forall i \in \mathbb{N})\ [r = i \in D]$.
   (b) $(\forall r \in \mathbf{RandVar})\ (\forall i, j \in \mathbb{N})\ [i \neq j \text{ implies } (r = i) \wedge (r = j) \vdash \mathtt{false}]$
4. $\vdash$ is decidable.

The last condition is necessary to have an effective operational semantics.

A *constraint* is an entailment closed subset of D. For any set of tokens S, we let $\overline{S}$ stand for the constraint $\{a \in D \mid \exists\{a_1, \ldots, a_k\} \subseteq S.\ a_1 \wedge \ldots \wedge a_k \vdash a\}$. For any token a, $\overline{a}$ is just the constraint $\overline{\{a\}}$. The set of constraints, written $|D|$, ordered by inclusion($\subseteq$), forms a complete algebraic lattice with least upper bounds induced by $\wedge$, least element $\mathtt{true} = \{a \mid \forall b \in D.\ b \vdash a\}$ and greatest element $\mathtt{false} = \overline{\mathtt{false}} = D$. Reverse inclusion is written $\supseteq$. $\exists, \vdash$ lift to operations on constraints.

An example of such a system is the system FD [HSD92]. In this system, variables are assumed to range over finite domains. In addition to tokens representing equality of variables, there are tokens that that restrict the range of a variable to some finite set.

In the rest of this paper we will assume that we are working in some constraint system $\langle D, \vdash, \mathbf{Var}, \mathbf{RandVar}, \{\exists_X \mid X \in \mathbf{Var}\}, \mathtt{false}\rangle$. We will let $a, b \ldots$ range over D. We use $u, v, w \ldots$ to range over constraints.

2.2 Modeling probability information

We model probability information using probability lattices. Given a set A let $L(A)$ be the free profinite lattice generated by it. In the following definition, one should think of A as the fixed-point set of constraints, and think of C as mapping each $x \in L(A)$ to the sum of the probabilities associated with the RV-valuations realizing x, where an RV-valuation is considered to realize $\bigvee\{x_i\}$ if it realizes some x_i and realize $\bigwedge\{x_i\}$ if it realizes each x_i. For instance, with this interpretation, the modularity condition below is seen to correspond to taking the union of two overlapping sets.

Definition 2. A probability lattice C on A is a function from $L(A) \rightarrow [0,1]$ satisfying:

Monotonicity: $x \leq y \Rightarrow C(x) \leq C(y)$.
Join Continuity: If $\{x_i\}$ is a directed set then $C(\vee x_i) = \sup C(x_i)$.
Meet Continuity: If $\{x_i\}$ is a filter then $C(\wedge_i x_i) = \inf C(x_i)$.
Normality: $C(\vee A) = 1$.
Modularity: $C(x \vee y) = C(x) + C(y) - C(x \wedge y)$.
Extensionality: If $C(x) = C(x') = C(x \vee x')$, then $(\forall y)\ [C(x \vee y) = C(x' \vee y)]$.

In what follows we will find useful the following definitions: For a probability lattice C on A, define $u \preceq_C v$ if $C(u) = C(u \vee v)$; intuitively, the set of RV-valuations realizing u is contained in the set of RV-valuations realizing v. Let $\equiv_C$ be the associated symmetric closure. Note that by extensionality, $\equiv_C$ is an equivalence relation. Say that $S \subseteq A$ is *C-consistent* if $C(\bigwedge S) > 0$; intuitively there is at least one RV-valuation that jointly realizes every element of a consistent set. Note that to specify a probability lattice f on A, it is enough to specify the values of f on all finite meets (or joins) of A; such an f can be uniquely extended (via monotonicity, continuity, modularity and extensionality) to a map on $L(A)$.
We define the following operations on probability lattice.

Quotient. Suppose C is a probability lattice on A, and $h : A \rightarrow B$ is a function. If $C(\vee(h^{-1}(B))$ is greater than 0, define $\frac{C}{h}$, the *quotient* of C by h, as follows. For b in the image of h, let $h^{-1}(y) = \bigvee\{x \in A \mid h(x) = y\}$ and freely extend it to the lattice $L(h(A))$ by $h^{-1}(y \wedge y') = h^{-1}(y) \wedge h^{-1}(y')$ and so on. (Alternatively we could have extended h to a homomorphism between $L(A)$ and $L(h(A))$, and then defined h^{-1}.) We can *quotient* C to a probability lattice C' on $h(A)$, by defining $C'(b) = C(h^{-1}(b))$. C' inherits monotonicity, modularity and extensionality from h^{-1}. Multiplying all values of $C'(b)$ by $\frac{1}{C(\vee h^{-1}(B))}$ normalizes the resulting probability lattice.

Expansion. Suppose C is a probability lattice on B, and $h : A \rightarrow B$ is a partial function. If $C(\vee h(A)) > 0$, define $C' = \mathtt{Exp}(C, h)$, the *expansion* of C by h, as follows. C' is a probability lattice on $\mathsf{dom}(h)$ (the domain of h) given by $C'(x) = C(h(x)), C'(\vee\{x_i\}) = C(\vee\{h(x_i)\}), C'(\wedge\{x_i\}) = C(\wedge\{h(x_i)\})$ etc. Multiplying all values of $C'(a)$ by $\frac{1}{C(\vee h(A))}$ normalizes the resulting probability lattice.

Product. The *product* of two probability lattices C_1 on A_1 and C_2 on A_2 is a probability lattice C on $A_1 \times A_2$. $C(\langle x, y\rangle) = C_1(x) \times C_2(y)$ for $\langle x, y\rangle \in A_1 \times A_2$. Similarly $C(\langle x, y\rangle \wedge \langle x', y'\rangle) = C_1(x \wedge x') \times C_2(y \wedge y')$; use modularity and continuity to define C on all elements of $L(A_1 \times A_2)$.

We can now define a process:

Definition 3 Process. A pcc *process* P is a pair (P_A, P_C) where $P_A \subseteq |D| - \{\mathtt{false}\}$ and P_C is a probability lattice on P_A that satisfies the following conditions:

Consistency: For every $u \in P_A$, $\{u\}$ is P_C-consistent, i.e. $P_C(u) > 0$.
Glb-closure: For every P_C-consistent subset S of P_A, $\sqcap S \in P_A$ and $\sqcap S \preceq_{P_C} \bigwedge S$.
Finiteness: The number of $\equiv_{P_C}$-equivalence classes are finite.

The first condition ensures that every fixed-point is consistent (generated by at least one RV-valuation). The second forces every P_C-consistent set S of fixed-points to have a glb that is realized by at least every RV-valuation which realizes S; this ensures that every P_C-consistent set of fixed-points can be consistently extended to the range of a closure operator. The third condition forces finiteness of the total number of possible closure operators that can thus be generated.

2.3 Semantics of combinators

Tell. $\mathcal{P}[\![c]\!]_A \stackrel{d}{=} \{u \in |D| \mid c \in u\}$. $\mathcal{P}[\![c]\!]_C$ is the constant function 1.

Ask. $\mathcal{P}[\![\textbf{if } c \textbf{ then } A]\!]_A \stackrel{d}{=} \{u \in |D| \mid c \in u \Rightarrow u \in \mathcal{P}[\![A]\!]_A\}$. If $c \notin u$, then $\mathcal{P}[\![\textbf{if } c \textbf{ then } A]\!]_C(u) = 1$, otherwise $\mathcal{P}[\![\textbf{if } c \textbf{ then } A]\!]_C(u) = \mathcal{P}[\![A]\!]_C(u)$. This is extended to the rest of the lattice in the usual way.

Parallel Composition. $\mathcal{P}[\![A_1, A_2]\!]_A \stackrel{d}{=} \mathcal{P}[\![A_1]\!]_A \cap \mathcal{P}[\![A_2]\!]_A$. The probability lattice is defined as $\texttt{Exp}(\mathcal{P}[\![A_1]\!]_C \times \mathcal{P}[\![A_2]\!]_C, \Delta)$ where $\Delta : |D| \rightarrow |D| \times |D|$ is the diagonal function.

Hiding. $\mathcal{P}[\![\textbf{new } X \textbf{ in } A]\!]_A \stackrel{d}{=} \{u \in |D| \mid \exists v \in \mathcal{P}[\![A]\!], \exists_X u = \exists_X v\}$. The probability lattice is defined as $\texttt{Exp}(\frac{\mathcal{P}[\![A]\!]_C}{\exists_X}, \exists_X)$, where $\exists_X : |D| \rightarrow |D|$ is the existential function on constraints from the given constraint system.

Distributions. Let f be a probability lattice of the domain of X[4]. Define $\texttt{Distr}(X, f)_A = \{u \in |D| \mid \exists r.(X = r) \in u, f(r) > 0\}$ and $\texttt{Distr}(X, f)_C = \texttt{Exp}(f, h)$, where $h : \texttt{Distr}(X, f)_A \rightarrow f$, and $h(u) = r$ if $(X = r) \in u$.

Now $\mathcal{P}[\![\textbf{new } (X, f) \textbf{ in } A]\!] \stackrel{d}{=} \mathcal{P}[\![\textbf{new } X \textbf{ in } (\texttt{Distr}(X, f), P)]\!]$.

Conservativity results. Let A be a cc program. Then, $\mathcal{P}[\![A]\!] = (Q, C)$, where Q is the set of quiescent points of A and C is the constant function 1. Conservativity of pcc over cc follows immediately.

2.4 Operational semantics

We define a transition relation to give the operational semantics of pcc programs, and then show that this operational semantics is equivalent to the denotational semantics. The transition relation is similar to the transition relation for cc. We assume that the program is operating in isolation —interaction with the environment can be coded as an observation and run in parallel with the program. A configuration is a multiset of agents Γ. $\sigma(\Gamma)$ is the lub of the tell constraints in Γ.

$$\frac{\sigma(\Gamma) \vdash a}{\Gamma, \textbf{if } a \textbf{ then } B \longrightarrow \Gamma, B} \qquad \Gamma, (A, B) \longrightarrow \Gamma, A, B$$

$$\Gamma, \textbf{new } X \textbf{ in } A \longrightarrow \Gamma, A[Y/X] \quad (Y \text{ not free in } \Gamma)$$

$$\frac{f(r) > 0}{\Gamma, \textbf{new } (X, f) \textbf{ in } A \longrightarrow \Gamma, Y = r, A[Y/X] \quad (Y \text{ not free in } \Gamma)}$$

[4] A probability mass function on a finite set extends to a probability lattice structure.

Consider $\{\Gamma_i \mid A, a \longrightarrow^* \Gamma_i \not\longrightarrow, \sigma(\Gamma_i) \not\approx \texttt{false}\}$. Define a probability lattice C on Γ_i by setting $C(\Gamma_i) = \Pi_{\mathbf{Y}} f_Y(r_Y)$, where the $\mathbf{Y}$ is the set of new variables introduced by the last rule, $Y = r_Y \in \Gamma_i$, and f_Y is the probability distribution corresponding to Y. $C(\Gamma_i \wedge \Gamma_j) = 0$, so we get a probability lattice by modularity and normalization.

The output of a process P on an input a, denoted $\texttt{OpsemIO}(P, a)$ is

$$\{\exists_{\mathbf{Y}}\sigma(\Gamma) \mid P, a \longrightarrow^* \Gamma \not\longrightarrow, \sigma(\Gamma) \not\approx \texttt{false}, \mathbf{Y} \text{ new vars in derivation}\}$$

with the probability lattice structure given by $\frac{C}{h}$, where $h(\Gamma) = \exists_{\mathbf{Y}}\sigma(\Gamma)$.

The operational semantics of a process P, denoted $\texttt{Opsem}(P)$ is a pair (P_A, P_C) where P_A is the set of quiescent points of the process P, *i.e*

$$P_A = \{c \mid P, a \longrightarrow^* \Gamma \not\longrightarrow, \exists_{\mathbf{Y}}\sigma(\Gamma) = c, \mathbf{Y} \text{ new vars in derivation}\}$$

P_C is the natural probability lattice structure on P_A induced by the valuations of (hidden) random variables correspoding to each quiescent point.

2.5 Correspondence Theorems

The key ingredient of the correspondence theorems relating the operational and denotational semantics is a representation theorem on pcc processes, sketched below. We show that each process corresponds to a set of closure operators with associated probability, and conversely, given such a set, we can recover a process.

Let P be a process. A *consistent closure operator* (cco) of P is any P_C-consistent subset of P closed under glbs of non-empty subsets. Note that to every cco S there corresponds at least one RV-valuation jointly realizing S. However, it could be that the valuation also realizes other constraints, that is, it realizes a cco $T \supset S$. Intuitively, the cco's exhibited by P are going to be those cco's S for which there is an RV-valuation realizing S and not any cco $T \supset S$. Such cco's can be determined as follows. Let $p(S) = P_C(\bigwedge S) - P_C(\bigvee\{\bigwedge T \mid T \supset S\})$. If $p(S) > 0$ then S is an exhibited cco. The probability of S is $p(S)$.

Conversely, given a set Z of closure operators, each associated with a probability $p : Z \to [0, 1]$, we can recover a process P as follows. $P_A = \bigcup\{S \mid S \in Z\}$. P_C is defined as follows. For any finite subset V of P_A, let $P_C(\wedge V) = \Sigma\{p(S) \mid S \in Z, S \supseteq V\}$. P_C can be extended to be a probability lattice in the usual way.

The input-output relation. The representation theorem permits the *semantic* recovery of the input output relation from a process P. Let c be an input. P will associate with c an output o iff there is closure operator f exhibited by P which maps c to o. The probability associated with o is the (normalized) sum of the probabilities associated with each closure operator that maps c to o.

Full abstraction. The operational and denotational semantics are equivalent. The proof exploits the representation theorem sketched above, and is omitted for lack of space.

Theorem 4. Computational Adequacy: *For any* pcc *program* A, $\texttt{IO}(\mathcal{P}[\![A]\!])(u) = \texttt{OpsemIO}(A, u)$

Full Abstraction: *For any* pcc *programs* A_1, A_2, *if* $\mathcal{P}[\![A_1]\!] \neq \mathcal{P}[\![A_2]\!]$ *then there is a context* C *such that* $\texttt{Opsem}(C[A_1]) \neq \texttt{Opsem}(C[A_2])$.

3 Adding time — Timed pcc

Timed pcc arises from pcc by adding a notion of discrete time. In adding time, we would also like to keep the characteristic properties of synchronous programming languages alluded to earlier. We ensure this by extending pcc to Timed pcc using the same method used to extend Default cc to Default tcc in [SJG, SJG94]. Concretely, we add a single temporal construct hence A — when this is invoked at time t, then a new copy of A is started at each time instant $t' > t$.

Notation. We will be working with sequences, *i.e.* partial functions on the natural numbers — their domains will be initial segments of the natural numbers of the form $0..n$. We let $s, t, s', s'', \ldots$ denote sequences. We use ϵ to denote the empty sequence. The concatenation of sequences is denoted by "$\cdot$"; for this purpose a singleton u is regarded as the one-element sequence $\langle u \rangle$. Given a subset of sequences S, and a sequence s, we will write S **after** s for the set $\{t \in \mathbf{Obs} \mid s \cdot t \in S\}$. $s(n)$ denotes its n'th element of s. We also define $S(0) = \{u \mid \exists s.\ u \cdot s \in S\}$.

We define a *sequence algebra* with the signature $\langle S, \text{Pref}_i, \text{length}() \rangle$, where S is the set of all sequences, $\text{length}(s) : S \to \mathbb{N}$ and $\text{Pref}_i : S \to S$, $\text{Pref}_i(s) = s$ if $\text{length}(s) \leq i$, otherwise $\text{Pref}_i(s) = \langle s(0), s(1), \ldots, s(i-1) \rangle$, the sequence consisting of the first i elements of s. Homomorphisms on sequence algebras will preserve prefixes and lengths.

Denotational Model. An observation of a Timed pcc program is a *quiescent sequence* of a program. Let **Obs** be the set of all finite sequences of consistent(*i.e.* not `false`) constraints. A process is a collection of observations that satisfies the condition that instantaneous execution at any time instant is modeled by a pcc process. The probability information is kept as a probability lattice for each sequence s in the process — this information is interpreted as the conditional probability information associated with the process at the first instant after the history s. Formally, we proceed as follows.

Definition 5. P is a Timed pcc process if $P_A \subseteq \mathbf{Obs}$, and for each $s \in P_A$ we are given a probability lattice P_s, satisfying the following conditions:

Non-emptiness: $\epsilon \in P_A$,
Prefix-closure: $s \in P_A$ whenever $s \cdot t \in P_A$,
Point execution: $(\forall s \in P_A), ((P_A \text{ **after** } s)(0), P_s)$ is a pcc process.

We can combine the probability lattices into a single indexed set of probability lattices by defining $P_C(s \cdot z) \stackrel{d}{=} P_s(z)$, and similarly for joins and meets in P_s.

Probability Lattice operations on P_C. We generalize the definitions of operations on probability lattices to indexed sets of probability lattices.

Quotienting. Let $h : A \to B$ be a sequence algebra homomorphism. Let P be an indexed set of probability lattices on A, we want to define an indexed set Q on the image of h. We will do this in an inductive fashion on the tree of sequences. The basic idea is that we will at each stage collapse the sequences identified by h, and assume that for any two sequences $t, t' \in A$, if $t \neq t'$ then the probability lattices P_t and $P_{t'}$ are independent.

For each sequence $s \in B$ we will also define inductively a probability lattice R^s on the set $\{t \cdot v \in A \mid h(t) = s\}$. R^s will be quotiented to produce Q_s.

Define $R^\epsilon = P_\epsilon$ and $Q_\epsilon = \frac{R^\epsilon}{h}$.

Assume we have defined Q_s and R^s for $s \in B$. Let $s \cdot u \in B$. If $h(t \cdot v) = s \cdot u$, define $R^{s \cdot u}(t \cdot v \cdot w) = R^s(t \cdot v) \times P_{t \cdot v}(w)$. Also, $R^{s \cdot u}(t \cdot v \cdot w \wedge t \cdot v \cdot w') = R^s(t \cdot v) \times P_{t \cdot v}(w \wedge w')$. If $h(t' \cdot v') = s \cdot u$, and $t' \cdot v' \neq t \cdot v$ then $R^{s \cdot u}(t \cdot v \cdot w \wedge t' \cdot v' \cdot w') = R^s(t \cdot v \wedge t' \cdot v') \times P_{t \cdot v}(w) \times P_{t' \cdot v'}(w')$. This follows from the independence assumption. Now $Q_{s \cdot u} = \frac{R^{s \cdot u}}{h'}$, where $h'(t \cdot v \cdot w) = u'$ if $h(t \cdot v \cdot w) = s \cdot u \cdot u'$.

Expansion. Let $h : A \to B$ be a partial sequence algebra homomorphism, i.e. the domain of h is a subalgebra of A. Let Q be an indexed set of probability lattices on B. Then we define an indexed set of probability lattices P on the domain of h by $P_s = \mathrm{Exp}(Q_s, h')$, where $h'(u) = h(s \cdot u)$.

Product. Let P_1 and P_2 be two indexed sets of probability lattices on A_1 and A_2. Define the fibered product of A_1 and A_2 as the set $\{s \cdot \langle u, v \rangle \mid s \cdot u \in A_1, s \cdot v \in A_2\}$. Define Q on this fibered product as $Q_s = P_{1_s} \times P_{2_s}$.

We will overload the symbols for quotient, expansion and product to stand for the corresponding operations on indexed sets of probability lattices also.

Combinators of Timed pcc. c, **if** c **then** A, (A, B) are inherited from pcc and their denotations are induced by their pcc definitions.

Tell. $\mathcal{D}[\![a]\!]_A \stackrel{d}{=} \{\epsilon\} \cup \{u \cdot s \in \mathbf{Obs} \mid a \in u\}$. $\mathcal{D}[\![a]\!]_C = 1$.

Ask. $\mathcal{D}[\![\mathbf{if}\ a\ \mathbf{then}\ A]\!]_A \stackrel{d}{=} \{\epsilon\} \cup \{u \cdot s \in \mathbf{Obs} \mid a \in u \Rightarrow u \cdot s \in \mathcal{D}[\![A]\!]_A\}$. For any sequence $u \cdot s$, if $a \in u$ then $\mathcal{D}[\![\mathbf{if}\ a\ \mathbf{then}\ A]\!]_C(u \cdot s) = \mathcal{D}[\![A]\!]_C(u \cdot s)$, otherwise $\mathcal{D}[\![\mathbf{if}\ a\ \mathbf{then}\ A]\!]_C(u \cdot s) = 1$. The rest of $\mathcal{D}[\![\mathbf{if}\ a\ \mathbf{then}\ A]\!]_C$ is defined by monotonicity, continuity and modularity.

Parallel Composition. $\mathcal{D}[\![A, B]\!]_A \stackrel{d}{=} \mathcal{D}[\![A]\!]_A \cap \mathcal{D}[\![B]\!]_A$. $\mathcal{D}[\![A, B]\!]_C$ is given as before by $\mathrm{Exp}(\mathcal{P}[\![A_1]\!]_C \times \mathcal{P}[\![A_2]\!]_C, \Delta)$ where $\Delta(\epsilon) = \epsilon$ and $\Delta(s \cdot u) = s \cdot \langle u, u \rangle$.

Hiding. Every observation $s \in \mathcal{D}[\![\mathbf{new}\ X\ \mathbf{in}\ A]\!]_A$ is induced by some observation $s' \in \mathcal{D}[\![A]\!]_A$, *i.e.* at every time instant t, $s(t)$ must equal the result of hiding X in the pcc process given by A at time t after history s^{t-1}.

Formally, let $\exists_X s = \exists_X s'$ denote $|s| = |s'|$, and $\forall i < |s|, \exists_X s(i) = \exists_X s'(i)$. Then

$$\mathcal{D}[\![\mathbf{new}\ X\ \mathbf{in}\ A]\!] \stackrel{d}{=} \{s \in \mathbf{Obs} \mid \exists s' \in \mathcal{D}[\![A]\!].\exists_X s = \exists_X s'\}$$

The set of probability lattices is defined as $\mathrm{Exp}(\frac{\mathcal{D}[\![A]\!]_C}{\exists_X}, \exists_X)$, where $\exists_X : |D| \to |D|$ is the existential on sequences.

Distributions. $\mathtt{Distr}(X, f)$ ensures that X follows distribution f for all time, *i.e.* after every sequence, we must get the pcc process $\mathtt{Distr}(X, f)$. Thus, we have: $\mathtt{Distr}(X, f)_A = \{s \in \mathbf{Obs} \mid \forall i < \text{length}(s).\ \exists r_i.\ (X = r_i) \in s(i), f(r_i) > 0\}$, and $\mathtt{Distr}(X, f)_C = \text{Exp}(F, h)$, where F is an indexed set of lattices defined by $F(s) = f$, $h(s \cdot u) = h(s) \cdot r$ if $(X = r) \in u$. As in pcc, define

$$\mathcal{D}[\![\textbf{new } (X, f) \textbf{ in } A]\!] \stackrel{d}{=} \mathcal{D}[\![\textbf{new } X \textbf{ in } (\mathtt{Distr}(X, f), A)]\!]$$

Hence. The definition for **hence** is as expected — observations have to "satisfy" A everywhere after the first instant; the probability lattice codes the fact that at time t there are $t - 1$ copies of B running in parallel.

$$\mathcal{D}[\![\textbf{hence } B]\!]_A \stackrel{d}{=} \{u \cdot s \in \mathbf{Obs} \mid (\forall s_1, s_2) s = s_1 \cdot s_2 \Rightarrow s_2 \in \mathcal{D}[\![B]\!]_A\}$$

$\mathcal{D}[\![\textbf{hence } B]\!]_C(u \cdot s) = 1$ if $s = \epsilon$, otherwise $\mathcal{D}[\![\textbf{hence } B]\!]_C(u \cdot s) = \Pi\{\mathcal{D}[\![B]\!]_C(s_2) \mid s = s_1 \cdot s_2\}$.

Definable combinators. Since all the basic combinators of Default tcc[SJG] are available here, (probabilistic approximations to) all the defined combinators of Default tcc are definable in Timed pcc demonstrating that Timed pcc is an expressive synchronous language.

next $_\epsilon A$	start A at the next instant with probability $1 - \epsilon$
first a **then** $_\epsilon A$	whenever a becomes true start A with probability $1 - \epsilon$
do A **watching** $_\epsilon c$	do A with probability $1 - \epsilon$ at each instant, until c becomes true
time $_\epsilon A$ **on** c	do A with probability $1 - \epsilon$ during the instants c holds

Operational semantics. The operational semantics for Timed pcc is built on the operational semantics for pcc — in this section, we focus on the aspects of the transition system that involve time. Following the synchronous paradigm, values of variables are not carried across time — in particular, a fresh "coin toss" is performed for random variables at each time instant.

A configuration consists of a pair(Γ, Δ) — the agents currently active and the "continuation" — the program to be executed at subsequent times. The rules for asks, hiding and parallel composition and new random variables are instantaneous and remain as before, in each case the Δ is unchanged after the transition. The rule for **hence** is also instantaneous and is given by

$$((\Gamma, \textbf{hence } A), \Delta) \longrightarrow (\Gamma, (A, \textbf{hence } A, \Delta))$$

The instantaneous outputs of Γ and the associated probability lattice C is derived as in pcc.

For a given possible instantaneous output u, let $\Delta_1 \ldots \Delta_n$ be such that $(\Gamma, \emptyset) \longrightarrow^* (\Gamma_i', \Delta_i) \not\longrightarrow$, $\mathbf{Y}_i$ are the new variables introduced in derivation, $\exists_{\mathbf{Y}_i} \sigma(\Gamma_i') = u$. Also, let $f = \frac{C}{h}$, where $h((\Gamma_i, \Delta_i)) = i$. For output u, the timestep transition relation $\leadsto$ is defined as

$$\Gamma \leadsto \textbf{new}\ (X, f)\ \textbf{in}\ (\ \textbf{if}\ X = 1\ \textbf{then new}\ \mathbf{Y}_1\ \textbf{in}\ \Delta_1,$$
$$\ldots$$
$$\textbf{if}\ X = n\ \textbf{then new}\ \mathbf{Y}_n\ \textbf{in}\ \Delta_n)$$

In the above, for all random variables in $\mathbf{Y}_i$, we write **new** (Y, g) **in** Δ_i, where g was the distribution in the prior time instant.

Correspondence theorems. As in pcc, the operational and denotational semantics are equivalent. The proof is essentially just a "lifting" of the proof for pcc, and is omitted lack of space.

Acknowledgements. We would like to thank Lise Getoor for bringing up the problem of probability modeling, and Daphne Koller, Moses Charikar and Fernando Pereira, for several discussions. This work was supported by grants from NSF, ARPA and ONR.

References

[Abr93] S. Abramsky. Interaction categories. Available by anonymous ftp from papers/Abramsky:theory.doc.ic.ac.uk, 1993.

[Abr94] Samson Abramsky. Interaction categories and communicating sequential processes. In A. W. Roscoe, editor, *A Classical Mind: Essays in honour of C. A. R. Hoare*, pages 1–16. Prentice Hall International, 1994.

[BB91] A. Benveniste and G. Berry. The synchronous approach to reactive and real-time systems. In *Special issue on Another Look at Real-time Systems*, Proceedings of the IEEE, September 1991.

[BLFG95] Albert Benveniste, Bernard C. Levy, Eric Fabre, and Paul Le Guernic. A calculus of stochastic systems for the specification, simulation, and hidden state estimation of mixed stochastic/nonstochastic systems. *Theoretical Computer Science*, 152(2):171–217, Dec 1995.

[CSZ92] R. Cleaveland, S. A. Smolka, and A. Zwarico. Testing preorders for probabilistic processes. *Lecture Notes in Computer Science*, 623, 1992.

[dKW89] Johan de Kleer and Brian C. Williams. Diagnosis with behavioral modes. In *Proceedings of the Eleventh International Joint Conference on Artificial Intelligence*, pages 1324–1330, August 1989.

[FBB+94] M. Fromherz, D. Bell, D. Bobrow, et al. RAPPER: The Copier Modeling Project. In *Working Papers of the Eighth International Workshop on Qualitative Reasoning About Physical Systems*, pages 1–12, June 1994.

[FJM90] R. Fagin, J.Y.Halpern, and N. Megiddo. A logic for reasoning about probabilities. *Information and Computation*, 87:78–128, 1990.

[FS95] Markus P.J. Fromherz and Vijay A. Saraswat. Model-based computing: Using concurrent constraint programming for modeling and model compilation. In U. Montanari and F. Rossi, editors, *Principles and Practice of Constraint Programming - CP'95*, pages 629–635. Springer-Verlag, LNCS 976, Sept. 1995.

[GJS] Vineet Gupta, Radha Jagadeesan, and Vijay Saraswat. Computing with continuous change. *Science of Computer Programming*. To appear.

[GSS95] Vineet Gupta, Vijay Saraswat, and Peter Struss. A model of a photocopier paper path. In *Proceedings of the 2nd IJCAI Workshop on Engineering Problems for Qualitative Reasoning*, August 1995.

[Hal93] N. Halbwachs. *Synchronous programming of reactive systems*. The Kluwer international series in Engineering and Computer Science. Kluwer Academic publishers, 1993.

[Har87] D. Harel. Statecharts: A visual approach to complex systems. *Science of Computer Programming*, 8:231 - 274, 1987.

[HJ90] H. Hansson and B. Jonsson. A calculus for communicating systems with time and probabilities. In *Proceedings of the 11th IEEE Real-Time Systems Symposium*, pages 278–287. IEEE Computer Society Press, 1990.

[HS86] S. Hart and M. Sharir. Probabilistic propositional temporal logics. *Information and Control*, 70:97–155, 1986.

[HSD92] Pascal Van Hentenryck, Vijay A. Saraswat, and Yves Deville. Constraint processing in cc(fd). Technical report, Computer Science Department, Brown University, 1992.

[Joh82] P. T. Johnstone. *Stone Spaces*, volume 3 of *Cambridge Studies in Advanced Mathematics*. Cambridge University Press, Cambridge, 1982.

[JP89] C. Jones and G. D. Plotkin. A probabilistic powerdomain of evaluations. In *Proceedings, Fourth Annual Symposium on Logic in Computer Science*, pages 186–195, Asilomar Conference Center, Pacific Grove, California, 1989.

[JY95] Bengt Jonsson and Wang Yi. Compositional testing preorders for probabilistic processes. In *Proceedings, Tenth Annual IEEE Symposium on Logic in Computer Science*, pages 431–441, San Diego, California, 1995.

[LS91] Kim G. Larsen and Arne Skou. Bisimulation through probabilistic testing. *Information and Computation*, 94(1):1–28, September 1991.

[Mar89] M. Ajmone Marsan. Stochastic petri nets: an elementary introduction. In *Advances in Petri Nets 1989*, pages 1–29. Springer, June 1989.

[MMS96] Carroll Morgan, Annabelle McIver, and Karen Seidel. Probabilistic predicate transformers. *ACM Transactions on Programming Languages and Systems*, 18(3):325–353, May 1996.

[Nil86] N.J. Nilsson. Probabilistic logic. *Artificial Intelligence*, 28:71–87, 1986.

[Pea88] J. Pearl. *Probabilistic Reasoning in Intelligent Systems*. Morgan-Kaufmann Publishers, 1988.

[Sar93] Vijay A. Saraswat. *Concurrent constraint programming*. Doctoral Dissertation Award and Logic Programming Series. MIT Press, 1993.

[SJG] V. A. Saraswat, R. Jagadeesan, and V. Gupta. Timed Default Concurrent Constraint Programming. *Journal of Symbolic Computation*. To appear. Extended abstract appeared in the *Proceedings of the 22nd ACM Symposium on Principles of Programming Languages*, San Francisco, January 1995.

[SJG94] V. A. Saraswat, R. Jagadeesan, and V. Gupta. Foundations of Timed Concurrent Constraint Programming. In Samson Abramsky, editor, *Proceedings of the Ninth Annual IEEE Symposium on Logic in Computer Science*. IEEE Computer Press, July 1994.

[SRP91] V. A. Saraswat, M. Rinard, and P. Panangaden. Semantic foundations of concurrent constraint programming. In *Proceedings of Eighteenth ACM Symposium on Principles of Programming Languages, Orlando*, January 1991.

[vGSST90] Rob van Glabbeek, S. A. Smolka, B. Steffen, and C. M. N. Tofts. Reactive, generative, and stratified models of probabilistic processes. In *Proceedings, Fifth Annual IEEE Symposium on Logic in Computer Science*, pages 130–141, Philadelphia, Pennsylvania, 1990.

[VN92] N. Viswanadham and Y. Narahari. *Performance Modeling of Automated Manufacturing Systems*. Prentice-Hall Inc., 1992.

On the Complexity of Verifying Concurrent Transition Systems*

David Harel[1] and Orna Kupferman[2]** and Moshe Y. Vardi[3]***

[1] Department of Applied Math. & Computer Science, The Weizmann Institute, Rehovot 76100, Israel.
Email: harel@wisdom.weizmann.ac.il
[2] EECS Department, UC Berkeley, Berkeley CA 94720-1770, U.S.A.
Email: orna@eecs.berkeley.edu
[3] Rice University, Department of Computer Science, Houston, TX 77251-1892, U.S.A.
Email: vardi@cs.rice.edu, URL: http://www.cs.rice.edu/~vardi

Abstract. In *implementation verification*, we check that an implementation is correct with respect to a specification by checking whether the behaviors of a transition system that models the program's implementation correlate with the behaviors of a transition system that models its specification. In this paper, we investigate the effect of concurrency on the complexity of implementation verification. We consider trace-based and tree-based approaches to the verification of concurrent transition systems, with and without fairness. Our results show that in almost all cases the complexity of the problem is exponentially harder than that of the sequential case. Thus, as in the model-checking verification methodology, the state-explosion problem cannot be avoided.

1 Introduction

While program verification has always been desirable but never easy, the advent of concurrent programming has made it significantly more necessary and difficult. We distinguish between two main methodologies for formal verification. The first is *temporal-logic model checking*. Here, we verify the correctness of a program with respect to a desired behavior by checking whether a state-transition graph that models the program satisfies a temporal-logic formula that specifies constraints on its behavior. The second methodology is *implementation verification*. Here, we check that an implementation is correct with respect to a specification by checking whether the behaviors of a state-transition graph that models the program's implementation correlate with the behaviors of a state-transition graph that models its specification.

The complexity of model checking is well known. For example, in the case of the temporal logics LTL and CTL, model checking can be carried out in space that is polynomial in $n \log m$, where n is the length of the formula and m is the size of the graph modeling the program [LP85, VW94, BVW94]. Keeping in mind that the formulas are usually small, it seems that model checking is easy and tractable. It suffers, however, acutely from the so-called *state-explosion problem*. In a concurrent setting, the program under consideration is typically the parallel composition of many processes, which implies that the size of the program graph is the product of the sizes of the graphs modeling the underlying processes. Accordingly, the model-checking problem for concurrent programs can be solved in space that is polynomial in nm,

* Part of this research was done in Bell Laboratories during the DIMACS special year on Logic and Algorithms.

** Supported in part by the ONR YIP award N00014-95-1-0520, by the NSF CAREER award CCR-9501708, by the NSF grant CCR-9504469, by the AFOSR contract F49620-93-1-0056, by the ARO MURI grant DAAH-04-96-1-0341, by the ARPA grant NAG2-892, and by the SRC contract 95-DC-324.036.

*** Supported in part by the NSF grant CCR-9628400.

where n is the length of the formula and m is the sum of the sizes of the graphs modeling the processes. Can we do better than this? Can we model-check a concurrent program and avoid the state-explosion problem? Unfortunately, the answer is no. Indeed, model checking of concurrent programs for LTL and CTL is PSPACE–complete even for a fixed formula [VW94, BVW94]. Hence, in the worst case we might need to traverse the exceedingly large state space introduced by the parallel composition. Coping with the state-explosion problem is one of the most important issues in computer-aided verification and is the subject of much active research (cf. [CGL93])

What about implementation verification? Is the state-explosion problem unavoidable there too? This is the subject of our work. We first describe implementation verification in more detail. Consider an implementation and a specification. Both describe possible behaviors of the program, but the implementation is more concrete than the specification, or, equivalently, the specification is more abstract than the implementation (cf. [AL91]). This basic notion suggests a top-down method for design development, called *hierarchical refinement* (cf. [LS84, Kur94]): Starting with a highly abstract specification, we construct a sequence of behavior descriptions, each of which refers to its predecessor as a specification, and is thus less abstract than the predecessor. At each stage the current implementation is verified to satisfy its specification. The last description in the sequence contains no abstractions, and constitutes the final implementation.

There are several ways of defining what it means for an implementation to satisfy a specification. The two main ones are *trace-based* and *tree-based*. The former requires each computation of the implementation to correlate with some computation of the specification, and the latter requires each computation tree embodied in the implementation to correlate with some computation tree embodied in the specification. The exact notion of correct implementation then depends on how we interpret correlation. Numerous proposals for this have been made and studied in the literature [Hen85, Mil89, AL91]. In this paper we adopt a simple interpretation, taking correlation to mean equivalence with respect to the variables joint to the implementation and the specification. One justification for this is the fact that the more concrete implementation is typically defined over a wider set of variables than the more abstract specification. With this interpretation, trace-based verification corresponds to establishing *containment* [Kur94] and tree-based verification corresponds to establishing *simulation* [Mil71]. As shown by Milner [Mil80], while simulation implies containment, the opposite direction is not true.

We model concurrent programs (and hence implementations and specifications) by what we shall call *concurrent transition systems*. The basic motivation for this comes from the *statecharts* of [Har87], which can be viewed as finite automata with both concurrency and hierarchy, though for simplicity we eliminate the hierarchy here. A concurrent transition system consists of *components*, which model the program's underlying processes. (The analogous parts of a statechart are called *orthogonal components* in [Har87].) Each component is a state-transition graph. Its states correspond to the possible positions of the process it models, and each state is labeled with the events that occur, or hold, in the corresponding position. The transitions of the graph correspond to the possible steps of the process, with branches representing nondeterminism. To model the cooperation of processes during execution, the transitions are made conditional and can depend on the states of the other components. This approach to modeling concurrency, called *bounded cooperative concurrency* in [Har89, DH94], is the dominating one in research on distributed systems (cf. [Kur94]).

A concurrent transition system with a single component models a program with no concurrency, and we call it a *sequential transition system*. By [DH94], a concurrent transition system can be translated into a sequential transition system with an exponential blow up in size. Indeed, it is the size of this sequential system that is referred to in current analyses of the complexity of verification. The question we want to address here is whether the exponential blow up that hides in these analyses can be avoided if the program to be verified is concurrent.

Before we turn to this question, let us review some known results for the implementation verification of sequential transition systems (for full details, see Section 2.3). We examine the complexity of the containment and the simulation problems in four different ways:

1. The *joint complexity* of containment and simulation. This measure considers the complexity in terms of both the implementation and the specification. The joint complexity of simulation is PTIME-complete [Mil80, BGS92], whereas that of containment is PSPACE-complete [SVW87].
2. The *implementation complexity* of containment and simulation. This measure considers the complexity in terms of the implementation, assuming the specification is fixed. Since the implementation is typically much larger than the specification, this measure is of particular interest. According to this measure, containment is easier than simulation [KV96].
3. The *joint complexity* of *fair containment* and *fair simulation*. When we consider *fair transition systems* [MP92], which enable the description of behaviors that satisfy both liveness and safety properties, containment and simulation are revised to consider only the fair computations of the implementation and the specification. The resulting problems, of fair containment and fair simulation [BBLS92, ASB$^+$94, GL94] are both PSPACE–complete [KV96].
4. The *implementation complexity* of *fair containment* and *fair simulation*. Here, the advantage of the trace-based approach reappears [KV96].

We address the question about the power of concurrency in program verification by examining the four measures when applied to concurrent transition systems. We first define containment and simulation with respect to such systems, and then consider the complexity and the implementation complexity of detecting their presence. We then turn to defining fair-containment and fair-simulation with respect to concurrent transition systems, and study their complexities too, employing *unconditional*, *weak*, and *strong* fairness (also known as *impartiality*, *justice*, and *compassion*, respectively) [LPS81, MP92].

Before saying a little more about the results themselves, we clarify what we feel are the paper's two main contributions. First, it continues the study of implementation verification in [Mil80, BGS92, KV96]. Unlike these papers, our complexity analysis addresses the state-explosion issue explicitly, by taking the size to be that of the concurrent systems themselves and not their sequential equivalents. In addition, our work continues the study of the power of bounded cooperative concurrency undertaken in [Har89, DH94, HH94, HRV90]. the results in these papers show that cooperative concurrency exhibits inherent exponential power. The power criteria considered there are succinctness of finite automata and pushdown automata, and the effect of the succinctness gap on the difficulty of reasoning about transition systems on a propositional level. In the present paper, the power criteria is the complexity of the verification problem.

Our results strengthen the observations in [Har89, DH94, KV96]. Specifically, the question of whether the exponential nature of concurrency carries over to the verification problem is answered in the affirmative. We show that verifying concurrent transition systems is exponentially harder than verifying sequential transition systems, and thus the state-explosion problem cannot be avoided. This result is robust: It is independent of the verification approach and the fairness constraint under consideration, and remains valid when we consider implementation complexity too. In particular, we show that the fair-containment and fair-simulation problems for concurrent transition systems are EXPSPACE–complete. These results join those of [KV96] in questioning the computational superiority of tree-based verification.

One exception to the inherent exponential power of cooperative concurrency is the fair-simulation problem for strongly-fair transition systems. While the implementation complexity of the problem is PTIME–complete for sequential transition systems [KV96], we show that it is PSPACE–complete (rather than EXPTIME–complete) for concurrent transition systems. The reason for this anomaly is the fact that translating a strongly fair concurrent system into a sequential one indeed involves an exponential blow up in the number of states, but involves no such blow up in the size of the fairness condition. Evidently, it is the size of the fairness condition that is the dominant factor when reasoning about strongly-fair transition systems. This suggests that strong fairness is the preferable fairness condition to use when specifying concurrent programs. Not only is it the most expressive condition, but it also suffers less than the others from the state-explosion problem.

2 Preliminaries

2.1 Fair Concurrent Transition Systems

A fair nondeterministic transition system with bounded concurrency (*concurrent transition system*, for short) is a tuple $S = \langle O, S_1, \ldots, S_n \rangle$ consisting of a finite set O of *observable events* and n *components* $S_1, \ldots, S_n$ for some $n \geq 1$. Each component S_i is a tuple $\langle O_i, W_i, W_i^0, \delta_i, L_i, \alpha_i \rangle$, where:

- $O_i \subseteq O$ is a set of local observable events. The O_j are not necessarily pairwise disjoint; hence, observable events may be shared by several components. We require that $O = \bigcup_{j=1}^n O_j$.
- W_i is a finite set of states, and we require that the W_j be pairwise disjoint. Also, we let $W = \bigcup_{j=1}^n W_j$.
- $W_i^0 \subseteq W_i$ is the set of initial states.
- $\delta_i \subseteq W_i \times \mathcal{B}(W) \times W_i$ is a transition relation, where $\mathcal{B}(W)$ denotes the set of all Boolean propositional formulas over W.
- $L_i : W_i \to 2^{O_i}$ is a labeling function that labels each state with a set of local observable events. The intuition is that $L_i(w)$ are the events that occur, or hold, in w.
- α_i is a fairness condition. We define three types of fairness conditions shortly. We require all the α_i's to be of the same type, which we refer to as the type of S.

Since states are labeled with sets of elements from O, we refer to $\Sigma = 2^O$ as the *alphabet* of S. While each component of S has its local observable events and its own states and transitions, these transitions depend not only on the component's current state but also on the current states of the other components. Also, as we shall now see, the labels of the components are required to agree on shared observable events.

A *configuration* of S is a tuple $c = \langle w_1, w_2, \ldots, w_n, \sigma \rangle \in W_1 \times W_2 \times \cdots \times W_n \times \Sigma$, satisfying $L_i(w_i) = \sigma \cap O_i$ for all $1 \leq i \leq n$. Note that, in particular, $\sigma = \bigcup_i L_i(w_i)$. Thus, a configuration describes the current state of each of the components, as well as the set of observable events labeling these states. The requirement on σ implies that these labels are *consistent*, i.e., for any S_i and S_j, and for each $o \in O_i \cap O_j$, either $o \in L_i(w_i) \cap L_j(w_j)$ (in which case, $o \in \sigma$), or $o \notin L_i(w_i) \cup L_j(w_j)$ (in which case, $o \notin \sigma$). For a configuration $c = \langle w_1, w_2, \ldots, w_n, \sigma \rangle$, we term $\langle w_1, w_2, \ldots, w_n \rangle$ the ***global state*** of c, and we term σ the ***label*** of c, and denote it by $L(c)$. A configuration is *initial* if for all $1 \leq i \leq n$, we have $w_i \in W_i^0$. We use C to denote the set of all configurations of a given system S, and C_0 to denote the set of all its initial configurations. We also use $c[i]$ to refer to S_i's state in c.

For a propositional formula θ in $\mathcal{B}(W)$ and a global state $p = \langle w_1, w_2, \ldots, w_n \rangle$, we say that *$p$ satisfies θ* if assigning **true** to states in p and **false** to states not in p makes θ true. For example, $s_1 \wedge (t_1 \vee t_2)$, with $s_1 \in W_1$ and $\{t_1, t_2\} \subseteq W_2$, is satisfied by every global state in which S_1 is in state s_1 and S_2 is in either t_1 or t_2. We shall sometimes write disjunctions as sets, so that the above formula can be written $\{s_1\} \wedge \{t_1, t_2\}$. Formulas in $\mathcal{B}(W)$ that appear in transitions are called *conditions*. If θ is equivalent to **true** in the transition $\langle w, \theta, w' \rangle$, we say that it is *unconditional*.

Given two configurations $c = \langle w_1, w_2, \ldots, w_n, \sigma \rangle$ and $c' = \langle w'_1, w'_2, \ldots, w'_n, \sigma' \rangle$, we say that c' is a *successor of c in S*, and write $succ_S(c, c')$, if for all $1 \leq i \leq n$ there is $\langle w_i, \theta_i, w'_i \rangle \in \delta_i$ such that $\langle w_1, w_2, \ldots, w_n \rangle$ satisfies θ_i. In other words, a successor configuration is obtained by simultaneously applying to all the components a transition that is enabled in the current configuration. Note that by requiring that successors are indeed configurations, we are saying that transitions can only lead to states satisfying the consistency criterion, to the effect that they agree on the labels for shared observable events.

Given a configuration c, a *c-computation* of S is an infinite sequence $\pi = c_0, c_1, \ldots$ of configurations, such that $c_0 = c$ and for all $i \geq 0$ we have $succ_S(c_i, c_{i+1})$. A *computation* of S is a c-computation for some $c \in C_0$. The c-computation $c_0, c_1, \ldots$ *generates* the infinite *trace* $\rho \in \Sigma^\omega$, defined by $\rho = L(c_0) \cdot L(c_1) \cdots$. Sometimes we want to exclude computations of S that do not meet some fairness criteria. This is particularly essential when we model concurrent programs and want to rule out computations that do not meet certain scheduling criteria. In order to determine whether a computation π is *fair*, we refer to the sets of states that each of the components visits infinitely often along π. For each $1 \leq i \leq n$, let $Inf(\pi, i)$ denote the set of states that S_i visits infinitely often. That is, $Inf(\pi, i) = \{w \in W_i \ : \ \text{for infinitely many } j \geq 0, \text{ we have } c_j[i] = w\}$. Note that the set $Inf(\pi, i)$ considers only the states of S_i and does not refer to the global states visited along π. The way we refer to $Inf(\pi, i)$ depends in the fairness condition of S. Several types of fairness conditions are studied in the literature. We consider here three: We consider three types of fairness conditions:

- *Unconditional* fairness (or *impartiality*), where for all components S_i we have $\alpha_i \subseteq 2^{W_i}$, and π is fair iff for all $1 \leq i \leq n$ and for every set $G \in \alpha_i$, we have $Inf(\pi, i) \cap G \neq \emptyset$.
- *Weak* fairness (or *justice*), where $\alpha_i \subseteq 2^{W_i} \times 2^{W_i}$, and π is fair iff for all $1 \leq i \leq n$ and for every pair $\langle G, B \rangle \in \alpha_i$, we have that $Inf(\pi, i) \cap (W_i \setminus G) = \emptyset$ implies $Inf(\pi, i) \cap B \neq \emptyset$.
- *Strong* fairness (or *fairness*), where $\alpha_i \subseteq 2^{W_i} \times 2^{W_i}$, and π is fair iff for all $1 \leq i \leq n$ and for every pair $\langle G, B \rangle \in \alpha_i$, we have that $Inf(\pi, i) \cap G \neq \emptyset$ implies $Inf(\pi, i) \cap B \neq \emptyset$.

In addition, we consider *non-fair concurrent transition systems*; i.e., concurrent transition systems in which all the computations are fair. For simplicity, we denote components of non-fair concurrent transition system by quintuplet, leaving α_i out.

We use $\mathcal{T}(S^c)$ to denote the set of all traces generated by fair c-computations, and the *trace set* $\mathcal{T}(S)$ of S is then defined as $\bigcup_{c \in C_0} \mathcal{T}(S^c)$. In this way, each concurrent transition system S defines a subset of Σ^ω. We say that S *accepts* a trace ρ if $\rho \in \mathcal{T}(S)$. Also, we say that S is *empty* if $\mathcal{T}(S) = \emptyset$; i.e., S has no fair computation. Note that for a non-fair concurrent transition system S, the trace set $\mathcal{T}(S)$ contains all traces $\rho \in \Sigma^\omega$ for which there exists a computation π with $L(\pi) = \rho$.

The *size* of a concurrent transition system S is the sum of the sizes of its components. Symbolically, $|S| = |S_1| + \cdots + |S_n|$. Here, for a component $S_i = \langle O_i, W_i, W_i^0, \delta_i, L_i, \alpha_i \rangle$, we define $|S_i| = |O_i| + |W_i| + |\delta_i| + |L_i| + |\alpha_i|$, where $|\delta_i| = \sum_{\langle w, \theta, w' \rangle \in \delta_i} |\theta|$, $|L_i| = |O_i| \cdot |W_i|$, and $|\alpha_i|$ is the sum of the cardinalities of the sets in α_i. Clearly, S can be stored in space $O(|S|)$.

When S has a single component, we say that it is a *sequential transition system*. Note that the transition relation of a sequential transition system can be really viewed as a subset of $W \times W$, and that a configuration of a sequential transition system is simply a labeled state.

Example 1. We construct a non-fair concurrent transition system S as a binary counter; it counts up to 2^n in base 2 using n components. Given n, let $S = \langle \{bit_1, \ldots, bit_n\}, S_1, \ldots, S_n \rangle$, where $S_i = \langle \{bit_i\}, \{w_i^0, w_i^1\}, \{w_i^0\}, \delta_i, L_i \rangle$, with δ_i and L_i defined as follows:

- $\delta_i = \{\langle w_i^0, \theta_i, w_i^0 \rangle, \langle w_i^0, \neg\theta_i, w_i^1 \rangle, \langle w_i^1, \theta_i, w_i^1 \rangle, \langle w_i^1, \neg\theta_i, w_i^0 \rangle\}$, where $\theta_i = \bigvee_{j<i} w_j^0$. Note that $\theta_1 \equiv$ **false**. Thus, S_1 corresponds to the least significant bit of the counter and always alternates between w_1^0 and w_1^1. The component S_i, for $i > 1$, switches between w_i^0 and w_i^1 whenever all the S_j with $j < i$ are in their w_j^1 states. Otherwise, S_i stays in its current state.
- For every S_i, we set $L_i(w_i^0) = \emptyset$ and $L_i(w_i^1) = \{bit_i\}$.

The trace $(\emptyset \cdot \{bit_1\} \cdot \{bit_2\} \cdot \{bit_2, bit_1\} \cdot \{bit_3\} \cdot \{bit_3, bit_1\} \cdots \{bit_n, bit_{n-1}, \ldots, bit_1\})^\omega$ is the single initial trace induced by the system S.

Note that although S has n components, its size is quadratic in n. Indeed, the size of each transition relation δ_i is $O(i)$. However, we can define a slightly more sophisticated version of this system that is of size $O(n)$. Each component S_i has four states, corresponding to the possible values of both the i'th bit of the counter and the i'th carry bit. The conditions in the transitions in δ_i then refer only to the states of S_{i-1}, and are of a constant size.

2.2 Trace-Based and Tree-Based Implementations

The problems that formalize correct trace-based and tree-based implementations of a system are *containment* and *simulation*, respectively. Once we add fairness to the systems, the corresponding problems are *fair containment* and *fair simulation*. These problems are defined below with respect to two concurrent transition systems $S = \langle O, S_1, \ldots, S_n \rangle$ and $S' = \langle O', S'_1, \ldots, S'_m \rangle$ with $O \supseteq O'$, and with possibly different numbers of components. For technical convenience, we assume that $O = O'$ and that S and S' have the same type of fairness conditions. [4]

Containment and Fair Containment. The *fair-containment problem* for S and S' is to determine whether $\mathcal{T}(S) \subseteq \mathcal{T}(S')$. That is, whether every trace accepted by S is also accepted by S'. When S and S' are non-fair, we call the problem *containment*. If $\mathcal{T}(S) \subseteq \mathcal{T}(S')$, we say that S' *contains* S and we write $S \subseteq S'$.

Simulation. While containment refers only to the set of computations of S and S', simulation refers also to the branching structure of the systems. Let c and c' be configurations of S and S', respectively. A relation $H \subseteq C \times C'$ is a *simulation relation* from $\langle S, c \rangle$ to $\langle S', c' \rangle$ iff the following conditions hold [Mil71].

1. $H(c, c')$.
2. For all configurations $a \in C$ and $a' \in C'$ with $H(a, a')$, we have $L(a) = L(a')$.
3. For all $a \in C$ and $a' \in C'$ with $H(a, a')$ and for every configuration $b \in C$ such that $succ_S(a, b)$, there exists a configuration $b' \in C'$ such that $succ_{S'}(a', b')$ and $H(b, b')$.

A simulation relation H is a *simulation from S to S'* iff for every $c \in C_0$ there exists $c' \in C'_0$ such that $H(c, c')$. If there exists a simulation from S to S', we say that S *simulates* S' and we write $S \preceq S'$. Intuitively, it means that the system S' has more behaviors than the system S. In fact, every tree embodied in S is also embodied in S'. The *simulation problem* is, given S and S', to determine whether $S \preceq S'$.

[4] Our results hold also for the general cases. Taking, for each $\sigma \in 2^O$, the letter $\sigma \cap O'$ instead the letter σ, adjusts all our algorithms to the case $O \supset O'$. Also, when S and S' have different types of fairness conditions, the type of S is dominant, and the complexity of the problem is the same as in the case where both systems have fairness conditions of S's type.

Fair Simulation. Let $H \subseteq C \times C'$ be a relation over the configurations of S and S'. It is convenient to extend H to relate also computations of S and S'. For two computations $\pi = c_0, c_1, \ldots$ in S, and $\pi' = c'_0, c'_1, \ldots$ in S', we say that $H(\pi, \pi')$ holds iff $H(c_i, c'_i)$ holds for all $i \geq 0$. Let c and c' be configurations in S and S', respectively. A relation $H \subseteq C \times C'$ is a *fair-simulation relation* from $\langle S, c\rangle$ to $\langle S', c'\rangle$ iff the following conditions hold [GL94].

1. $H(c, c')$.
2. For all configurations $a \in C$ and $a' \in C'$ with $H(a, a')$, we have $L(a) = L(a')$.
3. For all configurations $a \in C$ and $a' \in C'$ with $H(a, a')$, and for every fair c-computation π in S, there exists a fair c'-computation π' in S', such that $H(\pi, \pi')$.

A fair-simulation relation H is a *fair simulation from S to S'* iff for every $c \in C_0$ there exists $c' \in C'_0$ such that $H(c, c')$. If there exists a simulation from S to S', we say that S *fairly simulates* S' and we write $S \preceq S'$. Intuitively, it means that the concurrent transition system S' has more fair behaviors than the concurrent transition system S. The *fair-simulation problem* is, given S and S', to determine whether $S \preceq S'$.

We say that two concurrent transition systems S and S' are *equivalent* if they fairly simulate each other. Thus, if $S \preceq S'$ and $S' \preceq S$. Note that equivalent systems agree on their trace sets.

Theorem 1. *Every concurrent transition system S can be translated into an equivalent sequential transition system of the same type and of size $2^{O(|S|)}$.*

Proof (sketch): Drusinsky and Harel prove the theorem with respect to automata, where the observable events are input to the machine and where equivalence is defined as agreement on the trace set [DH94]. Yet, their proof holds also for transition systems with our definition of equivalence (mutual simulation), as follows. Consider a concurrent transition system S with n components. The state space of its equivalent sequential transition system S' is the Cartesian product of the state sets of the n components (this would be $W_1 \times W_2 \times \cdots \times W_n$ in the notation used earlier). Thus, each state of S' corresponds to a configuration of S. Accordingly, the transition relation of S' coincides with the relation $succ_S$ over the configurations of S. We now need to define the fairness condition of S' so that a computation of S' is fair iff the corresponding computation of S is fair. Let α' be such that for all $1 \leq i \leq n$, every set $G \in \alpha_i$ (pair $\langle G, B\rangle \in \alpha_i$) induces the set $W_1 \times \cdots \times W_{i-1} \times G \times W_{i+1} \times \cdots \times W_n$ (the pair $\langle W_1 \times \cdots \times W_{i-1} \times G \times W_{i+1} \times \cdots \times W_n, W_1 \times \cdots \times W_{i-1} \times B \times W_{i+1} \times \cdots \times W_n\rangle$, respectively) in α'. It is easy to see that S and S' agree on their trace sets, that they simulate each other, and that the size of S' is at most exponential in that of S. □

In the rest of this paper we examine the traced-based and the tree-based approaches from a *complexity-theoretic* point of view. We consider and compare the complexity of the four problems. The different levels of abstraction in the implementation and the specification are reflected in their sizes. The implementation is typically much larger than the specification and it is its size that is the computational bottleneck. Therefore, of particular interest to us is the *implementation complexity* of these problems; i.e., the complexity of checking whether $S \subseteq S'$ and $S \preceq S'$, in terms of the size of S, assuming S' is fixed.

2.3 Verification of Sequential Transition Systems

We mention here some known results on the verification of sequential transition systems.

Theorem 2. [SVW87, VW94, KV96] *The containment problem for sequential transition systems is PSPACE–complete; The implementation complexity of the problem is NLOGSPACE–complete.*

Theorem 3. [Mil80, BGS92, KV96] *The simulation problem for sequential transition systems is PTIME–complete; The implementation complexity of the problem is PTIME–complete.*

Theorem 4. [SVW87, VW94, KV96] *The fair-containment problem for sequential transition systems is PSPACE–complete; The implementation complexity of the problem is NLOGSPACE–complete for unconditionally-fair and weakly-fair systems, and is PTIME–complete for strongly-fair systems.*

Theorem 5. [KV96] *The fair-simulation problem for sequential transition systems is PSPACE–complete; The implementation complexity of the problem is PTIME–complete.*

It follows that, when comparing the trace-based and the tree-based approaches to verification from a complexity-theoretic point to view, there is no clear advantageous approach. While the joint complexity of simulation is lower than that of containment, it is containment that has lower implementation complexity. In addition, fair containment and fair simulation have the same joint complexity, with fair containment having lower implementation complexity for the case of unconditionally-fair and weakly-fair transition systems.

3 The Containment Problem

Theorem 6. *The containment problem for concurrent transition systems is EXPSPACE–complete.*

Proof (sketch): Membership in EXPSPACE follows from Theorems 1 and 2.

To prove hardness, we carry out a reduction from deterministic exponential-space-bounded Turing machines. Given a Turing machine T of exponential space complexity $s(n)$, we denote by Σ an alphabet for encoding T (the alphabet Σ and the encoding are defined later). We then construct a transition system S_T over the alphabet $\Sigma \cup \{\$\}$, for some $\$ \not\in \Sigma$, such that (i) the size of S_T is linear in $|T|$ and in $\log s(n)$, and (ii) $\Sigma^\omega + (\Sigma^* \cdot \$^\omega) \subseteq \mathcal{T}(S_T)$ iff T does not accept the empty tape.

We assume, without loss of generality, that once T reaches a final state it loops there forever. Typically, the transition system S_T accepts all traces in Σ^ω, and accepts a trace $w \cdot \$^\omega \in \Sigma^* \cdot \$^\omega$ if either (i) w is not an encoding of a prefix of a legal computation of T over the empty tape, (ii) w is an encoding of a prefix of a legal computation of T over the empty tape, but, within this prefix, the computation still has not reached a final state, or (iii) w is an encoding of a prefix of a legal, but rejecting, computation of T over the empty tape. Thus, S_T rejects a trace $w \cdot \$^\omega$ iff w encodes a prefix of a legal accepting computation of T over the empty tape and the computation has already reached a final state. Hence, S_T accepts all traces in $\Sigma^\omega + \Sigma^* \cdot \$^\omega$ iff T does not accept the empty tape.

In order to check whether a given trace w encodes a computation of T, the system S_T checks that each two successive configurations encoded in w are compatible with T's transition relation. For that, S_T needs to relate positions in w that are $s(n) + 1$ far from each other. Accordingly, one component of S_T, the one that performs the "compatibility check", cooperates with $\log s(n)$ other components, whose only task is to perform this count (as described in Example 1).

Now, we construct S to be a concurrent transition system that generates the language $\Sigma^\omega + (\Sigma^* \cdot \$^\omega)$. In fact, S can be easily taken to be a sequential transition system with $|\Sigma| + 1$ states. It follows that T does not accept the empty tape iff $S \subseteq S_T$. □

The reduction we present in the proof of Theorem 6 considers a simple implementation and an elaborated specification. We now show that the specification is indeed the dominant factor of the containment problem. Fixing it, the problem becomes significantly easier. Still, traversing the exponentially big state space of the implementation cannot be avoided.

Theorem 7. *The implementation complexity of containment for concurrent transition systems is PSPACE–complete.*

Proof (sketch): Membership in PSPACE follows from Theorems 1 and 2. For the lower-bound, we prove that the emptiness problem for concurrent transition systems is already PSPACE-hard. For that, we carry out a reduction from deterministic polynomial-space-bounded Turing machines. We show that given a Turing machine T of polynomial space complexity $s(n)$, it is possible to build, using a logarithmic amount of space, a concurrent transition system S_T of size $O(s(n))$ such that S_T is empty if and only if T does not accept the empty tape.

Let $T = \langle \Gamma, Q, \mapsto, q_0, F_{rej} \rangle$, where Γ is the alphabet, Q is the set of states, and $\mapsto: (Q \times \Gamma) \rightarrow (Q \times \Gamma \times \{L, R\})$ is the transition function. We write $(q, a) \mapsto (q', b, \Delta)$ for $\mapsto (q, a) = (q', b, \Delta)$, with the meaning that when in state q and reading a in the current tape cell, T moves to state q', writes b in the current tape cell and moves its head one cell to the left or right, depending on Δ. Finally, q_0 is T's initial state, and $F_{rej} \subseteq Q$ is the set of final rejecting states. The system S_T has $s(n)$ components, one for each tape cell that is used. For all $1 \leq i \leq s(n)$, the component $S_i = \langle \emptyset, W_i, W_i^0, \delta_i, L_i \rangle$ has all states labeled with $\emptyset$ and is defined as follows:

- $W_i = (((Q \setminus F_{rej}) \times \Gamma) \cup \Gamma) \times \{i\}$. A state of the form (q, a, i) indicates that T is in state q and its head is at the i'th cell, whose contents is a. A state of the form (a, i) indicates that the contents of the i'th cell is a but the head is not at that cell.
- A transition $(q, a) \mapsto (q', b, \Delta)$ of T, with $q' \notin F_{rej}$, induces the following transitions in δ_i.
  - An unconditional transition from (q, a, i) to (b, i); i.e., $\langle (q, a, i), \mathbf{true}, (b, i) \rangle \in \delta_i$. This transition corresponds to the head moving from cell i to cell $i + 1$ or $i - 1$.
  - A transition from every $(z, i) \in \Gamma \times \{i\}$ to (q', z, i), with a condition defined as follows: If $\Delta = R$, then the current state of S_{i-1} is $(q, a, i - 1)$; i.e., if $\Delta = R$, then $\langle (z, i), \{(q, a, i - 1)\}, (q', z, i) \rangle \in \delta_i$. Dually, if $\Delta = L$, then the current state of S_{i+1} is $(q, a, i + 1)$; i.e., if $\Delta = L$, then $\langle (z, i), \{(q, a, i + 1)\}, (q', z, i) \rangle \in \delta_i$. This transition corresponds to the head moving from cell number $i + 1$ or $i - 1$ to cell number i.

  In addition, we have a transition in δ_i from every $(z, i) \in \Gamma \times \{i\}$ to (z, i), with a condition stating that the head is not moving now to the i'th cell. Let W_R^i be the set of states $(q, a, i - 1)$ in W_{i-1} such that $(q, a) \mapsto (q', b, R)$ is a transition of T for some q' and b. In a dual way, let W_L^i be the set of states $(q, a, i + 1)$ in W_{i+1} such that $(q, a) \mapsto (q', b, L)$ is a transition of T for some q' and b. Then, $\langle (z, i), \neg(W_R^i \cup W_L^i), (z, i) \rangle \in \delta_i$.
- W_i^0, the set of initial states of S_i, is a singleton that corresponds to the initial contents of the i'th cell. Thus, $W_i^0 = \{(q_0, \beta, 1)\}$ for $i = 1$, and $W_0 = \{(\beta, i)\}$ for $1 < i \leq s(n)$.

Since T is deterministic, the system S_T proceeds in a deterministic fashion, which corresponds to the single computation of T on the empty tape. To see this, observe that each reachable configuration of S_T has exactly one component S_i which is in a state in $Q \times \Gamma \times \{i\}$. Thus, each reachable configuration of S_T corresponds to a configuration of T. Also, a transition in S_T from configuration c to c' corresponds to the single possible transition of T from its configuration corresponding to c to the one corresponding to c'. Since states in $F_{rej} \times \Gamma \times \{i\}$ are not reachable in W_i, the system S_T has no corresponding move whenever T moves to a final rejecting state. So, if T rejects the empty tape, then S_T is empty. In addition, if T accepts the empty tape, then, as T loops in its final state, S_T accepts the trace $\emptyset^\omega$. Hence, T rejects the empty tape iff S_T is empty. □

In view of the known PSPACE lower bound for emptiness in communicating finite state machines [Koz77], our PSPACE lower bound here is not surprising. Note, however, that the bound in [Koz77] does not directly imply our bound here, since concurrent transition systems generate *infinite* traces.

4 The Simulation Problem

Establishing simulation involves only local checks. One could hope that locality circumvents the state-explosion problem. We show here that while locality neutralizes the dominance of the specification, an exponential blow-up in the implementation cannot be avoided. Moreover, the branching nature of simulation can be used to encode alternation, making the implementation complexity of simulation higher than that of containment.

Theorem 8. *The simulation problem for concurrent transition systems is EXPTIME–complete.*

Proof (sketch): Membership in EXPTIME follows from Theorems 1 and 3. To prove hardness in EXPTIME, we carry out a reduction from alternating linear-space-bounded Turing machines, proved to be EXPTIME-hard in [CKS81]. Similarly to the construction in the proof of Theorem 7, we show that there exists a fixed concurrent transition system S', such that, given an alternating Turing machine T of space complexity $s(n)$, it is possible to build, using a logarithmic amount of space, a concurrent transition system S_T of size $O(s(n))$ such that $S \preceq S'$ if and only if T accepts the empty tape.

Consider an alternating Turing machine $T = \langle \Gamma, Q_u, Q_e, \mapsto, q_0, F_{acc}, F_{rej} \rangle$, where the four sets of states, Q_u, Q_e, F_{acc}, and F_{rej} are disjoint, and contain the universal, the existential, the accepting, and the rejecting states, respectively. We denote their union (the set of all states) by Q. Our model of alternation prescribes that $\mapsto \subseteq Q \times \Gamma \times Q \times \Gamma \times \{L, R, H\}$ has a binary branching degree, is universal in its even-numbered steps, and is existential in its odd-numbered ones (H means that the head of T stays on the same cell). In particular, $q_0 \in Q_e$. When a universal or existential state of T branches into two states, we distinguish between the left and the right branches. Accordingly, we use $(q, a) \mapsto \langle (q_l, b_l, \Delta_l), (q_r, b_r, \Delta_r) \rangle$ to indicate that when T is in state $q \in Q_u \cup Q_e$ reading input symbol a, it branches to the left with (q_l, b_l, Δ_l) and to the right with (q_r, b_r, Δ_r). (Note that the directions left and right here have nothing to do with the movement direction of the head; these are determined by Δ_l and Δ_r.) We term q_l the $\swarrow$*-child* of q, and q_r its $\searrow$*-child*. Finally, we assume that once T reaches a final state, it loops there forever in a deterministic fashion. Accordingly, we use $(q, a) \mapsto (q, a, H)$ to indicate that when T is in state $q \in F_{acc} \cup F_{rej}$ reading symbol a, it stays in the same configuration.

The possible computations of T on w induce an AND-OR graph, whose nodes are T's configurations. We say that a node *corresponds to* state q if T's state in the node's configuration is q. With each node in the graph we associate an *acceptance value* in $\{0, 1\}$ as follows. Nodes that correspond to states in F_{acc} (respectively, F_{rej}) have acceptance value 1 (respectively, 0). The acceptance value of an AND-node (which corresponds to a universal state) is the minimum of the acceptance values of its two children, and that of an OR-node (which corresponds to an existential state) is the maximum of the acceptance values of its children.

We now construct the fixed transition system S'. The intention is for S' to embody all possible AND-OR graphs that may be induced by accepting computations of all alternating Turing machines (using the model of alternation just described). The system S' has a single component (thus, it is really a sequential transition system), whose 20 states "model" states of such machines as follows: Eight states model the Turing machine's universal states. Each of these states matches an entry in the truth table of the operator AND, adorned with a direction, either $\swarrow$ or $\searrow$, and a flag $\wedge$ that indicates that this is a universal state. Thus, the *universal internal states* of S' are $\langle \wedge 000 \swarrow \rangle$, $\langle \wedge 010 \swarrow \rangle$, $\langle \wedge 100 \swarrow \rangle$, $\langle \wedge 111 \swarrow \rangle$, $\langle \wedge 000 \searrow \rangle$, $\langle \wedge 010 \searrow \rangle$, $\langle \wedge 100 \searrow \rangle$, and $\langle \wedge 111 \searrow \rangle$. Eight states model the Turing machine's existential states. These match the entries of the truth table of OR, adorned with a direction and a flag $\vee$. Thus, the *existential internal states* of S' are $\langle \vee 000 \swarrow \rangle$, $\langle \vee 011 \swarrow \rangle$, $\langle \vee 101 \swarrow \rangle$, $\langle \vee 111 \swarrow \rangle$, $\langle \vee 000 \searrow \rangle$, $\langle \vee 011 \searrow \rangle$, $\langle \vee 101 \searrow \rangle$, and $\langle \vee 111 \searrow \rangle$. Finally, four states model the Turing machine's final states. Each of these is a Boolean value, adorned with a direction. Thus, the *final states* of S' are $\langle 0 \swarrow \rangle$, $\langle 1 \swarrow \rangle$, $\langle 0 \searrow \rangle$, and $\langle 1 \searrow \rangle$.

The intuition is that an internal state $\langle *, l, r, val, d \rangle$ corresponds to a state of the Turing machine with the following properties: Its left child has acceptance value l, it right child has acceptance value r, its own acceptance value is, therefore, val, and it can be only a d-child of other states. Similarly, a final state $\langle val, d \rangle$ corresponds to a final state of the Turing machine with acceptance value val that can be only a d-child of other states.

Accordingly, the transitions in S' from an internal state $\langle *, l, r, val, d \rangle$ cover all the possible ways that l and r can be acceptance values of the left and right children, respectively. Thus, we have transitions from $\langle *, l, r, val, d \rangle$ to another state $w = \langle *', l', r', val', d' \rangle$ iff w is an internal state of the opposite type (i.e., either $* = \wedge$ and $*' = \vee$, or vice versa) or $w = \langle val', d' \rangle$ is a final state, and, in both cases, either $val' = l$ and $d' = \swarrow$, or $val' = r$ and $d' = \searrow$. For example, the internal state $\langle \wedge 100 \swarrow \rangle$ has transitions to states $\langle \vee 011 \swarrow \rangle$, $\langle \vee 101 \swarrow \rangle$, $\langle \vee 111 \swarrow \rangle$, $\langle \vee 000 \searrow \rangle$, $\langle 1 \swarrow \rangle$, and $\langle 0 \searrow \rangle$. It has transitions from all states $\langle \vee, l, r, val, d \rangle$ with $l = 0$. In addition, the final states have self loops.

The set of observable events of S' is $\{\swarrow, \searrow, 0, 1\}$. We label an internal state by $\swarrow$ or $\searrow$ according to its direction element. For example, the node $\langle \wedge 100 \swarrow \rangle$ is labeled $\{\swarrow\}$. We label a final state by its value and direction. For example, the node $\langle 1 \searrow \rangle$ is labeled $\{1, \searrow\}$. We define the initial states of S' to be the internal existential states with $val = 1$. This completes the definition of S'. Clearly, it's size is fixed.

Given a particular alternating Turing machine T, we now define the system S_T such that $S_T \leq S'$ iff T accepts the empty tape. In general, the construction of S_T is similar to that in the proof of Theorem 7. The main difference is that while T there was deterministic, T here is alternating, and it branches in each of its transitions. Therefore, moving from configuration to configuration we must take extra care to ensure that either all components move according to the left branch, or all components move according to the right branch.

Let $T = \langle \Gamma, Q_u, Q_e, \mapsto, q_0, F_{acc}, F_{rej} \rangle$ be an $s(n)$-space-bounded alternating Turing machine as described above. The concurrent transition system S_T has $s(n)$ components, one for each tape cell. For each $1 \leq i \leq s(n)$, the component S_i is defined as follows:

- $O_i = \{\swarrow, \searrow, 0, 1\}$. Thus, $O_i = O$, and the sets of observable events are thus independent of i. As we shall see below, the events $\swarrow$ and $\searrow$ guarantee that all components move according to the same branch.
- $W_i = ((Q \times \Gamma) \cup \Gamma) \times \{\swarrow, \searrow\} \times \{i\}$. A state of the form (q, a, d, i) is called a *head-content state*; it indicates that T is in state q, the head is at cell i, whose content is a, and q was reached by taking a d branch. A state of the form (a, d, i) is called a *content state*; it indicates that the content of cell i is a, the head is not at cell i, and if the previous state of S_i was a head-content state then the current state has become a content state as a result of a taking a d branch. For both types of states, we call d the *direction element*. The direction element of a content state is determined once there is a transition from some head-content state to it. The direction element is guaranteed to maintain the directionality of the branch taken in this transition only for the next configuration. Later, this direction element may be changed.

• S_T's transitions are induced by the transitions of T as follows (in the following description we ignore the borderline cases of $i = 1$ or $i = s(n)$, which are essentially the same but require a little more attention).

- Each transition $(q, a) \mapsto \langle(q_l, b_l, \Delta_l), (q_r, b_r, \Delta_r)\rangle$ of T induces the following transitions in δ_i:

1. Unconditional transitions that correspond to the head moving from cell i to cell $i+1$ or $i-1$. These transitions also determine the direction element of the new state of S_i. For $d \in \{\swarrow, \searrow\}$, we have $\langle(q, a, d, i), \mathbf{true}, (b_l, \swarrow, i)\rangle \in \delta_i$ and $\langle(q, a, d, i), \mathbf{true}, (b_r, \searrow, i)\rangle \in \delta_i$.
2. Transitions that correspond to the head moving from cell $i+1$ or $i-1$ to cell i, as a result of taking a left branch. This includes a transition from every state $(z, d, i) \in \Gamma \times \{\swarrow, \searrow\} \times \{i\}$ to the state $(q_l, z, \swarrow, i)$, with the following conditions: If $\Delta_l = R$, then the current state of S_{i-1} must be $(q, a, d', i-1)$ for some $d' \in \{\swarrow, \searrow\}$; i.e., if $\Delta_l = R$, then $\langle(z, d, i), \{(q, a, \swarrow, i-1), (q, a, \searrow, i-1)\}, (q_l, z, \swarrow, i)\rangle \in \delta_i$. Dually, if $\Delta_l = L$, then $\langle(z, d, i), \{(q, a, \swarrow, i+1), (q, a, \searrow, i+1)\}, (q_l, z, \swarrow, i)\rangle \in \delta_i$.
3. Dual transitions that correspond to the head moving from cell $i+1$ or $i-1$ to cell i, as a result of taking a right branch.

- For each transition $(q, a) \mapsto (q, a, H)$ of T, and for all $d \in \{\swarrow, \searrow\}$, we have an unconditional transition that corresponds to looping in the final state q; i.e., $\langle(q, a, d, i), \mathbf{true}, (q, a, d, i)\rangle \in \delta_i$.
- In addition, we have transitions that correspond to "passive" cells; that is, cells to which or from which the head does not move. We allow these cells to change their direction elements, so they can adjust themselves to the new configurations. This includes transitions from each state $(z, d, i) \in \Gamma \times \{\swarrow, \searrow\} \times \{i\}$ to states (z, d', i) for $d' \in \{\swarrow, \searrow\}$, with the condition that if a d' branch is currently taken, the head is not moving to cell i.

• The set of initial states of S_i is a singleton that corresponds to the initial content of cell i with (the arbitrarily chosen) direction element $\swarrow$. Thus, this set will be $\{(q_0, \beta, \swarrow, 1)\}$ for $i = 1$, and $\{(\beta, \swarrow, i)\}$ for $1 < i \leq s(n)$.

• The labeling function L_i is defined as follows:

- $\swarrow \in L_i(w)$ iff $w \in ((Q \times \Gamma) \cup \Gamma) \times \{\swarrow\} \times \{i\}$.
- $\searrow \in L_i(w)$ iff $w \in ((Q \times \Gamma) \cup \Gamma) \times \{\searrow\} \times \{i\}$.
- $0 \in L_i(w)$ iff $w \in F_{rej} \times \Gamma \times \{\swarrow, \searrow\} \times \{i\}$.
- $1 \in L_i(w)$ iff $w \in F_{acc} \times \Gamma \times \{\swarrow, \searrow\} \times \{i\}$.

We claim that the unwinding of the system S_T corresponds to the AND-OR graph induced by the possible computations of T on the empty tape and thus, T accepts the empty tape iff $S_T \preceq S'$. To see this, observe that each reachable configuration of S_T has exactly one component S_i in a head-content state. All other components are in content states. It is true that often two components can move into head-content states, but then, by the definition of δ_i, they will have different direction elements, which implies, by the definition of L_i, that there will be disagreement on the labeling of $\swarrow$ and $\searrow$. Thus, each reachable configuration of S_T corresponds to a legal configuration of T. Also, each configuration of S_T either corresponds to a universal or existential state of T (in which case it has exactly two possible successors, one for each possible branch) or corresponds to a final state of T (in which case it has one possible successor and is labeled by either 0 or 1). □

Theorem 9. *The implementation complexity of simulation for concurrent transition systems is EXPTIME–complete.*

Proof: Membership in EXPTIME follows from Theorem 8. Since the transition system S' used there is fixed, the proof of Theorems 8 provides an EXPTIME lower bound also for the implementation complexity of the simulation problem. □

5 The Fair-Containment and the Fair-Simulation Problems

So far, we saw that when we consider non-fair transition systems, verification of concurrent transition systems is exponentially harder than verification of sequential transition systems. We now turn to consider fair transition systems.

Theorem 10. *The fair-containment problem for concurrent transition systems is EXPSPACE–complete.*

Proof: Membership in EXPSPACE follows from Theorems 1 and 4. Hardness in EXPSPACE follows from Theorem 6. □

Theorem 10 shows that, as in the case of sequential transition systems, the trace-based approach to verification extends to fair systems at no cost. Indeed, the complexities of containment and fair containment coincide. An exception to this phenomenon are strongly fair transition systems. By Theorem 4, the implementation complexity of fair containment for strongly-fair systems is higher than the implementation complexity of containment. We now show that strongly-fair transition systems are exceptional also in their concurrent behavior: The implementation complexity of fair containment for concurrent strongly-fair systems is not exponentially harder than that of sequential strongly-fair systems.

Theorem 11. *The implementation complexity of the fair-containment problem for concurrent transition systems is PSPACE–complete.*

Proof (sketch): Hardness in PSPACE follows from Theorem 7. For unconditionally-fair and weakly-fair concurrent transition systems, membership in PSPACE follows from Theorems 1 and 4. For strongly-fair systems, a straightforward application of Theorems 1 and 4 results in an algorithm with exponential running time and space. To get the PSPACE bound, we suggest the following algorithm. Let S and S' be strongly fair concurrent transition systems, and let D be a strongly-fair sequential transition system equivalent to S. For each component S_i of S, let k_i and m_i denote the number of states and the number of pairs in the fairness condition of S_i, respectively. Assume that S has n components. Then, following the construction described in the proof of Theorem 1, the system D has $k = k_1 \cdot k_2 \cdots k_n$ states and $m = m_1 + m_2 + \cdots + m_k$ pairs in its fairness condition. By [KV96], we can translate D to an unconditionally-fair sequential transition system U with $k \cdot 2^{O(m)}$ states. Thus, the size of U is exponential in the size of S. We can also translate S' to an unconditionally-fair sequential transition system U' (this also involves an exponential blow up, which, as S' is fixed, is irrelevant to our proof). By Theorem 7, checking the containment of U in U' can be done nondeterministically in space logarithmic in U, thus polynomial in S, and we are done. □

Theorem 12. *The fair-simulation problem for concurrent transition systems is EXPSPACE–complete.*

Proof (sketch): Membership in EXPSPACE follows from Theorems 5 and 1. To prove hardness in EXPSPACE we do a reduction from exponential-space-bounded Turing machines. Our reduction is similar to the reduction described in [KV96] for proving a lower bound to the fair-simulation problem for sequential transition systems. The only change is that while there the Turing machines are polynomial-space bounded, yielding a PSPACE lower bound, here the machines are exponential-space bounded, yielding an EXPSPACE lower bound. Using bounded concurrency, we can handle the exponential size of the tape by n components that count to 2^n. The details of the reduction are given in the full paper. □

Theorem 13. *The implementation complexity of the fair-simulation problem for concurrent transition systems is EXPTIME–complete.*

Proof: Membership in EXPTIME follows from Theorems 5 and 1. Hardness in EXPTIME follows from Theorem 9. □

6 Discussion

Our results are illustrated by the cube figures below, in the style of [Har89, DH94]. All the complexities denote tight bounds. We use J to denote joint complexity (and its omission to denote implementation complexity), F to denote fair transition systems (and its omission to denote non-fair ones), and C to denote concurrent transition systems (and its omission to denote sequential ones). A bold arrow represents an exponential gap between the complexity classes, a dashed arrow represents a transition from a certain space-complexity class to the same time-complexity class, and a dotted line represents a transition from a certain time-complexity class to the space-complexity class it subsumes.

Containment:

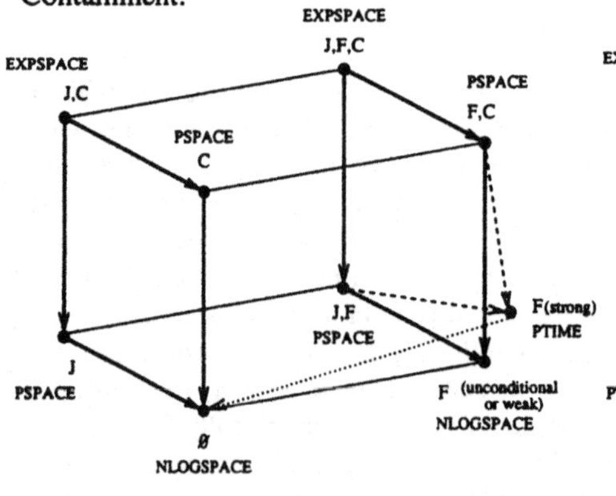

Simulation:

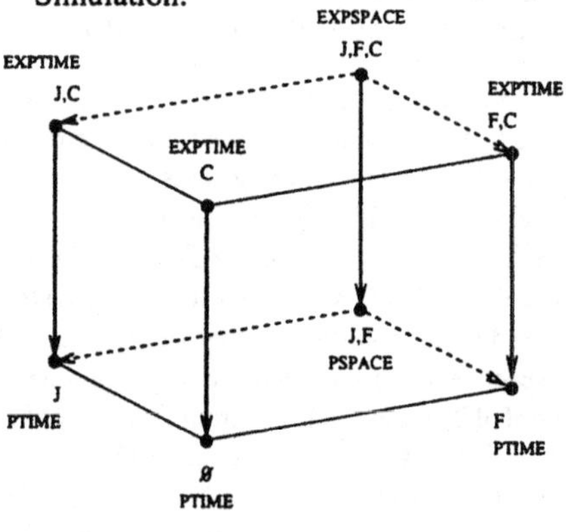

This paper considered the upper planes of the boxes. The vertical bold arrows illustrate the state-explosion problem, which is unavoidable. The protruding vertex on the lower level of the containment cube illustrates the anomaly of the strong fairness condition.

How robust are our results? Examining our lower-bound proofs, one can observe that they employ only a very humble kind of cooperation between the components. Indeed, in all the reductions, the conditions used in the transitions of a certain component S_i refer only to states of the components S_{i-1} and S_{i+1}. This suggests that a very weak, and local, model of concurrency is sufficient in order to cause the state-explosion problem. In particular, our results hold for the concurrency models presented in CSP and CCS.

References

[AL91] M. Abadi and L. Lamport. The existence of refinement mappings. *Theoretical Computer Science*, 82(2):253–284, 1991.

[ASB+94] A. Aziz, V. Singhal, F. Balarin, R. Brayton, and A.L. Sangiovanni-Vincentelli. Equivalences for fair kripke structures. In *Proc. 21st ICALP*, Jerusalem, 1994.

[BBLS92] S. Bensalem, A. Bouajjani, C. Loiseaux, and J. Sifakis. Property preserving simulations. In *Proc. 4th CAV*, LNCS 663, Montreal, 1992.

[BGS92] J. Balcazar, J. Gabarro, and M. Santha. Deciding bisimilarity is P-complete. *Formal Aspects of Computing*, 4(6):638–648, 1992.

[BVW94] O. Bernholtz, M.Y. Vardi, and P. Wolper. An automata-theoretic approach to branching-time model checking. In *Proc. 6th CAV*, LNCS 818, pages 142–155, Stanford, 1994.

[CGL93] E.M. Clarke and O. Grumberg and D. Long. Verification tools for finite-state concurrent systems. In *Decade of Concurrency – Reflections and Perspectives*, LNCS 803, pages 124–175, 1993.

[CKS81] A.K. Chandra, D.C. Kozen, and L.J. Stockmeyer. Alternation. *Journal of the Association for Computing Machinery*, 28(1):114–133, January 1981.

[DH94] D. Drusinsky and D. Harel. On the power of bounded concurrency I: Finite automata. *Journal of the ACM*, 41(3):517–539, 1994.

[GL94] O. Grumberg and D.E. Long. Model checking and modular verification. *ACM Trans. on Programming Languages and Systems*, 16(3):843–871, 1994.

[Har87] D. Harel. Statecharts: A visual formalism for complex systems. *Sci. Comp. Prog.*, 8:231–274, 1987.

[Har89] D. Harel. A thesis for bounded concurrency. In *Proc. 14th MFOCS*, LNCS 379, pages 35–48, New York, 1989.

[Hen85] M. Hennessy. *Algebraic theory of Processes*. MIT Press, Cambridge, 1985.

[HH94] T. Hirst and D. Harel. On the power of bounded concurrency II: Pushdown automata. *Journal of the ACM*, 41(3):540–554, 1994.

[HRV90] D. Harel, R. Rosner, and M.Y. Vardi. On the power of bounded concurrency iii: Reasoning about programs. In *Proc. 5th LICS*, Philadelphia, 1990.

[Koz77] D. Kozen. Lower bounds for natural proof systems. In *Proc. 18th FOCS*, pages 254–266, 1977.

[Kur94] R.P. Kurshan. *Computer Aided Verification of Coordinating Processes*. Princeton Univ. Press, 1994.

[KV96] O. Kupferman and M.Y. Vardi. Verification of fair transition systems. In *Proc. 8th CAV*, LNCS 1102, pages 372–382. Rutgers, 1996.

[LP85] O. Lichtenstein and A. Pnueli. Checking that finite state concurrent programs satisfy their linear specification. In *Proc. 12th POPL*, pages 97–107, New Orleans, 1985.

[LPS81] D. Lehman, A. Pnueli, and J. Stavi. Impartiality, justice, and fairness – the ethics of concurrent termination. In *Proc. 8th ICALP*, LNCS 115, pages 264–277. 1981.

[LS84] S.S. Lam and A.U. Shankar. Protocol verification via projection. *IEEE Trans. on Software Engineering*, 10:325–342, 1984.

[Mil71] R. Milner. An algebraic definition of simulation between programs. In *Proc. 2nd IJCAI*, pages 481–489, 1971.

[Mil80] R. Milner. *A Calculus of Communicating Systems*, LNCS 92, Springer Verlag, Berlin, 1980.

[Mil89] R. Milner. *Communication and Concurrecny*. Prentice-Hall, Englewood Clifs, 1989.

[MP92] Z. Manna and A. Pnueli. *The Temporal Logic of Reactive and Concurrent Systems: Specification*. Springer-Verlag, Berlin, January 1992.

[SVW87] A.P. Sistla, M.Y. Vardi, and P. Wolper. The complementation problem for Büchi automata with applications to temporal logic. *Theoretical Computer Science*, 49:217–237, 1987.

[VW94] M.Y. Vardi and P. Wolper. Reasoning about infinite computations. *Information and Computation*, 115(1):1–37, November 1994.

Fair Simulation*

Thomas A. Henzinger   Orna Kupferman   Sriram K. Rajamani

EECS Department, University of California, Berkeley, CA 94720-1770, U.S.A.
Email: {tah,orna,sriramr}@eecs.berkeley.edu

Abstract. The simulation preorder for labeled transition systems is defined locally as a game that relates states with their immediate successor states. Liveness assumptions about transition systems are typically modeled using fairness constraints. Existing notions of simulation for fair transition systems, however, are not local, and as a result, many appealing properties of the simulation preorder are lost. We extend the local definition of simulation to account for fairness: system $\mathcal{S}$ *fairly simulates* system $\mathcal{I}$ iff in the simulation game, there is a strategy that matches with each fair computation of $\mathcal{I}$ a fair computation of $\mathcal{S}$. Our definition enjoys a fully abstract semantics and has a logical characterization: $\mathcal{S}$ fairly simulates $\mathcal{I}$ iff every fair computation tree embedded in the unrolling of $\mathcal{I}$ can be embedded also in the unrolling of $\mathcal{S}$ or, equivalently, iff every Fair-∀AFMC formula satisfied by $\mathcal{I}$ is satisfied also by $\mathcal{S}$ (∀AFMC is the universal fragment of the alternation-free μ-calculus). The locality of the definition leads us to a polynomial-time algorithm for checking fair simulation for finite-state systems with weak and strong fairness constraints. Finally, fair simulation implies fair trace-containment, and is therefore useful as an efficiently-computable local criterion for proving linear-time abstraction hierarchies.

1 Introduction

In program verification, we check that an implementation satisfies a specification. Both the implementation and the specification describe the possible behaviors of a program at different levels of abstraction. We distinguish between two approaches to satisfaction of a specification by an implementation. In *trace-based* satisfaction, we require that every linear property (i.e., every property of computation sequences) which holds for the specification holds also for the implementation. In *tree-based satisfaction*, we require that every branching property (i.e., every property of computation trees) which holds for the specification holds also for the implementation [Pnu85].

If we represent the implementation $\mathcal{I}$ and the specification $\mathcal{S}$ using state-transition systems, then the formal relation that captures trace-based satisfaction is trace-containment: $\mathcal{S}$ *trace-contains* $\mathcal{I}$ iff it is possible to generate by $\mathcal{S}$ every sequence of observations that can be generated by $\mathcal{I}$. The notion of trace-containment is robust with respect to linear temporal logics such as LTL, in the sense that $\mathcal{S}$ trace-contains $\mathcal{I}$ iff every LTL formula that holds for $\mathcal{S}$ holds also for $\mathcal{I}$. Unfortunately, it is difficult to check trace-containment (complete for PSPACE [SM73]), and we are unlikely to find an efficient algorithm.

* This research was supported in part by the ONR YIP award N00014-95-1-0520, by the NSF CAREER award CCR-9501708, by the NSF grant CCR-9504469, by the AFOSR contract F49620-93-1-0056, by the ARO MURI grant DAAH-04-96-1-0341, by the ARPA grant NAG2-892, and by the SRC contract 95-DC-324.036.

The formal relation that captures tree-based satisfaction is tree-containment: $\mathcal{S}$ *tree-contains* $\mathcal{I}$ iff it is possible to embed in the unrolling of $\mathcal{S}$ every tree of observations that can be embedded in the unrolling of $\mathcal{I}$. The notion of tree-containment is equivalent to the notion of *simulation*, as defined by Milner [Mil71]: $\mathcal{S}$ tree-contains $\mathcal{I}$ iff $\mathcal{S}$ simulates $\mathcal{I}$; that is, we can relate each state of $\mathcal{I}$ to a state of $\mathcal{S}$ so that two related states i and s agree on their observations and every successor of i is related to some successor of s.

Simulation has several theoretically and practically appealing properties. First, like trace-containment, simulation is robust: for universal branching temporal logics (where only universal path quantification is allowed) such as ∀CTL (the universal fragment of Computation Tree Logic), ∀CTL*, and ∀AFMC (the universal fragment of the alternation free μ-calculus), $\mathcal{S}$ simulates $\mathcal{I}$ iff every formula that holds for $\mathcal{S}$ holds also for $\mathcal{I}$ [BBLS92, GL94]. Second, unlike trace-containment, the definition of simulation is local, as the relation between two states is based only on their successor states. As a result, it can be checked in polynomial time (quadratic in both $\mathcal{S}$ and $\mathcal{I}$) whether $\mathcal{S}$ simulates $\mathcal{I}$ [CPS93, BP96], and a witnessing relation for simulation can be computed using a symbolic fixpoint procedure [HHK95]. The locality advantage is so compelling as to make simulation useful also to researchers that favor trace-based specification: in automatic verification, simulation is widely used as an efficiently-computable sufficient condition for trace-containment [CPS93, Hoj96]; in manual verification, trace-containment is most naturally proved by exhibiting local witnesses such as simulation relations or refinement mappings (a restricted form of simulation relations) [Lam83, LT87, Lyn96].[2]

State-transition systems describe only the *safe* behaviors of programs. In order to model *liveness* assumptions, one typically augments state-transition systems with fairness constraints, which partition the infinite computations of a system into fair and unfair computations. The linear framework of trace-containment generalizes naturally to fair trace-containment: $\mathcal{S}$ *fairly trace-contains* $\mathcal{I}$ iff it is possible to fairly generate by $\mathcal{S}$ every sequence of observations that can be fairly generated by $\mathcal{I}$. Robustness with respect to LTL, and PSPACE-completeness extend to the fair case.

It is not so obvious how to generalize the branching framework of simulation to account for fairness. Indeed, several proposals can be found in the literature. The definition suggested by Grumberg and Long [GL94], and used among others by [ASB+94, KV96], rests on the motivation that $\mathcal{S}$ fairly simulates $\mathcal{I}$ iff every Fair-∀CTL* formula that holds for $\mathcal{S}$ holds also for $\mathcal{I}$ (the universal path quantifier of Fair-∀CTL* ranges over fair computations only). This definition, however, is neither robust (Fair-∀CTL induces a weaker preorder [ASB+94], and Fair-∀AFMC, as we show here, induces a stronger one) nor can it be checked efficiently (it is complete for PSPACE [KV96]). Following [Hoj96], we call the Grumberg-Long version of fair simulation ∃-*simulation*, because it can be defined as simulation where each fair computation of $\mathcal{I}$ is related to *some* fair computation of $\mathcal{S}$. In manual verification, by Lynch and others [LT87, Lyn96], usually a stronger notion of fair simulation is used, which we call ∀-*simulation* (see also [DHWT91]): for each fair computation of $\mathcal{I}$, *every* related computation of $\mathcal{S}$ is required to be fair.[3] Again, this definition is neither robust (no logical characterization

[2] In [AL91], it is shown that if auxiliary observable variables may be added to a system, then simulation is not only a sound proof technique but also complete for proving trace-containment.

[3] Using a similar proof technique, Lamport and others [Lam83, AL91] suggest a restricted,

is known) nor can it be checked efficiently (it is NP-complete [Hoj96]). While both ∃-simulation and ∀-simulation are sufficient conditions for fair trace-containment, they do not provide any computational advantage (indeed, algorithms for checking ∃-simulation use subroutines for checking fair trace-containment).

We introduce a new definition of *fair simulation*, and argue for its theoretical and practical merits and its advantages over existing definitions. In order to define fair simulation without losing the locality that makes simulation useful, we go back to the basis of the branching-time approach and view simulation as a generalization of tree-containment to *fair tree-containment*: we define that $\mathcal{S}$ *fairly simulates* $\mathcal{I}$ iff it is possible to fairly embed in the unrolling of $\mathcal{S}$ every tree of observations that can be fairly embedded in the unrolling of $\mathcal{I}$, where a tree embedding is fair if all infinite paths are mapped onto fair computations. This definition falls strictly between ∃-simulation and ∀-simulation.

Consider the implementation and specification appearing in Figure 1. The structures representing them are augmented with Büchi fairness constraints. In order to be fair, an infinite computation of $\mathcal{I}$ must visit the set $\{i_3, i_4\}$ infinitely often, and an infinite computation of $\mathcal{S}$ must visit the set $\{s_3, s'_4\}$ infinitely often. It is easy to see that $\mathcal{S}$ ∃-simulates $\mathcal{I}$. Indeed, the relation that maps each state in $\mathcal{I}$ to the set of states in $\mathcal{S}$ that agree with its observation is an ∃-simulation. Nevertheless, the infinite tree generated by unwinding $\mathcal{I}$ cannot be fairly embedded in an unwinding of $\mathcal{S}$. To see this, note that every occurrence of s_2 in any embedding must have both s_3 and s_4 as successors. Similarly, every occurrence of s'_2 must have both s'_3 and s'_4 as successors. Consequently, any embedding must have an infinite unfair computation.

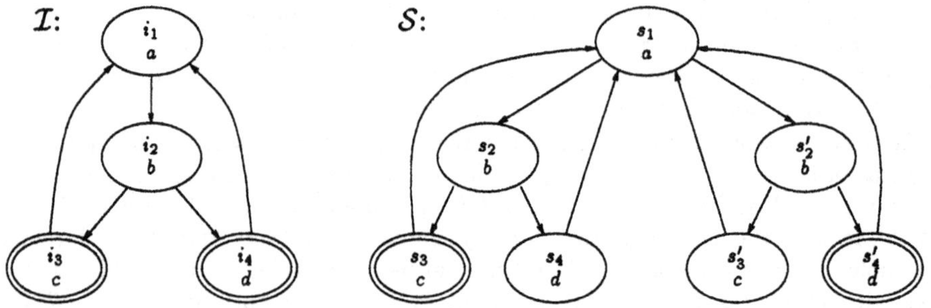

Fig. 1. Fair simulation is stronger than ∃-simulation

Consider now the implementation and specification appearing in Figure 2. Here, the infinite fair computations of $\mathcal{I}$ are those that visit i_6 infinitely often, and the infinite fair computations of $\mathcal{S}$ are those that visit s_6 infinitely often. Clearly, we can fairly embed in $\mathcal{S}$ the tree generated by unwinding $\mathcal{I}$. Hence, $\mathcal{S}$ fairly simulates $\mathcal{I}$. Still, $\mathcal{S}$ does not ∀-simulate $\mathcal{I}$. To see this, note that any candidate relation for ∀-simulation must relate i_6 to both s_4 and s_5. Then, however, the observations along the unfair

functional version of simulation, called *refinement mapping*. There, every computation of $\mathcal{I}$ is related to exactly one computation of $\mathcal{S}$; thus, ∃-simulation coincides with ∀-simulation.

computation $s_1 \cdot s_2 \cdot (s_4 \cdot s_5)^\omega$ of $\mathcal{S}$ agree with the observations of the fair computation $i_1 \cdot i_2 \cdot i_6^\omega$ of $\mathcal{I}$.

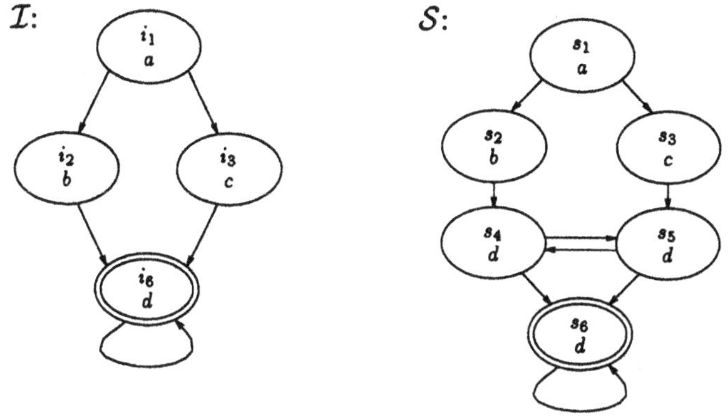

Fig. 2. ∀-simulation is stronger than fair simulation

The definition of fair simulation as fair tree-containment is equivalent to an alternative, local definition that is based on games. It is well-known that $\mathcal{S}$ simulates $\mathcal{I}$ iff in a game of the protagonist $\mathcal{S}$ against the adversary $\mathcal{I}$, the protagonist can match every move of the adversary by moving to a state with the same observation. Then, $\mathcal{S}$ fairly simulates $\mathcal{I}$ iff the protagonist has a strategy such that in the limit, after ω moves, if the adversary produces a fair computation of $\mathcal{I}$, then the protagonist produces a fair computation of $\mathcal{S}$. Consider again $\mathcal{I}$ and $\mathcal{S}$ of Figure 1, with the adversary starting at i_1 and the protagonist starting at s_1. We show that the adversary can produce a fair computation of $\mathcal{I}$ that the protagonist cannot match. The adversary first moves to i_2 and then uses the following strategy: if the protagonist replies with a move to s_2, then the adversary makes its next move to i_4, forcing the protagonist to reply with a move to s'_4. If, on the other hand, the protagonist replies with a move to s'_2, the adversary makes its next move to i_3, forcing the protagonist to reply with a move to s_3. Keeping this strategy, the adversary produces a fair computation (all computations of $\mathcal{I}$ are fair), while the protagonist, irrespective of the strategy used, produces an unfair computation, which never visits s_3 or s'_4. Hence, $\mathcal{S}$ does not fairly simulate $\mathcal{I}$. By contrast, recall, $\mathcal{S}$ ∃-simulates $\mathcal{I}$: while in ∃-simulation the protagonist can make use of information about the future moves of the adversary in order to produce a fair computation, in fair simulation the strategy of the protagonist must depend on the past and current moves only.

We argue that our definition of fair simulation is a suitable extension of simulation to fairness, as it preserves many of the appealing properties of simulation:

- Based on the locality in the game-theoretic definition of fair simulation, for two structures $\mathcal{I}$ and $\mathcal{S}$ with weak (Büchi) or strong (Streett) fairness constraints, it can be checked in time polynomial in $\mathcal{I}$ and $\mathcal{S}$ whether $\mathcal{S}$ fairly simulates $\mathcal{I}$. The algorithm, which employs tree automata, is presented in Section 3.

- Since fair simulation captures fair tree-containment, it allows a logical characterization: $\mathcal{S}$ fairly simulates $\mathcal{I}$ iff every Fair-∀AFMC formula that holds in $\mathcal{S}$ holds also in $\mathcal{I}$. This is shown in Section 4.
- Fair simulation implies fair trace-containment, and thus provides an efficiently-computable sufficient condition for checking fair trace-containment. There is evidence that most practical specifications fairly simulate their implementations. In particular, since fair simulation is implied by ∀-simulation, the fair simulation condition can be used as an efficient check to verify distributed protocols that have been verified using ∀-simulation [Lam83, LS93, Lyn96].
- In the degenerate case of vacuous fairness constraints, fair simulation coincides with simulation. In the degenerate case of deterministic systems, fair simulation coincides with fair trace-containment.

We note that in process algebra, several other preorders and equivalences on state-transition systems have been extended to account for fairness, including failure preorders [BKO87] and testing preorders [Hen87, BRV95, NC95]. From an algorithmic point of view, these preorders are closely related to (fair) trace-containment, and the problems of checking them are complete for PSPACE.

2 Definitions

A (*Kripke*) *structure* is a 5-tuple $K = \langle \Sigma, W, \hat{w}, R, L \rangle$ with the following components:

- A finite alphabet Σ of observations. Usually, we have a finite set P of propositions and $\Sigma = 2^P$.
- A finite set W of states.
- An initial state $\hat{w} \in W$.
- A transition relation $R \subseteq W \times W$.
- A labeling function $L\colon W \to \Sigma$ that maps each state to an observation.

The structure K is *deterministic* if whenever $R(w, w_1)$ and $R(w, w_2)$ for $w_1 \neq w_2$, then $L(w_1) \neq L(w_2)$. For a state $w \in W$, a *w-run* of K is a finite or infinite sequence $\overline{w} = w_0 \cdot w_1 \cdot w_2 \cdots$ of states $w_i \in W$ such that $w_0 = w$ and $R(w_i, w_{i+1})$ for all $i \geq 0$. We write $\inf(\overline{w})$ for the set of states that occur infinitely often in $\overline{w}$. A *run* of K is a $\hat{w}$-run, for the initial state $\hat{w}$. A *trace* of K is a finite or infinite sequence $\overline{\sigma} = \sigma_0 \cdot \sigma_1 \cdot \sigma_2 \cdots$ of observations $\sigma_i \in \Sigma$ such that there is a run $\overline{w}$ of K and $\sigma_i = L(w_i)$ for all $i \geq 0$; in this case we say that the run $\overline{w}$ *witnesses* the trace $\overline{\sigma}$.

A *fairness constraint* for K is a function that maps every run of K to the binary set $\{\mathit{fair}, \mathit{unfair}\}$. We consider three kinds of fairness constraints:

- The *vacuous* constraint maps every run of K to *fair*.
- A *Büchi* constraint F is specified by a set $F_B \subseteq W$ of states. Then $F(\overline{w}) = \mathit{fair}$ iff $\inf(\overline{w}) \cap F_B \neq \emptyset$.
- A *Streett* constraint F is specified by a set $F_S \subseteq 2^W \times 2^W$ of pairs of state sets. Then $F(\overline{w}) = \mathit{fair}$ iff for every pair $\langle l, r \rangle \in F_S$, if $\inf(\overline{w}) \cap l \neq \emptyset$ then $\inf(\overline{w}) \cap r \neq \emptyset$.

A *fair structure* $\mathcal{K} = \langle K, F \rangle$ consists of a structure K and a fairness constraint F for K. The fair structure $\mathcal{K}$ is a Büchi structure if F is a Büchi constraint, and $\mathcal{K}$ is a Streett structure if F is a Streett constraint. In particular, every Büchi structure is also a Streett structure. For a state $w \in W$, a *fair* w-run of $\mathcal{K}$ is either a finite w-run of K or an infinite w-run $\overline{w}$ of K such that $F(\overline{w}) = fair$. A fair run of $\mathcal{K}$ is a fair $\hat{w}$-run, for the initial state $\hat{w}$. A *fair trace* of $\mathcal{K}$ is a trace of K that is witnessed by a fair run of $\mathcal{K}$.

In the following, we consider two structures $K_1 = \langle \Sigma, W_1, \hat{w}_1, R_1, L_1 \rangle$ and $K_2 = \langle \Sigma, W_2, \hat{w}_2, R_2, L_2 \rangle$ over the same alphabet, and two fair structures $\mathcal{K}_1 = \langle K_1, F_1 \rangle$ and $\mathcal{K}_2 = \langle K_2, F_2 \rangle$.

Trace-containment and fair trace-containment

The structure K_1 *trace-contains* the structure K_2 if every trace of K_2 is also a trace of K_1 (or, equivalently, if every finite trace of K_2 is also a finite trace of K_1). The problem of checking if K_1 trace-contains K_2 is complete for PSPACE [SM73].

The fair structure $\mathcal{K}_1$ *fairly trace-contains* the fair structure $\mathcal{K}_2$ if every fair trace of $\mathcal{K}_2$ is also a fair trace of $\mathcal{K}_1$. For vacuous constraints F_1 and F_2, fair trace-containment coincides with trace-containment. For Büchi or Streett constraints F_1 and F_2, the problem of checking if $\mathcal{K}_1$ fairly trace-contains $\mathcal{K}_2$ is complete for PSPACE [SVW87, Saf88].

Simulation

A binary relation $S \subseteq W_1 \times W_2$ is a *simulation* of K_2 by K_1 if the following two conditions hold [Mil71]:

1. If $S(w_1, w_2)$, then $L_1(w_1) = L_2(w_2)$.
2. If $S(w_1, w_2)$ and $R_2(w_2, w_2')$, then there is a state $w_1' \in W_1$ such that $R_1(w_1, w_1')$ and $S(w_1', w_2')$.

The structure K_1 *simulates* the structure K_2 if there is a simulation S of K_2 by K_1 such that $S(\hat{w}_1, \hat{w}_2)$. The problem of checking if K_1 simulates K_2 can be solved in time $O((|W_1| + |W_2|) \cdot (|R_1| + |R_2|))$ [BP96, HHK95]. If K_1 simulates K_2, then K_1 trace-contains K_2. If K_1 and K_2 are both deterministic, then similarity coincides with trace-containment.

The following three alternative definitions of similarity are equivalent to the definition above.

The game-theoretic view. Consider a two-player game whose positions are pairs $\langle w_1, w_2 \rangle \in W_1 \times W_2$ of states. The initial position is $\langle \hat{w}_1, \hat{w}_2 \rangle$. The game is played between an adversary and a protagonist and it proceeds in a sequence of rounds. In each round, if $\langle w_1, w_2 \rangle$ is the current position, first the adversary updates the second component w_2 to any R_2-successor w_2', and then the protagonist updates the first component w_1 to some R_1-successor w_1' such that $L_1(w_1') = L_2(w_2')$. If no such w_1' exists, then the protagonist loses. If the game proceeds ad infinitum, for ω rounds, then the adversary loses. It is easy to see that K_1 simulates K_2 iff the protagonist has a winning strategy.

The tree-containment view. A (finite or infinite) *tree* is a set $t \subseteq \mathbb{N}^*$ such that if $xn \in t$, for $x \in \mathbb{N}^*$ and $n \in \mathbb{N}$, then $x \in t$ and $xm \in t$ for all $0 \leq m < n$. The elements of t represent nodes: the empty word ϵ is the root of t, and for each node x, the nodes of the form xn, for $n \in \mathbb{N}$, are the children of x. The number of children of the node x is denoted by $deg(x)$. A *path* ρ of t is a finite or infinite set $\rho \subseteq t$ of nodes that satisfies the following three conditions: (1) $\epsilon \in \rho$, (2) for each node $x \in \rho$, there exists at most one $n \in \mathbb{N}$ with $xn \in \rho$, and (3) if $xn \in \rho$, then $x \in \rho$. Given a set A, an *A-labeled tree* is a pair $\langle t, \lambda \rangle$, where t is a tree and $\lambda : t \to A$ is a labeling function that maps each node of t to an element in A. Then, every path $\rho = \{\epsilon, n_0, n_0n_1, n_0n_1n_2, \ldots\}$ of t generates a sequence $\lambda(\rho) = \lambda(\epsilon) \cdot \lambda(n_0) \cdot \lambda(n_0n_1) \cdots$ of elements in A.

Consider a structure $K = \langle \Sigma, W, \hat{w}, R, L \rangle$. A W-labeled tree $\langle t, \lambda \rangle$ is a *run-tree* of K if $\epsilon \in t$, $\lambda(\epsilon) = \hat{w}$, and for all nodes $x \in t$, if $xn \in t$ then $R(\lambda(x), \lambda(xn))$. A Σ-labeled tree $\langle t', \lambda' \rangle$ is a *trace-tree* of K if there is a run-tree $\langle t, \lambda \rangle$ of K such that $t' = t$ and $\lambda' = \lambda \circ L$ (that is, for every node $x \in t$, we have $\lambda'(x) = L(\lambda(x))$); in this case we say that the run-tree $\langle t, \lambda \rangle$ witnesses the trace-tree $\langle t', \lambda' \rangle$. It is easy to see that K_1 simulates K_2 iff every trace-tree of K_2 is also a trace-tree of K_1 (or, equivalently, iff every finite trace-tree of K_2 is also a finite trace-tree of K_1).

The temporal-logic view. The three branching-time logics ∀CTL, ∀CTL*, and ∀AFMC are the fragments of CTL, CTL*, and the alternation-free μ-calculus that do not contain existential path quantifiers [BBLS92, GL94]. It is well-known that K_1 simulates K_2 iff for every formula ψ of ∀CTL (or ∀CTL* or ∀AFMC), if K_1 satisfies ψ, then K_2 satisfies ψ. It follows that similarity is the coarsest abstraction that preserves any of these three logics.

Previous definitions of fair simulation

In the literature, we find several extensions of similarity that account for fairness constraints. In particular, the following two extensions have been studied and used extensively.

∃-simulation [GL94]. A binary relation $S \subseteq W_1 \times W_2$ is an *∃-simulation* of $\mathcal{K}_2$ by $\mathcal{K}_1$ if the following two conditions hold:

1. If $S(w_1, w_2)$, then $L_1(w_1) = L_2(w_2)$.
2. If $S(w_1, w_2)$, then for every fair w_1-run $\overline{w} = u_0 \cdot u_1 \cdot u_2 \cdots$ of $\mathcal{K}_2$, there is a fair w_2-run $\overline{w}' = u'_0 \cdot u'_1 \cdot u'_2 \cdots$ of $\mathcal{K}_1$ such that $\overline{w}'$ *S-matches* $\overline{w}$; that is, $|\overline{w}'| = |\overline{w}|$ and $S(u'_i, u_i)$ for all $0 \leq i \leq |\overline{w}|$.

Clearly, every ∃-simulation of $\mathcal{K}_2$ by $\mathcal{K}_1$ is a simulation of K_2 by K_1. The fair structure $\mathcal{K}_1$ *∃-simulates* the fair structure $\mathcal{K}_2$ if there is an ∃-simulation S of $\mathcal{K}_2$ by $\mathcal{K}_1$ such that $S(\hat{w}_1, \hat{w}_2)$.

For vacuous constraints F_1 and F_2, ∃-similarity coincides with similarity. For Büchi or Streett constraints F_1 and F_2, the problem of checking if $\mathcal{K}_1$ ∃-simulates $\mathcal{K}_2$ is complete for PSPACE [KV96]. ∃-similarity is the coarsest abstraction that preserves Fair-∀CTL*, where the universal path quantifiers range over the fair runs only: $\mathcal{K}_1$ ∃-simulates $\mathcal{K}_2$ iff for every formula ψ of Fair-∀CTL*, if K_1 satisfies ψ, then K_2 satisfies ψ [GL94]. By contrast, ∃-similarity is not the coarsest abstraction that preserves Fair-∀CTL: there are two Büchi structures $\mathcal{K}_1$ and $\mathcal{K}_2$ that satisfy the same formulas of ∀CTL, but $\mathcal{K}_1$ does not ∃-simulate $\mathcal{K}_2$ [ASB+94]. Moreover, ∃-similarity does not preserve Fair-∀AFMC: as we show in Section 4, there are two Büchi structures $\mathcal{K}_1$ and $\mathcal{K}_2$, and a Fair-∀AFMC formula ψ, such that $\mathcal{K}_1$ ∃-simulates $\mathcal{K}_2$, and $\mathcal{K}_1$ satisfies ψ, but $\mathcal{K}_2$ does not satisfy ψ.

∀-simulation [LT87, DHWT91]. A binary relation $S \subseteq W_1 \times W_2$ is a *∀-simulation* of $\mathcal{K}_2$ by $\mathcal{K}_1$ if the following two conditions hold:

1. S is a simulation of K_2 by K_1.
2. If $S(w_1, w_2)$, then for every fair w_1-run $\overline{w}$ of $\mathcal{K}_2$ and every w_2-run $\overline{w}'$ of K_1, if $\overline{w}'$ S-matches $\overline{w}$, then $\overline{w}'$ is a fair w_2-run of $\mathcal{K}_1$.

Clearly, every $\forall$-simulation of $\mathcal{K}_2$ by $\mathcal{K}_1$ is an $\exists$-simulation of $\mathcal{K}_2$ by $\mathcal{K}_1$. The fair structure $\mathcal{K}_1$ *$\forall$-simulates* the fair structure $\mathcal{K}_2$ if there is a $\forall$-simulation S of $\mathcal{K}_2$ by $\mathcal{K}_1$ such that $S(\hat{w}_1, \hat{w}_2)$.

For vacuous constraints F_1 and F_2, $\forall$-similarity coincides with similarity. For Büchi or Streett constraints F_1 and F_2, the problem of checking whether $\mathcal{K}_1$ $\forall$-simulates $\mathcal{K}_2$ is NP-complete [Hoj96]. $\forall$-simulation is widely used for proving abstraction hierarchies of distributed protocols [Lyn96]. In practice, Condition 2. is often replaced by a stronger condition that relates the two fairness constraints: for example, if F_1 and F_2 are both Büchi constraints, then a sufficient condition for 2. is that if $S(w_1, w_2)$ and $w_2 \in F_2$, then $w_1 \in F_1$. Particularly popular is a functional version of simulation: the simulation S is a *refinement mapping* if whenever $S(w_1, w_2)$ and $S(w'_1, w_2)$, then $w_1 = w'_1$ [AL91]. If S is a refinement mapping, then S is a $\forall$-simulation iff S is an $\exists$-simulation.

Our definition of fair simulation

Recall the simulation game of the protagonist K_1 against the adversary K_2. A *strategy* τ for the protagonist is a partial function from $(W_1 \times W_2)^* \times W_2$ to W_1: if the game so far has produced the sequence $\pi \in (W_1 \times W_2)^*$ of positions, and the adversary moves to w, then the strategy τ instructs the protagonist to move to $w' = \tau(\pi, w)$, thus resulting in the new position $\langle w', w\rangle$. Given a finite or an infinite sequence $\overline{w} = w_0 \cdot w_1 \cdot w_2 \cdots$ of states $w_i \in W_2$, the *outcome* $\tau[\overline{w}] = w'_0 \cdot w'_1 \cdot w'_2 \cdots$ of the strategy τ is the finite or the infinite sequence of states $w'_i \in W_1$ such that $|\tau[\overline{w}]| = |\overline{w}|$ and $w'_i = \tau(w'_0, w_0, \ldots, w'_{i-1}, w_{i-1}, w_i)$ for all $i \geq 0$. A binary relation $S \subseteq W_1 \times W_2$ is a *fair simulation* of $\mathcal{K}_2$ by $\mathcal{K}_1$ if the following two conditions hold:

1. If $S(w_1, w_2)$, then $L_1(w_1) = L_2(w_2)$.
2. If $S(w_1, w_2)$, then there exists a strategy τ such that for every fair w_2-run $\overline{w}$ of $\mathcal{K}_2$, the outcome $\tau[\overline{w}]$ is a fair w_1-run of $\mathcal{K}_1$ and $\tau[\overline{w}]$ S-matches $\overline{w}$.

Clearly, every fair simulation of $\mathcal{K}_2$ by $\mathcal{K}_1$ is an $\exists$-simulation of $\mathcal{K}_2$ by $\mathcal{K}_1$, and every $\forall$-simulation of $\mathcal{K}_2$ by $\mathcal{K}_1$ is a fair simulation of $\mathcal{K}_2$ by $\mathcal{K}_1$. The fair structure $\mathcal{K}_1$ *fairly simulates* the fair structure $\mathcal{K}_2$ if there is a fair simulation S of $\mathcal{K}_2$ by $\mathcal{K}_1$ such that $S(\hat{w}_1, \hat{w}_2)$.

In Section 3, we suggest an algorithm for checking whether two fair structures are fairly similar. The algorithm reduces the fair-similarity problem to the nonemptiness problem of tree automata. Known results about tree automata [Rab70, PR89] then imply that in Condition 2. above, if a required strategy exists, then there exists a *finite-state* strategy; that is, a strategy produced by a finite-state machine. Moreover, for Büchi structures, there exists a *memoryless* strategy; that is, a strategy that decides its next move based only on the current position and the current move of the adversary. On the other hand, for Streett structures, there may not exist a memoryless strategy. To see this, consider the two Streett structures shown below: the infinite fair runs of $\mathcal{I}$ are those that visit i_2 infinitely often, and the infinite fair runs of $\mathcal{S}$ are those that visit both s_2 and s'_2 infinitely often (i.e., $\mathcal{S}$ has the Streett constraint $\{\langle\{s_1\}, \{s_2\}\rangle, \langle\{s_1\}, \{s'_2\}\rangle\}$).

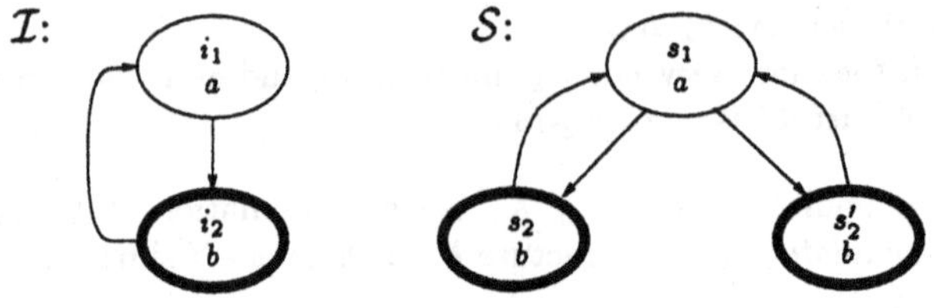

In order to satisfy Condition 2., the protagonist must visit both s_2 and s_2' infinitely often. Hence, it cannot follow a memoryless strategy.

As we demonstrated in Section 1, fair similarity falls strictly between ∃-similarity and ∀-similarity. Hence the following two propositions.

Proposition 1. *For all fair structures $\mathcal{K}_1$ and $\mathcal{K}_2$, if $\mathcal{K}_1$ fairly simulates $\mathcal{K}_2$, then $\mathcal{K}_1$ ∃-simulates $\mathcal{K}_2$. There are two Büchi structures $\mathcal{K}_1$ and $\mathcal{K}_2$ such that $\mathcal{K}_1$ ∃-simulates $\mathcal{K}_2$, but $\mathcal{K}_1$ does not fairly simulate $\mathcal{K}_2$.*

Proposition 2. *For all fair structures $\mathcal{K}_1$ and $\mathcal{K}_2$, if $\mathcal{K}_1$ ∀-simulates $\mathcal{K}_2$, then $\mathcal{K}_1$ fairly simulates $\mathcal{K}_2$. There are two Büchi structures $\mathcal{K}_1$ and $\mathcal{K}_2$ such that $\mathcal{K}_1$ fairly simulates $\mathcal{K}_2$, but $\mathcal{K}_1$ does not ∀-simulate $\mathcal{K}_2$.*

It is also worth noting that for vacuous fairness constraints, fair similarity, ∃-similarity, and ∀-similarity all coincide with similarity, and for deterministic structures, fair similarity, ∃-similarity, and ∀-similarity all coincide with fair trace-containment.

As with similarity, there are three alternative definitions of fair similarity that are equivalent to the definition above.

The game-theoretic view. If the simulation game is played for ω rounds, then the protagonist wins. In that case, the adversary produces an infinite run of K_2 and the protagonist produces an infinite run of K_1. In a fair game, the winning condition is modified as follows: if the game is played for ω rounds, then the protagonist wins iff either the adversary does not produce a fair run of $\mathcal{K}_2$, or the protagonist produces a fair run of $\mathcal{K}_1$. It is easy to see that $\mathcal{K}_1$ fairly simulates $\mathcal{K}_2$ iff the protagonist has a winning strategy in the fair game.

The tree-containment view. Given a fair structure $\mathcal{K} = \langle K, F \rangle$, a *fair run-tree* of $\mathcal{K}$ is a run-tree $\langle t, \lambda \rangle$ of K such that every path of t generates a fair run of $\mathcal{K}$. A *fair trace-tree* of $\mathcal{K}$ is a trace-tree of K that is witnessed by a fair run-tree of $\mathcal{K}$. The following proposition gives a fully abstract tree semantics to fair simulation.

Proposition 3. *A fair structure $\mathcal{K}_1$ fairly simulates a fair structure $\mathcal{K}_2$ iff every fair trace-tree of $\mathcal{K}_2$ is also a fair trace-tree of $\mathcal{K}_1$.*

The temporal-logic view. In Section 4, we show that $\mathcal{K}_1$ fairly simulates $\mathcal{K}_2$ iff for every formula ψ of Fair-∀AFMC, if $\mathcal{K}_1$ satisfies ψ, then $\mathcal{K}_2$ satisfies ψ. It follows that fair similarity is the coarsest abstraction that preserves the fair universal alternation-free μ-calculus.

3 Checking Fair Simulation

Given two fair structures $\mathcal{K}_1 = \langle K_1, F_1 \rangle$ and $\mathcal{K}_2 = \langle K_2, F_2 \rangle$, we present an automata-based algorithm that checks, in time polynomial in K_1 and K_2, whether $\mathcal{K}_1$ fairly simulates $\mathcal{K}_2$.

We begin with considering a weak version of fair simulations S, where the S-matching requirement is restricted to fair runs that start at the initial states of K_2 and K_1. Formally, a binary relation $S \subseteq W_1 \times W_2$ is an *init-fair simulation* of $\mathcal{K}_2$ by $\mathcal{K}_1$ if the following three conditions hold:

1. $S(\hat{w}_1, \hat{w}_2)$.
2. If $S(w_1, w_2)$, then $L_1(w_1) = L_2(w_2)$.
3. There exists a strategy τ such that for every fair run $\overline{w}$ of $\mathcal{K}_2$, the outcome $\tau[\overline{w}]$ is a fair run of $\mathcal{K}_1$ and $\tau[\overline{w}]$ S-matches $\overline{w}$.

Clearly, every fair simulation is an init-fair simulation. While the converse does not hold, the existence of an init-fair simulation between two fair structures implies the existence of a fair simulation. The fair structure $\mathcal{K}_1$ *init-fairly simulates* the fair structure $\mathcal{K}_2$ if there is an init-fair simulation S of $\mathcal{K}_2$ by $\mathcal{K}_1$.

Proposition 4. *A fair structure $\mathcal{K}_1$ init-fairly simulates a fair structure $\mathcal{K}_2$ iff $\mathcal{K}_1$ fairly simulates $\mathcal{K}_2$.*

Consequently, in order to check whether $\mathcal{K}_1$ fairly simulates $\mathcal{K}_2$, it suffices to check whether $\mathcal{K}_1$ init-fairly simulates $\mathcal{K}_2$. Init-fair simulations enjoy the following monotonicity property.

Proposition 5. *For all fair structures $\mathcal{K}_1 = \langle K_1, F_1 \rangle$ and $\mathcal{K}_2 = \langle K_2, F_2 \rangle$, if S is an init-fair simulation of $\mathcal{K}_2$ by $\mathcal{K}_1$, and $S' \supseteq S$ is a simulation of K_2 by K_1, then S' is also an init-fair simulation of $\mathcal{K}_2$ by $\mathcal{K}_1$.*

Consequently, in order to check whether $\mathcal{K}_1$ init-fairly simulates $\mathcal{K}_2$, we can first construct the (unique) maximal simulation $\hat{S}$ of K_2 by K_1, and then check if $\hat{S}$ is init-fair. The construction of $\hat{S}$ requires time $O((|W_1| + |W_2|) \cdot (|R_1| + |R_2|))$ [BP96, HHK95]. Hence we are left to find an algorithm that efficiently checks, given a relation $S \subseteq W_1 \times W_2$, if S is an init-fair simulation from $\mathcal{K}_2$ to $\mathcal{K}_1$.

For this purpose, consider the product structure $K_S = \langle \Sigma_S, W, \hat{w}, R, L \rangle$, with the following components:

- $\Sigma_S = W_1 \cup W_2$. Thus, each state of K is labeled by a state of K_1 or K_2.
- $W = (S \times \{\mathbf{a}\}) \cup (W_1 \times W_2 \times \{\mathbf{p}\})$. Thus, there are two types of states: adversary-states, in which the W_1-component is related by S to the W_2-component, and protagonist-states, which are not restricted. We regard the states of K_S as positions in a game, with the adversary moving in adversary-states and the protagonist moving in protagonist-states.
- $\hat{w} = \langle \hat{w}_1, \hat{w}_2, \mathbf{a} \rangle$. This is the initial game position.
- $R = \{\langle \langle w_1, w_2, \mathbf{a} \rangle, \langle w_1, w_2', \mathbf{p} \rangle \rangle \mid R_2(w_2, w_2')\} \cup \{\langle \langle w_1, w_2, \mathbf{p} \rangle, \langle w_1', w_2, \mathbf{a} \rangle \rangle \mid R_1(w_1, w_1')\}$. Thus, the adversary and the protagonist alternate moves. The adversary moves along transitions that correspond to transitions of K_2 and the protagonist moves along transitions that correspond to transitions of K_1. Since adversary-states consist only of pairs in S, the protagonist must reply to each move of the adversary to a state $\langle w_1, w_2', \mathbf{p} \rangle$ with a move to a state $\langle w_1', w_2', \mathbf{a} \rangle$ for which $S(w_1', w_2')$.

- We label an adversary-state by its W_2-component and we label a protagonist-state by its W_1-component; that is, $L(\langle w_1, w_2, \mathbf{a}\rangle) = \{w_2\}$ and $L(\langle w_1, w_2, \mathbf{p}\rangle) = \{w_1\}$.

The game on K_S is won by the protagonist if (1) whenever the game position is a protagonist-state, the protagonist can proceed with a move, and (2) whenever the game produces an infinite run of K_S, either the run does not satisfy F_2 or it satisfies both F_1 and F_2 (where a run $\overline{w}$ of K_S is considered to satisfy a fairness constraint F iff $F(L(\overline{w})) = \mathit{fair}$). Then, the protagonist has a winning strategy in this game iff S is an init-fair simulation from $\mathcal{K}_2$ to $\mathcal{K}_1$.

The problem of checking the existence of a winning strategy (and the synthesis of such a strategy [Rab70, PR89]) can be reduced to the nonemptiness problem for tree automata. We construct two automata:

1. $\mathcal{A}_S$, which accepts all infinite $(W_1 \cup W_2)$-labeled trees that can be obtained by unrolling K_S and pruning from it subtrees that have as a root an adversary-state so that each protagonist state has exactly one successor. The intuition is that each such tree corresponds to a strategy of the protagonist. The automaton $\mathcal{A}_S$ has $|W_1| \cdot |W_2|$ states, and it has a vacuous acceptance condition.
2. $\mathcal{A}_F$, which accepts all infinite trees labeled by $W_1 \cup W_2$ in in which all paths that satisfy F_2 satisfy F_1 as well. When $\mathcal{K}_1$ and $\mathcal{K}_2$ are Büchi structures, the automaton $\mathcal{A}_F$ can be defined as a Streett automaton with two states and a single pair in the Streett constraint. When $\mathcal{K}_1$ and $\mathcal{K}_2$ are Streett structures, the automaton $\mathcal{A}_F$ can be defined as the intersection of $|F_1|$ Streett automata, each with $2|F_2|$ states and a single pair. Thus, $\mathcal{A}_F$ has $(2|F_2|)^{|F_1|}$ states and $|F_1|$ pairs.

It is easy to see that the protagonist has a winning strategy iff the intersection of $\mathcal{A}_S$ and $\mathcal{A}_F$ is nonempty. Since checking the nonemptiness of a Streett tree automaton with n states and f pairs requires time $O((nf)^{3f})$ [EJ88], the theorem below follows.

Theorem 6. *Given two fair structures $\mathcal{K}_1$ and $\mathcal{K}_2$ with state sets W_1 and W_2, transition relations R_1 and R_2, and fairness constraints F_1 and F_2, we can check whether $\mathcal{K}_1$ fairly simulates $\mathcal{K}_2$ in time:*

- $O((|W_1| + |W_2|) \cdot (|R_1| + |R_2|) + (|W_1| \cdot |W_2|)^2)$, *for Büchi structures.*
- $O((|W_1| \cdot |W_2|)^{3|F_1|} \cdot |F_2|^{3|F_1|^2})$, *for Streett structures.*

4 A Logical Characterization of Fair Simulation

We show that fair simulation characterizes the distinguishing power of the fair universal fragment of the alternation free μ-calculus (Fair-∀AFMC); that is, for every two fair structures $\mathcal{K}_1$ and $\mathcal{K}_2$, every Fair-∀AFMC that is satisfied in $\mathcal{K}_1$ is satisfied also in $\mathcal{K}_2$ iff $\mathcal{K}_1$ simulates $\mathcal{K}_2$. For technical convenience, we consider ∃AFMC, the dual, existential fragment of the alternation-free μ-calculus.

Syntax and semantics of Fair-∃AFMC

The syntax of ∃AFMC is defined with respect to a set P of propositions and a set V of variables. A formula of ∃AFMC is one of the following:

- **true**, **false**, p, or $\neg p$, for $p \in P$.
- y, for $y \in V$.
- $\varphi_1 \vee \varphi_2$ or $\varphi_1 \wedge \varphi_2$, where φ_1 and φ_2 are ∃AFMC formulas.
- $\exists \bigcirc \varphi$, where φ is an ∃AFMC formula.
- $\mu y.f(y)$ or $\nu y.f(y)$, where $f(y)$ is a ∃AFMC formula. All occurrences of the variable y in $\mu y.f(y)$ and $\nu y.f(y)$ are bound.

The semantics of ∃AFMC is defined for formulas without free occurrences of variables. We interpret ∃AFMC formulas over *fair* structures, thus obtaining the logic Fair-∃AFMC. While there is no obvious interpretation of the full alternation-free μ-calculus over fair structures, ∃AFMC does not admit any switching between universal and existential path quantifiers within a fixed-point calculation. This enables us to limit all fixed-point calculations to fair paths.

The *closure* $cl(\psi)$ of a Fair-∃AFMC formula ψ is the least set of formulas that satisfies the following conditions:

- **true** $\in cl(\psi)$ and **false** $\in cl(\psi)$.
- $\psi \in cl(\psi)$.
- If $\varphi_1 \wedge \varphi_2$ or $\varphi_1 \vee \varphi_2$ is in $cl(\psi)$, then $\varphi_1 \in cl(\psi)$ and $\varphi_2 \in cl(\psi)$.
- If $\exists \bigcirc \varphi \in cl(\psi)$, then $\varphi \in cl(\psi)$.
- If $\mu y.f(y) \in cl(\psi)$, then $f(\mu y.f(y)) \in cl(\psi)$.
- If $\nu y.f(y) \in cl(\psi)$, then $f(\nu y.f(y)) \in cl(\psi)$.

Each Fair-∃AFMC formula ψ specifies a set of "obligations" —formulas in $cl(\psi)$— that need to be satisfied. The witness to the satisfaction of a formula is a tree called a sat-tree. Formally, given a fair structure $\mathcal{K} = \langle K, F \rangle$ with $K = \langle \Sigma, W, w, R, L \rangle$, and a Fair-∃AFMC formula ψ, a *sat-tree* $\langle t, \lambda \rangle$ of $\mathcal{K}$ for ψ is a $(W \times cl(\psi))$-labeled tree $\langle t, \lambda \rangle$ that satisfies the following conditions:

- $\lambda(\epsilon) = \langle \hat{w}, \psi \rangle$. Thus, the root of the tree, which corresponds to the initial obligation, is labeled by the initial state of K and ψ itself.
- If $\lambda(x) = \langle w, \mathbf{false} \rangle$, then $deg(x) = 0$.
- If $\lambda(x) = \langle w, \mathbf{true} \rangle$ and w has no successors in K, then $deg(x) = 0$.
- If $\lambda(x) = \langle w, \mathbf{true} \rangle$ and w has successors in K, then $deg(x) = 1$ and $\lambda(x0) \in \{\langle w', \mathbf{true} \rangle \mid R(w, w')\}$.
- If $\lambda(x) = \langle w, p \rangle$, where $p \in P$, then $deg(x) = 1$. If $p \in L(w)$, then $\lambda(x0) = \langle w, \mathbf{true} \rangle$, otherwise $\lambda(x0) = \langle w, \mathbf{false} \rangle$.
- If $\lambda(x) = \langle w, \neg p \rangle$, where $p \in P$, then $deg(x) = 1$. If $p \in L(w)$, then $\lambda(x0) = \langle w, \mathbf{false} \rangle$, otherwise $\lambda(x0) = \langle w, \mathbf{true} \rangle$.
- If $\lambda(x) = \langle w, \varphi_1 \vee \varphi_2 \rangle$, then $deg(x) = 1$ and $\lambda(x0) \in \{\langle w, \varphi_1 \rangle, \langle w, \varphi_2 \rangle\}$.
- If $\lambda(x) = \langle w, \varphi_1 \wedge \varphi_2 \rangle$, then $deg(x) = 2$, and $\lambda(x0) = \langle w, \varphi_1 \rangle$, and $\lambda(x1) = \langle w, \varphi_2 \rangle$.
- If $\lambda(x) = \langle w, \exists \bigcirc \varphi \rangle$, then $deg(x) = 1$ and $\lambda(x0) \in \{\langle w', \varphi \rangle \mid R(w, w')\}$.
- If $\lambda(x) = \langle w, \nu y.f(y) \rangle$, then $deg(x) = 1$ and $\lambda(x0) = \langle w, f(\nu y.f(y)) \rangle$.
- If $\lambda(x) = \langle w, \mu y.f(y) \rangle$, then $deg(x) = 1$ and $\lambda(x0) = \langle w, f(\mu y.f(y)) \rangle$.

Consider, for example, the fair structure $\mathcal{I}$ from Figure 1 and the Fair-∃AFMC formula

$$\varphi = \nu z.(a \wedge \exists \bigcirc (b \wedge \exists \bigcirc (c \wedge \exists \bigcirc z) \wedge \exists \bigcirc (d \wedge \exists \bigcirc z))).$$

Intuitively, a state of $\mathcal{I}$ belongs to the set defined by the variable z iff it is labeled a and it has a successor labeled b that has two successors, labeled c and d, both having a successor in z. The fact that z is calculated as a greatest fixed-point means that the set of states in z is the largest set that satisfies the above property. In addition, as φ is a Fair-∃AFMC formula, it is required that all runs of $\mathcal{I}$ that are embedded in z are fair. A sat-tree of $\mathcal{I}$ for φ is presented in Figure 3 (in the figure, we use the following abbreviations for formulas in $cl(\varphi)$: $\varphi_4 = d \wedge \exists\bigcirc\varphi$; $\varphi_3 = c \wedge \exists\bigcirc\varphi$; $\varphi_2 = b \wedge \exists\bigcirc\varphi_3 \wedge \exists\bigcirc\varphi_4$; and $\varphi_1 = a \wedge \exists\bigcirc\varphi_2$).

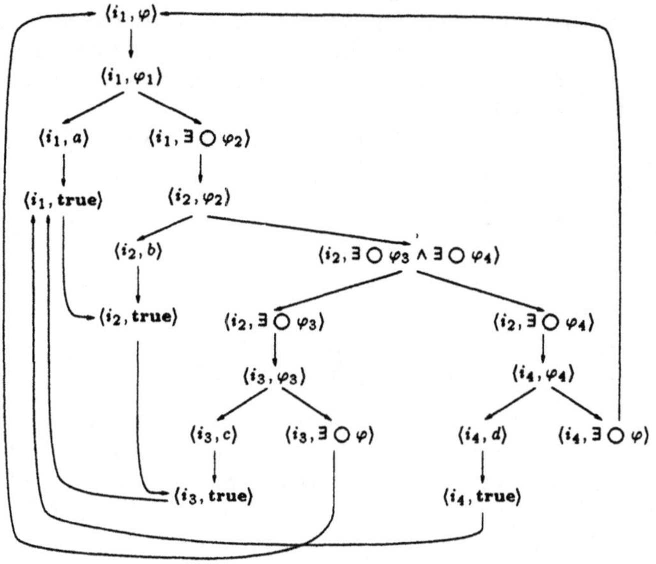

Fig. 3. A sat-tree of $\mathcal{I}$ (Figure 1) for φ

Consider a sat-tree $\langle t, \lambda \rangle$ of $\mathcal{K}$ for ψ. If $\langle t, \lambda \rangle$ contains no node labeled $\langle w, \mathbf{false} \rangle$, then it provides a witness to the satisfaction of all local obligations induced by ψ. In addition, we have to make sure that least fixed-point obligations are not propagated forever, and that existential obligations are satisfied along fair runs of $\mathcal{K}$. Formally, the sat-tree $\langle t, \lambda \rangle$ of $\mathcal{K}$ for ψ is *convincing* if the following three conditions hold:

1. The sat-tree $\langle t, \lambda \rangle$ contains no node labeled $\langle w, \mathbf{false} \rangle$. Thus, all local obligations induced by ψ are satisfied.
2. For all infinite paths ρ of $\langle t, \lambda \rangle$, the projection of $\lambda(\rho)$ on the $cl(\psi)$-component contains only finitely many formulas of the form $\mu y.f(y)$. Thus, no least fixed-point obligations are propagated forever.
3. For all infinite paths ρ of $\langle t, \lambda \rangle$, the projection of $\lambda(\rho)$ on the W-component satisfies the fairness constraint F of $\mathcal{K}$. Thus, all existential obligations are satisfied along fair runs.

Then, the fair structure $\mathcal{K}$ *satisfies* the Fair-∃AFMC formula ψ, written $\mathcal{K} \models \psi$, if there exists a convincing sat-tree of $\mathcal{K}$ for ψ. For example, the sat-tree from Figure 3 is convincing. This is because it contains no nodes labeled $\langle w, \mathbf{false}\rangle$, and because its two cycles are permissible. Hence, $\mathcal{I} \models \varphi$.

Our definition of Fair-∃AFMC is very similar to the automata-theoretic characterization of the alternation-free μ-calculus. Indeed, a convincing sat-tree of $\mathcal{K}$ for ψ can be viewed as a run of an alternating tree automaton for ψ on $\mathcal{K}$ [BVW94]. We also note that for the Fair-∃AFMC formulas that correspond to the existential fragment of Fair-CTL, our definition coincides with the usual semantics for Fair-CTL [CES86].

Fair simulation and Fair-∃AFMC

Before we show that fair simulation and Fair-∃AFMC induce the same relation on fair structures, we demonstrate that this is not the case for ∃-simulation. Consider again the fair structures from Figure 1. We saw that the Fair-∃AFMC formula φ is satisfied in $\mathcal{I}$. On the other hand, it is easy to check that although $\mathcal{S}$ ∃-simulates $\mathcal{I}$, the formula φ is not satisfied in $\mathcal{S}$.

Theorem 7. *For all fair structures $\mathcal{K}_1$ and $\mathcal{K}_2$, the following are equivalent:*

(1) *$\mathcal{K}_1$ fairly simulates $\mathcal{K}_2$.*
(2) *For every formula ψ of ∃AFMC, if $\mathcal{K}_2 \models \psi$ then $\mathcal{K}_1 \models \psi$.*

Proof. Assume first that $\mathcal{K}_1$ fairly simulates $\mathcal{K}_2$ and $\mathcal{K}_2 \models \psi$. Then, there exists a convincing sat-tree $\langle t, \lambda\rangle$ of $\mathcal{K}_2$ for ψ. Let $\langle t, \lambda'\rangle$ be the fair trace-tree of $\mathcal{K}_2$ induced by $\langle t, \lambda\rangle$. By Proposition 3, this trace-tree is also a fair trace-tree of $\mathcal{K}_1$. Thus, there exists a fair run-tree of $\mathcal{K}_1$ that witnesses $\langle t, \lambda'\rangle$ and which can be used to construct a convincing sat-tree of $\mathcal{K}_1$ for ψ. It follows that $\mathcal{K}_1 \models \psi$.

Assume now that $\mathcal{K}_1$ does not fairly simulate $\mathcal{K}_2$. Let $\mathcal{A}_1$ and $\mathcal{A}_2$ be tree automata that accept all fair trace-trees of $\mathcal{K}_1$ and $\mathcal{K}_2$, respectively. By Proposition 3, the language of $\mathcal{A}_1$ does not contain the language of $\mathcal{A}_2$. Hence, by [Rab70], there is a *regular* tree (i.e., a tree with only finitely many distinct subtrees) that is accepted by $\mathcal{A}_2$ and not accepted by $\mathcal{A}_1$. This tree can be encoded by a Fair-∃AFMC formula ψ such that $\mathcal{K}_2 \models \psi$ and $\mathcal{K}_1 \not\models \psi$. ■

Acknowledgment. We thank Ramin Hojati for very helpful comments.

References

[AL91] M. Abadi and L. Lamport. The existence of refinement mappings. *Theoretical Computer Science*, 82:253–284, 1991.

[ASB+94] A. Aziz, V. Singhal, F. Balarin, R.K. Brayton, and A.L. Sangiovanni-Vincentelli. Equivalences for fair Kripke structures. In *Proc. 21st ICALP*, Springer LNCS 820, pp. 364–375, 1994.

[BBLS92] S. Bensalem, A. Bouajjani, C. Loiseaux, and J. Sifakis. Property-preserving simulations. In *Proc. 4th CAV*, Springer LNCS 663, pp. 260–273, 1992.

[BKO87] J.A. Bergstra, J.W. Klop, and E.R. Olderog. Failures without chaos: a new process semantics for fair abstraction. In *Proc. 3rd IFIP FDPC*, Elsevier, pp. 77–103, 1987.

[BP96] B. Bloom and R. Paige. Transformational design and implementation of a new efficient solution to the ready simulation problem. *Science of Computer Programming*, 24:189–220, 1996.

[BRV95] E. Brinksma, A. Rensink, and W. Vogler. Fair testing. In *Proc. 6th CONCUR*, Springer LNCS 962, pp. 313–327, 1995.

[BVW94] O. Bernholtz, M.Y. Vardi, and P. Wolper. An automata-theoretic approach to branching-time model checking. In *Proc. 6th CAV*, Springer LNCS 818, pp. 142–155, 1994.

[CES86] E.M. Clarke, E.A. Emerson, and A.P. Sistla. Automatic verification of finite-state concurrent systems using temporal-logic specifications. ACM Transactions on Programming Languages and Systems, 8:244–263, 1986.

[CPS93] R.J. Cleaveland, J. Parrow, and B. Steffen. The Concurrency Workbench: a semantics-based tool for the verification of finite-state systems. *ACM Transactions on Programming Languages and Systems*, 15:36–72, 1993.

[DHWT91] D. Dill, A.J. Hu, and H. Wong-Toi. Checking for language inclusion using simulation relations. In *Proc. 3rd CAV*, Springer LNCS 575, pp. 255–265, 1991.

[EJ88] E.A. Emerson and C. Jutla. The complexity of tree automata and logics of programs. In *Proc. 29th FOCS*, IEEE Computer Society, pp. 368–377, 1988.

[GL94] O. Grumberg and D.E. Long. Model checking and modular verification. *ACM Transactions on Programming Languages and Systems*, 16:843–871, 1994.

[Hen87] M.C.B. Hennessy. An algebraic theory of fair asynchronous communicating processes. *Theoretical Computer Science*, 49:121–143, 1987.

[HHK95] M.R. Henzinger, T.A. Henzinger, and P.W. Kopke. Computing simulations on finite and infinite graphs. In *Proc. 36th FOCS*, IEEE Computer Society, pp. 453–462, 1995.

[Hoj96] R. Hojati. *A BDD-based Environment for Formal Verification of Hardware Systems*. PhD thesis, EECS Department, University of California, Berkeley, 1996.

[KV96] O. Kupferman and M.Y. Vardi. Verification of fair transition systems. In *Proc. 8th CAV*, Springer LNCS 1102, pp. 372–382, 1996.

[Lam83] L. Lamport. Specifying concurrent program modules. *ACM Transactions on Programming Languages and Systems*, 5:190–222, 1983.

[LS93] N.A. Lynch and R. Segala. A comparison of simulation techniques and algebraic techniques for verifying concurrent systems. Technical Report MIT/LCS/TM-499, Laboratory for Computer Science, MIT, 1993.

[LT87] N.A. Lynch and M.R. Tuttle. Hierarchical correctness proofs for distributed algorithms. In *Proc. 6th PODC*, ACM, pp. 137–151, 1987.

[Lyn96] N.A. Lynch. *Distributed Algorithms*. Morgan-Kaufmann, 1996.

[Mil71] R. Milner. An algebraic definition of simulation between programs. In *Proc. 2nd IJCAI*, British Computer Society, pp. 481–489, 1971.

[NC95] V. Natarajan and R.J. Cleaveland. Divergence and fair testing. In *Proc. 22nd ICALP*, Springer LNCS 944, pp. 648–659, 1995.

[Pnu85] A. Pnueli. Linear and branching structures in the semantics and logics of reactive systems. In *Proc. 12th ICALP*, Springer LNCS 194, pp. 15–32, 1985.

[PR89] A. Pnueli and R. Rosner. On the synthesis of a reactive module. In *Proc. 16th POPL*, ACM, pp. 179–190, 1989.

[Rab70] M.O. Rabin. Weakly definable relations and special automata. In *Proc. Mathematical Logic and Foundations of Set Theory*, Elsevier, pp. 1–23, 1970.

[Saf88] S. Safra. On the complexity of ω-automata. In *Proc. 29th FOCS*, IEEE Computer Society, pp. 319–327, 1988.

[SM73] L.J. Stockmeyer and A.R. Meyer. Word problems requiring exponential time. In *Proc. 5th STOC*, ACM, pp. 1–9, 1973.

[SVW87] A.P. Sistla, M.Y. Vardi, and P. Wolper. The complementation problem for Büchi automata with applications to temporal logic. *Theoretical Computer Science*, 49:217–237, 1987.

High Level Expressions with their SOS Semantics*

– Extended Abstract –

Hanna Klaudel[1] and Robert-C. Riemann[2]

[1] LRI, Université Paris-Sud, and IUT Paris XII, France
[2] LRI, Université Paris-Sud, France, and Universität Hildesheim, Germany

Abstract. A process algebra, called *M-expressions*, based on parameterised (multi-)actions is introduced. In the context of the *Petri Box Calculus*, it serves as a kind of high level counterpart to *Box expressions*. An operational semantics based on step sequences, similar to that given by Best, Esparza and Koutny for Box expressions is defined. The consistency and completeness of the semantics is proved with respect to the elementary case. The process algebra is applied as the semantic domain for a concurrent programming language. The consistency and completeness of the operational semantics is proved for this application with respect to an existing high level Petri net semantics.

1 Introduction

When modelling concurrent systems, the communication can be achieved in various ways. One way is the *handshake* communication, i.e., the direct transmission of values (as the rendezvous of Ada, input/output guards of (T)CSP [9] or synchronisations in CCS [12]). Another way is the common access to variables shared by two or more subprograms. One can also consider FIFO or LIFO buffers which are asynchronous versions of handshake communications. All these modes of communication are expressible in the *Petri Box Calculus* (PBC) [2], which can be seen for this respect as the common denominator for other process algebras.

The PBC is a basic process algebra which combines a number of ideas taken from CCS, CSP, ACP [1], etc., and provides a compositional Petri net semantics. Although the PBC has not specifically been defined as a common generalisation of other formalisms, it turns out that they can essentially be encoded in the PBC.

Originally, the PBC comprised a process algebra, called *Box expressions*, with a semantic domain of place/transition nets, called *Petri Boxes*. In the meantime a calculus based on high level Petri nets, called *M-nets* [5], has been introduced in order to cope with the net size problem encountered for Petri Boxes. The operations of M-nets are provably consistent in the strictest possible sense (through

* Supported by the French-German project POEM.

net unfoldings) [5]. Also, the introduction of M-nets (high level version of Petri Boxes) solved successfully the size explosion problem by giving "abbreviated" and more readable nets. In particular, it became possible to give a compositional (finite) net semantics to concurrent programming languages comprising various basic data types and process communication structures.

In this paper we propose a process algebra, called *M-expressions*, which can be seen as the high level counterpart of Box expressions. Its basic constituents are parameterised guarded actions and operators such as parallel composition ($\|$), sequence (;), choice ($\Box$), synchronisation (**sy**), restriction (**rs**), and iteration ($[\, \triangleright \triangleright]$). Each of them has basically its intuitive semantics known from PBC (and other process algebras). Like in the PBC, the synchronisation operator plays a crucial rôle in the formalism. Furthermore, a step sequential operational semantics in Plotkin style is given for the M-expressions algebra. On one hand, it allows to apply verification techniques for transition systems. On the other hand, it permits the comparisons of M-expressions with other models. Here, we characterise the relationship to M-nets and Box expressions.

Section 2 gives the syntax of M-expressions, defines their operational semantics, and concludes with results concerning the synchronisation operator and a comparison of Box expressions and M-expressions. Section 3 applies M-expressions as the semantic domain for a parallel programming language, which is also equiped with a high level Petri net semantics. The main results is the coherence of the M-expression and the existing Petri net based program semantics. This article is the extended abstract of [10]. Proofs, formal definitions concerning the M-net model, and examples can be found there.

2 Algebra of M-expressions

2.1 Notations and Preliminaries

Let *Val* be a fixed but suitable large set of *values*, and S and F disjoint sets of *storing*, respectively *free variables*; $S \cup F$ will be abbreviated by *Var*. In the set *Op* of *operators* we have, e.g., = to denote the equality of values, and operators like *not*, *and*, *or*, $+, -, \ldots$ The set of all well-formed *terms* over *Val*, *Var*, and *Op* is denoted by T.

We assume the existence of a fixed but sufficiently large set A of *actions*. Each action $A \in \mathsf{A}$ is assumed to have an arity $ar(A)$ which is a natural number describing the number of its parameters. The set A is, by definition, the carrier of a bijection:$\widehat{\ }$: $\mathsf{A} \rightarrow \mathsf{A}$, called *conjugation*, satisfying $\forall A \in \mathsf{A} : \hat{A} \neq A \wedge \hat{\hat{A}} = A$. That is, the mapping $\widehat{\ }$ groups the elements of A into pairwise conjugates. Conjugated actions will be used like in CCS to express synchronisation capabilities. It is assumed that $\forall A \in \mathsf{A} : ar(A) = ar(\widehat{A})$.

A construct $A(\tau_1, \ldots, \tau_{ar(A)})$, where A is an action and $\forall j : 1 \leq j \leq ar(A) : \tau_j \in Var \cup Val$, is a *parameterised action*. The set of all parameterised actions is denoted by P. A parameterised action $A(\tau_1, \ldots, \tau_{ar(A)})$, where $\forall j : 1 \leq j \leq ar(A) : \tau_j \in Val$, is called *elementary*. In that case we will abbreviate it as $A(\vec{\tau})$.

A parameterised action $A(\tau_1, \dots, \tau_{ar(A)})$ is *storing* if $\exists \tau \in \{\tau_1, \dots, \tau_{ar(A)}\} : \tau \in S$, otherwise it is *free*. A multiset of parameterised actions is *storing*, if one of its elements is storing. Note that each elementary parameterised action is free.
We consider finite multisets on a set B as functions $\mu: B \to \mathbb{N}$ such that $\mu(b) \neq 0$ only for finitely many $b \in B$. We denote by $\mathcal{M}_f(B)$ the set of all finite multisets on B, by $\emptyset$ the empty multiset, by $|\mu| = \sum_{b \in B} \mu(b)$ the cardinality of μ, and by $+$ the multiset sum: $(\mu + \mu')(b) = \mu(b) + \mu'(b)$. The *restriction* $\mu\lceil_b$ of a multiset μ to $b \in B$ is the multiset $\mu\lceil_b(a) = \mu(a)$, if $a = b$ and $\mu\lceil_b(a) = 0$, otherwise.
Substitutions are mappings $\theta : Var \to \mathsf{T}$ (different from the identity only for a finite subset of Var). Substitutions canonically extend to terms, sets and multisets of terms. They can be composed with each other: $\tau[\theta\theta'] = [\tau\theta]\theta'$. A renaming is a substitution which is a bijection on Var. A *binding* is a substitution $\sigma : Var \to (Var \cup Val)$, it can be written as a list $(a_1/v_1, a_2/v_2, \dots, a_n/v_n)$, where the a_j are mutually distinct variables and the v_j's are values, meaning that a_j is substituted by v_j. Whenever a variable a does not occur in a list then $\sigma(a) = a$. Variables which are mapped to a value are said to be *bound* to that value. The *domain* of a binding σ, denoted by $dom(\sigma)$, is the set $\{a \in Var \mid \sigma(a) \in Val\}$.
If τ is a term from T, then $\tau[\sigma]$ means the evaluation (and not only the substitution) of τ under σ. We will consider a multiset of terms μ to be *true* for a binding σ if $\mu[\sigma] \in \mathcal{M}_f(\{true\})$ (notice that $\mu[\sigma]$ may be empty).

2.2 Syntax of M-expressions

The basic constituent of the high level process algebra of *M-expressions* is a pair $\lambda.\alpha$, where λ is a multiset of parameterised actions, and α a multiset of terms. An M-expression E is defined according to the following syntax (where A is an action from A):

$$E ::= \lambda.\alpha \mid E;E \mid E \parallel E \mid E \,\square\, E \mid [E \rhd E \rhd E] \mid E\ \mathbf{sy}\ A \mid E\ \mathbf{rs}\ A.$$

Intuitively, λ, called the *label*, denotes the actions which can be performed if the evaluation of the parameters is such that α, called the *guard*, is true. M-expressions can be composed by sequential (;), or concurrent ($\parallel$) compositions, choice ($\square$) or iteration ($[\rhd \rhd]$), they also support synchronisation (**sy**) and restriction (**rs**) over some action A.
These operators are also part of formalisms like PBC, CCS, (T)CSP, or ACP, they have here the same intuitive meaning. We are especially interested in the slightly generalised (with respect to its previous version in [2, 11, 8, 3]) iteration operator $[E_1 \rhd E_2 \rhd E_3]$. In its usual interpretation E_1 is an initialisation which is executed once, after which zero or more repetition of the body E_2 may occur, after which exactly one execution of E_3 may complete the execution of the iteration. This operator allows us to model high level program constructs like loops or if-then-else statements. However, the behaviour of a program variable can be seen as some kind of iteration, namely: a variable changes arbitrarily often its value and is then terminated.

2.3 Operational Semantics of M-expressions

This section formalises the semantical intuitions for M-expressions by defining an operational semantics in Plotkin style [13], like this has already been done for Box expressions [11, 8, 3]. Generally, in process algebras, the action rule $E \xrightarrow{a} E'$ involves a change in the structure of E. Here we follow the approach defined by Koutny, Esparza and Best. In that approach, Box expressions encode a Petri Box where the execution of an action changes the marking and not the structure of the underlying Petri net. *Overbars* and *underbars* are introduced for Box expressions to express the marking (the current state) of the corresponding Petri Box. Intuitively, an overbared M-expression $\overline{E}$ indicates, that E is ready for execution, while an underbar signals that E has finished its execution.
We follow basically the same approach, but in addition, we will use bindings to encode arbitrary values for the parameters occurring in an M-expression. Even if M-expressions may not encode M-nets [5] in all generality, the operational semantics covers the intuition of evolving M-nets.
The step sequence semantics will be given by rules of the form:

$$\frac{P}{(\sigma)\ D \xrightarrow{\gamma} (\sigma')\ D',}$$

where P is a predicate, D and D' are M-expressions with some overbars and underbars, σ and σ' are bindings, and γ is a step (i.e., a multiset of multisets of elementary actions). An M-expression E with some overbars and underbars (denoted as D) with a binding describe some state of execution of E. If P is satisfied, the step γ can be infered and leads to a new state described by (possibly) another distribution of overbars and underbars of E (denoted by D') with a binding σ'.
A binding σ may bind some of the variables occurring in D, and links in some way combined subexpressions, i.e., the generated binding σ' stores the effect of the step γ. For reasons of brevity we will omit in the following the predicate P if it is always satisfied.
Formally, a *marked* M-expression D is an M-expression equiped with some overbars or underbars according to the following syntax, where E is an M-expression as defined above.

$$\begin{aligned} D ::= \overline{E}\ (\text{at } E) \mid \underline{E}\ (\text{after } E) \mid D;E \mid E;D \mid D \parallel D \mid D \square E \mid E \square D \mid \\ [D \rhd E \rhd E] \mid [E \rhd D \rhd E] \mid [E \rhd E \rhd D] \mid D\ \mathbf{sy}\ A \mid D\ \mathbf{rs}\ A. \end{aligned}$$

The given syntax for marked M-expressions is the same as for marked Box expressions, defined in [11, 8, 3]. In the following the letters $D, H, \ldots$ will be used to denote marked M-expressions. The notions of free and storing extend to M-expressions and marked M-expressions.
A marked M-expression D becomes *bound*, denoted by $(\sigma)\ D$, if we consider it together with some binding σ. In particular, $(id)\ D$ where $\forall a \in Var : id(a) = a$, is a bound M-expression. An *initially bound M-expression* is a marked M-expression together with some set of *initial bindings*, similar to the set of initial markings

in Petri net theory. Note that there is no standard initial binding, in fact, the choice of an initial binding is crucial for the behaviour of an M-expression. For a marked M-expression D, let $\lfloor D \rfloor$ be the underlying M-expression by leaving out all overbars and underbars. Formally, a *step* is a finite multiset $\gamma = \{\lambda_1, \dots, \lambda_n\}$, where each λ_i is a multiset of elementary parameterised actions, for instance $\{\{X(1,3), X(2,4)\}\}$ and $\emptyset$ are steps. The former contains an execution of the multiaction $\{X(1,3), X(2,4)\}$. The latter contains no multiaction at all and is therefore interpreted as *inaction*. Steps can be concatenated, yielding *step sequences*, where inaction plays the rôle of the empty word.
We are interested in the derivation/inference of step sequences from $(\sigma_{in})\,\overline{E}$, where σ_{in} is an *initial binding* of $\overline{E}$. All step sequences which can be derived from $(\sigma_{in})\,\overline{E}$ describe the behaviour of E. For basic M-expressions we define the basic inference rule RB, where σ, σ', and ϕ are bindings with pairwise disjoint domains, and $dom(\sigma\sigma'\phi) = Var(\lambda.\alpha)$, $dom(\sigma') \subseteq S$, and $dom(\phi) \subseteq F$, where $Var(\lambda.\alpha)$ denotes the set of all variables occurring in $\lambda.\alpha$.

$$\frac{\alpha[\sigma\sigma'\phi]}{(\sigma)\,\overline{\lambda.\alpha} \xrightarrow{\{\lambda[\sigma\sigma'\phi]\}} (\sigma')\,\underline{\lambda.\alpha}} \quad RB.$$

In general, the M-expression $\lambda.\alpha$ includes some free and some storing variables. Intuitively, a bound M-expression $(\sigma)\,\overline{\lambda.\alpha}$ describes the state where some of the variables are associated to values. If $\lambda.\alpha$ embodies only free variables, rule RB applies if there exists a binding ϕ, which satisfies the guard α. If $\lambda.\alpha$ embodies some storing variables and if σ associates values to some of them, then rule RB applies if there are bindings σ' and ϕ such that $\sigma\phi\sigma'$ satisfies the guard. In the latter case the rule requires to remove the mapping of values given by σ and to replace it by another mapping, given by σ', on the storing variables of $\lambda.\alpha$ not concerned by σ.[3]
Let $E = \{Z(a_s, b_s, c_f)\}.\{a_s = 0, b_s \in \{0,1,2\}, c_f = 2\}$, where $a_s, b_s \in S$ and $c_f \in F$, and $\sigma = (a_s/0)$ be given. In the new state b_s will be bound, hence, suppose we want to generate $(b_s/1)\,\underline{E}$, with $\sigma = (a_s/0)$, $\sigma' = (b_s/1)$ and $\phi = (c_f/2)$ rule RB is applicable and the step $\gamma = \{\{Z(0,1,2)\}\}$ can be derived, leading from $(\sigma)\,\overline{E}$ to $(\sigma')\,\underline{E}$. Considering instead $\sigma = (a_s/0, c_f/2)$ as the initial binding, we have $\phi = id$ and may again choose $\sigma' = (b_s/1)$. Rule RB is as well applicable with this setup and we may infer γ by entering the same new state as above.
The fact, that the given binding is used for the step derivations from more complex M-expressions is expressed by the *context rule* RCt, where σ, σ', and θ

[3] Notice the assymetry in the restrictions concerning the domain of the three bindings. While the initial binding σ may bind storing variables as well as free variables, the domain of the final binding σ' has to be a subset of storing variables S. Intuitively, each free variable occurring in $\lambda.\alpha$ should be bound by ϕ, i.e., the same restriction of the domain of σ to the set of storing variables, as there is for the domain of σ'. However, we don't want to restrict unnecessarily the set of possible initial bindings by such a condition, and allow to consider initial bindings, which bind equally free and storing variables.

are bindings, such that $dom(\theta) \cap (dom(\sigma) \cup dom(\sigma')) = \emptyset$, $dom(\theta) \cap Var(D) = \emptyset = dom(\theta) \cap Var(H) = \emptyset$, D and H are marked M-expressions, $Var(D)$ and $Var(H)$ are the sets of variables occurring in D, respectively H, and $C(\cdot)$ is some common context of D and H.

$$\frac{(\sigma)\, D \xrightarrow{\gamma} (\sigma')\, H}{(\theta\sigma)\, C(D) \xrightarrow{\gamma} (\theta\sigma')\, C(H)} \qquad RCt.$$

The context rule has to be read as follows: Consider three bindings σ, σ', and θ, respecting the following conditions: σ and σ' are related by some derivation $(\sigma)\, D \xrightarrow{\gamma} (\sigma')\, H$, and θ binds a disjoint set of variables than σ and σ', which do not occur neither in D nor in H. In that situation, the same derivation is also valid in a given common context $C(\cdot)$ of D and H, where θ represents the unchanged binding for variables in that context. RCt assures that for a complex M-expression a derivation for one of its subexpressions is also valid.
For marked M-expressions D and H we introduce like in [11, 8, 3] a set of *inaction rules*. They correspond basically to rewritings of marked M-expressions, according to its overbars and underbars. The rules describe an equivalence of states encoded by configurations of overbars and underbars. The reflexivity and symmetry of the equivalence is expressed by the two inaction rules $IN1$ and $IN2$.

$$D \xrightarrow{\emptyset} D \qquad IN1 \qquad\qquad \frac{D \xrightarrow{\emptyset} H}{H \xrightarrow{\emptyset} D} \qquad IN2.$$

Table 1 gives the other inaction rules for the M-expression algebra, they are identical to those given in [11, 8, 3] for Box expressions. However, we generalise the iteration operator by defining an additional inaction rule. Let D be a marked storing M-expression, then inaction rule $II6$ is defined as:

$$[E_1 \rhd D \rhd E_3] \xrightarrow{\emptyset} [E_1 \rhd \underline{\lfloor D \rfloor} \rhd \overline{E_3}] \qquad II6.$$

Intuitively speaking, $II6$ allows to abort a storing looping part at any stage. More precisely, from a given iteration construct with a storing subexpression and whatever configuration of overbars and underbars in the looping part, the termination part can directly be reached, by performing an inaction and removing all overbars and underbars from the subexpression in the looping part.
This (possible) behaviour will be needed when the iteration construct is used to express the semantics of program variables.
Table 1 defines as well the set of *inference rules*. For the sequence, choice, concurrent composition, and iteration operator, they pass the result of a rewriting or a step into a subexpression.
Consider the M-expression

$$E = (\{X(a,b)\}.\{a,b \in \{1,2\}\} \parallel \{\widehat{X}(c_s,d_s)\}.\{c_s = 1, d_s \in \{1,2\}\})\, \mathbf{sy}\, X,$$

where $a, b \in F$, and $c_s, d_s \in S$, hence, $X(a,b)$ is a free and $\widehat{X}(c_s,d_s)$ is a storing parameterised action. Furthermore, let $(c_s/1)$ be the initial binding. The following derivation proves the inferebility of the step $\gamma' = \{\emptyset\}$ from $(c_s/1)\,\overline{E}$.

	Inaction Rules	Inference Rules	
$IS1$	$\overline{E_1;E_2} \xrightarrow{\emptyset} \overline{E_1};E_2$	$\dfrac{D \xrightarrow{\gamma} H}{D;E \xrightarrow{\gamma} H;E}$	$RS1$
$IS2$	$\underline{E_1};E_2 \xrightarrow{\emptyset} E_1;\overline{E_2}$		
$IS3$	$E_1;\underline{E_2} \xrightarrow{\emptyset} \underline{E_1;E_2}$	$\dfrac{D \xrightarrow{\gamma} H}{E;D \xrightarrow{\gamma} E;H}$	$RS2$
		$\dfrac{D \xrightarrow{\gamma} D'}{D \parallel E \xrightarrow{\gamma} D' \parallel E}$	$RP1$
$IP1$	$\overline{E_1 \parallel E_2} \xrightarrow{\emptyset} \overline{E_1} \parallel \overline{E_2}$	$\dfrac{H \xrightarrow{\gamma} H'}{E \parallel H \xrightarrow{\gamma} E \parallel H'}$	$RP2$
$IP2$	$\underline{E_1} \parallel \underline{E_2} \xrightarrow{\emptyset} \underline{E_1 \parallel E_2}$		
		$\dfrac{D \xrightarrow{\gamma} D',\ H \xrightarrow{\delta} H'}{D \parallel H \xrightarrow{\gamma+\delta} D' \parallel H'}$	$RP3$
$IC1$	$\overline{E_1 \Box E_2} \xrightarrow{\emptyset} \overline{E_1} \Box E_2$	$\dfrac{D \xrightarrow{\gamma} H}{D \Box E \xrightarrow{\gamma} H \Box E}$	$RC1$
$IC2$	$\overline{E_1 \Box E_2} \xrightarrow{\emptyset} E_1 \Box \overline{E_2}$		
$IC3$	$\underline{E_1} \Box E_2 \xrightarrow{\emptyset} \underline{E_1 \Box E_2}$	$\dfrac{D \xrightarrow{\gamma} H}{E \Box D \xrightarrow{\gamma} E \Box H}$	$RC2$
$IC4$	$E_1 \Box \underline{E_2} \xrightarrow{\emptyset} \underline{E_1 \Box E_2}$		
$II1$	$\overline{[E_1 \rhd E_2 \rhd E_3]} \xrightarrow{\emptyset} [\overline{E_1} \rhd E_2 \rhd E_3]$	$\dfrac{D \xrightarrow{\gamma} H}{[D \rhd E \rhd F] \xrightarrow{\gamma} [H \rhd E \rhd F]}$	$RI1$
$II2$	$[\underline{E_1} \rhd E_2 \rhd E_3] \xrightarrow{\emptyset} [E_1 \rhd \overline{E_2} \rhd E_3]$		
$II3$	$[E_1 \rhd \underline{E_2} \rhd E_3] \xrightarrow{\emptyset} [E_1 \rhd \overline{E_2} \rhd E_3]$	$\dfrac{D \xrightarrow{\gamma} H}{[E \rhd D \rhd F] \xrightarrow{\gamma} [E \rhd H \rhd F]}$	$RI2$
$II4$	$[E_1 \rhd \underline{E_2} \rhd E_3] \xrightarrow{\emptyset} [E_1 \rhd E_2 \rhd \overline{E_3}]$	$\dfrac{D \xrightarrow{\gamma} H}{[E \rhd F \rhd D] \xrightarrow{\gamma} [E \rhd F \rhd H]}$	$RI3$
$II5$	$[E_1 \rhd E_2 \rhd \underline{E_3}] \xrightarrow{\emptyset} \underline{[E_1 \rhd E_2 \rhd E_3]}$		
$ISy1$	$\overline{[E\ \mathbf{sy}\ A]} \xrightarrow{\emptyset} [\overline{E}\ \mathbf{sy}\ A]$	$\dfrac{D \xrightarrow{\gamma} H}{D\ \mathbf{sy}\ A \xrightarrow{\gamma} H\ \mathbf{sy}\ A}$	$RSy1$
$ISy2$	$[\underline{E}\ \mathbf{sy}\ A] \xrightarrow{\emptyset} \underline{[E\ \mathbf{sy}\ A]}$	$\dfrac{D\ \mathbf{sy}\ A \xrightarrow{\gamma+\{\alpha+\{A(\vec{\tau})\}\}+\{\beta+\{\widehat{A}(\vec{\tau})\}\}} H\ \mathbf{sy}\ A}{D\ \mathbf{sy}\ A \xrightarrow{\gamma+\{\alpha+\beta\}} H\ \mathbf{sy}\ A}$	$RSy2$
$IRs1$	$\overline{[E\ \mathbf{rs}\ A]} \xrightarrow{\emptyset} [\overline{E}\ \mathbf{rs}\ A]$	$\dfrac{D \xrightarrow{\gamma} H,\ \gamma \in \mathcal{M}_f(\mathcal{M}_f(\mathsf{P}_{\vert \mathsf{A}\setminus\{A,\hat{A}\}}))}{D\ \mathbf{rs}\ A \xrightarrow{\gamma} H\ \mathbf{rs}\ A}$	RRs
$IRs2$	$[\underline{E}\ \mathbf{rs}\ A] \xrightarrow{\emptyset} \underline{[E\ \mathbf{rs}\ A]}$		

Table 1. Inaction and Inference Rules for bound M-expressions.

$$(c_s/1)\ \overline{(\{X(a,b)\}.\{a,b \in \{1,2\}\} \parallel \{\widehat{X}(c_s,d_s)\}.\{c_s = 1, d_s \in \{1,2\}\})}\ \mathbf{sy}\ X$$

$$\xrightarrow{\emptyset} (c_s/1)\ (\overline{\{X(a,b)\}.\{a,b \in \{1,2\}\}} \parallel \overline{\{\widehat{X}(c_s,d_s)\}.\{c_s = 1, d_s \in \{1,2\}\}})\ \mathbf{sy}\ X$$

$$\xrightarrow{\{\emptyset\}} (d_s/2)\ (\underline{\{X(a,b)\}.\{a,b \in \{1,2\}\}} \parallel \underline{\{\widehat{X}(c_s,d_s)\}.\{c_s = 1, d_s \in \{1,2\}\}})\ \mathbf{sy}\ X$$

$$\xrightarrow{\emptyset} (d_s/2)\ \underline{(\{X(a,b)\}.\{a,b \in \{1,2\}\} \parallel \{\widehat{X}(c_s,d_s)\}.\{c_s = 1, d_s \in \{1,2\}\})\ \mathbf{sy}\ X}.$$

In the third line, the step $\{\{\widehat{X}(1,2)\}\}$ can be infered by RB from the right side of the parallel operator. It leads from the initial binding $(c_s/1)$ to the successor binding $(d_s/2)$. In the same line the step $\{\{X(1,2)\}\}$ can be derived by RB from the left side of the operator (with binding $(a/1, b/2)$) and assuming the same pre- and post-bindings as in the previous derivation; note that rule RB was applied twice. By $RP3$ the infered step $\gamma'' = \{\{X(1,2), \widehat{X}(1,2)\}\}$ can be deduced. Since γ'' contains the pair $(X, \widehat{X})$ of conjugated actions, rule $RSy2$ is applicable (with $\gamma = \alpha = \beta = \emptyset$) and leads to $\gamma' = \{\emptyset\}$.
The following property of the synchronisation and restriction operator is needed in the application of M-expressions in section 3 (see [10] for the proof).

Theorem 1. *Synchronisation and restriction are commutative.*

2.4 M-expressions and Box Expressions

In this section we characterise the relationship of M-expressions and Box expressions with respect to their operational semantics. Intuitively, Box expressions are M-expressions of the 'lowest' possible level, i.e., without any variables which would allow potentially different evaluations.
We define *elementary M-expressions*, which are only a way to denote Box expressions syntactically in the domain of M-expressions. A basic M-expression $\lambda.\alpha$ is called *elementary* if λ is a multiset of elementary parameterised actions and $\alpha \in \mathcal{M}_f(\{true\})$. The definition extends canonically to composed M-expressions. Elementary M-expressions are actions without any variable parameters. Hence, they are free and the operational semantics for Box expressions [11, 8, 3] and the here defined semantics coincide for elementary M-expressions.
Our interest will now be focused on the problem, whether (non elementary) M-expressions could be 'unfolded' into elementary M-expressions. In general, elementary M-expressions are unable to mimic inferences from storing M-expressions[4]. Therefore, we restrict the definition of unfolding to bound free M-expressions.

[4] $E_1; E_2 = \{B(a,b)\}.\{a = 0, b = 1\}; \{B(b,a)\}.\{b \in \{0,1\}, a = 0\}$ with initial binding $(a/0)$. E_1 and $E_1' = \{B(0,1)\}.\emptyset$ on the one side, and E_2 and $E_2' = \{B(0,0)\}.\emptyset\Box\{B(1,0)\}.\emptyset$ on the other side allow the same step inferences. $E_1'; E_2'$ allows the inference of $\{\{B(1)\}\}\{\{B(0)\}\}$ which is not inferable from $E_1; E_2$ if b is not a free variable, i.e., $b \in S$, hence it would be false to consider $E_1'; E_2'$ as the unfolding of $E_1; E_2$.

The unfolding $\mathcal{U}(\cdot)$ is defined for a basic free M-expression $\lambda.\alpha$ by $\mathcal{U}(\lambda.\alpha) = \square\{\lambda[\sigma].\emptyset \mid \exists$ binding $\sigma : \alpha[\sigma]$ is true$\}$, and inductively for each operator of the M-expression algebra $(\mathcal{U}(E_1; E_2) = \mathcal{U}(E_1);\mathcal{U}(E_2)$, etc.). It extends to marked M-expressions by $\mathcal{U}(\overline{E}) = \overline{\mathcal{U}(E)}$, respectively $\mathcal{U}(\underline{E}) = \underline{\mathcal{U}(E)}$, and to bound M-expressions by $\mathcal{U}((\sigma)\ D) = (\sigma)\ \mathcal{U}(D)$. The unfolding of an M-expression may be infinite.

The following theorem relates free M-expression and their unfoldings (see [10] for the proof).

Theorem 2. *Let D and H be free marked M-expressions and σ, σ' be bindings, such that $(dom(\sigma) \cup dom(\sigma')) \cap F = \emptyset$. Then,*

$$(\sigma)\ D \xrightarrow{\gamma} (\sigma')\ H \iff (\sigma)\ \mathcal{U}(D) \xrightarrow{\gamma} (\sigma')\ \mathcal{U}(H).$$

3 The M-expression Semantics of a Parallel Programming Language

This section gives the $B(PN)^2$ (Basic Petri Net Programming Notation) [7] notation and its M-expression semantics by means of a mapping $Me(\cdot)$ which associates an M-expression to every $B(PN)^2$ construct.

3.1 $B(PN)^2$ Program Syntax

$B(PN)^2$ is a language for the specification of concurrent algorithms which incorporates within a simple syntax many of the constructs used in concurrent programming languages - (nested) parallel composition, iteration, guarded commands, and communication via both, handshake and buffered communication channels, as well as shared variables. The syntax of $B(PN)^2$ is defined as follows.

```
program ::= block
block   ::= begin scope end
scope   ::= decl; scope | com
decl    ::= var ident: type
type    ::= set init const | chan k of set (k ∈ ℕ₀ ∪ ω)
com     ::= ⟨expr⟩ | com; com | com || com | do alt-set od | block
alt-set ::= alt-set □ alt-set | com; exit | com; repeat
expr    ::= 'x | x' | c? | c! | const | expr op expr | op expr | (expr)
```

A command com is either an atomic command, ⟨expr⟩, a block comprising some declarations for a command, or one of a number of command compositions.

An atomic command is a $B(PN)^2$ expression, expr, which is a term over *Val* and *Op* with *program variable*, and *channel* identifiers.

A program variable x can appear in an expression as $'x$ (pre-value) and as x' (post-value), denoting respectively its value just before and just after evaluation of the expression during an execution of the program. A channel c can appear

in an expression as $c!$ (sending) and as $c?$ (receiving), denoting respectively the value which is sent and received in a communication on the channel c. An atomic action can execute if the expression evaluates to true. Thus, for example, $\langle 'x > 0 \wedge x' = c? \rangle$ corresponds to a guarded communication which requires x to be greater than zero and a communication to be available on channel c, in which case the value communicated on c is assigned to variable x.
A declaration `decl` of program variables and channels is made via the keyword **var** followed by an identifier with a type specification, **var ident : type**. A type specification, **type**, can be **set**, or **chan** k **of set**, where **set** identifies a set of values from *Val*. For a simple type declaration **set** the identifier describes an ordinary program variable which may carry values within **set**. The clause **chan** k **of set** declares a channel (FIFO buffer) of capacity k that may carry values within **set**. The capacity k can be equal to 0 (handshake communication), $1, 2, \ldots$ or ω (unbounded capacity).
The domain of relevance of a variable or channel identifier is limited to the part of a B(PN)^2 program, called **scope**, which follows its declaration.
Besides traditional constructs, sequence (;) and parallel (||) composition, there is a command **do** ... **od** which can be seen as a "merge" of the traditional '**if**' and '**while**'/'**repeat**' commands.
The core **alt-set** of the **do** ... **od** command is a set of clauses of two types: repeat commands, **com**; **repeat**, and exit commands, **com**; **exit**. During an execution, there can be zero or more iterations, each of them being an execution of one of the repeat commands; followed by an execution of one of the exit commands. Each repeat and exit command will typically be a sequence with an intial atomic command; the executability of which determines whether that repeat or exit command can start. If several can start, then there is a non-deterministic choice between them.

3.2 M-expression Semantics of B(PN)^2 Programs

Programs and Blocks: The main idea in describing a block is to juxtapose the M-expressions for its declarations and the M-expression for its command, followed by termination action(s), to synchronise over all matching actions of the data subexpression and the control subexpression, and then to restrict them in order to make local variables invisible outside the block.
The termination M-expression associated with declaration `decl` will be called τ(`decl`). If `decl` is the declaration of a variable v (plain or channel), then $\tau(\mathtt{decl}) = \{V_T\}.\emptyset$. The set of all actions pertaining to the declaration `decl` of a variable (plain or channel) will be denoted $\delta(\mathtt{decl})$. Thus, by definition, $\delta(\mathtt{decl}) = \{X, X_T\}$ if `decl` is a declaration of a plain variable, and $\delta(\mathtt{decl}) = \{C!, C?, C_T\}$ if `decl` is a declaration of a channel.
The semantical function $Me(\cdot)$ is defined as follows.

$$\begin{aligned}
Me(\mathtt{program}) &= Me(\mathtt{block}) \\
Me(\mathtt{block}) &= Me(\mathtt{scope}) \\
Me(\mathtt{decl};\, \mathtt{scope}) &= [\,((Me(\mathtt{decl}) \parallel Me(\mathtt{com}); \tau(\mathtt{decl}))\ \mathbf{sy}\ \delta(\mathtt{decl}))\ \mathbf{rs}\ \delta(\mathtt{decl})].
\end{aligned}$$

Declarations: Using the generalised iteration operator we define the semantics of B(PN)[2] variable declarations as follows, where $\{a_f, c_0, e_1, c^!, c^?\} \subseteq F$ and $\{a, b, c_1, d_1, q1, q2\} \subseteq S$ are variables, uniquely choosen for each declaration.

$$Me(\textbf{var}\ x:\ \textbf{set init const}) = [\{\widehat{X}(a_f, b)\}.\{a_f = \textbf{const}, b \in \textbf{set}\}$$
$$\rhd \{\widehat{X}(b,a)\}.\{a, b \in \textbf{set}\}; \{\widehat{X}(a,b)\}.\{a, b \in \textbf{set}\} \rhd \{\widehat{X_T}\}.\emptyset]$$

$$Me(\textbf{var}\ c_0:\ \textbf{chan 0 of set}) =$$
$$[\{\widehat{C}!(c_0), \widehat{C?}(c_0)\}.\{c_0 \in \textbf{set}\} \rhd \{\widehat{C}!(c_0), \widehat{C?}(c_0)\}.\{c_0 \in \textbf{set}\} \rhd \{\widehat{C_T}\}.\emptyset]$$

$$Me(\textbf{var}\ c:\ \textbf{chan 1 of set}) = [\{\widehat{C}!(c_1)\}.\{c_1 \in \textbf{set}, e_1 = \epsilon\}$$
$$\rhd \{\widehat{C?}(c_1)\}.\{c_1 \in \textbf{set}, e_1 = \epsilon\}; \{\widehat{C}!(c_1)\}.\{c_1 \in \textbf{set}, d_1 = \epsilon\} \rhd \{\widehat{C_T}\}.\emptyset]$$

$$Me(\textbf{var}\ c:\ \textbf{chan k of set}) = [\{\widehat{C}!(c^!)\}.\{c^! \in \textbf{set}, q1 = \epsilon, q2 = c^!\} \rhd$$
$$(\{\widehat{C?}(c^?)\}.\{q2 \neq \epsilon, q1 \cdot c^? = q2, c^? \in \textbf{set}\}$$
$$\Box \{\widehat{C}!(c^!)\}.\{lh(q2) < k, c^! \cdot q2 = q1, c^! \in \textbf{set}\}$$
$$\Box \{\widehat{C}!(c^!), \widehat{C?}(c^?)\}.\{q1 \cdot c^? = c^! \cdot q2, c^!, c^? \in \textbf{set}\});$$
$$(\{\widehat{C?}(c^?)\}.\{q1 \neq \epsilon, q2 \cdot c^? = q1, c^? \in \textbf{set}\}$$
$$\Box \{\widehat{C}!(c^!_v)\}.\{lh(q1) < k, c^! \cdot q1 = q2, c^! \in \textbf{set}\}$$
$$\Box \{\widehat{C}!(c^!), \widehat{C?}(c^?)\}.\{q2 \cdot c^? = c^! \cdot q1, c^!, c^? \in \textbf{set}\}) \rhd \{\widehat{C_T}\}.\emptyset]$$

To model the sequence of values in a channel we consider a complex type of all sequences with entries from **set**. A single value is identified with a sequence of length 1. The concatenation of sequences is denoted by a dot $\cdot$, ϵ denotes the empty sequence, and finally, the length of a sequence s is denoted by $lh(s)$. Consider the data M-expression for a channel with capacity $k > 1$. In the first choice construct of the looping part, the storing variables $q1$ and $q2$ are used to model the content of the channel before, respectively after, the corresponding basic M-expression, and vice versa in the second choice construct.
The choice of the variables is crucial for the program semantics. Therefore, a unique subset of variables occurs in each data M-expression of a program.
Notice that the looping part itself in each data M-expression is (sequentially) composed out of two subexpressions with the same structure, only the storing variables play a dual rôle.

Command Connectives: A command can be: a block, an atomic action, or a combination of commands by one of three connectives dealt with in this section, namely sequential composition, parallel composition and choice/iteration, which are subsumed in the **do–od** construct.

$$Me(\texttt{com};\ \texttt{com}) = Me(\texttt{com});\ Me(\texttt{com})$$
$$Me(\texttt{com} \parallel \texttt{com}) = Me(\texttt{com}) \parallel Me(\texttt{com}).$$

The semantics of the **do–od** construct involves two supplementary semantical functions relating to the iteration operator $[E_1 \rhd E_2 \rhd E_3]$ used, namely: $R(\cdot)$ to give the M-expression which is the choice over the M-expressions from all the repeat clauses, for use in the E_2 part, $E(\cdot)$ similarly for the exit clauses and the E_3 part. The E_1 part is the M-expression for a single silent action.

$$\begin{aligned}
&Me(\textbf{do alt-set od}) &&= [\emptyset.\emptyset \rhd \mathrm{R}(\texttt{alt-set}) \rhd \mathrm{E}(\texttt{alt-set})]\\
&\mathrm{R}(\texttt{alt-set}_1 \,\square\, \texttt{alt-set}_2) &&= \mathrm{R}(\texttt{alt-set}_1) \,\square\, \mathrm{R}(\texttt{alt-set}_2)\\
&\mathrm{E}(\texttt{alt-set}_1 \,\square\, \texttt{alt-set}_2) &&= \mathrm{E}(\texttt{alt-set}_1) \,\square\, \mathrm{E}(\texttt{alt-set}_2)\\
&\mathrm{E}(\texttt{com};\, \textbf{repeat}) = \mathrm{R}(\texttt{com};\, \mathrm{exit}) = \textbf{stop}^5\\
&\mathrm{E}(\texttt{com};\, \textbf{exit}) = \mathrm{R}(\texttt{com};\, \mathrm{repeat}) = Me(\texttt{com}).
\end{aligned}$$

Atomic Actions: We will assign to each atomic command $\langle\textbf{expr}\rangle$ a basic M-expression by a supplementary mapping $Ins(\cdot)$[6] to yield the semantics of an expression e (defined as **expr**). This semantics is defined as a pair (AS, G), where AS is a multiset of parameterised actions and G is a multiset of terms. The actions used in AS being X for access to a plain program variable x, $C?$ for input from, and $C!$ for output to a channel variable c. Action X is of arity 2, X_T is the termination action of arity 0, and actions $C!$, and $C?$ with arity 1 pertain to channel declarations. The terms in G are those from e appropriately replaced by value variables from F: x^i for $'x$, x^o for x', $c^?$ for $c?$, and $c^!$ for $c!$.

$$\begin{aligned}
&Ins('x) &&= (\{X(x^i, x^o)\}, x^i), \quad && Ins(c?) &&= (\{C?(c^?)\}, c^?)\\
&Ins(x') &&= (\{X(x^i, x^o)\}, x^o), \quad && Ins(c!) &&= (\{C!(c^!)\}, c^!)\\
&Ins(\textbf{const}) &&= (\emptyset, \textbf{const}) && Ins(op\, e) &&= (AS, op\, E) \text{ for } Ins(e) = (AS, E)\\
&Ins(e_1\, op\, e_2) &&= (AS_1 \cup AS_2, E_1\, op\, E_2) \text{ for } Ins(e_i) = (AS_i, E_i)
\end{aligned}$$

For $Ins(\textbf{expr}) = (AS, G)$ we define $Me(\langle\textbf{expr}\rangle) = AS.\{G\}$.

Initial Bindings: Intuitively, each initial binding σ_{in} for the semantics $Me(P)$ of a $\mathrm{B(PN)}^2$ program P assures, the initialisation of all data subexpressions of $Me(P)$.
More precisely, an initial binding σ_{in} bind the free variable a_f appearing in the parameter list of the initialisation action of the data subexpression for a plain variable, (no variable in the M-expression for a channel 0 variable,) the free variable e_1 in the guard of the subexpression for a channel 1 variable, and the free variable $q1$ in the initialisation part of a data subexpression for a channel variable with capacity $k \in \{\omega, 2, 3, \ldots\}$.
For a data M-expressions, each initial binding σ_{in} binds the free variable a for a plain variable, (none for a channel 0 variable,) e_1 for a channel 1 variable, and $q1$ for a channel with capacity $k \in \{\omega, 2, 3, \ldots\}$.

3.3 Consistency and Completeness of M-expressions and M-nets

We will now characterise the relationship of M-expressions as the semantic domain for $\mathrm{B(PN)}^2$ and the existing high level Petri net based program semantics. The reader is referred to [5, 6, 10] for introductions to the M-net model and

[5] Special M-expression with the same behaviour as $\emptyset.\{\mathit{false}\}$. It emphasises that there is no action.

[6] In fact, this is the mapping $Ins(\cdot)$ as defined in [6] to determine the inscription of transitions in the M-net semantics of $\mathrm{B(PN)}^2$.

the definition of the M-net based semantics. We denote by $Net_H(P)$ the M-net semantics of a B(PN)^2 program P, and by $\overline{Net_H(P)}$ the M-net of a program P with its initial marking.
Given a fragment of B(PN)^2 code, we want to show the equivalence of the two semantics, i.e., whatever actions can be performed by the M-net semantics can also be deduced from the M-expression semantics, and vice versa.

Theorem 3. *Let P be a $\underline{B(PN)^2}$ program*[7]*. If the step sequence γ can be infered from $(\sigma_{in})\,\overline{Me(P)}$ then $\overline{Net_H(P)}$ can perform the step sequence γ as well. Conversely, if $\overline{Net_H(P)}$ can perform the step sequence γ, then γ can be infered from $(\sigma_{in})\,\overline{Me(P)}$.*

The proof is done in [10] by relating the semantics $Net_H(\cdot)$ and $Me(\cdot)$ by mappings like $Mnet(\cdot)$ (giving an marked M-net from a bound free M-expressions) and $marking(\cdot)$ (giving a marking of an M-net from a bound M-expression).

4 Conclusions

The model proposed in this article defines the high level process algebra of M-expressions. An operational semantics is given for the algebra, which coincides with the SOS semantics of Koutny, Esparza and Best defined in [11, 8, 3] in the elementary case (Box expressions). The process algebra is applied to give a high level expression based semantics for the parallel programming language B(PN)^2. M-expressions and their operational semantics are shown to be just as powerful as the programming semantics in the domain of M-nets, a class of high level Petri nets.

Acknowledgements. The authors wish to thank Eike Best and Elisabeth Pelz for stating the problem and some helpful discussions, Hans Fleischhack and Maciej Koutny for helpful discussions, and last but not least Raymond Devillers and Stephan Melzer for their careful readings of draft versions of the paper.

References

1. J. Baeten and W.P. Weijland. Process Algebras. Cambridge Tracts in Theoretical Computer Science 18, 1990.
2. E. Best, R. Devillers, and J.G. Hall. The Box Calculus: a New Causal Algebra with Multi-Label Communication. In G. Rozenberg, Ed., *Advances in Petri Nets 92*, Vol. 609 of *Lecture Notes in Computer Science*, pages 21-69. Springer, 1992.
3. E. Best, R. Devillers, and M. Koutny. Petri Net Algebra. Book draft, 1997.
4. E. Best and H. Fleischhack, Eds. *PEP: Programming Environment Based on Petri Nets*. Number 14/95 in Hildesheimer Informatik-Berichte. Universitiät Hildesheim, May 1995.

[7] We consider either complete programs or any syntactically correct fragment, such as a declaration of a variable (without **begin–end** parentheses) or any command construct.

5. E. Best, H. Fleischhack, W. Fraczak, R.P. Hopkins, H. Klaudel, and E. Pelz. A Class of Composable High Level Petri Nets. In Michelis and Diaz, Eds., *Application and Theory of Petri Nets 1995*, Vol. 935 of *Lecture Notes in Computer Science*. Springer, June 1995.
6. E. Best, H. Fleischhack, W. Fraczak, R.P. Hopkins, H. Klaudel, and E. Pelz. An M-Net Semantics of $B(PN)^2$. In *STRICT*, WiC. Springer, 1995.
7. E. Best and R.P. Hopkins. $\mathrm{B(PN)}^2$ – a Basic Petri Net Programming Notation. In A. Bode, M. Reeve, and G. Wolf, Eds., *Proceedings of PARLE '93*, Vol. 694 of *Lecture Notes in Computer Science*, pages 379-390. Springer, 1993.
8. E. Best and M. Koutny. A Refined View of the Box Algebra. In Michelis and Diaz, Eds., *Application and Theory of Petri Nets 1995*, Vol. 935 of *Lecture Notes in Computer Science*, pages 1-20. Springer, June 1995.
9. C.A.R. Hoare. Communicating Sequential Processes. Prentice Hall (1985).
10. H. Klaudel and R.-C. Riemann. M-expressions – a High Level Process Algebra with an Application to a Parallel Programming Language. LRI, Université Paris-Sud, Rapport 1090, January 1997. (http://www.lri.fr/~robert/work.html).
11. M. Koutny, J. Esparza, and E. Best. Operational Semantics for the Petri Box Calculus. In B. Jonsson and J. Parrow, Eds., *CONCUR'94: Concurrency Theory*, Vol. 836 of *Lecture Notes in Computer Science*, pages 210-225. Springer, 1994.
12. R. Milner. *Communication and Concurrency*. Prentice-Hall, 1989.
13. G.D. Plotkin. A Structural Approach to Operational Semantics. Report DAIMI FN-19, Aarhus University, Computer Science Departement, September 1981.

How to Parallelize Sequential Processes

Antonín Kučera*
e-mail: tony@fi.muni.cz

Faculty of Informatics, Masaryk University
Botanická 68a, 60200 Brno
Czech Republic

Abstract. A process is prime if it cannot be decomposed into a parallel product of nontrivial processes. We characterize all non-prime normed BPA processes together with their decompositions by means of normal forms which are designed in this paper. Using this result we demonstrate decidability of the problem whether a given normed BPA process is prime; moreover, we show that non-prime normed BPA processes can be decomposed into primes effectively. This brings other positive decidability results. Finally, we prove that bisimilarity is decidable in a large subclass of normed PA processes.

1 Introduction

A general problem considered by many researchers is how to improve performance of sequential programs by parallelization. In this paper we study this problem within a framework of process algebras. They provide us with a pleasant formalism which allows to specify sequential as well as parallel programs.

Here we adopt normed BPA processes as a simple model of sequential behaviours (they are equipped with a binary sequential operator). We examine the problem of effective decomposability of normed BPA processes into a parallel product of primes (a process is prime if it cannot be decomposed into nontrivial components). We design special normal forms for normed BPA processes which allow us to characterize all non-prime normed BPA processes together with their decompositions up to bisimilarity. As a consequence we also obtain a refinement of the result achieved in [4].

Next we show that any normed BPA process can be decomposed into a parallel product of primes effectively. We also prove several related decidability results. Finally, we prove that bisimilarity is decidable in a large subclass of normed PA processes (see [2]), which consists of processes of the form $\Delta_1 \| \cdots \| \Delta_n$, where each Δ_i is a normed BPA or BPP process.

In many parts of our paper we rely on results established by other researchers. The question of possible decomposition of processes into a parallel product of primes was first addressed by Milner and Moller in [15]. A more general result was later proved by Christensen, Hirshfeld and Moller (see [8])—it says that

* supported by GA ČR, grant number 201/97/0456

each normed process has a unique decomposition into primes up to bisimilarity. However, the proof is non-constructive.

Bisimilarity was proved to be decidable for normed BPA processes (see [1, 11, 10]) and normed BPP processes (see [7, 9]). Blanco proved in [3] that bisimilarity is decidable even in the union of normed BPA and normed BPP processes. The same problem was independently examined by Černá, Křetínský and Kučera in [5]. They demonstrated decidability of the problem whether for a given normed BPA (or BPP) process Δ there is some unspecified normed BPP (or BPA) process Δ' such that $\Delta \sim \Delta'$. If the answer is positive, then it is also possible to *construct* an example of such Δ'. Decidability of bisimilarity in the union of normed BPA and normed BPP processes is an immediate consequence.

Another property of normed BPA and BPP processes which is important for us is *regularity*. A process is regular if it is bisimilar to a process with finitely many states. Kučera proved in [13] that regularity is decidable for normed BPA and normed BPP processes in polynomial time.

2 Preliminaries

Let $Act = \{a, b, c, \ldots\}$ be a countably infinite set of *atomic actions*. Let $Var = \{X, Y, Z, \ldots\}$ be a countably infinite set of *variables* such that $Var \cap Act = \emptyset$. The class of BPA (or BPP) expressions is composed of all terms over the signature $\{\epsilon, a, ., +\}$ (or $\{\epsilon, a, \|, +\}$) where 'ϵ' is a constant denoting the empty expression, 'a' is a unary operator of action prefixing ('a' ranges over Act), and '.', '$\|$' and '+' are binary operators of sequential composition, parallel composition and nondeterministic choice, respectively. In the rest of this paper we do not distinguish between expressions related by *structural congruence* which is the smallest congruence relation over BPA and BPP expressions such that the following laws hold: associativity and 'ϵ' as a unit for '.', '$\|$', '+' operators, and commutativity for '$\|$' and '+' operators. Moreover, we also abbreviate $a\epsilon$ as a.

As usual, we restrict our attention to *guarded* expressions. A BPA or BPP expression E is guarded if every variable occurrence in E is within the scope of an atomic action.

A *guarded BPA (or BPP) process* is defined by a finite family Δ of recursive process equations $\Delta = \{X_i = E_i \mid 1 \leq i \leq n\}$ where X_i are distinct elements of Var and E_i are guarded BPA (or BPP) expressions, containing variables from $\{X_1, \ldots, X_n\}$. The set of variables which appear in Δ is denoted by $Var(\Delta)$.

The variable X_1 plays a special role (X_1 is sometimes called *the leading variable*)—it is a root of a labelled transition system, defined by the process Δ and the rules of Figure 1.

Nodes of the transition system generated by Δ are BPA (or BPP) expressions, which are often called *states of* Δ, or just "states" when Δ is understood from the context. We also define the relation $\stackrel{w}{\rightarrow}^*$, where $w \in Act^*$, as the reflexive and transitive closure of $\stackrel{a}{\rightarrow}$ (we often write $E \rightarrow^* F$ instead of $E \stackrel{w}{\rightarrow}^* F$ if w is irrelevant). Given two states E, F, we say that F is *reachable from* E, if $E \rightarrow^* F$. States of Δ which are reachable from X_1 are said to be *reachable*.

$$\frac{}{aE \xrightarrow{a} E} \qquad \frac{E \xrightarrow{a} E'}{E.F \xrightarrow{a} E'.F} \qquad \frac{E \xrightarrow{a} E'}{E+F \xrightarrow{a} E'} \qquad \frac{F \xrightarrow{a} F'}{E+F \xrightarrow{a} F'}$$

$$\frac{E \xrightarrow{a} E'}{E\|F \xrightarrow{a} E'\|F} \qquad \frac{F \xrightarrow{a} F'}{E\|F \xrightarrow{a} E\|F'} \qquad \frac{E \xrightarrow{a} E'}{X \xrightarrow{a} E'} \; (X = E \in \Delta)$$

Fig. 1. SOS rules

Remark 1. Processes are often identified with their leading variables. Furthermore, if we assume fixed processes Δ_1, Δ_2 such that $Var(\Delta_1) \cap Var(\Delta_2) = \emptyset$, then we can view any process expression E (not necessarily guarded) whose variables are defined in Δ_1, Δ_2 as a process too—if we denote this process by Δ, then the leading equation of Δ is $X = E'$, where $X \notin Var(\Delta_1) \cup Var(\Delta_2)$ and E' is a process expression which is obtained from E by substituting each variable in E with the right-hand side of its corresponding defining equation in Δ_1 or Δ_2 (E' must be guarded now). Moreover, def. equations from Δ_1, Δ_2 are added to Δ. All notions originally defined for processes can be used for process expressions in this sense too.

Bisimulation The equivalence between process expressions (states) we are interested in here is *bisimilarity* [16], defined as follows: A binary relation R over process expressions is a *bisimulation* if whenever $(E, F) \in R$ then for each $a \in Act$

- if $E \xrightarrow{a} E'$, then $F \xrightarrow{a} F'$ for some F' such that $(E', F') \in R$
- if $F \xrightarrow{a} F'$, then $E \xrightarrow{a} E'$ for some E' such that $(E', F') \in R$

Processes Δ and Δ' are *bisimilar*, written $\Delta \sim \Delta'$, if their leading variables are related by some bisimulation.

Normed processes An important subclass of BPA and BPP processes can be obtained by an extra restriction of *normedness.* A variable $X \in Var(\Delta)$ is *normed* if there is $w \in Act^*$ such that $X \xrightarrow{w}{}^* \epsilon$. In that case we define the *norm* of X, written $|X|$, to be the length of the shortest such w. A process Δ is *normed* if all variables of $Var(\Delta)$ are normed. The norm of Δ is then defined to be the norm of X_1. Note that bisimilar normed processes must have the same norm which is easily computed by the following rules: $|a| = 1$, $|E+F| = \min\{|E|, |F|\}$, $|E.F| = |E|+|F|$, $|E\|F| = |E|+|F|$ and if $X_i = E_i$ and $|E_i| = n$, then $|X_i| = n$.

Greibach normal form Any BPA or BPP process Δ can be effectively presented in a special normal form which is called 3-Greibach normal form by analogy with CF grammars (see [1] and [6]). Before the definition we need to introduce the set $Var(\Delta)^*$ of all finite sequences of variables from $Var(\Delta)$, and the set $Var(\Delta)^{\otimes}$ of all finite multisets over $Var(\Delta)$. Each multiset of $Var(\Delta)^{\otimes}$ denotes a BPP expression by combining its elements in parallel using the '$\|$' operator.

A BPA (or BPP) process Δ is said to be in *Greibach normal form (GNF)* if all its equations are of the form $X = \sum_{j=1}^{n} a_j\alpha_j$ where $n \in N$, $a_j \in Act$ and $\alpha_j \in Var(\Delta)^*$ (or $\alpha_j \in Var(\Delta)^{\otimes}$). We also require that each $Y \in Var(\Delta)$ appears in some reachable state of Δ. If $length(\alpha_j) \leq 2$ (or $card(\alpha_j) \leq 2$) for each j, $1 \leq j \leq n$, then Δ is said to be in 3-GNF.

From now on we assume that all BPA and BPP processes we are working with are presented in GNF. This justifies also the assumption that all reachable states of a BPA process Δ are elements of $Var(\Delta)^*$ and all reachable states of a BPP process Δ' are elements of $Var(\Delta')^{\otimes}$.

Regular processes A process Δ is *regular* if there is a process Δ' with finitely many states such that $\Delta \sim \Delta'$. A regular process Δ is said to be in normal form if all its equations are of the form $X = \sum_{j=1}^{n} a_j X_j$ where $n \in N$, $a_j \in Act$ and $X_j \in Var(\Delta)$.

It is easy to see that a process is regular iff it can reach only finitely many states up to bisimilarity. In [14] it is shown, that regular processes can be represented in the normal form just defined. Thus a process Δ is regular iff there is a regular process Δ' in normal form such that $\Delta \sim \Delta'$. A proof of the following proposition can be found in [13].

Proposition 2. *Let Δ be a normed BPA or BPP process. The problem whether Δ is regular is decidable in polynomial time. Moreover, if Δ is regular then a regular process Δ' in normal form such that $\Delta \sim \Delta'$ can be effectively constructed.*

Special notation Here we summarize special notation used in this paper.

- **nBPA** and **nBPP** are abbreviations for normed BPA and normed BPP, respectively.
- if α is a state of a nBPA or nBPP process such that α is regular (see Remark 1), then $\Delta^{\mathcal{R}}(\alpha)$ denotes a bisimilar regular process in normal form, which can be effectively constructed due to Proposition 2. Furthermore, we always assume that $\Delta^{\mathcal{R}}(\alpha)$ contains completely fresh variables which are not contained in any other process we deal with.
- the class of all processes for which there is a bisimilar nBPA (or nBPP) process is denoted $\mathcal{S}(nBPA)$ (or $\mathcal{S}(nBPP)$).
- if $\Delta_1, \ldots, \Delta_n$ are processes from nBPA$\cup$nBPP and X_i is the leading variable of Δ_i for $1 \leq i \leq n$, then $\Delta_1 \| \cdots \| \Delta_n$ denotes the process $X_1 \| \cdots \| X_n$ in the sense of Remark 1.
- square brackets '[' and ']' indicate optional occurrence—if we say that some expression is of the form $a[A][B]$, we mean that this expression is either a, aA, aB or aAB.
- upper indexes are used heavily; they appear in two forms:

$$\alpha^i = \underbrace{\alpha \| \cdots \| \alpha}_{i} \qquad\qquad \alpha^{\cdot i} = \underbrace{\alpha . \cdots . \alpha}_{i}$$

Decidability of bisimilarity in nBPA ∪ nBPP Bisimilarity is known to be decidable for nBPA (see [1, 11, 10]) and nBPP (see [7, 9]) processes. The following result due to Černá, Křetínský and Kučera (see [5]) says that bisimilarity is decidable even in the union of nBPA and nBPP processes.

Proposition 3. *Let Δ be a nBPA (or nBPP) process. It is decidable, whether $\Delta \in S(nBPP)$ (or whether $\Delta \in S(nBPA)$) and if the answer is positive, then a bisimilar nBPP (or nBPA) process can be effectively constructed.*

Decomposability, prime processes Let *nil* be a special name for the process which cannot emit any action (i.e., $nil \sim \epsilon$). A nBPA or nBPP process Δ is *prime* if $\Delta \not\sim nil$ and whenever $\Delta \sim \Delta_1 \| \Delta_2$ we have that either $\Delta_1 \sim nil$ or $\Delta_2 \sim nil$.

Natural questions are, what processes have a decomposition into a finite parallel product of primes and whether this decomposition is unique. This problem was first examined by Milner and Moller in [15]. They proved that each normed finite-state process has a unique decomposition up to bisimilarity. A more general result is due to Christensen, Hirshfeld and Moller—they proved the following proposition (see [8]):

Proposition 4. *Each nBPP process has a unique decomposition into a parallel product of primes (up to bisimilarity).*

Remark 5. Proposition 4 holds for *any* normed process in fact (namely for nBPA). The proof is independent of a concrete syntax—it could be easily formulated in terms of normed transition systems. This proposition thus says that each normed process can be parallelized in the "best" way and that this way is in some sense unique. However, this nice theoretical result is non-constructive.

3 Decomposability of nBPP processes

Each nBPP processes Δ can be easily decomposed into a parallel product of primes—all what has to be done is a construction of a bisimilar *canonical* process (see [6]).

Theorem 6. *Let Δ be a nBPP process. It is decidable whether Δ is prime and if not, its decomposition into primes can be effectively constructed.*

Proof. By induction on $n = |\Delta|$:

- **n=1:** each nBPP process whose norm is 1 is prime.
- **Induction step:** Suppose $\Delta \sim \Delta_1 \| \Delta_2$. As Δ_1, Δ_2 are reachable states of $\Delta_1 \| \Delta_2$, there are $\alpha_1, \alpha_2 \in Var(\Delta)^{\otimes}$ such that $\Delta_1 \sim \alpha_1$ and $\Delta_2 \sim \alpha_2$, thus $\Delta \sim \alpha_1 \| \alpha_2$. Furthermore, $|\Delta| = |\alpha_1| + |\alpha_2|$. We show that there are only finitely many candidates for α_1, α_2. First, there are only finitely many pairs $[k_1, k_2] \in N \times N$ such that $k_1 + k_2 = |\Delta|$. For each such pair $[k_1, k_2]$ there are

only finitely many pairs $[\beta_1, \beta_2]$ such that $\beta_1, \beta_2 \in Var(\Delta)^{\otimes}$, $|\beta_1| = k_1$ and $|\beta_2| = k_2$. It is obvious that the set $\mathcal{M}$ of all such pairs can be effectively constructed. For each element $[\beta_1, \beta_2]$ of $\mathcal{M}$ we check whether $\Delta \sim \beta_1 \| \beta_2$ (it can be done because bisimilarity is decidable for nBPP processes). If there is no such pair then Δ is prime. Otherwise, we check whether β_1, β_2 are primes (it is possible by ind. hypothesis) and construct their decompositions. If we combine these decompositions in parallel, we get a decomposition of Δ. □

As each normed regular process in normal form can be seen as a nBPP process in GNF, Theorem 6 (and especially its constructive proof) can be also used for regular nBPA processes (see Proposition 2). In the next section we can thus concentrate on non-regular nBPA processes.

4 Decomposability of nBPA processes

It this section we give an exact characterization of non-prime nBPA processes. We design special normal forms which allow us to characterize all non-prime nBPA processes together with their decompositions (up to bisimilarity). Our results bring also interesting consequences—we obtain a refinement of the result achieved in [4] (see Remark 18) and we also show that any nBPA process can be decomposed into prime processes effectively. Further positive decidability results are discussed in the end of the second subsection. Finally, we demonstrate decidability of bisimilarity in a natural subclass of normed PA processes.

4.1 Normal forms for non-prime nBPA processes

In this subsection we design the promised normal forms for non-prime nBPA processes and for prime processes which appear in corresponding decompositions. As we already know from the previous section, the problem of possible decomposition of a nBPA process into a parallel product of primes is actually interesting only for non-regular nBPA processes, hence the main characterization theorem does not concern regular nBPA processes.

The layout of this subsection is as follows: first we present two technical lemmas (Lemma 7 and 8). Then we consider the following problem: if Δ is a non-regular nBPA process such that $\Delta \sim \Delta_1 \| \Delta_2$, where Δ_1, Δ_2 are some (unspecified) processes, how do the processes $\Delta, \Delta_1, \Delta_2$ look like? It is clear that $\Delta_1, \Delta_2 \in \mathcal{S}(nBPA)$, hence the assumption that Δ_1, Δ_2 are nBPA processes can be used w.l.o.g. This problem is solved by Proposition 11 and 16 with a help of several definitions. Having this, the proof of Theorem 21 is easy to complete.

Lemma 7. *Let Δ be a nBPA process. Let $\alpha, \gamma \in Var(\Delta)^{+}$, $Q, C \in Var(\Delta)$ such that $|Q| = |C| = 1$ and $\alpha \| Q \sim C.\gamma$. Then $\alpha \sim Q^{|\alpha|}$.*

Proof. We prove that for each $1 \leq i \leq |\alpha|$ there is $\beta \in Var(\Delta)^{*}$ such that $\beta \| Q^{i} \sim C.\gamma$. This is clearly sufficient, because then $\alpha \| Q \sim C.\gamma \sim Q^{|\alpha|+1}$ and thus $\alpha \sim Q^{|\alpha|}$. We proceed by induction on i.

- **i=1:** choose $\beta = \alpha$.
- **Induction step:** Let $\beta \| Q^i \sim C.\gamma$. As $|C| = 1$, all states which are reachable from $\beta \| Q^i$ in one norm-decreasing step are bisimilar. As Δ is normed, there is $\beta' \in Var(\Delta)^*$ such that $\beta \xrightarrow{a} \beta'$ where $|\beta| = |\beta'| + 1$. Hence $\beta \| Q^{i-1} \sim \beta' \| Q^i$ and by substitution we obtain $\beta \| Q^i \sim \beta' \| Q^{i+1}$. □

Lemma 8. *Let Δ be a nBPA process, $\alpha, \beta, \gamma \in Var(\Delta)^*$ such that α is non-regular and $\alpha \| \beta \sim \gamma$. Let $\beta \rightarrow^* Q$ where $|Q| = 1$. Then $\beta \sim Q^{|\beta|}$.*

The proof of Lemma 8 is omitted due to the lack of space (it is rather technical). It can be found in [12].

Definition 9 (simple processes). A nBPA process Δ is *simple* if $Var(\Delta)$ contains just one variable, i.e., $card(Var(\Delta)) = 1$.

We will often identify simple processes with their leading (and only) variables in the rest of this paper. Moreover, it is easy to see that a simple process Q is non-regular iff the def. equation for Q contains a summand of the form $aQ^{\cdot k}$ where $a \in Act$ and $k \geq 2$. The norm of Q is one, because Q could not be normed otherwise. Another important property of simple processes is presented in the remark below:

Remark 10. Each simple nBPA process Q belongs to $\mathcal{S}(nBPP)$—a bisimilar nBPP process can be obtained just by replacing the '.' operator with the '$\|$' operator in the def. equation for Q. Consequently, any process expressions built over k copies of Q using '.' and '$\|$' operators are bisimilar (e.g., $(Q.(Q\|Q))\|Q \sim (Q\|Q).(Q\|Q)$).

Proposition 11. *Let Δ_1, Δ_2 be non-regular nBPA processes. Then $\Delta_1 \| \Delta_2 \in \mathcal{S}(nBPA)$ iff $\Delta_1 \sim Q^{|\Delta_1|}$ and $\Delta_2 \sim Q^{|\Delta_2|}$ for some non-regular simple process Q.*

Proof.
"$\Leftarrow$" Easy—see Remark 10.
"$\Rightarrow$" Assume there is some nBPA process Δ such that $\Delta_1 \| \Delta_2 \sim \Delta$. Then there are $\alpha_1, \alpha_2 \in Var(\Delta)^*$ such that $\Delta_1 \sim \alpha_1$ and $\Delta_2 \sim \alpha_2$. Thus $\alpha_1 \| \alpha_2 \sim \Delta$ and as α_1, α_2 are non-regular, we can use Lemma 8 and conclude that there are $Q_1, Q_2 \in Var(\Delta)$ such that $|Q_1| = |Q_2| = 1$, $\alpha_1 \rightarrow^* Q_1$, $\alpha_2 \rightarrow^* Q_2$ and $\alpha_1 \sim Q_1^{|\alpha_1|}$, $\alpha_2 \sim Q_2^{|\alpha_2|}$. First we prove that $Q_1 \sim Q$ for some simple process Q. To do this, it suffices to prove that if $a\gamma$ is a summand in the def. equation for Q_1, then $\gamma \sim Q_1^{|\gamma|}$ (if this is the case, then also $\gamma \sim Q_1^{\cdot|\gamma|}$ — see Remark 10). As $\alpha_1 \| \alpha_2 \rightarrow^* Q_1 \| \alpha_2 \xrightarrow{a} \gamma \| \alpha_2$, the process $\gamma \| \alpha_2$ belongs to $\mathcal{S}(nBPA)$. Let $\gamma \rightarrow^* R$ where $|R| = 1$. Then $\gamma \sim R^{|\gamma|}$ (due to Lemma 8) and as $\alpha_1 \rightarrow^* \gamma \rightarrow^* R$, we also have $\alpha_1 \sim R^{|\alpha_1|}$. Hence $R \sim Q_1$ and $\gamma \sim Q_1^{|\gamma|}$.

To finish the proof we need to show that $Q_1 \sim Q_2$. Let $m = \max\{|X|, X \in Var(\Delta)\}$. As α_1 is non-regular, it can reach a state of an arbitrary norm—let $\alpha_1 \rightarrow^* \alpha_1'$ where $|\alpha_1'| = m$. Then $\alpha_1' \| Q_2 \sim \delta$ for some $\delta \in Var(\Delta)^*$ whose length is at least two—$\delta = A.B.\delta'$. Clearly $\alpha'_1 \sim Q_1^{|\alpha'_1|}$ (we can use the same argument as in the first part of this proof—Q_2 is non-regular and α' plays the role of γ), hence $Q_1^{|\alpha'_1|} \| Q_2 \sim A.B.\delta'$. As $Q_1^{|\alpha'_1|-|A|} \| Q_2 \sim B.\delta'$ and $Q_1^{|\alpha'_1|-|A|+1} \sim B.\delta'$, we have $Q_1^{|\alpha'_1|-|A|} \| Q_2 \sim Q_1^{|\alpha'_1|-|A|+1}$ by transitivity and thus $Q_1 \sim Q_2$. □

Proposition 11 in fact says that if Δ is a non-regular nBPA process such that $\Delta \sim \Delta_1 \| \Delta_2$, where Δ_1, Δ_2 are non-regular processes, then each of those three processes can be equivalently represented as a power of some non-regular simple process. This representation is very special and can be seen as normal form.

If Δ is a non-regular nBPA process such that $\Delta \sim \Delta_1 \| \Delta_2$, it is also possible that Δ_1 is non-regular and Δ_2 regular. Before we start to examine this sub-case, we introduce a special normal form for nBPA processes (as we shall see, Δ and Δ_1 can be represented in this normal form):

Definition 12 (DNF(Q)). Let Δ be a non-regular nBPA process in GNF, $Q \in Var(\Delta)$. We say that Δ is in $DNF(Q)$ if all summands in all defining equations from Δ are of the form $a([Y].[Q^{\cdot i}])$, where $Y \in Var(\Delta)$, $i \in N$ and $a \in Act$. Furthermore, all summands in the def. equation for Q must be of the form $a[Q]$, where $a \in Act$.

Example 13. The following process is in $DNF(Q)$:

$$X = a(Y.Q.Q) + bX + a(Q.Q.Q) + c$$
$$Y = bQ + cX + c(Y.Q) + b$$
$$Q = aQ + bQ + a + c$$

Remark 14. Reachable states of a process Δ in $DNF(Q)$ are of the form $[Y].[Q^{\cdot i}]$ where $Y \in Var(\Delta)$ and $i \in N \cup \{0\}$. As Δ is non-regular, the state $Q^{\cdot k}$ is reachable for each $k \in N$.

Note that the variable Q itself is a regular simple process. The next lemma says that if Δ is a process in $DNF(Q)$, then the variable Q is in some sense unique:

Lemma 15. *Let Δ and Δ' be processes in $DNF(Q)$ and $DNF(R)$, respectively. If $\Delta \sim \Delta'$, then $Q \sim R$.*

Proposition 16. *Let Δ_1, Δ_2 be nBPA processes such that Δ_1 is non-regular and Δ_2 is regular. Then $\Delta_1 \| \Delta_2 \in S(nBPA)$ iff there is a process Δ'_1 in $DNF(Q)$ such that $\Delta_1 \sim \Delta'_1$ and $\Delta_2 \sim Q^{|\Delta_2|}$.*

Proof.
"$\Rightarrow$" Let $\Delta_2 \to^* Q'$ where $Q' \in Var(\Delta_2)$, $|Q'| = 1$. Using the same kind of argument as in the proof of Proposition 11 we obtain that $Q' \sim Q$ for some regular simple process Q such that $\Delta_2 \sim Q^{|\Delta_2|}$. It remains to prove that there is a process Δ'_1 in $DNF(Q)$ such that $\Delta_1 \sim \Delta'_1$. We show that each summand of each defining equation from Δ_1 can be transformed to a form which is admitted by $DNF(Q)$. First, let us realize two facts about summands—if $a\alpha$ is a summand in a def. equation from Δ_1, then

1. If $\alpha = \beta.Y.\gamma$ where Y is a non-regular variable, then each variable P of γ is bisimilar to $Q^{|P|}$.
2. α contains at most one non-regular variable.

The first fact is a consequence of Lemma 7—let Δ be a nBPA process such that $\Delta_1 \| \Delta_2 \sim \Delta$. As Δ_1 is normed, $\Delta_1 \to^* Y.\gamma.\delta$ for some $\delta \in Var(\Delta_1)^*$. As Y is non-regular, it can reach a state of an arbitrary length—let $m = \max\{|X|, X \in Var(\Delta_1)\}$ and let $Y \to^* \omega$ where $length(\omega) = m$. As $\Delta_1 \| \Delta_2 \to^* \omega.\gamma.\delta \| Q'$, there is $\varphi \in Var(\Delta)^*$ such that $\omega.\gamma.\delta \| Q' \sim \varphi$. Let $\varphi = C.\varphi'$ and let s be a norm-decreasing sequence of actions such that $length(s) = |C| - 1$ and $\omega \xrightarrow{s}{}^* \omega'$. Then $\omega'.\gamma.\delta \| Q' \sim C'.\varphi'$ where $|C'| = 1$ and due to Lemma 7 (and the fact that $Q' \sim Q$) we have $\omega'.\gamma.\delta \sim Q^{|\omega'.\gamma.\delta|}$, hence $\gamma \sim Q^{|\gamma|}$ and $P \sim Q^{|P|}$ for each variable P which appears in γ.

The second fact is a consequence of the first one—assume that $\alpha = \beta.Y.\gamma.Z.\delta$ where Y, Z are non-regular. Then $Z \sim Q^{|Z|}$ and as Q is regular, $Q^{|Z|}$ is regular too. Hence Z is regular and we have a contradiction.

Now we can describe the promised transformation of Δ_1 to Δ_1': if $X = \sum_{i=1}^{n} a_i\alpha_i$ is a def. equation in Δ_1, then $X = \sum_{i=1}^{n} a_i\mathcal{T}(\alpha_i)$ is a def. equation in Δ_1', where $\mathcal{T}$ is defined as follows:

- If α_i does not contain any non-regular variable, then $\mathcal{T}(\alpha_i) = A$, where A is the leading variable of $\Delta^{\mathcal{R}}(\alpha_i)$. Moreover, defining equations of $\Delta^{\mathcal{R}}(\alpha_i)$ are added to Δ_1'.
- If $\alpha_i = \beta.Y.\gamma$ where Y is a non-regular variable, then $\mathcal{T}(\alpha_i) = A$, where A is the leading variable of the process Δ' which is obtained by the following modification of the process $\Delta^{\mathcal{R}}(\beta)$: each summand in each def. equation of $\Delta^{\mathcal{R}}(\beta)$ which is of the form b, where $b \in Act$, is replaced with $b(Y.Q^{\cdot|\gamma|})$ — remember $\gamma \sim Q^{|\gamma|} \sim Q^{\cdot|\gamma|}$. Moreover, def. equations of Δ' are added to Δ_1'.

The defining equation for Q is also added to Δ_1'. The resulting process is in $DNF(Q)$ and as $\mathcal{T}$ preserves bisimilarity, $\Delta_1 \sim \Delta_1'$.

"$\Leftarrow$" We show how to construct a nBPA process Δ which is bisimilar to $\Delta_1' \| Q^{|\Delta_2|}$. Let $k = |\Delta_2|$. The set of variables of Δ looks as follows:

$$Var(\Delta) = \{Q\} \cup \{Y_i,\ Y \in Var(\Delta_1'), Y \neq Q \text{ and } i \in \{0, \ldots, k\}\}$$

Defining equations of Δ are constructed using the following rules:

- the def. equation for Q is the same as in Δ_1'
- if $a(Y.Q^{\cdot j})$, where $j \in N \cup \{0\}$, $Y \neq Q$, is a summand in the def. equation for $Z \in Var(\Delta_1')$, then $a(Y_i.Q^{\cdot j})$ is a summand in the def. equation for Z_i for each $i \in \{0, \ldots, k\}$
- if $a(Q^{\cdot j})$ where $j \in N \cup \{0\}$ is a summand in the def. equation for $Z \in Var(\Delta_1')$, then $a(Q^{\cdot j+i})$ is a summand in the def. equation for Z_i for each $i \in \{0, \ldots, k\}$
- if aQ is a summand in the def. equation for Q and $Z \in Var(\Delta_1')$, $Z \neq Q$, then aZ_i is a summand in the def. equation for Z_i for each $i \in \{1, \ldots, k\}$

– if a is a summand in the def. equation for Q and $Z \in Var(\Delta_1')$, $Z \neq Q$, then aZ_{i-1} is a summand in the def. equation for Z_i for each $i \in \{1, \ldots, k\}$

The intuition which stands behind this construction is that lower indexes of variables indicate how many copies of Q in $Q^{|\Delta_2|}$ have not disappeared yet. The fact $\Delta_1' \| Q^{|\Delta_2|} \sim \Delta$ is easy to check. □

Example 17. If we apply the algorithm presented in the "⇐" part of the proof of Proposition 16 to the process $X \| Q^2$, where X, Q are variables of the process presented in Example 13, we obtain the following output:

$$\begin{aligned}
X_2 &= a(Y_2.Q.Q) + bX_2 + a(Q.Q.Q.Q.Q) + c(Q.Q) + aX_2 + bX_2 + aX_1 + cX_1 \\
X_1 &= a(Y_1.Q.Q) + bX_1 + a(Q.Q.Q.Q) + cQ + aX_1 + bX_1 + aX_0 + cX_0 \\
X_0 &= a(Y_0.Q.Q) + bX_0 + a(Q.Q.Q) + c \\
Y_2 &= b(Q.Q.Q) + cX_2 + c(Y_2.Q) + b(Q.Q) + aY_2 + bY_2 + aY_1 + cY_1 \\
Y_1 &= b(Q.Q) + cX_1 + c(Y_1.Q) + bQ + aY_1 + bY_1 + aY_0 + cY_0 \\
Y_0 &= bQ + cX_0 + c(Y_0.Q) + b \\
Q &= aQ + bQ + a + c
\end{aligned}$$

Remark 18. Proposition 16 can also be seen as a refinement of the result presented in [4]—Burkart and Steffen proved that PDA processes are closed under parallel composition with finite-state processes, while BPA processes lack this property. Proposition 16 says precisely, which nBPA processes can remain nBPA if they are combined in parallel with a regular process. Moreover, it also characterizes all such regular processes.

It is easy to see that the algorithm from the proof of Proposition 16 always outputs a process in $DNF(Q)$ (see Example 17). Moreover, the structure of this process is very specific; we can observe that each variable belongs to a special "level". This intuition is formally expressed by the following definition (it is a little complicated—but it pays because we will be able to characterize all non-prime nBPA processes):

Definition 19. Let Δ be a nBPA process in $DNF(Q)$. The *level* of Δ, denoted $Level(\Delta)$, is the maximal $l \in N$ such that the set $Var(\Delta) - \{Q\}$ can be divided into l disjoint linearly ordered subsets $L_1, \ldots, L_l$ of the same cardinality k. Moreover, the following conditions must be true (the jth element of L_i is denoted $A_{i,j}$):

- $A_{l,1}$ is the leading variable of Δ.
- Defining equations for variables of L_1 contain only variables from $L_1 \cup \{Q\}$
- The defining equation for $A_{i,j}$, where $i \geq 2$, $1 \leq j \leq k$, contains exactly those summands which can be derived by one of the following rules:
  1. If aQ is a summand in the defining equation for Q, then $aA_{i,j}$ is a summand in the defining equation for $A_{i,j}$ for each $2 \leq i \leq l$, $1 \leq j \leq k$.
  2. If a is a summand in the defining equation for Q, then $aA_{i-1,j}$ is a summand in the defining equation for $A_{i,j}$ for each $2 \leq i \leq l$, $1 \leq j \leq k$.

3. If $a(A_{1,m}.Q^{\cdot n})$ is a summand in the defining equation for $A_{1,j}$ such that $A_{1,m} \neq Q$, then $a(A_{i,m}.Q^{\cdot n})$ is a summand in the defining equation for $A_{i,j}$ for each $2 \leq i \leq l$.
4. If $aQ^{\cdot n}$ is a summand in the defining equation for $A_{1,j}$, then $aQ^{\cdot(n+i-1)}$ is a summand in the defining equation for $A_{i,j}$, where $2 \leq i \leq l$.

Example 20. The process of Example 17 has the level 3; $L_1 = \{X_0, Y_0\}$, $L_2 = \{X_1, Y_1\}$ and $L_3 = \{X_2, Y_2\}$.

Now we can present the first main theorem of this paper:

Theorem 21. *Let Δ be a non-regular nBPA process and let $\Delta \sim \Delta_1 \| \cdots \| \Delta_n$, where $n \geq 2$, Δ_i is a prime process for each $1 \leq i \leq n$ and Δ_1 is non-regular. Then one of the following possibilities holds:*

- *There is a non-regular simple process Q such that $\Delta \sim Q^{\cdot|\Delta|}$ and $\Delta_i \sim Q$ for each $1 \leq i \leq n$.*
- *There are nBPA processes Δ', Δ_1' in $DNF(Q)$ such that $\Delta \sim \Delta'$, $\Delta_1 \sim \Delta_1'$, $Level(\Delta') = n$, $Level(\Delta_1') = 1$ and $\Delta_i \sim Q$ for each $2 \leq i \leq n$.*

Proof. By a straightforward induction on n—see [12]. □

4.2 Decidability results

In this subsection we present several positive decidability results. We show that it is decidable whether a given nBPA process is prime and if the answer is negative, then its decomposition into primes can be effectively constructed. There are also other decidable properties which are summarized in Theorem 26. Finally, we demonstrate decidability of bisimilarity in a natural subclass of normed PA processes.

Lemma 22. *Let Δ be a nBPA process. It is decidable whether there is a nBPA process Δ' in $DNF(Q)$ such that $\Delta \sim \Delta'$. Moreover, if the answer to the previous question is positive, then the process Δ' can be effectively constructed.*

Proof. We can assume (w.l.o.g.) that Δ is in 3-GNF. If there is a process Δ' in $DNF(Q)$ such that $\Delta \sim \Delta'$, then there is $R \in Var(\Delta)$ such that $R \sim Q$, because Q is a reachable state of Δ'. As Q is a regular simple process, each summand in the def. equation for R must be of the form $a[P]$, where $R \sim P$. As bisimilarity is decidable for nBPA processes, we can construct the set $\mathcal{M}$ of all variables of $Var(\Delta)$ with this property. Each variable from this set is a potential candidate for the variable which is bisimilar to Q (if the set $\mathcal{M}$ is empty, then Δ cannot be bisimilar to any process in $DNF(Q)$).

For each variable $V \in \mathcal{M}$ we now modify the process Δ slightly—we replace each summand of the form aP in the def. equation for V with aV. The resulting process is denoted Δ_V (clearly $\Delta \sim \Delta_V$). For each Δ_V we check whether Δ_V can be transformed to a process in $DNF(V)$. To do this, we first need to realize the following fact: if there is Δ'_V in $DNF(V)$ such that $\Delta_V \sim \Delta'_V$ and $a(A.B)$ is a summand in a def. equation from Δ_V such that A is non-regular, then $B \sim V^{\cdot|B|}$. It is easy to prove by the technique we already used many times in this paper—as A is non-regular, it can reach a state of an arbitrary norm. Furthermore, there is a reachable state of Δ_V which is of the form $A.B.\gamma$ where $\gamma \in Var(\Delta_V)^*$. We choose sufficiently large α such that $A \to^* \alpha$ and $\alpha.B.\gamma$ must be bisimilar to a state of Δ'_V which is of the form $[Y].V^{\cdot i}$ where $i \geq |B.\gamma|$. From this we get $B \sim V^{\cdot|B|}$.

Now we can describe the promised transformation $\mathcal{T}$ of Δ_V to a process Δ'_V in $DNF(V)$. If this transformation fails, then there is *no* process in $DNF(V)$ bisimilar to Δ_V. $\mathcal{T}$ is invoked on each summand of each def. equation from Δ_V and works as follows:

- $\mathcal{T}(a) = a$
- $\mathcal{T}(aA) = aA$
- $\mathcal{T}(a(A.B)) = aN$ if A is regular. The variable N is the leading variable of $\Delta^{\mathcal{R}}(A)$, whose def. equations are also added to Δ'_V after the following modification: each summand in each def. equation of $\Delta^{\mathcal{R}}(A)$ which is of the form b where $b \in Act$ is replaced with bB.
- $\mathcal{T}(a(A.B)) = a(A.V^{\cdot|B|})$ if A is non-regular and $B \sim V^{\cdot|B|}$. If A is non-regular and $B \not\sim V^{\cdot|B|}$, then $\mathcal{T}$ *fails*.

If there is $V \in \mathcal{M}$ such that $\mathcal{T}$ succeeds for Δ_V, then the process $\Delta'_V \sim \Delta$ is the process we are looking for. Otherwise, there is no process in $DNF(Q)$ bisimilar to Δ. □

Proposition 23. *Let $\Delta_1, \ldots, \Delta_n$, $n \geq 2$ be nBPA processes. It is decidable whether $\Delta_1 \| \cdots \| \Delta_n \in S(nBPA)$. Moreover, if the answer to the previous question is positive, then a nBPA process Δ such that $\Delta_1 \| \cdots \| \Delta_n \sim \Delta$ can be effectively constructed.*

Proof. By induction on n:

- **n=2:** we distinguish three possibilities (it is decidable which one actually holds—see Proposition 2):
  1. Δ_1 and Δ_2 are regular. Then $\Delta_1 \| \Delta_2 \in S(nBPA)$ and a bisimilar regular process Δ in normal form can be easily constructed.
  2. Δ_1 and Δ_2 are non-regular. Proposition 11 says that there is a non-regular simple process Q such that $\Delta_1 \sim Q^{|\Delta_1|} \sim Q^{\cdot|\Delta_1|}$ and $\Delta_2 \sim Q^{|\Delta_2|} \sim Q^{\cdot|\Delta_2|}$. As Q is a reachable state of $Q^{\cdot|\Delta_2|}$, there is $R \in Var(\Delta_1)$ such that $Q \sim R$. As reachable states of Q are of the form $Q^{\cdot i}$ where $i \in N \cup \{0\}$, each summand $a\alpha$ in the def. equation for R has the property $\alpha \sim R^{\cdot|\alpha|}$. As bisimilarity is decidable for nBPA processes, we can find all variables of $Var(\Delta)$ having this property—we obtain a set of possible candidates for R (if this set is empty, then $\Delta_1 \| \Delta_2 \notin S(nBPA)$). Now we check whether the constructed set of candidates contains a variable R such that $\Delta_1 \sim R^{\cdot|\Delta_1|}$. If not, then $\Delta_1 \| \Delta_2 \notin S(nBPA)$. Otherwise we have R which is bisimilar to Q.

The same procedure is now applied to Δ_2. If it succeeds, it outputs some $S \in Var(\Delta)$. Now we check whether $R \sim S$. If not, then $\Delta_1 \| \Delta_2 \notin \mathcal{S}(nBPA)$. Otherwise $\Delta_1 \| \Delta_2 \in \mathcal{S}(nBPA)$ and $\Delta_1 \| \Delta_2 \sim R^{\cdot|\Delta_1|+|\Delta_2|}$.

3. Δ_1 is non-regular and Δ_2 is regular (or Δ_1 is regular and Δ_2 is non-regular—this is symmetric). Due to Proposition 16 we know that there is a regular simple process Q and a nBPA process Δ_1' in $DNF(Q)$ such that $\Delta_1 \sim \Delta_1'$ and $\Delta_2 \sim Q^{|\Delta_2|} \sim Q^{\cdot|\Delta_2|}$. An existence of Δ_1' can be checked effectively (see Lemma 22). If it does not exist, then $\Delta_1 \| \Delta_2 \notin \mathcal{S}(nBPA)$. If it exists, it can be also constructed and thus the only thing which remains is to test whether $\Delta_2 \sim Q^{\cdot|\Delta_2|}$. If this test succeeds, then $\Delta_1 \| \Delta_2 \in \mathcal{S}(nBPA)$ and we invoke the algorithm from the proof of Proposition 16 with $\Delta_1' \| Q^{|\Delta_2|}$ on input—it outputs a nBPA process which is bisimilar to $\Delta_1 \| \Delta_2$.

– **Induction step:** if $\Delta_1 \| \cdots \| \Delta_n \in \mathcal{S}(nBPA)$, then also $\Delta_1 \| \cdots \| \Delta_{n-1} \in \mathcal{S}(nBPA)$ and this is decidable by induction hypothesis—if the answer is negative, then $\Delta_1 \| \cdots \| \Delta_n \notin \mathcal{S}(nBPA)$ and if it is positive, then we can construct a nBPA process Δ' such that $\Delta_1 \| \cdots \| \Delta_{n-1} \sim \Delta'$. Now we check whether $\Delta' \| \Delta_n \in \mathcal{S}(nBPA)$ and construct a bisimilar nBPA process Δ. □

As an immediate consequence of Proposition 23 we get:

Proposition 24. *Let $\Delta, \Delta_1, \ldots, \Delta_n$ be nBPA processes. It is decidable whether $\Delta \sim \Delta_1 \| \cdots \| \Delta_n$.*

Theorem 25. *Let Δ be a nBPA process. It is decidable whether Δ is prime and if not, its decomposition into primes can be effectively constructed.*

Proof. The technique is the same as in the proof of Theorem 6. We can almost copy the whole proof—the crucial result which allows us to do so is Proposition 24. □

Decidability results which were proved in this subsection are summarized by the following theorem:

Theorem 26. *Let $\Delta, \Delta_1, \ldots, \Delta_n$ be nBPA processes. The following problems are decidable:*

- *Is Δ prime? (If not, its decomposition can be effectively constructed)*
- *Is Δ bisimilar to $\Delta_1 \| \cdots \| \Delta_n$?*
- *Does the process $\Delta_1 \| \cdots \| \Delta_n$ belong to $\mathcal{S}(nBPA)$?*
- *Is there any process Δ' such that $\Delta \| \Delta' \in \mathcal{S}(nBPA)$? (if so, an example of such a process can be effectively constructed).*
- *Is there any process Δ' such that $\Delta \sim \Delta_1 \| \cdots \| \Delta_n \| \Delta'$? (if so, Δ' can be effectively constructed).*

A "structural" way how to construct new processes from older ones is to combine them in parallel. If we do this with nBPA and nBPP processes, we obtain a natural subclass of normed PA processes denoted sPA (simple PA processes).

Definition 27 (sPA processes). The class of sPA processes is defined as follows: sPA $= \{\Delta_1 \| \cdots \| \Delta_n \mid n \in N,\ \Delta_i \in \text{nBPA} \cup \text{nBPP}$ for each $1 \le i \le n\}$

The class sPA is strictly greater than the union of nBPA and nBPP processes; it suffices to take a parallel composition of two "normed counters" specified by nBPA processes. The resulting sPA process is not bisimilar to any nBPA or nBPP process. It can be easily proved with the help of pumping lemmas for CF languages and for languages generated by nBPP processes—see [6].

Theorem 28. *Let $\Phi = \varphi_1 \| \cdots \| \varphi_n$, $\Psi = \psi_1 \| \cdots \| \psi_m$ be sPA processes. It is decidable whether $\Phi \sim \Psi$.*

Proof. As each φ_i, $1 \le i \le n$ and ψ_j, $1 \le j \le m$ can be effectively decomposed into a parallel product of primes, we can also construct the decompositions of Φ and Ψ. If $\Phi \sim \Psi$, then these decompositions must be the same up to bisimilarity (see Remark 5). In other words, there must be a one-to-one mapping between primes forming the two decompostions which preserves bisimilarity. An existence of such a mapping can be checked effectively, because bisimilarity is decidable in the union of nBPA and nBPP processes (see Proposition 3). □

5 Conclusions, future work

The main characterization theorem (Theorem 21) says that non-regular nBPA processes which are not prime can be divided into two groups:

1. processes which are bisimilar to a power of some non-regular simple process. It is obvious that each such nBPA process belongs to $S(nBPP)$—see Remark 10.
2. processes which are bisimilar to some process in $DNF(Q)$. It can be proved (with the help of results achieved in [5]) that each such process does *not* belong to $S(nBPP)$.

From this we can observe that our division based on normal forms corresponds to the membership to $S(nBPP)$.

We have also shown that the decomposition of non-prime nBPA processes can be effectively constructed. This algorithm can be interpreted as a construction of the "most parallel" version of a given sequential program. Finally, we proved that bisimilarity is decidable for sPA processes. (see Definition 27).

The first possible generalization of our results could be the replacement of the '$\|$' operator with the parallel operator of CCS which allows synchronizations on complementary actions. This should not be hard, but we can expect more complicated normal forms. Decidability results should be the same.

A natural question is whether our results can be extended to the class of all (not necessarily normed) BPA processes. The answer is no, because there are quite primitive BPA processes which do not have any decomposition at all—a simple example is the process $X = aX$.

Another related open problem is decidability of bisimilarity for normed PA processes. It seems that it should be possible to design at least rich subclasses of normed PA processes where bisimilarity remains decidable.

References

1. J.C.M. Baeten, J.A. Bergstra, and J.W. Klop. Decidability of bisimulation equivalence for processes generating context-free languages. In *Proceedings of PARLE'87*, volume 259 of *LNCS*, pages 93–114. Springer-Verlag, 1987.
2. J.C.M. Baeten and W.P. Weijland. *Process Algebra*. Number 18 in Cambridge Tracts in Theoretical Computer Science. Cambridge University Press, 1990.
3. J. Blanco. Normed BPP and BPA. In *Proceedings of ACP'94*, Workshops in Computing, pages 242–251. Springer-Verlag, 1995.
4. O. Burkart and B. Steffen. Pushdown processes: Parallel composition and model checking. In *Proceedings of CONCUR'94*, volume 836 of *LNCS*, pages 98–113. Springer-Verlag, 1994.
5. I. Černá, M. Křetínský, and A. Kučera. Bisimilarity is decidable in the union of normed BPA and normed BPP processes. In *Proceedings of INFINITY'96*, MIP-9614, pages 32–46. University of Passau, 1996.
6. S. Christensen. *Decidability and Decomposition in Process Algebras*. PhD thesis, The University of Edinburgh, 1993.
7. S. Christensen, Y. Hirshfeld, and F. Moller. Bisimulation is decidable for all basic parallel processes. In *Proceedings of CONCUR'93*, volume 715 of *LNCS*, pages 143–157. Springer-Verlag, 1993.
8. S. Christensen, Y. Hirshfeld, and F. Moller. Decomposability, decidability and axiomatisability for bisimulation equivalence on basic parallel processes. In *Proceedings of LICS'93*. IEEE Computer Society Press, 1993.
9. Y. Hirshfeld, M. Jerrum, and F. Moller. A polynomial algorithm for deciding bisimulation equivalence of normed basic parallel processes. Technical report ECS-LFCS-94-288, Department of Computer Science, University of Edinburgh, 1994.
10. Y. Hirshfeld, M. Jerrum, and F. Moller. A polynomial-time algorithm for deciding equivalence of normed context-free processes. In *Proceedings of 35th Annual Symposium on Foundations of Computer Science*, pages 623–631. IEEE Computer Society Press, 1994.
11. H. Hüttel and C. Stirling. Actions speak louder than words: Proving bisimilarity for context-free processes. In *Proceedings of LICS'91*, pages 376–386. IEEE Computer Society Press, 1991.
12. A. Kučera. How to parallelize sequential processes. Technical report FIMU-RS-96-05, Faculty of Informatics, Masaryk University, 1996.
13. A. Kučera. Regularity is decidable for normed BPA and normed BPP processes in polynomial time. In *Proceedings of SOFSEM'96*, volume 1175 of *LNCS*, pages 377–384. Springer-Verlag, 1996.
14. R. Milner. *Communication and Concurrency*. Prentice-Hall, 1989.
15. R. Milner and F. Moller. Unique decomposition of processes. *Theoretical Computer Science*, 107(2):357–363, 1993.
16. D.M.R. Park. Concurrency and automata on infinite sequences. In *Proceedings 5th GI Conference*, volume 104 of *LNCS*, pages 167–183. Springer-Verlag, 1981.

Causal Ambiguity and Partial Orders in Event Structures

Rom Langerak, Ed Brinksma *
University of Twente

Joost-Pieter Katoen†
Friedrich-Alexander University

March 1997

Abstract

Event structure models often have some constraint which ensures that for each system run it is clear what are the causal predecessors of an event (i.e. there is no causal ambiguity). In this contribution we study what happens if we remove such constraints. We define five different partial order semantics that are intentional in the sense that they refer to syntactic aspects of the model. We also define an observational partial order semantics, that derives a partial order from just the event traces.

It appears that this corresponds to the so-called early intentional semantics; the other intentional semantics cannot be observationally characterized. We study the equivalences induced by the different partial order definitions, and their interrelations.

1 Introduction

Prominent models for non-interleaving semantics are the *event structure* models. Event structures have as their basic objects labelled events together with relations representing causality and conflict. Originally event structures were used for giving a semantics to Petri nets [Win80]. They have been also used as a semantics for process algebraic languages like CCS [BC94], CSP [LG91] and LOTOS [Lan92]. Several different types of event structures exist: we mention prime event structures [Win80, Win89], stable event structures [Win89], flow event structures [BC94], and bundle event structures [Lan93, Lan92].

All these models are causally disambiguous, by which we mean the following: if an event has happened, there is exactly one set of causal predecessors of the

* {langerak,brinksma}@cs.utwente.nl, Department of Computer Science, PO Box 217, 7500 AE Enschede, The Netherlands

† katoen@informatik.uni-erlangen.de, Institut für Informatik VII, Martensstrasse 3, D-91058 Erlangen, Germany

event, i.e. there is never any ambiguity in deciding which are the causes of an event.
This is an important technical property, especially if one wants to relate an event structure model to the more fundamental model of partially ordered sets (or *posets*). Posets can be used as the underlying semantics of many different models; for an elaborate motivation of the importance of posets we refer to [Ren93]. Absence of causal ambiguity implies that there is exactly one poset corresponding to a system run.
Posets can be defined in two alternative ways: by referring to the causality representation in the model (we call this *intentional*), or by just referring to the system runs (we call this *observational*). Having corresponding intentional and observational characterizations of the posets is important for relating event structures to other models, where an explicit representation of causality may be absent.

In e.g. stable or bundle event structures the absence of causal ambiguity (this property is called *stability* in [Win89]) is due to a constraint on the model, which roughly says that if there are alternative causes for an event, then these causes should somehow be in conflict.

For certain application areas (e.g. business redesign) it can be argued that this constraint is too restrictive [Fer94]. Therefore the problem this paper addresses is the following: is it possible to define a partial order semantics for an event structure model with causal ambiguity ?

The organization of the paper is as follows. In section 2 we present an event structure model and sketch the problem of causal ambiguity. In section 3 we give five intentional poset definitions, and in section 4 we show that exactly one of them (the so-called early causality) has an observational characterization. In section 5 we look at the induced equivalence relations, and section 6 is for conclusions.

2 Event structures

Event structure models have as their basic ingredient events labelled with actions; an event models the occurrence of its action. Different events can have the same action label, implying that they model different occurrences of the action. Action labels do not play a role in this paper but are important when the model is used e.g. as a semantics for a language. We are in general not interested in the event identities as such (so implicitly we work modulo an event renaming morphism), as the events just serve to identify or distinguish action occurrences. Often we will denote an event by its action label, if no confusion arises.

Two events in a system are said to be in *conflict* if there is no system run in which both events happen. In this paper we will restrict ourselves to the representation of conflict by a binary relation between events. In that case the main difference between the models lies in the way they represent causality.

In prime event structures causality is modelled by a partial order on the set of

events. This model is mathematically very elegant and convenient. The drawback is that as a consequence each event has a unique enabling, so if an action can be caused in alternative ways we need to model the action by different events, harmful to the conciseness of models. In addition it may be rather complicated to define some operations on prime event structures, especially parallel synchronization.
For these reasons other models like stable, flow and bundle event structures model causality in a different way. Flow event structures model causality by a flow relation that (contrary to prime event structures) need not be transitive, thereby making it possible for an event to have alternative enablings. However, also for flow event structures parallel synchronization is a bit problematic as it is technically dependent on self-conflicting events (as we argued in [Lan92]).
The first event structure model that was defined in order to allow for multiple enablings is the model of *stable* event structures [Win89]. There causality is represented by a set $\vdash$ of *enablings*, which are pairs (X, e), with X a set of events and e an event, denoted by $X \vdash e$. The interpretation is that e can happen if for some enabling $X \vdash e$ all the events in X have happened already.
In this paper we use bundle event structures as our illustrative vehicle, since for them some necessary technical results are readily available. However, in the full version of this paper [LBK97] we have shown that the approach here applies to stable event structures just as well.
Since concepts, like well-foundedness [Win89], that address problems with infinite sets of events are orthogonal to the issues of this paper and need not bother us here, we conveniently restrict ourselves to finite sets of events.

2.1 Bundle event structures

In bundle event structures [Lan93, Lan92], causality is represented by *bundles*: a bundle is a pair (X, e) with X a set of events and e an event. The set of all bundles is denoted by $\mapsto$ and we denote a bundle (X, e) by $X \mapsto e$.
The meaning of a bundle $X \mapsto e$ is that X is a set of causal conditions for e, in the sense that if e happens, one of the events in X has to have happened before. If several bundles point to e, for each bundle set an event should have happened. In addition, we demand that for each bundle $X \mapsto e$, all the events in X are in mutual conflict with each other. In this way, if e has happened, exactly one event from X has happened before, so there is no doubt about which are the causal predecessors of e. In the next section we see what happens if we remove this condition.
The definition of bundle event structures:

Definition 2.1 A *bundle event structure* $\mathcal{E}$ is a 4-tuple
$\mathcal{E} = (E, \#, \mapsto, l)$ with :

- E a set of *events*
- $\# \subseteq E \times E$, the symmetric and irreflexive *conflict* relation
- $\mapsto \subseteq 2^E \times E$, the *bundle* set

- $l : E \rightarrow Act$, the *labelling* function

such that the following property holds:
P1: $X \mapsto e \Longrightarrow \forall e_1, e_2 \in X : (e_1 \neq e_2 \Longrightarrow e_1 \# e_2)$ □

We represent a bundle event structure graphically in the following way. Events are drawn as dots; near the dot we sometimes give the event name and/or the action. Conflicts are indicated by dotted lines. A bundle $X \mapsto e$ is indicated by drawing an arrow from each element of X to e and connecting all the arrows by small lines.
The following picture is an example of a bundle event structure, with a bundle $\{a, b, c\} \mapsto d$:

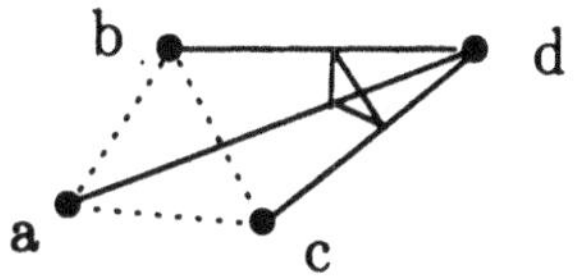

The bundle here means that for d to happen, either a, b or c should have happened already.

The concept of a system run for a bundle event structure is captured by the notion of an *event trace*, which is a conflict–free sequence of events, where each event is preceded by its causal predecessors:

Definition 2.2 Let $\mathcal{E} = (E, \#, \mapsto, l)$ be a bundle event structure. An *event trace* is a sequence of distinct events $e_1, \ldots, e_n$, with $e_1, \ldots, e_n \in E$, satisfying:

- $\{e_1, \ldots, e_n\}$ is conflict-free, i.e. $\forall e_i, e_j : \neg(e_i \# e_j)$.
- $X \mapsto e_i \Longrightarrow \{e_1, \ldots, e_{i-1}\} \cap X \neq \emptyset$

□

Notation: Let $\sigma = e_1 \ldots e_n$ be an event trace, then $\widehat{\sigma} = \{e_1, \ldots, e_n\}$ is the set of events in σ.
With the help of event traces we can define a semantics for bundle event structures in terms of (labelled) partial orders, abbreviated *posets* (not to be confused with *pomsets*, which are equivalence classes of posets modulo event renaming morphisms [Pra86]). Posets form a natural and attractive basic semantics for comparing true concurrency models [Ren93].
The next definition and theorem show how to obtain posets from event traces:

Definition 2.3 Let σ be an event trace of $\mathcal{E}$, with $\widehat{\sigma} = T$. We define the *precedence relation* $\prec_T \subseteq T \times T$ by $e \prec_T e'$ iff $\exists X \subseteq E : (e \in X \wedge X \mapsto e')$. The relation $\leq_T$ is defined as $\leq_T = \prec_T^*$, i.e. the reflexive and transitive closure of $\prec_T$. □

Theorem 2.4 $\leq_T$ is a partial order over T.

Proof : see [Lan92] □

Let $\mathcal{E}$ be a bundle event structure, then the set of posets we get by applying definition 2.3 to all event traces of $\mathcal{E}$ is denoted by $P(\mathcal{E})$, where P stands for posets.

2.2 Observational partial orders

We have called the above definitions of partial order (obtained from an event trace) *intentional*, as opposed to *observational*, because they refer to aspects of the model, viz. bundles, that are not observable as such. Therefore the question arises how to relate these partial orders to systems where the only observations that can be made are the event traces. As an answer to this question we give a definition of partial orders from event traces that is only based on event traces and does not need to take recourse to bundles. We call this definition observational, even though a rather strong notion of observation is assumed, namely the ability to observe events (so the occurrence of actions, instead of just actions).

It is easy to prove that each event trace is a linearization of the partial order we get by definition 2.3. This provides the basic intuition for the observational poset definition, which works as follows.
Let σ be an event trace of a bundle event structure $\mathcal{E}$, with set of events $\widehat{\sigma} = T$. Now consider all event traces of $\mathcal{E}$ with the same events as σ and suppose $\{\sigma' \mid \widehat{\sigma'} = T\} = \{\sigma_1, \ldots, \sigma_m\}$.
We associate with each event trace σ_i an ordering $\leq_i$ on its events, which is simply the order of the events in the event trace, so if $\sigma_i = e_{i1} \ldots e_{in}$ then $\leq_i$ is defined by $e_{i1} \leq_i e_{i2} \leq_i \ldots \leq_i e_{in}$.
Now define $\leq_T$ by $\leq_T = \leq_1 \cap \leq_2 \cap \ldots \cap \leq_m$. It is not hard to see that $\leq_T$ is a partial order over T, so $(T, \leq_T)$ is a partially ordered set or poset.
Let $\mathcal{E}$ be a bundle event structure, then the set of posets we get by applying the above definition to all event traces of $\mathcal{E}$ is denoted by $OP(\mathcal{E})$, where OP stands for *observational* posets.
In Corollary 7.5.4. in [Lan92] it is stated that $P(\mathcal{E}) = OP(\mathcal{E})$, i.e. the intentional posets are equal to the observational posets. This correspondence between the intentional and the observational definition makes it possible to relate bundle event structures to other models that can be defined to generate event traces, e.g. Petri nets or process algebras [Lan92].

2.3 The problem of causal ambiguity

Crucial for the definitions above is the constraint P1 (see definition 2.1), that says that from each bundle only one event can happen. If we would not have constraint P1, then the following would be a "bundle" event structure:

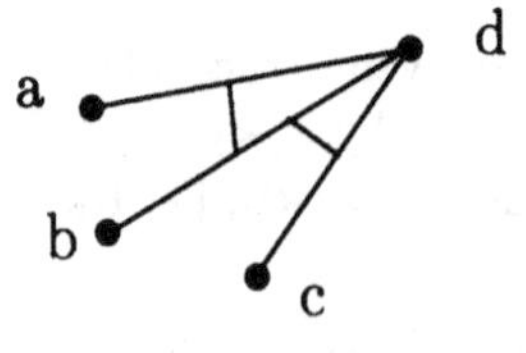

with bundles $\{a, b\} \mapsto d$ and $\{b, c\} \mapsto d$. Suppose we would take event trace *abcd* and would ask what partial order corresponds to this event trace. What are the causal predecessors of *d* ? With constraint P1 this question always has a unique answer, but now there are several candidates: $\{a, c\}$, $\{b\}$, $\{a, b\}$, $\{b, c\}$ and $\{a, b, c\}$ are all candidate sets of causal predecessors of *d*. We therefore have to adapt our definition of how to obtain a partial order from an event trace, and in the next section we will see that there are several ways of doing so.

Also the observational definition of the previous section does not work anymore. If we try the recipe given there for the above event structures, we obtain 14 event traces with events $\{a, b, c, d\}$; the intersection of these linear orders is a poset with just the identity as the ordering relation, which surely does not capture the causality information of the event structure.
Bundle event structures without constraint P1 have been baptized *dual* event structures in [Kat96]. Providing intentional and observational partial order definitions for dual event structures is the theme of the following sections.

3 Intentional partial order definitions

In this section we present several definitions of causality in possibly causally ambiguous situations. What definition is appropriate depends on considerations coming from the application area. In this respect the situation is very similar to the field of implementation relations [vG90], where many different implementation relations exist, each with its own (often observational) justification. In fact in section 5 we show how these different causality notions give rise to different partial order equivalences, and study their interrelations. In section 4 we show that only one of the notions in this section has an observational characterization in terms of event traces.

By a *cause* of e in σ we mean a set of causal predecessors of e, that is a set of events that enable e to happen. Each of the notions in this section gives an answer to the following question: suppose we have a dual event structure $\mathcal{E}$, with an event trace σ, and an event e in σ, what are the possible causes C in σ of e ? We do not demand that C is always unique, i.e. in principle we allow a set $\{C_i\}$ of possible causes as an answer to our question (some notions lead to a unique C though).

We can define partial orders on $\widehat{\sigma}$ in the following way: for each e in σ, choose a cause C_e. Now define for all $e, e' \in \widehat{\sigma}$: $e' \prec e$ iff $e' \in C_e$ and define the ordering relation on $\widehat{\sigma}$ to be the transitive and reflexive closure of $\prec$. If each cause C_e occurs before e in σ (and all notions we consider have this property, in agreement with the common sense idea that causes have to occur before effects) it is easy to see that this definition leads indeed to a partial order.

3.1 Liberal causality

The least restrictive notion of causality, which we call the *liberal* one, is the one saying that each set of events from bundles pointing to e that satisfies all bundles is a cause.

Definition 3.1 *Liberal:* Let σ be an event trace of $\mathcal{E}$, e an event in this trace, and all bundles pointing to e given by $X_1 \mapsto e, \ldots, X_n \mapsto e$.
A set C is a cause of e in σ iff the following conditions hold:

- each $e' \in C$ occurs before e in σ
- $C \subseteq X_1 \cup \ldots \cup X_n$
- for all i: $X_i \cap C \neq \emptyset$

The set of posets obtained in this way from σ is denoted by $P_{lib}(\sigma)$ □

Example 3.2 Consider event trace *abcd* of event structure

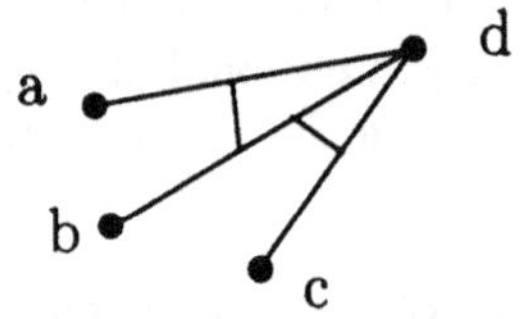

Then $P_{lib}(abcd)$ consists of the posets

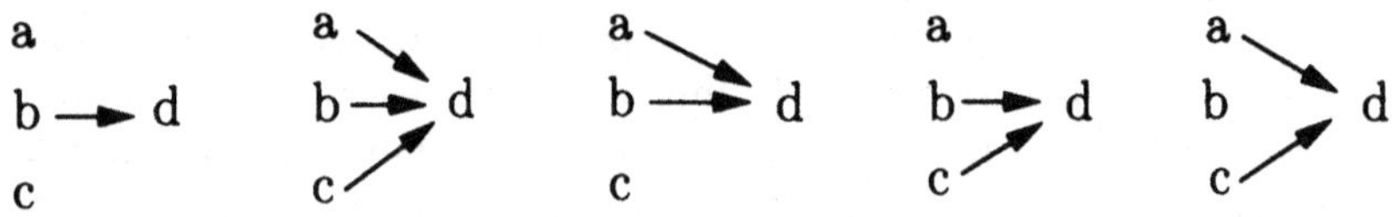

□

3.2 Bundle satisfaction causality

This causality notion is based on the idea that for an e in σ each bundle pointing to e is satisfied by exactly one event in a cause of e. This means that for all bundles pointing to e, each bundle can be mapped to an event in a cause C such that all events in C are being mapped upon, so the presence of each event e' in C should be justified by some bundle $X \mapsto e$, with $e' \in X$, that is associated to e'.

Definition 3.3 *Bundle satisfaction:* Let σ be an event trace of $\mathcal{E}$, e an event in this trace, and all bundles pointing to e given by $X_1 \mapsto e, \ldots, X_n \mapsto e$.
A set C is a cause of e in σ iff the following conditions hold:

- each $e' \in C$ occurs before e in σ
- There is a surjective mapping $f : \{X_i\} \to C$ such that $f(X_i) \in X_i$

The set of posets obtained in this way from σ is denoted by $P_{bsat}(\sigma)$ □

Example 3.4 Let $\mathcal{E}$ be the same dual event structure as in example 3.2. Now we allow e.g.

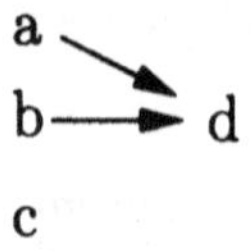

(where a satisfies bundle $\{a, b\} \mapsto d$ and b satisfies bundle $\{b, c\} \mapsto d$) and

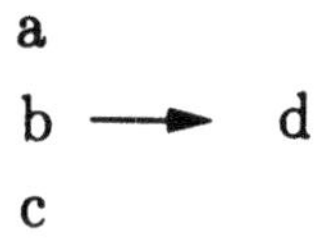

(where b satisfies both bundles $\{a,b\} \mapsto d$ and $\{b,c\} \mapsto d$). Notice that we do allow more events from one bundle, or several bundles satisfied by the same event.

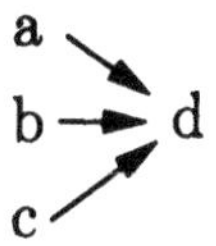

is not allowed as a poset, as d has three causal predecessors and there are only two bundles to be satisfied. □

Clearly each C satisfying definition 3.3 also satisfies definition 3.1, so for all event traces σ, $P_{bsat}(\sigma) \subseteq P_{lib}(\sigma)$.

3.3 Minimal causality

The next causality definition is based on the idea that each cause should be minimal, in the sense that there is no subset which is also a cause.

Definition 3.5 *Minimal:* Let σ be an event trace of $\mathcal{E}$, e an event in this trace, and all bundles pointing to e given by $X_1 \mapsto e, \ldots, X_n \mapsto e$.
A set C is a cause of e in σ iff the following conditions hold:

- each $e' \in C$ occurs before e in σ
- for all i: $X_i \cap C \neq \emptyset$
- there is no proper subset of C satisfying the previous two conditions

The set of posets obtained in this way from σ is denoted by $P_{min}(\sigma)$ □

Example 3.6 Let $\mathcal{E}$ be the same dual event structure as in example 3.2. Now the only posets for trace *abcd* are

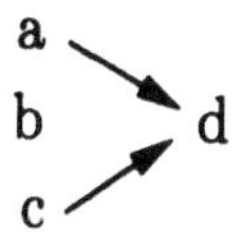

and

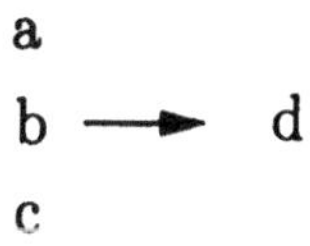

E.g.

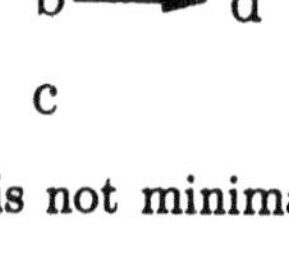

is not allowed anymore as $\{a,b\}$ is not minimal: also the subset $\{b\}$ would be sufficient for d to be enabled. □

Again it is easy to see that each C satisfying definition 3.5 also satisfies definition 3.3, so for all event traces σ, $P_{min}(\sigma) \subseteq P_{bsat}(\sigma)$.

3.4 Early causality

If one is trying to remove "superfluous" events from the causes, at first sight the minimal definition given above seems hard to improve upon. However, look at the following example.

Example 3.7 Consider trace abc from event structure

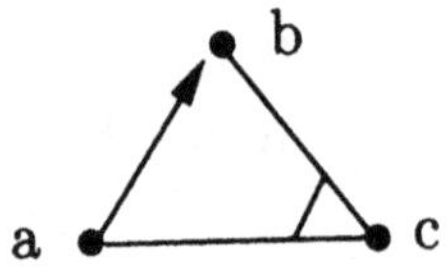

then $\{a\}$ is a minimal cause of b, and $\{b\}$ is a minimal cause of c, so we have a poset

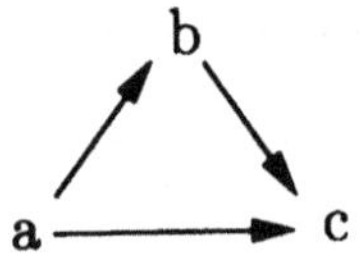

(with $a \leq c$ because of transitivity). However, if b happens, a has happened already, and a is enough to let c happen. So in a sense the causality relation between b and c is superfluous. □

In order to remove this superfluousness, we would like to demand that a cause is somehow the "earliest".

Definition 3.8 Let $\sigma = e_1 \dots e_n$ be an event trace, and let $C, C' \subseteq \{e_1 \dots e_n\}$. We say C is earlier than C', notation $C \ll C'$, iff the maximal index in σ of the events in $C \setminus C'$ is smaller than the maximal index in σ of the events in $C' \setminus C$ (we define the maximal index of $\emptyset$ to be 0). □

Lemma 3.9 Let σ be an event trace, let Id be the identity relation over all the subsets of $\widehat{\sigma}$. The relation $\ll \cup Id$ is a total order over all the subsets of $\widehat{\sigma}$.

Proof : Represent a subset C of $\widehat{\sigma}$ by a binary n-digit, where the ith digit is 1 iff $e_i \in C$, the nth digit being the most significant one. Call the resulting number $n(C)$, then it is easy to see that $C \ll C'$ iff $n(C) < n(C')$. □

Given a set of subsets of $\widehat{\sigma}$, lemma 3.9 ensures that it makes sense to talk of a unique earliest element of this set. Now we are ready for the definition of early causality:

Definition 3.10 *Early:* Let σ be an event trace of $\mathcal{E}$, e an event in this trace, and all bundles pointing to e given by $X_1 \mapsto e, \dots, X_n \mapsto e$.
A set C is a cause of e in σ iff the following conditions hold:

- each $e' \in C$ occurs before e in σ
- for all i: $X_i \cap C \neq \emptyset$

- C is the earliest set satisfying the previous two conditions.

The set of posets obtained in this way from σ is denoted by $P_{early}(\sigma)$ □

Note that due to the uniqueness of the earliest enabling, this definition leads to a unique cause in an event trace σ, and so to a unique poset for σ.

It is easy to check that if $C \subset C'$ then $C \ll C'$; this means that each earliest cause C is also minimal, so for all event traces σ, $P_{early}(\sigma) \subseteq P_{min}(\sigma)$.

3.5 Late causality

In the last section we defined an early causality, taking always the earliest cause. One might ask if it would also be possible to ask for the latest possible cause. Think for instance of a situation where events write values into variables; then it would be natural to consider the last write as a causal predecessor of e.g. an event that reads the variable.

We define C later C' iff $C' \ll C$. Now it is not the case that latest implies minimality (on the contrary, a superset of a set C will always be later). Therefore in the definition of late causality we have to explicitly state that the cause is a minimal one, whereas for early causality this was a consequence.

Definition 3.11 *Late:* Let σ be an event trace of $\mathcal{E}$, e an event in this trace, and all bundles pointing to e given by $X_1 \mapsto e, \ldots, X_n \mapsto e$.
A set C is a cause of e in σ iff the following conditions hold:

- each $e' \in C$ occurs before e in σ
- for all i: $X_i \cap C \neq \emptyset$
- there is no proper subset of C satisfying the previous two conditions
- C is the latest set satisfying the previous three conditions

The set of posets obtained in this way from σ is denoted by $P_{late}(\sigma)$ □

Each C satisfying definition 3.11 trivially satisfies definition 3.5, so for all event traces σ, $P_{late}(\sigma) \subseteq P_{min}(\sigma)$.

3.6 Comparisons

We saw that for each event trace σ, $P_{late}(\sigma), P_{early}(\sigma) \subseteq P_{min}(\sigma) \subseteq P_{bsat}(\sigma) \subseteq P_{lib}(\sigma)$.

We can extend the definition of P_x to dual event structures by having $P_x(\mathcal{E})$ denote the posets of all event traces of event structure $\mathcal{E}$.
The subset inclusions for the posets of a single event trace carry over to the subset relations for the posets of a dual event structure. These inclusions are strict because of the following reasons. For $\mathcal{E}$ in example 3.2 we have seen that $P_{min}(\mathcal{E}) \subset P_{bsat}(\mathcal{E}) \subset P_{lib}(\mathcal{E})$. For $\mathcal{E}$ in example 3.7 we have that $P_{early}(\mathcal{E}) \subset P_{min}(\mathcal{E})$. An example of a dual even structure that has a minimal poset that is not a late poset: let $\mathcal{E}$ be the following dual event structure:

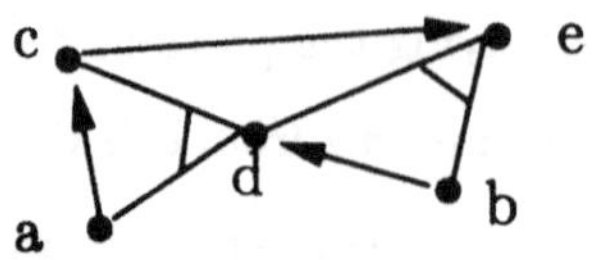

We invite the reader to check that

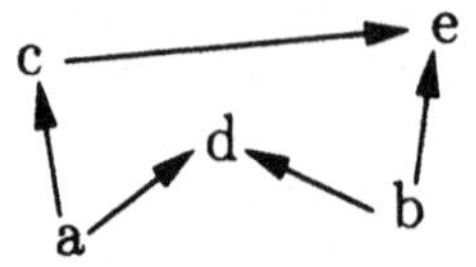

is a minimal poset for e.g. event trace *abcde*, but cannot be a late poset for any event trace of $\mathcal{E}$.

4 An observational partial order definition

We would like to have also for the dual or instable event structure an observational definition of partial order like the one in section 2.3 (cf. definition 2.3). As illustrated in section 3, we cannot use the technique of reconstructing the posets from their linearizations (the event traces) as we end up with posets that have too little ordering and do not model the causality in a satisfactory way. We therefore try another recipe.

The idea of this definition is the following: for an event e in σ, we look at all event traces with the same events as σ. We then look at the set of predecessors of e in some event trace (we call such a set a *securing* for e). From all these securings we now take the earliest securing for e in σ and define $e' \leq e$ for all e' in this earliest securing.

Definition 4.1 Let σ be an event trace of a dual event structure $\mathcal{E}$, and e an event in σ.

- let $[\sigma]$ be the set of all event traces of $\mathcal{E}$ with events $\widehat{\sigma}$
- the securings of e are defined as $\{\widehat{\sigma_1} | \exists \sigma_2 : \sigma_1 e \sigma_2 \in [\sigma]\}$
- take the earliest securing S in σ and define $e' \leq e$ iff $e' \in S \cup \{e\}$

□

The nice result is that $\leq$ as defined by the observational definition 4.1 is exactly the unique partial order as defined by the intentional one of *early* causality.
Let $\leq$ be the ordering defined by definition 4.1, then we write $OP(\sigma)$ (for *observational poset*) for $(\widehat{\sigma}, \leq)$.

Theorem 4.2 Let σ be an event trace of dual event structure $\mathcal{E}$. Then: $OP(\sigma) = P_{early}(\sigma)$.

Proof : See [LBK97] □

So early causality can also be characterized in an observational way. Is it possible to find a characterization for any of the other intentional causality concepts ? The answer is no, as can be learned from the following example.

Example 4.3 The dual event structures

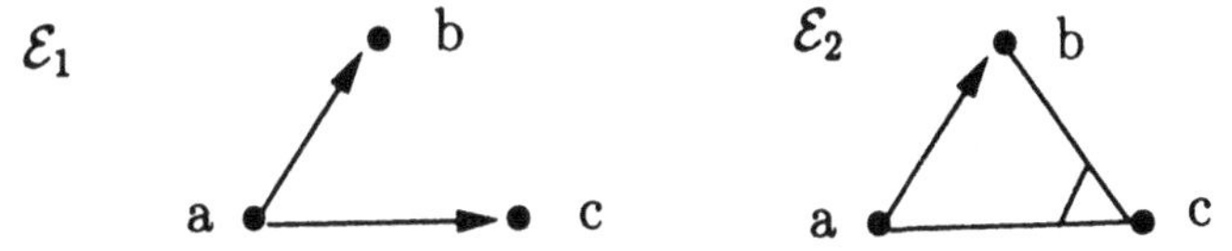

have the same event traces. $\mathcal{E}_2$ has for trace abc the poset

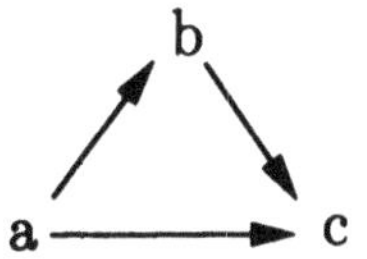

under liberal, bundle satisfaction, minimal and late causality, but this is not a poset of $\mathcal{E}_1$. □

Any observational definition of causality would have the same result for $\mathcal{E}_1$ and $\mathcal{E}_2$ above as they have the same traces. Since the other intentional causality concepts lead to different posets for $\mathcal{E}_1$ and $\mathcal{E}_2$ this shows that these intentional concepts cannot be observationally characterized.

So the result is that the early causality concept is the only one that can be observationally characterized.

5 Partial order equivalence relations

The causality notions defined in the previous sections induce equivalence relations in the following way:

Definition 5.1 Let $\mathcal{E}_1$, $\mathcal{E}_2$ be dual event structures. We define $\mathcal{E}_1 \approx_x \mathcal{E}_2$ iff $P_x(\mathcal{E}_1) = P_x(\mathcal{E}_2)$, where $x \in \{lib, bsat, min, early, late\}$. □

Now an obvious question is the relation between the different equivalence relations. First of all, we note that due to theorem 4.2, $\approx_{early}$ is equal to event trace equivalence (since equal event traces lead to the same observational posets so to the same early posets, and vice versa). We have the following two implications:

Theorem 5.2

1. $\mathcal{E}_1 \approx_x \mathcal{E}_2 \implies \mathcal{E}_1 \approx_{early} \mathcal{E}_2$ for $x \in \{lib, bsat, min, late\}$
2. $\mathcal{E}_1 \approx_{bsat} \mathcal{E}_2 \implies \mathcal{E}_1 \approx_{lib} \mathcal{E}_2$

Proof : See [LBK97] □

The two above implications are strict (i.e. the reverse does not hold). Moreover, no other implications hold. This can be seen from the following examples, where each pair of dual event structures is event trace equivalent and so early equivalent:

Example 5.3

as $\mathcal{E}_2$ can have $b \le c$ and $\mathcal{E}_1$ can not. □

Example 5.4

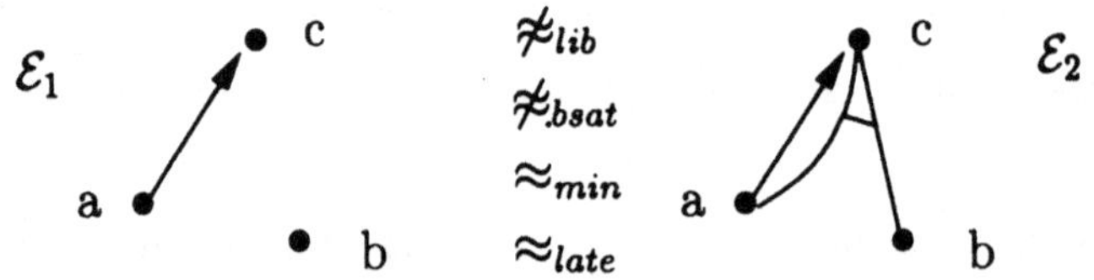

as $\mathcal{E}_2$ can have $b \le c$ in liberal and bundle satisfaction posets and $\mathcal{E}_1$ can not. For minimal and late causality, b will not be in a cause for c as a is sufficient. □

Example 5.5

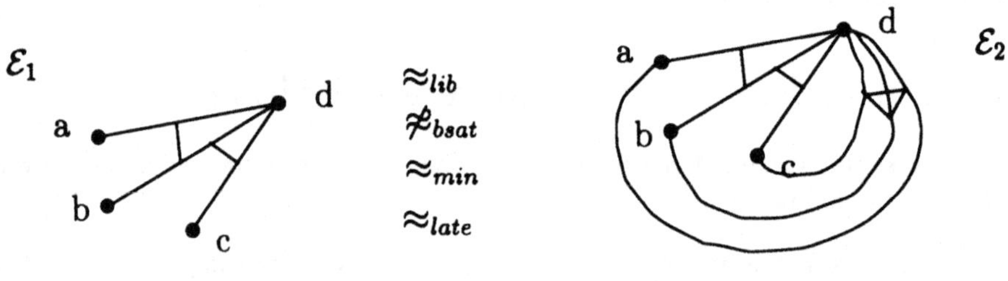

as the extra bundle $\{a, b, c\} \mapsto d$ has no influence on liberal, minimal and late causes, but $P_{bsat}(\mathcal{E}_2)$ has poset

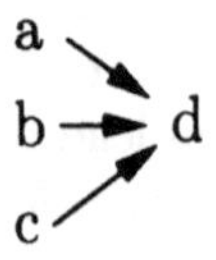

and $P_{bsat}(\mathcal{E}_1)$ has not. □

Example 5.6

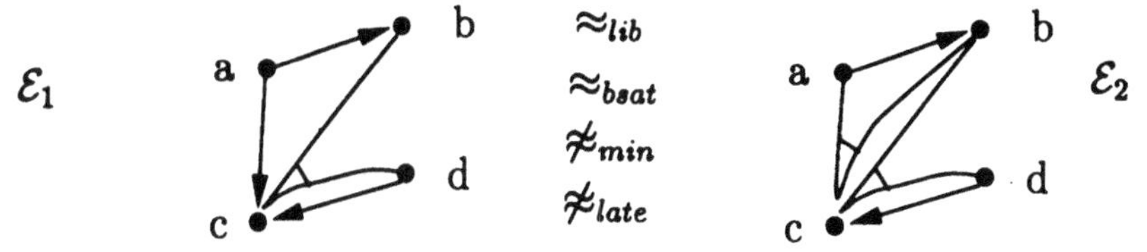

For minimal and late causality, $\mathcal{E}_2$ has poset

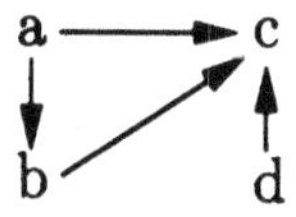

as $\{b, d\}$ is a minimal cause for c in e.g. trace $abdc$, which does not hold for $\mathcal{E}_1$. □

The only relationship we have not been able to clear up is between $\approx_{min}$ and $\approx_{late}$. We have not been able to produce an example of their difference, nor have we been able to prove that such an example does not exist.
If we leave that relation as an open question, we can resume our findings in the following diagram:

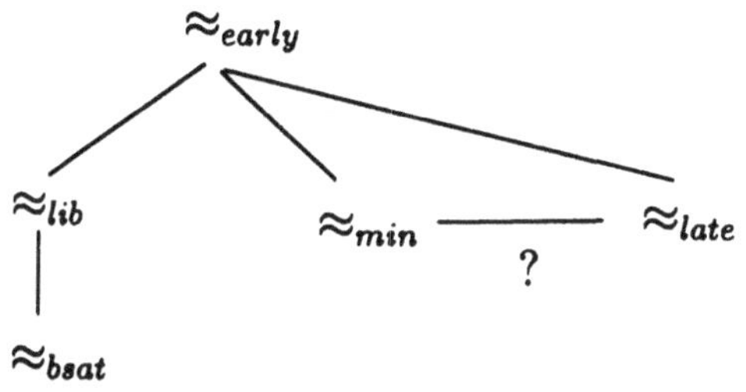

6 Conclusion

We have shown that it is possible to give a partial order semantics for a causally ambiguous event structure model. We have presented five intentional causality concepts (that make use of the way causality is represented in the model): liberal, bundle satisfaction, minimal, early and late causality. We have given an observational characterization (that makes use of just event traces) of one of them, namely the *early* causality, and have shown that for the other notions no observational characterization can be given.
Especially the fact that late causality, which at first sight seems a symmetric counterpart to early causality, cannot be observationally characterized is something that we did not expect beforehand.

We studied the induced equivalence relations and found that all equivalences imply early equivalence (which is equal to event trace equivalence), and that bundle satisfaction equivalence implies liberal equivalence.

We gave examples showing that apart from these implications the different equivalences are incomparable, except for the relation between minimal and late equivalence: the relation between these equivalences is an open question.

Another problem for further study would be to look at transformation laws preserving the various equivalences, in a similar way as has been done in [Lan92] for event trace equivalence.

Acknowledgements

This paper owes much to discussions with Rob van Glabbeek and Arend Rensink. Thanks to the anonymous referees for many suggestions for improvement.

References

[BC94] G. Boudol and I. Castellani. Flow models of distributed computations: three equivalent semantics for CCS. *Information and Computation*, 114:247–314, 1994.

[dBdRR89] J.W. de Bakker, W.-P. de Roever, and G. Rozenberg, editors. *Linear Time, Branching Time and Partial Order in Logics and Models for Concurrency*, volume 354 of *Lecture Notes in Computer Science*. Springer-Verlag, 1989.

[Fer94] L. Ferreira Pires. *Architectural Notes: A Framework for Distributed Systems Development*. PhD thesis, University of Twente, 1994.

[Kat96] J-P. Katoen. *Quantitative and Qualitative Extensions of Event Structures*. CTIT Ph. D-thesis series no. 96-09, University of Twente, 1996.

[Lan92] R. Langerak. *Transformations and Semantics for LOTOS*. PhD thesis, University of Twente, 1992.

[Lan93] R. Langerak. Bundle event structures: a non-interleaving semantics for LOTOS. In M. Diaz and R. Groz, editors, *Formal Description Techniques V*, volume C–10 of *IFIP Transactions*, pages 331–346. North-Holland, 1993.

[LBK97] R. Langerak, E. Brinksma, and J.-P. Katoen. Causal ambiguity and partial orders in event structures. CTIT technical report, University of Twente, 1997.

[LG91] R. Loogen and U. Goltz. Modelling nondeterministic concurrent processes with event structures. *Fundamentae Informaticae*, 14:39–74, 1991.

[Pra86] V.R. Pratt. Modeling concurrency with partial orders. *International Journal of Parallel Programming*, 15(1):33–71, 1986.

[Ren93] A. Rensink. *Models and Methods for Action Refinement*. PhD thesis, University of Twente, 1993.

[vG90] Rob van Glabbeek. *Comparative Concurrency Semantics and Refinement of Actions*. PhD thesis, Free University of Amsterdam, 1990.

[Win80] G. Winskel. *Events in Computation*. PhD thesis, University of Edinburgh, 1980. (also available as Technical Report CST-10-80).

[Win89] G. Winskel. An introduction to event structures. In de Bakker et al. [dBdRR89], pages 364–397.

Model Checking PA-Processes

Richard Mayr

Institut für Informatik, Technische Universität München,
Arcisstr. 21, D-80290 München, Germany;
e-mail: mayrri@informatik.tu-muenchen.de
Web: http://wwwbrauer.informatik.tu-muenchen.de/mitarbeiter/mayrri
fax: +49 (89) 289-28207/28483

Abstract. PA (Process algebra) is the name that has become common use to denote the algebra with a sequential and parallel operator (without communication), plus recursion. PA-processes subsume both Basic Parallel Processes (BPP) [Chr93] and context-free processes (BPA). They are a simple model for infinite state concurrent systems.
We show that the model checking problem for the branching time temporal logic *EF* is decidable for PA-processes.

Keywords: PA-processes, model checking, process algebras, tableau systems

1 Introduction

The Process Algebra PA is a simple model of infinite state concurrent systems. It has operators for nondeterministic choice, parallel composition, sequential composition and recursion. PA-processes and Petri nets are incomparable, meaning that neither model is more expressive than the other one. Unlike BPPs, PA is not a syntactical subset of CCS [Mil89], because CCS does not have an explicit operator for sequential composition. However, as CCS can simulate sequential composition by parallel composition and synchronization, PA is still a weaker model than CCS. PA-processes are a superset of both Basic Parallel Processes (BPP) [Chr93] and context-free processes (BPA).

Here we study the model checking problem for PA-processes. This is the problem of deciding if a given PA-process satisfies a property coded as a formula in a certain temporal logic.

For BPPs the situation is already fairly clear. It has been shown in [EK95] that the model checking problem for BPPs is undecidable for the branching time temporal logic EG, whose formulae are built out of the boolean operators, *EX* (for some successor) and EG (for some path always in the future). On the other hand the model checking problem is decidable for the logic *EF*, that uses the boolean operators, and the temporal operators *EX* and *EF* (for some path eventually in the future). Therefore, the logic *EF* (also called UB^- in [Esp] and [May96b]), seems to be the largest branching time logic with a decidable model checking problem. The model checking problem for BPPs and *EF* (UB^-) is PSPACE-complete [May96a, May96b].

Here we show that the model checking problem with the logic *EF* is decidable even for PA-processes. In section 2 we define PA-processes. In section 3 we describe the tableau system that solves the model checking problem, while in section 4 we prove its soundness and completeness. In Section 5 we describe a small example. Section 6 describes a possible extension of the logic *EF* by adding constraints on sequences of actions. The paper closes with a section on open problems and related work.

2 PA-Processes

The definition of PA is as follows: Assume a countably infinite set of atomic actions $Act = \{a, b, c, \ldots\}$ and a countably infinite set of process variables $Var = \{X, Y, Z, \ldots\}$. The class of PA expressions is defined by the following abstract syntax

$$E ::= \epsilon \mid X \mid aE \mid E + E \mid E \| E \mid E.E$$

Convention: We always work with equivalence classes of terms modulo commutativity of parallel composition. Also we define that $\epsilon.E = E$ and $E\|\epsilon = E$.

A PA is defined by a family of recursive equations $\{X_i := E_i \mid 1 \leq i \leq n\}$, where the X_i are distinct and the E_i are PA expressions at most containing the variables $\{X_1, \ldots, X_n\}$. We assume that every variable occurrence in the E_i is *guarded*, i.e. appears within the scope of an action prefix, which ensures that PA-processes generate finitely branching transition graphs. This would not be true if unguarded expressions were allowed. For example, the process $X := a + a\|X$ generates an infinitely branching transition graph. For every $a \in Act$ the transition relation $\xrightarrow{a}$ is the least relation satisfying the following inference rules:

$$aE \xrightarrow{a} E \qquad \frac{E \xrightarrow{a} E'}{E + F \xrightarrow{a} E'} \qquad \frac{F \xrightarrow{a} F'}{E + F \xrightarrow{a} F'} \qquad \frac{E \xrightarrow{a} E'}{X \xrightarrow{a} E'}(X := E)$$

$$\frac{E \xrightarrow{a} E'}{E\|F \xrightarrow{a} E'\|F} \qquad \frac{F \xrightarrow{a} F'}{E\|F \xrightarrow{a} E\|F'} \qquad \frac{E \xrightarrow{a} E'}{E.F \xrightarrow{a} E'.F}$$

Alternatively, PA-processes can be represented by a state described by a term of the form

$$G ::= \epsilon \mid X \mid G_1.G_2 \mid G_1\|G_2$$

and set of rules Δ of the form $X \xrightarrow{a} G$ whose application to states must respect sequential composition. This is described by the following inference rules:

$$X \xrightarrow{a} G \quad \text{if}\,(X \xrightarrow{a} G) \in \Delta$$

$$\frac{E \xrightarrow{a} E'}{E\|F \xrightarrow{a} E'\|F} \qquad \frac{F \xrightarrow{a} F'}{E\|F \xrightarrow{a} E\|F'} \qquad \frac{E \xrightarrow{a} E'}{E.F \xrightarrow{a} E'.F}$$

We assume w.r. that for every variable X there is at least one rule $X \xrightarrow{a} t$. The transition relation $\xrightarrow{a}$ is extended to sequences of actions $\xrightarrow{\sigma}$ in the standard way. If the sequence σ is of no account, then we just write $\xrightarrow{*}$.

BPPs are the subset of PA-processes without sequential composition, while context-free processes are the subset of PA-processes without parallel composition.

Unlike for PA-processes there is a one-to-one correspondence between BPPs and a class of labelled Petri nets, the *communication-free nets* [Esp]. In these nets every transition has exactly one input place with an arc labelled by 1.

3 The Tableau System

Model checking algorithms can be divided into two classes: iterative algorithms and tableau-based algorithms. The iterative algorithms compute all the states of the system which have the desired property, and usually yield higher efficiency in the worst case. The tableau-based algorithms are designed to check whether a particular expression has a temporal property. This is called local model checking which avoids the investigation of for the verification irrelevant parts of the process being verified. Therefore this method is applicable for the verification of systems with infinite state spaces. In local model checking the proof system is developed in a goal directed fashion (top down). A property holds iff there is a proof tree with a successful leaf which witnesses this truth. The algorithm for the following problem is tableau-based and decides the truth of an *EF*-formula for a PA-process by examining only finitely many states.

3.1 The Temporal Logic *EF*

The branching time temporal logic *EF* of [Esp, Esp96] is used to describe properties of PA-processes. We fix a countably infinite set of atomic actions *Act*. The syntax of the calculus is as follows:

$$\Phi \stackrel{\text{def}}{=} a \mid \neg\Phi \mid \Phi_1 \wedge \Phi_2 \mid \Diamond\Phi$$

where $a \in Act$ ranges over atomic actions. For convenience disjunction and another modal operator $\Box$ can be added by defining $\Box := \neg\Diamond\neg$.

Let $\mathcal{F}$ be the set of all *EF*-formulae. Let Ω be the set of all processes in the process algebra. The denotation $||\Phi||$ of a formula Φ is the set of processes inductively defined by the following rules:

$$\begin{aligned}
||a|| &:= \{t \mid \exists t \xrightarrow{a} t'\} \\
||\neg\Phi|| &:= \Omega - ||\Phi|| \\
||\Phi_1 \wedge \Phi_2|| &:= ||\Phi_1|| \cap ||\Phi_2|| \\
||\Diamond\Phi|| &:= \{t \mid \exists t \xrightarrow{\sigma} t'.\ t' \in ||\Phi||\}
\end{aligned}$$

The property $t \in ||\Phi||$ is also denoted by $t \models \Phi$. An instance of the model checking problem is a PA process algebra, a term t in the algebra and an *EF*-formula Φ. The question is if $t \models \Phi$.

In order to simplify the presentation we have left out the one-step nexttime-operator *EX* for now. In Section 6 we'll show that it can be added to the logic without causing any problems. In this framework this operator is often denoted by $\langle a \rangle$, with $a \in Act$ and defined by

$$||\langle a \rangle \Phi|| := \{t \mid \exists t \xrightarrow{a} t' \in ||\Phi||\}$$

The decidability results carry over to the logic that includes the nexttime-operator (see Section 6).

While the model checking problem with *EF* is undecidable for general Petri nets [Esp], it is decidable and PSPACE-complete for BPPs [May96a, May96b]. Here we show that model checking with the logic *EF* is decidable for PA-processes.

Definition 1. $\mathcal{F}_d \subset \mathcal{F}$ is defined as the set of all *EF*-formulae with a nesting-depth of modal operators $\Diamond$ of at most d. (It follows that formulae in $\mathcal{F}_0$ contain no modal operators.)

In order to simplify the notation we use some abbreviations:
Let $A = \{a_1, \ldots, a_n\} \subseteq Act$ be a set of atomic actions, then

$$t \models A \;:\Leftrightarrow\; t \models a_1 \wedge \ldots \wedge a_n$$

and

$$t \models -A \;:\Leftrightarrow\; t \models \neg a_1 \wedge \ldots \wedge \neg a_n$$

The decidability proof of the model checking problem is done by induction on the nesting depth d of modal operators in the formula. For a term t and a formula $\Phi \in \mathcal{F}_d$ the algorithm builds a finite tableau for $t \models \Phi$ by using properties of the form $t' \models F'$ with $F' \in \mathcal{F}_{d-1}$ as side conditions.

First we reduce the problem to a simpler form.

Definition 2. The set of conjunctive formulae $\mathcal{F}^c \subset \mathcal{F}$ is the smallest set of formulae satisfying the following conditions:

1. $A^+ \wedge -A^-$ is a conjunctive formula for $A^+, A^- \subseteq Act$
2. $A^+ \wedge -A^- \wedge \bigwedge_{i \in I} \Diamond \Psi_i \wedge \bigwedge_{j \in J} \neg \Diamond \Upsilon_j$ is a conjunctive formula if $A^+, A^- \subseteq Act$ and $\Psi_i \in \mathcal{F}^c$ and $\Upsilon_j \in \mathcal{F}^c$.

Let $\mathcal{F}_d^c := \mathcal{F}_d \cap \mathcal{F}^c$.

A formula Φ is in *normal form* if $\Phi = \bigvee_{i \in I} \Diamond \Psi_i$ s.t. the Ψ_i are conjunctive formulae. $\mathcal{F}_d^n \subset \mathcal{F}_d$ are the formulae in normal form in $\mathcal{F}_d$.

Lemma 3. *Any EF-formula $\Phi = \Diamond \Psi$ is equivalent to a formula in normal form.*

Proof By induction on the nesting-depth d of modal operators in Ψ.

1. If $d = 0$ then Ψ doesn't contain any modal operators, so it can be transformed into disjunctive normal form $\bigvee_{i \in I} A_i^+ \wedge -A_i^-$. Therefore Φ is equivalent to $\bigvee_{i \in I} \Diamond(A_i^+ \wedge -A_i^-)$. This is a formula in normal form.

2. Now $d > 0$. By induction hypothesis we can transform all subformulae $\Diamond\varphi$ of Ψ into normal from, obtaining a formula Ψ'. Then transform Ψ' into disjunctive normal form $\Psi'' = \bigvee_{i\in I}\gamma_i$. Thus Φ is equivalent to $\Phi' = \Diamond(\bigvee_{i\in I}\gamma_i) = \bigvee_{i\in I}\Diamond\gamma_i$. This is in normal form, because all γ_i are conjunctive formulae.

□

Lemma 4. *Every model checking problem for EF is decidable iff it is decidable for all formulae $\Diamond\Phi$ with $\Phi \in \mathcal{F}^c$.*

Proof If it is decidable for formulae of the form $\Diamond\Psi$ with $\Psi \in \mathcal{F}^c$, then it is decidable for formulae in normal form and thus by Lemma 3 for all formulae of the form $\Diamond\Phi$. Simple boolean operations yield the decidability of the whole model checking problem. The other direction is trivial. □

In the sequel all *EF*-formulae will be conjunctive formulae. Let $\Phi \in \mathcal{F}^c_d$. Then $\Diamond\Phi$ has the form $\Diamond(A^+ \wedge -A^- \wedge \bigwedge_{i\in I}\Diamond\Psi_i \wedge \bigwedge_{j\in J}\neg\Diamond\Upsilon_j)$ where $A^+ \subseteq Act$, $A^- \subseteq Act$ and $\Psi_i \in \mathcal{F}^c_{d-1}$ and $\Upsilon_j \in \mathcal{F}^c_{d-1}$.

Remark. In the definition of PA algebras we assumed that every occurring variable is defined. It follows that in the other representation there is at least one rule $X \xrightarrow{a} G$ in Δ for every X. Therefore a PA-process cannot perform any action if and only if it is empty. This means that $t \models \Diamond(-Act) \iff \exists t \xrightarrow{\sigma} \epsilon$.

3.2 Decomposition

For the construction of a finite tableau that solves the model checking problem it is necessary to split the problem into several smaller subproblems. We do this by showing that properties of a PA-process can be expressed by properties of its subprocesses.

Lemma 5. *Let t_1, t_2 be PA-terms and Φ in $\mathcal{F}^c_d$. Then a set I and terms $\Phi^1_i, \Phi^2_i \in \mathcal{F}^c_d$ can be effectively constructed s.t.*

$$t_1\|t_2 \models \Diamond\Phi \;\Leftrightarrow\; \bigvee_{i\in I} t_1 \models \Diamond\Phi^1_i \wedge t_2 \models \Diamond\Phi^2_i$$

Proof $\Diamond\Phi = \Diamond(A^+ \wedge -A^- \wedge \bigwedge_{i\in I}\Diamond\Psi_i \wedge \bigwedge_{j\in J}\neg\Diamond\Upsilon_j)$ with $A^+, A^- \subseteq Act$, $\Psi_i, \Upsilon_j \in \mathcal{F}^c_{d-1}$. The proof is done by induction on d.

$$t_1\|t_2 \models \Diamond(A^+ \wedge -A^- \wedge \bigwedge_{i\in I}\Diamond\Psi_i \wedge \bigwedge_{j\in J}\neg\Diamond\Upsilon_j)$$

By definition of *EF* this is equivalent to

$$\exists A_1^+ \cup A_2^+ = A^+.\ \exists t_1 \xrightarrow{*} t_1', t_2 \xrightarrow{*} t_2'.\ t_1' \models (A_1^+ \wedge -A^-) \wedge t_2' \models (A_2^+ \wedge -A^-) \wedge \\ \bigwedge_{i\in I} t_1'\|t_2' \models \Diamond\Psi_i \wedge \bigwedge_{j\in J} t_1'\|t_2' \models \neg\Diamond\Upsilon_j$$

By induction hypothesis there are K_i, L_j and $\varphi^1_{i,k}, \varphi^2_{i,k}, \delta^1_{j,l}, \delta^2_{i,l} \in \mathcal{F}^c_{d-1}$ s.t. the expression is equivalent to

$$\exists A_1^+ \cup A_2^+ = A^+ . \exists t_1 \xrightarrow{*} t_1', t_2 \xrightarrow{*} t_2'.\ t_1' \models (A_1^+ \wedge -A^-) \wedge t_2' \models (A_2^+ \wedge -A^-) \wedge \bigwedge_{i \in I}(\bigvee_{k \in K_i} t_1' \models \Diamond\varphi^1_{i,k} \wedge t_2' \models \Diamond\varphi^2_{i,k}) \wedge \bigwedge_{j \in J} \neg(\bigvee_{l \in L_j} t_1' \models \Diamond\delta^1_{j,l} \wedge t_2' \models \Diamond\delta^2_{j,l})$$

By De Morgan this is equivalent to

$$\exists A_1^+ \cup A_2^+ = A^+ . \exists t_1 \xrightarrow{*} t_1', t_2 \xrightarrow{*} t_2'.\ t_1' \models (A_1^+ \wedge -A^-) \wedge t_2' \models (A_2^+ \wedge -A^-) \wedge \bigwedge_{i \in I}(\bigvee_{k \in K_i} t_1' \models \Diamond\varphi^1_{i,k} \wedge t_2' \models \Diamond\varphi^2_{i,k}) \wedge \bigwedge_{j \in J} \bigwedge_{l \in L_j} (t_1' \models \neg\Diamond\delta^1_{j,l} \vee t_2' \models \neg\Diamond\delta^2_{j,l})$$

By transformation to disjunctive normal form we get

$$\exists A_1^+ \cup A_2^+ = A^+ . \exists t_1 \xrightarrow{*} t_1', t_2 \xrightarrow{*} t_2'.\ t_1' \models (A_1^+ \wedge -A^-) \wedge t_2' \models (A_2^+ \wedge -A^-) \wedge \bigvee_{F: I \mapsto K_i, G \times H \subset J \times L_j} \Big[\bigwedge_{i \in I} t_1' \models \Diamond\varphi^1_{i,F(i)} \wedge t_2' \models \Diamond\varphi^2_{i,F(i)} \wedge \bigwedge_{(j,l) \in G \times H} t_1' \models \neg\Diamond\delta^1_{j,l} \wedge \bigwedge_{(j,l) \in J \times L_j - G \times H} t_2' \models \neg\Diamond\delta^2_{j,l}\Big]$$

Here F is a total function $F : I \mapsto \bigcup_{i \in I} K_i$, s.t. $\forall i \in I.\ F(i) \in K_i$. G and H must satisfy the restriction that if $(j, l) \in G \times H$, then $l \in L_j$. Putting it together again yields

$$\bigvee_{A_1^+ \cup A_2^+ = A^+, F: I \mapsto K_i, G \times H \subset J \times L_j} t_1 \models \Diamond(A_1^+ \wedge -A^- \wedge \bigwedge_{i \in I} \Diamond\varphi^1_{i,F(i)} \bigwedge_{(j,l) \in G \times H} \neg\Diamond\delta^1_{j,l}) \wedge t_2 \models \Diamond(A_2^+ \wedge -A^- \wedge \bigwedge_{i \in I} \Diamond\varphi^2_{i,F(i)} \bigwedge_{(j,l) \in J \times L_j - G \times H} \neg\Diamond\delta^2_{j,l})$$

This is in normal form. □

Lemma 6. *Let t_1, t_2 be PA-terms and Φ in $\mathcal{F}^c_d$. Then sets N, P, Q and terms $\alpha, \beta_n \in \mathcal{F}^c_d$ and $\gamma_p, \delta_q \in \mathcal{F}^c_{d-1}$ can be effectively constructed s.t. $t_1.t_2 \models \Diamond\Phi$ iff*

$$t_1 \models \Diamond(-Act) \wedge t_2 \models \Diamond\Phi \vee$$
$$t_1 \models \neg\Diamond(-Act) \wedge t_1 \models \Diamond\Phi \vee$$
$$t_1 \models \Diamond\alpha \vee \bigvee_{n \in N} \Big[t_1 \models \Diamond\beta_n \wedge \bigwedge_{p \in P(n)} t_2 \models \Diamond\gamma_p \wedge \bigwedge_{q \in Q(n)} t_2 \models \neg\Diamond\delta_q\Big]$$

Proof by induction on d.
If $d = 0$ then $\Diamond\Phi = \Diamond(A^+ \wedge -A^-)$. The first two cases of the above disjunction

are clear. The only remaining case is $t_1 \rightarrow t_1' \neq \epsilon.\ t_1' \models (A^+ \wedge -A^-)$. (Here $\exists t_1' \xrightarrow{*} \epsilon$.) Choose $\alpha = \mathit{false}$, $N = Act$, $\beta_a = A^+ \cup \{a\} \wedge -A^-$, $P(a) = Q(a) = \emptyset$ for every $a \in Act$.

Now $d > 0$. We can assume that $\Diamond\Phi = \Diamond(A^+ \wedge -A^- \wedge \bigwedge_{i\in I} \Diamond\Psi_i \wedge \bigwedge_{j\in J} \neg\Diamond\Upsilon_j)$ with $A^+, A^- \subseteq Act$, $\Psi_i, \Upsilon_j \in \mathcal{F}^c_{d-1}$. The first two cases of the above disjunction are obvious. In the third case we have:

$$\exists t_1 \xrightarrow{*} t_1' \neq \epsilon.\ t_1' \models A^+ \wedge -A^- \wedge t_1'.t_2 \models \bigwedge_{i\in I} \Diamond\Psi_i \wedge \bigwedge_{j\in J} \neg\Diamond\Upsilon_j$$

This is equivalent to

$$\begin{aligned} & t_1 \models \Diamond(A^+ \wedge -A^- \wedge \neg\Diamond(-Act) \wedge \bigwedge_{i\in I} \Diamond\Psi_i \wedge \bigwedge_{j\in J} \neg\Diamond\Upsilon_j) \vee \\ & t_2 \models \bigwedge_{j\in J} \neg\Diamond\Upsilon_j \wedge \bigvee_{a\in Act} \exists t_1 \xrightarrow{*} t_1'.\Big[t_1' \models (A^+ \cup \{a\} \wedge -A^-) \wedge \\ & \qquad t_1' \models \bigwedge_{j\in J} \bigwedge_{b\in Act} \neg\Diamond(\Upsilon_j \wedge b) \wedge t_1'.t_2 \models \bigwedge_{i\in I} \Diamond\Psi_i\Big] \end{aligned}$$

As $\Psi_i \in \mathcal{F}^c_{d-1}$ there are (by induction hypothesis) $\alpha_i, \beta_n \in \mathcal{F}^c_{d-1}$ and $\gamma_p, \delta_q \in \mathcal{F}^c_{d-2}$ s.t. this is equivalent to

$$\begin{aligned} & t_1 \models \Diamond(A^+ \wedge -A^- \wedge \neg\Diamond(-Act) \wedge \bigwedge_{i\in I} \Diamond\Psi_i \wedge \bigwedge_{j\in J} \neg\Diamond\Upsilon_j) \vee \\ & \qquad t_2 \models \bigwedge_{j\in J} \neg\Diamond\Upsilon_j \wedge \\ & \bigvee_{a\in Act} \exists t_1 \xrightarrow{*} t_1'.\Big[t_1' \models (A^+ \cup \{a\} \wedge -A^-) \wedge t_1' \models \bigwedge_{j\in J} \bigwedge_{b\in Act} \neg\Diamond(\Upsilon_j \wedge b) \wedge \\ & \qquad \bigwedge_{i\in I} \Big(t_2 \models \Diamond\Psi_i \vee t_1' \models \Diamond\alpha_i \vee \\ & \qquad \bigvee_{n\in N_i} (t_1' \models \Diamond\beta_n \wedge \bigwedge_{p\in P(n)} t_2 \models \Diamond\gamma_p \wedge \bigwedge_{q\in Q(n)} t_2 \models \neg\Diamond\delta_q)\Big)\Big] \end{aligned}$$

This requires some explanation. The case that t_1' cannot be reduced to ϵ is already considered in the first line of this formula. So we can assume that $t_1' \models \Diamond(-Act)$. Therefore in the application of the induction hypothesis we only need to add the formula $t_2 \models \Diamond\Psi_i$.

By transformation to disjunctive normal form we get

$$\begin{aligned} & t_1 \models \Diamond(A^+ \wedge -A^- \wedge \neg\Diamond(-Act) \wedge \bigwedge_{i\in I} \Diamond\Psi_i \wedge \bigwedge_{j\in J} \neg\Diamond\Upsilon_j) \vee \\ & \qquad t_2 \models \bigwedge_{j\in J} \neg\Diamond\Upsilon_j \wedge \\ & \bigvee_{a\in Act} \exists t_1 \xrightarrow{*} t_1'.\Big[t_1' \models (A^+ \cup \{a\} \wedge -A^-) \wedge t_1' \models \bigwedge_{j\in J} \bigwedge_{b\in Act} \neg\Diamond(\Upsilon_j \wedge b) \wedge \end{aligned}$$

$$\bigvee_{I',I''\subseteq I, F:(I-(I'\cup I''))\mapsto N_i} \bigwedge_{i\in I'} t_2 \models \Diamond\Psi_i \bigwedge_{i\in I''} t_1' \models \Diamond\alpha_i$$

$$\bigwedge_{i\in I-(I'\cup I'')} t_1' \models \Diamond\beta_{F(i)} \bigwedge_{i\in I-(I'\cup I'')} \bigwedge_{k\in P(F(i))} t_2 \models \Diamond\gamma_k$$

$$\bigwedge_{i\in I-(I'\cup I'')} \bigwedge_{k\in Q(F(i))} t_2 \models \neg\Diamond\delta_k \Big]$$

Here F is a total function from $I - (I' \cup I'')$ to $\bigcup_{i\in I} N_i$ s.t. $\forall i.\ F(i) \in N_i$.

Putting it together again yields

$$t_1 \models \Diamond(A^+ \wedge -A^- \wedge \neg\Diamond(-Act) \wedge \bigwedge_{i\in I} \Diamond\Psi_i \wedge \bigwedge_{j\in J} \neg\Diamond\Upsilon_j) \vee$$

$$\bigvee_{a\in Act, I',I''\subseteq I, F:(I-(I'\cup I''))\mapsto N_i} \Big[\bigwedge_{j\in J} t_2 \models \neg\Diamond\Upsilon_j \wedge \bigwedge_{i\in I'} t_2 \models \Diamond\Psi_i$$

$$\bigwedge_{i\in I-(I'\cup I'')} \bigwedge_{k\in P(F(i))} t_2 \models \Diamond\gamma_k$$

$$\bigwedge_{i\in I-(I'\cup I'')} \bigwedge_{k\in Q(F(i))} t_2 \models \neg\Diamond\delta_k \ \wedge\ t_1 \models \Diamond(A^+ \cup \{a\} \wedge -A^- \wedge$$

$$\bigwedge_{j\in J} \bigwedge_{b\in Act} \neg\Diamond(\Upsilon_j \wedge b) \wedge$$

$$\bigwedge_{i\in I''} \Diamond\alpha_i \wedge \bigwedge_{i\in I-(I'\cup I'')} \Diamond\beta_{F(i)})\Big]$$

This has the desired form. □

3.3 The Tableau-rules

Now we can define the rules for the construction of a tableau that decides $t \models \Diamond\Phi$ for $\Phi \in \mathcal{F}_d^c$. In this construction we assume that we can already decide all problems of the form $t' \models \Diamond\Psi$ or $t' \models \neg\Diamond\Psi$ for any $\Psi \in \mathcal{F}_{d-1}^c$. In the base case of $d = 0$ this condition is trivially satisfied, as $\mathcal{F}_{-1}^c = \emptyset$. Also we assume that we can decide problems of the form $t \models \Diamond(-Act)$. (This is equivalent to $\exists t \xrightarrow{\sigma} \epsilon$).

Lemma 7. *Let t be a PA-term. It is decidable if $t \models \Diamond(-Act)$.*

Proof The algorithm proceeds by successively marking variables as being reducible to ϵ. First mark all variables X s.t. $\exists X \xrightarrow{a} \epsilon$. Then mark all variables Y s.t. $\exists X \xrightarrow{a} G$ where all variables occurring in G are already marked. Repeat this until no new variables can be marked. Then $t \models \Diamond(-Act)$ iff all variables occurring in t are marked. □

The nodes in the tableau are marked with sets of expressions of the form $t \vdash \Phi$, where t is a PA-term and Φ an EF-formula. Such sets are denoted by Γ. These sets of expressions at the nodes are interpreted conjunctively, while the branches in the tableau are interpreted disjunctively. The tableau is successful iff there is a successful branch.

$$\text{PAR}\quad \frac{\{t_1 \| t_2 \vdash \Diamond\Phi\} \cup \Gamma}{(\text{see Lemma 5}) \cup \Gamma}$$

$$\text{SEQ}\quad \frac{\{t_1 . t_2 \vdash \Diamond\Phi\} \cup \Gamma}{(\text{see Lemma 6}) \cup \Gamma}$$

$$\text{Step}\quad \frac{\{X \vdash \Diamond\Phi\} \cup \Gamma}{\{X \vdash \Phi\} \cup \Gamma \quad \{t_1 \vdash \Diamond\Phi\} \cup \Gamma \quad \ldots \quad \{t_n \vdash \Diamond\Phi\} \cup \Gamma} \quad \text{for } X \xrightarrow{a} t_i$$

$$\wedge\quad \frac{\{t \vdash \Phi \wedge \Psi\} \cup \Gamma}{\{t \vdash \Phi, t \vdash \Psi\} \cup \Gamma}$$

$$\vee\quad \frac{\{t \vdash \Phi \vee \Psi\} \cup \Gamma}{\{t \vdash \Phi\} \cup \Gamma \quad \{t \vdash \Psi\} \cup \Gamma}$$

$$\text{Induct1}\quad \frac{\{t \vdash \Diamond\Psi\} \cup \Gamma}{\Gamma} \quad \text{if } \Psi \in \mathcal{F}^c_{d-1} \text{ and } t \models \Diamond\Psi$$

$$\text{Induct2}\quad \frac{\{t \vdash \neg\Diamond\Psi\} \cup \Gamma}{\Gamma} \quad \text{if } \Psi \in \mathcal{F}^c_{d-1} \text{ and not } t \models \Diamond\Psi$$

$$\text{Term1}\quad \frac{\{t \vdash \Diamond(-Act)\} \cup \Gamma}{\Gamma} \quad \text{if } \exists t \xrightarrow{\sigma} \epsilon$$

$$\text{Term2}\quad \frac{\{t \vdash \neg\Diamond(-Act)\} \cup \Gamma}{\Gamma} \quad \text{if } \nexists t \xrightarrow{\sigma} \epsilon$$

$$\text{Act1}\quad \frac{\{t \vdash A^+\} \cup \Gamma}{\Gamma} \quad \text{if } \forall_{a \in A^+} \exists t \xrightarrow{a} t'$$

$$\text{Act2}\quad \frac{\{t \vdash -A^-\} \cup \Gamma}{\Gamma} \quad \text{if } \forall_{a \in A^-} \nexists t \xrightarrow{a} t'$$

To avoid any unnecessary growth of the proof tree we define that the rules $\wedge$, $\vee$, Induct1, Induct2, Term1, Term2, Act1 and Act2 take precedence over all the other rules (PAR, SEQ and Step).

The following property follows immediately from the definition of the tableau-rules and Lemma 5 and Lemma 6.

Proposition 8. *For any instance of a tableau-rule the antecedent is true iff one of the consequents is true.*

Definition 9. (Termination conditions) A node n consisting of a set of formulae Γ is a terminal node if one of the following conditions is satisfied:

1. Γ is empty
2. $t \vdash \Diamond\Psi \in \Gamma$ with $\Psi \in \mathcal{F}^c_{d-1}$ and $t \not\models \Diamond\Psi$
3. $t \vdash \neg\Diamond\Psi \in \Gamma$ with $\Psi \in \mathcal{F}^c_{d-1}$ and $t \models \Diamond\Psi$
4. $t \vdash \Diamond(-Act) \in \Gamma$ and $\not\exists t \xrightarrow{\sigma} \epsilon$
5. $t \vdash \neg\Diamond(-Act) \in \Gamma$ and $\exists t \xrightarrow{\sigma} \epsilon$
6. $t \vdash A^+ \in \Gamma$ and $\exists a \in A^+.\ \not\exists t \xrightarrow{a} t'$
7. $t \vdash -A^- \in \Gamma$ and $\exists a \in A^-.\ \exists t \xrightarrow{a} t'$
8. There is a previous node n' in the same branch that is marked with set Γ' s.t. $\Gamma = \Gamma'$

Terminals of type 1 are successful, while terminals of type 2–8 are unsuccessful.

4 Soundness and Completeness

Lemma 10. *If the root node has the form $t \vdash \Diamond\Phi$, then for every node n in the tableau at least one of the following conditions is satisfied:*

- *A tableau rule is applicable*
- *The node is a terminal node.*

Proof The only problematic cases are the formulae of the form $t \vdash \neg\Diamond\Phi$. If such a formula occurs, then it must be due to the rules SEQ or Step. By definition of the rule Step and Lemma 6 we know that $\Phi \in \mathcal{F}^c_{d-1}$. Therefore the node is a terminal node or one of the rules Induct2 or Term2 is applicable. □

Lemma 11. *The tableau is finite.*

Proof There are only finitely many formulae in $\mathcal{F}^c_d$ and only finitely many rules $X \xrightarrow{a} t$ with only finitely many subterms of the terms t. So there are only finitely many different sets of expressions of the form $t \vdash \Phi$ in the tableau. Therefore the branches of the tableau can only have finite length, because of termination condition 8. As the tableau is finitely branching, the result follows. □

Now we prove the soundness and completeness of the tableau.

Lemma 12. *Let $\Phi \in \mathcal{F}^c_d$. If there is a successful tableau with root $t \vdash \Diamond\Phi$, then $t \models \Diamond\Phi$.*

Proof A successful tableau has a successful branch ending with a node marked by the empty set of formulae. As these sets are interpreted conjunctively this node is true. By Proposition 8 all its ancestor-nodes must be true and thus the root-node must be true as well. □

Lemma 13. *Let t be a PA-term, $\Phi \in \mathcal{F}^c_d$ and Γ a set of formulae. If $t \models \Diamond\Phi$ then there is a sequence of rule applications s.t. there is a path from a node marked $\{t \vdash \Diamond\Phi\} \cup \Gamma$ to a node marked Γ.*

Proof by induction on lexicographically ordered pairs (x, y) where x is the length of the shortest sequence σ s.t. $t \xrightarrow{\sigma} t'$ and $t' \models \Phi$, and y is the size of t.

The construction of the tableau is done in rounds. Each round consists of an application of one of the rules SEQ, PAR or Step, followed by several applications of the rules $\wedge$, $\vee$, Induct1, Induct2, Term1 and Term2 to clear away unnecessary formulae (Remember that these rules take precedence over the rules SEQ, PAR and Step). As the node is true, at least one of its successors (at the end of the round) must be true.

SEQ If this rule was used, then the successor has the form $\Gamma \cup \Gamma'$, where all members of Γ' are of the form $t' \vdash \Diamond\Phi'$ where t' is smaller than t. This means that y is now smaller. An analysis of the proof of Lemma 6 shows that the value of x cannot have increased. The result follows from the induction hypothesis.

PAR In this case the successor has the form $\{t_1 \vdash \Diamond\Phi_1, t_2 \vdash \Diamond\Phi_2\} \cup \Gamma$ s.t. t_1 and t_2 are smaller than t. It follows from the proof of Lemma 5 that the value of x has not increased, while the value of y is smaller. Applying the induction hypothesis twice yields the desired result.

Step Here we have two subcases:

1. If the first branch of the Step-rule is true, then applications of the rules $\wedge$, $\vee$, Induct1, Induct2, Term1, Term2, Act1 and Act2 directly lead to a node marked by Γ.
2. Otherwise choose the true successor that corresponds to the shortest sequence σ (see above). Here the value of y may have increased, but the value of x has decreased by 1, and thus we can apply the induction hypothesis.

This construction cannot be stopped by termination condition 8, because this would contradict the minimality of the length of σ. □

Corollary 14. *If $t \models \Diamond\Phi$ for $\Phi \in \mathcal{F}_d^c$, then there is a successful tableau with root $t \vdash \Diamond\Phi$.*

Proof Applying Lemma 13 for the special case of an empty set Γ yields that a node can be reached that is marked by the empty set. The branch from the root-node to this node is successful and thus there is a successful tableau. □

Lemma 15. *Let t be a PA-term and $\Phi \in \mathcal{F}_d^c$. $t \models \Diamond\Phi$ iff there is a successful tableau for $t \vdash \Diamond\Phi$.*

Proof Directly from Lemma 12 and Corollary 14. □

Theorem 16. *The model checking problem for PA-processes and the logic EF is decidable.*

Proof By Lemma 4 it suffices to prove decidability for formulae of the form $\Diamond\Phi$ with Φ in $\mathcal{F}_d^c$ for any d. We prove this by induction on d. By Lemma 15 and Lemma 11 it suffices to construct a finite tableau. During the construction we need to decide problems of the form $t' \models \Diamond\Psi$ for $\Psi \in \mathcal{F}_{d-1}^c$ and problems of the form $t \models \Diamond(-Act)$. The first one is possible by induction hypothesis, and the second one by Lemma 7. □

5 Example

In this section we describe a tiny example of the model checking problem. Let a process algebra be described by the following set of rules Δ:

$$X \xrightarrow{a} X \| X$$

$$X \xrightarrow{c} \epsilon$$

$$Y \xrightarrow{b} X.Y$$

The operator $\Box$ (meaning always) can be expressed in the logic *EF* by defining $\Box := \neg\Diamond\neg$. By using the algorithm derived from the tableau system described in subsection 3.3 we can show a property of the process $(X \| Y)$.

$$(X \| Y) \models \Diamond(\Box\Diamond(a) \ \wedge \ \Box\Diamond(b) \ \wedge \ \neg\Diamond(a \wedge b))$$

This means that this process can reach a state s.t. from then on it can always get back into states where it can do action a or action b, but never both, as a and b are then mutually exclusive.

6 Extensions

In this section we extend the logic *EF* by constraints on sequences. So far the expression $t \models \Diamond\Phi$ only means that there is a sequence σ s.t. $t \xrightarrow{\sigma} t'$ and $t' \models \Phi$ without saying anything about σ. Now we generalize the operator $\Diamond$ to $\Diamond_C$, where $C : Act^* \mapsto \{true, false\}$ are predicates on finite sequences of actions. Here these functions are called constraints.

The semantics of the modified modal operator $\Diamond_C$ is defined by:

$$\|\Diamond_C\Phi\| = \{t \mid \exists\sigma, t'. \, t \xrightarrow{\sigma} t' \wedge t' \in \|\Phi\| \wedge C(\sigma)\}$$

We'll show that for a special class of constraints C the extended logic is still decidable for PA-processes.

Definition 17. (Decomposable constraints) Let $a \in Act$, $i, k \in \mathbb{N}$ and σ a sequence of actions. $[x]_k$ denotes x modulo k. Decomposable constraints are of the following form

$$C ::= W(\sigma) \geq i \mid W(\sigma) \leq i \mid [W(\sigma)]_k = i \mid C_1 \vee C_2 \mid C_1 \wedge C_2 \mid \mathit{first}(\sigma) = a$$

where $W : Act^* \mapsto \mathbb{N}$ is a function on sequences s.t. $W(\sigma_1\sigma_2) = W(\sigma_1) + W(\sigma_2)$ for all σ_1, σ_2. (This implies that if σ is the empty sequence, then $W(\sigma) = 0$).

These constraints are called "decomposable", because a constraint C on a sequence of actions σ performed by a sequential– or parallel composition of processes t_1 and t_2 can be expressed by constraints on sequences performed by t_1 and t_2.

For example let W be the function that counts the number of a-actions in a sequence. Now if $t_1 \| t_2 \xrightarrow{\sigma} t_1' \| t_2'$ and $[W(\sigma)]_3 = 0$ then there are sequences σ_1, σ_2 s.t. $t_1 \xrightarrow{\sigma_1} t_1'$ and $t_2 \xrightarrow{\sigma_2} t_2'$ and either $W(\sigma_1) = W(\sigma_2) = 0$ or $W(\sigma_1) = 1$ and $W(\sigma_2) = 2$ or $W(\sigma_1) = 2$ and $W(\sigma_2) = 1$.

Definition 18. Let EF_{DC} be the extension of EF by modal operators $\Diamond_C$, where C is a decomposable constraint.

By using decomposability of the constraints the Lemmas 5 and 6 can be extended to the logic EF_{DC}. The tableau method can be adjusted accordingly and thus the logic EF_{DC} is still decidable for PA-processes.

Let λ be the empty sequence of actions. The modified tableau rules are:

$$\text{PAR} \quad \frac{\{t_1 \| t_2 \vdash \Diamond_C \Phi\} \cup \Gamma}{\{\text{the modified Lemma 5}\} \cup \Gamma}$$

$$\text{SEQ} \quad \frac{\{t_1 . t_2 \vdash \Diamond_C \Phi\} \cup \Gamma}{\{\text{the modified Lemma 6}\} \cup \Gamma}$$

$$\text{Split} \quad \frac{\{t \vdash \Diamond_{C_1 \vee C_2} \Phi\} \cup \Gamma}{\{t \vdash \Diamond_{C_1} \Phi\} \cup \Gamma \quad \{t \vdash \Diamond_{C_2} \Phi\} \cup \Gamma}$$

$$\text{Clear} \quad \frac{\{t \vdash \Diamond_{C_1 \wedge C_2} \Phi\}}{t \vdash \Diamond_{C_1} \Phi} \quad \text{if } C_2 \text{ is equal to } \mathit{true}$$

$$\text{Step1} \quad \frac{\{X \vdash \Diamond_C \Phi\} \cup \Gamma}{\{X \vdash \Phi\} \cup \Gamma \quad \{t_1 \vdash \Diamond_{C_1} \Phi\} \cup \Gamma \quad \ldots \quad \{t_n \vdash \Diamond_{C_n} \Phi\} \cup \Gamma}$$

if $C(\lambda)$, $X \xrightarrow{a_i} t_i$ and $C_i = Cons(C, a_i)$

$$\text{Step2} \quad \frac{\{X \vdash \Diamond_C \Phi\} \cup \Gamma}{\{t_1 \vdash \Diamond_{C_1} \Phi\} \cup \Gamma \quad \ldots \quad \{t_n \vdash \Diamond_{C_n} \Phi\} \cup \Gamma}$$

if not $C(\lambda)$, $X \xrightarrow{a_i} t_i$ and $C_i = Cons(C, a_i)$

$$\wedge \quad \frac{\{t \vdash \Phi \wedge \Psi\} \cup \Gamma}{\{t \vdash \Phi, t \vdash \Psi\} \cup \Gamma}$$

$$\vee \quad \frac{\{t \vdash \Phi \vee \Psi\} \cup \Gamma}{\{t \vdash \Phi\} \cup \Gamma \quad \{t \vdash \Psi\} \cup \Gamma}$$

$$\text{Induct1} \quad \frac{\{t \vdash \Diamond_C \Psi\} \cup \Gamma}{\Gamma} \quad \text{if } \Psi \in \mathcal{F}^c_{d-1} \text{ and } t \models \Diamond_C \Psi$$

$$\text{Induct2} \quad \frac{\{t \vdash \neg\Diamond_C \Psi\} \cup \Gamma}{\Gamma} \quad \text{if } \Psi \in \mathcal{F}^c_{d-1} \text{ and not } t \models \Diamond_C \Psi$$

$$\text{Term1}\ \frac{\{t \vdash \Diamond_C(-Act)\} \cup \Gamma}{\Gamma} \quad \text{if } \exists t \xrightarrow{\sigma} \epsilon \text{ and } C(\sigma)$$

$$\text{Term2}\ \frac{\{t \vdash \neg\Diamond_C(-Act)\} \cup \Gamma}{\Gamma} \quad \text{if } \nexists t \xrightarrow{\sigma} \epsilon \text{ with } C(\sigma)$$

$$\text{Act1}\ \frac{\{t \vdash A^+\} \cup \Gamma}{\Gamma} \quad \text{if } \forall_{a \in A^+} \exists t \xrightarrow{a} t'$$

$$\text{Act2}\ \frac{\{t \vdash -A^-\} \cup \Gamma}{\Gamma} \quad \text{if } \forall_{a \in A^-} \nexists t \xrightarrow{a} t'$$

In the rules Step1 and Step2 the new constraints C_i are computed from the constraint C and the action a_i by

$$Cons(C_1 \wedge C_2, a) := Cons(C_1, a) \wedge Cons(C_2, a)$$

$$Cons(W(\sigma) \geq i, a) := W(\sigma) \geq i - W(a)$$

$$Cons(W(\sigma) \leq i, a) := W(\sigma) \leq i - W(a)$$

$$Cons([W(\sigma)]_k = j, a) := [W(\sigma)]_k = [j - W(a)]_k$$

$$Cons(first(\sigma) = b, a) := if\ a = b\ then\ true\ else\ false$$

The termination conditions are the same as in Definition 9 with the addition of one more unsuccessful one. A node of the form $t \vdash \Diamond_C \Phi$ is an unsuccessful terminal if C is equal to *false*, i.e. $C = C' \wedge false$ or $C = C' \wedge W(\sigma) \leq k$ for some $k < 0$.

Note that only finitely many different constraints can occur in a tableau, because of the definition of the function *Cons*, the rule *Clear* and this new termination condition. Thus the proofs of soundness and completeness of the tableau from section 3 carry over to the extended logic with constraints.

Theorem 19. *The model checking problem for PA-processes and the logic EF_{DC} is decidable.*

With decomposable constraints we can also express the usual one-step next operator by defining

$$\langle a \rangle := \Diamond_C$$

with $C := [first(\sigma) = a \wedge length(\sigma) = 1]$.

7 Conclusion

We have shown decidability of the model checking problem for the branching time temporal logic *EF* and PA-processes. The exact complexity of the problem is left open. While for the special case of BPPs the problem is PSPACE-complete [May96a, May96b] the algorithm described here for PA has superexponential complexity. The algorithm described here is not a generalization of the one for BPP in [May96b]. The PSPACE-algorithm for BPP of [May96b] uses a bounded search, while the algorithm for PA works by decomposition. For a formula of nesting-depth d the complexity of the algorithm derived from the tableau system is d-times exponential in the size of the process description. So the overall complexity of the algorithm is $O(tower(n))$, where $tower(0) := 0$ and $tower(i+1) := 2^{tower(i)}$.

It is interesting to compare the decidability results for branching time logics with the results for linear time logics like LTL and the linear time μ-calculus. While model checking PA-processes with *EF* is decidable, it is undecidable for LTL and the linear time μ-calculus [BH96]. For Petri nets the situation is just the other way round. While model checking Petri nets with *EF* is undecidable [Esp, Esp96], it is decidable for LTL and the linear time μ-calculus [Esp]. This emphasizes the fact that PA-processes and Petri nets are incomparable models of concurrent systems. For the modal μ-calculus the model checking problem is undecidable even for BPPs [Esp, Esp96].

	EF	LTL, linear time μ-calc.	modal μ-calc.
Petri nets	undecidable	decidable, EXPSPACE-hard	undecidable
PA	**decidable**	undecidable	undecidable
BPP	PSPACE-complete	decidable, EXPSPACE-hard	undecidable
finite LTS	polynomial	PSPACE-complete	$\in$ NP $\cap$ co-NP

References

[BH96] A. Bouajjani and P. Habermehl. Constrained properties, semilinear systems, and petri nets. In Ugo Montanari and Vladimiro Sassone, editors, *Proceedings of CONCUR'96*, number 1119 in LNCS. Springer Verlag, 1996.

[Chr93] S. Christensen. *Decidability and Decomposition in Process Algebras.* PhD thesis, Edinburgh University, 1993.

[EK95] J. Esparza and A. Kiehn. On the model checking problem for branching time logics and basic parallel processes. In *CAV'95*, number 939 in LNCS, pages 353–366. Springer Verlag, 1995.

[Esp] J. Esparza. Decidability of model checking for infinite-state concurrent systems. To appear in Acta Informatica.

[Esp96] J. Esparza. More infinite results. In B. Steffen and T. Margaria, editors, *Proceedings of INFINITY'96*, number MIP-9614 in Technical report series of the University of Passau. University of Passau, 1996.

[May96a] Richard Mayr. Some results on basic parallel processes. Technical Report TUM-I9616, TU-München, March 1996.

[May96b] Richard Mayr. Weak bisimulation and model checking for basic parallel processes. In *Foundations of Software Technology and Theoretical Computer Science (FSTTCS'96)*, number 1180 in LNCS. Springer Verlag, 1996.

[Mil89] R. Milner. *Communication and Concurrency.* Prentice Hall, 1989.

Bisimulation and Propositional Intuitionistic Logic

Anna Patterson

Computer Science Department, Stanford University
Stanford CA 94305, Email annap@cs.stanford.edu

Abstract. The Brouwer-Heyting-Kolmogorov interpretation of intuitionistic logic suggests that $p \supset q$ can be interpreted as a computation that given a proof of p constructs a proof of q. Dually, we show that every finite canonical model of q contains a finite canonical model of p. If q and p are interderivable, their canonical models contain each other. Using this insight, we are able to characterize validity in a Kripke structure in terms of *bisimilarity*.

THEOREM 1 Let K be a *finite* Kripke structure for propositional intuitionistic logic, then two worlds in K are bisimilar if and only if they satisfy the same set of formulas.

This theorem lifts to structures in the following manner.

THEOREM 2 Two *finite* Kripke structures K and K' are bisimilar if and only if they have the same set of valid formulas.

We then generalize these results to a variety of infinite structures; finite principal filter structures and saturated structures.

1 Background

The standard model theory for intuitionistic logic (Heyting 1966) was introduced by Kripke (1965). This model theory was originally introduced as a characterization of modal logics (Kripke 1963). A natural question that arises for any model theory is characterizing when two models satisfy the same set of formulas. A partial answer to this for modal logics was given by van Benthem, who showed that for well behaved modal structures the notion of bisimulation was appropriate.

We now apply the same techniques to intuitionistic logic. Although intuitionistic logic is not a traditional modal logic we can use the relationship between S4 and topology to provide a bridge.

The algebra of S4 (Lewis and Langford 1932) is a topological Boolean algebra (McKinsey and Tarski 1944) where the modality $\Box$ can be taken to be an interior operation and the modality $\Diamond$ is taken to be a closure operation (McKinsey 1941, Rasiowa and Sikorski 1963). It is well known (Birkhoff 1948) that the open subsets of a topological Boolean algebra form a relatively pseudo-complemented lattice. However, a relatively pseudo-complemented lattice with a bottom is a pseudo-complemented lattice, that is a Heyting algebra and hence an algebra of intuitionistic logic.

We prove that finite Kripke structures for intuitionistic logic are bisimilar exactly when they entail the same set of intuitionistic formulas. This means that two transitive monotonic modal models are bisimilar if and only if their associated finitely axiomatizable sets of valid intuitionistic formulas are equal. This can be interpreted as saying that all functions between open sets, the $\Box$-formulas, are definable in intuitionistic logic (McKinsey and Tarski 1946). Since functions between open sets are continuous and all operators in intuitionistic logic are computable, this result is perhaps better known in computer science as: continuous functions are computable (Scott 1972).

2 Intuitionistic Logic

We present a model theory for intuitionistic logic due to Kripke. For a nice overview of this model theory see Fitting (1969).

Definition 1. A Kripke structure for propositional intuitionistic logic over a set P of propositional atoms is a triple $\langle W, R, V\rangle$ where W is a non-empty set (the set of *worlds*), R is a binary reflexive and transitive relation on W and V is a function assigning to every world a set of propositional atoms from P where the assignment V satisfies, for every world w, $wRw' \to V(w) \subseteq V(w')$.

Thus, V is monotonic on propositional atoms.

Definition 2. The satisfaction relation $\models_K$ on a Kripke structure $K = \langle W, R, V\rangle$ over a set of propositional atoms P is a relation between worlds and propositional formulas. We define this relation inductively over the structure of a formula. Thus, for any $w \in W$,

$$
\begin{aligned}
w \models_K p &\equiv p \in V(w)\\
w \models_K \varphi \wedge \psi &\equiv w \models_K \varphi \text{ and } w \models_K \psi\\
w \models_K \varphi \vee \psi &\equiv w \models_K \varphi \text{ or } w \models_K \psi\\
w \models_K \varphi \supset \psi &\equiv \forall w' \in W \text{ such that } w\,R\,w',\ w' \models_K \varphi \text{ implies } w' \models_K \psi\\
w \models_K {\sim}\varphi &\equiv \forall w' \in W \text{ such that } w\,R\,w',\ w' \not\models_K \varphi
\end{aligned}
$$

Lemma 3. Monotonicity *Let $K = \langle W, R, V\rangle$ be a Kripke model. We have for all $w \in W$, and for all formula φ, if $w \models_K \varphi$, and wRw', then $w' \models_K \varphi$.*

Therefore, the satisfaction relation is monotonic for arbitrary formulas.

Definition 4. Let $K = \langle W, R, V\rangle$ be a Kripke structure, then a formula φ is *satisfied* in K if and only if $\exists w \in W.\ w \models_K \varphi$. A formula φ is *valid in* K if and only if $\forall w \in W.\ w \models_K \varphi$. A formula φ is *valid* if and only if φ is valid in all Kripke structures.

A formula φ is *refuted* at a world, w, in K if and only if $w \not\models_K \varphi$. A formula φ is *refuted in* K if and only if $\exists w \in W.\ w \not\models_K \varphi$.

Definition 5. – A set of formulas Θ is a propositional intuitionistic *theory* if it is closed under the intuitionistic inference rules.

- A theory Θ is *consistent* if Θ does not include a contradiction.
- A set of formulas Θ has the *disjunction property* if $\varphi \vee \psi \in \Theta$ implies $\varphi \in \Theta$ or $\psi \in \Theta$.
- The theory of a world w in a Kripke structure is the set of formulas satisfied at w in K, i.e. $\mathcal{T}h(w) = \{\varphi \mid w \models_K \varphi\}$.
- Two worlds w, w' are *theory equivalent*, denoted $w \approx w'$, if $\mathcal{T}h(w) = \mathcal{T}h(w')$.
- The *theory of a structure* K is the set of formulas valid in K.

We say that a Kripke structure is *finite* if the cardinality of W is finite. Studying finite Kripke structures is not particularly restrictive because it is well known that an intuitionistic formula is valid if and only if it is valid in all finite Kripke structures.

Theorem 6. *Let $K = \langle W, R, V\rangle$ be a* finite *Kripke structure over P and let Θ be a consistent intuitionistic theory satisfying the disjunction property whose propositional atoms are in P. Let w be a world in W.*

$$\mathcal{T}h(w) \subseteq \Theta \text{ if and only if } \exists w' \in W \text{ such that } (wRw' \text{ and } \mathcal{T}h(w') = \Theta).$$

Proof. The direction from right to left is a restatement of monotonicity (Lemma 3).

Now from left to right, we need a world above w with exactly the theory Θ.

1. We are going to define a formula γ as the conjunction of some subset of Θ which *in* K implies every other formula in Θ.
   Let $W_<$ be the set of worlds in K that do not satisfy all of Θ. For each world $w_<$ in $W_<$, pick some formula $\phi_{w_<}$ in Θ such that $w_< \not\models_K \phi_{w_<}$. As $W_<$ is finite, we can define γ as the finite conjunction $\bigwedge_{w_< \in W_<} \phi_{w_<}$. *In* K, by construction, every world which satisfies γ satisfies Θ.
   The theory Θ contains γ, hence $w \not\models_K \sim \gamma$. Otherwise $\sim \gamma$ would be in Θ contrary to the consistency of Θ. Therefore there is a world accessible from w that satisfies all of Θ.
2. We are going to define a formula δ as the disjunction of some subset of the complement of Θ and use the formula $\gamma \supset \delta$ to force the satisfaction of *only* the formulas in Θ.
   Let $W_>$ be the set of worlds in K that satisfy a formula not in Θ. For each world $w_>$ in $W_>$, pick some formula $\psi_{w_>}$ which is not in Θ such that $w_> \models_K \psi_{w_>}$. As $W_>$ is finite, let δ be the finite disjunction $\bigvee_{w_> \in W_>} \psi_{w_>}$. In K, by construction, in every world where δ is refuted, only formulas in Θ could be satisfied.
   Now we have $w \not\models_K \gamma \supset \delta$. Otherwise the formula $\gamma \supset \delta$ would be in Θ. Since Θ is a theory satisfying the disjunction property, we would have δ and one $\psi_{w_>}$ in Θ — contrary to the construction. Therefore there is a world accessible from w that satisfies γ and refutes δ. This means that there is a world w' accessible from w which satisfies exactly Θ. ∎

By a simplification of the above proof we obtain the following theorem.

Theorem 7. *Let $K = \langle W, R, V\rangle$ be a finite Kripke structure over P and let Θ be a consistent intuitionistic theory satisfying the disjunction property whose propositional atoms are in P.*

$$\mathcal{T}h(K) \subseteq \Theta \text{ if and only if } \exists w \in W \text{ such that } \mathcal{T}h(w) = \Theta.$$

Definition 8. A Kripke structure K is a *canonical* model for a theory Θ if every formula in Θ is valid in K and every formula not in Θ is refuted in K.

Definition 9. Let $K = \langle W, R, V\rangle$ be a Kripke structure, and let w be an element of W, then $K \uparrow w$ is the structure, $\langle \uparrow (w), R\restriction_{\uparrow(w)}, V\restriction_{\uparrow(w)}\rangle$, where the *principal filter of* w is $\uparrow (w) = \{w' \mid wRw'\}$.

This is simply the restriction of K to the worlds above w. Technically we should prove that $K \uparrow w$ is a Kripke structure, but this is immediate. Likewise, for any $X \subseteq W$, we can construct a *sub-Kripke structure* $K \uparrow X$ from the upwards closed elements generated from X, $\uparrow (X) = \bigcup_{w \in X} \uparrow (w)$.

Theorem 10. *If K is a finite canonical model for a theory Φ and Φ is included in some consistent theory Θ and Φ and Θ have the same set of propositional atoms, then a finite* canonical *model for Θ is a sub-structure of K.*

Proof. Let $\Delta = \{\Psi \mid \Psi$ a consistent theory extending Θ satisfying the disjunction property$\}$. By Theorem 7, for all theories Ψ in Δ, there exists a world w_Ψ in K satisfying exactly Ψ. Let X be the union of such worlds i.e. $X = \bigcup_{\Psi \in \Delta} w_\Psi$, then $K \uparrow X$ is the required sub-structure. ∎

3 Bisimulation within a structure

Bisimulation was introduced by Milner (1980) as a way of defining an equivalence notion for a process algebra. There bisimulation characterized equivalences between labeled transition systems. Earlier, van Benthem showed the close connection between bisimulation (or more precisely *p-morphisms*) and definability in modal logics (1976). Using the classical transformation of modal formulas to first order formulas, he showed that a first order formula is preserved under bisimulation exactly when it is equivalent to the translation of a modal formula. Bisimulation has been used in a variety of other ways; Aczel (1988) for instance showed that bisimulation provided a natural identity condition for non-well-founded sets.

Bisimulation is usually defined over labeled transition systems. In structures for intuitionistic logic, we do not really have labels on transitions. Therefore, we consider labeled transition systems with just one label; in addition, the states of these labeled transition systems are decorated with the set of propositional atoms "true" at that world.

The following is the definition of bisimulation in such a structure.

Definition 11. Let $K = \langle W, R, V\rangle$ be a Kripke structure, then we say that two worlds $w, w' \in W$ are *bisimilar*, denoted $w \leftrightarrows w'$, in K if there exists a relation $B \subseteq W \times W$ (a *bisimulation*) such that

$$\begin{array}{lll} wBw' & & \text{and} \\ xBy & \Rightarrow V(x) = V(y) & \text{and} \\ xBy & \Rightarrow \forall x'.\,(x\,R\,x' \rightarrow \exists y'.\,y\,R\,y' \text{ and } x'\,B\,y') & \text{and} \\ xBy & \Rightarrow \forall y'.\,(y\,R\,y' \rightarrow \exists x'.\,x\,R\,x' \text{ and } x'\,B\,y') & \end{array}$$

Note that bisimilarity is the largest such bisimulation relation. The set of equivalence classes under $\leftrightarrows$ is denoted $W/\leftrightarrows$ and the equivalence class of w is denoted $[w]$.

We can make a smaller structure using this equivalence relation on worlds.

Definition 12. Let $K = \langle W, R, V\rangle$ be a Kripke structure, then $K/\leftrightarrows = \langle W/\leftrightarrows, R/\leftrightarrows, V/\leftrightarrows\rangle$ is a Kripke structure where $V/\leftrightarrows([w]) = V(w)$ and

$$[w]R/\leftrightarrows[w'] \equiv \exists w_1 \in [w], \exists w_1' \in [w'] \text{ such that } w_1\,R\,w_1'.$$

Technically, we have to show that $K/\leftrightarrows$ is a Kripke structure. To this end one should notice that $V/\leftrightarrows$ is monotonic with respect to propositional atoms.

3.1 Bisimulation and Finite Kripke Models

The following theorem states that bisimulation is truth preserving and does not strengthen the structure to prove any extra formulas. This is a result also found in modal logics (Benthem 1976). The forward direction of this theorem for intuitionistic logic appears as a lemma in Rodenburg's thesis (1986). The backward direction is an easy exercise in structural induction.

Theorem 13. *Let $K = \langle W, R, V\rangle$ be a* Kripke *structure, then $\forall w \in W$,*

$$w \models_K \alpha \textit{ if and only if } [w] \models_{K/\leftrightarrows} \alpha.$$

Next we show that if two worlds in a finite Kripke structure are theory equivalent, then they are bisimilar. This result also holds for modal logics (Benthem 1976).

Theorem 14. *Let $K = \langle W, R, V\rangle$ be a* finite *Kripke structure, then $\forall w_1, w_2 \in W$. $w_1 \approx w_2$ implies that $w_1 \leftrightarrows w_2$.*

Proof. It suffices to show that $\approx$ is a bisimulation. By definition, $V(w_1) = V(w_2)$. Since $\approx$ is symmetric, we only need to show one more clause of the bisimulation definition; for all $w_1' \in W$ such that $w_1\,R\,w_1'$ there is a $w_2' \in W$ such that $w_2\,R\,w_2'$ and $w_1' \approx w_2'$.

Let Θ be the set of formulas satisfied at w_1'. By monotonicity and theory equivalence, Θ is a superset of formulas satisfied at w_2. Thus $Th(w_2) \subseteq Th(w_1')$ and we apply Theorem 6 to find a w_2' such that $w_2' \approx w_1'$. ∎

Corollary 15. *Let $K = \langle W, R, V\rangle$ be a finite Kripke structure, then for all $w, w' \in W$.*

$$w \leftrightarrows w' \textit{ if and only if } w \approx w'$$

Proof. This follows from Theorems 13 and 14. ∎

3.2 Extending Beyond the Finite

We extend this study beyond finite Kripke structures because we wish to study structures which correspond to intuitionistic theories, not simply structures which correspond to an intuitionistic formula.

We define two extensions and prove theorems that are tailored to intuitionistic Kripke models. There are similarities and differences with the modal case. In the modal case the *non-finite* Kripke structures where a correspondence between bisimilarity and theory equivalence has been discovered are the *image-finite* and the *saturated* Kripke structures. The definitions of those concepts are specific to Kripke models for modal logic. In this section, we examine similar conditions for Kripke models for intuitionistic logic.

Finite Principal Filter Structures *Finite principal filter structures* are a candidate for an intuitionistic version of *image-finite* Kripke structures for modal logic. But as we shall see, there are other candidates as well.

Definition 16. Let $K = \langle W, R, V \rangle$ be a Kripke structure. K has *finite principal filters* when $\forall w \in W$ the *principal filter*, $\uparrow(w)$, is finite.

Insisting that the set of worlds accessible from any world be a finite set seems like a quite restrictive condition. However, this condition does not imply that the entire structure is finite, for there could exist an infinite set of incomparable worlds. Finite principal filter structures have the advantage over finite structures in that they can describe a canonical model for any intuitionistic theory over a finite number of propositional atoms.

It follows from the work of Riger and Nishimura (1957, 1960) that there are no *finite* canonical Kripke models for the entire theory of propositional intuitionistic logic even if the cardinality of the set of propositional atoms is only 1. However, there is a canonical Kripke model with the finite principal filter property. In fact, every theory over a finite set of propositional atoms has a model which is a finite principal filter model.

Moreover, for each *finite* set of propositional atoms (Bellissima 1986) constructed such a model which has the property that no two distinct worlds in this structure are bisimilar. In other words, this structure is the bisimulation class representative as well as the canonical model.

Theorem 17. *Let* $K = \langle W, R, V \rangle$ *be a Kripke structure with* finite principal filters, *then* $\forall w_1, w_2 \in W.\ w_1 \approx w_2$ *if and only if that* $w_1 \leftrightarrow w_2$.

Proof. From right to left is simply an application of Theorem 13. From left to right, consider the filter generated by $\{w_1, w_2\}$. This equals $\uparrow(w_1) \cup \uparrow(w_2)$. Since $\uparrow(w_1)$ is finite and $\uparrow(w_2)$ is finite, also $\uparrow(w_1) \cup \uparrow(w_2)$ is finite. We apply Theorem 14 to conclude that $w_1 \leftrightarrow w_2$ in $K \uparrow \{w_1, w_2\}$. However, a bisimulation between w_1 and w_2 in $K \uparrow \{w_1, w_2\}$ is also a bisimulation in K. ∎

Saturation Now we attempt to generalize to *saturated* structures in the lines of what has been accomplished in the modal setting. See Hollenberg (1994) for an excellent overview and de Rijke (1996) for a collection of papers pertinent to the following generalizations.

We now give a definition which is similar in spirit to m-saturation found in (Hollenberg 1994).

Definition 18. Let $K = \langle W, R, V\rangle$ be a Kripke structure, then K is

- *weakly conjunctively saturated* if for every set of formulas Θ_s, if for every finite subset θ_f of Θ_s there is world in K which satisfies $\wedge\theta_f$ (the conjunction of formulas in θ_f), then there is a world in K which satisfies all of Θ_s, i.e.

$$\forall\Theta_s.(\forall \text{ finite } \theta_f \subseteq \Theta_s.\exists w.\forall\theta \in \theta_f.w \models_K \theta) \to \exists w'.\forall\theta \in \Theta_s.w' \models_K \theta,$$

- *weakly disjunctively saturated* if for every set of formulas Θ_r, if for every finite subset θ_f of Θ_r there is world in K which refutes $\vee\theta_f$ (the disjunction of the formulas in θ_f), then there is a world in K which refutes all of Θ_r.

$$\forall\Theta_r.(\forall \text{ finite } \theta_f \subseteq \Theta_r.\exists w.\forall\theta \in \theta_f.w \not\models_K \theta) \to \exists w'.\forall\theta \in \Theta_r.w' \not\models_K \theta,$$

- *weakly saturated* if for every pair of disjoint sets of formulas Θ_s and Θ_r, if for every finite subset θ_s, θ_r, in Θ_s and Θ_r respectively, there is a world in K which satisfies $\wedge\theta_s$, and a world in K which refutes $\vee\theta_r$, then there is a world in K which satisfies all of Θ_s and refutes all of Θ_r,

$$\begin{aligned}\forall\Theta_s.\forall\Theta_r.\ \Theta_s \cap \Theta_r = \emptyset \quad &\to \\ [((\forall \text{ finite } \theta_f \subseteq \Theta_s.\ &\exists w.\forall\theta \in \theta_f.w \models_K \theta)\wedge \\ (\forall \text{ finite } \theta_f \subseteq \Theta_r.\ &\exists w.\forall\theta \in \theta_f.w \not\models_K \theta)) \\ \to \quad &\exists w'.\forall\theta \in \Theta_s.\forall\theta' \in \Theta_r.\ w' \models_K \theta \text{ and } w' \not\models_K \theta'].\end{aligned}$$

Definition 19. Let $K = \langle W, R, V\rangle$ be a Kripke structure, then K is

- *locally conjunctively saturated* if for every $w \in W$, $K \uparrow w$ is weakly conjunctively saturated,
- *locally disjunctively saturated* if for every $w \in W$, $K \uparrow w$ is weakly disjunctively saturated, and
- *locally saturated* for every $w \in W$, $K \uparrow w$ is weakly saturated.

Definition 20. Let $K = \langle W, R, V\rangle$ be a Kripke structure, then K is

- *conjunctively saturated* if K is weakly conjunctively saturated and locally conjunctively saturated,
- *disjunctively saturated* if K is weakly disjunctively saturated and locally disjunctively saturated, and
- *saturated* if K is weakly saturated and locally saturated.

Theorem 21. *Let* $K = \langle W, R, V\rangle$ *be a* saturated *Kripke structure, then* $\forall w_1, w_2 \in W.\ w_1 \approx w_2$ *if and only if* $w_1 \leftrightarrows w_2$.

Proof. From right to left, we simply use the fact that bisimulation is truth preserving and apply Theorem 13. From left to right assume $w_1 R w_1'$. Let $\Theta = \mathcal{T}h(w_1')$ and Θ_r be the complement of Θ. Let $\Phi = \{\wedge\theta_f \supset \vee\varphi_f \mid \theta_f \subseteq \Theta$ where θ_f is finite and $\varphi_f \subseteq \Theta_r$ where φ_f is finite$\}$.

All of Φ is refuted at w_2, by construction, and for every θ_f, $w_2 \not\models_K \sim (\wedge\theta_f)$. This means that for every $\phi = (\wedge\theta_f) \supset (\vee\varphi_f)$ there is a world w' above w_2 such that $w' \models_K \wedge\theta_f$ and $w' \not\models_K \vee\varphi_f$.

By conjunctive saturation, there is a world w_2' in $K \uparrow w_2$ which satisfies all of Θ, by disjunctive saturation, there is a world w_2' in $K \uparrow w_2$ which refutes all of Θ_r. By saturation, we can use the same world w_2' to satisfy Θ and refute Θ_r. Therefore, w_2' has theory exactly Θ as needed. ∎

We need both clauses in the definition of saturation to generalize this result to bisimulation between structures. In the proof above, K need only be a locally saturated structure.

Lemma 22. *Let K be a Kripke structure.*

1. *If K is locally saturated, it is not necessarily weakly saturated.*
2. *If K is weakly saturated, it is not necessarily locally saturated.*

Proof. Counterexample to 1) Let this structure be denoted K_1.

$$w_1 = \{q_1\} \quad w_2 = \{q_2\} \quad \ldots \quad w_n = \{q_n\} \quad \ldots$$

Counterexample to 2) Add to K_1 a bottom world connected to all worlds w_i and call it w_b. Also add a world w disconnected from K_1. The world which witnesses the saturation of $K \uparrow w_b$ is not above w_b.

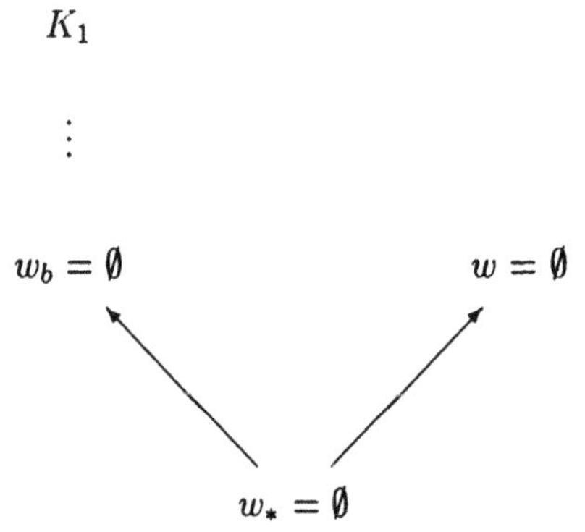

∎

When drawing Kripke structures, we show the name of the world and the value of the valuation function V at that world. The arcs represent the accessibility relation where arcs derivable by transitivity or reflexivity are not shown.

4 Comparison with the Modal Case

Our definitions of finite principal filter structures and saturated structures are not their modal counterparts applied to intuitionistic Kripke models. In the modal case, the series of structures,

1. finite,
2. image-finite, and
3. saturated structures

are generalizations of each other in numerical order. Since finite principal filter structures are a candidate for an analogue of image-finite structures we might assume that they are saturated. Here we provide a counterexample.

Lemma 23. *1. Finite principal filter structures are not necessarily saturated.*

Proof. K_1 from Lemma 22 is neither

1. *conjunctively saturated*, namely for every finite subset of $Q = \{q_i \mid i \in \mathbb{N}\}$, a world in K satisfies the conjunction of intuitionistic negations of each element in that subset, but no world satisfies $\bigwedge_i \sim q_i \quad i \in \mathbb{N}$,
2. nor *disjunctively saturated*, because no world refutes $\bigvee_i q_i \; i \in \mathbb{N}$. ∎

We could rectify the problem with saturation by adding a new world w_0.

$$w_0 = \emptyset \quad w_1 = \{q_1\} \quad w_2 = \{q_2\} \quad \ldots \quad w_n = \{q_n\} \quad \ldots$$

There is another counterexample which only uses two propositional atoms.

Lemma 24. *Finite principal filter structures over a finite set of propositional atoms are not necessarily saturated.*

Proof. We take K_2 the free Kripke model on two generators $\{p, q\}$. It has the theory *True*. From (Bellissima 1986) we know that this is a finite filter model with an infinite anti-chain given by the w_i's.

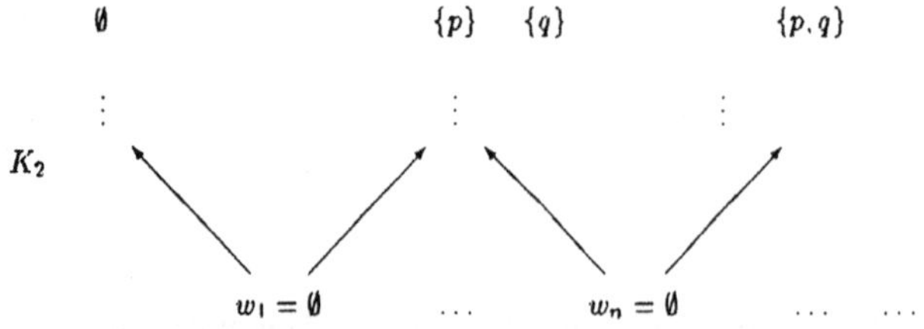

Take Θ now to be the theory of intuitionistic logic over two generators (the theory *True*). Every subset of Θ is satisfied in this structure, and every subset of non-valid formulas is refuted in this structure, but there is no world which is a witness to this fact. For the theory *True* in K_2 to be witnessed at a world, we would need to add a point w_*.

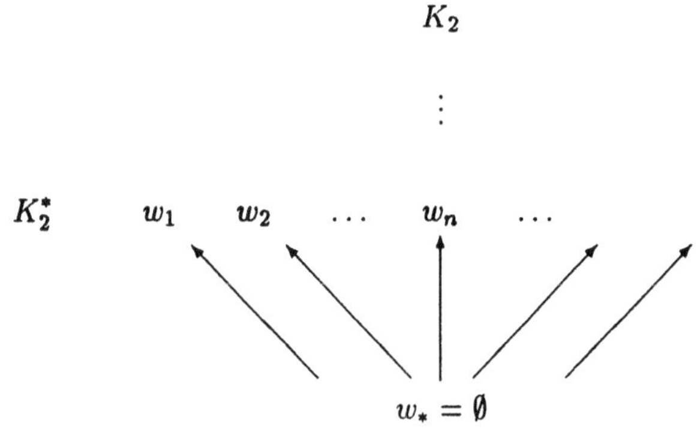

■

Once we have added that w_*, we cannot stop there. We would need to add a continuum of points; one for every subset of the infinite anti-chain in order to saturate this structure. Saturatedness must hold for all Θ. This means that for arbitrary infinite structures, we cannot always obtain a correspondence between structures which have the same set of *valid* formulas and bisimilar structures.

4.1 Image Finite Structures?

Another result in modal logics is that bisimilarity and theory equivalence correspond for image finite structures. There are two manners in which we could define image finite structures. When we view Kripke structures as annotated labeled transitions systems with only a single label then, because of transitivity, image finite structures are simply the finite principal filter structures. In the preceding text, we have just studied this form of image finite structure. Another quite reasonable reading of an image finite structure requires an alternate transformation from a Kripke structure to a labeled transition system. This alternate transformation labels transitions between Kripke worlds with the set of propositional atoms that have "just become true". That is for each pair of worlds w, w' such that wRw' let us label the transition with the difference among the propositional atoms.

Definition 25. A Kripke structure, $K = \langle W, R, V \rangle$ is *image finite* when for every world w and for every propositional atom p, the set $\{w' \mid p \in V(w') - V(w) \wedge w' \text{ is an immediate successor of } w\}$ is finite.

Using the previous definition, the following serves as a counterexample to the proposed result that two image finite structures with the same theory are bisimilar.

Theorem 26. *(Bellissima 1986) If the number of propositional atoms is greater than 1, then every canonical Kripke model has an infinite anti-chain.*

Proposition 27. *Two image finite structures with the same theory are not necessarily bisimilar.*

Proof. Take K_2^* (from Lemma 23), as one structure. Let K' be a variation of the structure K_2 in which every infinite subset of the antichain has a world representing the infinite meet. These new worlds are above the bottom world w'_* which is the meet of every element of the infinite anti-chain. The worlds w_* and w'_* both have the same theory. However w_* and w'_* are not bisimilar. Hence K' and K_2^* are not bisimilar.

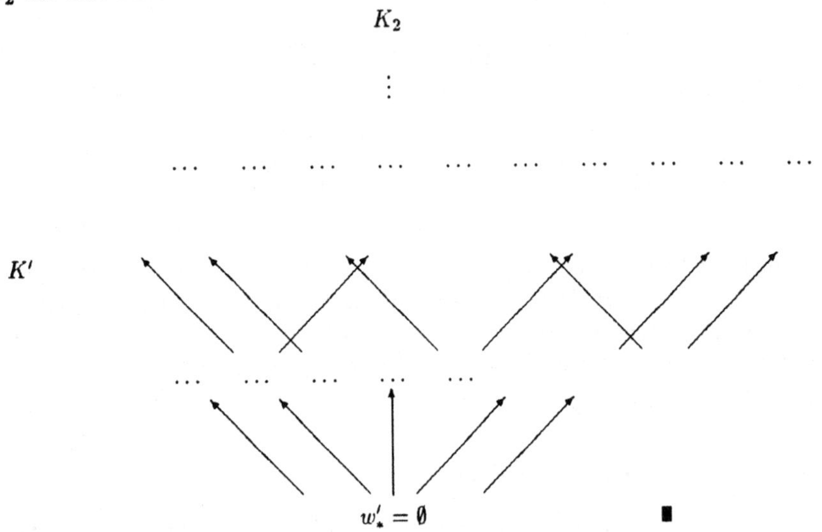

∎

4.2 Modal Saturation

Modal m-saturation (Hollenberg 1994) is most similar to *locally saturated* because the modal case concerns itself with only pointed modal structures, i.e. structures which contain a world w_* from which all other worlds are accessible. If we insist that the intuitionistic Kripke structures are pointed, then locally saturated is the same as saturated. However, as we saw, some very natural structures like the canonical Kripke model, K_2, for propositional intuitionistic logic over two generators are not pointed. K_2 cannot be made saturated and pointed without adding a continuum of points. Hence structures which are not necessarily pointed arise naturally in intuitionistic logic. Given this, to obtain a correspondence between structures with the same theory and bisimilar structures we need the global view of saturation given in Definition 20.

5 Bisimulation between structures

The definition of bisimulation can be extended slightly to include the equivalence of two worlds from different structures.

Definition 28. Let $K = \langle W, R, V\rangle$ and $K' = \langle W', R', V'\rangle$ be two Kripke structures over P, then K is bisimilar to K', $K \leftrightarroweq K'$, if there is a relation $S \subseteq W \times W'$ such that

- $\forall w \in W\ \exists w' \in W'$ such that $w\ S\ w'$, and
- $\forall w' \in W'\ \exists w \in W$ such that $w\ S\ w'$, and
- $x\ S\ y$ implies $V(x) = V'(y)$, and
- $x\ S\ y$ implies $\forall x' \in W.\ x\ R\ x' \rightarrow (\exists y' \in W'.\ \ y\ R'\ y' \wedge x'\ S\ y')$, and
- $x\ S\ y$ implies $\forall y' \in W'.\ y\ R'\ y' \rightarrow (\exists x' \in W.\ \ x\ R\ x' \wedge x'\ S\ y')$.

Definition 29. Let $K = \langle W, R, V\rangle, K' = \langle W', R', V'\rangle$ be two Kripke structures. K is a logical substructure of K', written $K \subseteq K'$, when for any valid formula φ in K, φ is valid in K'.

K and K' are elementarily equivalent, $K \approx K'$, when $K \subseteq K'$ and $K' \subseteq K$.

Lemma 30. *Let K and K' be two finite/finite principal filter/saturated structures.*

K is a logical substructure of K' if and only if K' is bisimilar to some sub-Kripke structure of K.

That is whenever the theory of $K = \langle W, R, V\rangle$ is included in the theory of $K' = \langle W', R', V'\rangle$, then there exists a $U \subseteq W$ such that K' is bisimilar to $K \uparrow U$.

Definition 31. Let $K = \langle W, R, V\rangle$ and $K' = \langle W', R', V'\rangle$ be two Kripke structures over P. We say that K is isomorphic to K', denoted $K \cong K'$, if there is a bijection on worlds, $f\colon W \rightarrow W'$, such that

- $\forall w, w' \in W.\ \ w\ R\ w'$ if and only if $f(w)\ R'\ f(w')$, and
- $\forall w \in W.\ \ V(w) = V'(f(w))$.

We can make a quotient structure using theory equivalence on worlds where the set of equivalences classes under $\approx$ is $W/\approx$ and apply Lemma 12 to produce $K/\approx$. The following is a corollary to Corollary 15/ Theorem 17/Theorem 21.

Corollary 32. *Let $K = \langle W, R, V\rangle$ be a finite/finite principal filter/saturated Kripke structure, then $K/\leftrightarroweq\ \cong\ K/\approx$.*

Lemma 33. *Let $K = \langle W, R, V\rangle$ and $K' = \langle W', R', V'\rangle$ be two finite/finite principal filter/ saturated Kripke structures over P, then K and K' are bisimilar, $K \leftrightarroweq K'$, if and only if $K/\leftrightarroweq$ is isomorphic to $K'/\leftrightarroweq$.*

Theorem 34. *Let $K = \langle W, R, V\rangle$ and $K' = \langle W', R', V'\rangle$ be two finite/finite principal filter/saturated Kripke structures over P, then K and K' have the same set of valid formulas, $K \approx K'$, if and only if $K/\approx$ is isomorphic to $K'/\approx$.*

Corollary 35. *Let* $K = \langle W, R, V\rangle$ *and* $K' = \langle W', R', V'\rangle$ *be two finite/finite principal filter/saturated Kripke structures over* P*, then the following are all equivalent,*

$$(1)\ K \approx K' \quad (2)\ K \leftrightarrow K' \quad (3)\ K/\leftrightarrow\ \cong\ K'/\leftrightarrow$$

$$(4)\ K/\approx\ \cong\ K'/\approx \quad (5)\ K/\approx\ \cong\ K'/\leftrightarrow$$

∎

6 Conclusion

Bisimulation has been examined in conjunction with modal logics starting with van Benthem's correspondence theory (1976). It has been shown that two finite Kripke structures for modal systems have the same set of valid formulas if and only if the two Kripke structures are bisimilar. Although the forward direction of our correspondence (Theorem 13) can be obtained as a corollary of the corresponding results for modal logic, the backwards direction (Theorem 14) strengthens the traditional modal results.

Goldblatt has also studied validity preserving constructions for modal logics and a survey is found in (Goldblatt 1993). We considered a similar problem for intuitionistic logic. This is non-trivial, as the translations from intuitionistic logic into modal logics (Feferman 1986) are not onto. There is further difficulty because it has been shown that bisimulation is characterized by $\Diamond$ and negation and conjunction. However there is no definable intuitionistic connective which corresponds to $\Diamond$ nor to classical negation. Therefore we would expect a stronger notion than bisimulation to characterize intuitionistic logic. Two structures could differ on a modal formula but not on any intuitionistic formula.

There is however extra structure in intuitionistic models, namely monotonicity. There are deep connections between monotonicity, computability and intuitionistic logic (McKinsey 1941, McKinsey and Tarski 1946, Birkhoff 1948, Scott 1972). It is this connection that allows the reduct of the models to the monotonic ones to exactly parallel the reduct of the modal logic to intuitionistic logic. Restricting our language to intuitionistic logic and restricting our model to open sets is orthogonal to elementary equivalence and thus bisimulation.

Nonetheless, we have obtained a correspondence between theory equivalence and bisimilarity for finite structures, for finite principal filter structures and for saturated structures.

7 Acknowledgments

The author is deeply indebted to Rob van Glabbeek and Tom Costello for helpful discussions and reading the manuscript. This research also benefited from discussions with Johan van Benthem, Albert Visser, Solomon Feferman and an anonymous referee.

References

Aczel, P. 1988. *Non-Well-Founded Sets*. Vol. 14 of *Lecture Notes*. CSLI.

Bellissima, F. 1986. Finitely generated free Heyting algebras. *Journal of Symbolic Logic* 51(1):152–165.

Benthem, J. v. 1976. *Modal Correspondence theory*. PhD thesis, Mathematical Institute, University of Amsterdam. See also *Correspondence Theory*, Handbook of philosophical logic, Vol. II, Reidel, Dordrecht 1984.

Birkhoff, G. 1948. *Lattice Theory*. Vol. 25. A.M.S. Colloq. Publications.

Feferman, S. (Ed.). 1986. *Kurt Gödel Collected Works*. Oxford, UK: Oxford University Press.

Fitting, M. C. 1969. *Intuitionistic logic, model theory and forcing*. North-Holland.

Goldblatt, R. 1993. *Mathematics of modality*. Vol. 43 of *Lecture Notes*. CSLI.

Heyting, A. 1966. *Intuitionism - An Introduction*. North-Holland.

Hollenberg, M. 1994. Hennessy-Milner classes and process algebra. Technical Report 124, Utrecht Research Institute for Philosophy.

Kripke, S. 1963. A semantical analysis of modal logic I: normal modal propositional calculi. *Zeitschrift für Mathematische Logik und Grundlagen der Mathematik* 9:67–96. Announced in *Journal of Symbolic Logic*, **24**, 1959, p. 323.

Kripke, S. A. 1965. Semantical analysis of intuitionistic logic I. In *Formal Systems and Recursive Functions*, 92–130. Amsterdam: (Proc. 8th Logic Colloq. Oxford 1963) North-Holland.

Lewis, C., and C. Langford. 1932. *Symbolic Logic*. The Century Company. 2nd ed. 1959, Dover Publications, Inc.

McKinsey, J. 1941. A solution to the decision problem for the Lewis systems S.2 and S.4 with an application to topology. *Journal of Symbolic Logic* 6:117–134.

McKinsey, J., and A. Tarski. 1944. The algebra of topology. *Annals of Mathematics* 45:141–191.

McKinsey, J., and A. Tarski. 1946. On closed elements in closure algebras. *Annals of Mathematics* 47:122–162.

Milner, R. 1980. *A Calculus of Communicating Systems, LNCS 92*. Springer-Verlag.

Nishimura, I. 1960. On formulas in one variable in intuitionistic propositional calculus. *Journal of Symbolic Logic* 25:327–331.

Rasiowa, H., and R. Sikorski. 1963. *The Mathematics of Metamathematics*. Vol. 41 of *Polska Akademia Nauk. Monografie matematyczne*. Warsaw.

Ríger, L. 1957. Zamétka o t. naz. svobodnyh algébrah c zamykaniámi. *Czechoslovak Mathematical Journal* 7(82):16–20.

Rijke, M. d. 1996. *Modal Logics and Process Algebra*. Cambridge University Press and CSLI.

Rodenburg, P. 1986. *Intuitionistic Correspondence Theory*. PhD thesis, University of Amsterdam.

Scott, D. 1972. Continuous lattices. In *Proc. 1971 Dalhousie Conference: LNM 274*, 97–136. Springer-Verlag.

A Rigorous Analysis of Concurrent Operations on B-Trees

Anna Philippou and David Walker

Department of Computer Science, University of Warwick
Coventry CV4 7AL, U.K.

Abstract. An account is given of a rigorous study of concurrent operations on a variant of the B-tree in the framework of a general theory of concurrent systems, an extension of the π-calculus. The assertion of correctness of the algorithms is that the agent representing the system is behaviourally equivalent to an agent whose observable behaviour describes simply the expected interactions of the system with its environment. An outline of the proofs of correctness of algorithms for insertion and search is given. Algorithms for deletion and compression are considered briefly. The main theoretical contribution is an extension of the theory of partial confluence of agents.

1 Introduction

The B-tree [2] and variants of it are widely used as index structures. Concurrent operations on such structures have been studied in many papers including [3, 5, 8, 9, 12, 17, 18]. The aim of this paper is to give an account of a rigorous study of concurrent operations on one such structure in the framework of a general theory of concurrent systems. The structure is the B^{link}-tree of [9], itself a variant of the B^*-tree introduced in [22]. The algorithms studied are those of [17] which, as explained below, improve on those described in [9]. In [9] and [17] the structure is described and explained using prose and diagrams, the algorithms are described using pseudo-code, and the arguments for their correctness are informal, though detailed. It is widely recognized that it is often very difficult to give convincing informal arguments that a concurrent system enjoys desired properties. Indeed, without a formal model of the system in question, it can be difficult even to express clearly and precisely what the desired properties are. In the case of database concurrency control in particular, many varieties of 'serializability' have been proposed and used as criteria by which to judge algorithms. For instance, in [17] a criterion of correctness for the algorithms considered is that any 'schedule of operations' arising by executing them is 'data equivalent to a serial schedule and [preserves] the validity of the search structure'.

The general theory of concurrent systems we use is an extension of the π-calculus [14], a process calculus in which one may express succinctly and directly systems whose structure may change during computation. The B^{link}-system is of this kind: requests for operations result in creations of processes which act concurrently on a graph, creating nodes and altering the pointer structure among nodes as they carry out their tasks. Among the features of the process-calculus theory is a precise account of behavioural equivalence of systems. We use this to express the correctness of the algorithms. We model the system consisting of the data structure and the algorithms in a structured way as an agent. We define a simple agent whose observable behaviour describes the expected interactions of the system with its environment, i.e. the receipt of requests to carry out operations and the return of the results of doing so. The assertion of correctness is that these two agents are behaviourally equivalent. Thus the criterion of correctness is in terms of the observable behaviour of the system. This is in contrast to the situation with forms of serializability. However, the principle that concurrent systems should be compared on the basis of their observable behaviours is widely held, and has been elaborated in depth in concurrency theory. The principle has been argued to be sound specifically for database concurrency control systems in the extensive study of atomic transactions in [11]. That study employs I/O-automata, which are themselves very closely related to process calculus [20]. I/O-automata do not, however, allow direct representation of systems with changing structure. A further important point is that process calculus provides an accessible, unifying and simplifying framework within which concepts and techniques originating in one domain may be abstracted and generalized and hence applied in others. Indeed in this paper we will make use of, and significantly extend, some process-calculus theory introduced to show the correctness of program transformation rules for concurrent object-oriented languages [10, 16].

The operations considered in [9] are insertion, search, and a simple form of deletion. The insertion algorithm may require a process to hold exclusive locks on two or three nodes simultaneously. The insertion algorithm of [17] improves on this in that any process need lock at most one node at any time. Further, as observed in [17], [9] neglects to consider two important cases: when the root node in the structure must be split, and when an inserting process needs to give one node a pointer to another node but is unable to do so as the node which was the root when the process was created is no longer the root and so the process cannot access the node in question. The deletion algorithm of [17] is much more sophisticated than that of the earlier paper as it involves compression of the tree to avoid proliferation of sparsely-occupied nodes. In this paper we describe the rigorous analysis we have undertaken of the insertion and search algorithms of [17]. In fact, we began with the algorithms of [9] and, in formalising and analysing them, independently discovered the defects and improvement described above and previously published in [17]. We have also carried out a rigorous analysis of the deletion and compression algorithms of [17]. In doing so we discovered an improvement to these algorithms. Due to lack of space it is not possible to describe this here; see [15]. In our view, the rigorous proofs are perspicuous and give valuable insight into why the algorithms are correct.

The main theoretical contribution of this paper is an extension of the theory of partial confluence of agents. In [13] a theory of confluence of agents was developed in the setting of the process calculus CCS. The essence of confluence is that of any two possible actions, the occurrence of one will never preclude that of the other. In [19, 10, 16] notions of partial confluence were introduced and studied. The idea is that in a partial-confluent agent, the occurrence of *some* actions will never preclude that of *some* others. A key observation is that in reasoning about the behaviour of a (partial-) confluent system in certain contexts, it may be sufficient to examine in detail only a part of that behaviour: from this and the fact of the system's (partial) confluence, it may be possible to deduce properties of the remaining behaviour. As mentioned earlier, the theory of [10, 16] was used to prove the soundness of program transformation rules for concurrent object-oriented languages. The systems considered there could be viewed as consisting of two agents, Q and A, which interact in a question-answer fashion, with possibly many questions outstanding at any moment. An important property was that on accepting a question from Q, A immediately assumed a state in which the answer to that question was determined, up to behavioural equivalence. This property does not hold of the B^{link}-system: the result of an operation is not determined when the operation is requested as other operations may be in progress but not yet have 'committed', and operations may begin later and 'overtake' the operation in question. This extension and the theory of [10, 16] are also used to show that the full system, in which several search processes may access a node concurrently, has the same behaviour as two simplifications of it: when each node allows at most one access at a time, and when the whole tree allows at most one operation to be active at a time. These observations allow us to obtain results about the full system by analysing the simpler systems.

The following section contains a brief account of the process calculus, section 3 a description of the index structure and the insertion and search algorithms, section 4 an outline of the analysis of those algorithms, and section 5 concluding remarks. Due to space limitations this paper gives only an outline of the analysis; see [15] for a full account.

2 Background

Process calculi are general theories of concurrent systems. The calculus of interest here is an extension of the π-calculus with first-order data other than names [21]. It has a small but expressive language for describing systems. Terms of the language are interpreted as labelled transition systems whose nodes represent states and whose arrows carry information pertinent to state change. An equivalence on transition systems induces an equivalence on terms capturing when two terms express the same observable behaviour. The first-order data part of the language may be tailored to the application at hand. Here we assume it contains names, Booleans, integers, tuples, records and variants; we omit the syntax of expressions. The names may be thought of as names of communication links between components of systems. Components use names to interact; and by passing names in interactions, components may pass to one another the ability to interact with other components. Important features of the theory are its treatment of the creation of names and of the scoping of names. Names are categorized according to the ways they may be used. This gives structure to the descriptions, making them clearer and providing information useful in reasoning about systems. Technically, each name is assigned a *sort*, and a *sorting* is fixed which prescribes the types of values names of each sort may carry. We use variants so that values of several types may be passed via names of a given sort; we omit the details.

The terms of the language, the *agents*, are given as follows:

$$P \ ::= \ \Sigma_{j \in J}\, \pi_j . P_j \ \mid \ P|Q \ \mid \ (\nu x)P \ \mid \ K\langle v\rangle \ \mid \ \mathsf{cond}\,(b_1 \triangleright P_1, \ldots, b_n \triangleright P_n).$$

Here the π_j are *prefixes* of three kinds. First *input* prefixes of the form $a(z)$: an agent $a(z).P$ is able to receive via the name a a value v of any type allowed by the sorting and then continue as $P\{v/z\}$, that is P with v substituted for the pattern z in P; we omit the syntax of patterns. Secondly, *output* prefixes of the form $\overline{a}\langle e\rangle$: an agent $\overline{a}\langle e\rangle.P$ may send the value of the expression e via the name a and then continue as P. Finally, the *internal* prefix τ: an agent $\tau.P$ may evolve autonomously and invisibly into P. The agent $\Sigma_{j \in J}\, \pi_j . P_j$, a finite sum, represents a choice of the prefixed summands; we write $\mathbf{0}$ for the empty sum, the inactive agent. The agent $P \mid Q$ describes the concurrent composition of P and Q: the component agents may proceed independently and may also interact with one another using shared names. In $(\nu x)P$ the scope of the name x is restricted to P: components of P may use it to interact with one another but not with P's environment. However, the scope of x may change by its being sent in a communication. K is an agent constant with an associated definition $K \stackrel{\mathrm{def}}{=} (z)P$: the agent $K\langle v\rangle$ behaves as $P\{v/z\}$. Further, $\mathsf{cond}\,(b_1 \triangleright P_1, \ldots, b_n \triangleright P_n)$ is a nested-conditional agent with Boolean conditions b_i guarding the alternatives P_i. We use also the derived replicator form, $!\,a(z).\,P$, which may generate instances of P indefinitely by interacting via a: $!\,a(z).\,P \stackrel{\mathrm{def}}{=} a(z).\,(P \mid !\,a(z).\,P)$.

The informal account of behaviour just given is made precise via a family of rules which define the (early) labelled transition relations $\stackrel{\alpha}{\longrightarrow}$ on agents. The labels (*actions*) α are of three kinds with the following interpretations (in the first two a is the *subject*, $\mathsf{subj}(\alpha)$, of α; also $\mathsf{subj}(\tau) = \tau$): (1) $P \stackrel{a(v)}{\longrightarrow} Q$ means that P may receive the value v via the name a and thereby evolve into Q; (2) $P \stackrel{\overline{a}\langle v\rangle}{\longrightarrow} Q$ means that P may send the value v via the name a and thereby evolve into Q; (3) $P \stackrel{\tau}{\longrightarrow} Q$ means that P may evolve invisibly into Q, without interacting with its environment. Such a transition will arise either from a silent prefix or from a communication between two of P's components via some name which they share. In the space available we can not give the rules; see [14, 21] for details and further explanation.

Many notions of behavioural equivalence of agents have been studied. Here we employ a well-studied equivalence called *branching bisimilarity* [13, 6]. An important feature is that it abstracts from silent actions. It is one of the most demanding reasonable notions of equivalence. We adopt it here first as it enables us to give a precise description of the behaviour of the system we consider, and secondly because the techniques for reasoning with it are powerful. First some notation: we write $\Longrightarrow$ for the reflexive and transitive closure of $\xrightarrow{\tau}$.

Definition 1. *Branching bisimilarity*, $\simeq$, is the largest *branching bisimulation*, i.e. symmetric relation $\mathcal{B}$ on agents such that if $P\mathcal{B}Q$ then for all actions α, if $P \xrightarrow{\alpha} P'$ then (1) for some Q'', Q', $Q \Longrightarrow Q'' \xrightarrow{\alpha} Q'$, $P\mathcal{B}Q''$ and $P'\mathcal{B}Q'$, or (2) $\alpha = \tau$ and $P'\mathcal{B}Q$.

Thus any transition of either of a pair of branching-bisimilar agents can be matched by a computation of the other with the same visible content and which respects the branching structure of the agents. To show that a pair of agents are branching bisimilar, it suffices to find a branching bisimulation relating them.

3 The structure

This section contains the process-calculus descriptions of the B^{link}-tree of [9] and of simplified versions of the concurrent insertion and search algorithms presented in [17]; we consider deletion and compression briefly in section 5. The simplification is that at most one inserting or searching process may access a given node of the tree at any time. As mentioned earlier and explained in detail in section 5, by analysing this system and applying the theory of partial confluence, we are able to obtain results about the full system which allows many searches to proceed concurrently in a node. The process-calculus description is at a higher level of abstraction, and is therefore clearer and more readily comprehended, than the descriptions using prose and pseudo-code given in [9, 17]. However, it is helpful to begin with a brief informal description of the structure.

A B^{link}-tree indexes a database by storing in its leaves pairs $\langle k, b\rangle$ with k an integer key associated with a record and b a pointer to the record. All of its leaves are at the same distance from the root. Each of its internal nodes has j keys and j pointers where $2 \leq j \leq 2m+1$ if the node is the root, and $m+1 \leq j \leq 2m+1$ otherwise (for some tree-parameter m). A node's keys are stored in ascending order. It is intended that a node's greatest key, its *high key*, is the largest key in the subtree rooted at the node. All but the last pointer of an internal node point to children of the node. All but the last of a leaf's pointers point to records of the database. The last pointer of a node or leaf, its *link*, points to the next node at the same level of the tree, if it exists. The purpose of links is to provide additional paths through the structure. The rightmost node at each level has high key ∞ and link nil. If an internal node has keys $\widetilde{k} = k_1, \ldots, k_j$ and non-nil pointers $\widetilde{p} = p_1, \ldots, p_j$, an intended invariant is that for $i < j$, pointer p_i points to a subtree whose leaves contain all keys k with $k_i < k \leq k_{i+1}$.

As mentioned earlier, the process-calculus sorting is important in organising the description of the system. The process-calculus representation of a pointer to a node is a value of the record type $\{ins : \mathsf{P}^I, srch : \mathsf{P}^S\}$ which we abbreviate to P. If p is a node name, $p : ins$ and $p : srch$ are the names, of sorts P^I and P^S respectively, via which insertions and searches may be initiated. The sorting decrees that a name of sort P^S carries a pair consisting of an integer (a key to be searched for) and a name of sort R^S (via which the result of the search should be returned). Similarly, a name of sort P^I carries a triple consisting of a key and a pointer to a database record (to be inserted) and a name of sort R^I (via which the outcome of the insertion should be communicated). We use a function f_N which given a triple $(k, \widetilde{k}, \widetilde{p})$ as argument returns the pointer p_i such that $k_i < k \leq k_{i+1}$, the link $last\,\widetilde{p}$ if $k > last\,\widetilde{k}$, and p_1 otherwise. The definition of the agent $\mathsf{NODE} \equiv \mathsf{NODE}\langle p, \widetilde{k}, \widetilde{p}\rangle$ representing a non-root, non-leaf node with name p storing keys $\widetilde{k} = k_1 \ldots k_j$ and pointers $\widetilde{p} = p_1 \ldots p_j$ is:

$$\begin{aligned}
\mathsf{NODE} \stackrel{\text{def}}{=} \; & p : srch(k, r).\ \mathsf{cond}\ (\ k > last\,\widetilde{k} \rhd \overline{r}\langle link, \mathsf{f}_N(k, \widetilde{k}, \widetilde{p})\rangle.\, \mathsf{NODE}, \\
& \qquad\qquad\qquad\qquad\ \ k \leq last\,\widetilde{k} \rhd \overline{r}\langle \mathsf{f}_N(k, \widetilde{k}, \widetilde{p})\rangle.\, \mathsf{NODE}) \\
+ \; & p : ins(k, q, r).\ \mathsf{cond}\ (\ k > last\,\widetilde{k} \rhd \overline{r}\langle \mathsf{f}_N(k, \widetilde{k}, \widetilde{p})\rangle.\, \mathsf{NODE}, \\
& \qquad\qquad\qquad\qquad\ \ k \in \widetilde{k} \qquad \rhd \overline{r}.\, \mathsf{NODE}\langle p, \widetilde{k}, \widetilde{p}''\rangle, \\
& \qquad\qquad\qquad\qquad\ \ notfull \quad \rhd \overline{r}.\, \mathsf{NODE}\langle p, \widetilde{k}', \widetilde{p}'\rangle, \\
& \qquad\qquad\qquad\qquad\ \ full \qquad\ \rhd (\nu p')(\overline{r}\langle p', k_{m+1}\rangle. \\
& \qquad\qquad\qquad\qquad\qquad\qquad\qquad (\mathsf{NODE}\langle p, \widetilde{k}_1, \widetilde{p}_1\rangle \\
& \qquad\qquad\qquad\qquad\qquad\qquad\qquad \mid \mathsf{NODE}\langle p', \widetilde{k}_2, \widetilde{p}_2\rangle))).
\end{aligned}$$

In its quiescent state a node may accept a search request via the name $p : srch$ and an insertion request via the name $p : ins$. In response to a search request it returns the appropriate pointer together with an indication of whether it is its link. Suppose insertion of k, q is requested with return name r thus: $\mathsf{NODE} \xrightarrow{p:ins(k,q,r)} P$ where P is the continuation agent. If k is greater than the high key of the node then the node returns its link and resumes its quiescent state. Otherwise, if $k = k_h$ a pointer is changed ($\widetilde{p}'' = p_1 \cdots p_{h-1} q p_{h+1} \cdots p_j$), else if the node is not full the pair is inserted ($\widetilde{k}' = k_1 \ldots k_h\, k\, k_{h+1} \ldots k_j$, $\widetilde{p}' = p_1 \cdots p_h\, q\, p_{h+1} \cdots p_j$ where $k_h < k < k_{h+1}$) and a signal is sent via r indicating completion of the insertion. Otherwise, the node is split, represented by the concurrent composition of two nodes: $\mathsf{NODE}\langle p, \widetilde{k}_1, \widetilde{p}_1\rangle$ and $\mathsf{NODE}\langle p', \widetilde{k}_2, \widetilde{p}_2\rangle$ where p' is a new name. The data of the original node is divided between the two and the new pair added to the appropriate node (we omit the precise definitions of $\widetilde{k}_1$ etc.). The high key of the first node becomes the value k_{m+1} and its link becomes name p'. The second node which contains the larger keys of the original node also assumes its link and high key. Via r is returned the pair $\langle p', k_{m+1}\rangle$ consisting of the name of the new node and its smallest key k_{m+1}. The recipient of this pair, the agent responsible for initiating the insertion, will use this pair to add a new pointer to the tree: see below.

The definition of the agent $\mathsf{LEAF} \equiv \mathsf{LEAF}\langle p, \widetilde{k}, \widetilde{b}q\rangle$ representing a leaf is similar. Here $\widetilde{b}$ are pointers to the records of the database and q is the leaf's link. It uses a function f_L which given a triple $(k, \widetilde{k}, \widetilde{b})$ as argument returns b_i if $k = k_i$ and nil otherwise.

$$\begin{aligned}
\mathsf{LEAF} \stackrel{\text{def}}{=} \; & p : srch(k, r).\ \mathsf{cond}\ (\ k > last\,\widetilde{k} \rhd \overline{r}\langle link, q\rangle.\, \mathsf{LEAF}, \\
& \qquad\qquad\qquad\qquad\ \ k \leq last\,\widetilde{k} \rhd \overline{r}\langle done, \mathsf{f}_L(k, \widetilde{k}, \widetilde{b})\rangle.\, \mathsf{LEAF})
\end{aligned}$$

$$\begin{aligned} + p : ins(k, b, r).\ \mathsf{cond}\ (\ & k > last\ \widetilde{k} \rhd \overline{r}\langle q\rangle.\ \mathsf{LEAF}, \\ & k \in \widetilde{k} \quad\ \rhd \overline{r}.\ \mathsf{LEAF}\langle p, \widetilde{k}, \widetilde{b}''q\rangle, \\ & notfull \rhd \overline{r}.\ \mathsf{LEAF}\langle p, \widetilde{k}', \widetilde{b}'q\rangle, \\ & full \quad\ \rhd (\nu p')(\overline{r}\langle p', k_{m+1}\rangle. \\ & \qquad\qquad (\mathsf{LEAF}\langle p, \widetilde{k}_1, \widetilde{b}_1 p'\rangle \\ & \qquad\qquad \mid \mathsf{LEAF}\langle p', \widetilde{k}_2, \widetilde{b}_2 q\rangle)), \end{aligned}$$

where again we omit the definitions of $\widetilde{k}'$ etc. Note that when a search terminates in a leaf, then the value *done* is returned along with the result to indicate this.

The definition of the agent $\mathsf{ROOT} \equiv \mathsf{ROOT}\langle p, \widetilde{k}, \widetilde{p}, put\rangle$ representing a root node with name p, keys $\widetilde{k}$, pointers $\widetilde{p}$ and name put to be used when the root is split is as follows:

$$\begin{aligned} \mathsf{ROOT} \stackrel{\text{def}}{=}\ & p : srch(k, r).\ \overline{r}\langle f_N(k, \widetilde{k}, \widetilde{p})\rangle.\ \mathsf{ROOT} \\ & + p : ins(k, q, r).\ \mathsf{cond}\ (k \in \widetilde{k} \rhd \overline{r}.\ \mathsf{ROOT}\langle p, \widetilde{k}, \widetilde{p}''\rangle, \\ & \qquad notfull \rhd \overline{r}.\ \mathsf{ROOT}\langle p, \widetilde{k}', \widetilde{p}'\rangle, \\ & \qquad full \quad\ \rhd (\nu p_0, p')(\overline{put}\langle p_0\rangle.\ \overline{r}. \\ & \qquad\qquad (\mathsf{NODE}\langle p, \widetilde{k}_1, \widetilde{p}_1\rangle \\ & \qquad\qquad \mid \mathsf{NODE}\langle p', \widetilde{k}_2, \widetilde{p}_2\rangle \\ & \qquad\qquad \mid \mathsf{NEWROOT}))) \end{aligned}$$

where $\mathsf{NEWROOT} \equiv \mathsf{ROOT}\langle p_0, \langle -\infty, k_{m+1}, \infty\rangle, \langle p, p', \mathrm{nil}\rangle, put\rangle$, and the definitions of $\widetilde{k}'$ etc. are again omitted. This third clause of the conditional describes the behaviour of a full root when an insertion is requested. The root assumes node status and a new sibling node (with new name p') and a new root (with new name p_0) are created, the latter with pointers to the old root and its new sibling. Note that the restriction $(\nu p_0, p')$ ensures that the names are indeed new and different from all others. Before the three nodes become accessible, the name of the new root is sent via name *put* to the following agent, $\mathsf{STORE} \equiv \mathsf{STORE}\langle \widetilde{p}, get, put, que\rangle$, which is responsible for recording the names of the current and previous roots:

$$\mathsf{STORE} \stackrel{\text{def}}{=} \overline{get}\langle last\ \widetilde{p}\rangle.\ \mathsf{STORE} + put(p_0).\ \mathsf{STORE}\langle \widetilde{p}\, p_0, \ldots\rangle + que(p, r).\overline{r}\langle \widetilde{p}_1\rangle.\ \mathsf{STORE}$$

where $\widetilde{p} = \widetilde{p}_2\, p\, \widetilde{p}_1$. Here $\widetilde{p}$ is the list of names (in order of creation) which have been roots of the tree, $last\ \widetilde{p}$ thus being the name of the current root. The names *get* and *put* are links via which the current root can be read and updated. Finally, *que* may be used to discover which names named the root after the parameter p did. The B^{link}-tree in its initial state is represented by the agent

$$\begin{aligned} T_0 \stackrel{\text{def}}{=} (get\ que)\,(\nu p, p', put)\ (& \mathsf{STORE}\langle\langle p\rangle, get, put, que\rangle \\ & \mid \mathsf{ROOT}\langle p, \langle -\infty, \infty\rangle, \langle p', \mathrm{nil}\rangle, put\rangle \\ & \mid \mathsf{LEAF}\langle p', \varepsilon, \varepsilon\, \mathrm{nil}\rangle). \end{aligned}$$

It remains to describe the search and insertion operations. The searcher $S \equiv S\langle s, get\rangle$ is defined as follows:

$$S \stackrel{\text{def}}{=} !\, s(k,a).\, get(p).\, Search\langle k,p,a\rangle$$

$$\begin{aligned} Search \stackrel{\text{def}}{=} (k\,p\,a)\,(\nu r)\overline{p : srch}\langle k,r\rangle.\,(r(p').\, Search\langle k,p',a\rangle + r(done,b).\,\overline{a}\langle b\rangle.\,\mathbf{0} \\ + r(link,p').\, Search\langle k,p',a\rangle)\end{aligned}$$

The agent S may repeatedly spin off searchers when supplied via s with a key k to search for and a link a via which to send the answer; thus for instance

$$S \xrightarrow{s(k,a)}\xrightarrow{get(p)} Search\langle k,p,a\rangle \mid S \xrightarrow{s(k',a')}\xrightarrow{get(p')} Search\langle k,p,a\rangle \mid Search\langle k',p',a'\rangle \mid S\,.$$

On initiation of a search, the searcher reads from the STORE via get the name of the root of the structure. It then traces a path through the structure until it reaches some LEAF which synchronizes with it by performing an action $\overline{r}\langle done,b\rangle$ returning the result b of the search (which may be nil) which is then emitted via the name a. The searcher then becomes inactive.

The inserter $I \equiv I\langle i, get, que\rangle$ is defined as follows:

$$\begin{aligned}
I \quad & \stackrel{\text{def}}{=} !\, i(k,b,a).\, get(q).\, Down\langle k,a,b,q,\varepsilon\rangle \\
Down \quad & \stackrel{\text{def}}{=} (k\,a\,b\,q\,\widetilde{p})\,(\nu r)\,\overline{q : srch}\langle k,r\rangle.\,(\; r(link,q').\, Down\langle k,a,b,q',\widetilde{p}\rangle \\
& \qquad + r(q').\, Down\langle k,a,b,q',q\widetilde{p}\rangle \\
& \qquad + r(done,b').\, Add\langle k,a,b,q,\widetilde{p}\rangle) \\
Add \quad & \stackrel{\text{def}}{=} (k\,a\,b\,q\,\widetilde{p})\,(\nu r)\;\overline{q : ins}\langle k,b,r\rangle.\;\; (r(p',k').\,\overline{a}.\; Up\langle k',p',hd\,\widetilde{p},tl\,\widetilde{p}\rangle, \\
& \qquad + r.\,\overline{a}.\,\mathbf{0}, \\
& \qquad + r(q').\, Add\langle k,a,b,q',\widetilde{p}\rangle) \\
Up \quad & \stackrel{\text{def}}{=} (k\,p\,q\,\widetilde{p})\;(\nu r)\,\overline{q : ins}\langle k,p,r\rangle. \\
& \quad \mathsf{cond}\;(\widetilde{p} \neq \varepsilon \;\triangleright\; (r(p',k').\; Up\langle k',p',hd\,\widetilde{p},tl\,\widetilde{p}\rangle, \\
& \qquad + r.\,\mathbf{0}, \\
& \qquad + r(q').\; Up\langle k,p,q',\widetilde{p}\rangle) \\
& \quad \widetilde{p} = \varepsilon \;\triangleright\; (r(p',k').\,(\nu r)\overline{que}\langle q,r\rangle.r(\widetilde{p'}). \\
& \qquad\qquad Up\langle k',p',hd\,\widetilde{p'},tl\,\widetilde{p'}\rangle, \\
& \qquad + r.\,\mathbf{0}, \\
& \qquad + r(q').\; Up\langle k,p,q',\widetilde{p}\rangle))\,.
\end{aligned}$$

The replicator I may repeatedly spin off inserters when supplied via i with a pair $\langle k,b\rangle$ to insert and an answer name a via which a confirmation that the insertion has been done is to be sent. The inserter obtains the name of the root from the STORE and searches until the appropriate leaf is reached. Note that the names of the rightmost nodes in the path followed are recorded in the last parameter $\widetilde{p}$. An insertion within a leaf may result in it splitting. The inserter is informed of this by being sent a pair $\langle p',k'\rangle$. In such a case the continuation agent Up is responsible for inserting this pair in the level above. This process may be repeated by Up in several levels of the tree and may result in the creation of a new root. This is the reason that the node-names $\widetilde{p}$ of the rightmost nodes visited are recorded during the searching phase. It is possible that $\widetilde{p}$ may become empty although an insertion is required at a higher level of the tree: new levels may have been created after the individual inserter began its task. If this happens the inserter queries the STORE via *que* to obtain the names of the leftmost nodes at each of the new levels.

The system consisting of the structure and the operations is represented by the agent

$$P_0 \stackrel{\text{def}}{=} (\nu get, que)(S \mid I \mid T_0).$$

A state reachable from this has the form $(\nu\tilde{z})(Q_1 \mid \ldots \mid Q_n \mid S \mid I \mid T)$ where each Q_i is an individual searcher or inserter in some state and T is reachable from T_0.

4 Correctness

We now define an agent which gives a succinct description of the intended observable behaviour of the B^{link}-system P_0. This agent is parametrized on: the names i and s via which the operations may be initiated; a function f recording the key-pointer associations held in the leaves of the tree; a set ι (the *insertions*) of triples consisting of a key k, a pointer b and a name a via which a signal is to be made to the environment when the insertion of the $\langle k, b\rangle$-pair has been completed; a set ι^c (the *completed insertions*) of names a whose key-pointer pairs have been inserted but which have not been used to signal this; a set σ (the *searches*) of pairs consisting of a key k to be searched for and a name a to be used to return to the environment the pointer found; and a set σ^c (the *completed searches*) of pairs consisting of a name a and a pointer b found but not yet returned.

We define $B \equiv B\langle i, s, f, \iota, \iota^c, \sigma, \sigma^c\rangle$ as follows highlighting the changes by eliding the unchanged parameters:

$$\begin{aligned} B \stackrel{\text{def}}{=} & \; i(k,b,a).\, B\langle \ldots, \iota \cup \{\langle k,b,a\rangle\}, \ldots\rangle \\ & + s(k,a).\, B\langle \ldots, \sigma \cup \{\langle k,a\rangle\}, \ldots\rangle \\ & + \Sigma_{\langle k,b,a\rangle \in \iota}\, \tau.\, B\langle \ldots, f[b/k], \iota - \{\langle k,b,a\rangle\}, \iota^c \cup \{a\}, \ldots\rangle \\ & + \Sigma_{\langle k,a\rangle \in \sigma}\, \tau.\, B\langle \ldots, \sigma - \{\langle k,a\rangle\}, \sigma^c \cup \{\langle a, f(k)\rangle\}\rangle \\ & + \Sigma_{a \in \iota^c}\, \overline{a}.\, B\langle \ldots, \iota^c - \{a\}, \ldots\rangle \\ & + \Sigma_{\langle a,b\rangle \in \sigma^c}\, \overline{a}\langle b\rangle.\, B\langle \ldots, \sigma^c - \{\langle a,b\rangle\}\rangle\,. \end{aligned}$$

The first and second summands represent initiation of new operations, the third and fourth invisible completion of outstanding operations (with appropriate update of the association in the case of insertion), and the fifth and sixth returns of results to the environment.

Let $B_0 \equiv B\langle i, s, \lambda k.\,\text{nil}, \varepsilon, \varepsilon, \varepsilon, \varepsilon\rangle$. The result asserting the correctness of the operations is the following.

Theorem 2. $P_0 \simeq B_0$.

Let Q (for 'question') be the sorts of the names i, s used by the environment for initiating insertions and searches, and A (for 'answer') the sorts of names to be used by the system for returning the results of the operations to the environment.

Let Q^- (resp. Q^+) be the set of actions which are outputs (resp. inputs) via a name in Q, and similarly for A^- (resp. A^+) for sort A; let $Q = Q^- \cup Q^+$ and $A = A^- \cup A^+$. Thus, for instance, the actions in Q^+ have the forms $s\langle k, a\rangle$ and $i\langle k, b, a\rangle$ where a is of sort A.

The theorem above is strong: it asserts that P_0 and B_0 cannot be distinguished even if different requests for operations supply the same name for return of the answer, thus allowing the possibility, for instance, that each of two processes may receive the result of the other's request. It may be argued that a weaker result would be adequate:

Theorem 3. $P_0 \simeq_{\mathsf{A}} B_0$.

Here $\simeq_{\mathsf{A}}$ is defined like $\simeq$ except that in each action in Q, the A-component is a fresh name, i.e. in comparing two agents R, R', only actions $s\langle k, a\rangle$ etc. are considered where a does not occur in R, R'. This restriction captures the assumption that when an operation is invoked in the system, the name which is supplied for return of the answer is distinct from answer names supplied in other operation invocations. It corresponds, for instance, to the use in [11] of integers to distinguish 'operation instances'. The partial-confluence theory required to prove the $\simeq_{\mathsf{A}}$-result is simpler than that needed for the full result. We outline the simpler theory and indicate how it may be extended.

Some further notation is convenient: $P \Longrightarrow\xrightarrow{\alpha} P'$ means that $P \Longrightarrow P'' \xrightarrow{\alpha} P'$ for some P'' with $P'' \simeq P$ and moreover if $\alpha = \tau$ then $P' \not\simeq P$. We can now define partial confluence.

Definition 4. An agent R_0 is A-*confluent* if for each agent R reachable from it,

1. if $R \xrightarrow{\alpha} R_1$ and $R \Longrightarrow\xrightarrow{\alpha} R_2$ where $\alpha \in A^+$, then $R_1 \simeq R_2$,
2. if $R \xrightarrow{\alpha} R_1$ and $R \Longrightarrow\xrightarrow{\alpha'} R_2$ where $\alpha, \alpha' \in A^-$ and $\mathsf{subj}(\alpha) = \mathsf{subj}(\alpha')$, then $\alpha = \alpha'$ and $R_1 \simeq R_2$, and
3. if $\alpha \in A$, $\mathsf{subj}(\beta) \neq \mathsf{subj}(\alpha)$, $R \xrightarrow{\alpha} R_1$ and $R \Longrightarrow\xrightarrow{\beta} R_2$, then $R_2 \Longrightarrow\xrightarrow{\alpha} R_2'$ and $R_1 \Longrightarrow\xrightarrow{\beta} R_1'$ with $R_1' \simeq R_2'$.

It is required of an A-confluent agent that each agent reachable from it be $\simeq$-determinate under A-actions (clauses 1 and 2) and enjoy a confluence property with respect to A-actions and other actions (clause 3). The following definition is useful in recording which questions are outstanding in the question-answer dialogue between the B^{link}-system and its environment.

Definition 5. An agent R_0 which is A-confluent and Q-confluent is (Q^+, A^-)-*tidy* if there is a partition $\{\mathcal{R}^{\tilde{a}} \mid \tilde{a}$ a finite set of A-names$\}$ of its state space $\mathcal{R}$, a (Q^+, A^-)-*tidy partition*, such that:

1. if $R \in \mathcal{R}^{\tilde{a}}$ and $R \xrightarrow{\alpha} R'$ where $\alpha \notin Q^+ \cup A^-$ then $R' \in \mathcal{R}^{\tilde{a}}$,
2. if $R \in \mathcal{R}^{\tilde{a}}$ and $R \xrightarrow{\alpha} R'$ where $\alpha = q\langle v, a\rangle \in Q^+$ with a a fresh name then $R' \in \mathcal{R}^{\tilde{a},a}$,

3. if $R \in \mathcal{R}^{\tilde{a}}$ and $R \xrightarrow{\alpha} R'$ where $\alpha \in A^-$ then $\alpha = \overline{a}\langle v \rangle$ for some $a \in \tilde{a}$ and $R' \in \mathcal{R}^{\tilde{a}-a}$.

It is straightforward to show that B_0 and P_0 have this property: their state spaces $\mathcal{B}$ and $\mathcal{P}$ are partitioned according to the A-names occurring in the agents in them. The notion (Q^-, A^+)-*tidy* is defined in a dual way.

The following definition isolates some further properties enjoyed by B_0 and P_0, though in the case of P_0 it is not obvious that this is so.

Definition 6. An agent R_0 is a (Q^+, A^-)-*server* if there is a (Q^+, A^-)-tidy partition $\{\mathcal{R}^{\tilde{a}}\}_{\tilde{a}}$ of its state space $\mathcal{R}$ such that:

1. if $R \in \mathcal{R}^a$ (where a is a singleton) then $R \Longrightarrow\xrightarrow{\alpha}$ or $R \Longrightarrow\xrightarrow{\tau} R' \Longrightarrow\xrightarrow{\alpha}$ for some $\alpha = \overline{a}\langle v \rangle$,
2. if $R \Longrightarrow\xrightarrow{\tau} R'$ then there exists $\alpha \in A^-$ such that $R' \Longrightarrow\xrightarrow{\alpha}$ but not $(R \Longrightarrow\xrightarrow{\alpha'})$ for any α' with $\mathsf{subj}(\alpha') = \mathsf{subj}(\alpha)$,
3. if not $(R \Longrightarrow\xrightarrow{\alpha})$, $R \Longrightarrow\xrightarrow{\tau} R_1 \Longrightarrow\xrightarrow{\alpha}$ and $R \Longrightarrow\xrightarrow{\tau} R_2 \Longrightarrow\xrightarrow{\alpha'}$ where $\alpha, \alpha' \in A^-$ with $\mathsf{subj}(\alpha') = \mathsf{subj}(\alpha)$, then $R_1 \simeq R_2$,
4. if $R \Longrightarrow\xrightarrow{\alpha} R_1 \Longrightarrow\xrightarrow{\beta} R_2$ where either $\alpha \notin Q \cup \{\tau\}$ or $\beta \notin A \cup \{\tau\}$, then $R \Longrightarrow\xrightarrow{\beta} R_1' \Longrightarrow\xrightarrow{\alpha} R_2'$ with $R_2 \simeq R_2'$.

To grasp the motivation for this definition think of R_0 as B_0 above. The clauses concern the occurrence of decisive τ-actions, those which represent the significant moment in an insertion or a search, and commutation of actions The first expresses that an answer to an outstanding question is already available or may become available after a single decisive τ-action. The second captures that each decisive τ-action results in a new answer becoming available. The third says that the determination of an answer results in a uniquely-determined state. The last says that certain pairs of actions commute up to $\simeq$.

For an agent R_0 with state space $\mathcal{R}$ of this kind, let $\underset{\sim}{\mathcal{R}}^\flat$ be the transition system obtained from $\mathcal{R}$ by deleting all points not in an $\mathcal{R}^{\tilde{a}}$ with $|\,\tilde{a}\,| \leq 1$ (i.e. all points in which there is more than one outstanding question) and all arrows incident on such points. Let $R^\flat$ be the point in $\mathcal{R}^\flat$ corresponding to R in $\mathcal{R}$ (if it exists). In order to understand the behaviour of R_0 in certain contexts, it suffices to examine the behaviour of $R_0^\flat$. The contexts are those which satisfy the following complementary property.

Definition 7. An agent E_0 is a (Q^-, A^+)-*client* if there is a (Q^-, A^+)-tidy partition $\{\mathcal{E}^{\tilde{a}}\}_{\tilde{a}}$ of its state space $\mathcal{E}$ such that:

1. if $E \in \mathcal{E}^{\tilde{a}}$ and $\alpha = a\langle v \rangle$ where $a \in \tilde{a}$ then $E \xrightarrow{\alpha}$,
2. if $E \Longrightarrow\xrightarrow{\alpha} E_1 \Longrightarrow\xrightarrow{\beta} E_2$ where either $\alpha \notin Q \cup \{\tau\}$ or $\beta \notin A \cup \{\tau\}$, then $E \Longrightarrow\xrightarrow{\beta} E_1' \Longrightarrow\xrightarrow{\alpha} E_2'$ with $E_2 \simeq E_2'$.

The first condition requires that E be able immediately to accept an answer to an outstanding question. The second concerns commutation up to $\simeq$ of certain pairs of actions.

The main result about partial confluence is the following.

Theorem 8. Suppose R_0 is a (Q^+, A^-)-server, E is a (Q^-, A^+)-client and $\tilde{z}$ contains all Q-names and A-names. Then $(\nu\tilde{z})(E \mid R_0) \simeq (\nu\tilde{z})(E \mid R_0^\flat)$.

That is, in a client context, a server agent is indistinguishable from the truncation of it in which at most one operation may be active at any time. The proof of this theorem is difficult and is omitted.

Outline of proof of Theorem 4.2 The proof involves establishing:

1. B_0 is a (Q^+, A^-)-server,
2. P_0 is a (Q^+, A^-)-server,
3. $P_0^\flat \simeq B_0^\flat$.

Then, from 2 and 1 by Theorem 4.7 we have that for any (Q^-, A^+)-client context of the form $C[\cdot] \equiv (\nu\tilde{z})(E \mid \cdot)$, $C[P_0] \simeq C[P_0^\flat]$ and $C[B_0^\flat] \simeq C[B_0]$. Moreover, by 3 it follows, since $\simeq$ is preserved by the operators in question, that $C[P_0^\flat] \simeq C[B_0^\flat]$. Hence we have

$$C[P_0] \simeq C[P_0^\flat] \simeq C[B_0^\flat] \simeq C[B_0]\,.$$

By constructing an appropriate E it can be shown that $C[P_0] \simeq C[B_0]$ implies $P_0 \simeq_{\mathsf{A}} B_0$.

The proof of 1 is straightforward. In very broad outline the proofs of 2 and 3 are based on showing that certain invariants hold of P_0. Among these are that any search or insertion which has been begun but has not yet been completed *can* be completed. Moreover there are indeed 'decisive' τ-actions as highlighted in the abstract description B on whose occurrence the state changes. It is in carrying out this analysis that the simplification that at most one inserting or searching process may access a node of the tree at any time is helpful. This completes the outline of the proof of Theorem 4.2.

In order to prove the stronger Theorem 4.1 it is necessary to generalize the theory. The definitions of 'A-confluence', '(Q^+, A^-)-server' and '(Q^-, A^+)-client' must be modified to take into account the relaxation of the requirement on A-names, and the theory reworked accordingly. This can be done and the analogue of Theorem 4.7 proved. The argument is then completed on the lines just outlined.

5 Concluding remarks

As mentioned earlier, the analysis of the system in which each node allows at most one operation at a time may be used to deduce the correctness of the full system in which many searches may proceed concurrently in a node. Let NODE', LEAF' and ROOT' be process-calculus agents representing nodes that allow multiple reads and a single write to take place simultaneously. Let

$$T_0' \stackrel{\text{def}}{=} (get\ que)\,(\nu p, q, put)(\mathsf{STORE}\langle\langle p\rangle, get, put, que\rangle \\ \mid \mathsf{ROOT}'\langle p, \langle -\infty, \infty\rangle, \langle q, \text{nil}\rangle, put\rangle \\ \mid \mathsf{LEAF}'\langle q, \varepsilon, \varepsilon\rangle)\,.$$

It is fairly straightforward to show that $T_0'^{\flat} \simeq T_0^{\flat}$ where $T_0'^{\flat}$ represents the truncation of the full system in which at most one operation may be active in the tree at any time. Hence $(\nu\tilde{z})(S \mid I \mid T_0'^{\flat}) \simeq (\nu\tilde{z})(S \mid I \mid T_0^{\flat})$. Further, for the appropriate sorts P and R it can be shown that T_0' and T_0 are (P^+, R^-)-tidy and $S \mid I$ is (P^-, R^+)-tidy. Moreover, T_0', T_0 and $S \mid I$ enjoy further properties studied in connection with partial confluence in [10, 16]. Using that theory it may be shown that $(\nu\tilde{z})(S \mid I \mid T_0') \simeq (\nu\tilde{z})(S \mid I \mid T_0'^{\flat})$ and similarly for T_0. Hence $(\nu\tilde{z})(S \mid I \mid T_0') \simeq (\nu\tilde{z})(S \mid I \mid T_0)$ as required.

We have also studied the deletion and compression operations in [17] and in doing so discovered an improvement to the latter. Due to lack of space we can only give the briefest outline of this here. First we note that the definitions of NODE, LEAF and ROOT must be changed to accommodate the additional operations. In particular, the process-calculus representation of a pointer to a node becomes a value of the record type $\{ins : \mathsf{P}^I, srch : \mathsf{P}^S, del : \mathsf{P}^D, com : \mathsf{P}^C\}$ so that if p is a node name, $p : del$ and $p : com$ are names of sorts P^D and P^C via which deletions and compressions may be initiated. The deletion algorithm involves locating the leaf where the key to be deleted is and then removing it and the pointer associated with it. Thus execution of a deletion is somewhat similar to that of an insertion where no splitting occurs. The agent $D \equiv D\langle d, get\rangle$ is defined as follows:

$$\begin{aligned} D &\stackrel{\text{def}}{=} !\,d(k,a).\,get(q).\,Delete\langle q, k, a, \varepsilon\rangle \\ Delete &\stackrel{\text{def}}{=} (q\,k\,a\,\tilde{p})\,(\nu r)\overline{q : srch}\langle k, r\rangle.\,(r(q').\,Delete\langle q', k, a, q\,\tilde{p}\rangle \\ &\qquad\qquad + r(done, b).\,Del\langle q, k, a, \tilde{p}\rangle \\ &\qquad\qquad + r(link, q').\,Delete\langle q', k, a, \tilde{p}\rangle) \\ Del &\stackrel{\text{def}}{=} (q\,k\,a\,\tilde{p})\,(\nu r)\overline{q : del}\langle k, r\rangle. \\ &\qquad (r(q').\,Del\langle q', k, a, \tilde{p}\rangle \ +\ r.\,\overline{a}.\,\mathbf{0} +\ r(empty, k').\,\overline{a}.\,\overline{c}\langle q, k', \tilde{p}\rangle.\,\mathbf{0})\,. \end{aligned}$$

The agent D may repeatedly generate deletion processes when supplied via name d with a key k to be deleted and a name a via which to signal completion of the deletion. *Delete* follows a path through the tree, recording the rightmost node visited at each level. When the appropriate leaf is found, it requests deletion of the appropriate key using the selector *del*. If the deletion results in the leaf becoming less than half full, the deletion process is informed of this by the appropriate LEAF agent sending it the value *empty* and a key. In that case, via the name c a compression process is activated to redistribute the leaf's data or delete it if it has become empty; this may lead to activation of other compression processes. When the compression agent $C \equiv C\langle c\rangle$ below is supplied with the pointer to the half-empty node, one of its keys, and the path recorded by the deletion process, it activates a compressor:

$$C \stackrel{\text{def}}{=} !\,c(q, k, \tilde{p}).\,Compress\langle q, k, \tilde{p}\rangle\,.$$

Although sharing properties with the *Up* phase of the insertion operation, *Compress* has a much more complicated and subtle behaviour. This can be expressed precisely and succinctly (but not here) in the process calculus.

Let C_0 be the system composed from a tree in its initial state and the operations S, I, D and C. The correctness of the algorithms may then be expressed by comparison with an agent B^+ which gives a succinct description of the intended observable behaviour of the system. B^+ is similar to agent B in the previous section and it takes the following additional parameters: the name d via which deletions may be initiated; a set δ (the *deletions*) of pairs consisting of a key k to be deleted and a name a via which the completion of the deletion may be signalled; and a set δ^c (the *completed deletions*) of names a whose keys have been deleted but which have not been used to signal this. We define $B^+ \equiv B^+\langle i, s, d, f, \iota, \iota^c, \sigma, \sigma^c, \delta, \delta^c\rangle$ as follows:

$$
\begin{aligned}
B^+ \stackrel{\text{def}}{=}\ & i(k,b,a).\, B^+\langle \ldots, \iota \cup \{\langle k,b,a\rangle\}, \ldots\rangle \\
& + s(k,a).\, B^+\langle \ldots, \sigma \cup \{\langle k,a\rangle\}, \ldots\rangle \\
& + d(k,a).\, B^+\langle \ldots, \delta \cup \{\langle k,a\rangle\}, \ldots\rangle \\
& + \Sigma_{\langle k,b,a\rangle \in \iota}\ \tau.\, B^+\langle \ldots, f[b/k], \iota - \{\langle k,p,a\rangle\},\ \iota^c \cup \{a\}, \ldots\rangle \\
& + \Sigma_{\langle k,a\rangle \in \sigma}\ \tau.\, B^+\langle \ldots, \sigma - \{\langle k,a\rangle\},\ \sigma^c \cup \{\langle a, f(k)\rangle\}, \ldots\rangle \\
& + \Sigma_{\langle k,a\rangle \in \delta}\ \tau.\, B^+\langle \ldots, f[\mathrm{nil}/k], \ldots, \delta - \{\langle k,a\rangle\},\ \delta^c \cup \{\langle a\rangle\}\rangle \\
& + \Sigma_{a \in \iota^c}\ \overline{a}.\, B^+\langle \ldots, \iota^c - \{\langle a\rangle\}, \ldots\rangle \\
& + \Sigma_{\langle a,b\rangle \in \sigma^c}\ \overline{a}\langle b\rangle.\, B^+\langle \ldots, \sigma^c - \{\langle a,b\rangle\}, \ldots\rangle \\
& + \Sigma_{a \in \delta^c}\ \overline{a}.\, B^+\langle \ldots, \delta^c - \{\langle a\rangle\}\rangle\,.
\end{aligned}
$$

Let $B_0^+ \equiv B^+\langle i, s, d, \lambda k.\,\mathrm{nil}, \varepsilon, \varepsilon, \varepsilon, \varepsilon, \varepsilon, \varepsilon\rangle$. The result asserting the correctness of the operations is the following:

Theorem 9. $C_0 \simeq B_0^+$.

To prove this theorem we extend the proof of the corresponding result for the insertion and search algorithms. The main additions are proofs that the deletion algorithm does indeed perform a single 'decisive' τ-action as highlighted in the abstract description B^+, and that the compression algorithm does not alter the state of the system up to branching bisimilarity.

We believe the partial-confluence theory presented in this paper should be useful in understanding and reasoning about a variety of systems. Further development of the theory and study of its applicability, in particular to database concurrency-control systems, seems worthwhile. Specifically, one might examine whether the requirements on (Q^-, A^+)-clients and (Q^+, A^-)-servers can be relaxed to allow analysis of, for instance, sequential consistency [1, 4, 7] where systems may perform several decisive silent actions before returning an answer.

References

1. Y. Afek, G. Brown, and M. Merritt. Lazy caching. *ACM Transactions on Programming Languages and Systems*, 15(1):182–205, 1993.

2. R. Bayer and E. McCreight. Organisation and maintenance of large ordered indexes. *Acta Informatica*, 1:173–189, 1972.
3. R. Bayer and M. Schkolnick. Concurrency of operations on B-trees. *Acta Informatica*, 9:1–21, 1977.
4. E. Brinksma. Cache consistency by design. *Distributed Computing*, to appear.
5. C. Ellis. Concurrency in linear hashing. *ACM Transactions on Database Systems*, 12:195–217, 1987.
6. R.van Glabbeek and P. Weijland. Branching time and abstraction in bisimulation semantics. In *Information Processing '89*, pages 613–618, 1989.
7. W. Janssen, M. Poel, and J. Zwiers. The compositional approach to sequential consistency and lazy caching. Technical report, Universiteit Twente, 1994.
8. Y. S. Kwong and D. Wood. A new method for concurrency in B-trees. *IEEE Transactions on Software Engineering*, SE-8:211–222, 1982.
9. P. Lehman and S. B. Yao. Efficient locking for concurrent operations on B-trees. *ACM Transactions on Database Systems*, 6:650–670, 1981.
10. X. Liu and D. Walker. Confluence of processes and systems of objects. In *Proceedings of TAPSOFT'95*, pages 217–231. Springer, 1995.
11. N. Lynch, M. Merritt, W. Weihl, and A. Fekete. *Atomic Transactions*. Morgan Kaufmann, 1994.
12. R. Miller and L. Snyder. Multiple access to B-trees. In *Information Science and Systems, Baltimore*, 1978.
13. R. Milner. *Communication and Concurrency*. Prentice-Hall, 1989.
14. R. Milner, J. Parrow, and D. Walker. A calculus of mobile processes, parts 1 and 2. *Information and Computation*, 100:1–77, 1992.
15. A. Philippou. *Reasoning about systems with evolving structure*. PhD thesis, University of Warwick, 1996.
16. A. Philippou and D. Walker. On transformations of concurrent object programs. In *Proceedings of CONCUR'96*, pages 131–146. Springer, 1996.
17. Y. Sagiv. Concurrent operations on B^*-trees with overtaking. *Journal of Computer and System Sciences*, 33:275–296, 1986.
18. B. Samadi. B-trees in a system with multiple users. *Information Processing Letters*, 5:107–112, 1976.
19. C. Tofts. *Proof methods and pragmatics for parallel programming*. PhD thesis, University of Edinburgh, 1990.
20. F. Vaandrager. On the relationship between process algebra and input/output automata. In *Proceedings of LICS'91*, pages 387–398. Springer, 1991.
21. D. Walker. Algebraic proofs of properties of objects. In *Proceedings of ESOP'94*, pages 501–516. Springer, 1994.
22. H. Wedekind. On the selection of access paths in a data base system. In *Data base managememt*, pages 385–397. North-Holland, 1974.

First-Order Axioms for Asynchrony

Peter Selinger*
Department of Mathematics
University of Pennsylvania
Philadelphia, PA 19104-6395

Abstract. We study properties of asynchronous communication independently of any concrete concurrent process paradigm. We give a general-purpose, mathematically rigorous definition of several notions of asynchrony in a natural setting where an agent is asynchronous if its input and/or output is filtered through a buffer or a queue, possibly with feedback. In a series of theorems, we give necessary and sufficient conditions for each of these notions in the form of simple first-order or second-order axioms. We illustrate the formalism by applying it to asynchronous CCS and the core join calculus.

Introduction

The distinction between *synchronous* and *asynchronous* communication is a relevant issue in the design and analysis of distributed and concurrent networks. Intuitively, communication is said to be synchronous if messages are sent and received simultaneously, via a 'handshake' or 'rendez-vous' of sender and receiver. It is asynchronous if messages travel through a communication medium with possible delay, such that the sender cannot be certain if or when a message has been received.

Asynchronous communication is often studied in the framework of concurrent process paradigms such as the asynchronous π-calculus, which was originally introduced by Honda and Tokoro [9], and was independently discovered by Boudol [6] as a result of his work with Berry on chemical abstract machines [5]. Another such asynchronous paradigm is the join calculus, which was recently proposed by Fournet and Gonthier as a calculus of mobile agents in distributed networks with locality and failure [7, 8].

In this paper, we study properties of asynchronous communication in general, not with regard to any particular process calculus. We give a general-purpose, mathematically rigorous definition of asynchrony, and we then show that this notion can be axiomatized. We model processes by labeled transition systems with input and output, a framework that is sufficiently general to fit concurrent process paradigms such as the π-calculus or the join calculus, as well as data flow models and other such formalisms. These transition systems are similar to Lynch and Stark's input/output automata [10], but our treatment is more category-theoretical and close in spirit to Abramsky's interaction categories [1, 2].

Various properties of asynchrony have been exploited in different contexts by many authors. For instance, Lynch and Stark [10] postulate a form of *input receptivity* for

*This research was supported by an Alfred P. Sloan Doctoral Dissertation Fellowship.

their automata. Palamidessi [13] makes use of a certain *confluence* property to prove that the expressive power of the asynchronous π-calculus is strictly less than that of the synchronous π-calculus. Axioms similar to ours have been postulated by [4] and by [14] for a notion of asynchronous labeled transition systems, but without the input/output distinction which is central to the our approach.

The main novelty of this paper is that our axioms are not postulated *a priori*, but derived from more primitive notions. We define asynchrony in elementary terms: an agent is asynchronous if its input and/or output is filtered through a communication medium, such as a buffer or a queue, possibly with feedback. We then show that our first- and second-order axioms precisely capture each of these notions. This characterization justifies the axioms *a posteriori*. As a testbed and for illustration, we apply these axioms to an asynchronous version of Milner's CCS, and to the core join calculus.

Due to limitations of space, most proofs are omitted in this abbreviated version of the paper. Only the proof of Theorem 2.1 is included as a typical example of the type of reasoning that is employed here. A full version of the paper is available from the author and will also appear as part of his Ph.D. Thesis.

Acknowledgments. I would like to thank Catuscia Palamidessi, Davide Sangiorgi, Benjamin Pierce, Dale Miller, Steve Brookes, Ian Stark, and Glynn Winskel for discussions and helpful comments on this work.

1 An Elementary Definition of Asynchrony

If R is a binary relation, we write R^{-1} for the inverse relation and R^* for the reflexive, transitive closure of R. We also write $\leftarrow$ for $\rightarrow^{-1}$, etc. The binary identity relation on a set is denoted Δ. The composition of two binary relations R and Q is written $R \circ Q$ or simply RQ, *i.e.* $xRQz$ if there exists y such that $xRyQz$. The disjoint union of two sets X and Y is denoted by $X + Y$.

1.1 Labeled Transition Systems and Bisimulation

To keep this paper self-contained, we summarize the standard definitions for labeled transition systems and weak and strong bisimulation.

Definition. A ***labeled transition system (LTS)*** is a tuple $\mathbf{S} = \langle S, A, \rightarrow_{\mathbf{S}}, s_0 \rangle$, where S is a set of ***states***, A is a set of ***actions***, $\rightarrow_{\mathbf{S}} \subseteq S \times A \times S$ is a ***transition relation*** and $s_0 \in S$ is an ***initial state***. We call A the ***type*** of $\mathbf{S}$, and we write $\mathbf{S}\colon A$.

We often omit the subscript on $\rightarrow_{\mathbf{S}}$, and we write $|\mathbf{S}|$ for the set of states S. For $\alpha \in A$, we regard $\xrightarrow{\alpha}$ as a binary relation on $|\mathbf{S}|$ via $s \xrightarrow{\alpha} s'$ iff $\langle s, \alpha, s' \rangle \in \rightarrow$.

Definition. Let $\mathbf{S}$ and $\mathbf{T}$ be LTSs of type A. A binary relation $R \subseteq |\mathbf{S}| \times |\mathbf{T}|$ is a ***strong bisimulation*** if for all $\alpha \in A$, $R\xrightarrow{\alpha} \subseteq \xrightarrow{\alpha}R$ and $R^{-1}\xrightarrow{\alpha} \subseteq \xrightarrow{\alpha}R^{-1}$. In diagrams:

$$\begin{array}{ccc} s\,R\,t & & \\ \downarrow^{\alpha} & & \\ t' & & \end{array} \Rightarrow \exists s'.\ \begin{array}{ccc} s & R & t \\ {}_{\alpha}\downarrow & & \downarrow^{\alpha} \\ s' & R & t' \end{array} \quad \text{and} \quad \begin{array}{c} s\,R\,t \\ {}_{\alpha}\downarrow \\ s' \end{array} \Rightarrow \exists t'.\ \begin{array}{ccc} s & R & t \\ {}_{\alpha}\downarrow & & \downarrow^{\alpha} \\ s' & R & t' \end{array}$$

Next, we consider LTSs with a distinguished action $\tau \in A$, called the ***silent*** or the ***unobservable*** action. Let $\stackrel{\tau}{\Rightarrow}$ be the relation $\stackrel{\tau}{\rightarrow}^*$. For $a \in A \setminus \tau$, let $\stackrel{a}{\Rightarrow}$ be the relation $\stackrel{\tau}{\rightarrow}^*\stackrel{a}{\rightarrow}\stackrel{\tau}{\rightarrow}^*$. A binary relation $R \subseteq |\mathbf{S}| \times |\mathbf{T}|$ is a ***weak bisimulation*** if for all $\alpha \in A$, $R\stackrel{\alpha}{\rightarrow} \subseteq \stackrel{\alpha}{\Rightarrow}R$ and $R^{-1}\stackrel{\alpha}{\rightarrow} \subseteq \stackrel{\alpha}{\Rightarrow}R^{-1}$. In diagrams:

$$\begin{array}{ccc} s\ R\ t & & s\ R\ t \\ \downarrow\alpha & \Rightarrow \exists s'.\ \alpha\Downarrow & \downarrow\alpha \\ t' & & s'\ R\ t' \end{array} \qquad \text{and} \qquad \begin{array}{ccc} s\ R\ t & & s\ R\ t \\ \alpha\downarrow & \Rightarrow \exists t'.\ \alpha\downarrow & \Downarrow\alpha \\ s' & & s'\ R\ t' \end{array}$$

It is well-known that there is a maximal strong bisimulation, which we denote by $\sim$, and a maximal weak bisimulation, which we denote by $\approx$. We say that $s \in |\mathbf{S}|$ and $t \in |\mathbf{T}|$ are ***strongly (weakly) bisimilar*** if $s \sim t$ ($s \approx t$). Finally, $\mathbf{S}$ and $\mathbf{T}$ are said to be strongly (weakly) bisimilar if $s_0 \sim t_0$ ($s_0 \approx t_0$).

The relations $\sim$ and $\approx$, as binary relations on an LTS $\mathbf{S}$, are equivalence relations. We denote the respective equivalence classes of a state s by $[s]_\sim$ and $[s]_\approx$. On the quotient $\mathbf{S}/\!\sim$, we define transitions $[s]_\sim \stackrel{a}{\rightarrow} [t]_\sim$ iff $s \stackrel{a}{\rightarrow}\sim t$, making it into a well-defined transition system. Similarly, on $\mathbf{S}/\!\approx$, we define $[s]_\approx \stackrel{a}{\rightarrow} [t]_\approx$ iff $s \stackrel{a}{\rightarrow}\approx t$. For all $s \in \mathbf{S}$, one has $s \sim [s]_\sim$ and $s \approx [s]_\approx$, and hence $\mathbf{S} \sim (\mathbf{S}/\!\sim)$ and $\mathbf{S} \approx (\mathbf{S}/\!\approx)$. We say that $\mathbf{S}$ is ***$\sim$-reduced*** if $\mathbf{S} = \mathbf{S}/\!\sim$, and ***$\approx$-reduced*** if $\mathbf{S} = \mathbf{S}/\!\approx$.

1.2 Input, Output and Sequential Composition

So far we have distinguished only one action: the silent action τ. We will now add further structure to the set of actions by distinguishing input and output actions. Let *in* and *out* be constants. For any sets X and Y, define a set of ***input actions*** $\mathit{In}\,X := \{\mathit{in}\} \times X$, and a set of ***output actions*** $\mathit{Out}\,Y := \{\mathit{out}\} \times Y$. Note that $\mathit{In}\,X$ and $\mathit{Out}\,Y$ are disjoint. We will write input and output actions as $\mathit{in}\,x$ and $\mathit{out}\,x$ instead of $\langle \mathit{in}, x\rangle$ and $\langle \mathit{out}, x\rangle$, respectively. Let B be a set whose elements are not of the form $\mathit{in}\,x$, $\mathit{out}\,y$ or τ. The elements of $\mathrm{B} + \{\tau\}$ are called ***internal actions***.

Definition. We define $X \rightarrow_B Y$ to be the set $\mathit{In}\,X + \mathit{Out}\,Y + B + \{\tau\}$. A labeled transition system $\mathbf{S}$ of type $X \rightarrow_B Y$ is called an ***LTS with input and output***, or simply an ***agent***. If B is empty, we will omit the subscript in $X \rightarrow_B Y$.

Our labeled transition systems with input and output are similar to the input/output automata of Lynch and Stark [10]. However, we consider a notion of sequential composition that is more in the spirit of Abramsky's interaction categories [1, 2]. Given two agents $\mathbf{S}\colon X \rightarrow_B Y$ and $\mathbf{T}\colon Y \rightarrow_B Z$, we define $\mathbf{S};\mathbf{T}\colon X \rightarrow_B Z$ by feeding the output of $\mathbf{S}$ into the input of $\mathbf{T}$. This is a special case of parallel composition and hiding. Notice that this notion of sequential composition is different from the one of CSP or ACP, where $\mathbf{T}$ cannot start execution until $\mathbf{S}$ is finished.

Definition 1.1. Let $\mathbf{S}\colon X \rightarrow_B Y$ and $\mathbf{T}\colon Y \rightarrow_B Z$ be agents with respective initial states s_0 and t_0. The ***sequential composition*** $\mathbf{S};\mathbf{T}$ is of type $X \rightarrow_B Z$. It has states $|\mathbf{S}| \times |\mathbf{T}|$ and initial state $\langle s_0, t_0\rangle$. The transitions are given by the following rules:

$$\frac{s \stackrel{\alpha}{\rightarrow}_{\mathbf{S}} s' \quad \alpha \text{ not output}}{\langle s,t\rangle \stackrel{\alpha}{\rightarrow}_{\mathbf{S};\mathbf{T}} \langle s',t\rangle} \qquad \frac{t \stackrel{\alpha}{\rightarrow}_{\mathbf{T}} t' \quad \alpha \text{ not input}}{\langle s,t\rangle \stackrel{\alpha}{\rightarrow}_{\mathbf{S};\mathbf{T}} \langle s,t'\rangle} \qquad \frac{s \stackrel{\mathit{out}\,y}{\longrightarrow}_{\mathbf{S}} s' \quad t \stackrel{\mathit{in}\,y}{\longrightarrow}_{\mathbf{T}} t'}{\langle s,t\rangle \stackrel{\tau}{\rightarrow}_{\mathbf{S};\mathbf{T}} \langle s',t'\rangle}$$

Example 1.2. For any set X, define an agent $\mathcal{I}_X$ of type $X \rightarrow X$ with states $X + \{\bot\}$, initial state $\bot$ and transitions $\bot \xrightarrow{in\ x} x$ and $x \xrightarrow{out\ x} \bot$, for all $x \in X$. $\mathcal{I}_X$ acts as a buffer of capacity one: A possible sequence of transitions is

$$\bot \xrightarrow{in\ x} x \xrightarrow{out\ x} \bot \xrightarrow{in\ y} y \xrightarrow{out\ y} \bot \xrightarrow{in\ z} z \xrightarrow{out\ z} \bot \ldots$$

Let $X = \{x\}$. Then $\mathcal{I}_X$ and $\mathcal{I}_X;\mathcal{I}_X$ are the following agents:

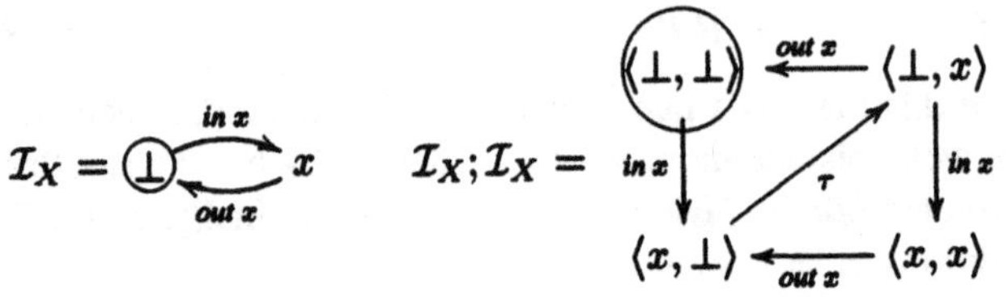

Here the initial state of each agent is circled. When representing agents in diagrams like these, it is often convenient to omit the names of the states, and to identify weakly bisimilar states. With that convention, we write:

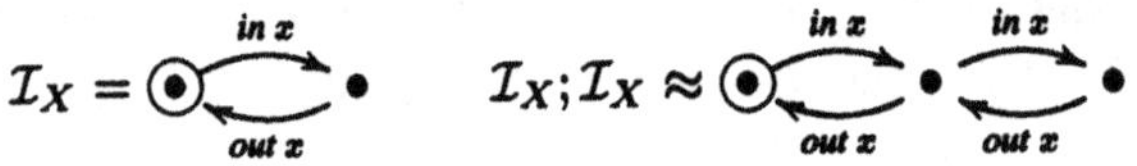

Note that $\mathcal{I}_X;\mathcal{I}_X$ is a queue of capacity 2. In general, for any set Y, $\mathcal{I}_Y;\mathcal{I}_Y$ is a first-in, first-out queue of capacity 2.

Two LTSs $\mathbf{S}$ and $\mathbf{T}$ of type A are ***isomorphic*** if there is a bijection between $|\mathbf{S}|$ and $|\mathbf{T}|$ preserving $\rightarrow$ and initial states.

Lemma 1.3. *1. Sequential Composition of labeled transition systems is associative up to isomorphism.*

2. Sequential Composition of agents respects both weak and strong bisimulation, i.e.

$$\frac{\mathbf{S}_1 \approx \mathbf{S}_2 \qquad \mathbf{T}_1 \approx \mathbf{T}_2}{\mathbf{S}_1;\mathbf{T}_1 \approx \mathbf{S}_2;\mathbf{T}_2} \quad \text{and} \quad \frac{\mathbf{S}_1 \sim \mathbf{S}_2 \qquad \mathbf{T}_1 \sim \mathbf{T}_2}{\mathbf{S}_1;\mathbf{T}_1 \sim \mathbf{S}_2;\mathbf{T}_2}$$

Unfortunately, agents do not form a category under sequential composition: there are no identity morphisms. In Section 1.4, we will introduce two categories of agents, one of which has unbounded buffers as its identity morphisms, and the other one queues.

1.3 Buffers and Queues

For any set X, let X^* be the free monoid and X^{**} the free commutative monoid generated by X. The elements of X^* are finite sequences. The empty sequence is denoted by ϵ. The elements of X^{**} are finite multisets. The empty multiset is denoted by $\emptyset$. We define the following agents of type $X \rightarrow_B X$:

1. The ***buffer*** $\mathcal{B}_X$ has states X^{**}, initial state $\emptyset$, and transitions $w \xrightarrow{in\ x} wx$ and $xw \xrightarrow{out\ x} w$, for all $w \in X^{**}$ and $x \in X$.

2. The ***queue*** $\mathcal{Q}_X$ has states X^*, initial state ϵ, and transitions $w \xrightarrow{in\,x} wx$ and $xw \xrightarrow{out\,x} w$, for all $w \in X^*$ and $x \in X$.

The only difference between the definitions of $\mathcal{B}_X$ and $\mathcal{Q}_X$ is whether the states are considered as sequences or multisets. We will write $\mathcal{B}$ and $\mathcal{Q}$ without subscript if X is clear from the context. $\mathcal{B}$ acts as an infinite capacity buffer which does not preserve the order of messages. For example, one possible sequence of transitions is

$$\emptyset \xrightarrow{in\,x} x \xrightarrow{in\,y} xy \xrightarrow{in\,z} xyz \xrightarrow{out\,y} xz \xrightarrow{out\,x} z \xrightarrow{in\,w} wz \ldots$$

$\mathcal{Q}$ acts as an infinite capacity first-in, first-out queue. A possible sequence of transitions is

$$\epsilon \xrightarrow{in\,x} x \xrightarrow{in\,y} xy \xrightarrow{out\,x} y \xrightarrow{in\,z} yz \xrightarrow{in\,w} yzw \xrightarrow{out\,y} zw \ldots$$

Lemma 1.4. *1. $\mathcal{B};\mathcal{B} \approx \mathcal{B}$ and $\mathcal{B};\mathcal{B} \not\sim \mathcal{B}$.*

2. $\mathcal{Q};\mathcal{Q} \approx \mathcal{Q}$ and $\mathcal{Q};\mathcal{Q} \not\sim \mathcal{Q}$.

3. $\mathcal{Q};\mathcal{B} \approx \mathcal{B}$ and $\mathcal{Q};\mathcal{B} \not\sim \mathcal{B}$.

4. If $|X| \geq 2$, then $\mathcal{B};\mathcal{Q} \not\approx \mathcal{B}$ and $\mathcal{B};\mathcal{Q} \not\approx \mathcal{Q}$.

The remainder of this paper is devoted to examining the effect of composing arbitrary agents with buffers and queues.

1.4 Notions of Asynchrony

In the asynchronous model of communication, messages are assumed to travel through a communication medium or *ether*. Sometimes, the medium is assumed to be first-in, first-out (a queue); sometimes, as in the asynchronous π-calculus, messages might be received in any order (a buffer).

Our approach is simple: we model the medium explicitly. An asynchronous agent is one whose output and/or input behaves as if filtered through either a buffer $\mathcal{B}$ or a queue $\mathcal{Q}$.

Definition 1.5. An agent $\mathbf{S}: X \rightarrow_B Y$ is

out-buffered	if	$\mathbf{S} \approx \mathbf{S};\mathcal{B}$	***out-queued***	if	$\mathbf{S} \approx \mathbf{S};\mathcal{Q}$
in-buffered	if	$\mathbf{S} \approx \mathcal{B};\mathbf{S}$	***in-queued***	if	$\mathbf{S} \approx \mathcal{Q};\mathbf{S}$
buffered	if	$\mathbf{S} \approx \mathcal{B};\mathbf{S};\mathcal{B}$	***queued***	if	$\mathbf{S} \approx \mathcal{Q};\mathbf{S};\mathcal{Q}$

We use the word ***asynchrony*** as a generic term to stand for any such property. Distinguishing these six different notions will allow us to study them separately. Yet another notion of asynchrony, incorporating feedback, will be defined in Section 3.2.

Remark. Because of Lemma 1.4, the operation of pre- or post-composing an agent with $\mathcal{B}$ or $\mathcal{Q}$ is idempotent up to $\approx$. Consequently, any agent of the form $\mathbf{S};\mathcal{B}$ is out-buffered, any agent of the form $\mathcal{B};\mathbf{S}$ is in-buffered, an agent is buffered iff it is in- and out-buffered, and so on. Also, each of the six properties is invariant under weak bisimulation.

Let B be a set. Buffered agents $\mathbf{S}\colon X \to_B Y$ form the morphisms of a category $\mathbf{Buf}_B$, whose objects are sets X, Y, etc.; the identity morphism on X is given by the buffer $\mathcal{B}_X$. Similarly, queued agents form a category $\mathbf{Que}_B$. These categories have a symmetric monoidal structure, which will be described in Section 3.1.

1.5 Examples

Example 1.6. The first example shows the effect of post-composing different agents with the buffer $\mathcal{B}$. Notice that although $\mathcal{B}$ has infinitely many states, $\mathbf{S}; \mathcal{B}$ may have only finitely many states up to weak bisimulation.

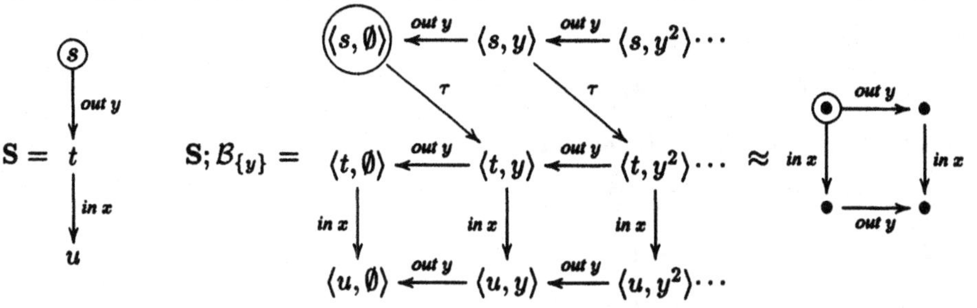

Example 1.7.

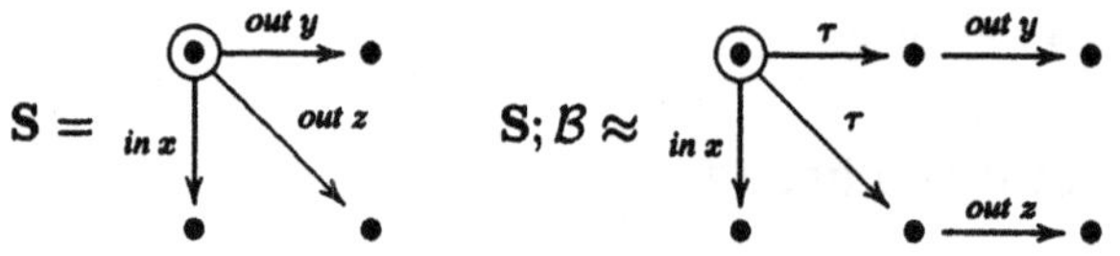

Example 1.8. Here is an example on in-bufferedness. Notice that an input action is possible at every state of $\mathcal{B}; \mathbf{S}$.

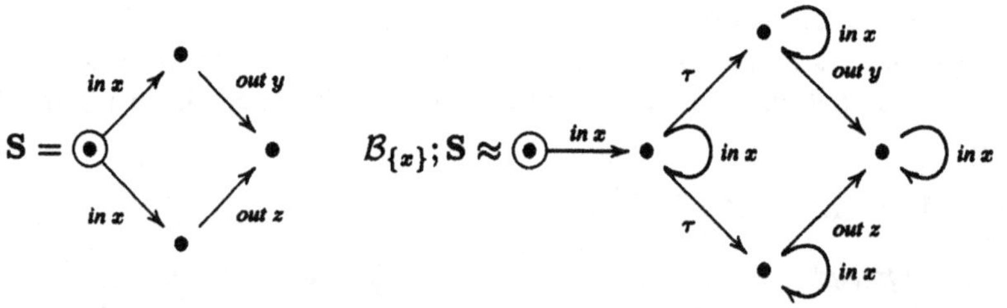

2 First-Order Axioms for Asynchrony

In this section, we will give necessary and sufficient conditions for each of the notions of asynchrony from Definition 1.5. These conditions take the form of *first-order axioms*, by which we mean axioms that use quantification only over states and actions, but not over subsets of states or actions. The axioms, which are shown in Tables 1 through 2, characterize each of our notions of asynchrony *up to weak bisimulation*; this means, an LTS is asynchronous iff it is weakly bisimilar to one satisfying the axioms. It is possible to lift the condition "up to weak bisimulation" at the cost of introducing second-order axioms; this is the subject of Section 6.

Table 1: First-order axioms for out-buffered agents

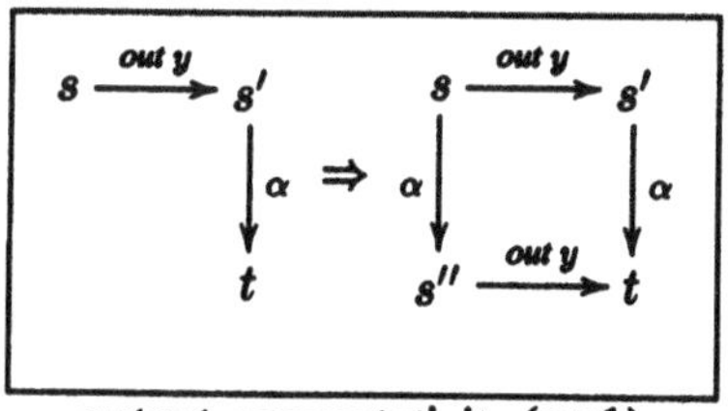

output-commutativity (OB1)

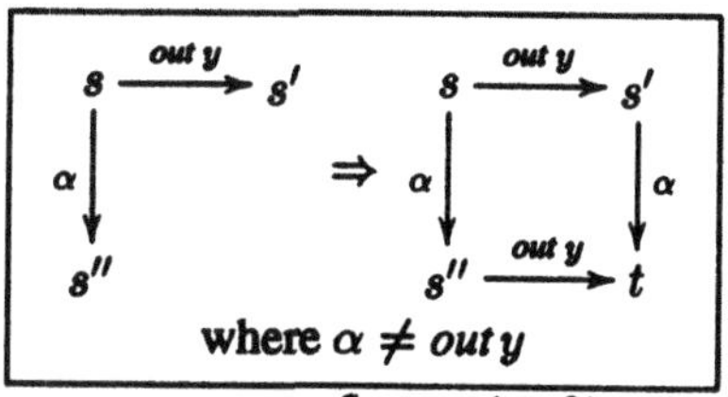

output-confluence (OB2)

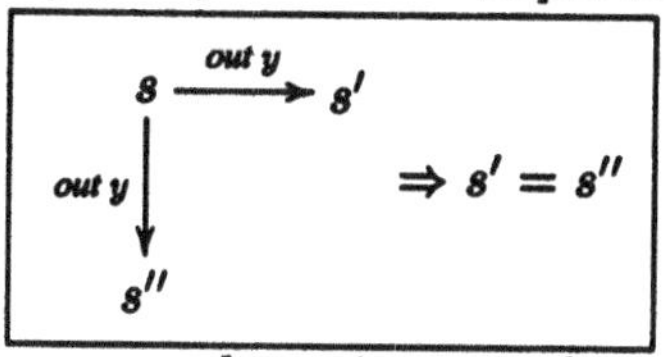

output-determinacy (OB3)

2.1 Out-Buffered Agents

Table 1 lists three axioms for out-buffered agents. We use the convention that variables are implicitly existentially quantified if they occur only on the right-hand-side of an implication, and all other variables are implicitly universally quantified. Thus the axioms are:

(OB1) *Output-commutativity*: output actions can always be delayed.

(OB2) *Output-confluence*: when an output action and some other action are possible, then they can be performed in either order with the same result. In particular, neither action precludes the other.

(OB3) *Output-determinacy*: from any state s, there is at most one transition $out\, y$ for each $y \in Y$.

Each of these axioms is plausible for the behavior of a buffer. Output-determinacy is maybe the least intuitive of the three properties; the idea is that once an output action is stored in a buffer, there is only one way of retrieving it. Together, these axioms characterize out-bufferedness up to weak bisimulation:

Theorem 2.1 (Characterization of out-buffered agents). *An agent* $\mathbf{S}$ *is out-buffered if and only if* $\mathbf{S} \approx \mathbf{T}$ *for some* $\mathbf{T}$ *satisfying* (OB1)–(OB3).

This is a direct consequence of the following proposition:

Proposition 2.2. *1. Every agent of the form* $\mathbf{S}; \mathcal{B}$ *satisfies* (OB1)–(OB3).

2. *If* $\mathbf{S}$ *satisfies* (OB1)–(OB3), *then* $\mathbf{S} \approx \mathbf{S}; \mathcal{B}$.

Proof. 1. Clearly, the buffer $\mathcal{B}$ satisfies (OB1)–(OB3). Moreover, these conditions are preserved by arbitrary sequential composition from the left.

Table 2: First-order axioms for in-buffered agents

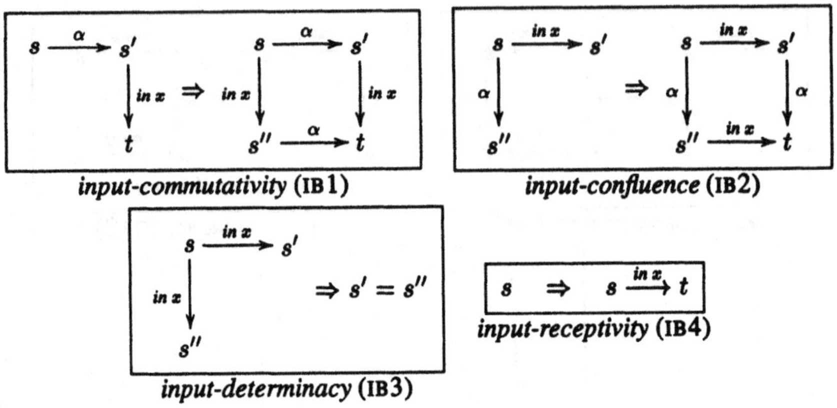
input-commutativity (IB1)
input-confluence (IB2)
input-determinacy (IB3)
input-receptivity (IB4)

2. Suppose $\mathbf{S}\colon X \to_B Y$ satisfies (OB1)–(OB3). For a sequence $w = y_1 y_2 \cdots y_n \in Y^*$, we write $s \xrightarrow{out\,w} t$ if $s \xrightarrow{out\,y_1}\xrightarrow{out\,y_2} \cdots \xrightarrow{out\,y_n} t$ $(n \geq 0)$. Note that if $w' \in Y^*$ is a permutation of w, then $s \xrightarrow{out\,w'} t$ iff $s \xrightarrow{out\,w} t$ by (OB1). Consider the relation $R \subseteq |\mathbf{S}| \times |\mathbf{S}; B|$ given by $sR\langle t, w\rangle$ iff $s \xrightarrow{out\,w} t$. Clearly, R relates initial states. We show that R is a weak bisimulation. In one direction, suppose

$$\begin{array}{l} s \; R \; \langle t, w\rangle \\ {\scriptstyle\alpha}\big\downarrow \\ s'. \end{array}$$

Two cases arise:

Case 1: $\alpha = out\,y$ for some $y \in w$. By the definition of R, $s \xrightarrow{out\,y} s'' \xrightarrow{out\,w'} t$, where $w = yw'$. By (OB3), we have $s' = s''$. Therefore $s'R\langle t, w'\rangle$, and also $\langle t, w\rangle \xrightarrow{\alpha} \langle t, w'\rangle$.✓

Case 2: $\alpha \neq out\,y$ for all $y \in w$. From $s \xrightarrow{out\,w} t$ and $s \xrightarrow{\alpha} s'$, we get $s' \xrightarrow{out\,w} t'$ and $t \xrightarrow{\alpha} t'$ by repeated application of (OB2). Therefore $s'R\langle t', w\rangle$ and $\langle t, w\rangle \overset{\alpha}{\Rightarrow} \langle t', w\rangle$ (notice the use of $\Rightarrow$ here, which is necessary in case α is an output action).✓

In the other direction, suppose

$$\begin{array}{c} s \; R \; \langle t, w\rangle \\ \big\downarrow{\scriptstyle\alpha} \\ \langle t', w'\rangle. \end{array}$$

We distinguish three cases for $\langle t, w\rangle \xrightarrow{\alpha} \langle t', w'\rangle$, depending on which rule in Definition 1.1 was used.

Case 1: $t \xrightarrow{\alpha} t'$, $w = w'$ and α not output. Then $s \xrightarrow{out\,w} t \xrightarrow{\alpha} t'$, which implies $s \xrightarrow{\alpha} s' \xrightarrow{out\,w} t'$ by repeated application of (OB1), *i.e.* $s \xrightarrow{\alpha} s'R\langle t', w\rangle$.✓

Case 2: $t = t'$, $w \xrightarrow{\alpha} w'$ and α not input. Since $\mathcal{B}$ has only input and output transitions, α must be $out\, y$ for some $y \in Y$ with $w = yw'$. Then $s \xrightarrow{out\, y} s' \xrightarrow{out\, w'} t$, *i.e.* $s \xrightarrow{\alpha} s' R\langle t, w'\rangle$.✓

Case 3: $t \xrightarrow{out\, y} t'$, $w \xrightarrow{in\, y} w'$ and $\alpha = \tau$. In this case, $w' = wy$ and $s \xrightarrow{out\, w} t \xrightarrow{out\, y} t'$, hence $sR\langle t', w'\rangle$.✓ □

Remark 2.3. Theorem 2.1 generalizes to other notions of equivalence of processes, as long as they are coarser than weak bisimulation. Indeed, if $\cong$ is an equivalence of processes such that $\approx\ \subseteq\ \cong$, then for any agent $\mathbf{S}$, there exists some out-buffered $\mathbf{T}$ with $\mathbf{S} \cong \mathbf{T}$ iff there exists $\mathbf{T}'$ satisfying (OB1)–(OB3) and $\mathbf{S} \cong \mathbf{T}'$. This is a trivial consequence of Theorem 2.1. Similar remarks apply to the other results in this section and in Section 3.

2.2 In-Buffered Agents and Queues

The axioms for in-buffered agents are listed in Table 2. The main difference to the out-buffered case is the property *input-receptivity*: an in-buffered agent can perform any input action at any time. This was illustrated in Example 1.8. The input/output automata of Lynch and Stark [10] have this property, and so does Honda and Tokoro's original version of the asynchronous π-calculus [9].

Remark. Somewhat surprisingly, the axioms in Table 2 are not independent. In fact, (IB1) and (IB2) are equivalent in the presence of (IB3) and (IB4). We present all four axioms in order to highlight the analogy to the output case.

Theorem 2.4 (Characterization of in-buffered agents). *An agent* $\mathbf{S}$ *is in-buffered if and only if* $\mathbf{S} \approx \mathbf{T}$ *for some* $\mathbf{T}$ *satisfying* (IB1)–(IB4).

The axioms can be adjusted to accommodate queues rather than buffers: In (OB1) and (OB2), change the side conditions to "α not output". Change (OB3) to "if $s \xrightarrow{out\, y} s'$ and $s \xrightarrow{out\, z} s''$ then $y = z$ and $s' = s''$". In (IB1) and (IB2), change the side conditions to "α not input". Then the analogs of Theorems 2.1 and 2.4 hold.

3 More Constructors and Asynchrony with Feedback

3.1 Agent Constructors

In this section, we will introduce some operations on agents, such as renaming and hiding of actions, parallel composition and feedback.

1. *Domain extension.* If $\mathbf{S}$ is an LTS of type A, and if $A \subseteq A'$, then $\mathbf{S}$ can also be regarded as an LTS of type A'.

2. *Domain restriction (hiding).* If $\mathbf{S}$ is an LTS of type A, and if $\tau \in A' \subseteq A$, then $\mathbf{S}|_{A'}$ is defined to be the LTS of type A' which has the same states as $\mathbf{S}$, and whose transitions are those of $\mathbf{S}$ restricted to $|\mathbf{S}| \times A' \times |\mathbf{S}|$.

Domain extension and domain restriction are special cases of the following, general renaming construct:

3. *General renaming and hiding.* Let $\mathbf{S}$ be an LTS of type A and let $r \subseteq A \times A'$ be a relation such that $\tau r \alpha'$ iff $\tau = \alpha'$. Define $\mathbf{S}_r$ to be the LTS of type A' that has the same states and initial state as $\mathbf{S}$ and transitions $s \xrightarrow{\alpha}_{\mathbf{S}_r} t$ iff $s \xrightarrow{\alpha'}_{\mathbf{S}} t$ for some $\alpha r \alpha'$.

Let us now turn to various forms of parallel composition.

4. *Parallel composition without interaction.* Let $\mathbf{S}$ and $\mathbf{T}$ be LTSs of type A. Then $\mathbf{S}\|\mathbf{T}$ is the LTS of type A with states $|\mathbf{S}| \times |\mathbf{T}|$ and initial state $\langle s_0, t_0 \rangle$, and whose transitions are given by the rules

$$\frac{s \xrightarrow{\alpha}_{\mathbf{S}} s'}{\langle s, t\rangle \xrightarrow{\alpha}_{\mathbf{S}\|\mathbf{T}} \langle s', t\rangle} \qquad \frac{t \xrightarrow{\alpha}_{\mathbf{T}} t'}{\langle s, t\rangle \xrightarrow{\alpha}_{\mathbf{S}\|\mathbf{T}} \langle s, t'\rangle}.$$

5. *Symmetric monoidal structure.* Let $X \oplus X'$ be the disjoint union of sets. For $\mathbf{S}\colon X \to_B Y$ and $\mathbf{T}\colon X' \to_B Y'$, define $\mathbf{S} \oplus \mathbf{T}\colon X \oplus X' \to_B Y \oplus Y'$ to be the agent $\mathbf{S}_r \| \mathbf{T}_q$, where r and q are the inclusions of $X \to_B Y$, respectively $X' \to_B Y'$ into $X \oplus X' \to_B Y \oplus Y'$. Then $\oplus$ defines a symmetric monoidal structure on the categories **Buf** and **Que**. The tensor unit is given by the agent $\mathbf{I}$ of type $\emptyset \to \emptyset$ with one state and no transitions.

The constructors we have considered so far, including sequential composition, are not sufficient to build arbitrary networks. What is missing is the ability to construct loops. The next constructor allows the output of an agent to be connected to its own input:

6. *Self-composition (feedback).* Let $\mathbf{S}\colon X \to_B Y$. Let $O \subseteq Y \times X$ be a set of pairs. Define $\mathbf{S} \circlearrowleft O$, the self-composition of $\mathbf{S}$ along O, to be the LTS of type $X \to_B Y$ whose states are identical with those of $\mathbf{S}$, and whose transitions are given by the rules

$$\frac{s \xrightarrow{\alpha}_{\mathbf{S}} t}{s \xrightarrow{\alpha}_{\mathbf{S} \circlearrowleft O} t} \qquad \frac{s \xrightarrow{out\, y} \overset{\tau}{\Rightarrow} \xrightarrow{in\, x}_{\mathbf{S}} t \qquad \langle y, x\rangle \in O}{s \xrightarrow{\tau}_{\mathbf{S} \circlearrowleft O} t}.$$

In the common case where $\mathbf{S}\colon X \to_B X$ and $O = \{\langle x, x\rangle \mid x \in X\}$, we will write $\mathbf{S}^\circ$ instead of $\mathbf{S} \circlearrowleft O$.

We can use self-composition to define both sequential and parallel composition.

7. *Sequential composition.* The sequential composition of agents was defined in Definition 1.1. Alternatively, one can define it from the more primitive notions of direct sum, feedback and hiding: Let $\mathbf{S}\colon X \to_B Y$ and $\mathbf{T}\colon Y \to_B Z$. Then $\mathbf{S} \oplus \mathbf{T}\colon X \oplus Y \to_B Y \oplus Z$, and with $\Delta Y = \{\langle y, y\rangle \mid y \in Y\}$, one gets $\mathbf{S};\mathbf{T} \approx ((\mathbf{S} \oplus \mathbf{T}) \circlearrowleft \Delta Y)|_{X \to_B Z}$.

8. *Parallel composition (with interaction).* Let $\mathbf{S}, \mathbf{T}\colon X \to_B X$. The parallel composition $\mathbf{S}|\mathbf{T}$ is defined to be the agent $(\mathbf{S}\|\mathbf{T})^\circ$.

Proposition 3.1. *All of the agent constructors in this section respect weak bisimulation. For instance, if* $\mathbf{S} \approx \mathbf{S}'$ *and* $\mathbf{T} \approx \mathbf{T}'$*, then* $\mathbf{S}_r \approx \mathbf{S}'_r$ *and* $\mathbf{S}\|\mathbf{T} \approx \mathbf{S}'\|\mathbf{T}'$*, etc.*

Table 3: First-order axioms for out-buffered agents with feedback

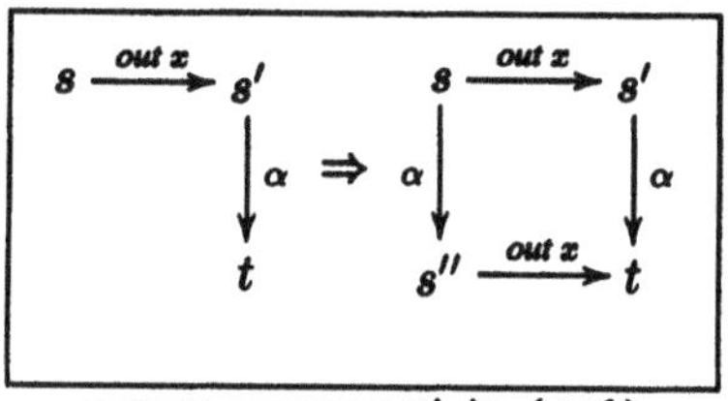

output-commutativity (FB1)

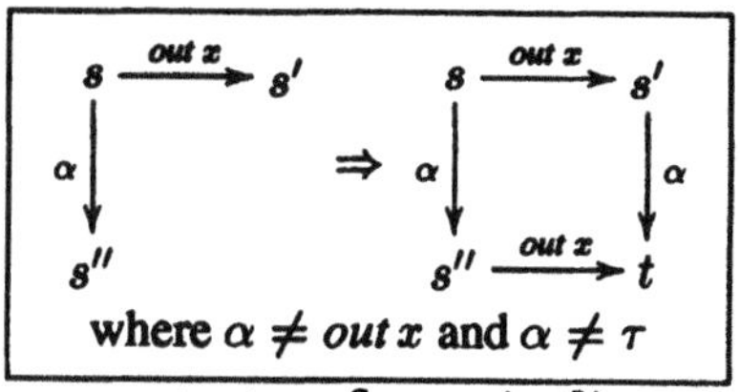

output-confluence (FB2)

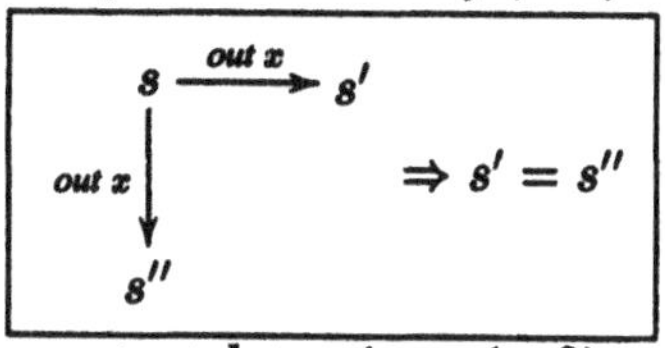

output-determinacy (FB3)

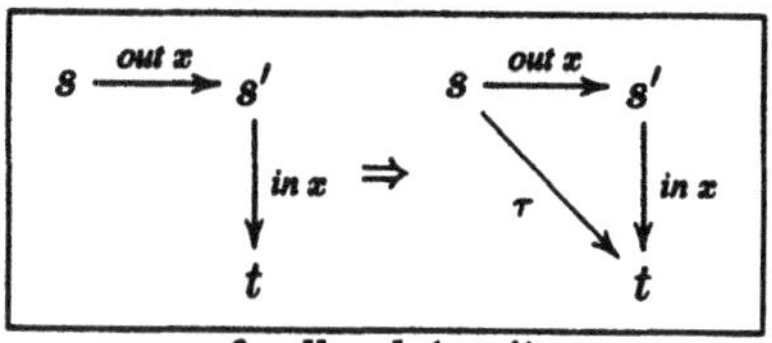

feedback (FB4)

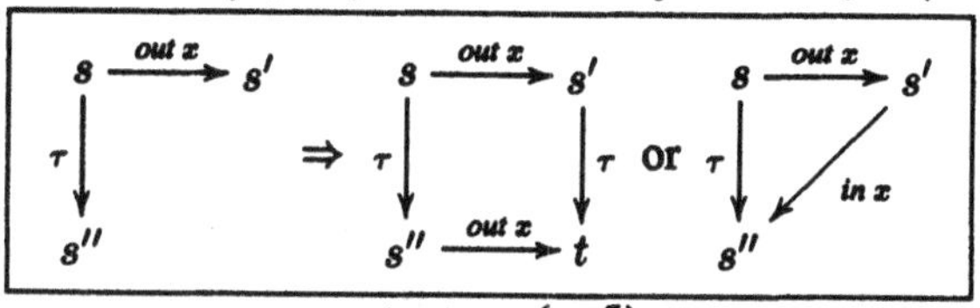

output-tau (FB5)

3.2 Asynchrony with Feedback

In concurrent process calculi such as CCS or the π-calculus, messages that are emitted from a process are immediately available as input to all processes, including the sending process itself. In our setting, this is best modeled by requiring that all processes are of type $X \to X$ for one fixed set X, and by using self-composition to feed the output back to the input.

In the presence of feedback, out-bufferedness takes a slightly different form, which is expressed in the following definition.

Definition. An agent $\mathbf{S}: X \to_B X$ is ***out-buffered with feedback*** if $\mathbf{S} \approx \mathbf{R}^\circ$ for some out-buffered agent $\mathbf{R}$.

Example 3.2. The following agent **S** is out-buffered with feedback but not out-buffered:

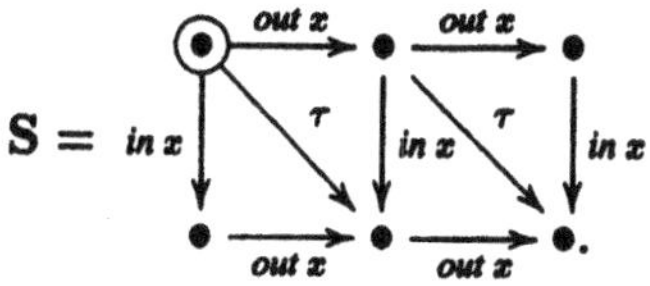

Remark. Recently, Amadio, Castellani and Sangiorgi [3] have given a definition of asynchronous bisimulation, which accounts for the fact that an agent of type $X \to X$

Table 4: Transitions for asynchronous CCS

$$(act)\ \frac{}{\alpha.P \xrightarrow{\alpha} P} \qquad (synch)\ \frac{P \xrightarrow{\alpha} P' \quad Q \xrightarrow{\bar{\alpha}} Q'}{P|Q \xrightarrow{\tau} P'|Q'}$$

$$(sum)\ \frac{G \xrightarrow{\alpha} P}{G+G' \xrightarrow{\alpha} P} \qquad (res)\ \frac{P \xrightarrow{\alpha} P' \quad \alpha \notin L \cup \bar{L}}{P \setminus L \xrightarrow{\alpha} P' \setminus L}$$

$$(sum')\ \frac{G' \xrightarrow{\alpha} P}{G+G' \xrightarrow{\alpha} P} \qquad (rel)\ \frac{P \xrightarrow{\alpha} P'}{P[f] \xrightarrow{f\alpha} P'[f]}$$

$$(comp)\ \frac{P \xrightarrow{\alpha} P'}{P|Q \xrightarrow{\alpha} P'|Q} \qquad (rec)\ \frac{P \xrightarrow{\alpha} P' \quad A \stackrel{\text{def}}{=} P}{A \xrightarrow{\alpha} P'}$$

$$(comp')\ \frac{Q \xrightarrow{\alpha} Q'}{P|Q \xrightarrow{\alpha} P|Q'}$$

might receive a message, and then immediately send it again, without this interaction being observable on the outside. Feedback is concerned with the dual phenomenon, namely a process that sends a message and then immediately receives it again.

Out-bufferedness with feedback is characterized up to weak bisimulation by the first-order axioms that are listed in Table 3.

Theorem 3.3 (Characterization of out-buffered agents with feedback).
An agent $\mathbf{S}\colon X \to_B X$ *is out-buffered with feedback if and only if* $\mathbf{S} \approx \mathbf{T}$ *for some agent* $\mathbf{T}$ *satisfying* (FB1)–(FB5).

4 Example: Asynchronous CCS

In this section, we will show that an asynchronous version of Milner's Calculus of Communicating Systems (CCS) [11, 12] fits into the framework outlined in the previous section of out-buffered labeled transition systems with feedback.

Let $X = \{a, b, c, \dots\}$ be an infinite set of ***names***, and let $\bar{X} = \{\bar{a}, \bar{b}, \bar{c}, \dots\}$ be a corresponding set of ***co-names***, such that X and $\bar{X}$ are disjoint and in one-to-one correspondence via $(\bar{\ })$. We also write $\bar{\bar{a}} = a$. Names correspond to input-actions, and co-names to output-actions. Let $\tau \notin X + \bar{X}$, and let $Act = X + \bar{X} + \{\tau\}$ be the set of ***actions***, ranged over by the letters $\alpha, \beta, \dots$; Let the letter L range over subsets of X, and write $\bar{L}$ for $\{\bar{a} \mid a \in L\}$. Let the letter f range over ***relabeling functions***, which are functions $f : X \to X$. Any relabeling function extends to $f : Act \to Act$ by letting $f\bar{a} = \overline{fa}$ and $f\tau = \tau$.

Let $A, B, C, \dots$ range over a fixed set of ***process constants***. Asynchronous CCS ***processes*** $P, Q, \dots$ and ***guards*** $G, H, \dots$ are given by the following grammars:

$$P ::= \bar{a}.0 \mid P|P \mid P \setminus L \mid P[f] \mid A \mid G$$

$$G ::= a.P \mid \tau.P \mid G+G \mid \mathbf{0}$$

Assume a set of ***defining equations*** $A \stackrel{\text{def}}{=} P$, one for each process constant A. The operational semantics of asynchronous CCS is given in terms of a labeled transition system $S_{CCS} = \langle S, Act, \rightarrow \rangle$, which is defined in Table 4. The states are CCS processes. Notice that we have not specified a distinguished initial state; this is more convenient in this context, and no harm is done. Also notice that there is no rule for $\mathbf{0}$. This is because the process $\mathbf{0}$ is inert, *i.e.* there are no transitions $\mathbf{0} \xrightarrow{\alpha} P$.

Theorem 4.1. *The labeled transition system* S_{CCS} *is out-buffered with feedback.*

5 Example: The Core Join Calculus

The join calculus was introduced by Fournet and Gonthier in [7] and further developed in [8]. It is a concurrent, message passing calculus like the π-calculus. However, the reaction rule is simpler and closer to the semantics of a chemical abstract machine. Here, we will only be concerned with the *core* join calculus.

Let $x, y, \ldots$ range over a countable set $\mathcal{N}$ of ***names***. Let $\tilde{x}, \tilde{y}, \ldots$ range over sequences of names. Core join calculus ***processes*** $P, Q, \ldots$ and ***rules*** $R, S, \ldots$ are given by the following grammars:

$$P ::= x\langle\tilde{y}\rangle \mid P|P \mid \textbf{def } R_1 \wedge \ldots \wedge R_m \textbf{ in } P \qquad R ::= x_1(\tilde{v}_1)|\ldots|x_n(\tilde{v}_n) \triangleright P$$

A process of the form $x\langle\tilde{v}\rangle$ is called a ***message***. In the rule $R = x_1(\tilde{v}_1)|\ldots|x_n(\tilde{v}_n) \triangleright P$, the names $\tilde{v}_1 \ldots \tilde{v}_n$ are bound, and they are assumed to be distinct. The names $x_1 \ldots x_n$ are called the ***defined names*** of R, denoted $dn(R)$. Finally, all of the defined names of $R_1, \ldots, R_m$ are bound in the process $\textbf{def } R_1 \wedge \ldots \wedge R_m \textbf{ in } P$. For a more comprehensive treatment, see [7, 8].

The semantics of the core join calculus is given in the style of a chemical abstract machine. A ***state*** $\Delta \vdash_N \Pi$ is a multiset Δ of rules together with a multiset Π of processes. N is a set of names, such that $fn(\Delta, \Pi) \subseteq N$. We identify states up to α-equivalence, *i.e.* up to renaming of bound variables. The transitions of this machine follow a simple idea: the processes on the right hand side evolve according to the rules on the left-hand side. There are two kinds of transitions: ***structural*** transitions, denoted $\rightharpoonup$, and ***reactions***, denoted $\mapsto$:

$$(str1) \qquad \Delta \vdash_N \Pi, P|Q \rightharpoonup \Delta \vdash_N \Pi, P, Q$$

$$(str2) \quad \Delta \vdash_N \Pi, \textbf{def } R_1 \wedge \ldots \wedge R_m \textbf{ in } P \rightharpoonup \Delta, R_1, \ldots, R_m \vdash_{N'} \Pi, P$$

$$\text{where } N' = N + dn(R_1, \ldots, R_m)$$

$$(join) \quad \Delta \vdash_N \Pi, x_1\langle\tilde{y_1}\rangle, \ldots, x_n\langle\tilde{y_n}\rangle \mapsto \Delta \vdash_N \Pi, [\tilde{y_1}/\tilde{v}_1, \ldots, \tilde{y_n}/\tilde{v}_n]P$$

$$\text{where } (x_1(\tilde{v}_1)|\ldots|x_n(\tilde{v}_n) \triangleright P) \in \Delta$$

The rule $(join)$ is of course only applicable is the length of $\tilde{y}_i$ and $\tilde{v}_i$ are the same, for all i. Note that in the rule $(str2)$, the sets N and $dn(R_1, \ldots, R_m)$ must be disjoint; this may necessitate renaming some bound variables in $\textbf{def } R_1 \wedge \ldots \wedge R_m \textbf{ in } P$.

Table 5: Second-order axioms for out-buffered agents

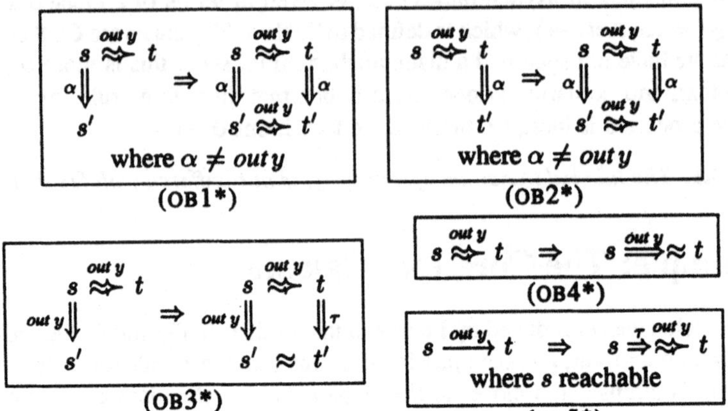

$$
\left(
\begin{array}{c}
s \overset{out\,y}{\approx\!\!\!\!\rightarrow} t \\
\alpha \big\Downarrow \\
s'
\end{array}
\;\Rightarrow\;
\begin{array}{c}
s \overset{out\,y}{\approx\!\!\!\!\rightarrow} t \\
\alpha \big\Downarrow \quad \big\Downarrow \alpha \\
s' \overset{out\,y}{\approx\!\!\!\!\rightarrow} t'
\end{array}
\right)
$$
where $\alpha \neq out\,y$
(OB1*)

$$
\left(
\begin{array}{c}
s \overset{out\,y}{\approx\!\!\!\!\rightarrow} t \\
\big\Downarrow \alpha \\
t'
\end{array}
\;\Rightarrow\;
\begin{array}{c}
s \overset{out\,y}{\approx\!\!\!\!\rightarrow} t \\
\alpha \big\Downarrow \quad \big\Downarrow \alpha \\
s' \overset{out\,y}{\approx\!\!\!\!\rightarrow} t'
\end{array}
\right)
$$
where $\alpha \neq out\,y$
(OB2*)

$$
\left(
\begin{array}{c}
s \overset{out\,y}{\approx\!\!\!\!\rightarrow} t \\
out\,y \big\Downarrow \\
s'
\end{array}
\;\Rightarrow\;
\begin{array}{c}
s \overset{out\,y}{\approx\!\!\!\!\rightarrow} t \\
out\,y \big\Downarrow \quad \big\Downarrow \tau \\
s' \approx t'
\end{array}
\right)
$$
(OB3*)

$$
s \overset{out\,y}{\approx\!\!\!\!\rightarrow} t \;\Rightarrow\; s \overset{out\,y}{\Longrightarrow} \approx t
$$
(OB4*)

$$
s \overset{out\,y}{\longrightarrow} t \;\Rightarrow\; s \overset{\tau}{\Rightarrow} \overset{out\,y}{\approx\!\!\!\!\rightarrow} t
$$
where s reachable
(OB5*)

Remark. In the original formulation of the join calculus [7, 8], the structural rules are assumed to be reversible. We adopt a different convention here.

To fit the join calculus into our framework, we make it into a labeled transition system with input and output. Let $X = \{x\langle\tilde{y}\rangle \mid x \in \mathcal{N}, \tilde{y} \in \mathcal{N}^*\}$ be the set of messages. We add input and output transitions:

$$(in) \qquad \Delta \vdash_N \Pi \xrightarrow{in\,x\langle\tilde{y}\rangle} \Delta \vdash_{N \cup \{x,\tilde{y}\}} \Pi, x\langle\tilde{y}\rangle$$

$$(out) \quad \Delta \vdash_N \Pi, x\langle\tilde{y}\rangle \xrightarrow{out\,x\langle\tilde{y}\rangle} \Delta \vdash_N \Pi$$

Further, we let $\xrightarrow{\tau} = \rightarrow \cup \mapsto$. With these definitions, the join calculus defines a labeled transition system $S_{join} \colon X \to X$.

Theorem 5.1. *The labeled transition system S_{join} defined by the core join calculus is out-buffered with feedback.*

6 Other Characterizations of Asynchrony

In Sections 2 and 3, we have characterized notions of asynchrony by first-order axioms *up to weak bisimulation*. It is possible to remove the words "up to weak bisimulation", *i.e.* to characterize asynchrony directly. This happens at the cost of introducing second-order axioms. The shift to second-order seems to be inevitable, since weak bisimulation itself is a second-order notion.

The axioms for out-buffered agents are given in Tables 5. It is possible to give corresponding axioms for in-bufferedness, out-queuedness and in-queuedness.

Theorem 6.1. *An agent $S \colon X \to_B Y$ is out-buffered if and only if for each $y \in Y$ there exists a binary relation $\overset{out\,y}{\approx\!\!\!\!\rightarrow} \subseteq |S| \times |S|$ satisfying (OB1*)–(OB5*).*

7 Conclusions and Future Work

We have shown how to abstractly characterize various notions of asynchrony in a general-purpose framework, independently of any particular process paradigm. This can be done by first-order axioms up to weak bisimulation, or by higher-order axioms "on the nose". The present framework of labeled transition systems with input and output can be used to model asynchronous communication in CCS, as well as the join calculus. To give an adequate treatment of calculi with explicit, dynamic scoping operators, such as the π-calculus, one should equip these labeled transition systems with the ability to handle dynamically created names. Work is in progress on a notion of fibered labeled transition system that can be used to model this more general situation.

References

[1] S. Abramsky. Interaction categories and communicating sequential processes. In A. W. Roscoe, editor, *A Classical Mind: Essays in honour of C. A. R. Hoare*, pages 1–16. Prentice Hall International, 1994.

[2] S. Abramsky, S. Gay, and R. Nagarajan. Interaction categories and typed concurrent programming. In *Proceedings of the 1994 Marktoberdorf Summer School*. Springer, 1994.

[3] R. M. Amadio, I. Castellani, and D. Sangiorgi. On bisimulations for the asynchronous π-calculus. In *CONCUR '96*, Springer LNCS 1119, pages 147–162, 1996.

[4] M. A. Bednarczyk. *Categories of asynchronous systems*. PhD thesis, University of Sussex, 1988.

[5] G. Berry and G. Boudol. The chemical abstract machine. *Theoretical Computer Science*, 96:217–248, 1992.

[6] G. Boudol. Asynchrony and the π-calculus. Technical Report 1702, INRIA, Sophia-Antipolis, 1992.

[7] C. Fournet and G. Gonthier. The reflexive cham and the join-calculus. In *POPL '96*, 1996.

[8] C. Fournet, G. Gonthier, J.-J. Levy, L. Maranget, and D. Remy. A calculus of mobile agents. In *CONCUR '96*, Springer LNCS 1119, pages 406–421, 1996.

[9] K. Honda and M. Tokoro. An object calculus for asynchronous communication. In *Proc. ECOOP 91, Geneve*, 1991.

[10] N. A. Lynch and E. W. Stark. A proof of the Kahn principle for input/output automata. *Information and Computation*, 82:81–92, 1989.

[11] R. Milner. *A Calculus of Communicationg Systems*. Springer LNCS 92. 1980.

[12] R. Milner. Operational and algebraic semantics of concurrent processes. Technical report, University of Edinburgh, Nov. 1987. Chapter for the Handbook of Theoretical Computer Science.

[13] C. Palamidessi. Comparing the expressive power of the synchronous and the asynchronous π-calculus. In *POPL '97 (Paris)*, 1997.

[14] M. W. Shields. Concurrent machines. *Theoretical Computer Science*, 28:449–465, 1985.

On Implementations and Semantics of a Concurrent Programming Language

Peter Sewell[1]

Abstract The concurrency theory literature contains many proposals for models of process algebras. We consider an example application of the π-calculus, the programming language Pict of Pierce and Turner, primarily in order to see how far it is possible to argue, from facts about the application, that some model is the most appropriate. We discuss informally the sense in which the semantics of Pict relates to the behaviour of actual implementations. Based on this we give an operational model of the interactions between a Pict implementation (considered as the abstract behaviour of a C program) and its environment (modelling an operating system and user). We then give a class of abstract machines and a definition of abstract machine correctness, using an adapted notion of testing, and prove that a sample abstract machine is indeed correct. We briefly discuss the standard of correctness appropriate for program transformations and the induced precongruence. Many of the semantic choices do indeed turn out to be determined by facts about Pict.

1 Introduction

The concurrency theory literature contains many proposals for models of process algebras, as can be seen for example from the surveys by van Glabeek [Gla90, Gla93] of certain models that are quotients of labelled transition systems (LTS's). This diversity poses a problem: for any particular application of a process algebra how can an appropriate model be selected? In this paper the problem is addressed for an example application of the π-calculus of Milner, Parrow and Walker [MPW92], primarily in order to see how far it is possible to argue, from facts about the application, that some model is the most appropriate. The application is the Pict programming language, based on the π-calculus, of Pierce and Turner [PT97]. We consider models that are quotients of the terms by congruence relations defined using notions of observation. The core of the paper is devoted to defining a notion of observation that can be seen to be appropriate for Pict. We discuss in detail the interactions between an actual Pict implementation and a user, together with their relationship to the structured operational semantics (SOS). This discussion is, in the absence of a semantics for the implementation language, necessarily informal. We then incorporate a number of simple but essential facts about the interactions into a formal model, giving precise definitions of a class of abstract machines and of a notion of observation suitable for defining abstract machine correctness. These are used to define an appropriate observational precongruence. We prove that a sample abstract machine is indeed correct and give some characterisation results, relating the observational preorder and precongruence to standard notions of testing and bisimulation.

[1] Computer Laboratory, University of Cambridge. Email: `Peter.Sewell@cl.cam.ac.uk`

Some of the discussion and technical work is necessarily specific to Pict. Much, however, should be applicable to other concurrent programming languages that do not prescribe a particular implementation scheduling strategy, for example Facile [TLK96], CML [Rep92], Concurrent Haskell [JGF96], and the Join calculus [FG96].

To define what is a correct abstract machine one must specify the required relationship between the LTS semantics of programs, as given by a π-calculus structured operational semantics, and their behaviour when executed. It is thus an essential part of the language definition, together with definitions of the syntax, type system, SOS and libraries. It must satisfy three rather pragmatic criteria. Firstly, it must be strong enough to give programmers sufficient guarantees about the behaviour of programs. Secondly, it must be loose enough to admit any 'reasonable' implementation and 'reasonable' compiler optimisations. Thirdly, it must be sufficiently mathematically tractable to allow correctness proofs for abstract machines and program transformations to be carried out. Our approach to defining abstract machine correctness is as follows. In §2 we introduce Pict and discuss informally the relationship between the SOS and implementation behaviour. The current implementation compiles a Pict program to a C program which is then compiled and executed. In §3 we give an operational model of the interaction between such a C program and the operating system which forms its immediate environment. We then give an analogous model of the interaction between the LTS semantics of programs given by the SOS and an environment. In §4 we relate the two, defining abstract machine correctness via an adaptation of the *testing preorder* of De Nicola and Hennessy [DH84] (we show that the standard notion is inappropriate). We also give a sample abstract machine, closely based on the current implementation, and prove it correct. Finally in §5 we consider program transformation, defining an observational preorder, giving some examples and proving that the induced precongruence is refined by a simple notion of bisimulation.

There is an extensive theoretical literature discussing behavioural equivalences of process calculi that are induced by some kind of tests or observations of processes, e.g. [HM80, Mil81, DH84, Hoa85, Abr87, AV93, Gla90, Gla93, San93]. The argument that the testing scenario we adopt is appropriate for Pict relies on some essential differences between Pict and any process calculus considered only in the abstract. Firstly, Pict is a *programming language*, with a fixed interpretation of nondeterminism (as a loose specification of the required implementation behaviour). It is not a modelling or simulation language, which would fix other interpretations, or a pure process calculus, which would not be committed to any interpretation. Secondly, Pict is *implemented and used.* There are clear intuitions for the intended use of the language and the behaviour of 'reasonable' implementations that can be appealed to. Further, there are libraries providing specific primitives by which a Pict program can interact with its immediate environment. The behaviour of these primitives in any reasonable implementation is well understood, giving us a solid foundation upon which to base our formal model and argue for its accuracy.

2 Pict: SOS and Implementation

Pict has a rich type system and high level syntax. This syntax is translated (in both the semantics and the implementation) into a core syntax which is a mild extension of an asynchronous choice-free π-calculus. For discussion of the design decisions underlying Pict, and of the implementation issues, we refer the reader to [PT97] and [Tur96]. For this paper we are largely concerned with the behaviour of whole programs. These interact with their environment only by communicating on channels (provided by the libraries) of rather simple types. We work with an idealized Pict, taking only these rather simple types and only the core syntax. In fact, we omit also nested tuples, records and polymorphic packages from the core, and add an equality test at base types (to replace library routines providing case analysis). These idealizations should not significantly affect the behaviours expressible by whole programs.

We take an infinite set $\mathcal{X}$, of *names*, with $\tau \notin \mathcal{X}$, and a set $\mathcal{T}$, of *base types* provided by the libraries (including e.g. the naturals), ranged over by t. The *types* are given by $T ::= t \mid !\langle T_1, \ldots, T_n\rangle \mid ?\langle T_1, \ldots, T_n\rangle \mid \updownarrow\langle T_1, \ldots, T_n\rangle$. The latter three are the types of names (or channels) along which a program can respectively output, input, and output or input tuples of names, of types $T_1, \ldots, T_n$. We write $\vec{T}$ for a tuple $T_1, \ldots, T_n$. We order types by $\leq$, which is the least preorder such that $\updownarrow\vec{T} \leq !\vec{T}$ and $\updownarrow\vec{T} \leq ?\vec{T}$. This is simply a notational convenience, we will not have substantive subtyping. *Type contexts* Γ are partial functions from $\mathcal{X}$ to types with $\mathcal{X} - \mathrm{dom}(\Gamma)$ infinite. We write Γ, Δ for the union of partial functions Γ and Δ with disjoint domains and $\mathcal{X} - \mathrm{dom}(\Gamma) - \mathrm{dom}(\Delta)$ infinite. *Process terms* are

$$P \quad ::= \quad 0 \;\Big|\; \overline{x}\langle\vec{z}\rangle \;\Big|\; x(\vec{y}).P \;\Big|\; !\,x(\vec{y}).P \;\Big|\; P \,|\, P \;\Big|\; (\nu y : T)P \;\Big|\; [x = z]P$$

where $x, y, z \in \mathcal{X}$ and $\vec{z}, \vec{y} \in \mathcal{X}^*$. The names $\vec{y}$ and y bind in the respective continuation process P. Here and below we suppose $\vec{y}$ contains no duplicated names. Process terms are taken up to alpha conversion. The typing rules, defining a judgement $\Gamma \vdash P$ to be read as 'P is typable with respect to Γ, structural congruence, written $\equiv$, and SOS are given in Figure 1. The SOS is similar to the 'early' definition of Sangiorgi [San93]. It differs in that it defines transitions of process terms equipped with a type context instead of partitioning the names into a subset for each type. This removes the need for side conditions on the free names of processes and simplifies the definitions of operational equivalences, as processes need only be compared with respect to the same type context. The *labels*, ranged over by α, are $\{\, \overline{x}\langle\vec{z}\rangle \mid x \in \mathcal{X} \wedge \vec{z} \in \mathcal{X}^* \,\} \cup \{\, x\langle\vec{z}\rangle \mid x \in \mathcal{X} \wedge \vec{z} \in \mathcal{X}^* \,\} \cup \{\tau\}$. The *names* of a label are $\mathrm{n}(\overline{x}\langle\vec{z}\rangle) = \{x\} \cup \vec{z}$, $\mathrm{n}(x\langle\vec{z}\rangle) = \{x\} \cup \vec{z}$ and $\mathrm{n}(\tau) = \{\}$. We define transition relations

$$\Gamma \vdash P \xrightarrow[\Delta]{\alpha} Q$$

where $\Gamma \vdash P$, the type context Δ contains names only at channel types, $\mathrm{dom}(\Gamma) \cap \mathrm{dom}(\Delta) = \{\}$, and Q is a process term. Intuitively Δ is the type context for the new names intruded or extruded by the transition (in the absence of subtyping Δ is determined by the other data). For example, if $\alpha = \overline{x}\langle z\rangle$ and $\Delta = \{z : \updownarrow\langle\rangle\}$

the transition above corresponds to a transition of [San93] with label $(\nu z)\overline{x}\langle z\rangle$, where z would be a name in the $\updownarrow\langle\rangle$ partition.

Proposition 1 *(Subject reduction) If* $\Gamma \vdash P \xrightarrow[\Delta]{\alpha} Q$ *then* $\Gamma, \Delta \vdash Q$. *Moreover,* $\mathrm{dom}(\Delta) \subseteq \mathrm{n}(\alpha)$, *if* $\alpha = \overline{x}\langle\vec{z}\rangle$ *then* $\Gamma(x) \leq\ !(\Gamma,\Delta)(\vec{z})$ *and if* $\alpha = x\langle\vec{z}\rangle$ *then* $\Gamma(x) \leq\ ?(\Gamma,\Delta)(\vec{z})$.

Proposition 2 (CONG-L) *If* $P' \equiv P$ *and* $\Gamma \vdash P \xrightarrow[\Delta]{\alpha} Q$ *then* $\Gamma \vdash P' \xrightarrow[\Delta]{\alpha} Q$.

The current Pict libraries provide a rich set of primitives for interacting with Unix and the X window system. They are made available to programs by providing a pervasive type context Γ_{p} of certain channels along which a program can input and/or output. This includes, for example, a channel $\mathrm{print} : !\langle\mathrm{String}\rangle$ on which a program can output strings. The implementation will send these to standard output. *Programs* are process terms P such that $\Gamma_{\mathrm{p}} \vdash P$.

We now briefly describe the behaviour of the current Pict implementation. After type checking a Pict program is compiled to a C program which is then executed as a single Unix process. The implementation is thus sequential — the intended use of concurrency in Pict is for expressiveness, not for distributed or parallel programming (work on distribution is in progress). It maintains a *state* consisting of a *run queue* of processes to be scheduled (round robin) together with *channel queues* of processes waiting to communicate. It executes in steps, in each of which the process at the front of the run queue is removed and processed. This internal behaviour of the implementation is described by Turner in [Tur96, Ch. 7] and incorporated into the abstract machine given in §4. When an output or input on a library channel reaches the front of the run queue some special processing takes place. For many library channels this consists of a single call to a corresponding Unix IO routine. For example, processing $\overline{\mathrm{print}}\langle\text{“Ping”}\rangle$ involves an invocation of the C library call `printf(...)`. There are a number of facts that must be taken into account in order to accurately formalise a model of implementations and relate it to the SOS. We discuss them informally here, incorporating them into precise definitions in the following two sections.

Linear/Branching time The Pict SOS is nondeterministic. Any realistic implementation will be largely deterministic, however, as requiring that any nondeterministic path may be taken (stochastically, or as determined by an oracle) has a prohibitive performance cost for a programming language. Nonetheless, we do not wish to prescribe a particular scheduling strategy, as that would unduly prevent compiler optimisations. The SOS must therefore be regarded as a loose specification of the required implementation behaviour, so any definition of implementation correctness based on branching time, such as any notion of bisimulation, would render realistic implementations ‘incorrect’. Moreover, the strong forms of copying required to observe branching time distinctions [Mil81, Abr87] are not applicable to executing Pict implementations. One could, of course, examine an executing Pict implementation with a machine-level debugger. This would reveal many implementation-dependent details which the programmer

$$\textsc{Out}\ \frac{\Gamma(x) \leq\ !\langle \Gamma(z_1), \ldots, \Gamma(z_n)\rangle}{\Gamma \vdash \overline{x}\langle z_1, \ldots, z_n\rangle} \qquad (\textsc{Rep-})\textsc{In}\ \frac{\begin{array}{c}\Gamma(x) \leq ?\langle T_1, \ldots, T_n\rangle \\ \Gamma, y_1 : T_1, \ldots, y_n : T_n \vdash P\end{array}}{\begin{array}{c}\Gamma \vdash x(y_1, \ldots, y_n).P \\ \text{and}\quad \Gamma \vdash\ !x(y_1, \ldots, y_n).P\end{array}}$$

$$\textsc{Par}\ \frac{\Gamma \vdash P \quad \Gamma \vdash Q}{\Gamma \vdash P \mid Q} \qquad \textsc{Nil}\ \frac{}{\Gamma \vdash 0}$$

$$\textsc{Res}\ \frac{\begin{array}{c}\Gamma, x : T \vdash P \\ T \notin \mathcal{T}\end{array}}{\Gamma \vdash (\nu x : T)P} \qquad \textsc{Match}\ \frac{\begin{array}{c}\Gamma \vdash P \\ \Gamma(x) = \Gamma(y) \in \mathcal{T}\end{array}}{\Gamma \vdash [x = y]P}$$

$$\begin{array}{rcll}
P \mid 0 & \equiv & P & \\
P \mid Q & \equiv & Q \mid P & \\
P \mid (Q \mid R) & \equiv & (P \mid Q) \mid R & \\
(\nu x : T)(\nu y : T')P & \equiv & (\nu y : T')(\nu x : T)P & x \neq y \\
P \mid (\nu x : T)Q & \equiv & (\nu x : T)(P \mid Q) & x \notin \mathrm{fn}(P)
\end{array}$$

$$\textsc{Out}\ \frac{}{\Gamma \vdash \overline{x}\langle \vec{z}\rangle \xrightarrow[\{\}]{\overline{x}\langle \vec{z}\rangle} 0} \qquad (\textsc{Rep-})\textsc{In}\ \frac{\begin{array}{c}\Gamma(x) \leq ?\vec{T} \\ (\Gamma, \Delta)(\vec{z}) = \vec{T} \\ \mathrm{dom}(\Delta) \subseteq \vec{z}\end{array}}{\begin{array}{c}\Gamma \vdash x(\vec{y}).P \xrightarrow[\Delta]{x\langle \vec{z}\rangle} P[\vec{z}/\vec{y}] \\ \text{and}\ \Gamma \vdash\ !x(\vec{y}).P \xrightarrow[\Delta]{x\langle \vec{z}\rangle} P[\vec{z}/\vec{y}] \mid !x(\vec{y}).P\end{array}}$$

$$\textsc{Par}\ \frac{\Gamma \vdash P \xrightarrow[\Delta]{\alpha} P'}{\Gamma \vdash P \mid Q \xrightarrow[\Delta]{\alpha} P' \mid Q} \qquad \textsc{Com}\ \frac{\Gamma \vdash P \xrightarrow[\Delta]{\overline{x}\langle \vec{z}\rangle} P' \quad \Gamma \vdash Q \xrightarrow[\Delta]{x\langle \vec{z}\rangle} Q'}{\Gamma \vdash P \mid Q \xrightarrow[\{\}]{\tau} (\nu\Delta)(P' \mid Q')}$$

$$\textsc{Res}\ \frac{\Gamma, x : T \vdash P \xrightarrow[\Delta]{\alpha} P' \quad x \notin \mathrm{n}(\alpha)}{\Gamma \vdash (\nu x : T)P \xrightarrow[\Delta]{\alpha} (\nu x : T)P'} \qquad \textsc{Open}\ \frac{\Gamma, x : T \vdash P \xrightarrow[\Delta]{\overline{w}\langle \vec{z}\rangle} P' \quad w \neq x \in \vec{z}}{\Gamma \vdash (\nu x : T)P \xrightarrow[\Delta, x : T]{\overline{w}\langle \vec{z}\rangle} P'}$$

$$\textsc{Match}\ \frac{\Gamma \vdash P \xrightarrow[\Delta]{\alpha} P'}{\Gamma \vdash [x = x]P \xrightarrow[\Delta]{\alpha} P'} \qquad \textsc{Cong-R}\ \frac{\Gamma \vdash P \xrightarrow[\Delta]{\alpha} P' \quad P' \equiv P''}{\Gamma \vdash P \xrightarrow[\Delta]{\alpha} P''}$$

Figure 1: Typing, structural congruence and structured operational semantics. Symmetrical versions of PAR and COM are omitted.

and the language definition should abstract from, so we regard it as outside the intended use of the language.

Non-refusable communication All interaction between a Pict implementation and the operating system (which forms its immediate environment) occurs via invocations of C library calls, such as `printf(...)`, by the implementation. These calls cannot be 'refused' by the operating system and their return cannot be 'refused' by the implementation.

Blocking communication A Pict implementation should satisfy the following progress criterion: if a Pict program has at least one possible transition, i.e. a transition that is either an external input for which a value is available, an external output or an internal communication, then the implementation should perform one of the corresponding steps in a reasonable time. Now, some C library calls can potentially never return, e.g. `getchar()` if no characters become available. Such calls should therefore not be invoked unless either they can be guaranteed to return or the Pict program has no possible transitions. Consider, for example, the putative program $(\mathrm{getchar}(c).0 \mid \overline{\mathrm{print}}\langle\text{“Ping”}\rangle)$. An implementation should guarantee that the "Ping" is printed and so must not call `getchar()` first unless a character is available. (In fact we will consider only the most interesting potentially non-returning library call, for getting events from the X window system. Dealing with the others should not involve significant complication.)

External nondeterminism A C program cannot simultaneously 'offer' two library calls for the operating system to select between. An accurate model of implementations must therefore forbid external nondeterminism.

Termination When a Pict program terminates, i.e. when it has no more transitions in the SOS, the implementation Unix process terminates, typically returning the user to a Unix shell prompt. The user is therefore concerned with the termination of programs, despite the fact that there is no Pict language context that can 'detect' termination of an arbitrary subprogram.

Divergence Pict programs may diverge, i.e. have an infinite sequence of internal actions in the SOS. The user is concerned with the distinction between programs that diverge and programs that do not. Moreover, we cannot simply regard divergence as catastrophic, identifying divergent programs that are otherwise significantly different [Hoa85, Wal88]. To do so would allow an implementation to behave arbitrarily for any divergent program, which would be unduly confusing, particularly for programs which are unintentionally divergent. The testing scenario must therefore be divergence-sensitive.

Compositionality Much work on process calculi has been concerned with defining behavioural relations with good mathematical properties, e.g. congruence properties, axiomatisations, and coinductive characterisations. For this paper we take the problem of the development of tractable proof techniques to be secondary to that of giving a good language definition for Pict, although it must ultimately influence the language design. Now, Pict subprograms can only be composed (by parallel composition etc.) before they are compiled and only have behaviour when they are compiled and executing. There is therefore no reason to include congruence properties in the definition of correct program transformation, so it will be expressed simply in terms of a preorder over whole programs. For reasoning about particular programs one will obviously be concerned with *observational precongruence*, defined to be the largest precongruence contained in this preorder, and might ideally like a direct characterisation of it. We expect, however, that many program transformations are correct up to rather fine equivalences (see e.g. [PW96, NP96]) so for many purposes it will be preferable to have congruences with simple coinductive definitions that can be shown to be finer than observational precongruence.

X events Communication from the X window system to a C program, e.g. notification of mouse clicks, takes place via *X events*. These are generated and buffered within X. Two C library routines are provided; `XPending` returns the number of events in the buffer and `XNextEvent` returns the first available event. The latter may block, so access to it should not be provided directly to Pict programs (otherwise the progress criterion above will not be satisfiable). We therefore assume that access to X events is provided to Pict programs via a library channel getXEvent. Inputs on this channel should not block the implementation unless there are no possible transitions.

Asynchrony Pict is based on an asynchronous π-calculus, in which outputs do not have continuation processes. This means that explicit acknowledgement signals must be used to control the sequencing of external IO. For example, instead of the program $\overline{\text{print}}\langle\text{“Hello”}\rangle \mid \overline{\text{print}}\langle\text{“World”}\rangle$, which could output “HelloWorld” or “WorldHello”, one can write $(\nu a : \updownarrow\langle\rangle)\ (\overline{\text{pr}}\langle\text{“Hello”}, a\rangle \mid a().\overline{\text{print}}\langle\text{“World”}\rangle)$. Here pr is a channel of type $!\langle \text{String}, \updownarrow\langle\rangle\rangle$ provided by the libraries. An implementation executing the subprogram $\overline{\text{pr}}\langle\text{“Hello”}, a\rangle$ must invoke the appropriate C library call and also add an acknowledgement $\overline{a}\langle\rangle$ to the program.

Fairness This paper leaves fairness properties for future work. Substantial effort has gone into ensuring that the current implementation is reasonably fair, as this is necessary for some natural programs. A good definition of implementation correctness should, therefore, require that the implementation is fair in some precise sense. One could also give a more accurate model of the interaction of a user and an implementation by taking the composition $\_ \| \_$, defined in §3, to be a fair composition. In the distributed case the appropriate fairness properties will be more subtle, as will the issues of compositionality and external nondeterminism.

3 Implementation Model and Test Harnesses

In this section we give an abstract operational semantics of C programs, their environments, and the interactions between them. We define a class of models of the behaviour of C programs, ranged over by C, a test harness $\mathrm{H}_{\mathrm{am}}(\_)$ for these models, a class of models of the environments of C programs, ranged over by E, and a composition $\_ \| \_$ of an environment and a C behaviour in the test harness. The behaviour of a composition $E \| \mathrm{H}_{\mathrm{am}}(C)$ thus models the behaviour of an actual implementation. We then define a test harness $\mathrm{H}_{\mathrm{sos}}(\_)$ for Pict programs with the SOS semantics so that any $\mathrm{H}_{\mathrm{sos}}(P)$ and $\mathrm{H}_{\mathrm{am}}(C)$ are comparable. The definitions are given explicitly, rather than by encoding into some calculus, so that the facts from §2 can be incorporated directly.

We suppose that a C program and its environment can only interact in two ways. Firstly, the program can invoke an operating system (OS) routine, e.g. by executing a statement `y = f(a)` for an OS routine `f` that takes an argument `a` and returns a result to be stored in `y`. Arguments and results may be values of some C structured types. We will assume that arguments and results are elements of the Pict base types, and so associate a pair of base types to each OS routine. This is obviously a major idealization for arbitrary C programs — we are not dealing with communication via shared memory or callback functions. For Pict implementations, however, it does not appear to be too serious. Secondly, the program can terminate by executing a statement `return`. A C program is single-threaded, so while an OS routine is executing the rest of the program is blocked. We can therefore model the program by a labelled transition system in which a single transition models a complete invocation of an OS routine.

We suppose, for each base type $t \in \mathcal{T}$, a non-empty set $|t|$ of its values. We assume that $\{\text{Unit}, \text{Nat}, \text{XEvent}\} \subseteq \mathcal{T}$, $|\text{Unit}| = \{\bullet\}$ and $|\text{Nat}| = \mathbb{N}$. For technical simplicity we treat return as an OS routine of type $\langle \text{Unit}, \text{Unit} \rangle$. We use an 'early' LTS and do not distinguish input and output labels. We take a *C interface type context* Γ to be a finite partial function from $\mathcal{X}$ to pairs of base types. The *labels* over a C interface type context Γ are $\mathcal{L}(\Gamma) = \{\, x\langle a, r\rangle \mid \Gamma(x) = \langle A, R\rangle \wedge a \in |A| \wedge r \in |R| \,\} \cup \{\tau\}$. We take a labelled transition system S over a C interface type context Γ (a Γ-LTS) to consist of a set of states S, an initial state $\text{root}(S) \in S$, and transitions $\xrightarrow{l} \subseteq S \times S$ for $l \in \mathcal{L}(\Gamma)$.

We will treat most OS routines uniformly, taking an arbitrary C interface type context Γ_u (strictly, with $\text{dom}(\Gamma_u)$ not intersecting $\{\text{return}, \text{XPending}, \text{XNextEvent}, \text{XInsertEvent}\}$). X events and `return` must be treated specially, however. Letting Γ_c be $\Gamma_u, \text{return}:\langle \text{Unit}, \text{Unit}\rangle, \text{XPending}:\langle \text{Unit}, \text{Nat}\rangle, \text{XNextEvent}:\langle \text{Unit}, \text{XEvent}\rangle$, a C program behaviour will be modelled by a Γ_c-LTS. For $f:\langle A, R\rangle \in \Gamma_c$, $a \in |A|$ and $r \in |R|$ a transition $c \xrightarrow{f\langle a,r\rangle} c'$ will model an invocation by the program in state c, of OS routine `f`, with argument a, returning result r, and with c' being the program state in which r has been returned.

Definition A *C-behaviour* C is a Γ_c-LTS satisfying conditions

1. If $f:\langle A, R\rangle \in \Gamma_c$ and $c \xrightarrow{f\langle a,r\rangle} c_1$ then $\forall r' \in |R| \,.\, \exists c' \,.\, c \xrightarrow{f\langle a,r'\rangle} c'$.

2. If $\text{root}(C) \xrightarrow{\mathcal{L}(\Gamma_c - \text{return})^*} \xrightarrow{\text{return}\langle \bullet,\bullet\rangle} c'$ then $c' \not\rightarrow$.

3. If $\text{root}(C) \xrightarrow{\mathcal{L}(\Gamma_c - \text{return})^*} c$ then $c \longrightarrow$.

4. If $c \xrightarrow{l_1} c_1$ and $c \xrightarrow{l_2} c_2 \neq c_1$ then either $l_1 = l_2 = \tau$ or $\exists f, a, r_1, r_2 \,.\, l_1 = f\langle a, r_1\rangle \wedge l_2 = f\langle a, r_2\rangle \wedge r_1 \neq r_2$.

The conditions reflect the facts that a C program cannot 'refuse' a particular result value; that after an execution of `return` a C program has no behaviour; that a C program cannot 'halt' and that a C program cannot simultaneously 'offer' two OS routine calls for the OS to select between. It is arguable that one should also forbid internal nondeterminism (up to strong bisimilarity).

In order to compare a C-behaviour and the Pict SOS some semantic mismatches between them, involving X events, asynchrony and termination, must be addressed. Simply relating transitions labelled $\mathrm{XNextEvent}\langle \bullet, ev \rangle$ of C-behaviours to transitions labelled $\mathrm{getXEvent}\langle ev \rangle$ of the Pict SOS would have two undesirable consequences. Firstly, it would allow an implementation to be 'correct' even though it could invoke `XNextEvent` with no events available and with other steps possible (hence not satisfying the progress criterion). Secondly, it would render some reasonable implementations, that get and internally buffer X events before the executing Pict program can input them, 'incorrect'. Instead, therefore, we will compare C-behaviours and the SOS in test harnesses that include explicit models of the X event buffer, allowing the OS to insert events at any time and a C-behaviour or SOS to remove events using their respective internal interfaces to the buffer. The test harness for C-behaviours is as follows, in which Γ_e is $\Gamma_\mathrm{u}, \mathrm{return} : \langle \mathrm{Unit}, \mathrm{Unit} \rangle, \mathrm{XInsertEvent} : \langle \mathrm{XEvent}, \mathrm{Unit} \rangle$, we write $|evs|$ for the length of the list evs and write $ev :: evs$ and $evs :: ev$ for the concatenation of the list evs with the singleton list ev.

Definition For a C-behaviour C we define $\mathrm{H_{am}}(C)$ to be the Γ_e-LTS with states $\{\bullet\} \cup \{\, evs, c \mid evs \in |\mathrm{XEvent}|^* \wedge c \in C\,\}$, root $\langle \mathrm{nil}, \mathrm{root}(C) \rangle$ and transitions

$$\frac{c \xrightarrow{x\langle a,r \rangle} c' \quad x \in \mathrm{dom}(\Gamma_\mathrm{u})}{evs, c \xrightarrow{x\langle a,r \rangle} evs, c'} \qquad \frac{c \xrightarrow{\tau} c'}{evs, c \xrightarrow{\tau} evs, c'} \qquad \frac{c \xrightarrow{\mathrm{return}\langle \bullet,\bullet \rangle} c'}{evs, c \xrightarrow{\mathrm{return}\langle \bullet,\bullet \rangle} \bullet}$$

$$\frac{}{evs, c \xrightarrow{\mathrm{XInsertEvent}\langle ev,\bullet \rangle} (evs :: ev), c} \qquad \frac{c \xrightarrow{\mathrm{XPending}\langle \bullet,|evs| \rangle} c'}{evs, c \xrightarrow{\tau} evs, c'} \qquad \frac{c \xrightarrow{\mathrm{XNextEvent}\langle \bullet,ev \rangle} c'}{(ev :: evs), c \xrightarrow{\tau} evs, c'}$$

The environment of a C program, comprising Unix, the X window system (without its event buffer), a terminal etc., will also be modelled by an Γ_e-LTS. Its transitions model invocations by the program of non-X-event library routines, the program's final return and the insertion of events into the buffer by X.

Definition An *environment* E is a Γ_e-LTS satisfying

1. If $\mathrm{root}(E) \xrightarrow{\mathcal{L}(\Gamma_\mathrm{e} - \mathrm{return})^*} e$ then $\forall x : \langle A, R \rangle \in (\Gamma_\mathrm{e} - \mathrm{XInsertEvent}) \,.\, \forall a \in |A| \,.$ $\exists r \in |R|, e' \,.\, e \xrightarrow{x\langle a,r \rangle} e'$.

2. If $\mathrm{root}(E) \xrightarrow{\mathcal{L}(\Gamma_\mathrm{e} - \mathrm{return})^*} \xrightarrow{\mathrm{return}\langle \bullet,\bullet \rangle} e$ then $e \not\rightarrow$.

Condition 1 reflects the fact that Unix cannot 'refuse' a particular argument value of an OS routine call, or a `return`. Condition 2 reflects the fact that after an execution of `return` the environment has no further interaction with the program.

The model of interactions between C programs and their environments is completed by a parallel composition operator:

Definition For an environment E and a Γ_e-LTS H we define $E \,||\, H$ to be the $\{\}$-LTS with states pairs e, h of states of E and H, root $\langle \mathrm{root}(E), \mathrm{root}(H) \rangle$ and transitions

$$\frac{e \xrightarrow{x\langle a,r\rangle} e' \quad h \xrightarrow{x\langle a,r\rangle} h'}{e, h \xrightarrow{\tau} e', h'} \qquad \frac{e \xrightarrow{\tau} e'}{e, h \xrightarrow{\tau} e', h} \qquad \frac{h \xrightarrow{\tau} h'}{e, h \xrightarrow{\tau} e, h'}$$

Turning to the SOS, the pervasive Pict type context Γ_p will be taken to have a name $x : !\langle A, \updownarrow\langle R\rangle\rangle$ for each $x : \langle A, R\rangle$ in Γ_u, together with $\mathrm{getXEvent} : ?\langle \mathrm{XEvent}\rangle$ and a name $x : t$ for each base type $t \in \mathcal{T}$ and $x \in |t|$. In example programs the types $!\langle A, \updownarrow\langle \mathrm{Unit}\rangle\rangle$ and $!\langle A, \updownarrow\langle\rangle\rangle$ will be confused. The test harness for the SOS must include a model of the X event buffer, must detect termination and must generate acknowledgements for asynchronous external IO.

Definition For a program P we define $\mathrm{H_{sos}}(P)$ to be the Γ_e-LTS with states $\{\bullet\} \cup \{\, evs, P' \mid evs \in |\mathrm{XEvent}|^* \text{ and } P' \text{ is a } \equiv\text{-class of programs}\,\}$, root $\langle \mathrm{nil}, P\rangle$ and transitions

$$\frac{\Gamma_p \vdash P_1 \xrightarrow[y:\updownarrow\langle R\rangle]{\overline{x}\langle a,y\rangle} Q \qquad r \in |R|}{evs, P_1 \xrightarrow{x\langle a,r\rangle} evs, (\nu y : \updownarrow\langle R\rangle)(\overline{y}\langle r\rangle \mid Q)} \qquad \frac{\Gamma_p \vdash P_1 \xrightarrow[\{\}]{\tau} P_2}{evs, P_1 \xrightarrow{\tau} evs, P_2} \qquad \frac{\Gamma_p \vdash P_1 \not\rightarrow}{evs, P_1 \xrightarrow{\mathrm{return}\langle\bullet,\bullet\rangle} \bullet}$$

$$\frac{}{evs, P_1 \xrightarrow{\mathrm{XInsertEvent}\langle ev,\bullet\rangle} (evs :: ev), P_1} \qquad \frac{\Gamma_p \vdash P_1 \xrightarrow[\{\}]{\mathrm{getXEvent}\langle ev\rangle} P_2}{(ev :: evs), P_1 \xrightarrow{\tau} evs, P_2}$$

4 Testing

We would like to describe, to programmers and implementers, the behaviour of correct Pict implementations in terms of the SOS. The desired intuition is:

An implementation is correct if, for all programs P, a user interacting with the implementation running P cannot tell that he/she is not interacting with the LTS semantics of P given by the SOS.

To formalise 'user interacting with ... cannot tell ...' we consider the environments of §3 to be modelling the user of a Pict system, together with a terminal, Unix, and all of X except its event buffer. As the user is also the pertinent observer of the combined system, we can take observations based on changes of environment state. Letting H range over Γ_e-LTS's of the forms $\mathrm{H_{am}}(C)$ and $\mathrm{H_{sos}}(P)$, for C-behaviours C and programs P, and $\langle e, h\rangle$ range over states of $E \,||\, H$, we define:

$$\begin{aligned}
\langle e, h\rangle \rightharpoonup \langle e', h'\rangle &\overset{def}{\Leftrightarrow} e = e' \wedge \langle e, h\rangle \xrightarrow{\tau} \langle e', h'\rangle \\
\langle e, h\rangle \rightharpoondown \langle e', h'\rangle &\overset{def}{\Leftrightarrow} e \neq e' \wedge \langle e, h\rangle \xrightarrow{\tau} \langle e', h'\rangle \\
\langle e, h\rangle \Rightarrow \langle e', h'\rangle &\overset{def}{\Leftrightarrow} \langle e, h\rangle \rightharpoonup^* \rightharpoondown \rightharpoonup^* \langle e', h'\rangle
\end{aligned}$$

As discussed in §2 the definitions of correctness should be linear time and sensitive to termination and divergence. We therefore take *tests* o to be $\langle E,\vec{e},\mathrm{par}\rangle$, $\langle E,\vec{e},\mathrm{term}\rangle$, $\langle E,\vec{e},\mathrm{div}\rangle$ and $\langle E,\tilde{e}\rangle$, where E is an environment, $\vec{e} \in E^*$ and $\tilde{e} \in E^\omega$. We define a may-testing preorder $\sqsubseteq$ as follows.

$$
\begin{aligned}
H \;\mathbf{may}\; \langle E,\vec{e},\mathrm{par}\rangle &\overset{def}{\Leftrightarrow} \exists \vec{h} \,.\, \langle \mathrm{root}(E),\mathrm{root}(H)\rangle \Rightarrow \langle e_1,h_1\rangle \ldots \Rightarrow \langle e_n,h_n\rangle \\
H \;\mathbf{may}\; \langle E,\vec{e},\mathrm{term}\rangle &\overset{def}{\Leftrightarrow} \exists \vec{h} \,.\, \langle \mathrm{root}(E),\mathrm{root}(H)\rangle \Rightarrow \ldots \Rightarrow \langle e_n,h_n\rangle \rightharpoonup^* \not\rightharpoonup \\
H \;\mathbf{may}\; \langle E,\vec{e},\mathrm{div}\rangle &\overset{def}{\Leftrightarrow} \exists \vec{h} \,.\, \langle \mathrm{root}(E),\mathrm{root}(H)\rangle \Rightarrow \ldots \Rightarrow \langle e_n,h_n\rangle \rightharpoonup^\omega \\
H \;\mathbf{may}\; \langle E,\tilde{e}\rangle &\overset{def}{\Leftrightarrow} \exists \tilde{h} \,.\, \langle \mathrm{root}(E),\mathrm{root}(H)\rangle \Rightarrow \langle e_1,h_1\rangle \Rightarrow \langle e_2,h_2\rangle \ldots \\
H \sqsubseteq H' &\overset{def}{\Leftrightarrow} \forall o \,.\, H \;\mathbf{may}\; o \Rightarrow H' \;\mathbf{may}\; o
\end{aligned}
$$

Finally we can give our central definition:

Definition An *abstract machine* M is a function from programs to C-behaviours. It is *correct* if for all programs P we have $\mathrm{H}_{\mathrm{am}}(M(P)) \sqsubseteq \mathrm{H}_{\mathrm{sos}}(P)$.

We now briefly discuss $\sqsubseteq$ and some conceivable alternatives. It is perhaps the finest appropriate notion. There are two obvious ways in which its definition could be weakened, by amalgamating the termination and divergence tests and by omitting the infinite tests. We have chosen not to do either, as we expect that any reasonable abstract machine will be correct up to the stronger notion given (this is supported by Theorem 1 below). We therefore might as well provide programmers with the stronger guarantees about behaviour. The preorder is not affected by the omission of the tests $\langle E,\vec{e},\mathrm{par}\rangle$. It can be given a direct characterization as an annotated trace inclusion. For $k \in \mathcal{L}(\Gamma_\mathrm{e}) - \{\tau\}$ we take $\overset{k}{\Longrightarrow} \overset{def}{=} \overset{\tau}{\longrightarrow}^* \overset{k}{\longrightarrow} \overset{\tau}{\longrightarrow}^*$ as usual.

$$
\begin{aligned}
\mathrm{tr}_{\mathrm{dead}}(H) &\overset{def}{=} \{ k_1 \ldots k_n \mid \exists h \,.\, \mathrm{root}(H) \overset{k_1}{\Longrightarrow} \ldots \overset{k_n}{\Longrightarrow} \overset{\tau}{\longrightarrow}^* h \\
&\qquad\qquad \wedge \neg \exists l \in \mathcal{L}(\Gamma_\mathrm{e} - \mathrm{XInsertEvent}) \,.\, h \overset{l}{\longrightarrow} \} \\
\mathrm{tr}_{\mathrm{div}}(H) &\overset{def}{=} \{ k_1 \ldots k_n \mid \mathrm{root}(H) \overset{k_1}{\Longrightarrow} \ldots \overset{k_n}{\Longrightarrow} \overset{\tau}{\longrightarrow}^\omega \} \\
\mathrm{tr}_{\mathrm{inf}}(H) &\overset{def}{=} \{ k_1 k_2 \ldots \mid \mathrm{root}(H) \overset{k_1}{\Longrightarrow} \overset{k_2}{\Longrightarrow} \ldots \}
\end{aligned}
$$

Proposition 3 *$H \sqsubseteq H'$ iff $\forall \kappa \in \{\mathrm{dead},\mathrm{div},\mathrm{inf}\} \,.\, \mathrm{tr}_\kappa(H) \subseteq \mathrm{tr}_\kappa(H')$.*

The proof of this uses standard techniques, involving discriminating environments constructed from traces over $\mathcal{L}(\Gamma_\mathrm{e}) - \{\tau\}$. The preorder $\sqsubseteq$ is intuitively closely related to the annotated trace inclusions of Hoare [Hoa85] and the testing of De Nicola and Hennessy [DH84]. We give an exact comparison with the latter. Instantiating their definitions, say a *DH-test* d is a pair $\langle E,\surd\rangle$ of an environment E and set of 'successful' states $\surd \subseteq E$. Letting $e_0 = \mathrm{root}(E)$:

$$
\begin{aligned}
H \;\mathbf{may}\; \langle E,\surd\rangle &\overset{def}{\Leftrightarrow} \exists e \in \surd, h \,.\, \langle e_0,\mathrm{root}(H)\rangle \longrightarrow^* \langle e,h\rangle \\
H \;\mathbf{must}\; \langle E,\surd\rangle &\overset{def}{\Leftrightarrow} \langle e_0,\mathrm{root}(H)\rangle \overset{\tau}{\longrightarrow} \ldots \overset{\tau}{\longrightarrow} \langle e_n,h_n\rangle \not\longrightarrow \Rightarrow \exists i \in 0..n \,.\, e_i \surd \\
&\qquad \wedge \langle e_0,\mathrm{root}(H)\rangle \overset{\tau}{\longrightarrow} \langle e_1,h_1\rangle \overset{\tau}{\longrightarrow} \ldots \Rightarrow \exists i \geq 0 \,.\, e_i \surd
\end{aligned}
$$

$$H \sqsubseteq_{\mathrm{DH-may}} H' \overset{def}{\Leftrightarrow} \forall d \,.\, H \textbf{ may } d \Rightarrow H' \textbf{ may } d$$
$$H \sqsubseteq_{\mathrm{DH-must}} H' \overset{def}{\Leftrightarrow} \forall d \,.\, H \textbf{ must } d \Rightarrow H' \textbf{ must } d$$

It is straightforward to check that $\sqsubseteq \subsetneq (\sqsubseteq_{\mathrm{DH-may}} \cap \sqsubseteq_{\mathrm{DH-must}}^{-1})$. For forwards must-testing, however, one has $\sqsubseteq \not\subseteq \sqsubseteq_{\mathrm{DH-must}}$. Moreover, including forwards must-testing would render reasonable abstract machines 'incorrect', e.g. abstract machines that, given the program $(\nu x : \updownarrow\langle\rangle)(\overline{x}\langle\rangle \mid x().0 \mid x().(\nu y : \updownarrow\langle\rangle)(\overline{y}\langle\rangle \mid !\, y().\overline{y}\langle\rangle))$, always return.

One could imagine taking tests based on Pict contexts (following e.g. [Hen91, BD95]) rather than on our test harnesses and $||$. It is hard to see how the facts about Pict could be introduced, particularly given that termination detection is required. More generally, there is no reason to suppose that the interactions between a Pict implementation and its environment are of the same kind as the interactions between two Pict subprograms. Several authors have considered restricting to observations that are in some sense effective. A user may indeed only be concerned with effective *real time* properties of implementations, however we do not wish to incorporate these properties into the language definition. We must therefore either allow 'infinite' observations or neglect divergence despite the fact that users are concerned with it.

We give an example abstract machine M_1, closely based on the actual Pict implementation, in Figure 2. It has states $\langle\Gamma\,;\, rq\,;\, cqs\rangle$ consisting of a type context Γ, a run queue rq and a collection of channel queues cqs. The rules for internal transitions follow those of Turner [Tur96, Ch. 7], although without certain optimisations. For external communication X is polled periodically for new X events (whenever the token $\mathbb{X}$ reaches the front of the run queue). The rules ensure that no potentially blocking XNextEvent call is performed except when all processes are waiting for an event, in which case a blocking call *is* made (to avoid busy-waiting). Other non-blocking IO occurs immediately, and the machine returns when there are no processes left in the run queue or left waiting for X events.

Theorem 1 *M_1 is a correct abstract machine.*

The proof of this uses a decompilation function from states of $\mathrm{H_{am}}(M_1(P))$ to states of $\mathrm{H_{sos}}(P)$, using which one can prove that $\mathrm{H_{am}}(M_1(P))$ simulates (in a specialised sense that refines $\sqsupseteq$) $\mathrm{H_{sos}}(P)$. The treatment of events and divergence is delicate; the rest is reasonably straightforward (as one would hope, as M_1 is not optimised).

5 The Observational Precongruence

The same testing scenario can be used to define an observational preorder over programs that is appropriate as a standard of correctness for program transformations, such as those considered by Jones [Jon96], Philippou and Walker [PW96], and Nestmann and Pierce [NP96]. The desired intuition is:

STATES: $\langle \Gamma\, ; rq\, ; cqs \rangle$ where

- Γ is a finite type context with names only at channel types such that $\mathrm{dom}(\Gamma_{\mathrm{p}}) \cap \mathrm{dom}(\Gamma) = \{\}$
- $\Gamma'_{\mathrm{p}} = (\Gamma_{\mathrm{p}} - \mathrm{getXEvent}), \mathrm{getXEvent} : \updownarrow\langle \mathrm{XEvent} \rangle$
- $\mathrm{outs}(x, \Gamma) = \{\, \overline{x}\langle \vec{z} \rangle \mid \Gamma'_{\mathrm{p}}, \Gamma \vdash \overline{x}\langle \vec{z} \rangle \,\}^{+}$
- $\mathrm{ins}(x, \Gamma) = (\{\, x(\vec{y}).P \mid \Gamma'_{\mathrm{p}}, \Gamma \vdash x(\vec{y}).P \,\} \cup \{\, !x(\vec{y}).P \mid \Gamma'_{\mathrm{p}}, \Gamma \vdash !x(\vec{y}).P \,\})^{+}$
- $rq \in (\{\mathbb{X}, \mathbb{X}'\} \cup \{\, P \mid \Gamma'_{\mathrm{p}}, \Gamma \vdash P \,\})^{*}$
- $cqs \in \Pi x \in \mathrm{dom}(\Gamma) \cup \{\mathrm{getXEvent}\} \,.\, \{\mathrm{nil}\} \cup \mathrm{outs}(x, \Gamma) \cup \mathrm{ins}(x, \Gamma)$

INITIAL STATE: $\mathrm{root}(M_1(P_0)) \stackrel{\mathit{def}}{=} \langle \{\}\, ; P_0 :: \mathbb{X} :: \mathrm{nil}\, ; \{\mathrm{getXEvent} \mapsto \mathrm{nil}\} \rangle$.

TRANSITIONS:

$$
\begin{array}{llr}
\langle \Gamma ; 0 :: rq ; cqs \rangle & \xrightarrow{\tau} \langle \Gamma ; rq ; cqs \rangle & \\
\langle \Gamma ; \overline{x}\langle \vec{z} \rangle :: rq ; cqs, x \mapsto x(\vec{y}).P :: cq \rangle & \xrightarrow{\tau} \langle \Gamma ; rq :: P[\vec{z}/\vec{y}] ; cqs, x \mapsto cq \rangle & \\
\langle \Gamma ; \overline{x}\langle \vec{z} \rangle :: rq ; cqs, x \mapsto !x(\vec{y}).P :: cq \rangle & \xrightarrow{\tau} \langle \Gamma ; rq :: P[\vec{z}/\vec{y}] :: !x(\vec{y}).P ; cqs, x \mapsto cq \rangle & \\
\langle \Gamma ; \overline{x}\langle \vec{z} \rangle :: rq ; cqs, x \mapsto cq \rangle & \xrightarrow{\tau} \langle \Gamma ; rq ; cqs, x \mapsto cq :: \overline{x}\langle \vec{z} \rangle \rangle & 1 \\
\langle \Gamma ; x(\vec{y}).P :: rq ; cqs, x \mapsto \overline{x}\langle \vec{z} \rangle.P :: cq \rangle & \xrightarrow{\tau} \langle \Gamma ; rq :: P[\vec{z}/\vec{y}] ; cqs, x \mapsto cq \rangle & \\
\langle \Gamma ; x(\vec{y}).P :: rq ; cqs, x \mapsto cq \rangle & \xrightarrow{\tau} \langle \Gamma ; rq ; cqs, x \mapsto cq :: x(\vec{y}).P \rangle & 2 \\
\langle \Gamma ; !x(\vec{y}).P :: rq ; cqs, x \mapsto \overline{x}\langle \vec{z} \rangle.P :: cq \rangle & \xrightarrow{\tau} \langle \Gamma ; rq :: P[\vec{z}/\vec{y}] :: !x(\vec{y}).P ; cqs, x \mapsto cq \rangle & \\
\langle \Gamma ; !x(\vec{y}).P :: rq ; cqs, x \mapsto cq \rangle & \xrightarrow{\tau} \langle \Gamma ; rq ; cqs, x \mapsto cq :: !x(\vec{y}).P \rangle & 2 \\
\langle \Gamma ; (P \mid Q) :: rq ; cqs \rangle & \xrightarrow{\tau} \langle \Gamma ; rq :: P :: Q ; cqs \rangle & \\
\langle \Gamma ; (\nu x : T)P :: rq ; cqs \rangle & \xrightarrow{\tau} \langle (\Gamma, x : T) ; rq :: P ; cqs, x \mapsto \mathrm{nil} \rangle & 3 \\
\langle \Gamma ; [x = x]P :: rq ; cqs \rangle & \xrightarrow{\tau} \langle \Gamma ; rq :: P ; cqs \rangle & \\
\langle \Gamma ; [x = y]P :: rq ; cqs \rangle & \xrightarrow{\tau} \langle \Gamma ; rq ; cqs \rangle & 4 \\
 & & \\
\langle \Gamma ; \overline{x}\langle a, y \rangle :: rq ; cqs \rangle & \xrightarrow{x\langle a, r \rangle} \langle \Gamma ; rq :: \overline{y}\langle r \rangle ; cqs \rangle & 5 \\
 & & \\
\langle \Gamma ; \mathbb{X} :: P :: rq ; cqs \rangle & \xrightarrow{\mathrm{XPending}\langle \bullet, 0 \rangle} \langle \Gamma ; P :: rq :: \mathbb{X} ; cqs \rangle & \\
\langle \Gamma ; \mathbb{X} :: P :: rq ; cqs \rangle & \xrightarrow{\mathrm{XPending}\langle \bullet, n+1 \rangle} \langle \Gamma ; \mathbb{X}' :: P :: rq ; cqs \rangle & \\
\langle \Gamma ; \mathbb{X}' :: P :: rq ; cqs \rangle & \xrightarrow{\mathrm{XNextEvent}\langle \bullet, ev \rangle} \langle \Gamma ; \overline{\mathrm{getXEvent}}\langle ev \rangle :: P :: rq :: \mathbb{X} ; cqs \rangle & \\
\langle \Gamma ; \mathbb{X} :: \mathrm{nil} ; cqs \rangle & \xrightarrow{\mathrm{XNextEvent}\langle \bullet, ev \rangle} \langle \Gamma ; \overline{\mathrm{getXEvent}}\langle ev \rangle :: \mathbb{X} :: \mathrm{nil} ; cqs \rangle & 6 \\
\langle \Gamma ; \mathbb{X} :: \mathrm{nil} ; cqs \rangle & \xrightarrow{\mathrm{return}\langle \bullet, \bullet \rangle} \langle \Gamma ; \mathrm{nil} ; cqs \rangle & 7
\end{array}
$$

Side conditions 1: $cq \notin \mathrm{ins}(x, \Gamma)$, 2: $cq \notin \mathrm{outs}(x, \Gamma)$, 3: $x \notin \mathrm{dom}(\Gamma_{\mathrm{p}}, \Gamma)$, 4: $x \neq y$, 5: $\Gamma_{\mathrm{p}}(x) = !\langle A, \updownarrow\langle R \rangle \rangle \wedge r \in |R|$, 6: $cqs(\mathrm{getXEvent}) \in \mathrm{ins}(\mathrm{getXEvent}, \Gamma)$, 7: $cqs(\mathrm{getXEvent}) \notin \mathrm{ins}(\mathrm{getXEvent}, \Gamma)$.

Figure 2: The abstract machine M_1 executing a program P_0

A program P can be transformed to a program P' if, for all correct abstract machines M, a user interacting with $\mathrm{H_{am}}(M(P'))$ cannot tell that he/she is not interacting with $\mathrm{H_{sos}}(P)$.

This is formalised by the *observational preorder* $\dot{\gtrsim}$ over programs, where $P \dot{\gtrsim} P'$ iff for all correct abstract machines M we have $\mathrm{H_{am}}(M(P')) \sqsubseteq \mathrm{H_{sos}}(P)$. (Transitivity requires a brief argument.) The observational preorder reflects the realities of Pict implementations, with for example $(\nu x : \updownarrow\langle\rangle)\overline{\mathrm{pr}}\langle\text{“Ping”}, x\rangle \quad (\dot{\gtrsim} \cap \dot{\gtrsim}^{-1}) \quad (\nu x : \updownarrow\langle\rangle)(\overline{\mathrm{pr}}\langle\text{“Ping”}, x\rangle \mid x().x().P)$, $(\nu x : \updownarrow\langle\rangle)(\overline{x}\langle\rangle \mid x().0 \mid x().\overline{\mathrm{pr}}\langle\text{“Ping”}, x\rangle) \ \dot{\gtrsim}\ 0$ and $(\nu x : \updownarrow\langle\rangle)\overline{\mathrm{pr}}\langle\text{“Ping”}, x\rangle \dot{\not\gtrsim} 0$. These confirm that $\dot{\gtrsim}$ differs from standard π-calculus notions. As correctness does not fix a particular scheduling strategy, a correct abstract machine may have completely different behaviour when executing structurally congruent programs, let alone those related by $\dot{\gtrsim}$. Further, different correct abstract machines may behave completely differently when executing the same program. A programmer should therefore only write programs for which any execution path (from those given by the SOS) would be acceptable. This is obviously problematic, accentuating the need for formal development techniques and the identification of well behaved (especially, confluent) idioms.

The observational preorder induces an *observational precongruence* $\gtrsim$ and hence a term model for Pict. Say a *typed precongruence* $>$ is a family of relations, indexed by type contexts, such that each $>_\Gamma$ is an preorder over $\{ P \mid \Gamma \vdash P \}$ and $>$ satisfies the evident congruence rules. $\gtrsim$ is defined to be the largest typed precongruence such that $\gtrsim_{\Gamma_P} \subseteq \dot{\gtrsim}$. We conclude by giving a typed congruence with a tractable definition that refines $\gtrsim$ and may suffice for many program transformations. Further work should take into account the asynchronous nature of Pict and a larger fragment of its type system, building on [ACS96, PS96]. Say *weak divergence bisimulation*, written $\dot{\approx}$, is the largest type context indexed family of relations such that each $\dot{\approx}_\Gamma$ is a symmetric relation over $\{ P \mid \Gamma \vdash P \}$ and, for all $P \dot{\approx}_\Gamma Q$: if $\Gamma \vdash P \xrightarrow[\Delta]{\alpha} P'$ then $\exists Q' \,.\, \Gamma \vdash Q \xRightarrow[\Delta]{\hat{\alpha}} Q' \wedge P' \dot{\approx}_{\Gamma,\Delta} Q'$ and if $\Gamma \vdash P \xrightarrow[\{\}]{\tau}{}^{\omega}$ then $\Gamma \vdash Q \xrightarrow[\{\}]{\tau}{}^{\omega}$, where $\xRightarrow[\Delta]{\hat{\alpha}} \stackrel{def}{=} \xrightarrow[\{\}]{\tau}{}^{*} \xrightarrow[\Delta]{\alpha} \xrightarrow[\{\}]{\tau}{}^{*}$, for $\alpha \neq \tau$, and $\xRightarrow[\{\}]{\hat{\tau}} \stackrel{def}{=} \xrightarrow[\{\}]{\tau}{}^{*}$. We define $\approx$ by $P \approx_\Gamma Q$ iff for all substitutions $[\vec{z}/\vec{y}]$, such that $\forall i \,.\, \Gamma(z_i) = \Gamma(y_i)$, we have $P[\vec{z}/\vec{y}] \dot{\approx}_\Gamma Q[\vec{z}/\vec{y}]$.

Proposition 4 $\approx$ *is a typed congruence.*

Theorem 2 $\approx \subseteq \gtrsim$.

Acknowledgements I would like to thank Benjamin Pierce for many interesting discussions on this work and the EPSRC for support via grant GR/K 38403.

References

[Abr87] Samson Abramsky. Observation equivalence as a testing equivalence. *Theoretical Computer Science*, 53:225–241, 1987.

[ACS96] Roberto M. Amadio, Ilaria Castellani, and Davide Sangiorgi. On bisimulations for the asynchronous π-calculus. In Montanari and Sassone [MS96], pages 147–162.

[AV93] S. Abramsky and S. J. Vickers. Quantales, observational logic and process semantics. *Mathematical Structures in Computer Science*, 3:161–227, 1993.

[BD95] Michele Boreale and Rocco De Nicola. Testing equivalences for mobile processes. *Information and Computation*, 120:279–303, 1995.

[DH84] R. De Nicola and M. C. B. Hennessy. Testing equivalences for processes. *Theoretical Computer Science*, 34:83–133, 1984.

[FG96] Cédric Fournet and Georges Gonthier. The reflexive CHAM and the join-calculus. In POPL'96 [POP96], pages 372–385.

[Gla90] R. J. van Glabeek. The linear time — branching time spectrum. In *Proceedings CONCUR '90, LNCS 458*, pages 278–297, 1990.

[Gla93] R. J. van Glabbeek. The linear time — branching time spectrum II (the semantics of sequential systems with silent moves). In *Proceedings of CONCUR '93, LNCS 715*, pages 66–81, 1993.

[Hen91] M. Hennessy. A model for the π-calculus. Technical Report 91:08, University of Sussex, 1991.

[HM80] Matthew Hennessy and Robin Milner. On observing nondeterminism and concurrency. In *Proceedings 7th ICALP, LNCS 85*, pages 299–309, 1980.

[Hoa85] C. A. R. Hoare. *Communicating Sequential Processes*. Series in Computer Science. Prentice-Hall International, 1985.

[JGF96] Simon Peyton Jones, Andrew Gordon, and Sigbjorn Finne. Concurrent Haskell. In POPL'96 [POP96], pages 295–308.

[Jon96] C. B. Jones. Accommodating interference in the formal design of concurrent object-based programs. *Formal Methods in System Design*, 8(2):105–122, March 1996.

[Mil81] Robin Milner. A modal characterisation of observable machine-behaviour. In *Proceedings CAAP '81, LNCS 112*, pages 25–34, 1981.

[MPW92] R. Milner, J. Parrow, and D. Walker. A calculus of mobile processes, Parts I + II. *Information and Computation*, 100(1):1–77, 1992.

[MS96] Ugo Montanari and Vladimiro Sassone, editors. *Proceedings CONCUR 96*, Pisa, Italy, volume 1119 of *Lecture Notes in Computer Science*. Springer-Verlag, 1996.

[NP96] Uwe Nestmann and Benjamin C. Pierce. Decoding choice encodings. In Montanari and Sassone [MS96], pages 179–194.

[POP96] *Conference Record of the* 23rd *ACM Symposium on Principles of Programming Languages*, 1996.

[PS96] Benjamin Pierce and Davide Sangiorgi. Typing and subtyping for mobile processes. *Mathematical Structures in Computer Science*, 6(5), 1996.

[PT97] Benjamin C. Pierce and David N. Turner. Pict: A programming language based on the pi-calculus. Technical report, Computer Science Department, Indiana University, 1997. To appear in Milner *festschrift*, MIT Press.

[PW96] Anna Philippou and David Walker. On transformations of concurrent object programs. In Montanari and Sassone [MS96], pages 131–146.

[Rep92] John Hamilton Reppy. *Higher-Order Concurrency*. PhD thesis, Cornell University, June 1992. Technical Report TR 92-1285.

[San93] Davide Sangiorgi. *Expressing Mobility in Process Algebras: First-Order and Higher-Order Paradigms*. PhD thesis, University of Edinburgh, 1993.

[TLK96] Bent Thomsen, Lone Leth, and Tsung-Min Kuo. A Facile tutorial. In Montanari and Sassone [MS96], pages 278–298.

[Tur96] David N. Turner. *The Polymorphic Pi-calculus: Theory and Implementation*. PhD thesis, University of Edinburgh, 1996.

[Wal88] D. J. Walker. Bisimulations and divergence. In *Proc. 3rd IEEE Symposium on Logic in Computer Science*, pages 186–192, 1988.

Algebraic Characterization of Petri Net Pomset Semantics

Harro Wimmel Lutz Priese

Universität Koblenz–Landau
D-56075 Koblenz, Germany
wimmel,priese@uni-koblenz.de

Abstract. Sets of pomsets are frequently used as a true-concurrency, linear-time semantics of Petri nets. For a Petri net N, let $\mathcal{P}(N)$, a set of pomsets, denote the pomset behaviour of N, and let $\mathcal{P} := \{\mathcal{P}(N) \mid N$ is a Petri net$\}$ denote the class of pomset behaviours of Petri nets, a generalization of $\mathcal{L}$, the class of all Petri net languages. We present here an algebraic characterization for $\mathcal{P}$, similar to the known algebraic characterizations for $\mathcal{L}$.

1 Introduction

We assume the reader is familiar with Petri nets and to some extent with the definition of their interleaving behaviour, Petri net languages. Interleaving languages of Petri nets, consisting of linear words of firing sequences or their labellings, have been intensively studied. Famous results are found e.g. in [5], [6], [7], or [10]. Especially Hack [6] has proved several characterizations for interleaving behaviours. He distinguishes between *terminal behaviours* where a firing sequence must reach some predefined terminal marking, and *prefix-closed behaviours* where any firing sequence contributes to the behaviour. Also, a distinction is made between behaviours based on nets with unobservable τ-transitions and nets without such τ-transitions. We will take a closer look at the prefix-closed behaviour of Petri nets with τ-transitions in this paper. Hack's characterization for prefix-closed behaviours with τ-transitions may be written as

$$\mathcal{L} = \bar{Cl}^{\sqcup\!\sqcup, h_\ell, h^{-1}, \cap}(\text{Pref } D_1, \{\epsilon, a\}),$$

where $\bar{Cl}^{op_1,\ldots,op_m}(L_1,\ldots,L_n)$ means the smallest family closed under $op_1,\ldots,$ op_m and containing $L_1,\ldots,L_n$. D_1 is the *Dyck-language* containing all correct parenthesis expressions over one pair of parentheses, and Pref D_1 is the language of all prefixes of D_1. $\sqcup\!\sqcup$ denotes the *shuffle*, h_ℓ the *letter homomorphism* (which maps each letter to another letter or ϵ), h^{-1} the *inverse homomorphism*, and $\cap$ the set theoretic *intersection*. Thus, $\mathcal{L}$ is the smallest family that contains Pref D_1 and $\{\epsilon, a\}$ and is closed under the above operations.

To obtain true-concurrency we generalize words to partially ordered multisets, *pomsets* for short. Any pomset consists of a number of letters and a partial order on them. Sets of such pomsets are generalizations of languages. We shall characterize sets of pomsets describing the behaviour of Petri nets by a formula very similar to that of Hack. For a closer look at pomsets the reader is referred to [2], [11], or [14]. A categorical characterization of Petri net semantics can be found in [3] and [8], where several concurrent behaviours like processes and unfoldings are compared.

We shall present an algebraic characterization for the class of pomset behaviours of Petri nets with τ-transitions. In section 2 we define the pomset behaviour of Petri nets. In section 3 we introduce algebraic operations on pomsets and prove the family of pomset behaviours of Petri nets to be closed under them. In section 4 we present a compositional pomset semantics using only our algebraic operators and a fixed set of pomset behaviours. Finally, in section 5 we conclude our algebraic characterization and show that Hack's result is a special case.

2 Petri Nets and their Pomsets

Definition 1 (Preliminaries) Let *Act* denote some fixed, infinite, countable set of *actions*. We frequently use a, b, ... as names for actions. Let $Act_\tau := Act \cup \{\tau\}$, where τ is an *invisible* action. For sets A and B we denote by $A \dot{\cup} B$ the *disjoint union* of A and B. If A and B are not disjoint we assume the elements of one of the sets to be renamed. For a relation R on some set A, $R \subseteq A \times A$, let R^+ denote the transitive closure of R. Any mapping $h : A \to B$ with arbitrary sets A and B may be canonically extended to a mapping on multisets $h' : (A \to \mathbb{N}) \to (B \to \mathbb{N})$ by defining $h'(f)(b) := \sum_{a \in h^{-1}(b)} f(a)$ for any $f : A \to \mathbb{N}$ and $b \in B$. As any set A may be viewed as a mapping $A \to \{1\}$ we do not distinguish between h and h'. □

We shall define the pomset behaviour of a standard Petri net and present a smooth algebraic characterization of the class of pomset semantics for standard Petri nets. However, to do so we need Petri nets with an *interface*. An interface of a Petri net, N, is an ordered set of some places and transitions of N that are declared as *public*. This means that the algebra of Petri nets, which is introduced in section 4, contains operators working on public places and transitions only, plus operations for removing places and transitions from the interface.

Definition 2 (Petri Net) A finite labelled Petri net with an interface, *Petri net* for short, is a 7–tuple $N = (P_N, T_N, F_N, \lambda_N, s_N, \mathbf{p}, \mathbf{t})$, where

- P_N is a finite set of *places*, T_N is a finite set of *transitions*, and $P_N \cap T_N = \emptyset$,
- $F_N : (P_N \times T_N) \cup (T_N \times P_N) \to \mathbb{N}$ is a mapping defining directed *(multi)arcs* between transitions and places,
- $\lambda_N : T_N \to Act_\tau$ is a *labelling function*,
- $s_N : P_N \to \mathbb{N}$ is the *initial state* (or *marking*),
- $\mathbf{p} = p_1 \ldots p_m$ is a word of distinct places in P_N, the word of ordered *interface places*,
- $\mathbf{t} = t_1 \ldots t_n$ is a word of distinct transitions in T_N, the word of ordered *interface transitions*, such that $\lambda_N(t_i) \neq \tau$ for $1 \leq i \leq n$.

For an element $x \in P_N \cup T_N$ we also use the notation ${}^\bullet x := F_N(\cdot, x)$ and $x^\bullet := F_N(x, \cdot)$. For some interface word $\mathbf{w}$ let $\mathbf{w}(i)$ denote the i-th letter of $\mathbf{w}$. We write $x \in \mathbf{w}$ if $x = \mathbf{w}(i)$ for some i. We denote the class of (finite, labelled) *Petri nets* (with an interface) by $\mathcal{PNI}$. A *classical Petri net* is a Petri net with an empty interface, $\mathbf{p} = \epsilon = \mathbf{t}$. $\mathcal{PN}$ denotes the class of classical Petri nets. $(|\mathbf{p}|, |\mathbf{t}|)$ is called the *dimension* of N. □

Definition 3 (Posets, Causality Structures, Pomsets) A *partially ordered set (poset)* is a pair (σ, R) of a finite set σ and an irreflexive, transitive, antisymmetric relation, a partial order, $R \subseteq \sigma \times \sigma$. We call e_1 a *predecessor* of e_2 if $e_1 R e_2$ holds. e_1 is a *direct predecessor* of e_2 if additionally there is no e with $e_1 R e$ and $e R e_2$. In this case, e_2 is the (*direct*) *successor* of e_1. A *causality structure κ over Act* is a triple $\kappa = (\sigma_\kappa, R_\kappa, \lambda_\kappa)$ consisting of a poset $(\sigma_\kappa, R_\kappa)$ and a labelling function $\lambda_\kappa : \sigma_\kappa \rightarrow Act$. Two causality structures κ_1, κ_2 are *isomorphic* if there is a bijection $\alpha\colon \sigma_{\kappa_1} \rightarrow \sigma_{\kappa_2}$ with $\alpha(e_1) R_{\kappa_2} \alpha(e_2) \iff e_1 R_{\kappa_1} e_2$ for all $e_1, e_2 \in \sigma_{\kappa_1}$ and $\lambda_{\kappa_2} \circ \alpha = \lambda_{\kappa_1}$. A *pomset (partially ordered multiset)* p is an isomorphism class of causality structures. By $[\kappa]$ we denote the pomset containing the causality structure κ as a representative. $\mathcal{POM}$ denotes the class of pomsets. □

Graphically, a pomset $[(\sigma, R, \lambda)]$ will be presented as a directed graph whose nodes are labelled by elements of the set $\lambda(\sigma)$ and whose directed arcs, $\longrightarrow$, represent the direct predecessor relation. For an example see figure 1.

$p = [(\sigma, R^+, \lambda)]$ with
$\sigma = \{1, 2, 3, 4, 5, 6, 7, 8\}$,
$R = \{(1,4), (2,4), (1,5), (4,5), (5,7), (4,6), (3,6), (6,8)\}$,
λ: $1, 7 \mapsto a$; $2, 4 \mapsto b$; $5, 6 \mapsto c$; $3 \mapsto d$; $8 \mapsto e$.

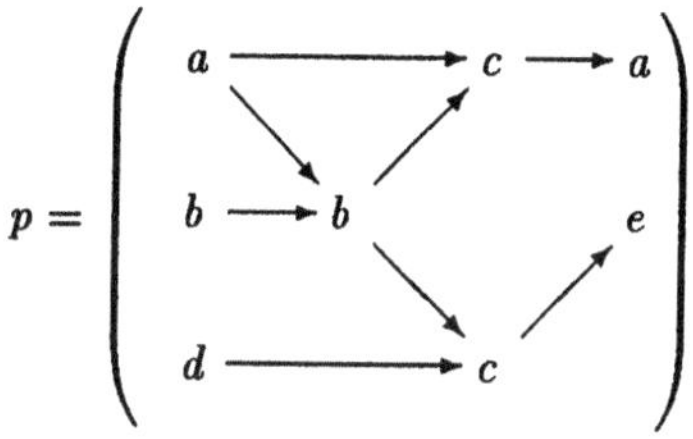

Fig. 1. Formal and graphical view of a pomset p

Some authors use pomsets of infinite size, though they generally will put some restrictions on them. In [2], for example, pomsets may contain infinitely many actions but must have a finite "breadth". We use pomsets as a generalization of finite words, thus we do not consider pomsets with an infinite number of actions at all. Our formalization of the pomset semantics of a Petri net is very similar to that of Pomello et al [10]. Pomsets are seen as an abstraction of processes. A process reflects an actual simulation of the token game of a Petri net.

Definition 4 (Occurrence Net) A (finite) *Occurrence net*, *O-net* for short, is a triple (B, E, F) fulfilling the following conditions:

1. B and E are finite sets of *conditions* and *events* with $B \cap E = \emptyset$,
2. $F \subseteq (B \times E) \cup (E \times B)$ describes directed arcs between B and E,
3. F^+ is acyclic,
4. $\forall b \in B$: $|{}^\bullet b| \leq 1 \wedge |b^\bullet| \leq 1$.

We also write $F(x, y) = 1$ for xFy and $F(x, y) = 0$ for $\neg xFy$. □

Definition 5 (Process) A process π_N of a Petri net $N = (P, T, F_N, \lambda_N, s_0, \mathbf{p}, \mathbf{t})$ is a triple (O, r, λ), where

1. $O = (B, E, F)$ is an O-net,
2. $\lambda : E \rightarrow Act_\tau$ is defined as $\lambda := \lambda_N \circ r|_E$,
3. $r : B \cup E \rightarrow P \cup T$ with $r(B) \subseteq P$ and $r(E) \subseteq T$, is a projection which "folds" the O-net O onto the Petri net N, obeying the following two rules:
4. $\forall e \in E$: $r({}^\bullet e) = {}^\bullet r(e) \wedge r(e^\bullet) = r(e)^\bullet$, and
5. $r(\{b \in B \mid {}^\bullet b = \emptyset\}) = s_0$.

Let $Proc(N)$ denote the class of all processes of N. □

As a pomset is supposed to describe a possible, observable behaviour, we consider only the observable events and their relations in a process.

Definition 6 (A Pomset of a Petri net) Φ: $\bigcup_{N \in \mathcal{PNI}} Proc(N) \rightarrow \mathcal{POM}$ is defined as $\Phi((O, r, \lambda)) := [(\sigma_p, R_p, \lambda_p)]$ with $\sigma_p := \{e \in E \mid \lambda(e) \neq \tau\}$, $R_p := F^+|_{\sigma_p \times \sigma_p}$, and $\lambda_p := \lambda|_{\sigma_p}$ for $O = (B, E, F)$. □

Thus, the pomset $\Phi(\pi)$ is an abstraction from the process π. We allow for autoconcurrency here, i.e. multiple instances of the same action may occur in a pomset $\Phi(\pi)$ without any causal ordering between them. Another property that can be derived from the processes of a net N is prefix-closure. We define prefixes of pomsets recursively, any pomset p being prefix of itself, and if $[(\sigma, R, \lambda)]$ is a prefix of p and some $e \in \sigma$ is maximal with respect to R then $[(\sigma - \{e\}, R|_{(\sigma-\{e\})\times(\sigma-\{e\})}, \lambda|_{\sigma-\{e\}})]$ is a prefix of p, too. As the set $Proc(N)$ is known to be prefix-closed, so is the set of all pomsets of a Petri net N.

Definition 7 (Pomset Behaviour) We define the set of all pomsets, or *pomset behaviour*, of a given Petri net N by

$$\mathcal{P}(N) := \{\Phi(\pi) \mid \pi \text{ is a process of } N\}.$$

$\mathcal{P} := \{\mathcal{P}(N) \mid N \text{ is a Petri net}\}$ denotes the class of these pomset behaviours of Petri nets, i.e. $\mathcal{P} \subseteq 2^{\mathcal{POM}}$. □

Some examples of Petri nets with typical pomsets from their respective behaviours can be seen in figure 2. For any pomset behaviour $L \in \mathcal{P}$ let Act_L denote the set of all actions from Act actually appearing in some pomset $p \in L$.

3 Algebraic Operations on Pomsets

We now define four algebraic operations on sets of pomsets that we need for our algebraic characterization of the class of Petri net pomset behaviours. We shall prove that $\mathcal{P}$ is closed under each of these operations.

Definition 8 (Shuffle) For pomsets $p = [(\sigma_p, R_p, \lambda_p)]$ and $q = [(\sigma_q, R_q, \lambda_q)]$ the *shuffle* of p and q is defined by $p \sqcup\!\sqcup q := [(\sigma_p \dot{\cup} \sigma_q, R_p \cup R_q, \lambda_p \cup \lambda_q)]$. In addition, we define a *big shuffle* on a set of pomsets L inductively by $\bigsqcup\!\!\!\sqcup^0 L := \{(\epsilon)\} := \{[(\emptyset, \emptyset, \emptyset)]\}$, $\bigsqcup\!\!\!\sqcup^{n+1} L := L \sqcup\!\sqcup \bigsqcup\!\!\!\sqcup^n L$, and $\bigsqcup\!\!\!\sqcup L := \bigcup_{n \in \mathbb{N}} \bigsqcup\!\!\!\sqcup^n L$. □

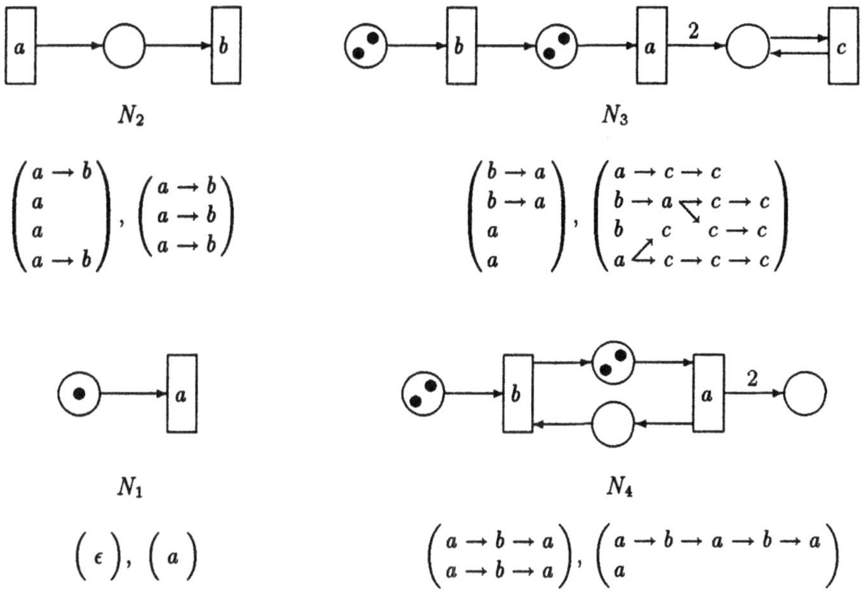

Fig. 2. Some Petri nets with some pomsets

We can use the big shuffle for a short description of a pomset behaviour. E.g., the pomset behaviour of the net N_2 of figure 2 is $\biguplus\{(a \rightarrow b), (a)\}$.

Lemma 1 ($\mathcal{P}$ is closed under shuffle) For any two Petri nets $N_i = (P_i, T_i, F_i, \lambda_i, s_{0i}, \mathbf{p}_i, \mathbf{t}_i)$, $i \in \{1, 2\}$, there is a Petri net N such that $\mathcal{P}(N) = \mathcal{P}(N_1) \uplus \mathcal{P}(N_2)$ holds.

Proof: Choose $N = (P_1 \dot\cup P_2, T_1 \dot\cup T_2, F_1 \cup F_2, \lambda_1 \cup \lambda_2, s_{01} + s_{02}, \mathbf{p}_1\mathbf{p}_2, \mathbf{t}_1\mathbf{t}_2)$. ■

Definition 9 (Letter Homomorphism) Let h_ℓ: $Act \rightarrow Act_\tau$ be a mapping. For a pomset $p = [(\sigma_p, R_p, \lambda_p)]$ the *letter homomorphism* h_ℓ applied to p is defined by $h_\ell(p) := [(\sigma'_p, R_p|_{\sigma'_p \times \sigma'_p}, h_\ell \circ \lambda_p|_{\sigma'_p})]$ with $\sigma'_p := \{e \in \sigma_p \mid h_\ell \circ \lambda_p(e) \neq \tau\}$. □

A letter homomorphism is just a renaming of the labels of a pomset where we drop the τ-labels.

Lemma 2 ($\mathcal{P}$ is closed under letter homomorphism) For any Petri net $N = (P, T, F, \lambda, s_0, \mathbf{p}, \mathbf{t})$ and mapping $h_\ell : Act \rightarrow Act_\tau$, there is a Petri net N' with $\mathcal{P}(N') = h_\ell(\mathcal{P}(N))$.

Proof: Extend h_ℓ to Act_τ by defining $h_\ell(\tau) := \tau$. $N' := (P, T, F, \lambda', s_0, \mathbf{p}, \mathbf{t})$ with $\lambda' := h_\ell \circ \lambda$. Obviously, $\mathcal{P}(N') = h_\ell(\mathcal{P}(N))$ holds. ■

Definition 10 (Inverse Renaming) Let $r : A \rightarrow Act$ be a mapping with a finite set $A \subseteq Act$. For any pomset $p = [(\sigma_p, R_p, \lambda_p)]$ we define the *inverse renaming* $r^{-1}(p)$ by $r^{-1}(p) := \{[(\sigma_p, R_p, \lambda)] \mid r \circ \lambda = \lambda_p\}$. □

We might note that an inverse renaming is an inverse homomorphism, as used in the introduction, where each letter is mapped to a letter only, and not to a word or, fitting better here, a pomset.

Lemma 3 ($\mathcal{P}$ is closed under inverse renaming) For any Petri net $N = (P, T, F, \lambda, s_0, \mathbf{p}, \mathbf{t})$ and inverse renaming r^{-1} there is a Petri net N' such that $\mathcal{P}(N') = r^{-1}(\mathcal{P}(N))$ holds.
Proof: We construct N' from N by replacing each transition t with the label a by $|r^{-1}(a)|$ transitions, each labelled with one of the symbols in $r^{-1}(a)$, all having the same pre- and postset as t. We get $N' = (P, T', F', s_0, \lambda', \epsilon, \epsilon)$ where $T' := \{t_a \,|\, t \in T,\ a \in r^{-1}(\lambda(t))\}$, $F'(p, t_a) := F(p, t)$ and $F'(t_a, p) := F(t, p)$ for all $p \in P$ and $t_a \in T'$, $\lambda'(t_a) := a$ for all $t_a \in T'$. Since r has a finite domain, T' is finite and N' is a Petri net. Obviously, each action a in some pomset $p \in \mathcal{P}(N)$ corresponds to a firing of some transition t of the Petri net N which is labelled by a. In N' each of the replacement transitions for such a t may fire for the same reasons as t may do in N. Thus, a pomset of N' results from a pomset of N by replacing any action a by an arbitrary element of $r^{-1}(a)$. ∎

Definition 11 (Intersection) For two pomsets $p = [(\sigma_p, R_p, \lambda_p)]$ and $q = [(\sigma_q, R_q, \lambda_q)]$ we define the intersection of p and q by

$$p \Cap q := \{[(\sigma_p, (R_p \cup \alpha^{-1} R_q \alpha)^+, \lambda_p)] \mid \alpha \text{ is a bijection from } \sigma_p \text{ to } \sigma_q \text{ with } 1.\ \lambda_p = \lambda_q \alpha \text{ and } 2.\ (R_p \cup \alpha^{-1} R_q \alpha)^+ \text{ is acyclic } \}. \square$$

This definition is sound as other representations of the pomset p (respectively q) are expressed via a bijection on σ_p (or σ_q), just leading to some different bijection α in the above definition.

An intersection of two pomsets p_1, p_2 is the set of all those pomsets p that intuitively contain p_1 and p_2 simultaneously. As our intersection is defined with the help of a union ($R_p \cup \alpha^{-1} R_q \alpha$) both "order restrictions" R_p <u>and</u> R_q must hold. As an example the pomsets of N_4 in figure 2 are in the intersection of the first pomset of N_2 and N_3. This is not a coincidence, as N_4 forms the "intersection" of N_2 and N_3 according to the following lemma. If the pomsets of N_2 and N_3 are rewritten as $\left(\begin{smallmatrix} a \to b & a \\ a \to b & a \end{smallmatrix}\right)$ and $\left(\begin{smallmatrix} a & b \to a \\ a & b \to a \end{smallmatrix}\right)$ it becomes obvious that they are "contained" in $\left(\begin{smallmatrix} a \to b \to a \\ a \to b \to a \end{smallmatrix}\right)$. We may again rewrite them as $\left(\begin{smallmatrix} a \to b & a \to b & a \\ a & & \end{smallmatrix}\right)$ and $\left(\begin{smallmatrix} a & b \to a & b \to a \\ a & & \end{smallmatrix}\right)$ to see how they form $\left(\begin{smallmatrix} a \to b \to a \to b \to a \\ a \end{smallmatrix}\right)$. On the other hand, the intersection of $\left(\begin{smallmatrix} a \to b & a \to b \\ a \to b & \end{smallmatrix}\right)$ with $\left(\begin{smallmatrix} a & b \to a \\ a & b \to a \end{smallmatrix}\right)$ is empty as the sets of actions in both pomsets are not isomorphic.

Though this is obviously not the usual set-theoretic intersection, it is still justified to call this operation an intersection, as both "order restrictions" must now be obeyed. Further, if we identify linear words with totally ordered pomsets, then the pomset intersection will coincide on words with the set-theoretic intersection. For a proof, see section 5. Obviously, the intersection is commutative and associative due to the fact that a bijection has an inverse and the composition of two bijections again forms a bijection.

Lemma 4 ($\mathcal{P}$ is closed under intersection) For two Petri nets $N_i = (P_i, T_i, F_{N_i}, \lambda_{N_i}, s_{0i}, \mathbf{p}_i, \mathbf{t}_i)$, $i \in \{1, 2\}$, there is a Petri net N such that $\mathcal{P}(N) = \mathcal{P}(N_1) \Cap \mathcal{P}(N_2)$ holds.
Proof: We follow the idea of the constructional approach of [5], proving that Petri net languages are closed under standard intersection. The Petri net N is

defined as the "synchronization" of the Petri nets N_1 and N_2. A transition from N_1 is synchronized with a transition from N_2 if both have the same label and this label is not τ. Thus, the synchronized transitions are $T^\times := \{(t_1,t_2) \in T_1 \times T_2 \mid \lambda_{N_1}(t_1) = \lambda_{N_2}(t_2) \neq \tau\}$. A transition $(t_1,t_2) \in T^\times$ gets the union of the pre-/postsets of t_1 and t_2 as its pre-/postset. Leaving the τ-transitions as they are, $T_i^\tau := \{t \in T_i \mid \lambda_{N_i}(t) = \tau\}$ for $i \in \{1,2\}$, and keeping their original pre- and postsets, we define the Petri net N by $N = (P_1 \dot{\cup} P_2,\ T_1^\tau \dot{\cup} T^\times \dot{\cup} T_2^\tau,\ F_N,\ \lambda_N,\ s_{01}+s_{02},\ \epsilon,\ \epsilon)$, where $\forall t=(t_1,t_2)\in T^\times$: $F_N(\cdot,t):=F_{N_1}(\cdot,t_1)+F_{N_2}(\cdot,t_2)$, $F_N(t,\cdot) := F_{N_1}(t_1,\cdot)+F_{N_2}(t_2,\cdot)$, and $\lambda_N(t) := \lambda_{N_1}(t_1)$, as well as $\forall t \in T_i^\tau, i \in \{1,2\}$: $F_N(\cdot,t):=F_{N_i}(\cdot,t)$, $F_N(t,\cdot):=F_{N_i}(t,\cdot)$, and $\lambda_N(t):=\tau$.

We have to prove that $\mathcal{P}(N) = \mathcal{P}(N_1) \cap \mathcal{P}(N_2)$ holds.

"$\mathcal{P}(N) \subseteq \mathcal{P}(N_1) \cap \mathcal{P}(N_2)$":
Given some $p = [(\sigma_p, R_p, \ell_p)] \in \mathcal{P}(N)$, we have to construct $p_1 = [(\sigma_1, R_1, \ell_1)] \in \mathcal{P}(N_1)$ and $p_2 = [(\sigma_2, R_2, \ell_2)] \in \mathcal{P}(N_2)$ such that $p \in p_1 \cap p_2$ holds. By definition 7, there is a process $\pi = (O_p, r_p, \lambda_p)$ with an O-net $O_p = (B_p, E_p, F_p)$ such that $\Phi(\pi) = p$ holds. We create processes $\pi_i = (O_i, r_i, \lambda_i)$ with $O_i = (B_i, E_i, F_i)$, $i \in \{1,2\}$, supplying us with the pomsets $p_i := \Phi(\pi_i)$. As a first step, we define the O-nets O_i, $i \in \{1,2\}$, by: $B_i := \{b \in B_p \mid r_p(b) \in P_i\}$, $E_i := \{e \in E_p \mid r_p(e) \in T_i^\tau \dot{\cup} T^\times\}$, and $F_i := F_p|_{(B_i \times E_i) \cup (E_i \times B_i)}$. Trivially, as $B_i \subseteq B_p$ and $E_i \subseteq E_p$, O_1 and O_2 are O-nets. Note that $B_1 \dot{\cup} B_2 = B_p$ and $r_p(E_1 \cap E_2) \subseteq T^\times$. Furthermore, $F_p = F_1 \cup F_2$ holds as there are, in O_p, no arcs between elements of B_1 and $E_p - E_1$ on the one hand and B_2 and $E_p - E_2$ on the other hand:

$$\begin{aligned} F_p &= F_p|_{(B_1 \times E_p) \cup (E_p \times B_1)} \dot{\cup} F_p|_{(B_2 \times E_p) \cup (E_p \times B_2)} \\ &= F_p|_{(B_1 \times E_1) \cup (E_1 \times B_1)} \dot{\cup} F_p|_{(B_2 \times E_2) \cup (E_2 \times B_2)} = F_1 \dot{\cup} F_2. \end{aligned}$$

For the processes π_i, $i \in \{1,2\}$, we further define mappings $r_i : B_i \dot{\cup} E_i \to P_i \dot{\cup} T_i$ and $\lambda_i : E_i \to Act_\tau$ by $r_i(b) := r_p(b)$, $\forall b \in B_i$, $r_i(e) := r_p(e)$, if $r_p(e) \in T_i^\tau$, $r_i(e) := t_i$, if $r_p(e) = (t_1,t_2) \in T^\times$, $\forall e \in E_i$, and $\lambda_i := \lambda_{N_i} \circ r_i|_{E_i}$.

To prove that π_i is a process of N_i, $i \in \{1,2\}$, the requirements of definition 5 can easily be checked. Let $p_i = [(\sigma_i, R_i, \ell_i)] := \Phi(\pi_i)$ for $i \in \{1,2\}$. To prove $p \in p_1 \cap p_2$ we choose a bijection α for the intersection (compare definition 11) and show that $\ell_p = \ell_1 = \ell_2\alpha$ and $R_p = (R_1 \cup \alpha^{-1}R_2\alpha)^+$ holds. Acyclicity of the latter term automatically follows from the fact that R_p is the causal ordering relation of a pomset.

As a first step, notice that from definition of E_i and r_i we can show $\sigma_i = \{e \in E_i \mid \lambda_i(e) \neq \tau\} = \{e \in E_i \mid r_i(e) \notin T_i^\tau\} = \{e \in E_p \mid r_p(e) \in T^\times\} = \{e \in E_p \mid \lambda_p(e) \neq \tau\} = \sigma_p$ for $i \in \{1,2\}$. Thus the bijection $\alpha : \sigma_p \to \sigma_p$ may be chosen as the identity, $\alpha := id_{\sigma_p}$, as $\ell_1 = \lambda_1|_{\sigma_p} = \lambda_{N_1} \circ r_1|_{\sigma_p} = \lambda_N \circ r_p|_{\sigma_p} = \lambda_{N_2} \circ r_2|_{\sigma_p} = \lambda_2|_{\sigma_p} = \ell_2 = \ell_2\alpha$ and $\lambda_N \circ r_p|_{\sigma_p} = \lambda_p|_{\sigma_p} = \ell_p$.

Finally we show $R = (R_1 \cup \alpha^{-1}R_2\alpha)^+$:

$$\begin{aligned} R &= F^+|_{\sigma_p \times \sigma_p} = (F_1 \cup F_2)^+|_{\sigma_p \times \sigma_p} = (F_1^+ \cup F_2^+)^+|_{\sigma_p \times \sigma_p} \\ &= ((F_1^+ \cup F_2^+)^+|_{\sigma_p \times \sigma_p})^+ \overset{(*)}{=} ((F_1^+ \cup F_2^+)|_{\sigma_p \times \sigma_p})^+ \\ &= (F_1^+|_{\sigma_p \times \sigma_p} \cup F_2^+|_{\sigma_p \times \sigma_p})^+ = (R_1 \cup R_2)^+ = (R_1 \cup \alpha^{-1}R_2\alpha)^+. \end{aligned}$$

While most of the equivalences are obvious, the one marked by $(*)$ has to be shown explicitly: "$\supseteq$" is clear. For "$\subseteq$", take elements $a, c \in \sigma_p$ with $a((F_1^+ \cup$

$F_2^+)^+|_{\sigma_p\times\sigma_p})^+c$. We can find $b_1,\ldots,b_n \in B_p \cup E_p$ such that $aF_i^+b_1F_j^+b_2F_i^+b_3\ldots b_nF_{i/j}^+c$ with alternating F_i^+ and F_j^+ holds for either $i=1\wedge j=2$ or $j=1\wedge i=2$. Each b_k, $1\leq k\leq n$ contributes to both F_1 and F_2, so one of two cases holds:
Case 1: $b_k \in B_1\cap B_2 \Longrightarrow r_p(b_k)\in P_1\cap P_2=\emptyset$, a contradiction.
Case 2: $b_k\in E_1\cap E_2 \Longrightarrow r_p(b_k)\in (T_1^\tau\cup T^\times)\cap(T_2^\tau\cup T^\times)=T^\times \Longrightarrow b_k\in\sigma_p$.
Thus, $a((F_1^+\cup F_2^+)|_{\sigma_p\times\sigma_p})^+c$ holds.

"$\mathcal{P}(N)\supseteq\mathcal{P}(N_1)\Cap\mathcal{P}(N_2)$":
Given arbitrary pomsets $p_i=[(\sigma_i,R_i,\ell_i)]\in\mathcal{P}(N_i)$ for $i\in\{1,2\}$, by definition there are processes of N_i, $\pi_i=(O_i,r_i,\lambda_i)$ with $O_i=(B_i,E_i,F_i)$ for $i\in\{1,2\}$ such that $p_i=\Phi(\pi_i)$ holds. If $p_1\Cap p_2=\emptyset$ we are done. Suppose there is a $p=[(\sigma_p,R_p,\ell_p)]\in p_1\Cap p_2$. Without loss of generality, we may assume $B_1\cap B_2=\emptyset$, $E_1\cap E_2=\{e\in E_1\mid\lambda_1(e)\neq\tau\}=\{e\in E_2\mid\lambda_2(e)\neq\tau\}$, and $\forall e\in E_1\cap E_2$: $\lambda_1(e)=\lambda_2(e)$. If the events of E_1 and E_2 could not be chosen this way, the resulting pomsets p_1, p_2 would not contain the same labels and therefore the intersection would have been empty. We immediately conclude $\sigma_1=\sigma_2=E_1\cap E_2=\sigma_p$ and $\ell_1=\ell_2=\ell_p$. Now, from the definition of the intersection we know that p has the form $p=[(\sigma_p,(R_1\cup\alpha^{-1}R_2\alpha)^+,\ell_p)]$ with a bijection $\alpha:\sigma_p\to\sigma_p$, $\ell_p=\ell_p\alpha$, and an acyclic relation $(R_1\cup\alpha^{-1}R_2\alpha)^+$. Let $E_i^\tau:=\{e\in E_i\mid\lambda_i(e)=\tau\}$ for $i\in\{1,2\}$. We extend α to $B_1\cup B_2\cup E_1\cup E_2$ by setting $\forall e\in E_1^\tau\cup E_2^\tau$: $\alpha(e):=e$ and $\forall b\in B_1\cup B_2$: $\alpha(b):=b$. Still, $\alpha:B_1\cup B_2\cup E_1\cup E_2\to B_1\cup B_2\cup E_1\cup E_2$ is a bijection.

We have to prove that the pomset p is in $\mathcal{P}(N)$. Therefore, we construct a process of N, $\pi:=(O_p,r_p,\lambda_p)$ with an occurrence net $O_p=(B_p,E_p,F_p)$, such that $\Phi(\pi)=p$ holds. Firstly, we define $B_p:=B_1\dot\cup B_2$, $E_p:=\sigma_p\dot\cup E_1^\tau\dot\cup E_2^\tau=E_1\cup E_2$, and $F_p:=F_1\cup\alpha^{-1}F_2\alpha$. All conditions for O_p being an O-net (see definition 4) except the acyclicity of F_p^+ are obviously fulfilled. Suppose F_p^+ is not acyclic. Since O_p is a bipartite graph, a cycle consists of at least an element of B_p and an element of E_p.
Case 1: $\nexists e\in\sigma_p$: eF_p^+e. Only elements of σ_p contribute to F_p both via F_1 and $\alpha^{-1}F_2\alpha$. Therefore a cycle must lie completely in either F_1^+ or $(\alpha^{-1}F_2\alpha)^+$. Now by definition, F_1^+ and F_2^+ (and thus $(\alpha^{-1}F_2\alpha)^+$) are acyclic, which is a contradiction.
Case 2: $\exists e\in\sigma_p$: eF_p^+e. We conclude $F_p^+|_{\sigma_p\times\sigma_p}$ is not acyclic, but we also know

$$\begin{aligned}F_p^+|_{\sigma_p\times\sigma_p}&=(F_1\cup\alpha^{-1}F_2\alpha)^+|_{\sigma_p\times\sigma_p}=(F_1^+\cup\alpha^{-1}F_2^+\alpha)^+|_{\sigma_p\times\sigma_p}\\&=((F_1^+\cup\alpha^{-1}F_2^+\alpha)^+|_{\sigma_p\times\sigma_p})^+=((F_1^+\cup\alpha^{-1}F_2^+\alpha)|_{\sigma_p\times\sigma_p})^+\\&=(F_1^+|_{\sigma_p\times\sigma_p}\cup\alpha^{-1}F_2^+\alpha|_{\sigma_p\times\sigma_p})^+=(F_1^+|_{\sigma_p\times\sigma_p}\cup\alpha^{-1}F_2^+|_{\sigma_p\times\sigma_p}\alpha)^+\\&=(R_1\cup\alpha^{-1}R_2\alpha)^+,\end{aligned}$$

where the latter is acyclic because of the definition of the intersection. Again, this is a contradiction, so F_p^+ must have been acyclic in the first place and O_p is an O-net.

To define $\pi=(O_p,r_p,\lambda_p)$ it remains to define $r_p:B_p\cup E_p\to P_1\cup P_2\cup T_1^\tau\cup T^\times\cup T_2^\tau$ by $\forall b\in B_1$: $r_p(b):=r_1(b)$, $\forall b\in B_2$: $r_p(b):=r_2(b)$, $\forall e\in E_1^\tau$: $r_p(e):=r_1(e)$, $\forall e\in E_2^\tau$: $r_p(e):=r_2(e)$, $\forall e\in\sigma_p$: $r_p(e):=(r_1(e),r_2(\alpha(e)))$, and $\lambda_p:=\lambda_N\circ r_p|_{E_p}$. To prove that $\pi=(O_p,r_p,\lambda_p)$ is a process of N the properties 1 to 5 of definition 5

are easily checked. Thus, it only remains to prove $p = \Phi(\pi)$, compare definition 6:
1. $\{e \in E_p \mid \lambda_p(e) \neq \tau\} = \{e \in E_p \mid \lambda_N \circ r_p(e) \neq \tau\} = \{e \in E_p \mid \lambda_{N_1} \circ r_1(e) \neq \tau\} = \sigma_p$,
2. In case 2 of the proof that O_p is an O-net, we have already shown $F_p^+|_{\sigma_p \times \sigma_p} = (R_1 \cup \alpha^{-1} R_2 \alpha)^+$.
3. $\lambda_p|_{\sigma_p} = \lambda_N \circ r|_E|_{\sigma_p} = \lambda_N \circ r_p|_{\sigma_p} = \lambda_{N_1} \circ r_1|_{\sigma_p} = \lambda_{N_1} \circ r_1|_{E_1}|_{\sigma_p} = \lambda_1|_{\sigma_p} = \ell_1 = \ell_p$. ■

4 Compositional Pomset Semantics

In this section we present an algebra for free Petri nets and a compositional semantics for this algebra that coincides with the pomset behaviour for classical Petri nets. We call a Petri net *free* if the labelling function λ is one-to-one and $\lambda(t) \neq \tau$ for all transitions t. As is known, any interleaving Petri net language can be expressed as the application of a letter homomorphism (on words) to the interleaving Petri net language of a free Petri net. An analogous fact obviously holds for sets of pomsets of Petri nets, too: any $\mathcal{P}(N)$ is a letter-homomorphic image of $\mathcal{P}(N')$, where N' is a free version of N (e.g., $\lambda_{N'} = id_T$).

We introduce an algebra on free Petri nets with interfaces such that any free Petri net with a tokenless interface (and, thus, also any classical free Petri net with an empty interface) can be described by an expression of the algebra in a straightforward way.

Definition 12 (Petri Net Operators)
place $:= (\{p\}, \emptyset, \emptyset, \emptyset, \emptyset, p, \epsilon)$ is the Petri net that consists of exactly one place, becoming the first and only place of the ordered interface.

a-trans $:= (\emptyset, \{t\}, \emptyset, \lambda(t) = a, \emptyset, \epsilon, t)$, for $a \in Act$, is the net that consists of exactly one transition, labelled by a. t becomes the first transition of the ordered interface.

$$add_{i \to a}(N) := \begin{cases} (P_N, T_N, F', \lambda_N, s_N, \mathbf{p}_N, \mathbf{t}_N), & \text{if } 1 \leq i \leq |\mathbf{p}_N| \\ & \wedge \exists! t \in T_N\colon \lambda_N(t) = a \wedge t \in \mathbf{t}_N, \\ \bot & \text{, otherwise,} \end{cases}$$

$$\text{with } F'(x,y) := \begin{cases} F_N(x,y) + 1, & \text{if } x = \mathbf{p}_N(i) \wedge y = \lambda_N^{-1}(a), \\ F_N(x,y) & \text{, otherwise.} \end{cases}$$

$add_{i \to a}(N)$ denotes the net resulting from adding one arc from the i-th interface place of N to the unique transition labelled with a in the interface of N.

$$add_{a \to i}(N) := \begin{cases} (P_N, T_N, F', \lambda_N, s_N, \mathbf{p}_N, \mathbf{t}_N), & \text{if } 1 \leq i \leq |\mathbf{p}_N| \\ & \wedge \exists! t \in T_N\colon \lambda_N(t) = a \wedge t \in \mathbf{t}_N, \\ \bot & \text{, otherwise,} \end{cases}$$

$$\text{with } F'(x,y) := \begin{cases} F_N(x,y) + 1, & \text{if } x = \lambda_N^{-1}(a) \wedge y = \mathbf{p}_N(i), \\ F_N(x,y) & \text{, otherwise.} \end{cases}$$

$add_{a \to i}(N)$ denotes the net that results from adding one arc from the unique transition in the interface of N labelled with a to the i-th interface place.

$$hidemark_{i,n}(N) := \begin{cases} (P_N, T_N, F_N, \lambda_N, s_N + n \cdot \mathbf{p}_N(i), h_i(\mathbf{p}_N), \mathbf{t}_N), & \text{if } 1 \le i \le |\mathbf{p}_N| \wedge n \in \mathbb{N}, \\ \bot, & \text{otherwise,} \end{cases}$$

with $h_i(w_1 \ldots w_n) := w_1 \ldots w_{i-1} w_{i+1} \ldots w_n$.

$hidemark_{i,n}(N)$ adds n tokens onto the i-th interface place of N and removes this place from the interface (but it stays in N).

$$hide_a(N) := \begin{cases} (P_N, T_N, F_N, \lambda_N, s_N, \mathbf{p}_N, h_i(\mathbf{t}_N)), & \text{if } \exists! t \in T_N \colon \lambda_N(t) = a \wedge \mathbf{t}_N(i) = t, \\ \bot, & \text{otherwise,} \end{cases}$$

with the same h_i as above.

$hide_a(N)$ removes the unique transition labelled with a from the interface of N, but leaves it in N.

$N_1 \| N_2 := (P_1 \dot\cup P_2, T_1 \dot\cup T_2, F_1 \cup F_2, \lambda_1 \cup \lambda_2, s_1 \cup s_2, \mathbf{p}_1\mathbf{p}_2, \mathbf{t}_1\mathbf{t}_2)$.

$N_1 \| N_2$ is the shuffle-product of N_1 and N_2, where the interface of N_1 is ordered before the interface of N_2 in $N_1 \| N_2$. □

Thus, $N_1 = a\text{-}trans \,\|\, b\text{-}trans \,\|\, c\text{-}trans$ and $N_2 = b\text{-}trans \,\|\, c\text{-}trans \,\|\, a\text{-}trans$ are two different Petri nets. The transition labelled with a is the first one in the ordered interface of N_1 but the third one in the ordered interface of N_2.

We now define a calculus for generating free Petri nets using these operations.

Definition 13 (A Calculus for free Petri nets) Let $\mathcal{E}$ be the calculus over *Act* given by: $\forall a \in Act\colon \forall i, n \in \mathbb{N}$:

$$N :\equiv place \;\Big|\; a\text{-}trans \;\Big|\; N \| N \;\Big|\; add_{i \to a}(N) \;\Big|\; add_{a \to i}(N) \;\Big|\; hidemark_{i,n}(N) \;\Big|\; hide_a(N)$$

By $\mathcal{F}$ we denote the subcalculus of $\mathcal{E}$ that allows the operators a-*trans* to be used at most once for each $a \in Act$. □

Obviously, there is, for any free Petri net with a tokenless interface, at least one expression of $\mathcal{F}$ describing the net. One such expression for the classical free Petri net N_4 of figure 2 is $hidemark_{1,2}\ hidemark_{2,2}\ hidemark_{3,0}\ hidemark_{4,0}\ hide_a\ hide_b\ add_{a \to 4}\ add_{a \to 4}\ add_{a \to 3}\ add_{b \to 2}\ add_{3 \to b}\ add_{2 \to a}(add_{1 \to b}(place \,\|\, b\text{-}trans) \,\|\, (place \,\|\, place \,\|\, a\text{-}trans \,\|\, place))$. Petri nets can communicate with some *environment* via their interface. Such an environment, also called *context*, can itself be defined as an expression in our calculus with some additional variable, $\bullet$.

Definition 14 (Petri Net Context) A *Petri net context*, C, is an expression in $\mathcal{F}^\bullet$, where $\mathcal{F}^\bullet$ is the calculus $\mathcal{F}$ over *Act* extended by a variable $\bullet$. For $C \in \mathcal{F}^\bullet$ and $N \in \mathcal{F}$ let $C[N]$ denote the expression resulting from replacing each occurrence of $\bullet$ in C by N. *Con* denotes the class of all contexts. □

Definition 15 (Universal Context) Let $\mathcal{X} := \{x_i^+, x_i^- \mid i \in \mathbb{N}\} \subseteq Act$ be a set of special action names solely used by the *universal context* $U_{m,n}$ (*of dimension* (m,n)), for $m, n \in \mathbb{N}$, where $U_{m,n}$ is defined as the $\mathcal{F}^\bullet$-expression

$$U_{m,n} := hide_{x_1^+} add_{x_1^+ \to 1} hide_{x_1^-} add_{1 \to x_1^-} \ldots hide_{x_m^+} add_{x_m^+ \to m} hide_{x_m^-} add_{m \to x_m^-}$$
$$\left(x_1^+\text{-}trans \;\Big\|\; x_1^-\text{-}trans \;\Big\|\; \ldots \;\Big\|\; x_m^+\text{-}trans \;\Big\|\; x_m^-\text{-}trans \;\Big\|\; \bullet\right)$$

For a Petri net N of dimension (m,n) we abbreviate $U_{m,n}[N]$ to $U[N]$. □

$\widehat{a\text{-}trans} := \biguplus(a)$, since $U[a\text{-}trans] = a\text{-}trans$ is a single transition with empty pre- and postconditions.

If N_1 and N_2 are Petri nets of dimension (m_i, n_i), $i = 1, 2$, then $N_1||N_2$ is of dimension $(m_1 + m_2, n_1 + n_2)$ and the i-th interface place of N_2 becomes the $(n_1 + i)$-th interface place of $N_1||N_2$. Thus, we have to rename the labels $x_1^{\pm}, \ldots, x_{n_2}^{\pm}$ of $U_{m_2,n_2}[N_2]$ to $x_{i+n_1}^{\pm}$ in $U_{m_1+m_2,n_1+n_2}[N_1||N_2]$, which is done by a letter homomorphism (actually a renaming) h_{L_1}. Observe that $\widehat{||}$ operates on behaviours and not nets, so the renaming of the $x_i^{\pm}$ has to be done using only the information available in $L_1 := \mathcal{S}(N_1)$ and $L_2 := \mathcal{S}(N_2)$. Fortunately, the universal context allows us to determine the number of places in the interface of N_1 by just looking at L_1: it is the highest number j for which (x_j^+) appears as a pomset in L_1. Thus, we define

$$L_1 \,\widehat{||}\, L_2 := L_1 \uplus h_{L_1}(L_2) \text{ with}$$

$$h_{L_1} : a \mapsto \begin{cases} x_{i+n_1}^+, & \text{if } a = x_i^+ \text{ and } n_1 = max\{j \mid (x_j^+) \in L_1\}, \\ x_{i+n_1}^-, & \text{if } a = x_i^- \text{ and } n_1 = max\{j \mid (x_j^+) \in L_1\}, \\ a & , \text{otherwise.} \end{cases}$$

For the $hidemark_{i,n}$-operator, which puts n tokens on the i-th interface place and then removes this place from the interface, notice that each firing of the x_i^+-transition generates one token on the interface place. Thus, if we allow at most n firings of x_i^+ in any pomset and map x_i^+ to ϵ right afterwards, we can simulate an initial marking of n tokens on the i-th interface place and simultaneously hide this place from the interface. We must also inhibit firings of the x_i^--transition, as this transition is also removed from the universal context when hiding the i-th interface place. This is an easy task for our intersection. We construct a set in which all pomsets fulfil two conditions: first, the ordering relation of a pomset must be empty, and second, a pomset must contain no more than n x_i^+'s and no x_i^-'s but may contain any number of other labels. If we intersect this set with some behaviour L, all pomsets from L that have more than n x_i^+'s or any x_i^-'s at all will be automatically excluded. On the other hand, pomsets that are not excluded will not be changed due to the empty ordering relation in the set we construct.

$$\widehat{hidemark}_{i,n}(L) := h_{x_i}(L \,\widehat{\cap}\, (\biguplus(Act_L - \{x_i^+, x_i^-\}) \uplus \biguplus^n\{(\epsilon), (x_i^+)\})),$$

$$\text{with } h_{x_i} : c \mapsto \begin{cases} \epsilon & , \text{if } c = x_i^+, \\ x_{j-1}^+, & \text{if } c = x_j^+ \text{ with } j > i, \\ x_{j-1}^-, & \text{if } c = x_j^- \text{ with } j > i, \\ c & , \text{otherwise.} \end{cases}$$

$\widehat{hide}_a(L) := L$. Hiding a transition will only remove the transition from the interface of the net. Obviously, this has no effect on the behaviour.

For the $add_{a\rightarrow i}$-operator, we have to simulate an arc from an a-transition to the i-th interface place. The obvious solution is to force a firing of an $\hat{x}_i^+$ (an x_i^+ renamed for this purpose) after each a in any pomset and "hide" these $\hat{x}_i^+$'s afterwards, by mapping them to ϵ. Therefore, we will add new elements $a \rightarrow \hat{x}_i^+$ to the predecessor relation of each pomset. This can easily be done by

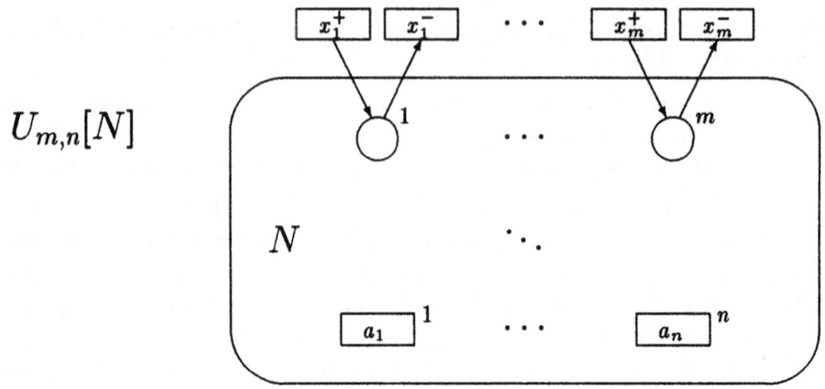

Fig. 3. A Petri net N of dimension (m, n) embedded into its universal context $U_{m,n}$

The reader may be surprised why the number n of transitions in an interface of N is completely ignored by U. The reason is that in a *free* Petri net a firing of a letter a uniquely determines the transition that has fired. A universal context for general Petri nets is slightly more involved, cf. [8] or [11].
Figure 3 presents an example of a Petri net N of dimension (m, n) embedded into $U_{m,n}$. The position of a place/transition in the interface is denoted by the number next to the circle/bar it is represented by.
We are now able to explain our semantics for Petri nets and show its compositionality.

Definition 16 (A Semantics for free Petri nets) For any free Petri net N we define the semantics of N to be $\mathcal{S}(N) := \mathcal{P}(U[N])$. □

The reason why we call U *universal* is the following. One can prove that two free Petri nets cannot be separated in any context if they cannot be separated by U: $\forall N_1, N_2$ free Petri nets: $(\forall C \in \mathit{Con}\colon \mathcal{S}(C[N_1]) = \mathcal{S}(C[N_2]) \iff \mathcal{S}(U[N_1]) = \mathcal{S}(U[N_2]))$. One may get a proof of the universality of U for free Petri nets following the techniques in [11]. However, we do not need these facts in this paper where we shall use $\mathcal{S}$ and its compositionality solely to obtain an algebraic characterization of $\mathcal{P}$.

Theorem 1 (Compositionality of $\mathcal{S}$) The semantics $\mathcal{S} : \mathcal{F} \to \mathcal{P}$ is compositional for $\mathcal{F}$.

Proof: We present for each k-ary operator, op^k, in $\mathcal{F}$ a k-ary operation, $\widehat{op}^k : \mathcal{P}^k \to \mathcal{P}$, such that for all $N_1, \ldots, N_k \in \mathcal{F}$ the equation

$$\mathcal{S}(op^k(N_1, \ldots, N_k))) = \widehat{op}^k(\mathcal{S}(N_1), \ldots, \mathcal{S}(N_k))$$

holds:

$\widehat{place} := \bigsqcup\{(x_1^+), (x_1^+ \to x_1^-)\}$, since $\mathcal{S}(place) = \mathcal{P}(U[place]) =$

$= \mathcal{P}($ 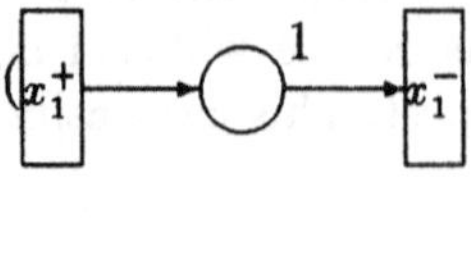 $) = \bigsqcup\{(x_1^+), (x_1^+ \to x_1^-)\}$.

an intersection with special pomsets as the intersection unifies the predecessor relations of the intersected pomsets. As the last step, we hide the $\hat{x}_i^+$'s by a letter homomorphism. Sometimes an a may not be followed by a $\hat{x}_i^+$. In this case the token additionally produced by a will never be consumed, which is allowed in prefix-closed behaviours.

$$\widehat{add}_{a\to i}(L) := h(r^{-1}(L) \Cap (\coprod\{(a \to \hat{x}_i^+), (a)\} \sqcup \coprod Act_L - \{a\})),$$
$$\text{with } h : c \mapsto \begin{cases} \epsilon, & \text{if } c = \hat{x}_i^+ \\ c, & \text{otherwise,} \end{cases} \quad \text{and } r : c \mapsto \begin{cases} x_i^+, & \text{if } c = \hat{x}_i^+ \\ c\ , & \text{otherwise.} \end{cases}$$

For the $add_{i\to a}$-operator, we analogously have to simulate an arc from the i-th interface place to an a-transition. This time, we force a firing of an $\hat{x}_i^-$ (a renamed x_i^-) before each a in any pomset and "hide" the $\hat{x}_i^-$'s afterwards (once again by mapping them to ϵ). We do this by adding new elements $\hat{x}_i^- \to a$ to the predecessor relation of each pomset; as before we use an intersection with special pomsets for this purpose. After that, we hide these $\hat{x}_i^-$'s by a letter homomorphism. The following formula might remove too many x_i^-'s, but again this just represents tokens that are never consumed.

$$\widehat{add}_{i\to a}(L) := h(r^{-1}(L) \Cap (\coprod\{(\hat{x}_i^- \to a), (\hat{x}_i^-)\} \sqcup \coprod Act_L - \{a\})),$$
$$\text{with } h : c \mapsto \begin{cases} \epsilon, & \text{if } c = \hat{x}_i^- \\ c, & \text{otherwise,} \end{cases} \quad \text{and } r : c \mapsto \begin{cases} x_i^-, & \text{if } c = \hat{x}_i^- \\ c\ , & \text{otherwise.} \end{cases} \quad \blacksquare$$

Let N be a classical free Petri net, i.e., a free Petri net with an interface of dimension $(0,0)$. Thus, $U_{0,0} = \bullet$ and $\mathcal{S}(N) = \mathcal{P}(N)$. As a consequence, we exploit the compositionality of $\mathcal{S}$ with respect to the calculus $\mathcal{F}$ to get a smooth algebraic description of $\mathcal{P}$ in the following section.

5 Algebraic Characterization of $\mathcal{P}$

As a result of the previous sections we may now conclude our algebraic characterization theorem:

Theorem 2 (Algebraic Characterization)

$$\mathcal{P} = \bar{Cl}^{\sqcup, h_\ell, r^{-1}, \Cap}(\coprod\{(a \to b), (a)\}, \{(\epsilon), (a)\}).$$

Proof: As figure 2 shows, the above sets $\coprod\{(a \to b), (a)\}$ and $\{(\epsilon), (a)\}$ of pomsets are indeed pomset behaviours of Petri nets, namely of N_2 and N_1, respectively. From section 3 we know that $\mathcal{P}$ is closed under $\sqcup$, h_ℓ, r^{-1}, and $\Cap$. Thus, the "$\supseteq$"-part holds.
"$\subseteq$": We have expressed the semantic operations of theorem 1 solely using the four algebraic operators $\Cap$, $\sqcup$, h_ℓ, and r^{-1}, and the pomset behaviours $\coprod A$ for some $A \subseteq Act$, and $\{(\epsilon), (a)\}$ and $\coprod\{(a \to b), (a)\}$ for some $a, b \in Act$. Except for $\coprod A$, all these operations and behaviours appear in our characterization. $\coprod A$ may be generated from the behaviour $\coprod\{(a \to b), (a)\}$ by mapping b to ϵ and then applying an inverse renaming with $r^{-1}(a) = A$ to the result. $\blacksquare$

Definition 17 (Linearizations of a Pomset) For any pomset $p = [(\sigma_p, R_p, \lambda_p)]$ let $\text{lin}(p) := \{[(\sigma_p, R, \lambda_p)] \mid R_p \subseteq R \land \forall e_1, e_2 \in \sigma_p : e_1 R e_2 \lor e_2 R e_1\}$ be the set of all *linearizations* of p, where R is a total ordering. For a behaviour $L \in \mathcal{P}$ we define $\text{lin}(L) := \{\text{lin}(p) \mid p \in L\}$. □

If we identify the totally ordered pomsets in $\text{lin}(p)$ with words we easily get versions of the operators $\Cap$, $\sqcup\!\sqcup$, h_ℓ, and r^{-1} for interleaving languages. These interleaved versions of our operators coincide with well-known operators for interleaving languages.

Lemma 5 (Linearizations of Operators) Let $L_1, L_2 \in 2^{\mathcal{POM}}$. The following equations hold:

1. $\text{lin}(L_1 \Cap L_2) = \text{lin}(L_1) \cap \text{lin}(L_2)$,
2. $\text{lin}(L_1 \sqcup\!\sqcup L_2) = \text{lin}(\text{lin}(L_1) \sqcup\!\sqcup \text{lin}(L_2))$,
3. $\text{lin}(h_\ell(L_1)) = h_\ell(\text{lin}(L_1))$,
4. $\text{lin}(r^{-1}(L_1)) = r^{-1}(\text{lin}(L_1))$,
5. $\text{lin}(\bigsqcup\!\sqcup\{(a \to b), (a)\}) = \text{Pref } D_1$ (with a and b as parentheses),
6. $\text{lin}(\{(\epsilon), (a)\}) = \{\epsilon, a\}$.

Proof: As the equations 2 to 6 are rather obvious only the first equation remains to be proven. Notice that for two totally ordered pomsets p and q either $|p \Cap q| = 1$ (which means p and q are identified with the same word, and so $p \Cap q = \{p\} = \{q\}$), or $p \Cap q = \emptyset$ holds. Thus, for interleaving behaviours L_1, L_2, we get $L_1 \Cap L_2 = L_1 \cap L_2$. Now, as $\Cap$ is commutative and associative, and as we obviously may express lin by $\text{lin}(L) = L \Cap Act_L^*$ for $L \in 2^{\mathcal{POM}}$, we get for L_1, $L_2 \in 2^{\mathcal{POM}}$: $\text{lin}(L_1 \Cap L_2) = L_1 \Cap L_2 \Cap (Act_{L_1} \cup Act_{L_2})^* = (L_1 \Cap Act_{L_1}^*) \Cap (L_2 \Cap Act_{L_2}^*) = \text{lin}(L_1) \Cap \text{lin}(L_2) = \text{lin}(L_1) \cap \text{lin}(L_2)$. ■

As we know $\mathcal{L} = \text{lin}(\mathcal{P})$, we may calculate $\mathcal{L}$ from the characterization of theorem 2. Since r^{-1} is a special case of the inverse homomorphism h^{-1} on interleaving behaviours, we may conclude:

Corollary 1 Theorem 2 is a generalization of Hack's characterization of Petri net languages $\mathcal{L} = \bar{Cl}^{\sqcup\!\sqcup, h_\ell, h^{-1}, \cap}(\text{Pref } D_1, \{\epsilon, a\})$.

6 Summary

We have proposed an algebraic characterization for a true-concurrency behaviour of Petri nets. A compositional semantics over an algebra for Petri nets with interfaces yields the desired behaviour for free, classical Petri nets and can be expressed using several newly introduced algebraic operators. Especially the pomset intersection has been highly effective for our purposes and should prove useful generally. Hack's characterization of an interleaving behaviour of Petri nets, as found in [5], has turned out to be a special case of ours, with a proof very different from that of Hack.

Other classes of sets of pomsets seem worth consideration. Safe nets, e.g., yield regular languages as an interleaving semantics, so their pomset behaviours can possibly be seen as regular pomset languages. A modified calculus $\mathcal{F}'$ allows for the generation and therefore a characterization of regular pomset behaviours. Adding a generalized form of stack gets us access to what could be called contextfree pomset languages. A comparison to the classification of Esparza [3] seems an interesting goal for future work.

References

1. E. Best, C. Fernandéz, *"Nonsequential Processes: A Petri Net View"*, Monographs on Theoretical Computer Science Vol. 13, Springer Verlag, 1988.
2. J.W. de Bakker, J.H.A. Warmerdam, *"Metric Pomset Semantics for a Concurrent Language with Recursion"*, Lecture Notes in Computer Science Vol. 469, Springer Verlag, 1990.
3. P. Degano, J. Meseguer, U. Montanari, *"Axiomatizing the algebra of net computations and processes"*, Acta Informatica 33, pp.641–667, 1996.
4. J. Esparza, *"More infinite results"*, Proceedings of INFINITY, First International Workshop on Verification of Infinite State Systems, pp.4–20, 1996.
5. S.A. Greibach, *"Remarks on Blind and Partially Blind One-Way Multicounter Machines"*, Theoretical Computer Science Vol. 7, pp. 311–324, 1978.
6. M. Hack, *"Petri Net Languages"*, Computation Structures Group Memo 124, Project MAC, M.I.T., 1975.
7. M. Jantzen, *"Language Theory of Petri Nets"*, Lecture Notes in Computer Science Vol. 254, pp. 397–412, Springer Verlag, 1987.
8. J. Meseguer, U. Montanari, V. Sassone, *"Process versus unfolding semantics for Place/Transition Petri nets"*, Theoretical Computer Science Vol. 153, pp. 171–210, 1996.
9. M. Nielsen, L. Priese, V. Sassone, *"Characterizing Behavioural Congruences for Petri Nets"*, Lecture Notes in Computer Science Vol. 962, Proceedings CONCUR '95, eds. I. Lee, S. Smolka, pp. 175–189, 1995.
10. J.L. Peterson, *"Petri Nets"*, Computing Surveys Vol. 9, No. 3, pp. 223–252, 1977.
11. L. Pomello, G. Rozenberg, C. Simone, *"A Survey of Equivalence Notions for Net Based Systems"*, Lecture Notes in Computer Science Vol. 609, pp.410-472, 1992.
12. L. Priese, H. Wimmel, *"A Uniform Approach to True-Concurrency and Interleaving Semantics for Petri Nets"*, to appear in Theoretical Computer Science.
13. L. Priese, H. Wimmel, *"An Application of Compositional Petri Net Semantics"*, Technical Report, Fachberichte Informatik 14/96, Institut für Informatik, Fachbereich Informatik, Universität Koblenz
14. W. Vogler, *"Partial Words versus Processes: A Short Comparison"*, Lecture Notes in Computer Science Vol. 609, pp. 292–303, 1992.

Author Index

Lecture Notes in Computer Science

For information about Vols. 1–1170

please contact your bookseller or Springer-Verlag

Vol. 1171: A. Franz, Automatic Ambiguity Resolution in Natural Language Processing. XIX, 155 pages. 1996. (Subseries LNAI).

Vol. 1172: J. Pieprzyk, J. Seberry (Eds.), Information Security and Privacy. Proceedings, 1996. IX, 333 pages. 1996.

Vol. 1173: W. Rucklidge, Efficient Visual Recognition Using the Hausdorff Distance. XIII, 178 pages. 1996.

Vol. 1174: R. Anderson (Ed.), Information Hiding. Proceedings, 1996. VIII, 351 pages. 1996.

Vol. 1175: K.G. Jeffery, J. Král, M. Bartošek (Eds.), SOFSEM'96: Theory and Practice of Informatics. Proceedings, 1996. XII, 491 pages. 1996.

Vol. 1176: S. Miguet, A. Montanvert, S. Ubéda (Eds.), Discrete Geometry for Computer Imagery. Proceedings, 1996. XI, 349 pages. 1996.

Vol. 1177: J.P. Müller, The Design of Intelligent Agents. XV, 227 pages. 1996. (Subseries LNAI).

Vol. 1178: T. Asano, Y. Igarashi, H. Nagamochi, S. Miyano, S. Suri (Eds.), Algorithms and Computation. Proceedings, 1996. X, 448 pages. 1996.

Vol. 1179: J. Jaffar, R.H.C. Yap (Eds.), Concurrency and Parallelism, Programming, Networking, and Security. Proceedings, 1996. XIII, 394 pages. 1996.

Vol. 1180: V. Chandru, V. Vinay (Eds.), Foundations of Software Technology and Theoretical Computer Science. Proceedings, 1996. XI, 387 pages. 1996.

Vol. 1181: D. Bjørner, M. Broy, I.V. Pottosin (Eds.), Perspectives of System Informatics. Proceedings, 1996. XVII, 447 pages. 1996.

Vol. 1182: W. Hasan, Optimization of SQL Queries for Parallel Machines. XVIII, 133 pages. 1996.

Vol. 1183: A. Wierse, G.G. Grinstein, U. Lang (Eds.), Database Issues for Data Visualization. Proceedings, 1995. XIV, 219 pages. 1996.

Vol. 1184: J. Waśniewski, J. Dongarra, K. Madsen, D. Olesen (Eds.), Applied Parallel Computing. Proceedings, 1996. XIII, 722 pages. 1996.

Vol. 1185: G. Ventre, J. Domingo-Pascual, A. Danthine (Eds.), Multimedia Telecommunications and Applications. Proceedings, 1996. XII, 267 pages. 1996.

Vol. 1186: F. Afrati, P. Kolaitis (Eds.), Database Theory - ICDT'97. Proceedings, 1997. XIII, 477 pages. 1997.

Vol. 1187: K. Schlechta, Nonmonotonic Logics. IX, 243 pages. 1997. (Subseries LNAI).

Vol. 1188: T. Martin, A.L. Ralescu (Eds.), Fuzzy Logic in Artificial Intelligence. Proceedings, 1995. VIII, 272 pages. 1997. (Subseries LNAI).

Vol. 1189: M. Lomas (Ed.), Security Protocols. Proceedings, 1996. VIII, 203 pages. 1997.

Vol. 1190: S. North (Ed.), Graph Drawing. Proceedings, 1996. XI, 409 pages. 1997.

Vol. 1191: V. Gaede, A. Brodsky, O. Günther, D. Srivastava, V. Vianu, M. Wallace (Eds.), Constraint Databases and Applications. Proceedings, 1996. X, 345 pages. 1996.

Vol. 1192: M. Dam (Ed.), Analysis and Verification of Multiple-Agent Languages. Proceedings, 1996. VIII, 435 pages. 1997.

Vol. 1193: J.P. Müller, M.J. Wooldridge, N.R. Jennings (Eds.), Intelligent Agents III. XV, 401 pages. 1997. (Subseries LNAI).

Vol. 1194: M. Sipper, Evolution of Parallel Cellular Machines. XIII, 199 pages. 1997.

Vol. 1195: R. Trappl, P. Petta (Eds.), Creating Personalities for Synthetic Actors. VII, 251 pages. 1997. (Subseries LNAI).

Vol. 1196: L. Vulkov, J. Waśniewski, P. Yalamov (Eds.), Numerical Analysis and Its Applications. Proceedings, 1996. XIII, 608 pages. 1997.

Vol. 1197: F. d'Amore, P.G. Franciosa, A. Marchetti-Spaccamela (Eds.), Graph-Theoretic Concepts in Computer Science. Proceedings, 1996. XI, 410 pages. 1997.

Vol. 1198: H.S. Nwana, N. Azarmi (Eds.), Software Agents and Soft Computing: Towards Enhancing Machine Intelligence. XIV, 298 pages. 1997. (Subseries LNAI).

Vol. 1199: D.K. Panda, C.B. Stunkel (Eds.), Communication and Architectural Support for Network-Based Parallel Computing. Proceedings, 1997. X, 269 pages. 1997.

Vol. 1200: R. Reischuk, M. Morvan (Eds.), STACS 97. Proceedings, 1997. XIII, 614 pages. 1997.

Vol. 1201: O. Maler (Ed.), Hybrid and Real-Time Systems. Proceedings, 1997. IX, 417 pages. 1997.

Vol. 1203: G. Bongiovanni, D.P. Bovet, G. Di Battista (Eds.), Algorithms and Complexity. Proceedings, 1997. VIII, 311 pages. 1997.

Vol. 1204: H. Mössenböck (Ed.), Modular Programming Languages. Proceedings, 1997. X, 379 pages. 1997.

Vol. 1205: J. Troccaz, E. Grimson, R. Mösges (Eds.), CVRMed-MRCAS'97. Proceedings, 1997. XIX, 834 pages. 1997.

Vol. 1206: J. Bigün, G. Chollet, G. Borgefors (Eds.), Audio- and Video-based Biometric Person Authentication. Proceedings, 1997. XII, 450 pages. 1997.

Vol. 1207: J. Gallagher (Ed.), Logic Program Synthesis and Transformation. Proceedings, 1996. VII, 325 pages. 1997.

Vol. 1208: S. Ben-David (Ed.), Computational Learning Theory. Proceedings, 1997. VIII, 331 pages. 1997. (Subseries LNAI).

Vol. 1209: L. Cavedon, A. Rao, W. Wobcke (Eds.), Intelligent Agent Systems. Proceedings, 1996. IX, 188 pages. 1997. (Subseries LNAI).

Vol. 1210: P. de Groote, J.R. Hindley (Eds.), Typed Lambda Calculi and Applications. Proceedings, 1997. VIII, 405 pages. 1997.

Vol. 1211: E. Keravnou, C. Garbay, R. Baud, J. Wyatt (Eds.), Artificial Intelligence in Medicine. Proceedings, 1997. XIII, 526 pages. 1997. (Subseries LNAI).

Vol. 1212: J. P. Bowen, M.G. Hinchey, D. Till (Eds.), ZUM '97: The Z Formal Specification Notation. Proceedings, 1997. X, 435 pages. 1997.

Vol. 1213: P. J. Angeline, R. G. Reynolds, J. R. McDonnell, R. Eberhart (Eds.), Evolutionary Programming VI. Proceedings, 1997. X, 457 pages. 1997.

Vol. 1214: M. Bidoit, M. Dauchet (Eds.), TAPSOFT '97: Theory and Practice of Software Development. Proceedings, 1997. XV, 884 pages. 1997.

Vol. 1215: J. M. L. M. Palma, J. Dongarra (Eds.), Vector and Parallel Processing – VECPAR'96. Proceedings, 1996. XI, 471 pages. 1997.

Vol. 1216: J. Dix, L. Moniz Pereira, T.C. Przymusinski (Eds.), Non-Monotonic Extensions of Logic Programming. Proceedings, 1996. XI, 224 pages. 1997. (Subseries LNAI).

Vol. 1217: E. Brinksma (Ed.), Tools and Algorithms for the Construction and Analysis of Systems. Proceedings, 1997. X, 433 pages. 1997.

Vol. 1218: G. Păun, A. Salomaa (Eds.), New Trends in Formal Languages. IX, 465 pages. 1997.

Vol. 1219: K. Rothermel, R. Popescu-Zeletin (Eds.), Mobile Agents. Proceedings, 1997. VIII, 223 pages. 1997.

Vol. 1220: P. Brezany, Input/Output Intensive Massively Parallel Computing. XIV, 288 pages. 1997.

Vol. 1221: G. Weiß (Ed.), Distributed Artificial Intelligence Meets Machine Learning. Proceedings, 1996. X, 294 pages. 1997. (Subseries LNAI).

Vol. 1222: J. Vitek, C. Tschudin (Eds.), Mobile Object Systems. Proceedings, 1996. X, 319 pages. 1997.

Vol. 1223: M. Pelillo, E.R. Hancock (Eds.), Energy Minimization Methods in Computer Vision and Pattern Recognition. Proceedings, 1997. XII, 549 pages. 1997.

Vol. 1224: M. van Someren, G. Widmer (Eds.), Machine Learning: ECML-97. Proceedings, 1997. XI, 361 pages. 1997. (Subseries LNAI).

Vol. 1225: B. Hertzberger, P. Sloot (Eds.), High-Performance Computing and Networking. Proceedings, 1997. XXI, 1066 pages. 1997.

Vol. 1226: B. Reusch (Ed.), Computational Intelligence. Proceedings, 1997. XIII, 609 pages. 1997.

Vol. 1227: D. Galmiche (Ed.), Automated Reasoning with Analytic Tableaux and Related Methods. Proceedings, 1997. XI, 373 pages. 1997. (Subseries LNAI).

Vol. 1228: S.-H. Nienhuys-Cheng, R. de Wolf, Foundations of Inductive Logic Programming. XVII, 404 pages. 1997. (Subseries LNAI).

Vol. 1230: J. Duncan, G. Gindi (Eds.), Information Processing in Medical Imaging. Proceedings, 1997. XVI, 557 pages. 1997.

Vol. 1231: M. Bertran, T. Rus (Eds.), Transformation-Based Reactive Systems Development. Proceedings, 1997. XI, 431 pages. 1997.

Vol. 1232: H. Comon (Ed.), Rewriting Techniques and Applications. Proceedings, 1997. XI, 339 pages. 1997.

Vol. 1233: W. Fumy (Ed.), Advances in Cryptology — EUROCRYPT '97. Proceedings, 1997. XI, 509 pages. 1997.

Vol 1234: S. Adian, A. Nerode (Eds.), Logical Foundations of Computer Science. Proceedings, 1997. IX, 431 pages. 1997.

Vol. 1235: R. Conradi (Ed.), Software Configuration Management. Proceedings, 1997. VIII, 234 pages. 1997.

Vol. 1238: A. Mullery, M. Besson, M. Campolargo, R. Gobbi, R. Reed (Eds.), Intelligence in Services and Networks: Technology for Cooperative Competition. Proceedings, 1997. XII, 480 pages. 1997.

Vol. 1239: D. Sehr, U. Banerjee, D. Gelernter, A. Nicolau, D. Padua (Eds.), Languages and Compilers for Parallel Computing. Proceedings, 1996. XIII, 612 pages. 1997.

Vol. 1240: J. Mira, R. Moreno-Díaz, J. Cabestany (Eds.), Biological and Artificial Computation: From Neuroscience to Technology. Proceedings, 1997. XXI, 1401 pages. 1997.

Vol. 1241: M. Akşit, S. Matsuoka (Eds.), ECOOP'97 – Object-Oriented Programming. Proceedings, 1997. XI, 531 pages. 1997.

Vol. 1242: S. Fdida, M. Morganti (Eds.), Multimedia Applications, Services and Techniques – ECMAST '97. Proceedings, 1997. XIV, 772 pages. 1997.

Vol. 1243: A. Mazurkiewicz, J. Winkowski (Eds.), CONCUR'97: Concurrency Theory. Proceedings, 1997. VIII, 421 pages. 1997.

Vol. 1244: D. M. Gabbay, R. Kruse, A. Nonnengart, H.J. Ohlbach (Eds.), Qualitative and Quantitative Practical Reasoning. Proceedings, 1997. X, 621 pages. 1997. (Subseries LNAI).

Vol. 1245: M. Calzarossa, R. Marie, B. Plateau, G. Rubino (Eds.), Computer Performance Evaluation. Proceedings, 1997. VIII, 231 pages. 1997.

Vol. 1246: S. Tucker Taft, R. A. Duff (Eds.), Ada 95 Reference Manual. XXII, 526 pages. 1997.

Vol. 1247: J. Barnes (Ed.), Ada 95 Rationale. XVI, 458 pages. 1997.

Vol. 1248: P. Azéma, G. Balbo (Eds.), Application and Theory of Petri Nets 1997. Proceedings, 1997. VIII, 467 pages. 1997.

Vol. 1249: W. McCune (Ed.), Automated Deduction – Cade-14. Proceedings, 1997. XIV, 462 pages. 1997.

Vol. 1250: A. Olivé, J.A. Pastor (Eds.), Advanced Information Systems Engineering. Proceedings, 1997. XI, 451 pages. 1997.

Vol. 1251: K. Hardy, J. Briggs (Eds.), Reliable Software Technologies – Ada-Europe '97. Proceedings, 1997. VIII, 293 pages. 1997.

Vol. 1253: G. Bilardi, A. Ferreira, R. Lüling, J. Rolim (Eds.), Solving Irregularly Structured Problems in Parallel. Proceedings, 1997. X, 287 pages. 1997.